KEYBOARD MUSICIANSHIP

piano for adults

BOOK ONE

Tenth Edition
By

James Lyke
Professor of Music, Emeritus
University of Illinois, Urbana-Champaign, IL

Tony Caramia
Eastman School of Music, Rochester, NY

Reid Alexander
University of Illinois, Urbana-Champaign, IL

Geoffrey Haydon
Georgia State University, Atlanta, GA

Ronald Chioldi
Northeastern State University, Tahlequah, OK

Published by
STIPES PUBLISHING COMPANY
204 West University Avenue
Champaign, Illinois 61820

To Rita and Walter

DESIGN, LAYOUT AND ARTWORK BY IS PRODUCTIONS, CHICAGO, ILLINOIS

STIPES PUBLISHING COMPANY

ISBN 978-1-60904-307-0

Preface

Keyboard Musicianship, Piano For Adults, Book One provides the first-year adult pianist in college group instruction with the necessary unified musical materials to develop into a well-rounded keyboard musician. A well-rounded keyboard musician reads well, plays in all keys, harmonizes folk and popular melodies, plays by ear, improvises, composes, and notates music with skill. In addition, a knowledgeable keyboard musician plays repertoire from all the eras of keyboard literature with taste and intelligence. Good keyboard musicians function well in ensemble and accompanying situations. Their bodies work in a natural way at the keyboard. With these things in mind, this book is organized sequentially thus enabling skill and understanding to unfold in a logical manner.

The tenth edition follows a basic plan in each chapter. As new musical elements are introduced, they are reinforced through a variety of keyboard activities. These include analyzing (melodies, rhythms, harmonies, etc.), sight reading, transposing, harmonizing melodies, improvising and composing short pieces. Piano solos, ensemble works, and accompaniments are all interrelated with the new elements along with technical patterns requiring a certain amount of drill. Evaluation of progress is assisted with suggested playing exam topics that appear at the end of each chapter. If students can successfully master these playing topics, they are ready to move on to the next chapter.

The text's eight chapters and appendices reflect a typical first-year college secondary piano curriculum for music majors who are not pianists. Normally, a first semester class (15 or 16 weeks) would cover Chapters One through Four. If the first four chapters are covered in the fall term, students could do additional work in Appendix C that includes holiday music (Christmas carols and Hanukkah music). Second semester classes would complete Chapters Five through Eight. Helpful supplementary materials include: *Essential Melodic and Harmonic Patterns for Group Piano Students* by Lyke and Haydon (4th ed.) and *Ensemble Music For Group Piano* by Lyke and Haydon (4th ed.). These revised publications are available from the publisher of this text, Stipes Publishing Company.

The tenth edition of *Keyboard Musicianship, Book One*, contains American Song Repertoire commencing with Chapter Two. Students are introduced to the music of great American songwriters such as Jerome Kern, Irving Berlin, George Gershwin, and Richard Rodgers. These song arrangements complement the many ethnic song arrangements contained in each chapter.

The tenth edition includes a play-along CD containing both audio tracks and embedded Standard MIDI Files. The tracks have been digitally recorded by co-author Dr. Geoffrey Haydon. Dr. Reid Alexander organized the repertoire sections and Dr. Ronald Chioldi was responsible for the technical and theory sections of each chapter.

Composers Professor Tony Caramia and Céline Bussières-Lessard have contributed selections to highlight specific musical topics introduced in various chapters. Dr. Haydon and Dr. Lyke have arranged solo works, ensemble works, and accompaniments.

Note to the instructor: *Keyboard Musicianship, Book One*, is designed to assist the creative college teacher to plan a variety of activities for each class. This book is not intended as a "page by page" method. Rather, it provides all the necessary materials to make planning and evaluating a painless process. The teacher remains the key person for providing excitement, fun, leadership, encouragement, and effective instruction thus enabling students to reach their full potential at the keyboard. Once the semester is under way, teachers may find that alternating musicianship activities with the checking of repertoire, technical work, sight reading, and theory will achieve good results.

Table of Contents

CHAPTER ONE

CHAPTER TWO

CHAPTER THREE

CHAPTER FOUR

CHAPTER FIVE

CHAPTER SIX

CHAPTER SEVEN

CHAPTER EIGHT

APPENDICES

Note to the Instructor

It is likely that music majors (vocalists and instrumentalists) will move rapidly through the material in Chapter One. For those students who are bass clef readers, emphasis should be placed on reading the treble clef. Treble clef readers should work on the bass clef. Experience reading in both clefs can be found in the sight reading, solo and ensemble sections.

One of the challenges facing group teaching focuses on building a solid technique at the keyboard. At the end of each chapter, exercises are given to devleop skill with many keyboard patterns. Scales, arpeggios, chords and other essential studies appear at the end of each chapter. Be sure to assign these studies early on when beginning a new chapter.

Harmonization studies are presented in a sequential manner and tied to chord pattern practice. In the first semester, emphasis is placed on I-IV-V^7 harmony in major and minor. The final four chapters (5-8) introduce secondary chords and secondary dominants. At the end of the first year, students become acquainted with major and minor scales, the chromatic scale, the pentatonic scale, the whole tone scale and the blues scale. In addition they learn chord progressions using vi, ii and iii and secondary dominants. Chapters 5-8 stress harmonization in four voices with the chord in the RH and single bass tones in the LH. LH chords are replaced with a more open texture.

Sight reading sections appear in every chapter and are tied to the topics covered in each chapter. There is a mixture of styles and suggestions for transposition. Five or more minutes of class time should be devoted to sight reading.

Each chapter contains solos, duets and accompaniments. Students select what they want to learn and play. It is important to allow the student to have a voice in the selection process. Each chapter takes approximately three and half weeks to cover. Chapters 1-4 are intended for a semester's work; Chapters 5-8 are intended for the second semester. The repertoire seciton contains at least 8 solos; some are simple and others challenging. At the close of each chapter, **Suggested Playing Exam Topics** should be used at the discretion of the instructor. These topics are meant to guide the instuctor and assist in the evaluation process.

1
chapter

Keyboard Basics, Counting, Melody Playing, Pattern Recognition, Reading Studies, Repertoire, Musicianship Activities, and Technical Studies

Note to Music Majors: The first several pages of Chapter 1 serve as a quick review of keyboard music essentials.

Exploring the Piano Keyboard

On the piano keyboard, high sounds or low sounds may be produced. These sounds, or *pitches*, become higher as you play keys to the right.

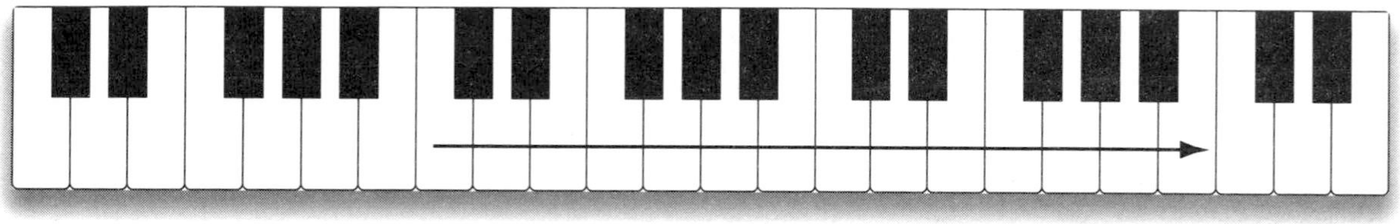

Pitches become lower as you play keys to the left.

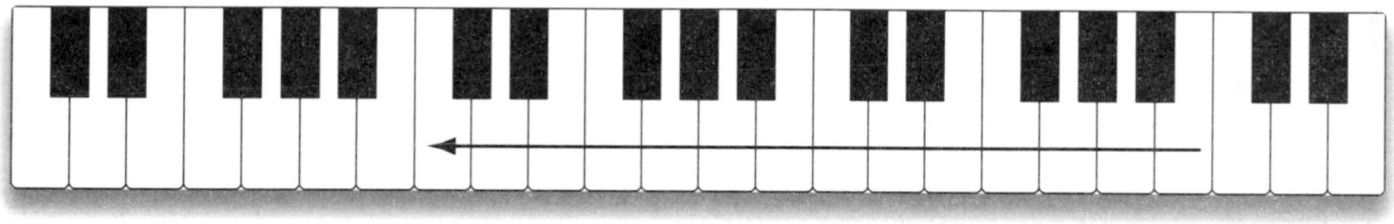

Find two black keys in the middle of the keyboard. Using your right hand (RH) pointer finger and middle finger, push down these two black keys, then move to the right and push down the next set; finally, move right again to push down one last set of black keys.

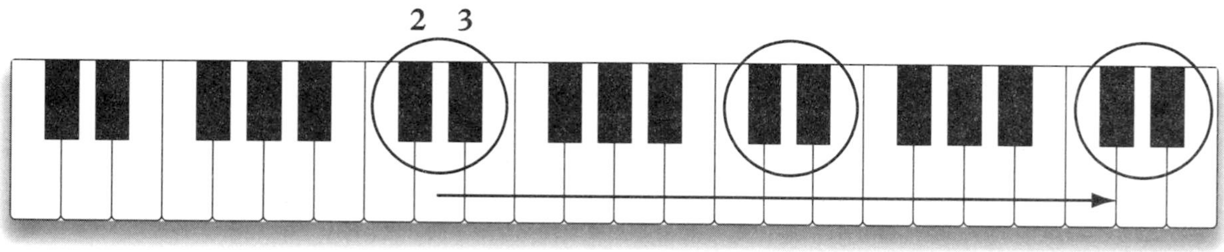

Using your left hand (LH) middle finger and pointer finger, find two black keys in the middle of the keyboard. Push these two black keys down; move left and repeat with the next set; and move left again to push down one last set of black keys.

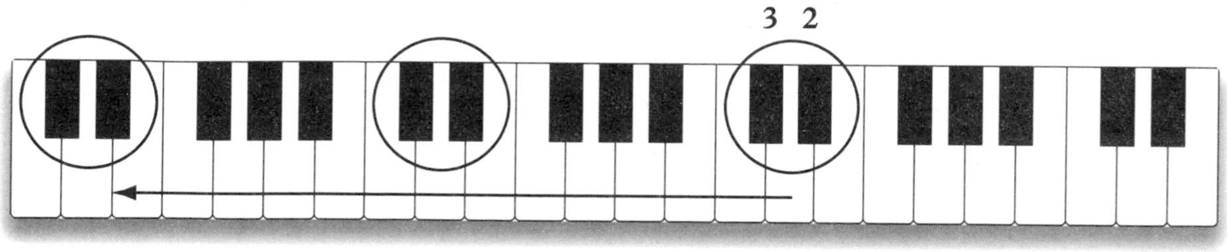

Finger Numbers

The fingers of each hand are indicated by numbers.

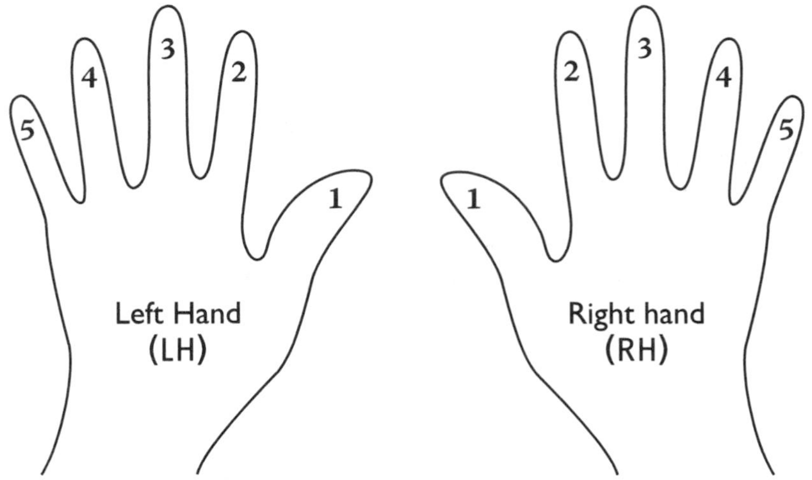

Hand Position

Build a "bridge" with the knuckles of each hand. Allow the fingers to taper to the keys. Bring the thumb up to the tip of the second finger. Let the fingers that are not playing rest on the adjacent key tops.

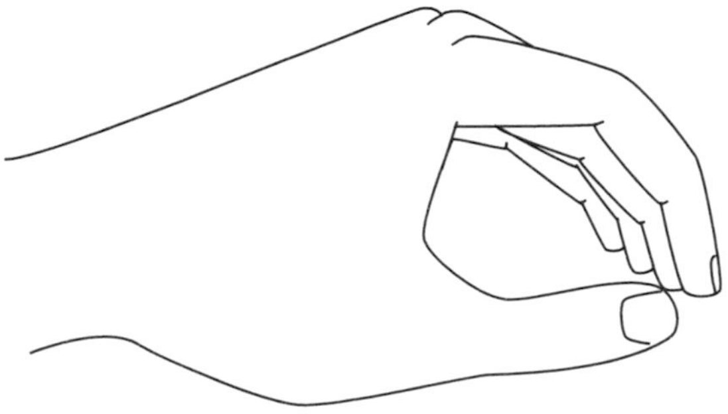

Sitting Position

Sit forward on the piano bench and lean slightly toward the keyboard. Arms should hang loosely from the shoulders. Hands should be placed level with the keyboard. Elbows need to be flexible to accommodate various movements. Feet should be placed squarely on the floor with the left foot slightly behind the right.

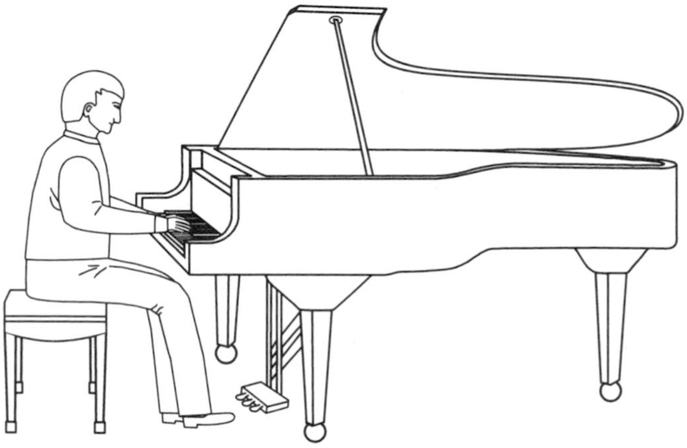

Black Keys

Find three black keys just to the right of the middle of the keyboard. Using RH fingers 2-3-4, push down all three black keys; then move to the right and push down the next set; finally, move right again to push down one last set of black keys.

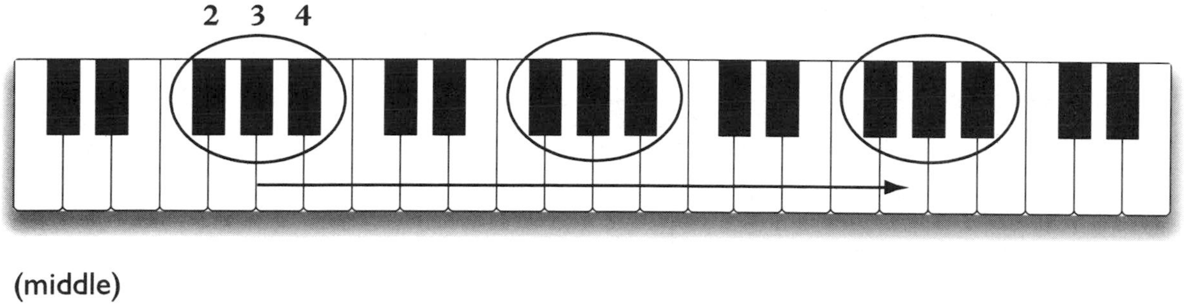

Using LH fingers 4-3-2, push down the set of three black keys to the left of the middle of the keyboard; move left and repeat with the next set; and move left again to push down one last set of black keys.

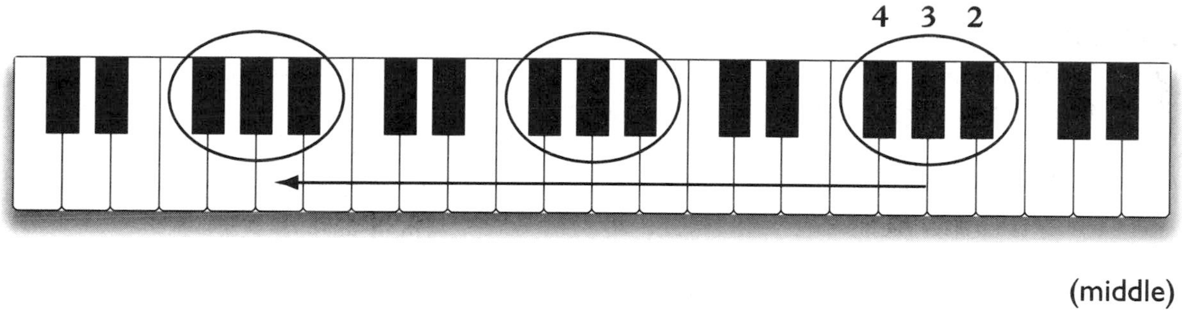

White Keys

White keys are easily named by their relationship to the group of two black keys and the group of three black keys.

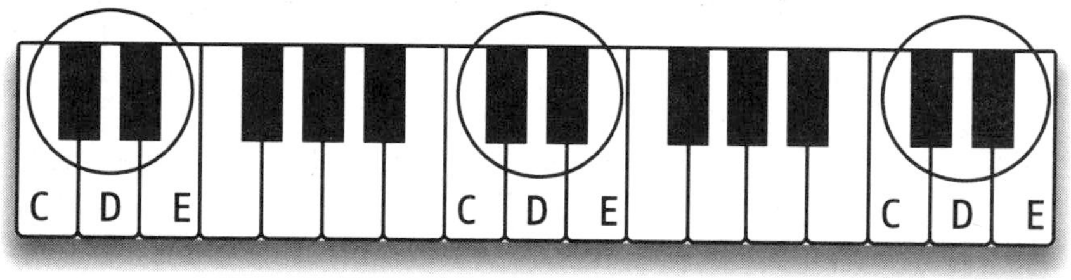

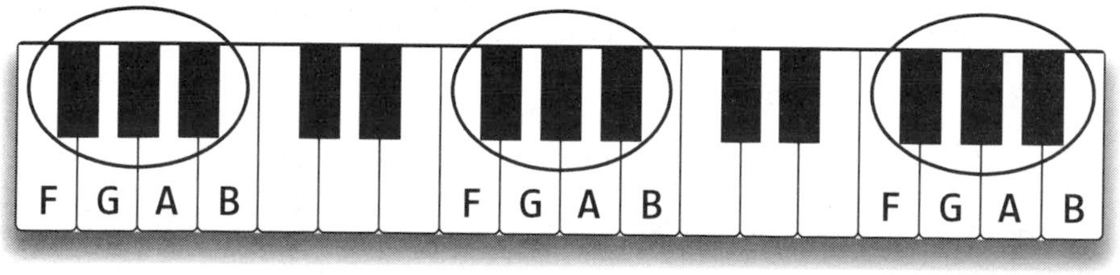

Staffs

Piano music is writen on two five-line *staffs* which are joined together. The upper staff is called the *treble staff*; the lower staff is called the *bass staff*. In most of our beginning tunes and pieces, the right hand will play in the treble staff while the left hand plays in the bass staff.

Grand Staff

When the treble and bass clef staffs are joined, the *Grand Staff* is formed. The treble clef, or *G clef* (𝄞), names the treble staff G line (above middle C). The bass clef, or *F clef* (𝄢), names the bass staff F line (below middle C).

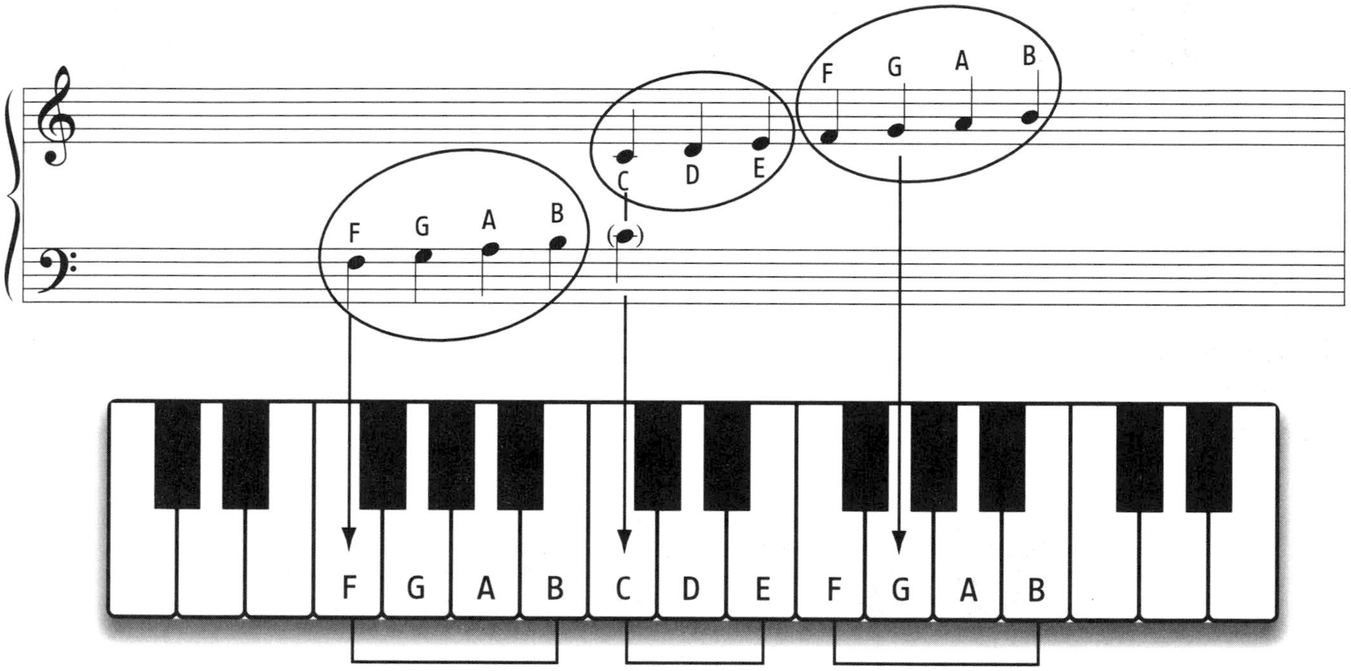

Line Notes and Space Notes

Music is written (notated) on *lines* and in *spaces*. With line notes, the line goes through the middle of the notehead. With space notes, the note head is in a space. Notes can repeat, notes can step and notes can skip. Note stems may extend up or down from the note head (♩ or 𝅘𝅥 stem down).

Note Values

A *quarter note* (♩) lasts for one count. A *half note* (𝅗𝅥) lasts for two counts. A *dotted half note* (𝅗𝅥.) lasts for three counts. A *whole note* (𝅝) lasts for four counts. Chant and tap the following rhythm pattern with both hands.

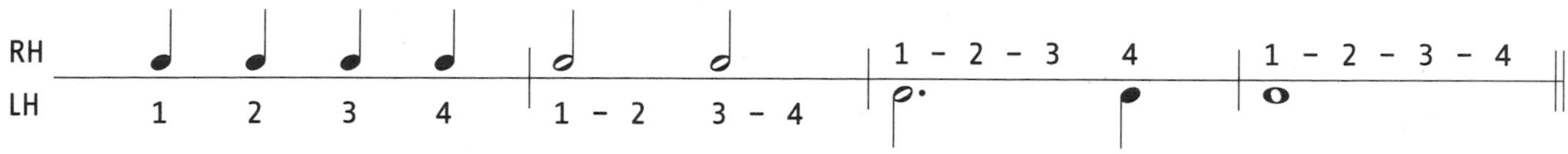

Measure Bars and Time Signatures

Music is much easier to read when divided into *measures*. Measures are marked off with single *bar lines*. The last measure of every piece has a double bar line. *Meter* in music is shown at the beginning of every piece with a *time signature*. The top number indicates the number of pulses in each measure. The bottom number shows which kind of note receives one pulse, or count. Tap the rhythm pattern once again with each hand; observe the time signature and measure bars.

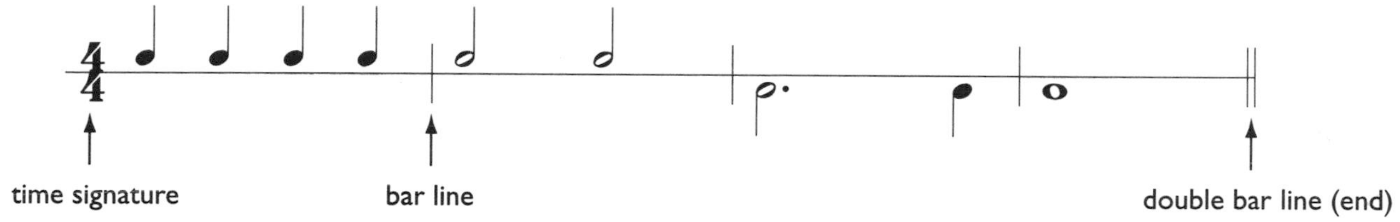

Rests

Rests are symbols for silence. Every note value has a corresponding rest. Study the chart below.

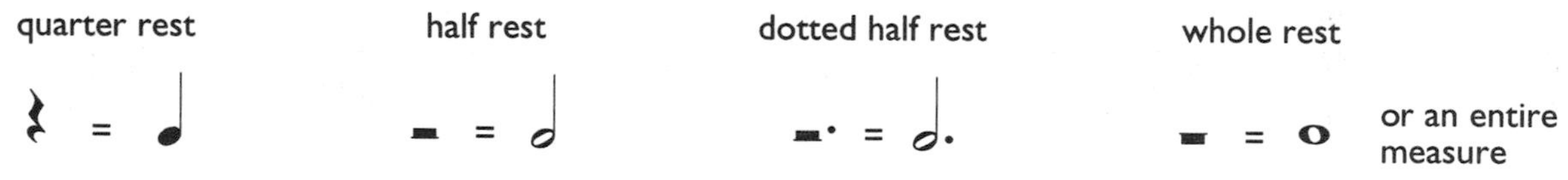

Tap the following rhythm patterns observing all rests.

1. 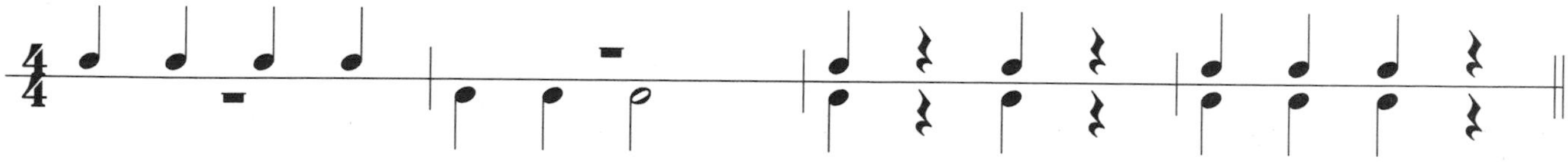

2. 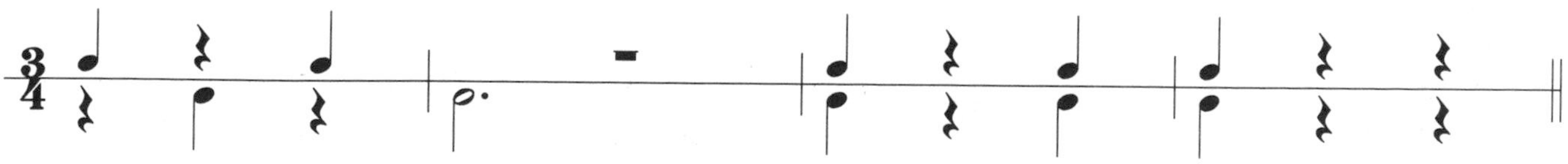

Playing Treble CDE Groups

Play the three CDE groups shown below. Start on Middle C. Count and say the names of the notes as you play. *8va* means to play one octave (eight notes) higher than written. *Loco* means to return to the actual written notes.

Playing Bass CDE Groups and Using Leger Lines

Occasionally, added lines (*leger lines*) appear above and below each staff. Leger lines facilitate reading. Play the following melody which utilizes leger lines above the 𝄢 staff. An *8va* sign below the staff means to play those notes one octave lower than written.

Playing CDE Groups Using Both Hands

Play the melodies below which use CDE groups in each hand. Observe the *8va* signs. The *repeat sign* (:‖) means the tune is to be played a second time with no interruption in the rhythm.

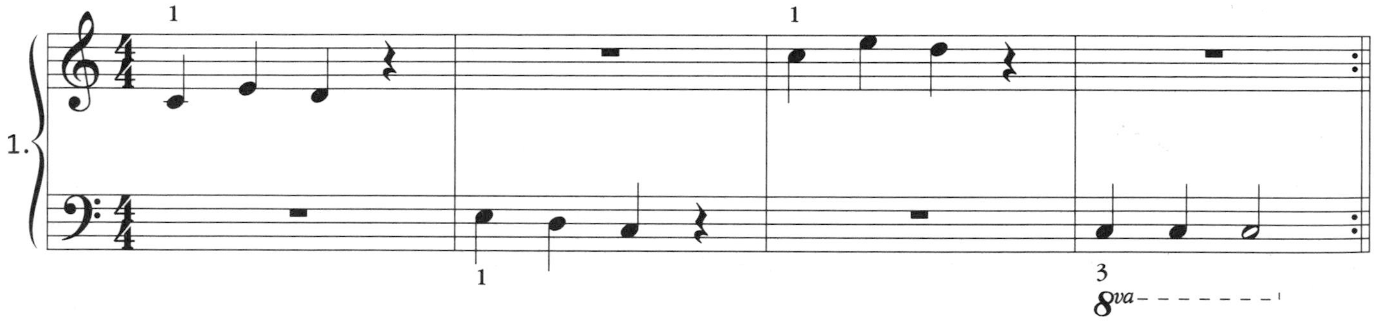

Sharps, Flats, and Naturals

A *sharp* (♯) placed before a note indicates that note be played one half-step *higher*. It lasts through the remainder of the measure *unless cancelled by a natural* (♮).

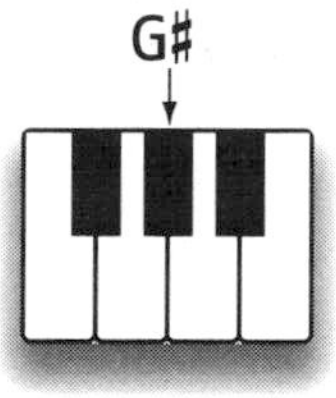

A *flat* (♭) placed before a note indicates that note be played one half-step *lower*. It lasts through the remainder of the measure *unless cancelled by a natural* (♮).

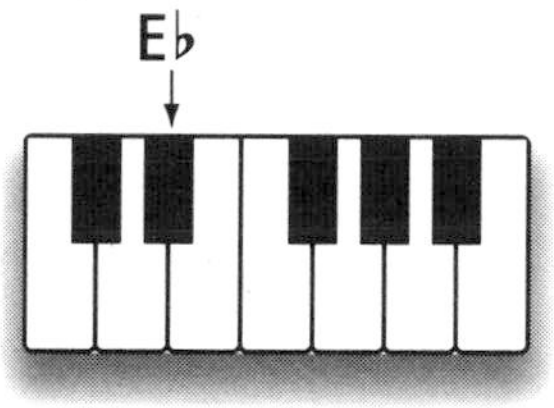

A *natural* (♮) shows a cancellation of a sharp or flat and a return to the natural (white key).

Study and play the various sharps and flats shown below. A knowledge of sharps and flats becomes necessary when building various major pentachords, or 5-finger patterns.

♯ Sharp: one key up from the closest white key. This may be a black key or a white key.

♭ Flat: one key down from the closest white key. This may be a black key or a white key.

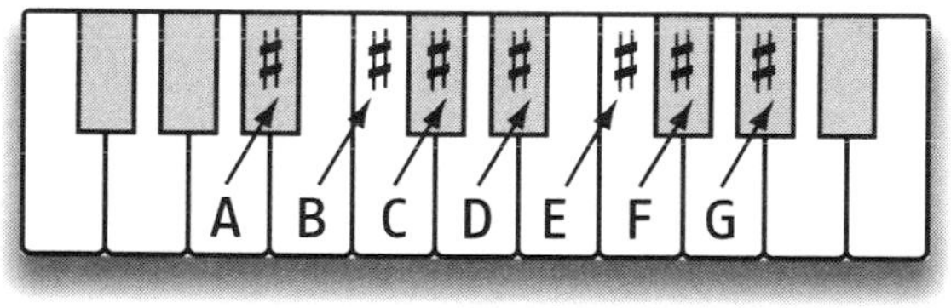

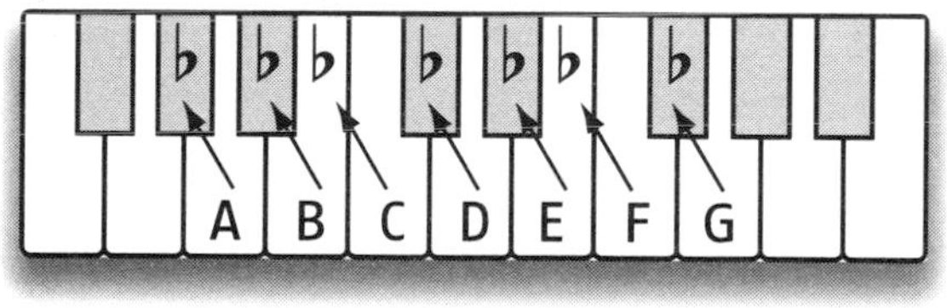

Playing Tune Fragments That Use Sharp, Flat, and Natural Signs

Study and play the following tunes written for either RH or LH at a moderate tempo. Locate the starting note by studying the landmark notes (C, F or G). Some start on the landmark note. Others start from a note near the landmark note. Chant letter names in rhythm. The slur marks (‿ ⁀) indicate connection of one note to another. This enhances smooth or *legato* playing. Place each hand in a 5-finger pattern according to the fingering. Sharps, flats, or naturals introduced at the beginning of a measure lasts through the remainder of the measure.

from a **British Tune**

1. 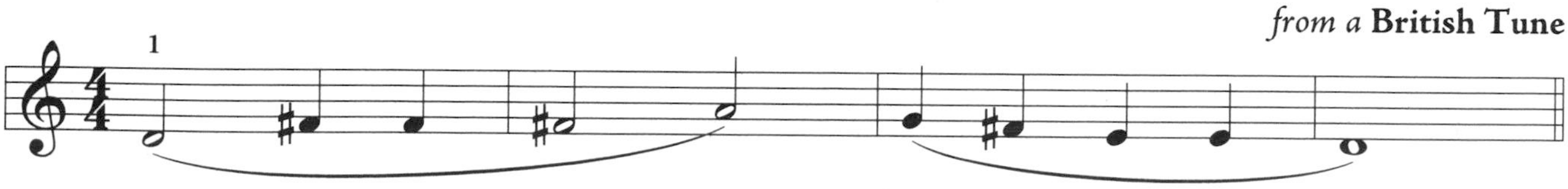

from a **French Tune**

2. 

from a **Polish Tune**

3. 

from a **German Tune**

4. 

from a **British Tune**

5. 

from a **German Tune**

6. 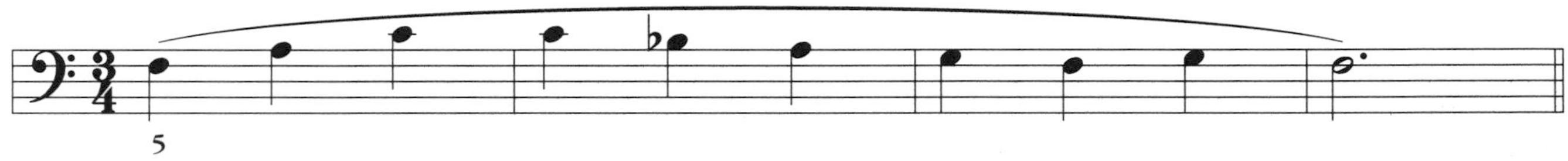

from a **British Tune**

7. 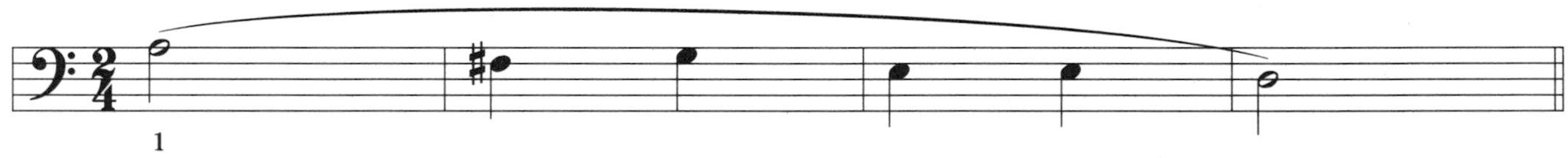

8. 

9. 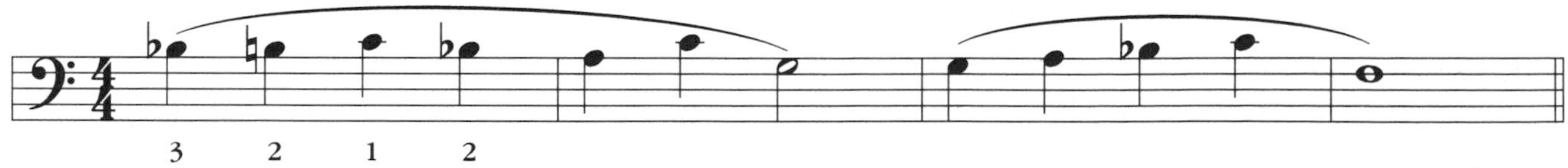

10. 

Combining FGAB and CDE

The following melody combines 𝄢 FGAB with 𝄞 CDE. Observe the slur marks.

1.

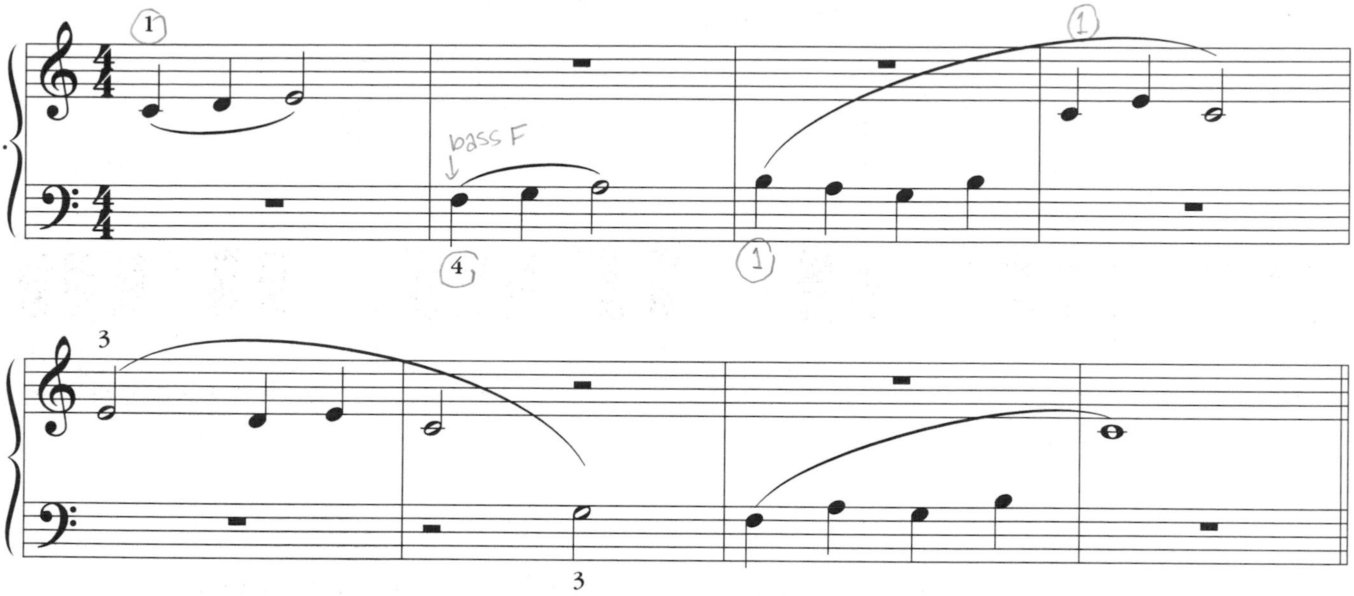

Adding F, G, and A to the Right Hand (RH)

2.

Intervals (Unison – 5th)

An interval represents the distance in pitch between two tones. Study the intervals below as they look on both the staff and on the keyboard.

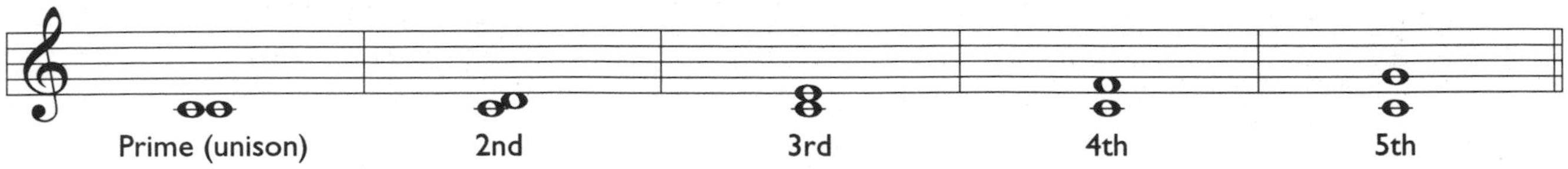

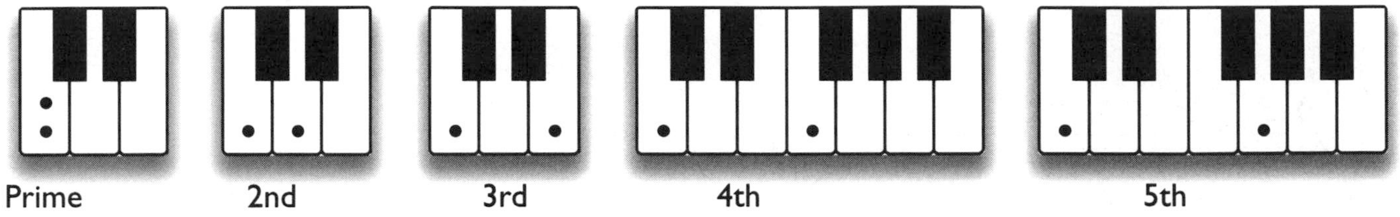

Intervallic Reading

The following melodies encompass either a CDE group or an FGAB group (with a few notes added). Some melodies are for RH; others are for LH. A variety of time signatures and note values is used. Observe the fingering and count. Analyze the intervals that are bracketed. Chant note names in rhythm. You have played these intervals. Now you have a specific designation, e.g., 2nds, 3rds, etc. Write the correct interval within each bracket as shown in measure 2 of No. 1.

1.
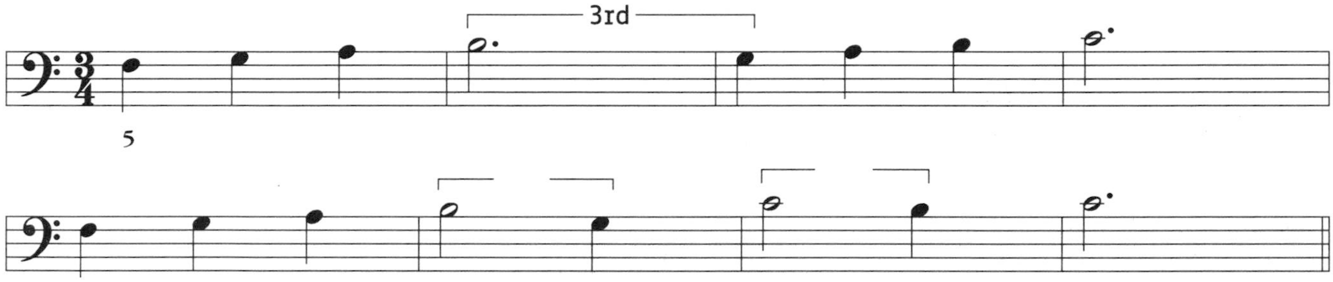

2.
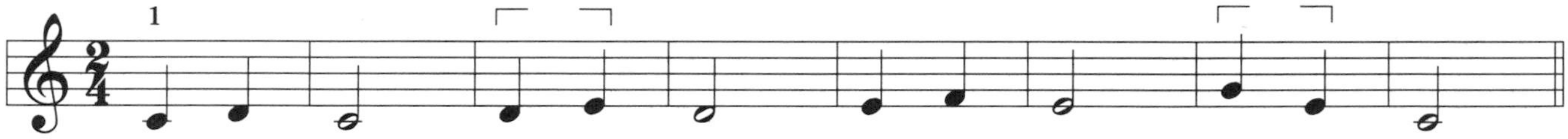

3.

4.

Music for Sight Reading

Before sight reading the following studies, establish the following procedures. Identify landmark notes (𝄢 F, middle C and 𝄞 G). Then place the hands in the patterns suggested by the fingering (given at the beginning). Find CDE groups and FGAB groups. Count and play at reasonable tempos (speeds). Do NOT go back to correct errors. In beginning reading it helps to chant letter names of notes. For example, in No. 1, chant E G C E | C A G–2 | etc. Dynamic marks are used in the tunes for reading: ***f*** = loud, ***p*** = soft, ***mf*** = medium loud, and ***mp*** = medium soft.

Moderately bright

3.

Moderately

4.

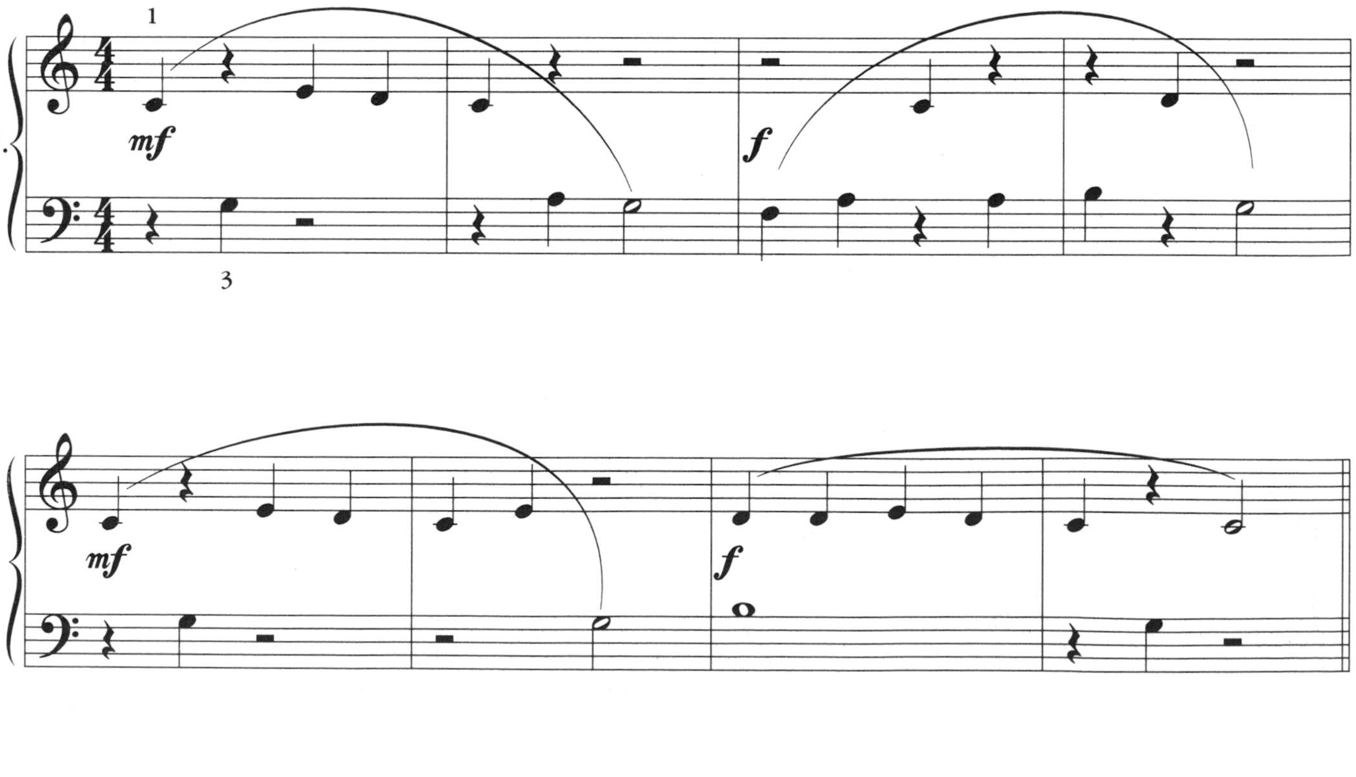

Moderate waltz time

5.

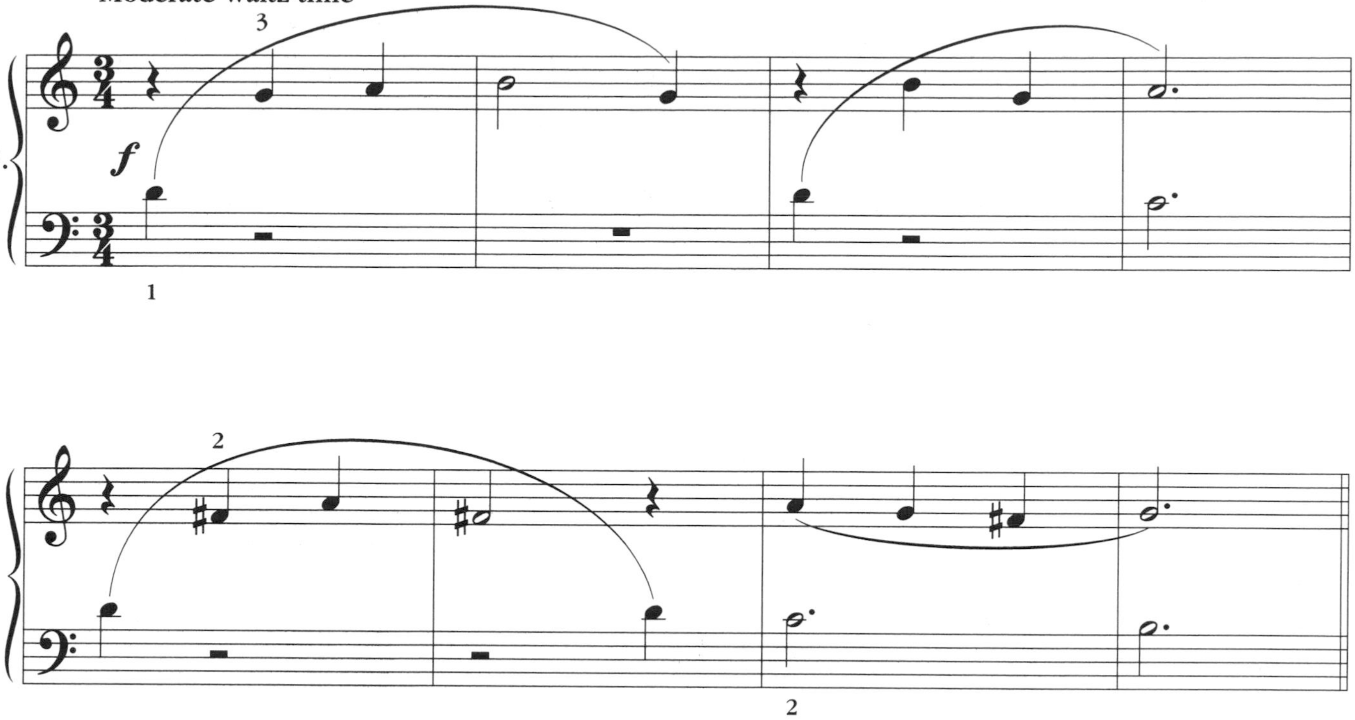

March tempo

6.

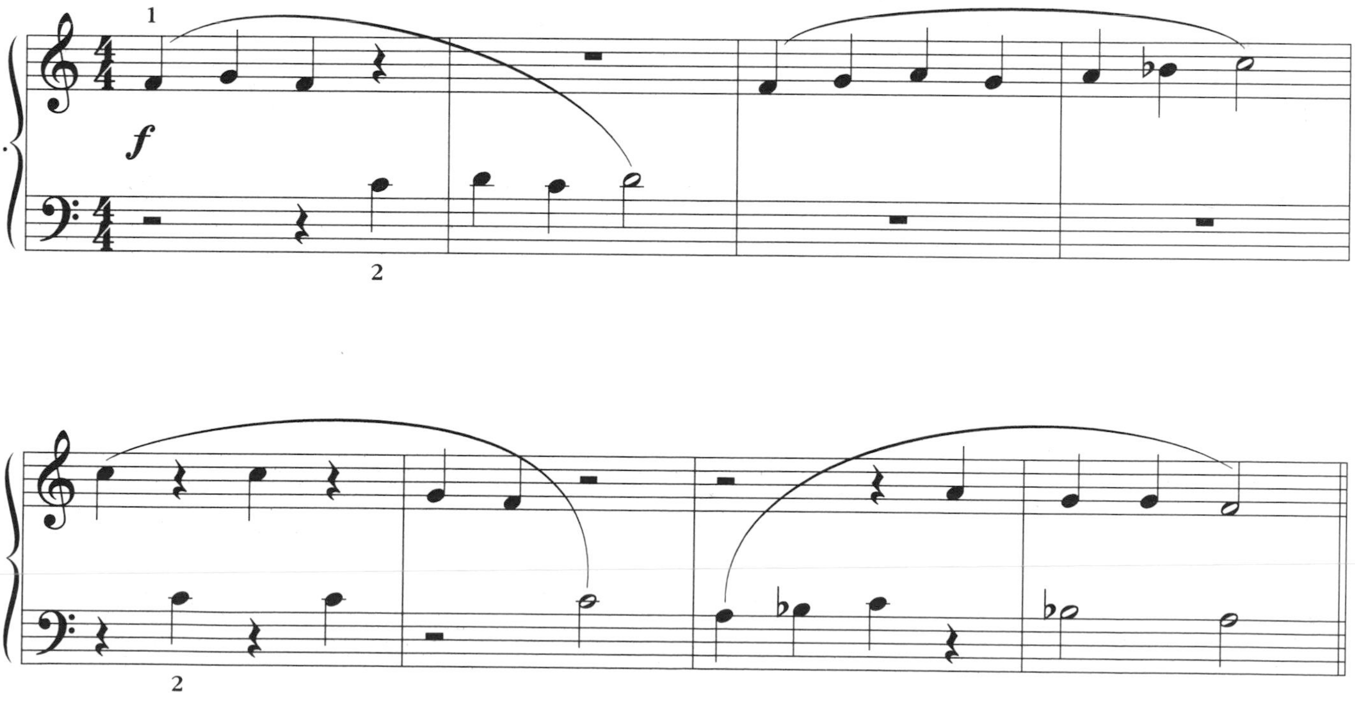

Moderately bright

7.

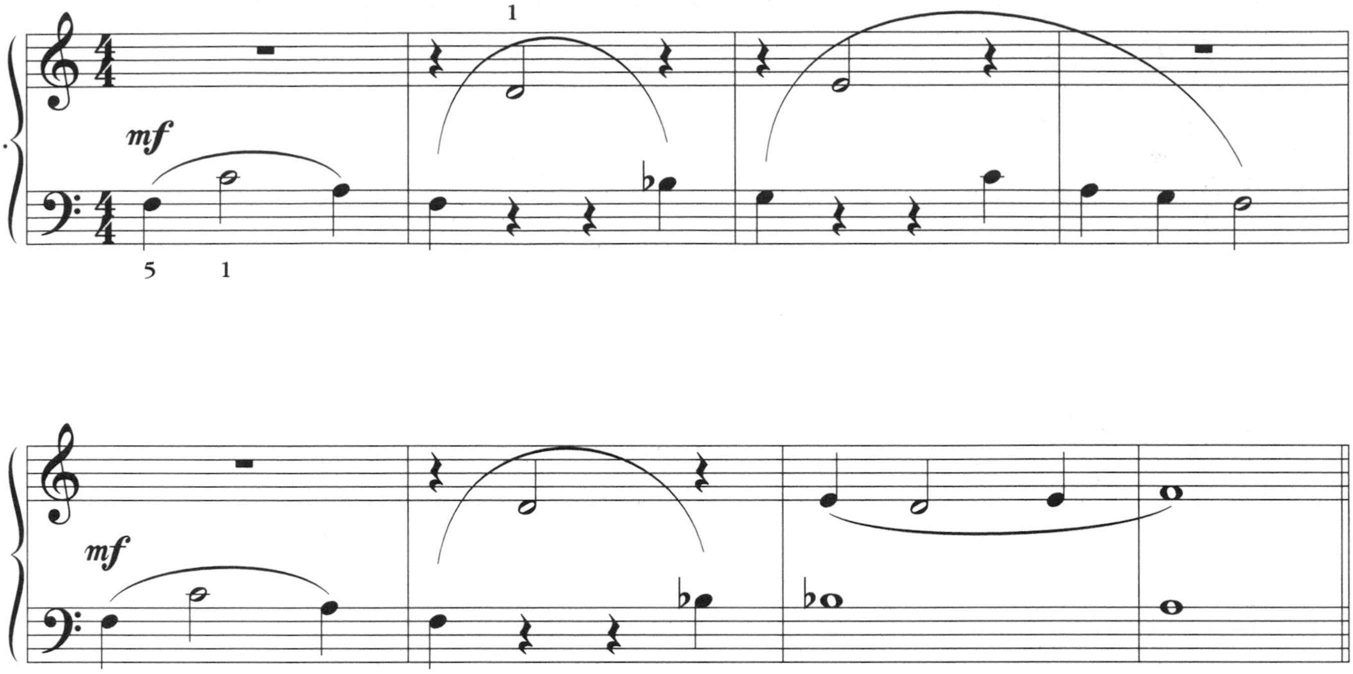

Slowly

8.

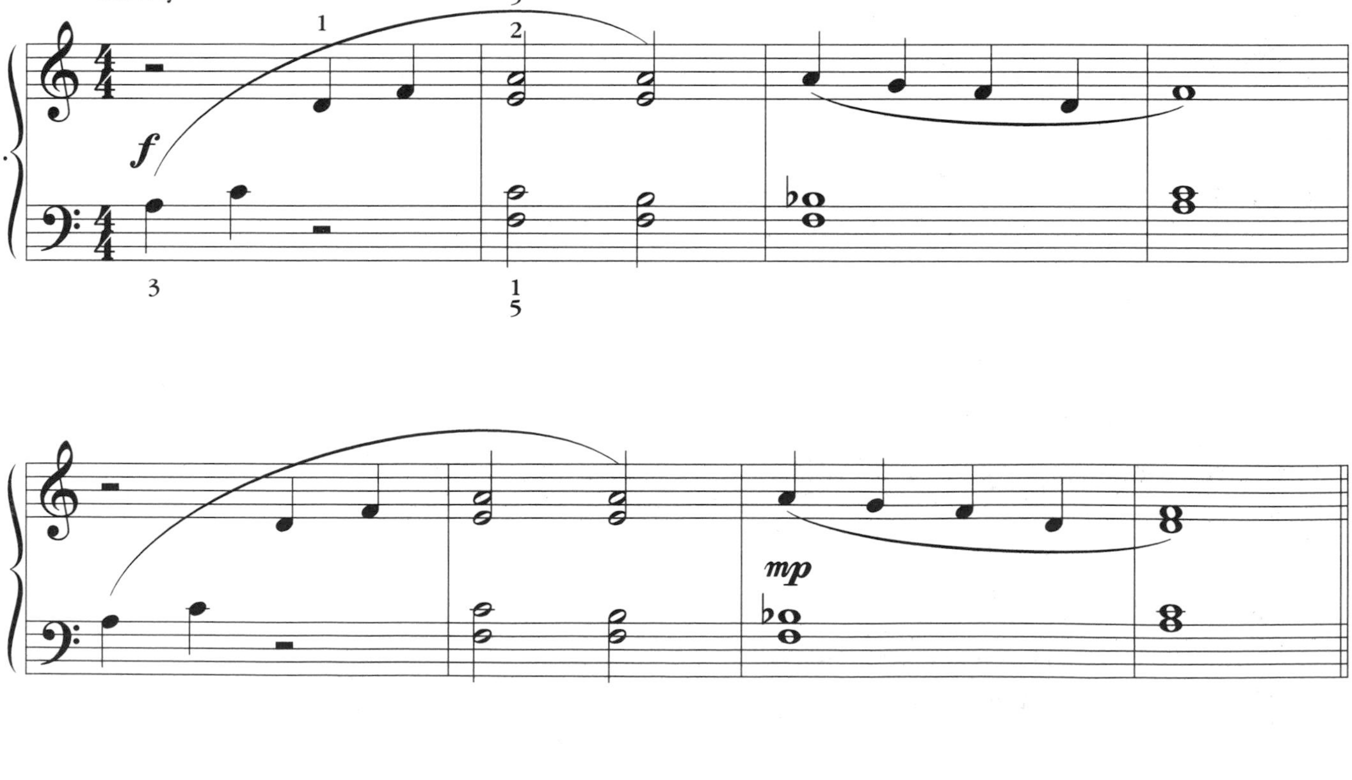

One-Hand Reading in 5-Finger Patterns (Pentachords)

Play the following melodies at an easy tempo (rate of speed). The starting notes should be determined from land mark notes and from CDE / FGAB groupings. Observe the repeat signs (:‖).

RIGHT HAND MELODIES

1. 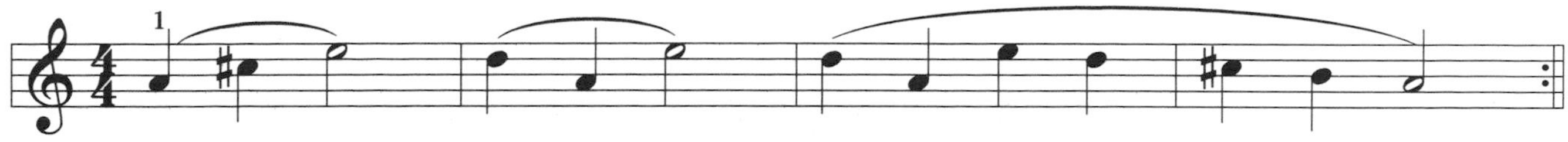

2. 

3. 

4. 

LEFT HAND MELODIES

5. 

6. 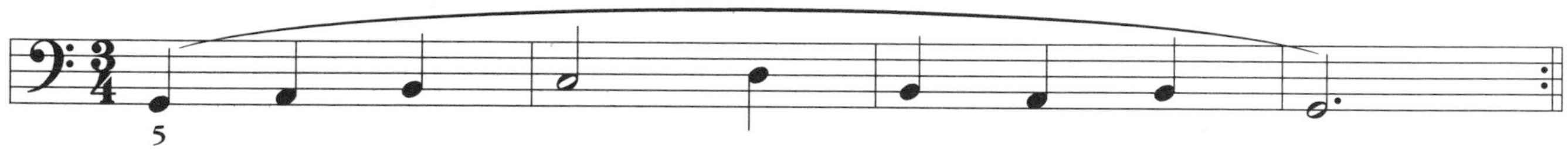

7. 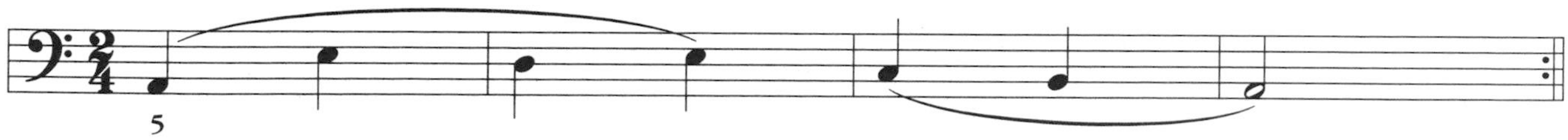

8. 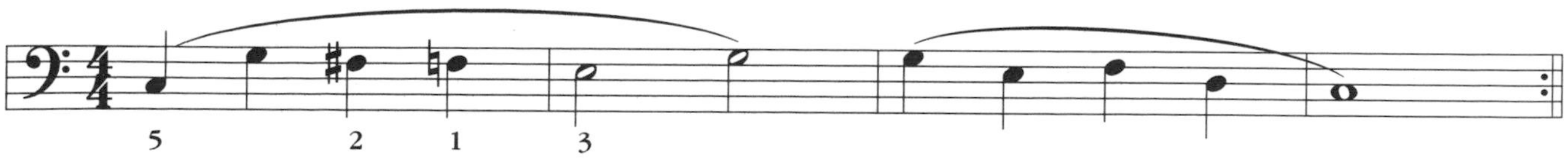

ACCOMPANYING

Play the accompanying part (S) to *The More We Get Together*. Your teacher (T) will play the melody. Study the handsets. The combination of the LH bass notes and the RH intervals creates chords. Hence, you will be playing a chordal accompaniment.

THE MORE WE GET TOGETHER

Germany
***arr.* James Lyke**

*Teacher: Double the melody with RH playing two octaves higher.

S: In RH position keep 5th finger on B♭

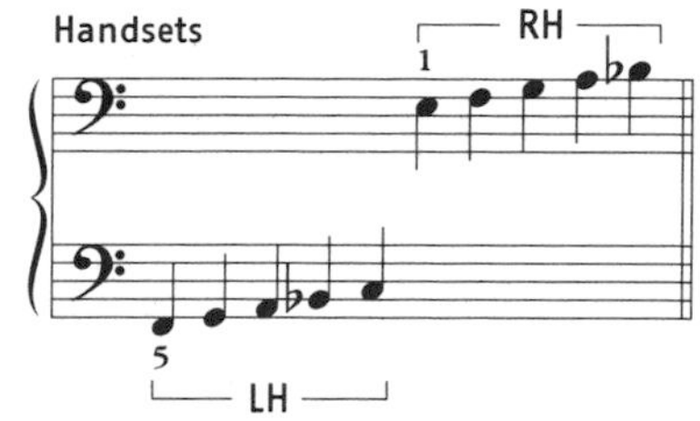

CRADLE SONG

Franz Schubert
***arr.* James Lyke**

Slowly

*Teacher: Double the melody with RH playing two octaves higher.

SCARBOROUGH FAIR

Secondo – Teacher

English
arr. **James Lyke**

S: Play both hands 8va when joined by the secondo at one piano.

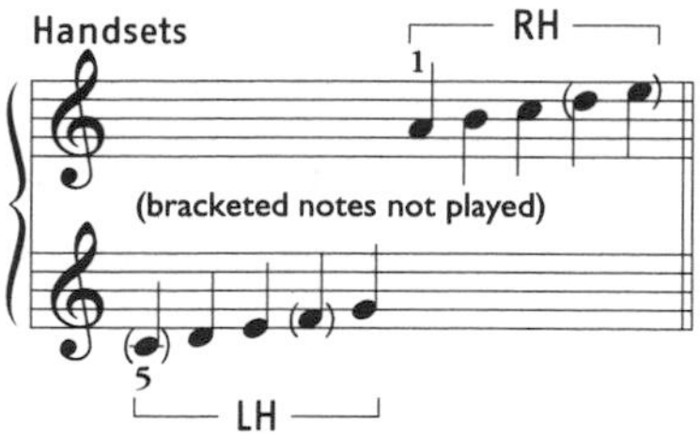

SCARBOROUGH FAIR

Primo – Student

English
arr. James Lyke

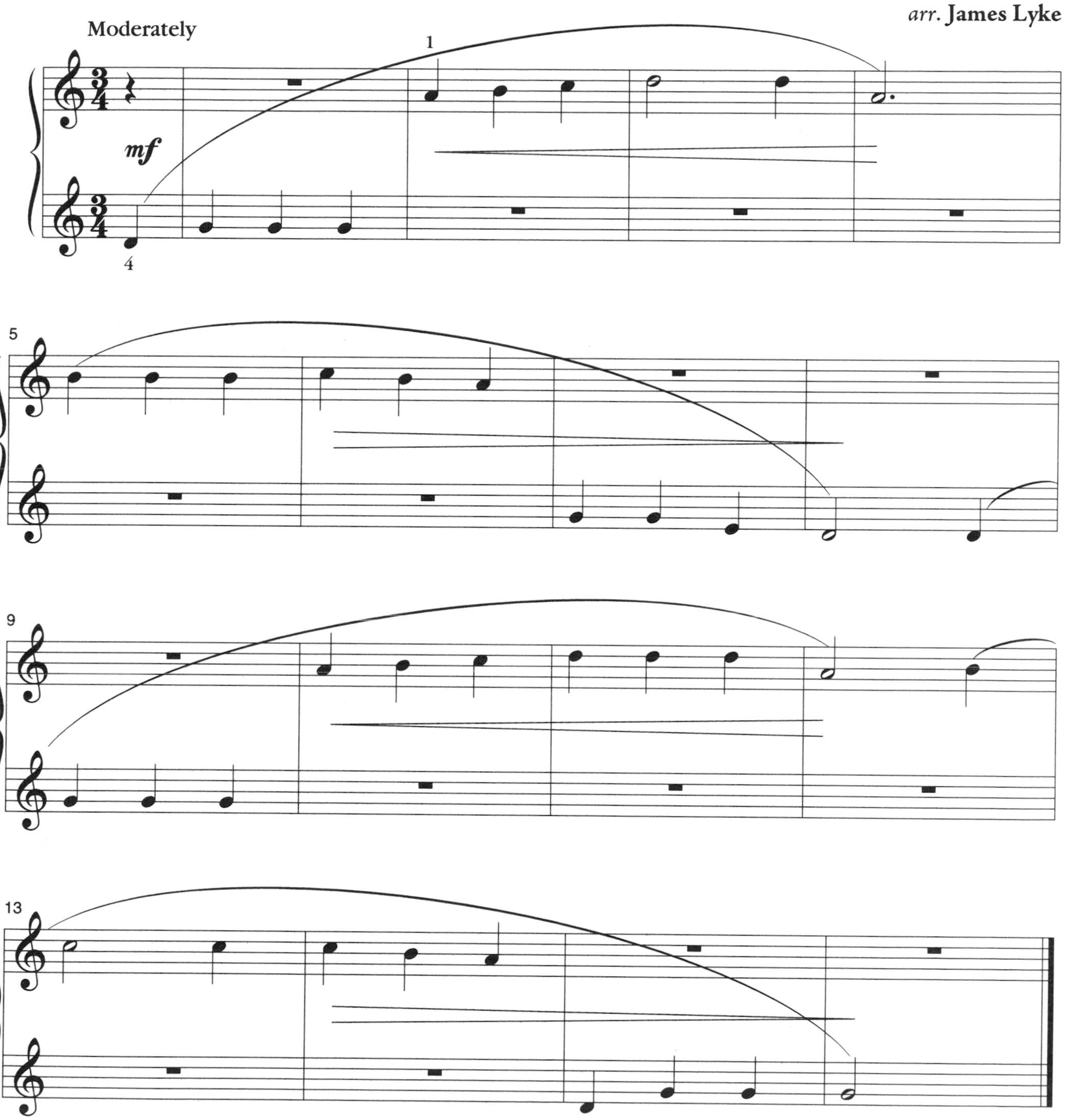

A *crescendo* mark means gradually become louder.

A *decrescendo* mark means gradually become softer.

The quarter note that begins *Scarborough Fair* illustrates an upbeat. It's value is subtracted from the final measure.

4 CD

GOODBYE OL' PAINT

Secondo – Teacher

American Cowboy
***arr.* James Lyke**

Slowly

S: If played at one piano, consider moving the entire primo part up one octave (8va).

4 CD

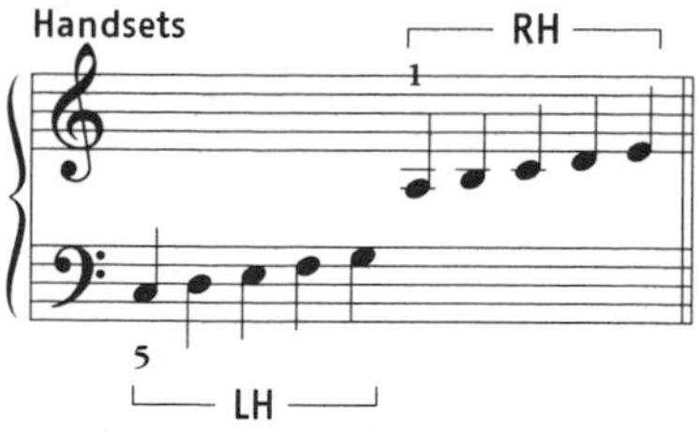

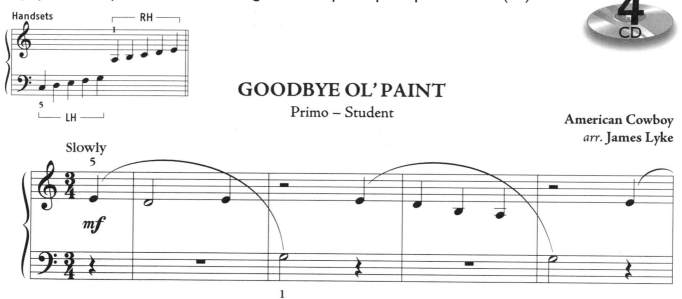

GOODBYE OL' PAINT

Primo – Student

American Cowboy
arr. James Lyke

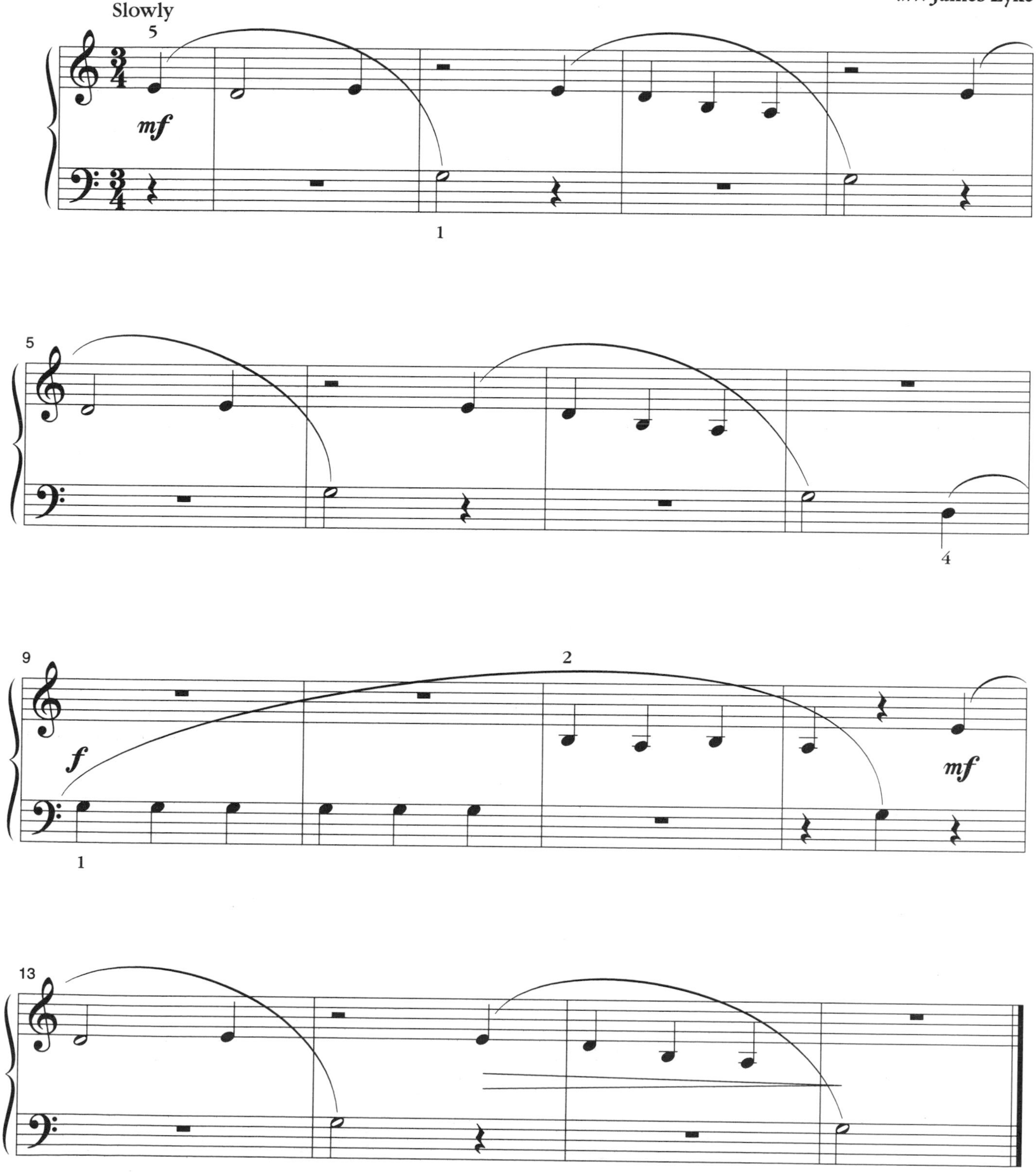

SOLO REPERTOIRE

Before beginning to learn solo selections, review white key groups, intervals, and sharps, flats and naturals. Pay close attention to dynamic marks and slurs. A few new elements will be introduced in this section.

White Key Groups – A Review

Knowing how to locate FGAB and CDE groups will help you learn the names of lines and spaces on each staff. Moreover, it will help you place your hands in the proper position for playing. Study the groups below. Play each group in the proper register.

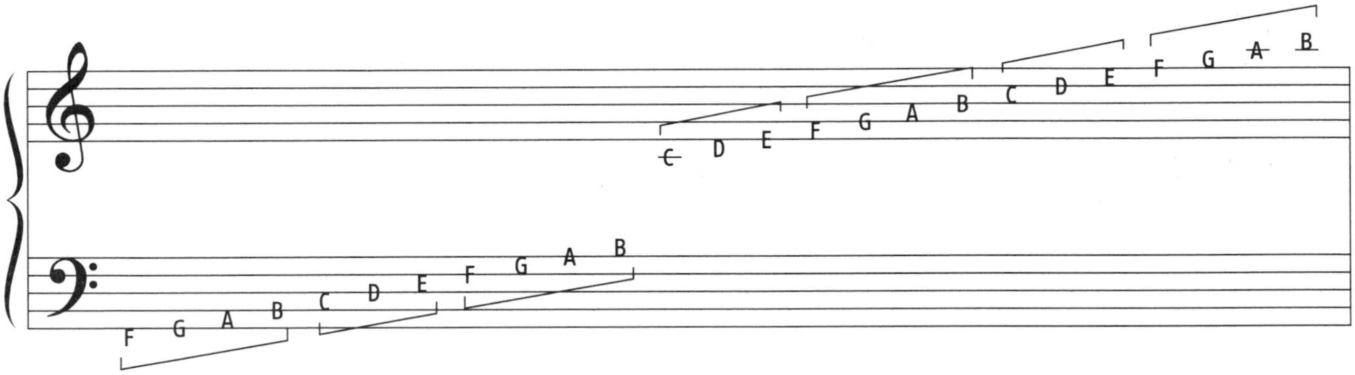

Intervals – A Review

You will recall that an *interval* is the distance between two notes. In your pieces so far, you have played all the intervals shown below. Study these intervals that are pictured as *blocked*, or *harmonic* intervals. Play the intervals with the LH, also.

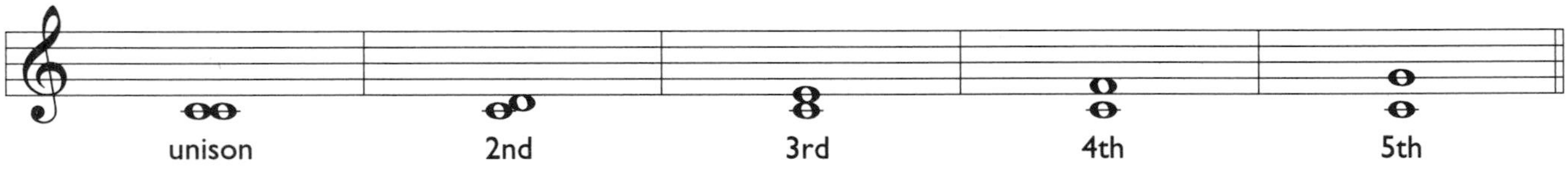

A CONVERSATION

Céline Bussières-Lessard

Identify the intervals in bar 1 (RH), bars 3 and 4 (RH) and bar 1 (LH).

BREEZING ALONG

Céline Bussières-Lessard

You will note that thumbs will be side by side (a second apart) throughout this piece. Practice shifting to each new pattern by "blocking" the 5ths in each measure. The final bar will require special attention. Practice sliding the thumb from B to A while holding the E with the 4th finger.

FIFTHS

James Lyke

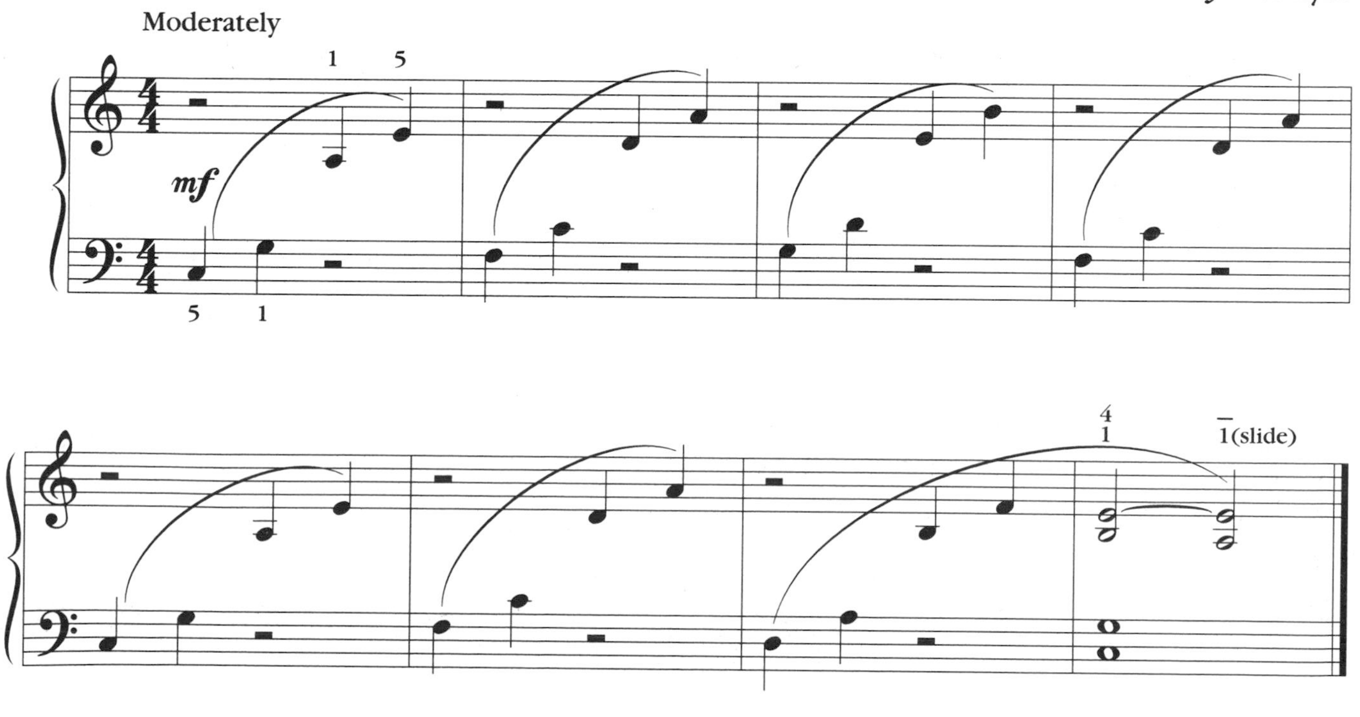

Fermata 𝄐

A *fermata* (hold sign) indicates that the note or chord should be held longer than its normal value.

PENSIVE

Tony Caramia

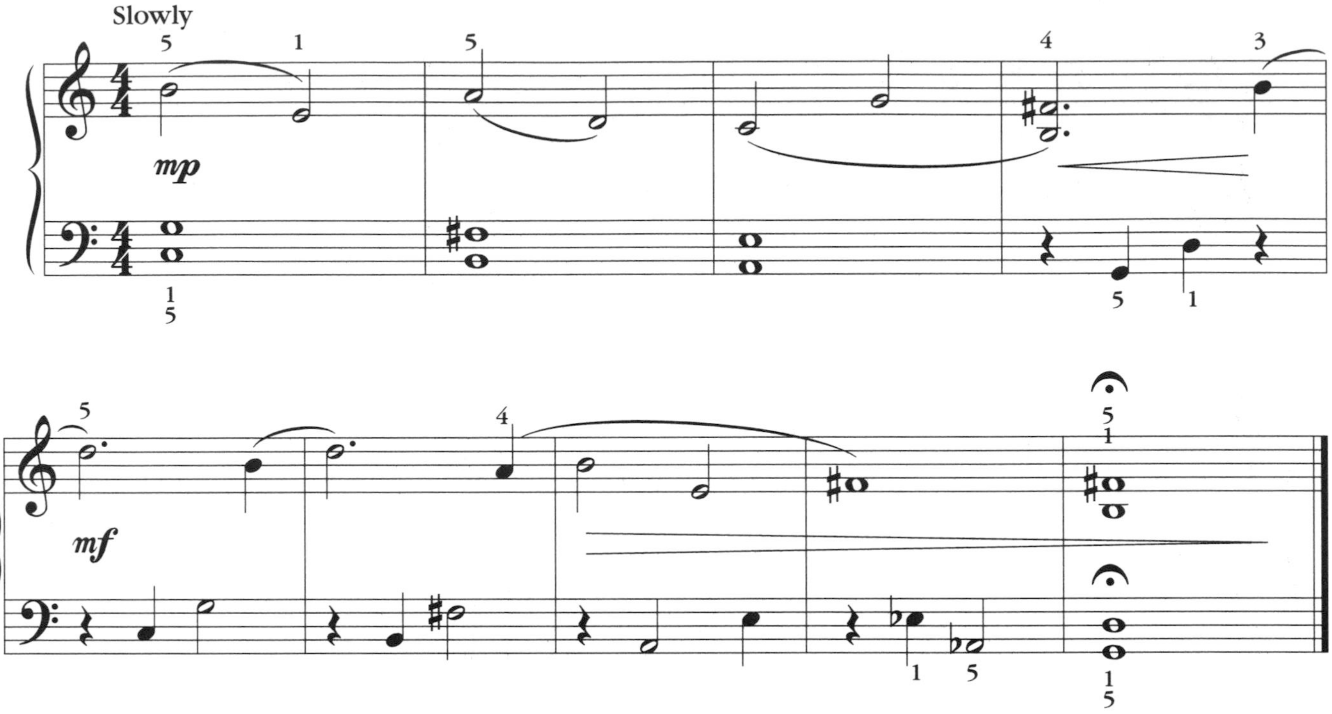

Staccato

A dot placed above or below a note indicates that the note is to be played short (half of the time value). Learn *A Second Chance* slowly and calculate the leaps (up and down). Then play quickly as indicated.

A SECOND CHANCE

Tony Caramia

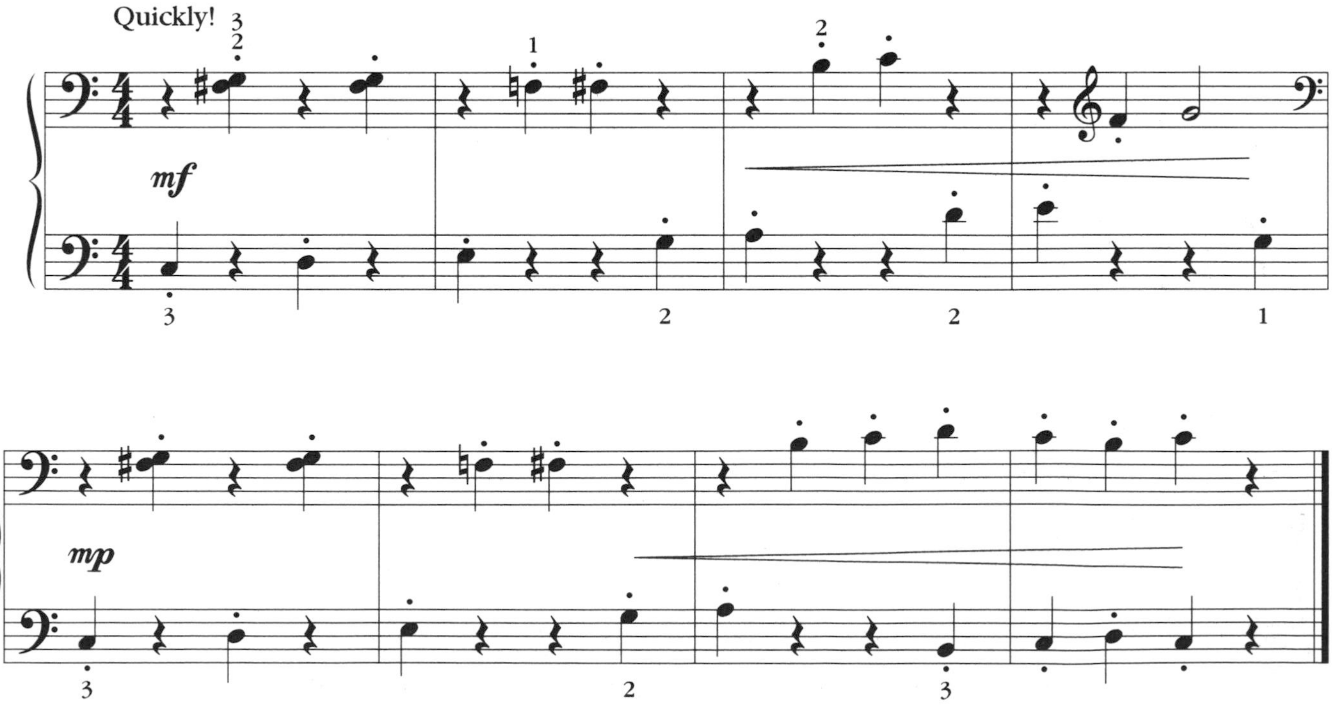

Tied Notes 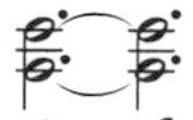

Tied notes consist of a curved line joining two or more notes of the same pitch. The duration is that of the combined note values.

GENTLE LEAVES

Céline Bussières-Lessard

Questions

1. What are the "accompanying" intervals?
2. What is the melodic interval which begins phrases 1 and 3?
3. What do you find when comparing the melody in phrase 1 (RH) to the melody in phrase 2 (LH)?

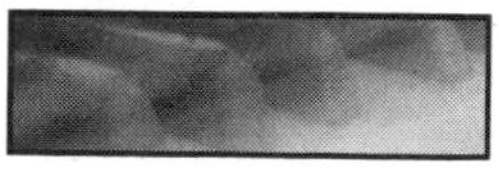

Modal Memory requires shifting to new 5-finger positions. Practice hands separately with careful attention to fingering.

MODAL MEMORY

Tony Caramia

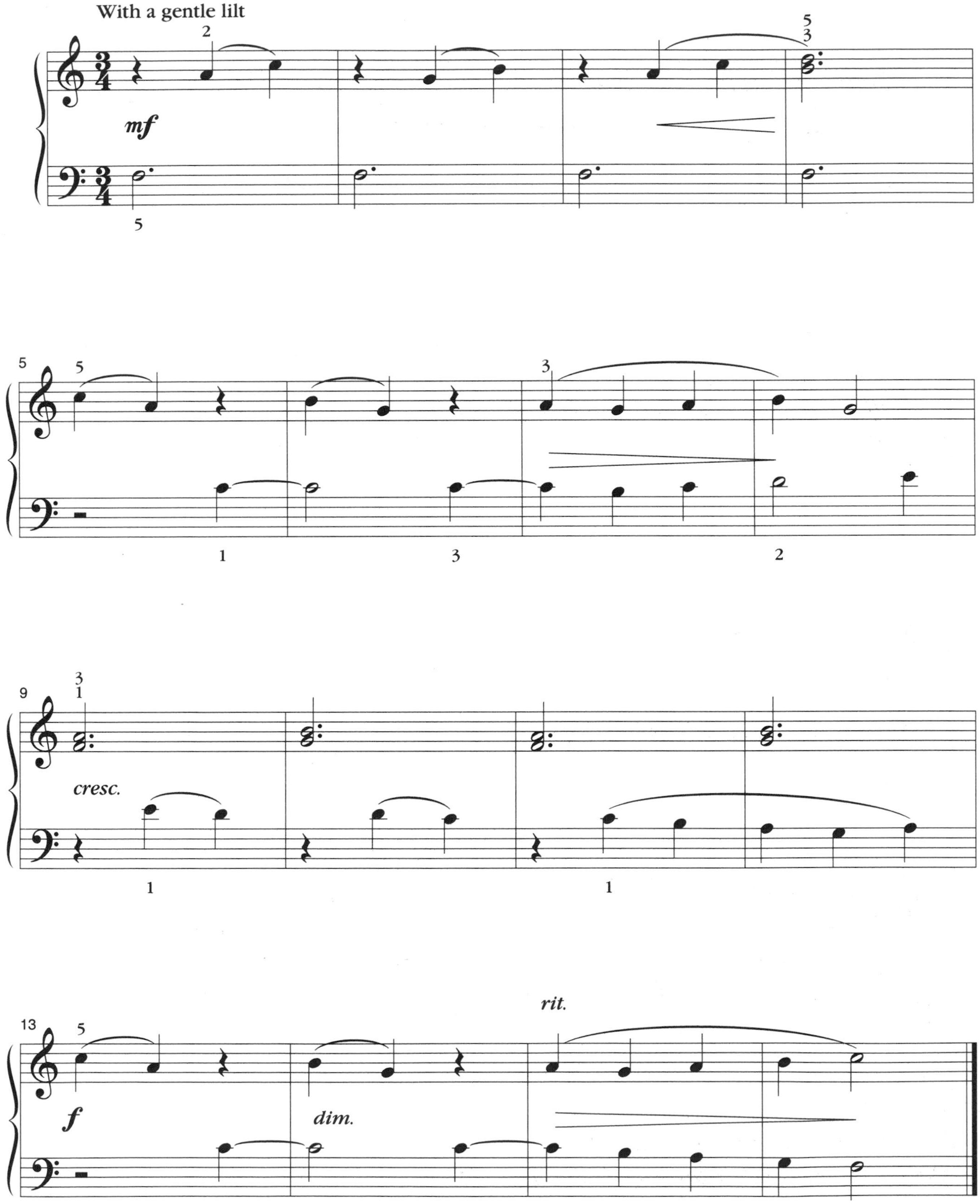

A Thoughtful Gesture gives practice reading in two bass clefts. Both hands are in 5-finger patterns.

A THOUGHTFUL GESTURE

Céline Bussières-Lessard

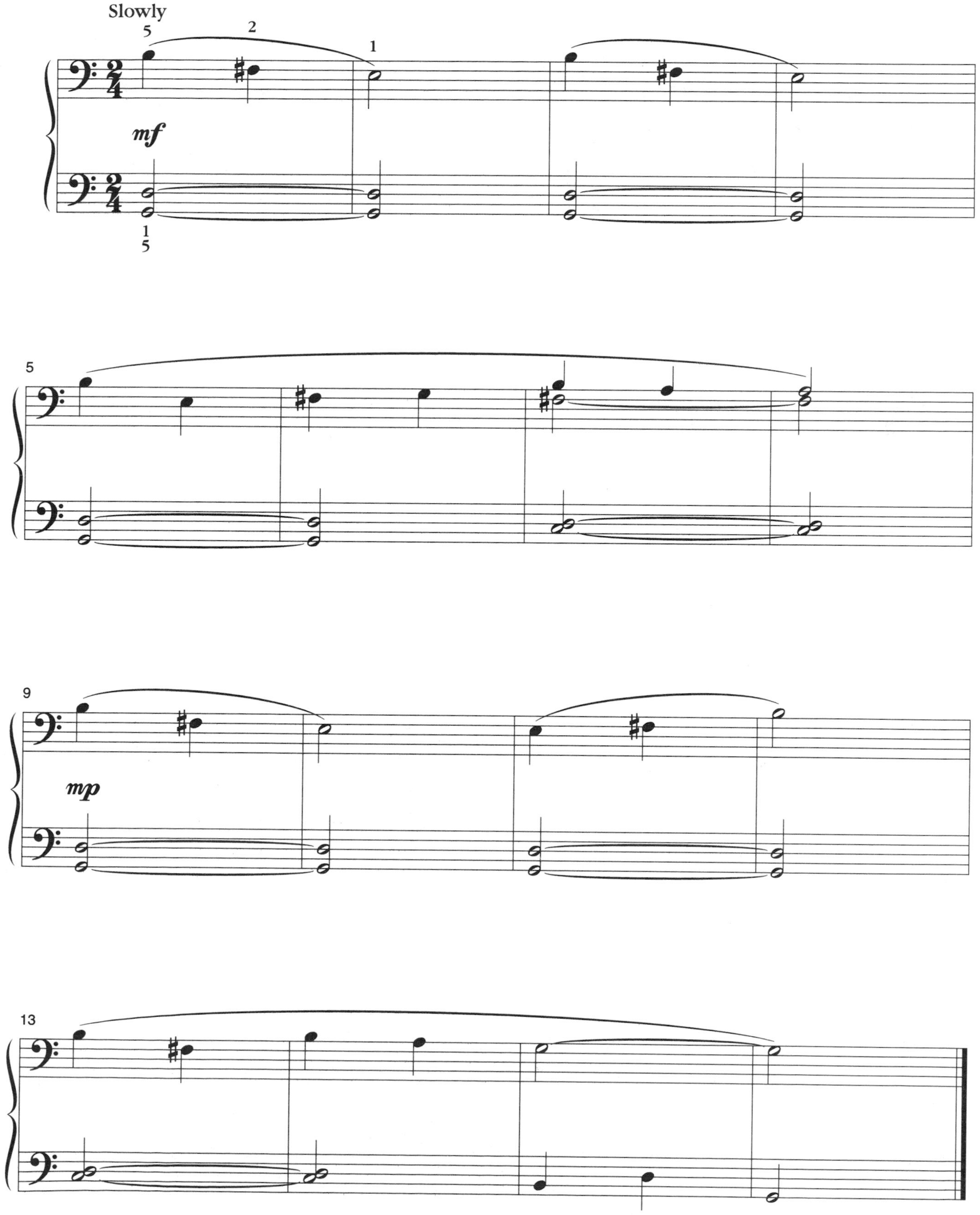

In *Ties That Bind* note the downward shifts of the LH 5ths. Play hands separately with attention to the tied notes.

TIES THAT BIND

Tony Caramia

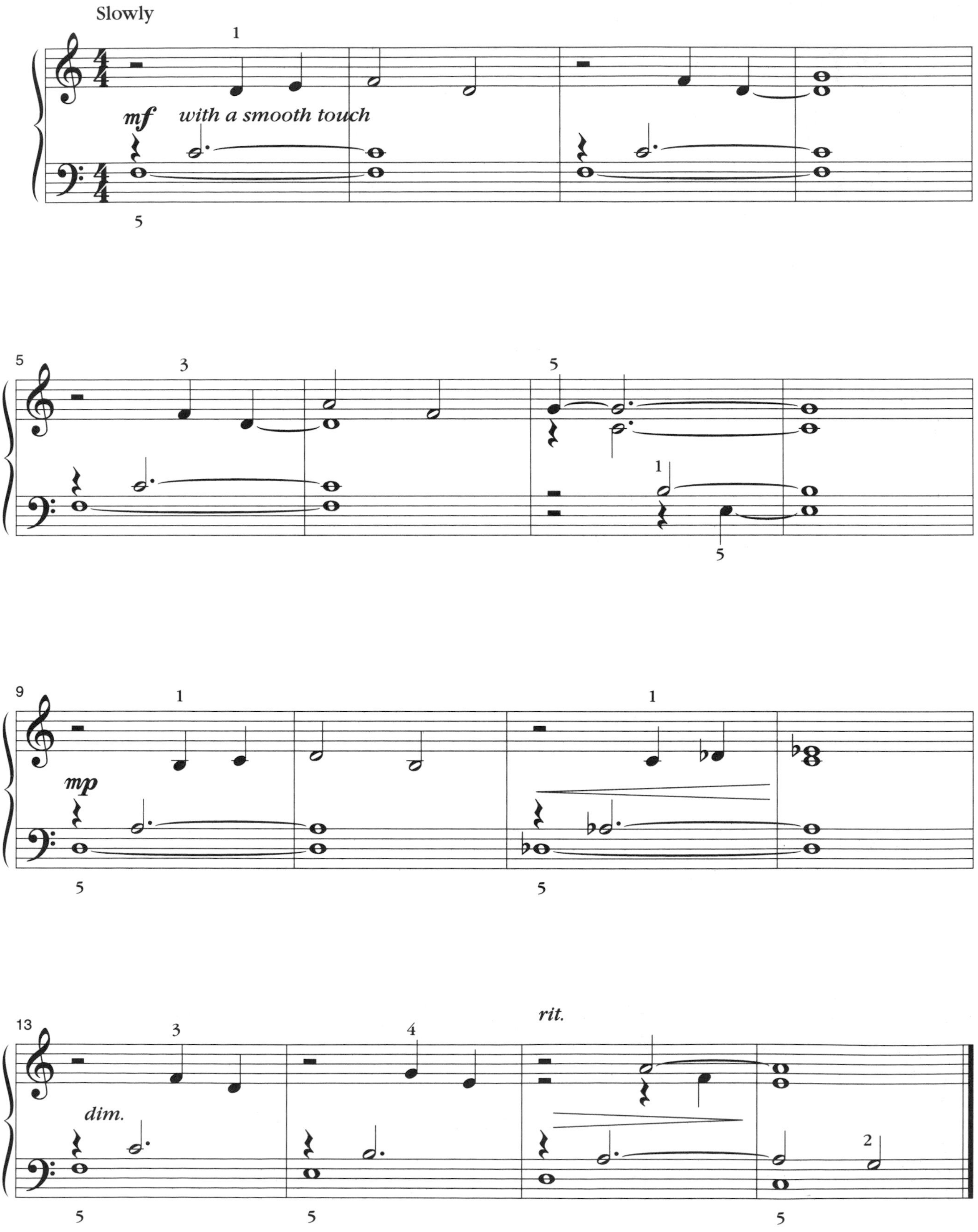

MUSICIANSHIP ACTIVITIES

Complete the following exercises which review various topics introduced in Chapter One.

Harmonic and Melodic Intervals

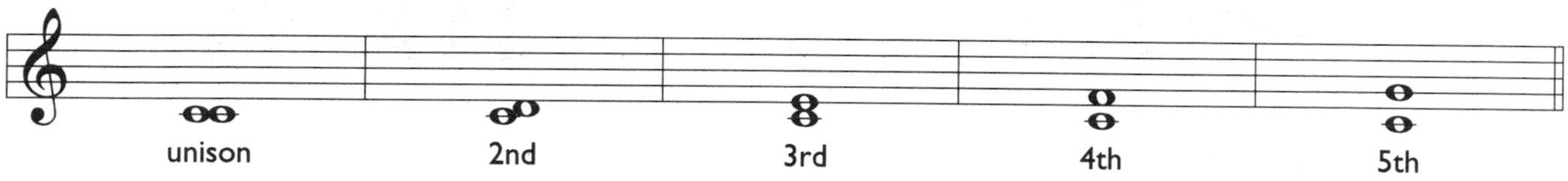

Intervals may also be played as *melodic* intervals, e.g., one tone follows another. Study and identify the melodic intervals below.

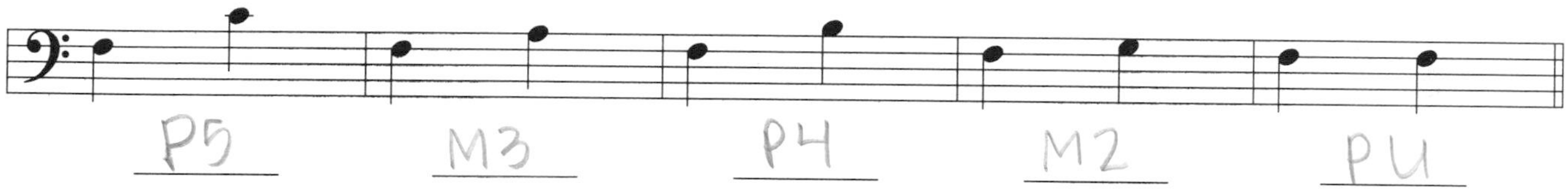

Study and identify the harmonic intervals below.

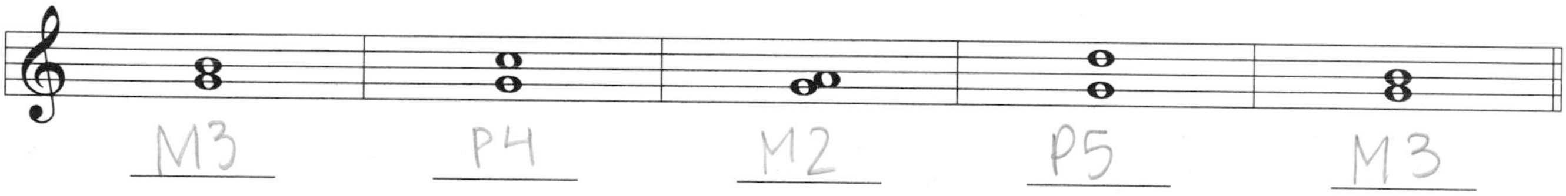

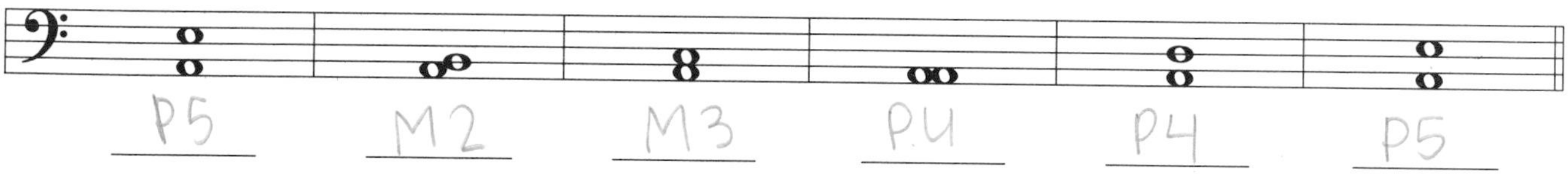

Write notes to create the given harmonic intervals above AND below the given note.

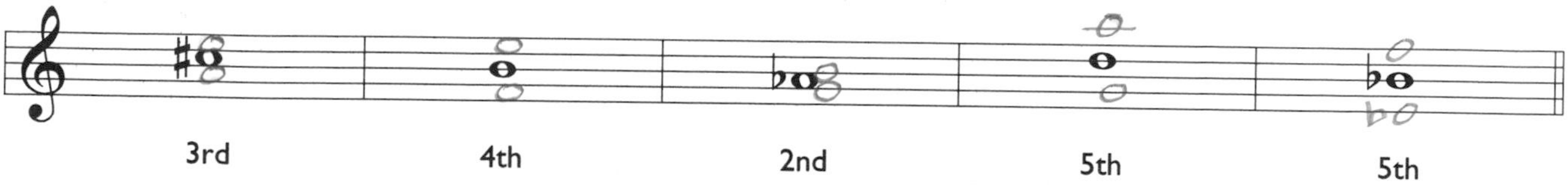

Improvising

Improvise melodies using the black key pentatonic scales shown below. Note the fingering of each pattern. The teacher accompaniments stress various moods. Use elements of repetition, sequence (same idea on different pitches) and contrast (change in the melody). Use ♩, 𝅗𝅥, 𝅗𝅥. and 𝅝 notes. Develop four-bar phrases in the beginning. Later, expand the length of the improvisation.

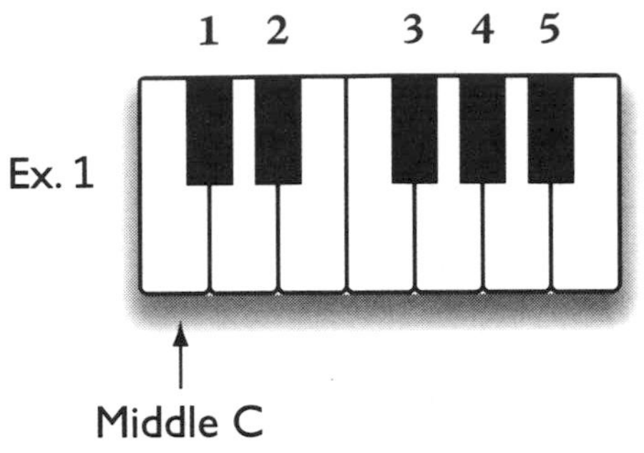

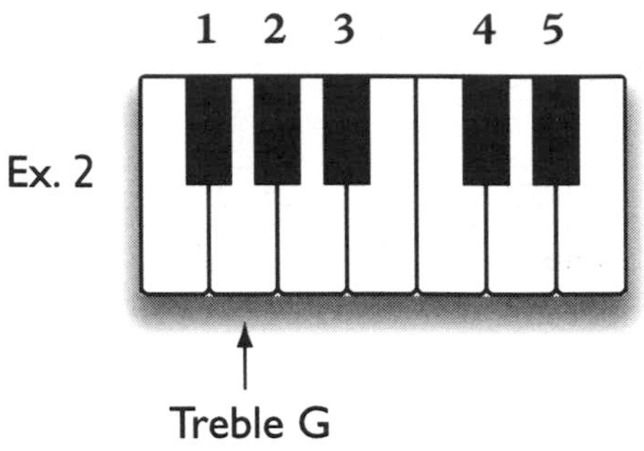

Teacher Patterns (will work for either Ex. 1 or Ex. 2)
Keep repeating each pattern until the improvisation comes to a logical conclusion.

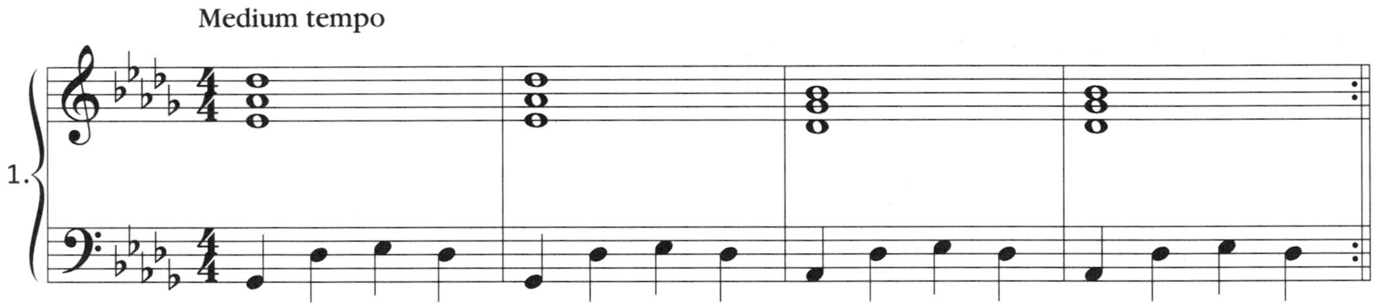

Technical Studies

The following exercises emphasize ease in playing. Avoid any tension. Drop into the keys with a natural follow-through (slight drop) of the wrist.

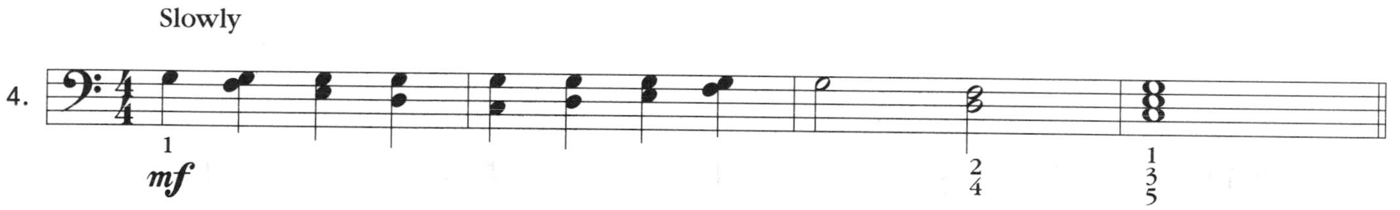

Repeat with 12321 and 34543

Repeat with 12321 and 34543

SUGGESTED PLAYING EXAM TOPICS
CHAPTER ONE

1. Play any sight reading study with good accuracy, pages 11–14.

2. Play at least one accompaniment fluently. Select from pages 16 or 17.

3. Play one duet with good ensemble skills. Select from pages 19–21.

4. Play a selected piece from the *Solo Repertoire* section found on pages 22–28. (Two short pieces on one page count as one piece.)

5. Play harmonic intervals found on page 31 from *Technical Studies*.

6. Improvise a short melody using the black key pentatonic scale on page 30.

2 chapter Major Pentachords, Major Triads, Eighth Notes, Harmonization, Keyboard Touches, Pedaling, Repertoire, Musicianship Activities, and Technical Studies

The Major Pentachord (Major 5-Finger Pattern)

Play the following two examples which illustrate an important structure called the *major pentachord*, or *major 5-finger pattern*. Chant the letter names in rhythm as you play each example.

C Major Pentachord – RH

G Major Pentachord – LH

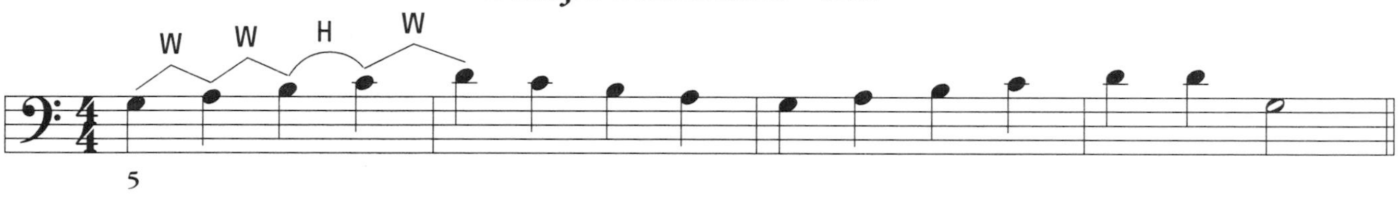

Whole Steps and Half Steps

The *major pentachord* consists of a certain step arrangement of piano keys. A *half step* is the distance from one key to the very next key. A *whole step* consists of two half steps, with one key skipped. Study the diagrams below. H = half step; W = whole step.

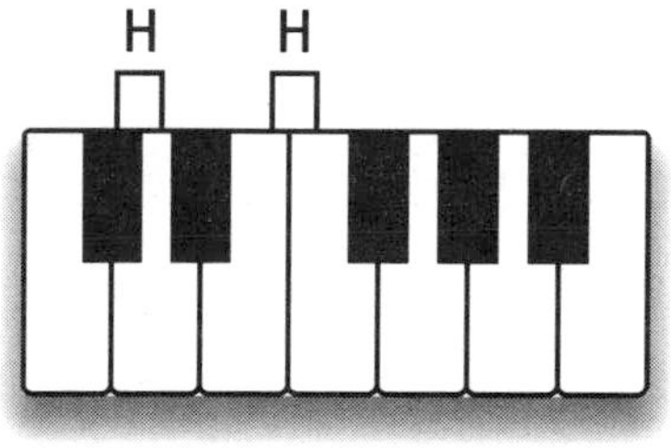

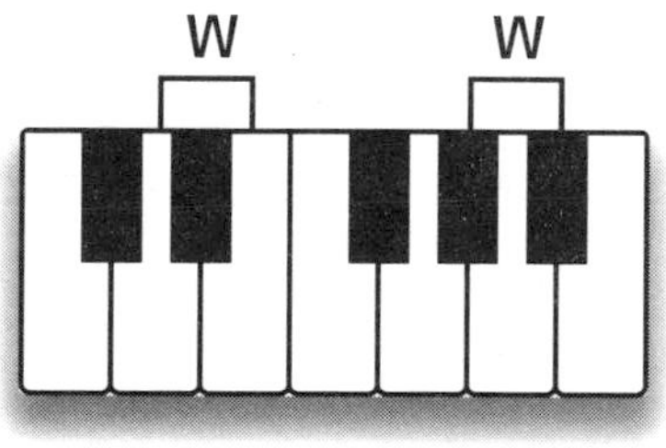

A major pentachord (major 5-finger pattern or major pentascale) consists of the following: whole step, whole step, half step, whole step. Memorize this pattern. Each pentachord starts with a keynote which names the pattern (C major pentachord, G major pentachord, etc.).

Pentachord Tunes

Before playing *A Russian Tune* and *A Danish Tune,* identify the pentachords used. Tap the rhythm in each hand before playing. Chant letter names while playing.

A RUSSIAN TUNE

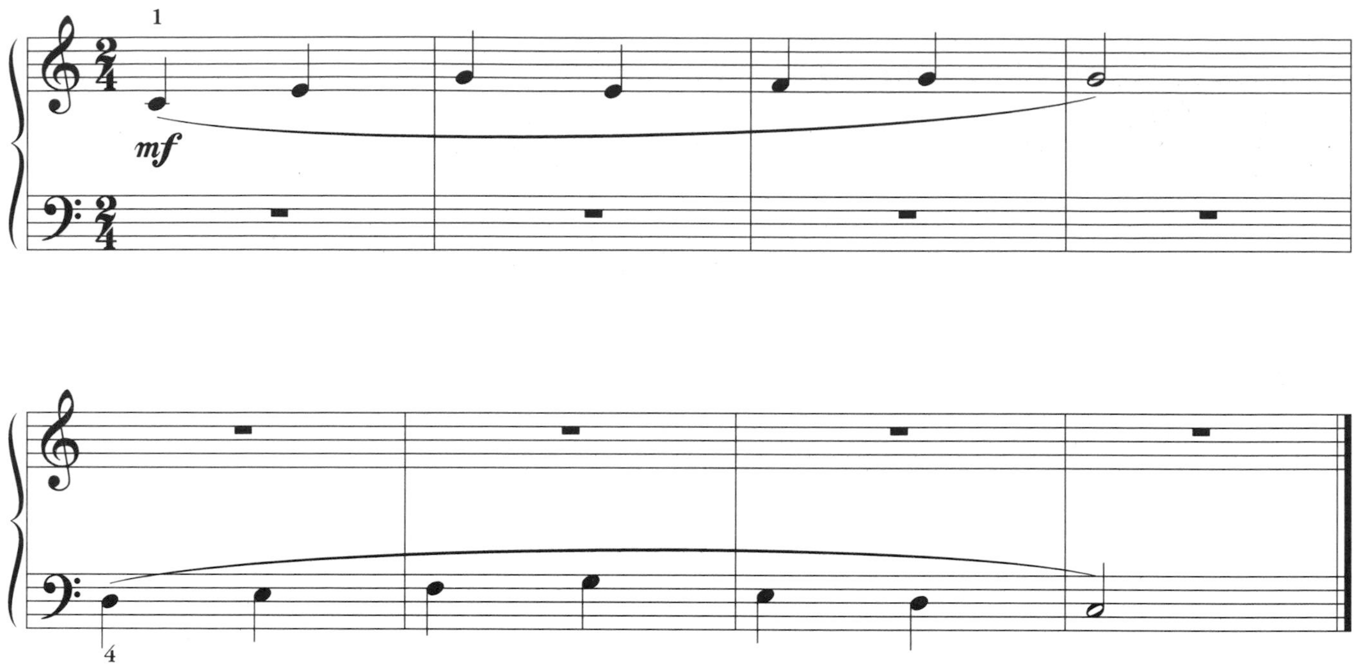

The quarter note that begins *A Danish Tune* is another illustration of an upbeat. See the explanation of an upbeat on page 19 of Chapter One.

A DANISH TUNE

Before playing each of the following tunes, name the keynote, check the arrangement of whole and half steps, tap and chant letter names in rhythm, and set a moderate tempo. Identify the pentachord used in *A Hungarian Tune*. What sharp is used? Why?

A HUNGARIAN TUNE

A FRENCH TUNE

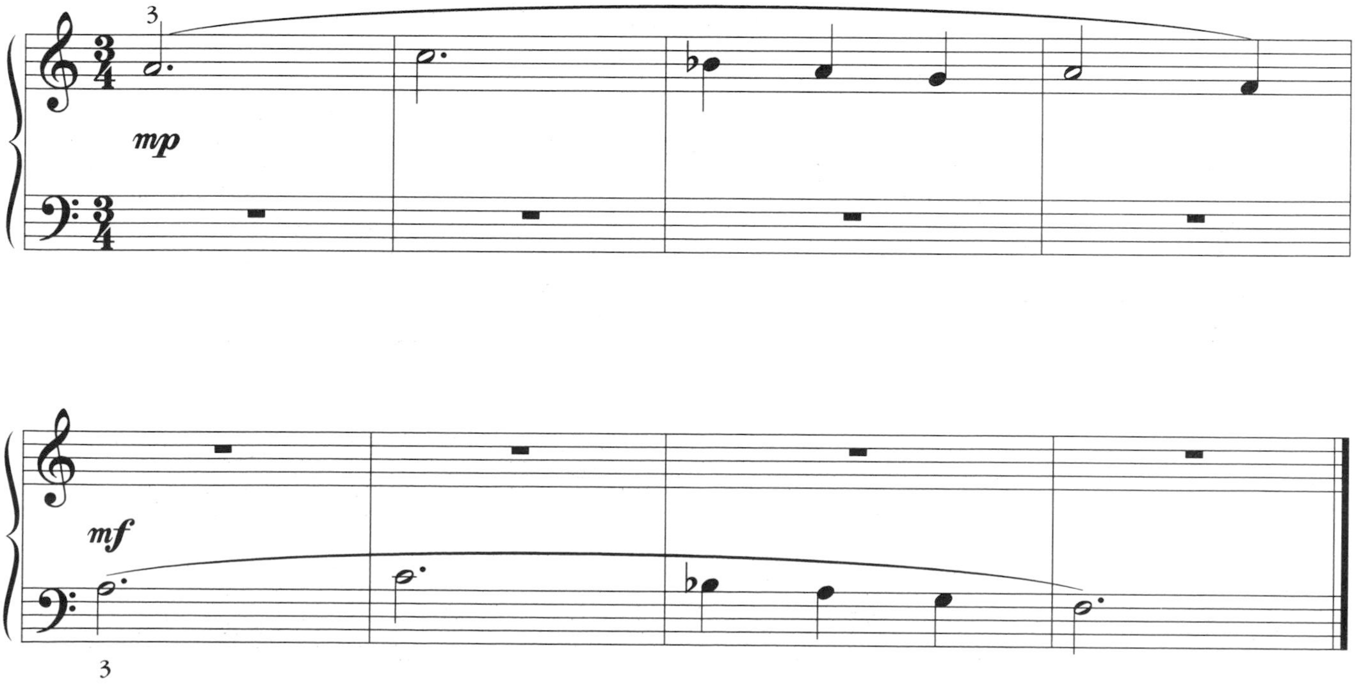

Major Triads (Chords)

In a major pentachord, the first, third and fifth tones form a major triad.

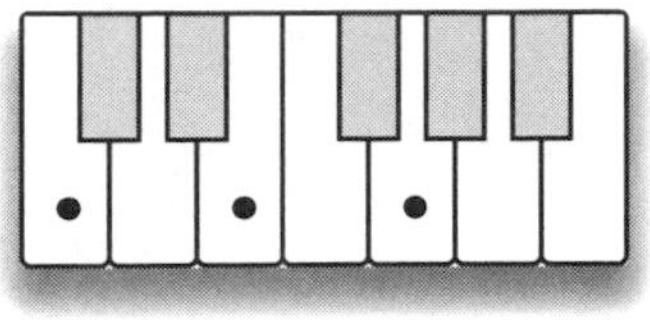

C Major Triad

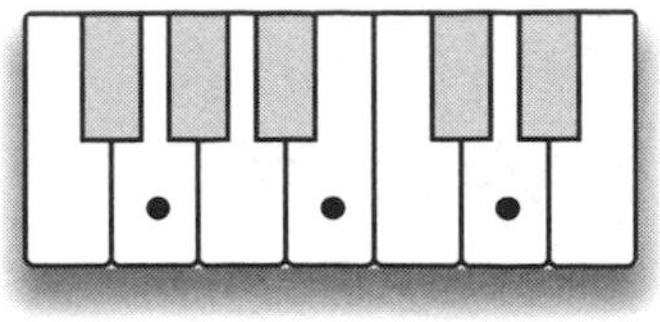

G Major Triad

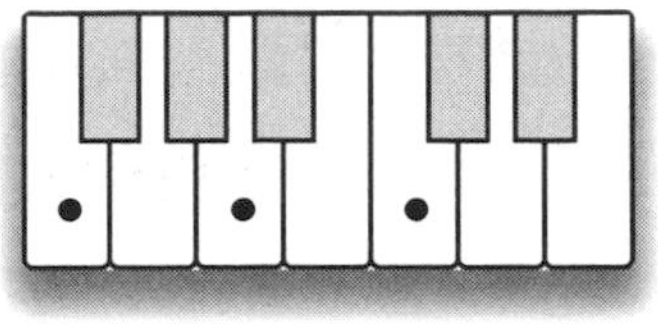

F Major Triad

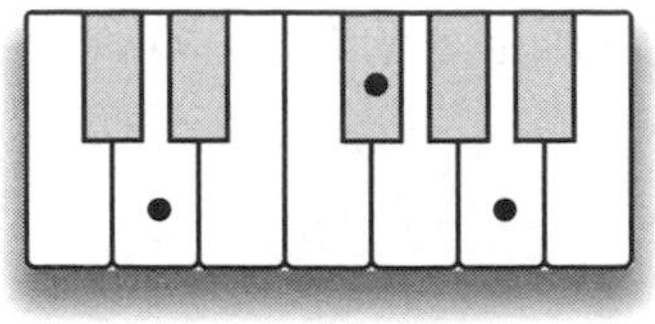

D Major Triad

Triads may be outlined in melodies, or may be "blocked" (all tones sounding at once). A triad is a three-note *chord*. Triads are added to enrich the melody.

AMERICAN MELODY

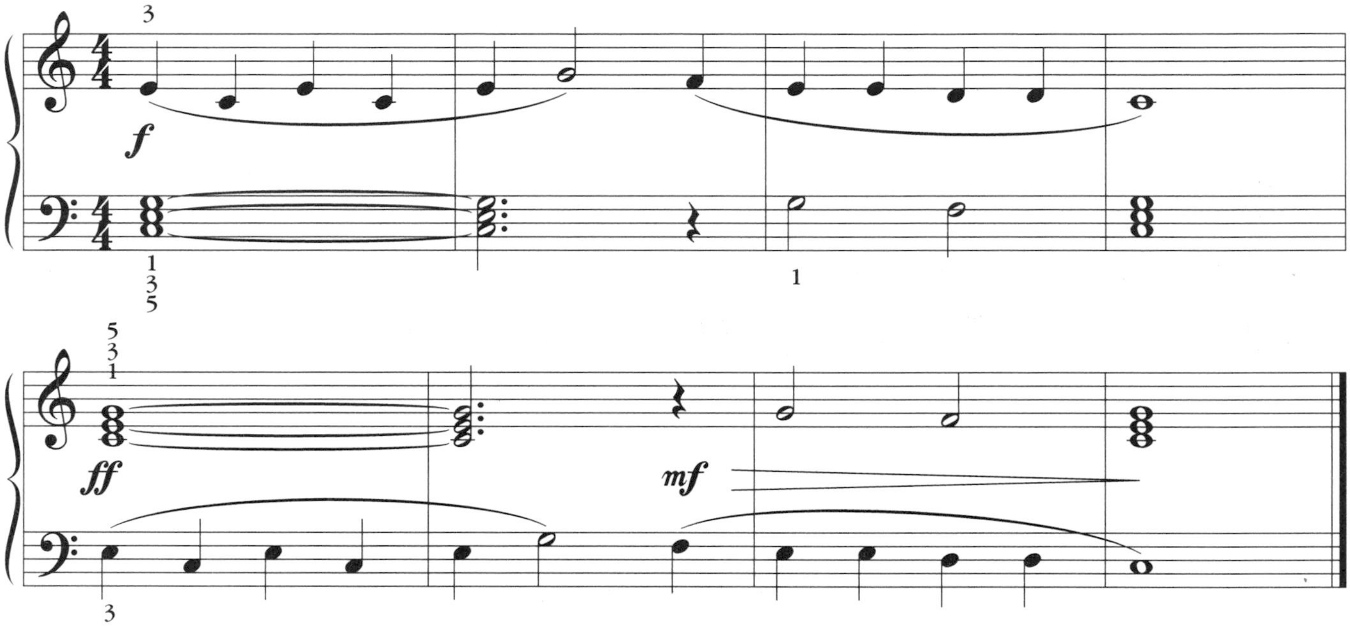

FOLK MELODY

In *American Melody* and *A Latin Melody* lighten your touch on the chords so that the melody sings out.

AMERICAN MELODY

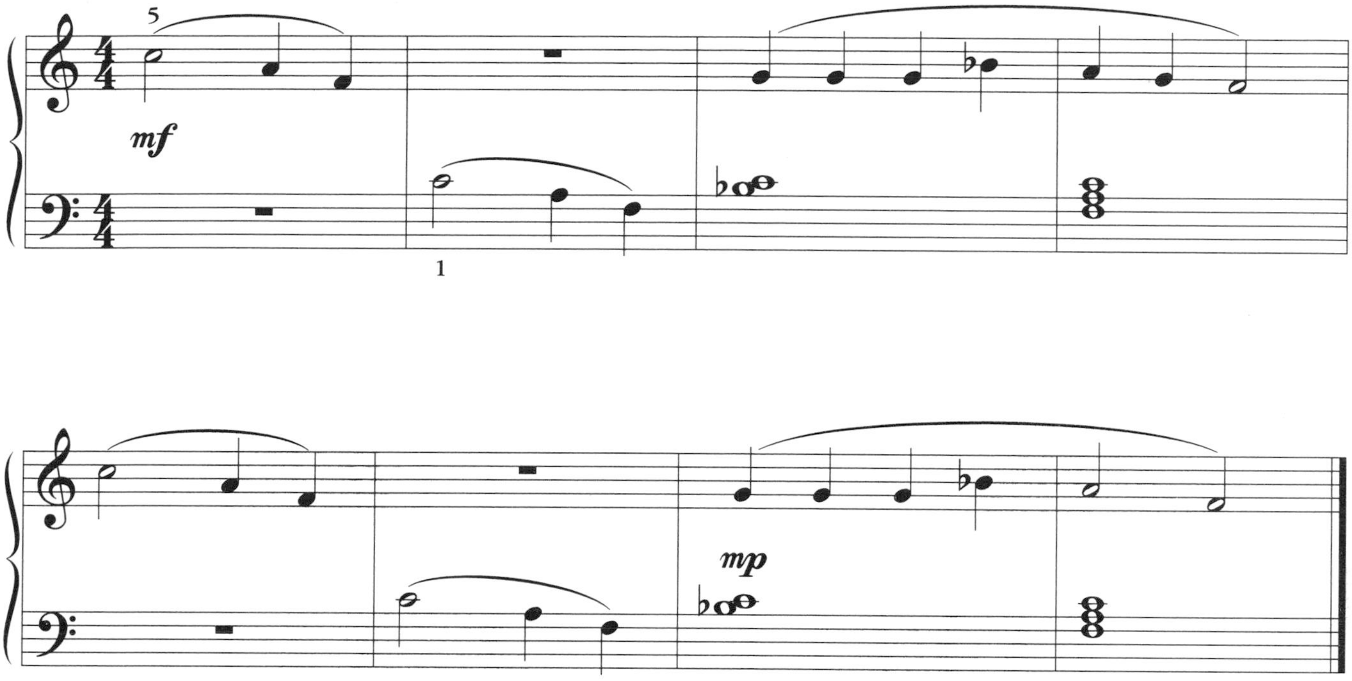

A LATIN MELODY

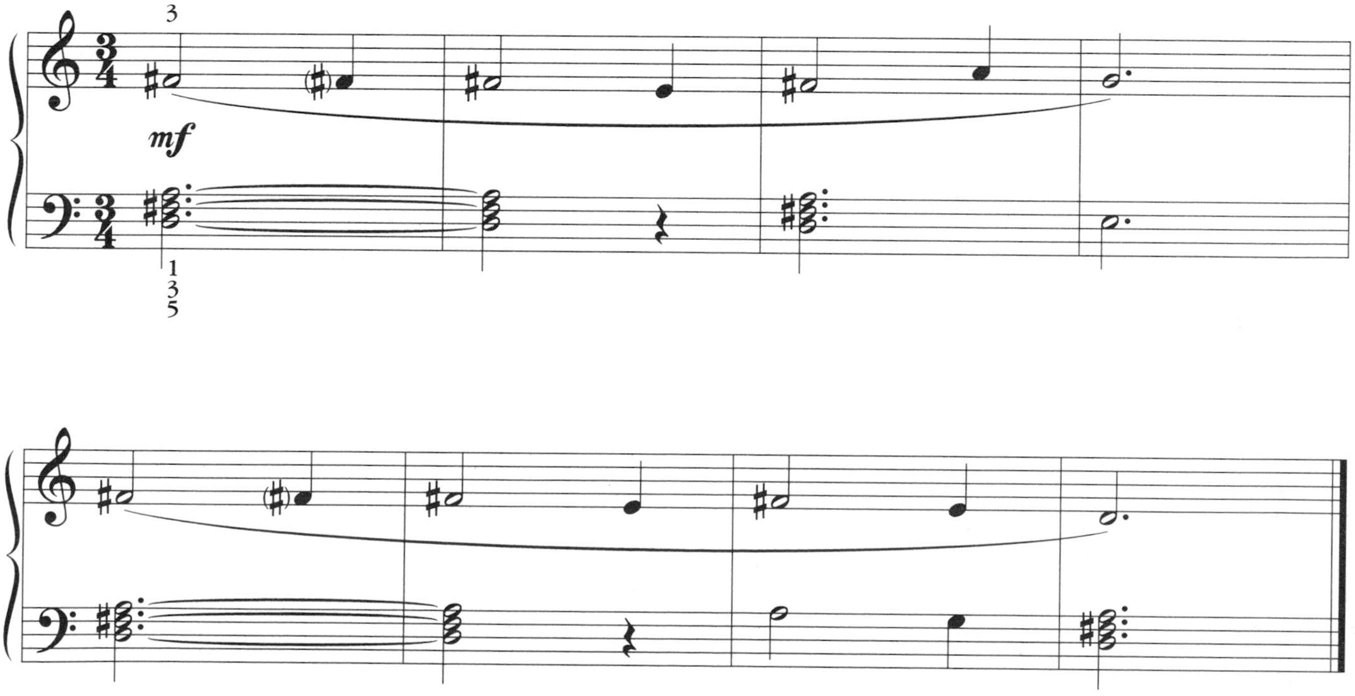

Unison Playing

Freight Train illustrates both hands playing in *unison*. You will notice that the LH plays the same tones an octave lower than the RH. Follow the fingering; hands are in various 5-finger patterns.

FREIGHT TRAIN

American Folk Song

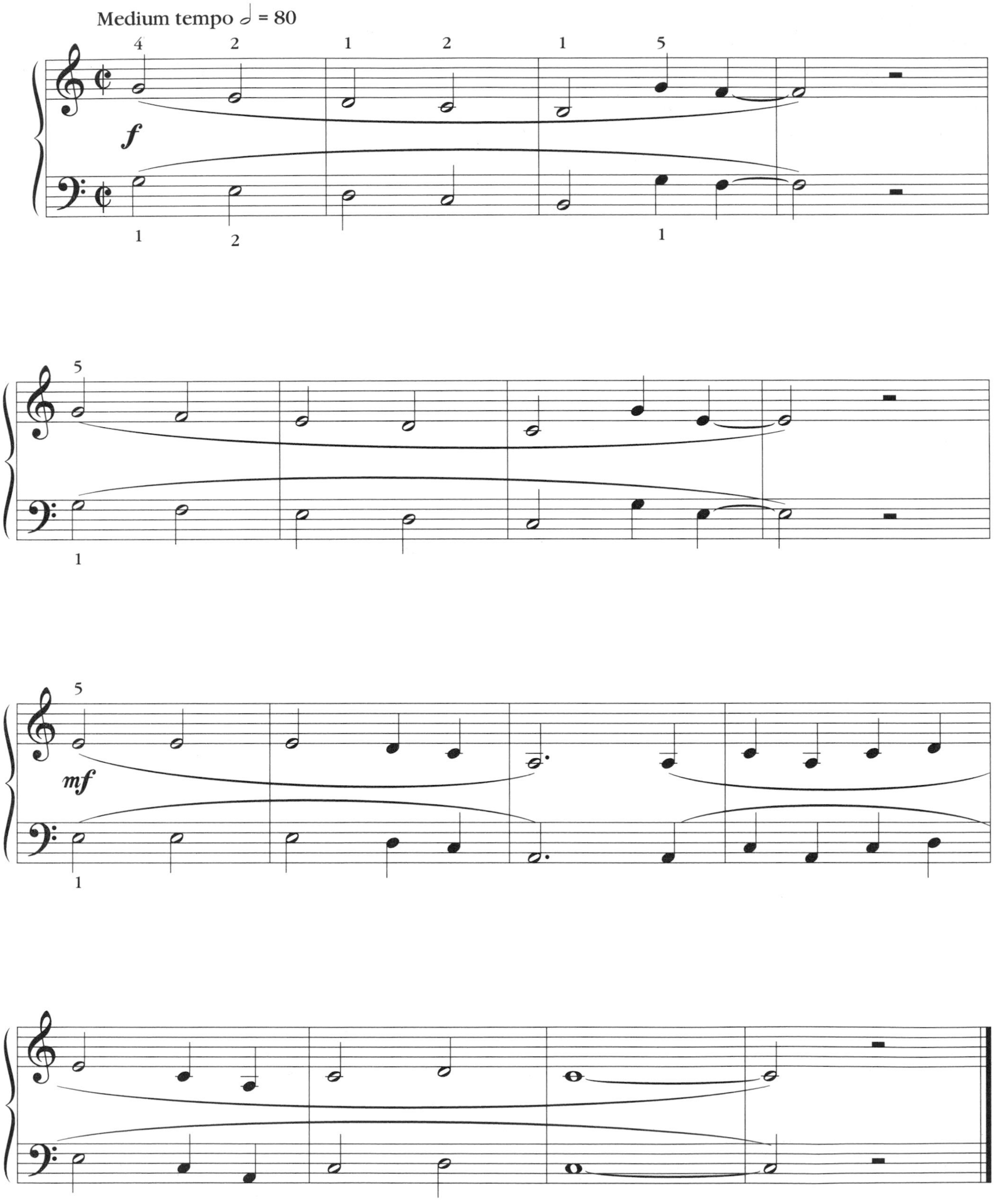

Additional 5-Finger Melodies in Unison with Occasional Triads

Play the following melodies which feature unison playing (both hands playing the melody) and the use of chords.

RUSSIAN MELODY

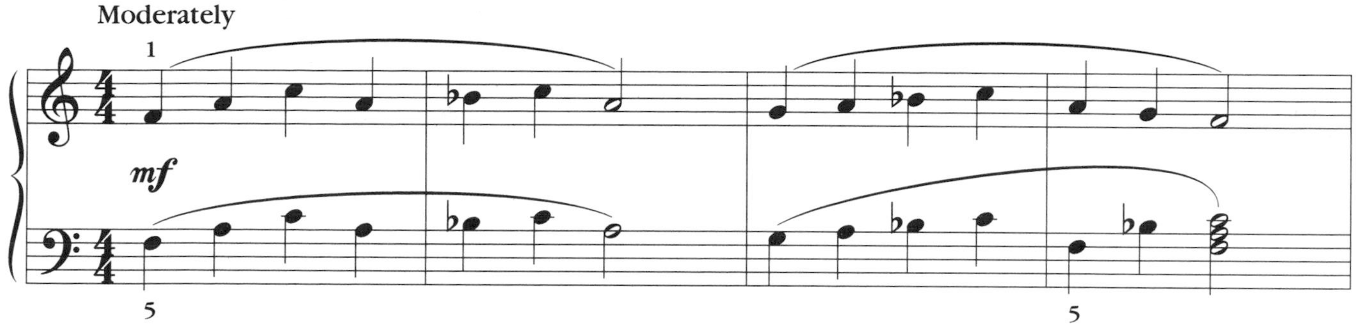

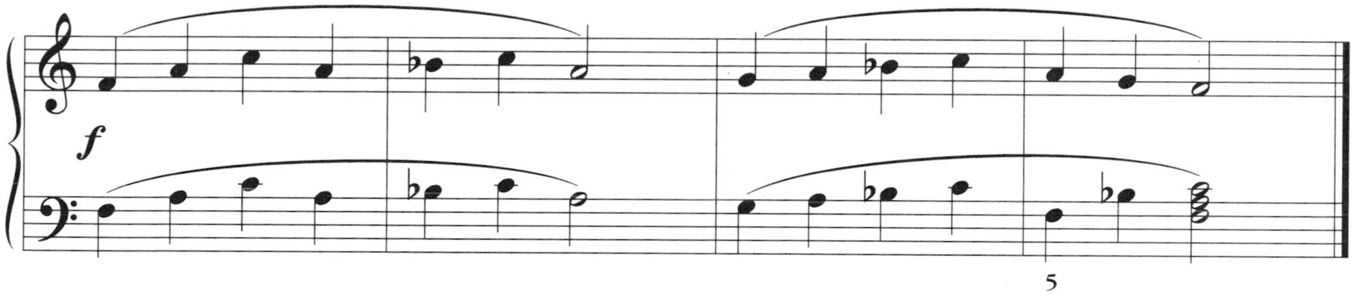

DUTCH MELODY

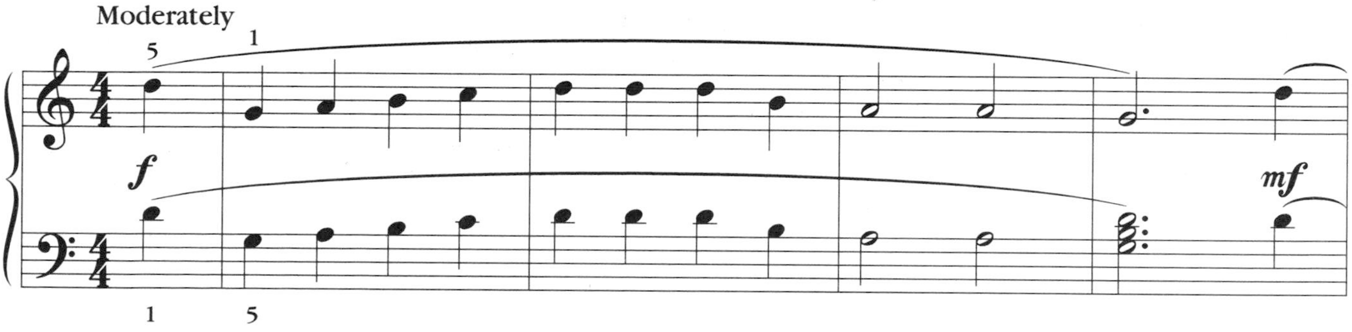

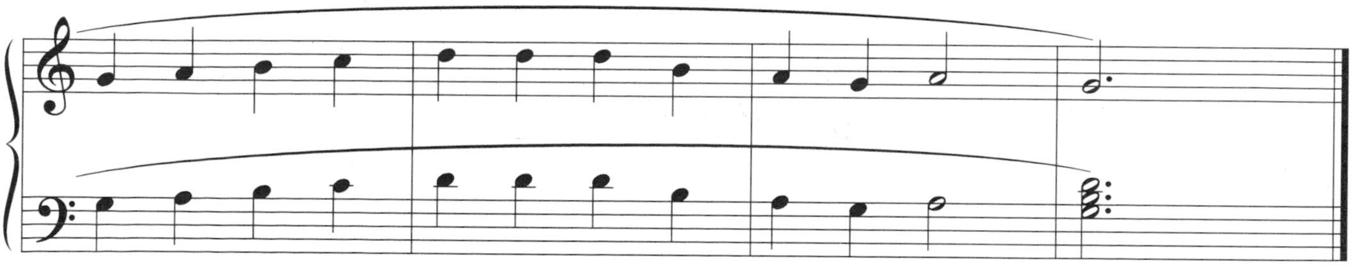

BRITISH MELODY

In *French Melody* circle the chord outlines.

FRENCH MELODY

FOLK MELODY

Andante

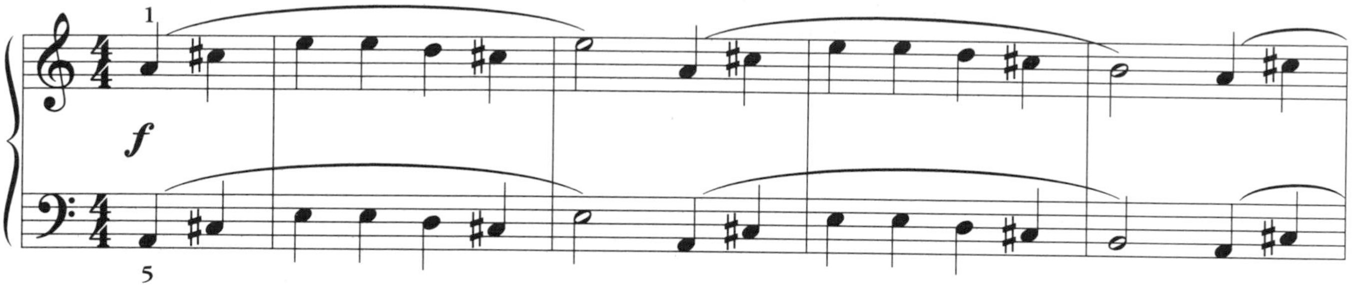

AUSTRIAN MELODY

Moderato

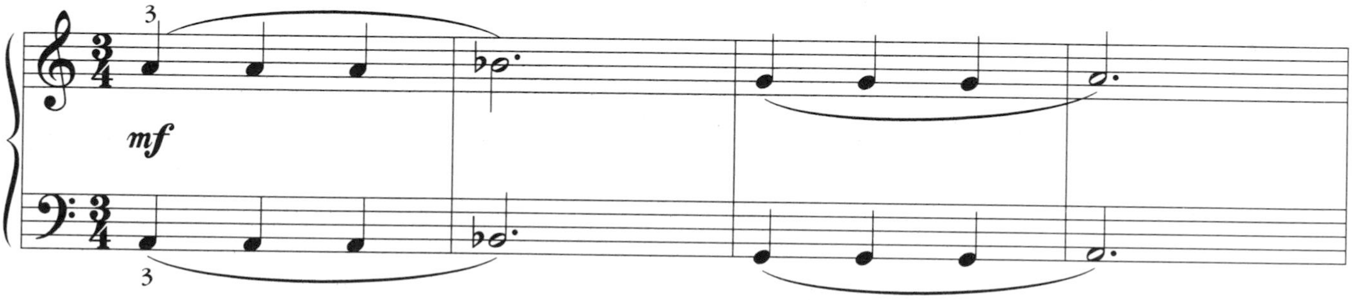

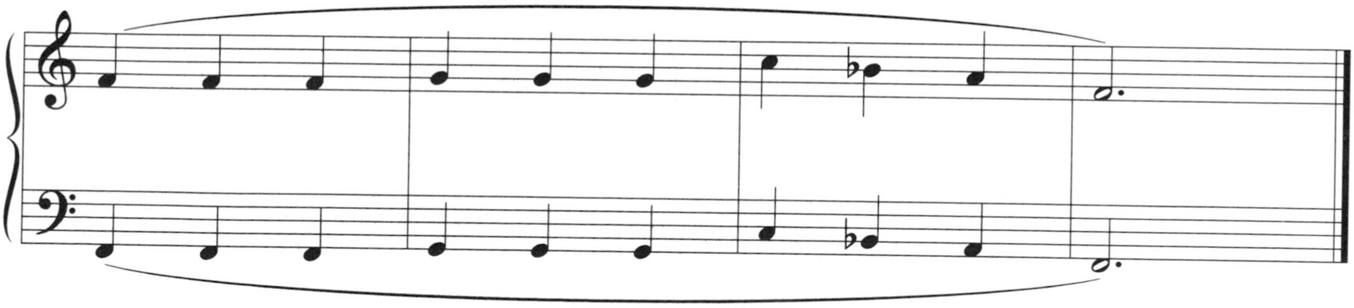

Eighth Notes

In meters with a **4** as the bottom number, eighth notes (♫ or ♪♪) are grouped two to a beat (♫ = ♩). Tap the rhythms of each hand found in *Casey Jones* directly below. Note that hands come together at the end and outline the major pentachord. Chant eighth notes as "1–a" or "1–and." Play each hand an octave higher when the accompaniment is added.

CASEY JONES

U.S. Railroad Song

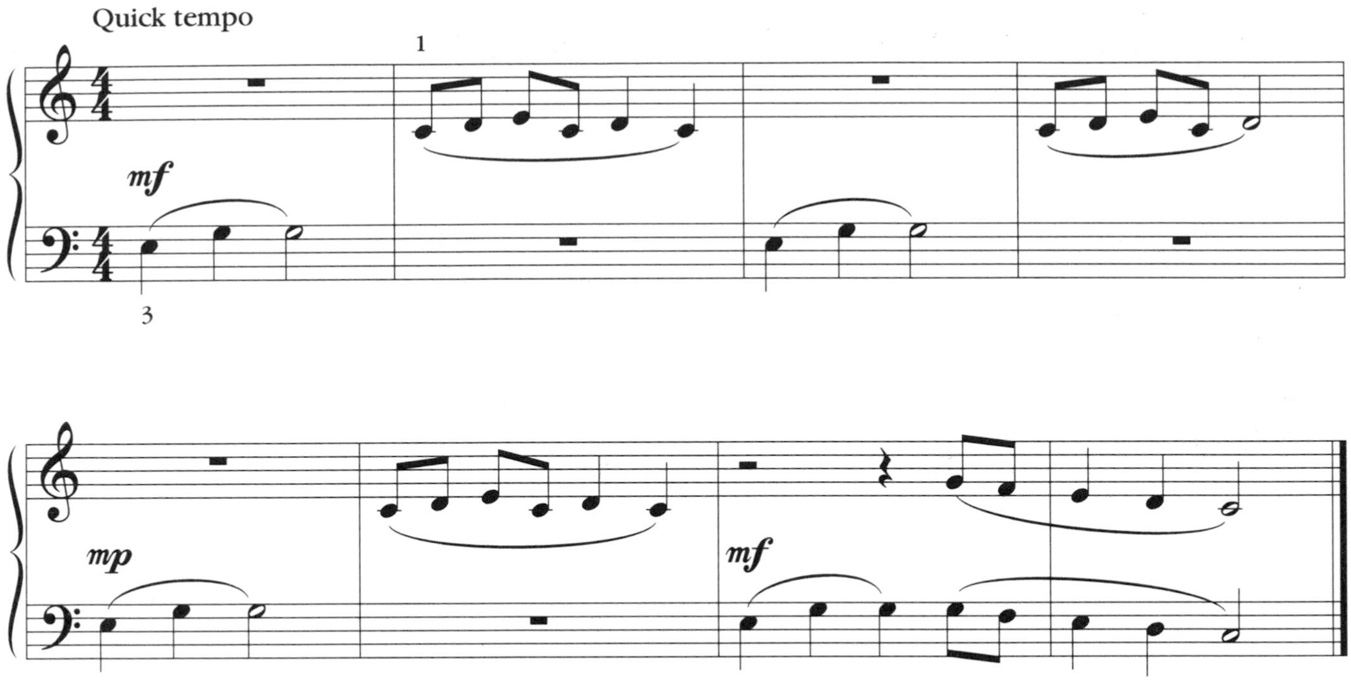

Teacher accompaniment for *Casey Jones*.

arr. **James Lyke**

Melodies with Eighth Notes

Play the following melodies. Tap and count the rhythm before playing.

DUTCH MELODY

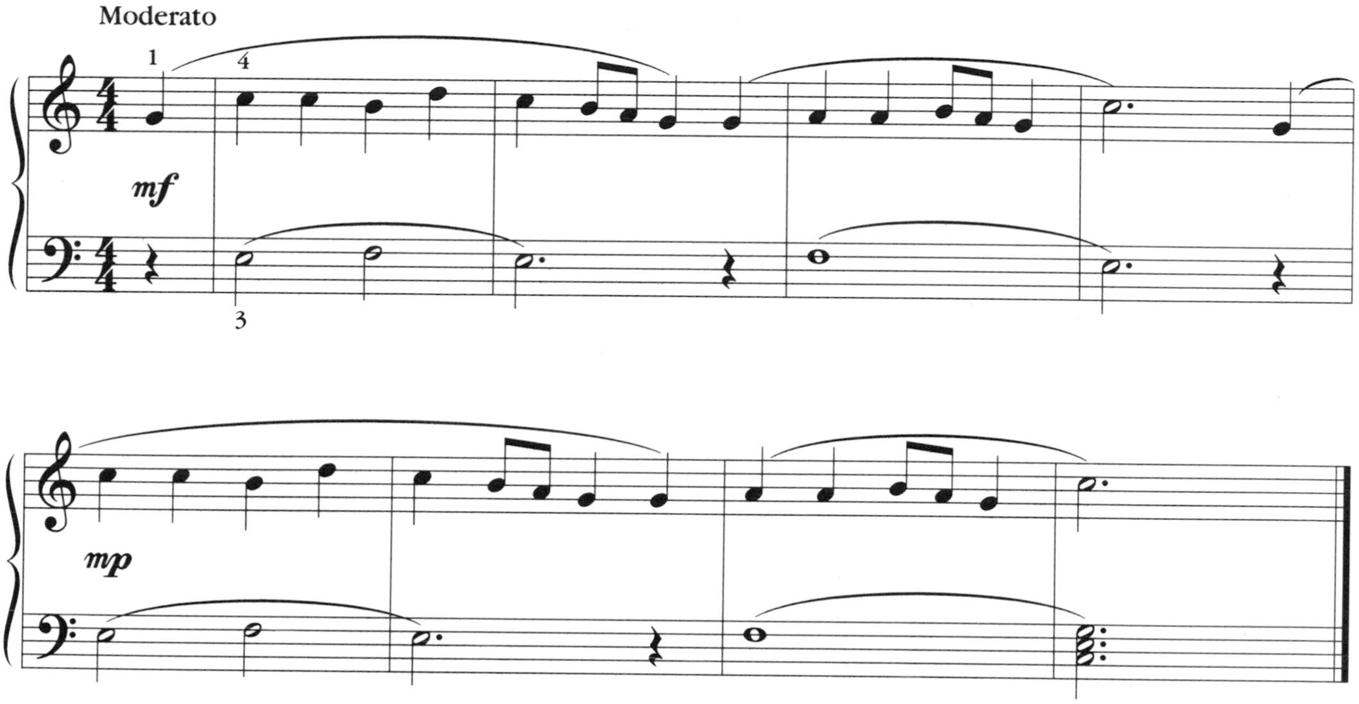

AUSTRIAN MELODY

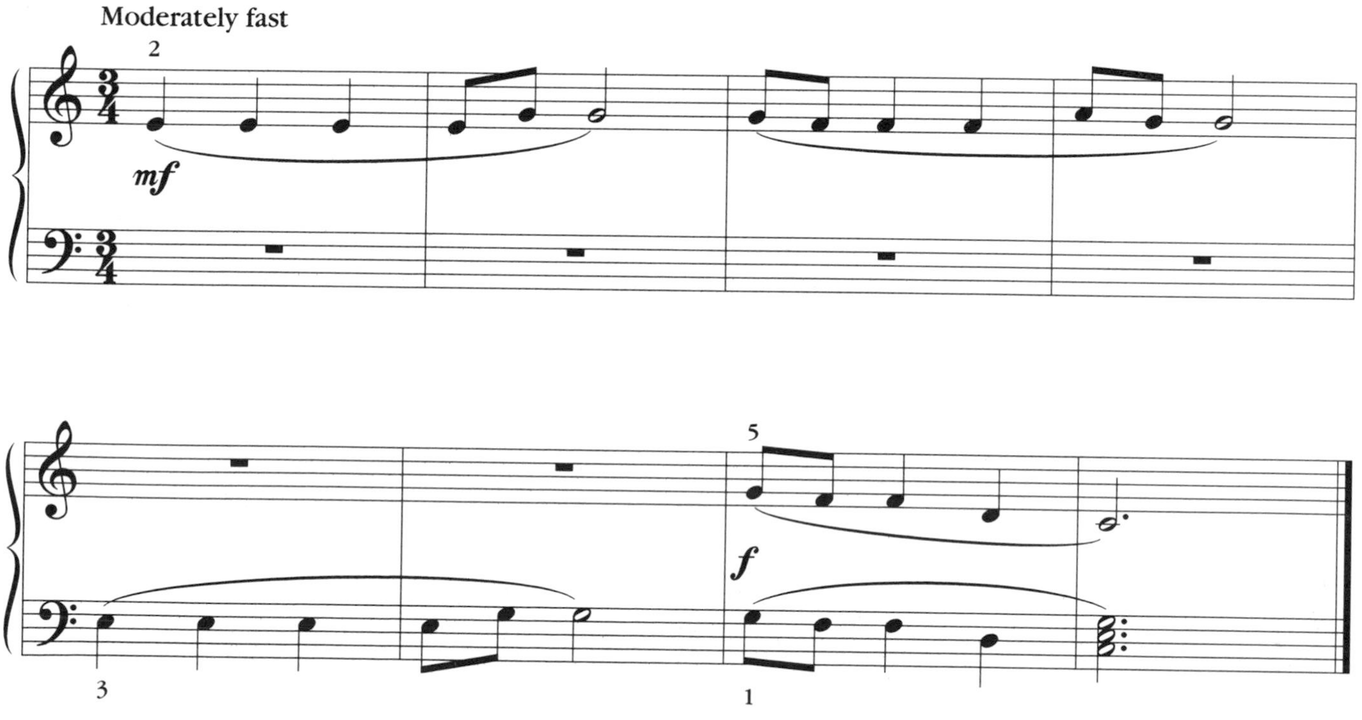

Triad Outlines: Two Versions of *Green Gravel* and Two New 5-Finger Patterns

Folk melodies are often handed down in varied versions. Compare the British version of *Green Gravel* to the New England version. Find triad outlines in each melody. *Two new pentachords are introduced.* Identify each major pentachord. Place hands over the proper notes, count, and play. Observe the slur marks.

GREEN GRAVEL

British

GREEN GRAVEL

New England

Staccato Touch: A Review

Dots above or below noteheads (♩ = ♪𝄾) indicate *staccato touch*. *Staccato* is an Italian term meaning detached.

POLISH TUNE

WHO'S THAT TAPPING AT THE WINDOW?

Virginia

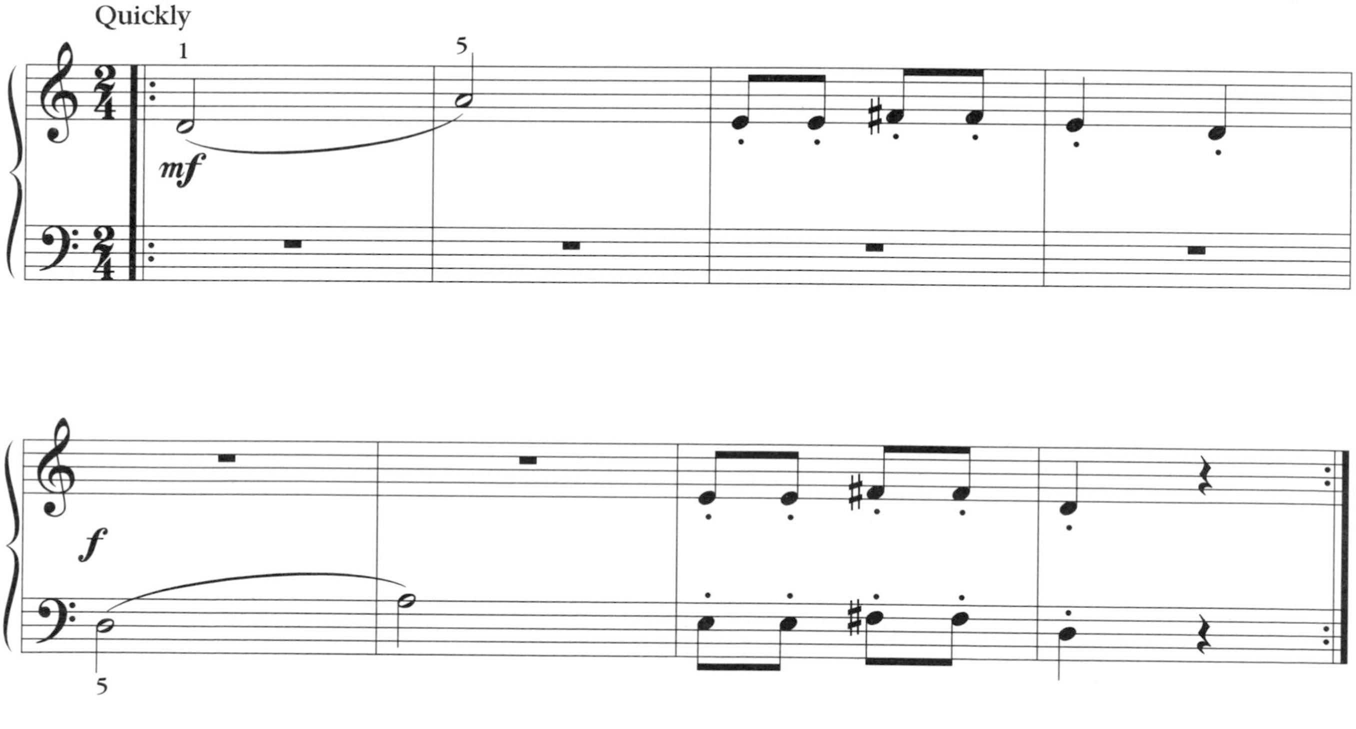

Ukrainian

With spirit

Céline Bussières-Lessard

Moderately slow

Using the Pedals*

Damper Pedal: When the right pedal on an acoustic piano is depressed, the dampers are lifted from the strings. This allows the strings to continue to vibrate – and the tones to sound – even after the fingers have left the keys. The *damper* pedal produces a sustained *legato* effect between melody notes and chordal figures. On digital pianos, the same effect is created electronically.

Sostenuto Pedal: The middle pedal is called the *sostenuto* pedal (*sost.* or *s.p.*). This pedal catches and holds any dampers that are raised at the moment it is depressed. While this pedal is held down, it doesn't interfere with any other dampers raised while playing their notes or using the damper (right) pedal. On moderately priced upright pianos, this pedal may not function.

Una Corda Pedal: The left pedal is called the *una corda* pedal (*u.c.*). It is somethimes referred to as the soft pedal. Depressing this pedal shifts the hammers so that only two of the three strings are struck. The release of this pedal is indicated by the words *tre corde* (*t.c.*) which mean that three strings are sounded again.

Syncopated Pedal: Chordal music is easier to pedal than purely melodic music because both melody and accompanying chords are based on the same chord formation. When passing from one tone or chord to the next we use the *syncopated* or *legato* pedal in order to achieve an unbroken, *legato* effect. Play the tone first, then quickly change the pedal. The pedal is depressed *after* the tone begins to sound, and connections are made without a blur. As each change is indicated, the pedal is released and depressed immediately after the key goes down. This stops the sound of the preceding tone. Change quickly in order to retain the sustained *legato* effect.

Melodic Pedaling

Brace RH finger 2 with the thumb behind it while playing the following pedal exercise.

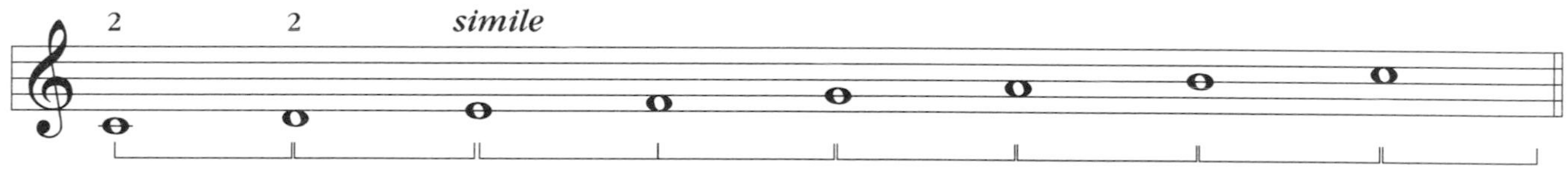

Pedal Markings

Pedal markings are indicated in several ways.

down (depress) hold up (release)

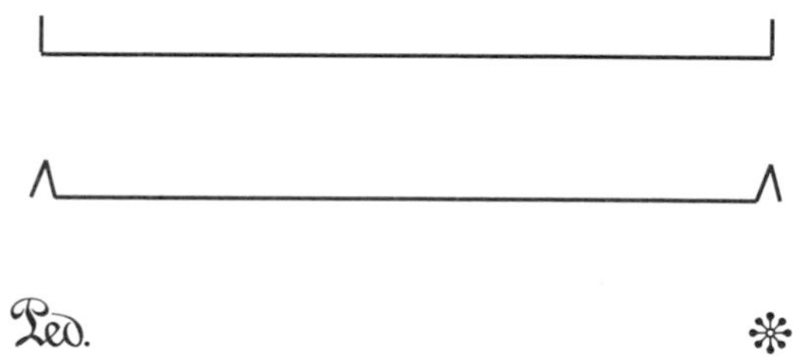

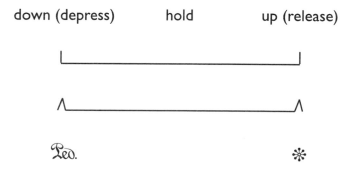

* In addition to the two pedal studies on the next page, there are several pieces in the Solo Reprtoire section that require the use of the damper pedal.

Two Pedal Studies

Both pedal studies employ the damper (right) pedal. At first, practice each piece without using the pedal.

PEDAL STUDY NO. 1

Tony Caramia

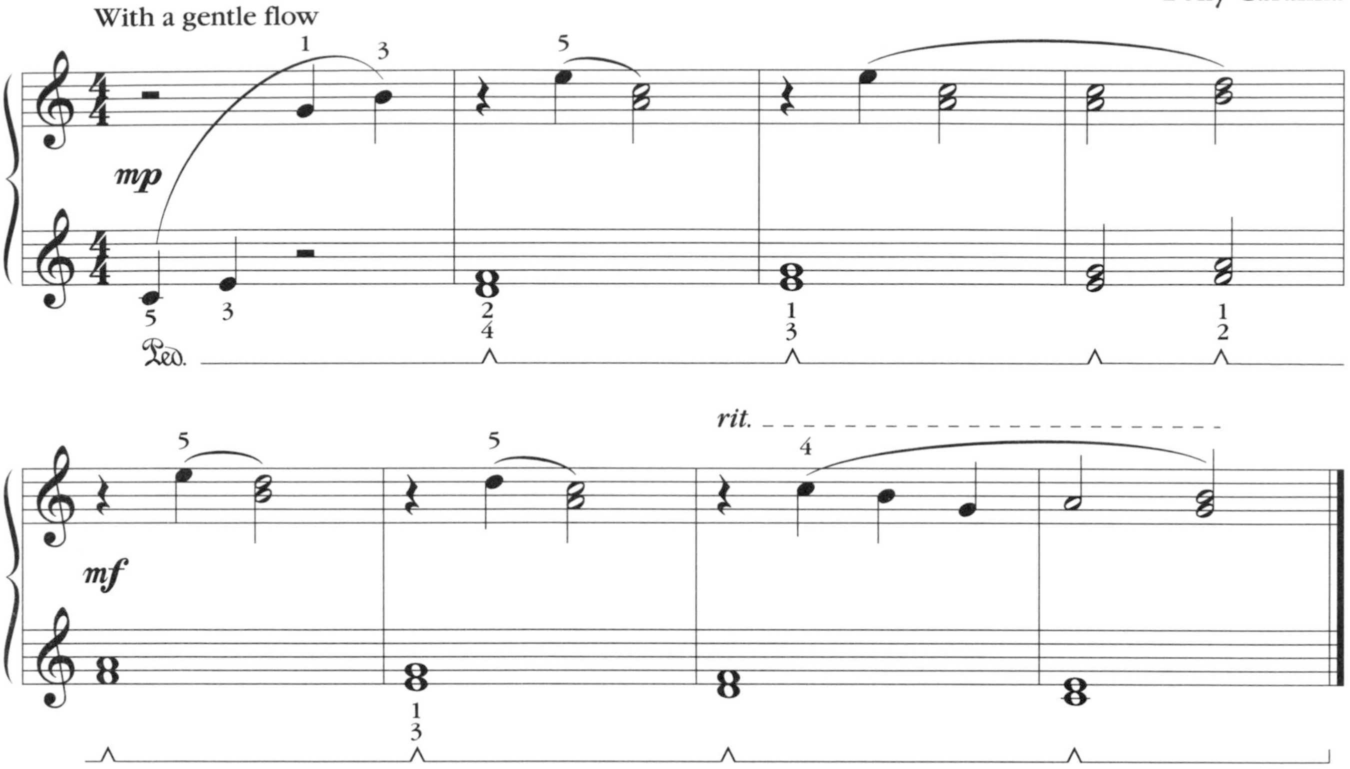

Pedal Study No. 2 uses a new time signature, $\frac{6}{4}$. Count 6 beats to a measure.

PEDAL STUDY NO. 2

Tony Caramia

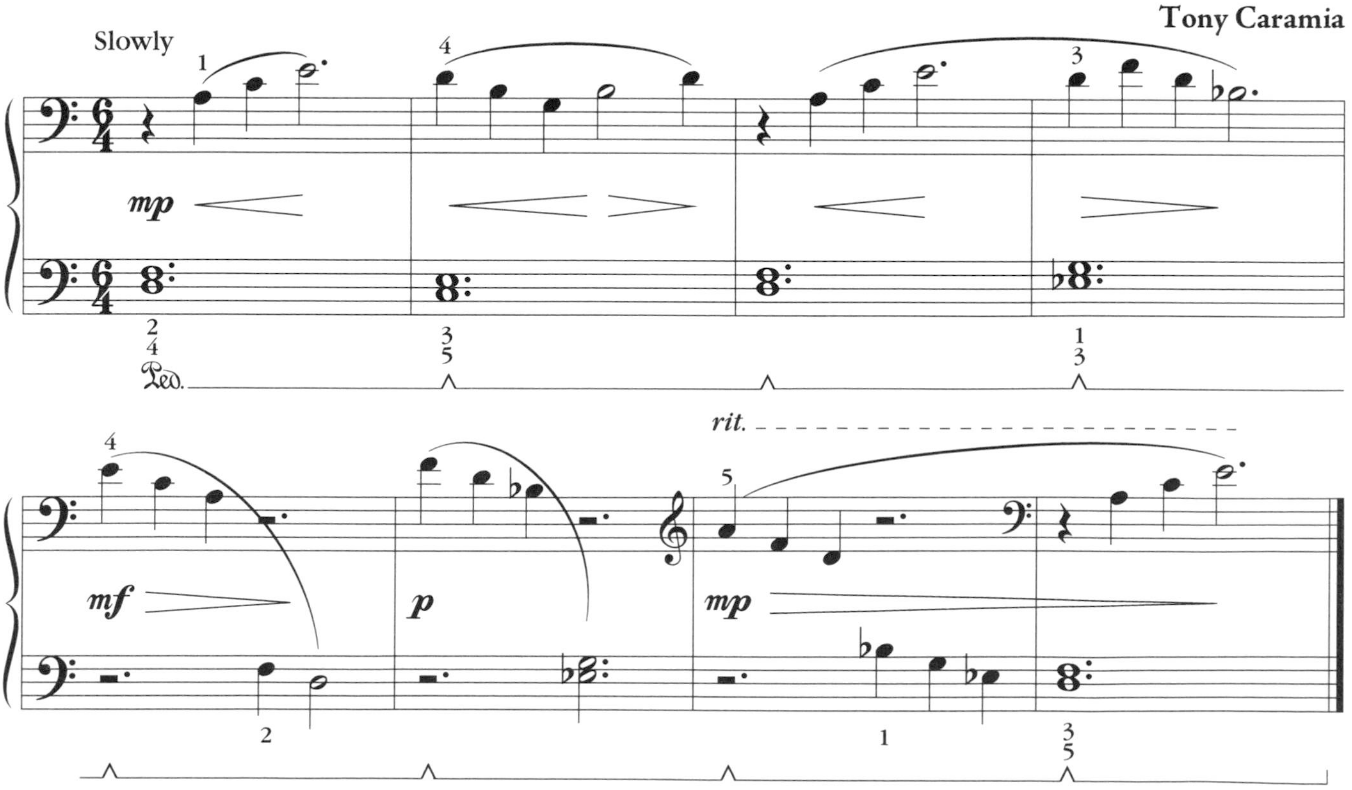

Music for Sight Reading and Transposing

Before reading the following studies, establish a routine which includes: 1) tapping and chanting the rhythm of each hand, 2) locating starting positions from the given fingering, 3) identifying helpful landmark notes, and 4) analyzing melodic and chordal shapes after a preliminary scan of the music. Take note of any errors in your playing and determine the cause.

James Lyke

Moderately bright

Transpose to the G pentachord.

Folk Song

Moderately slow

Transpose to the C pentachord.

German

With spirit

Transpose to the D pentachord.

Geoffrey Haydon

Moderately fast

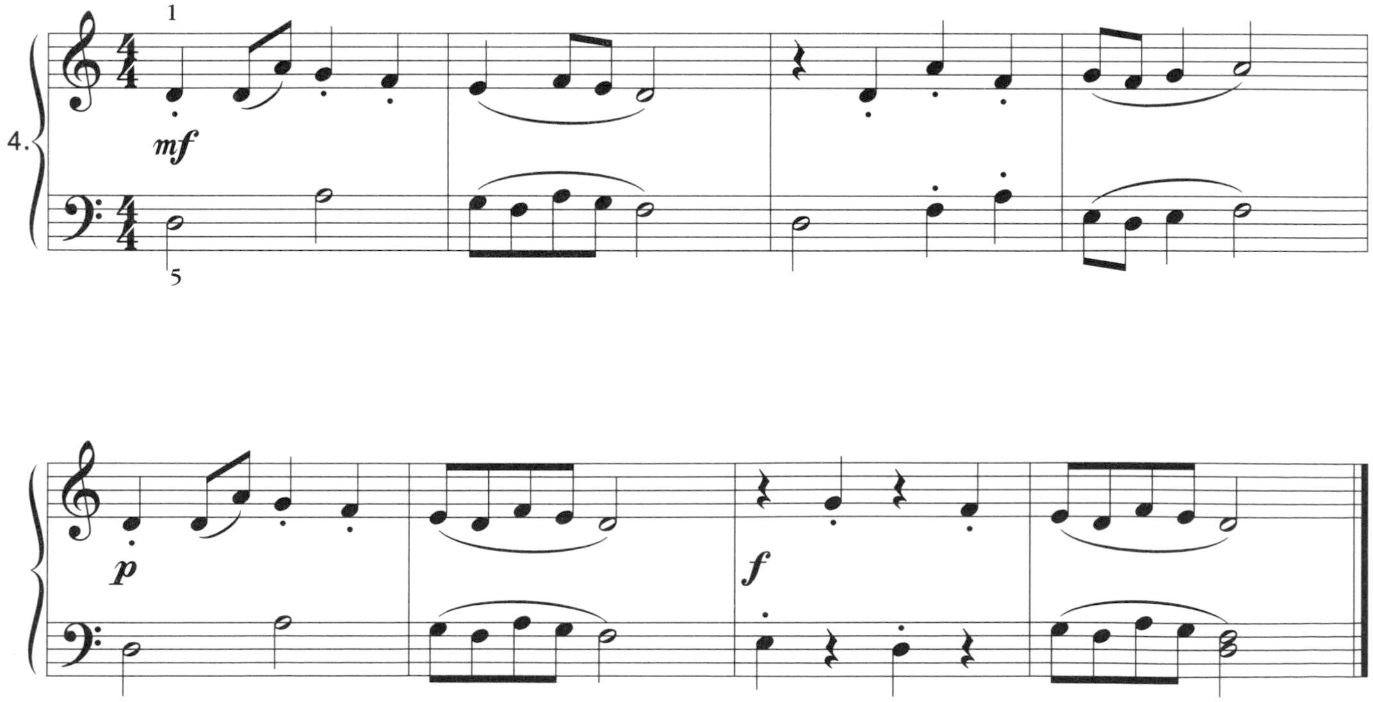

German

Moderately slow

Transpose to the F pentachord.

Study No. 6 requires *rapid shifts* in both hands. Use the measure of rest to prepare for the new position.

Slow march

James Lyke

German

Transpose to the C pentachord.

Note the new pentachord (A♭ major) in *Study No. 8.* How far apart are the hands?

American

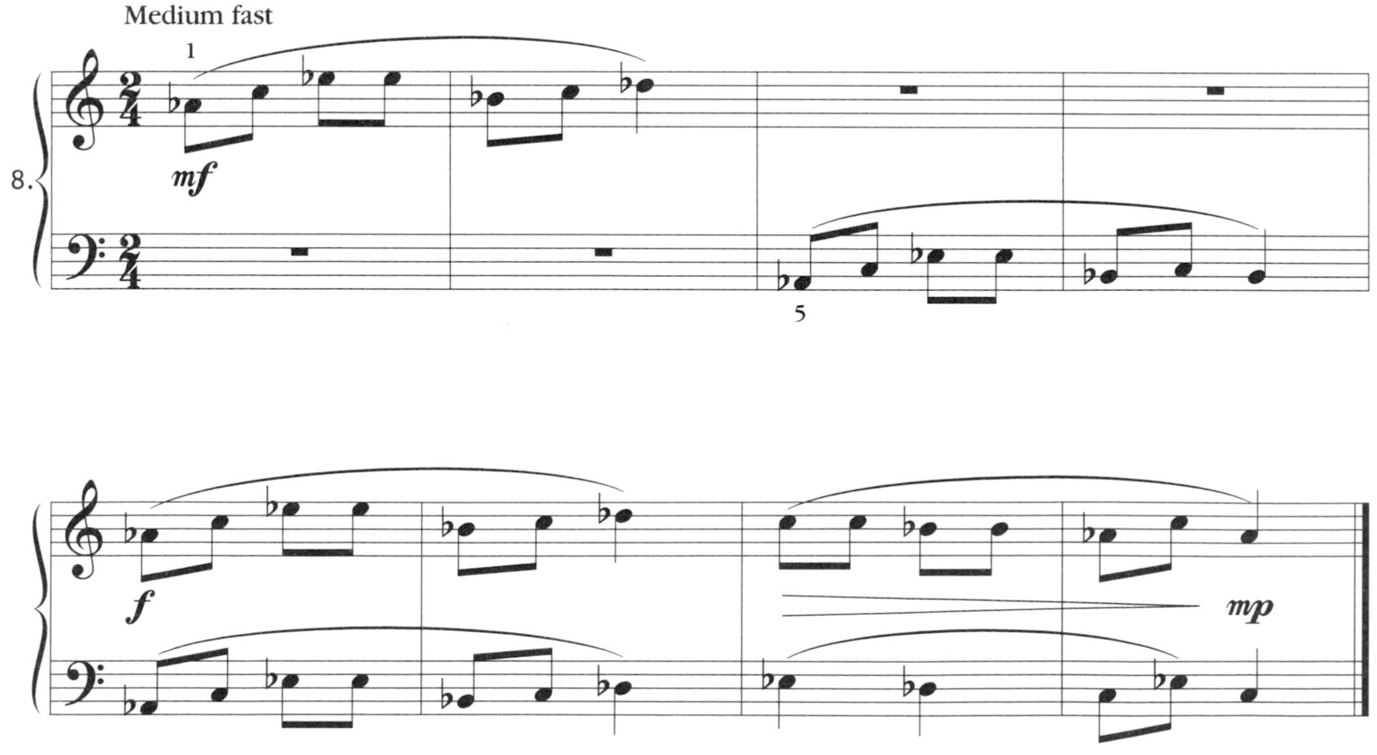

Be aware of the contrasting touches in *Study No. 9.* The two-note slur requires a "drop-lift" gesture.

Slovakian

Transpose to the B♭ pentachord.

melody by **Mozart**

ACCOMPANYING

In chapters 2-8, student accompaniments become an integral part of study. Examine the "**S**" part. Place your hands over the notes in the chords (see the "Handsets"). Before playing, block the chords in quarter-note rhythm (see examples below). There should be very little hand motion from one chord to the next. Move your hands *into* the keys. Alternate LH with RH in preparation.

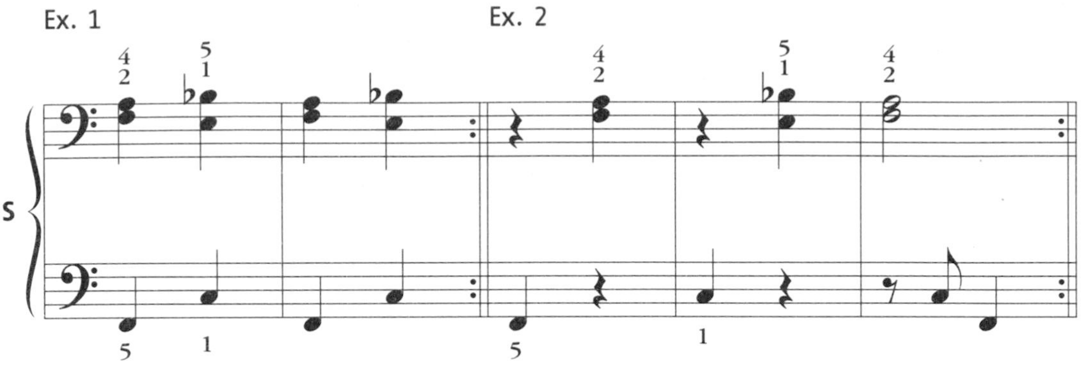

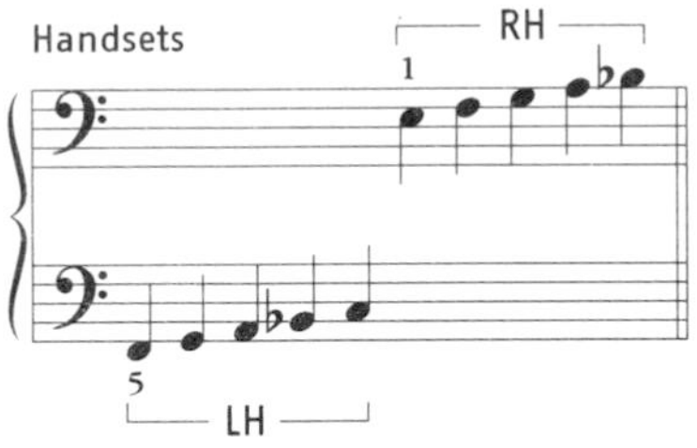

Repeat Signs (𝄆 𝄇) are used to indicate the repeat of an entire section.

BOW BELINDA

American
arr. **James Lyke**

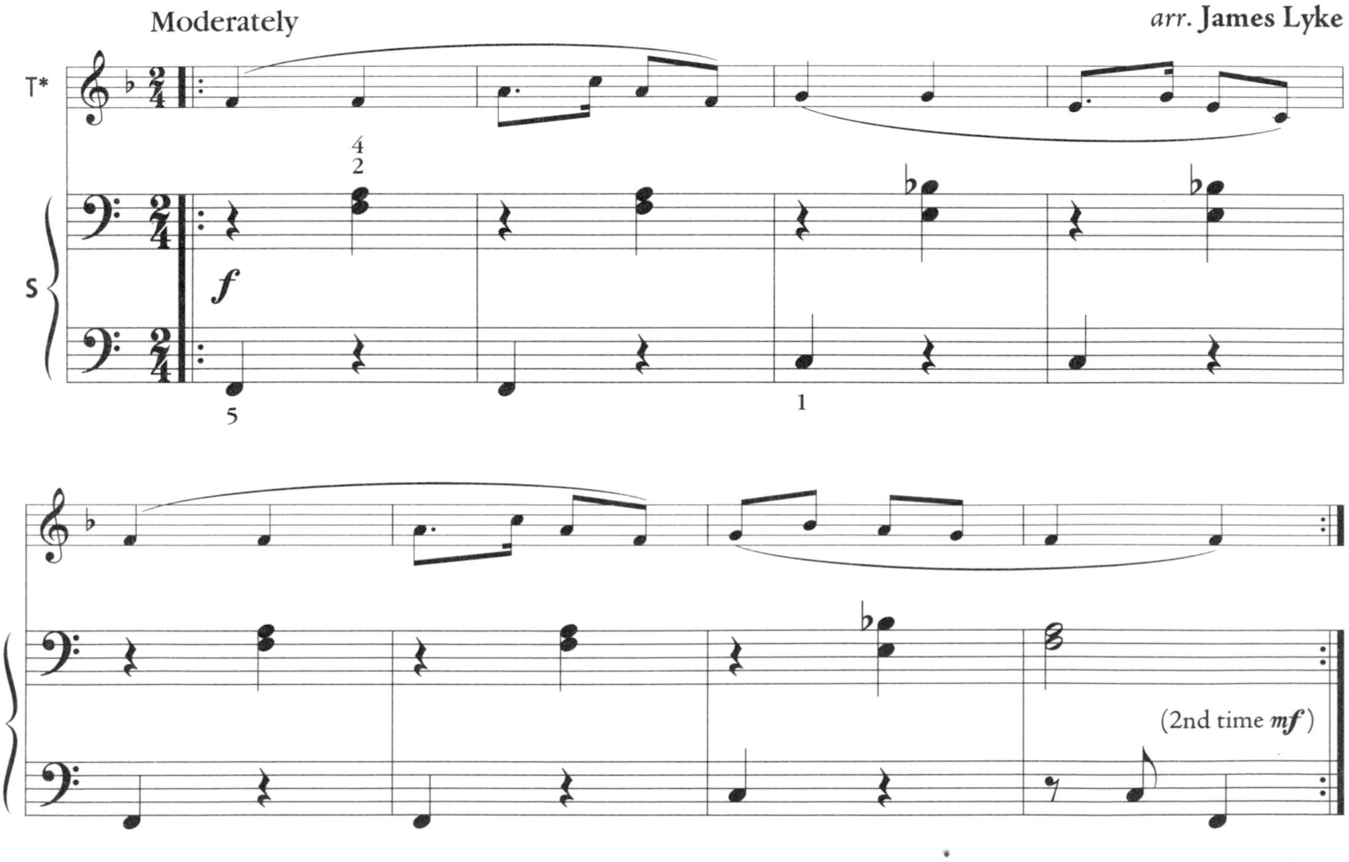

*Teacher: Double the melody with RH playing two octaves higher.

Use practice steps similar to those shown on page 54.

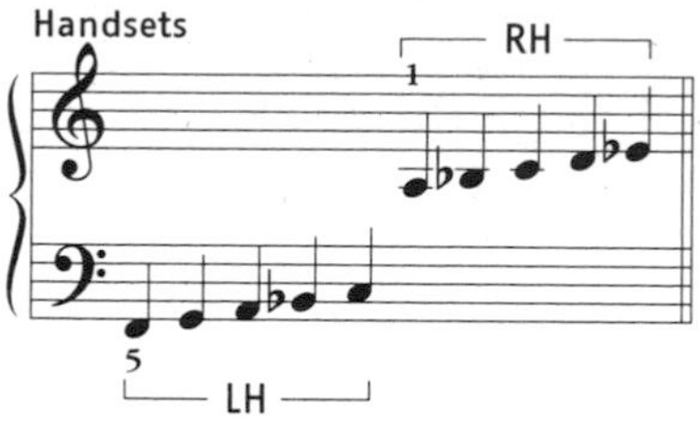

6 CD

THE JUNIPER TREE

Arkansas
arr. James Lyke

Vigorously

AMERICAN SONG REPERTOIRE

Beginning in Chapter Two, works of the great classic American Songwriters will appear. Composers such as Jerome Kern, Irving Berlin, Cole Porter, George Gershwin, and Richard Rodgers will be featured. Their melodies are fashioned into easy-to-play arrangements. As you move through the book, typical jazz rhythms and harmonies will be introduced in these pieces. Each has a CD/MIDI disk accompaniment.

7 CD

PLAY A SIMPLE MELODY

Irving Berlin

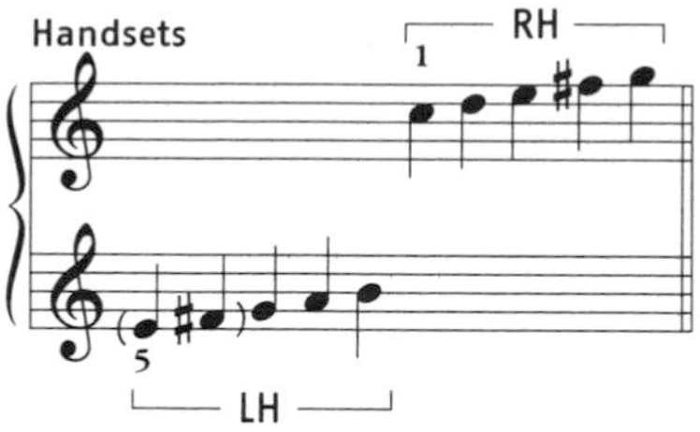

EVERY DAY

Jerome Kern

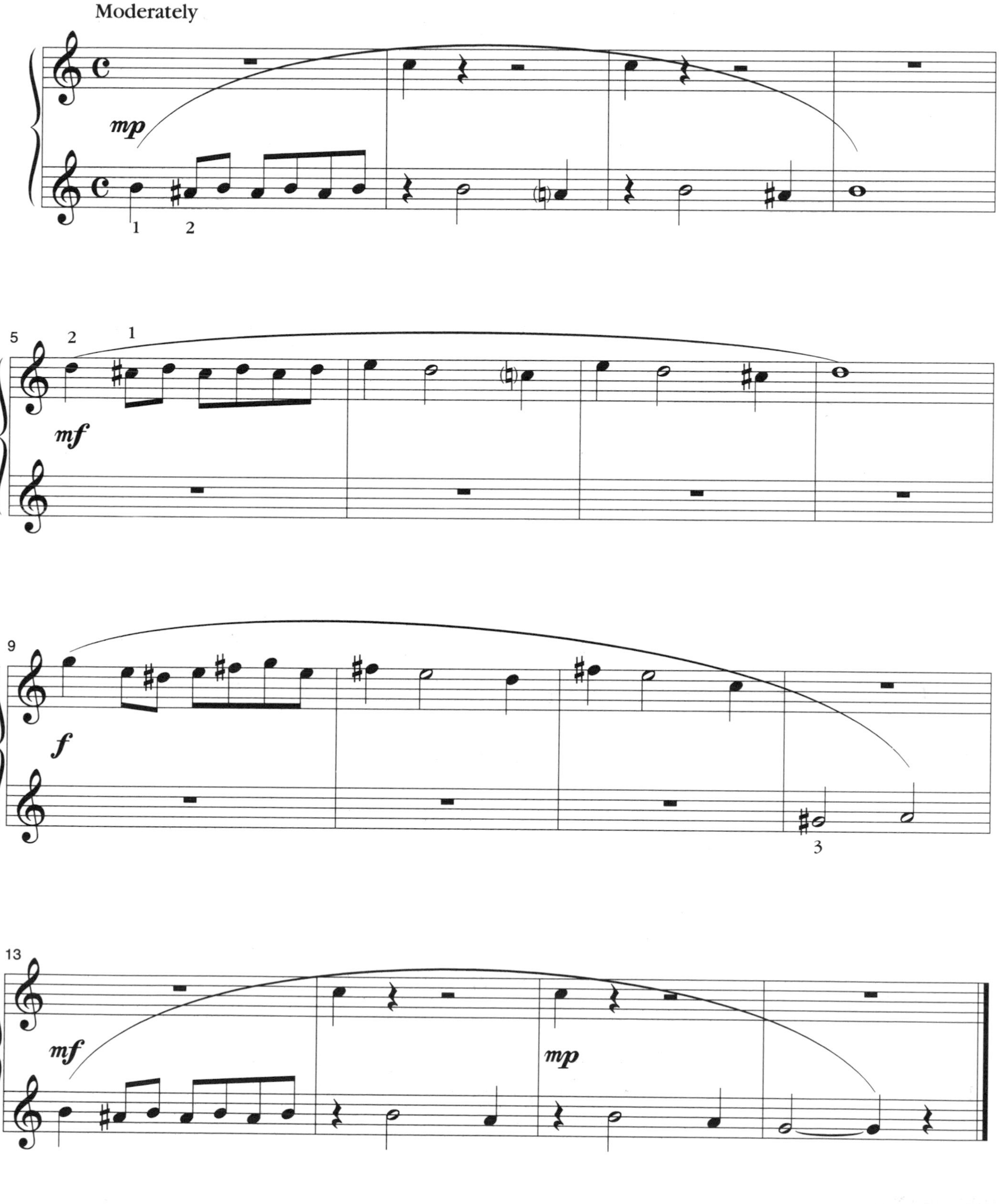

ENSEMBLE REPERTOIRE

9 CD

WHEN THE CURTAIN FALLS

Secondo – Teacher

music by **Irving Berlin**
arr. **James Lyke**

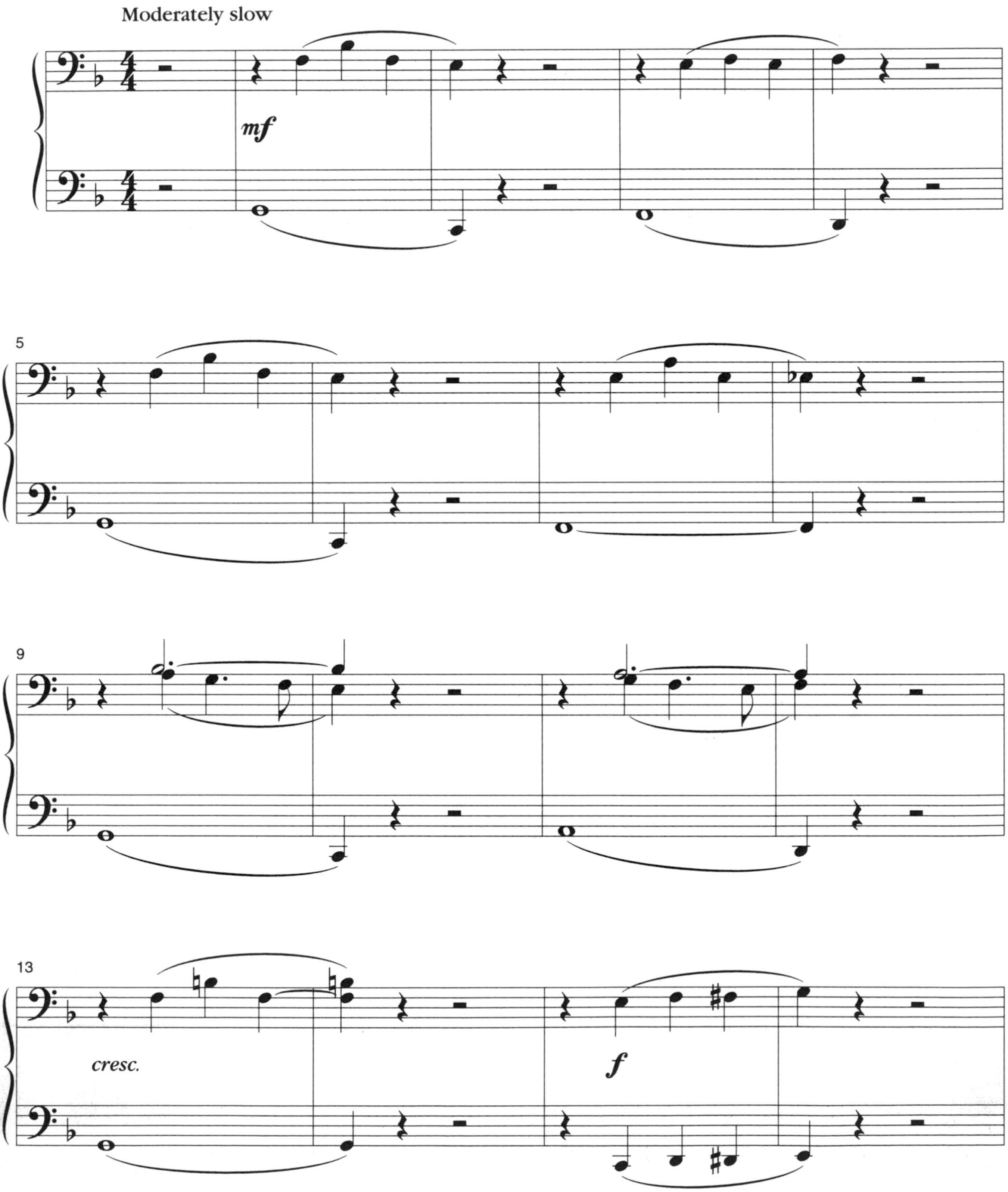

WHEN THE CURTAIN FALLS

Primo – Student

music by **Irving Berlin**
arr. **James Lyke**

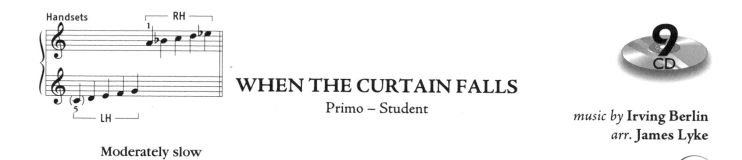

Secondo

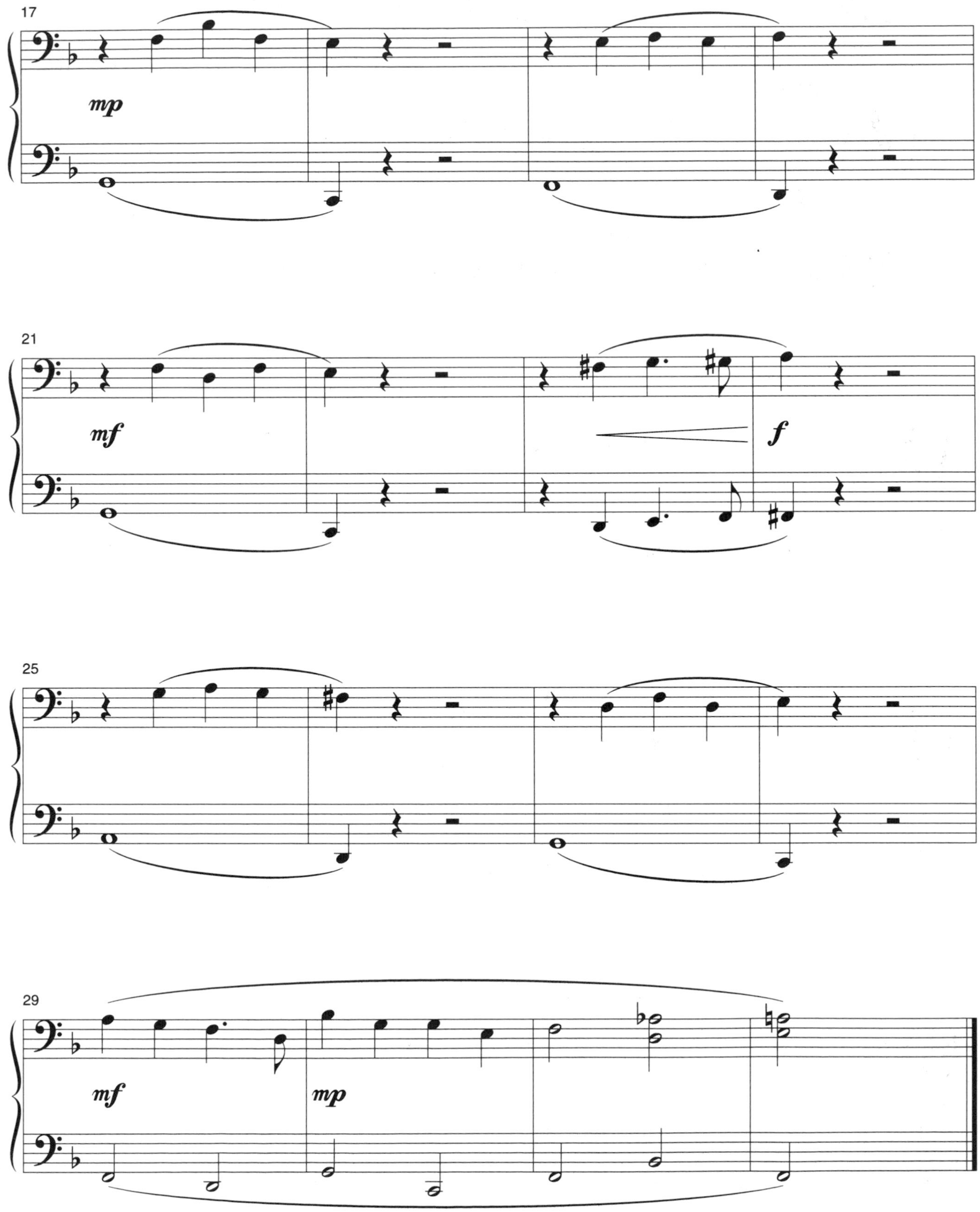

Primo

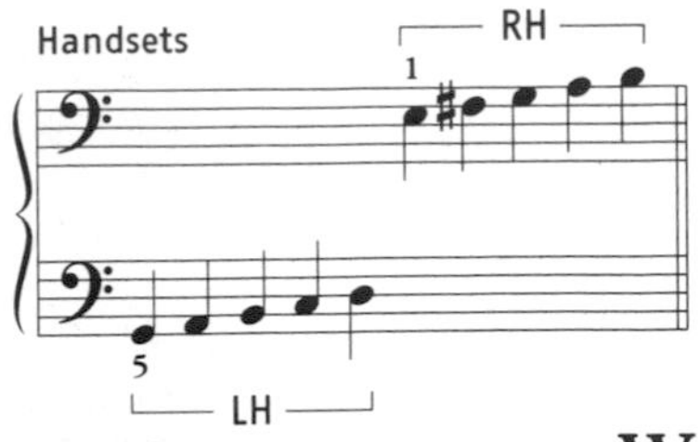

WALKING HOME WITH ANGELINE

Secondo – Student

music by **George Gershwin**
arr. **James Lyke**

Andante 𝅗𝅥 = 72

10 CD

WALKING HOME WITH ANGELINE

Primo – Teacher

music by **George Gershwin**
arr. **James Lyke**

Andante 𝅗𝅥 = 72

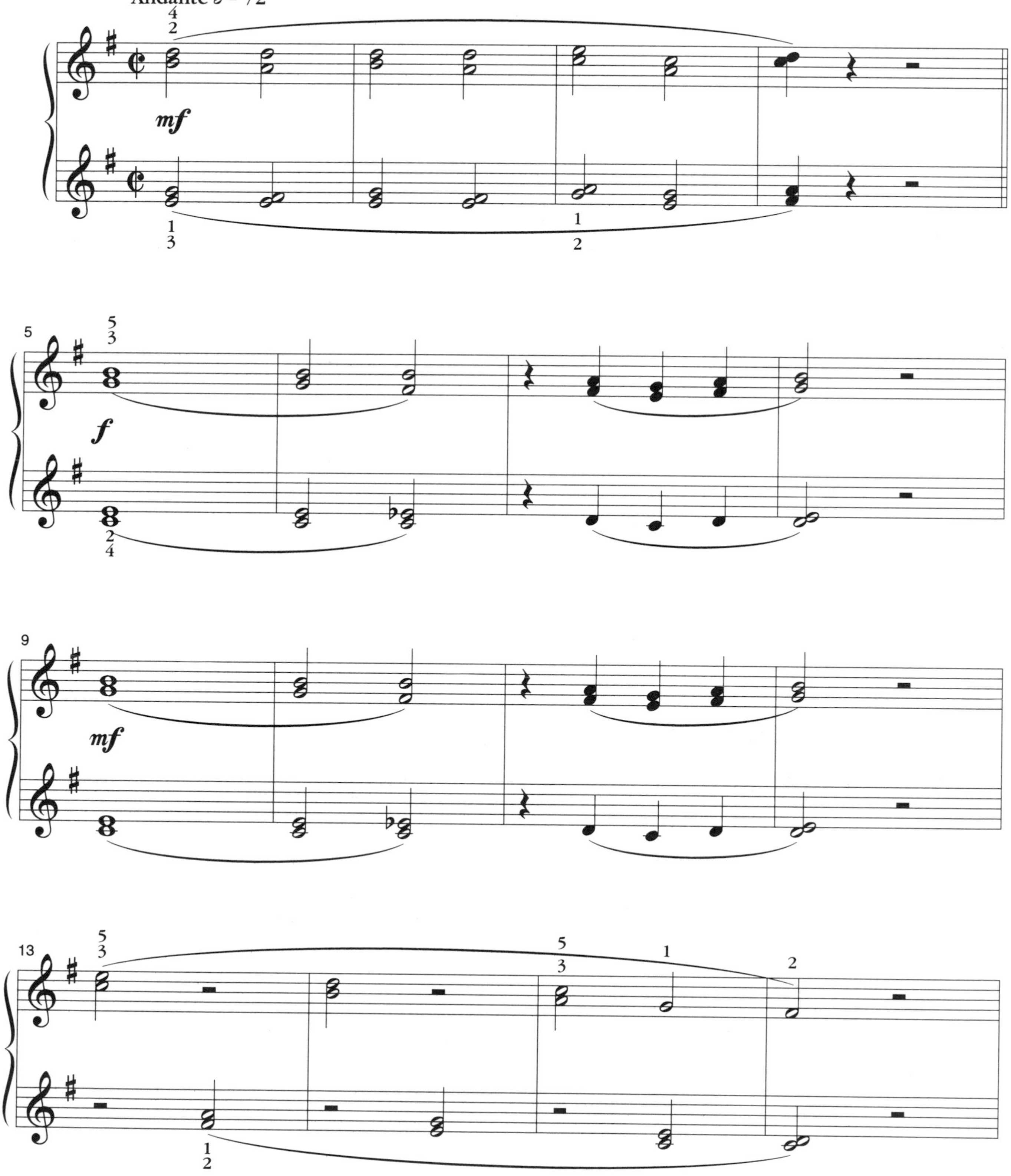

< A *crescendo* mark means gradually become louder.

> A *decrescendo* mark means gradually become softer.

Secondo

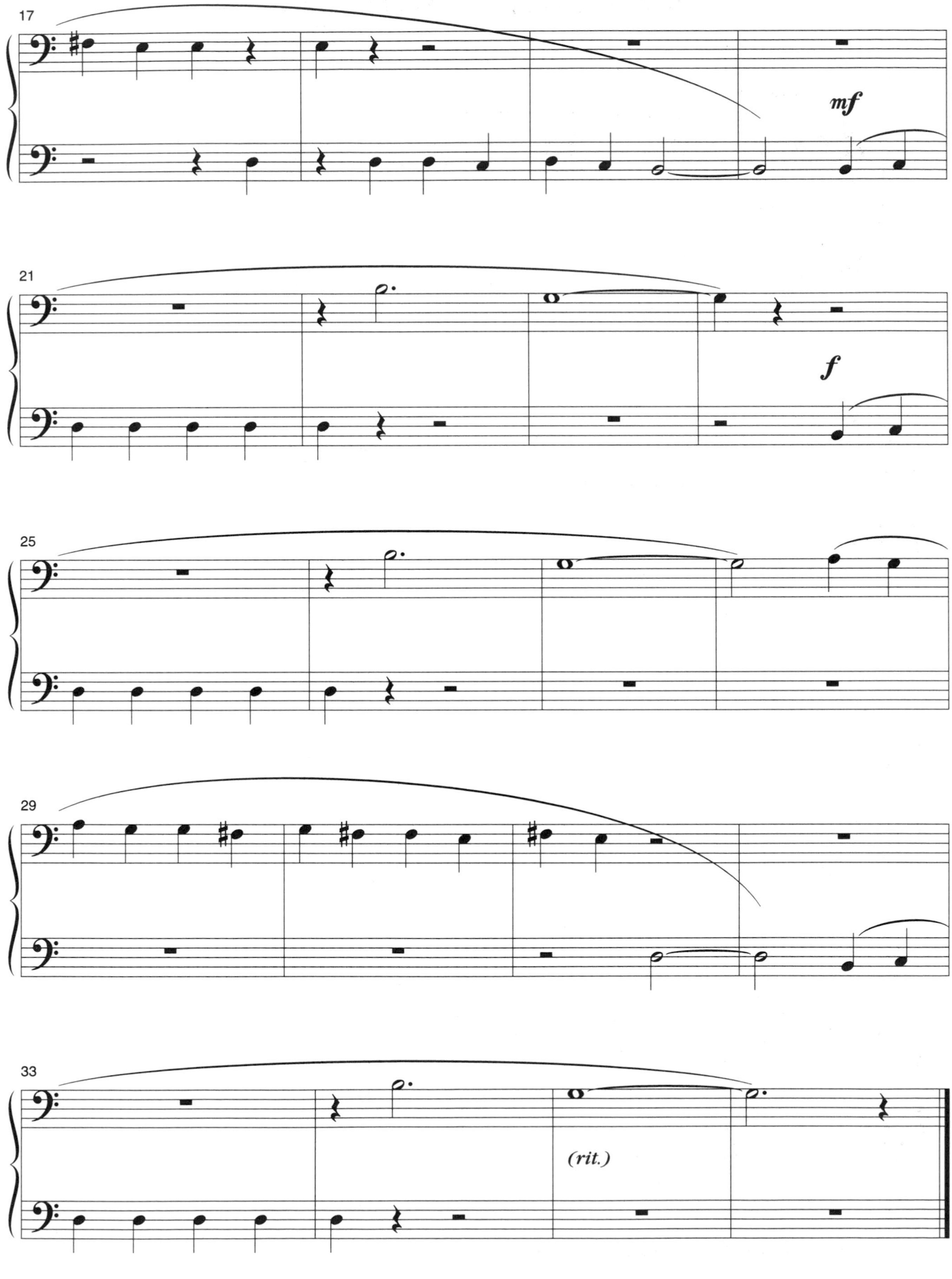

Primo

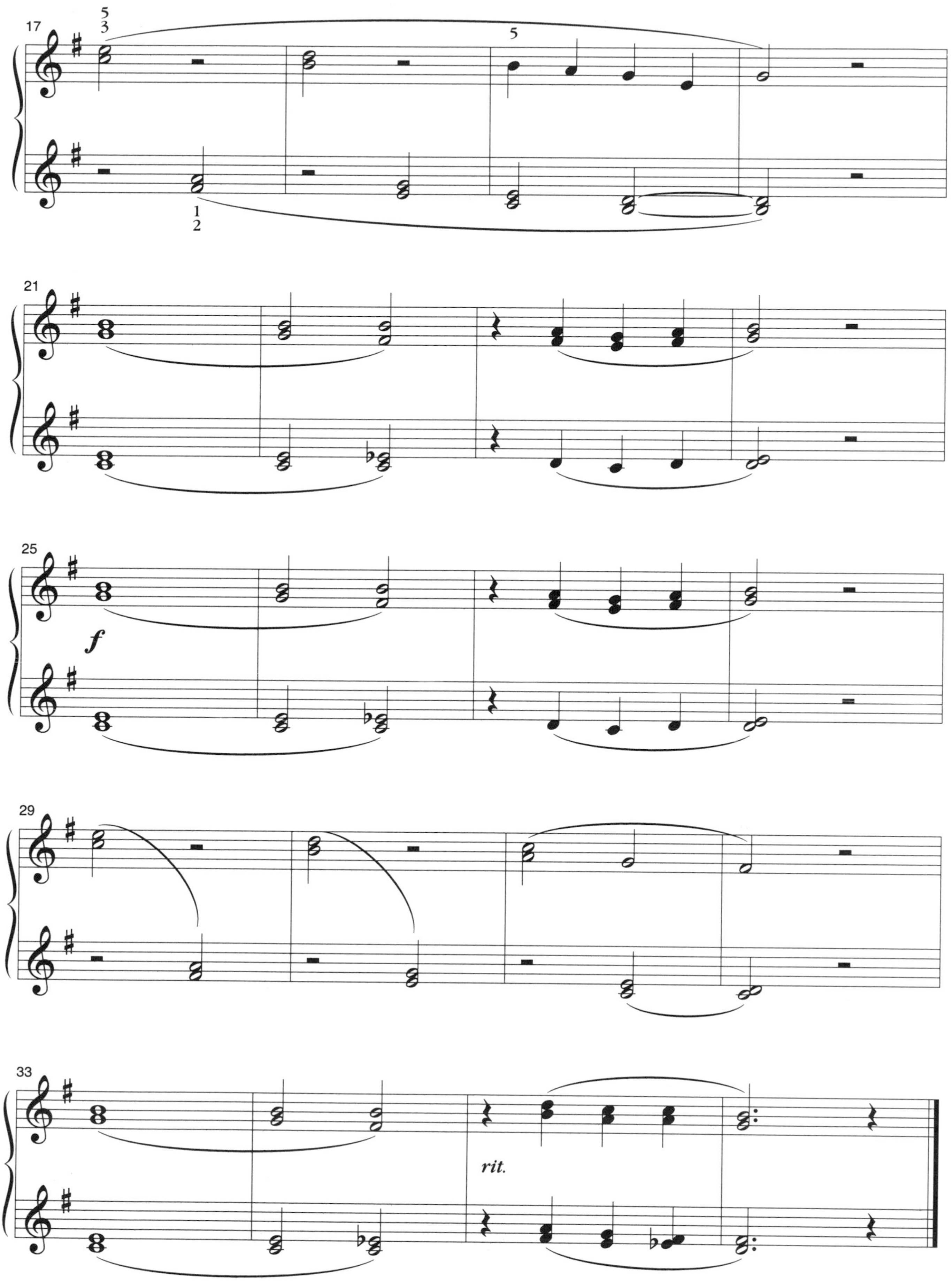

SOLO REPERTOIRE

In learning the following pieces, develop an effective practice plan with the help of the teacher. Isolate difficulties, such as shifts and problem fingerings, for special study. Block figures, observe expressive markings, and play evenly. Smooth playing may require a *slow* tempo until everything comes together. Above all, *listen* and make judgments about your own playing. Find various sections of a piece and study their similarities and differences. Several pieces will require hands alone practice before combining hands. This will ensure secure fingering, proper position, and details of touch and sound.
EMPHASIS: intervals, triads and pedaling.

Practice Plan: *Staccatos* should be performed crisply and with firm fingertips. Observe all two-note slurs.

SECONDS, ANYONE?

Quickly

Tony Caramia

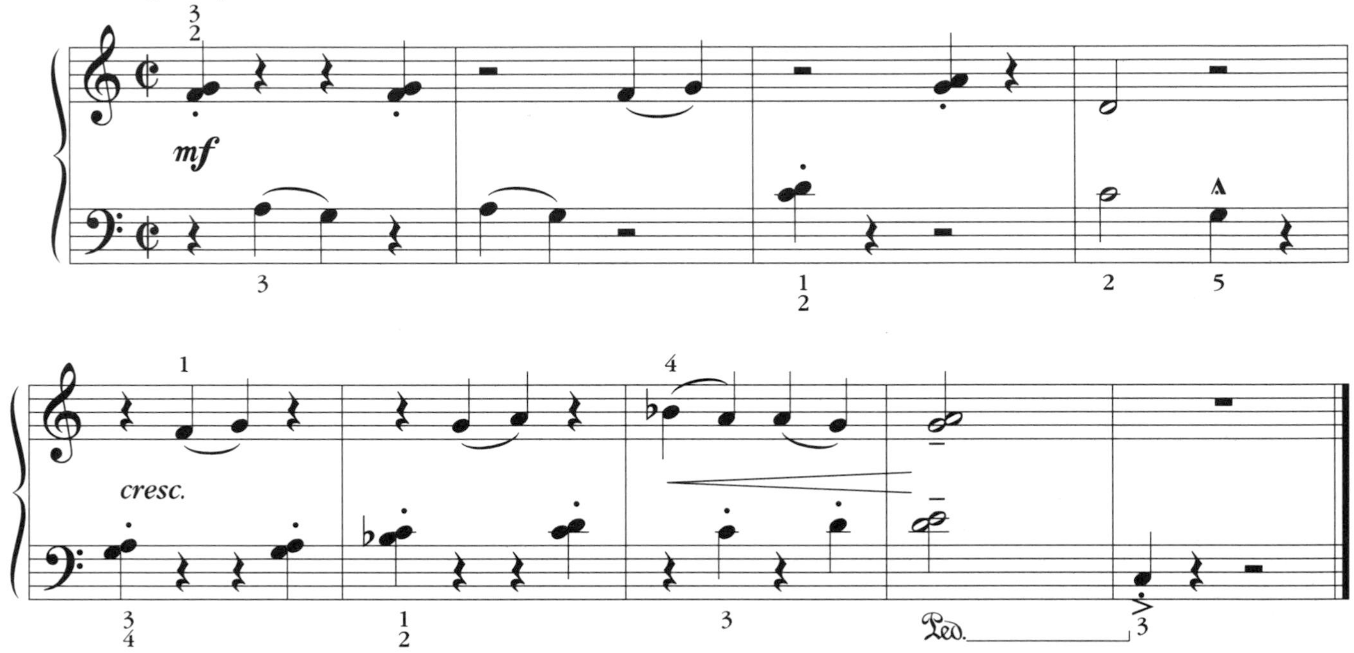

Practice Plan: Practice hands alone. Pay special attention to LH shift of positions in measures 5–8.

GOING FOURTH

Tenderly

Tony Caramia

Practice Plan: Perform eighth notes evenly. The final three measures should be practiced slowly in order to achieve the correct coordination.

from "FIRST TERM AT THE PIANO"

Béla Bartók

Moderato

Practice Plan: Exaggerate RH *staccato* and *legato* touches. Strive for even eighth notes.

DRONE PIECE

Jan Valastan Dolinsky

Animato ♩ = 138

Practice Plan: Isolate the first measure of *Touches Blanches (White Keys)*. Chant "con–nect short" while playing  several times.

TOUCHES BLANCHES

Tony Caramia

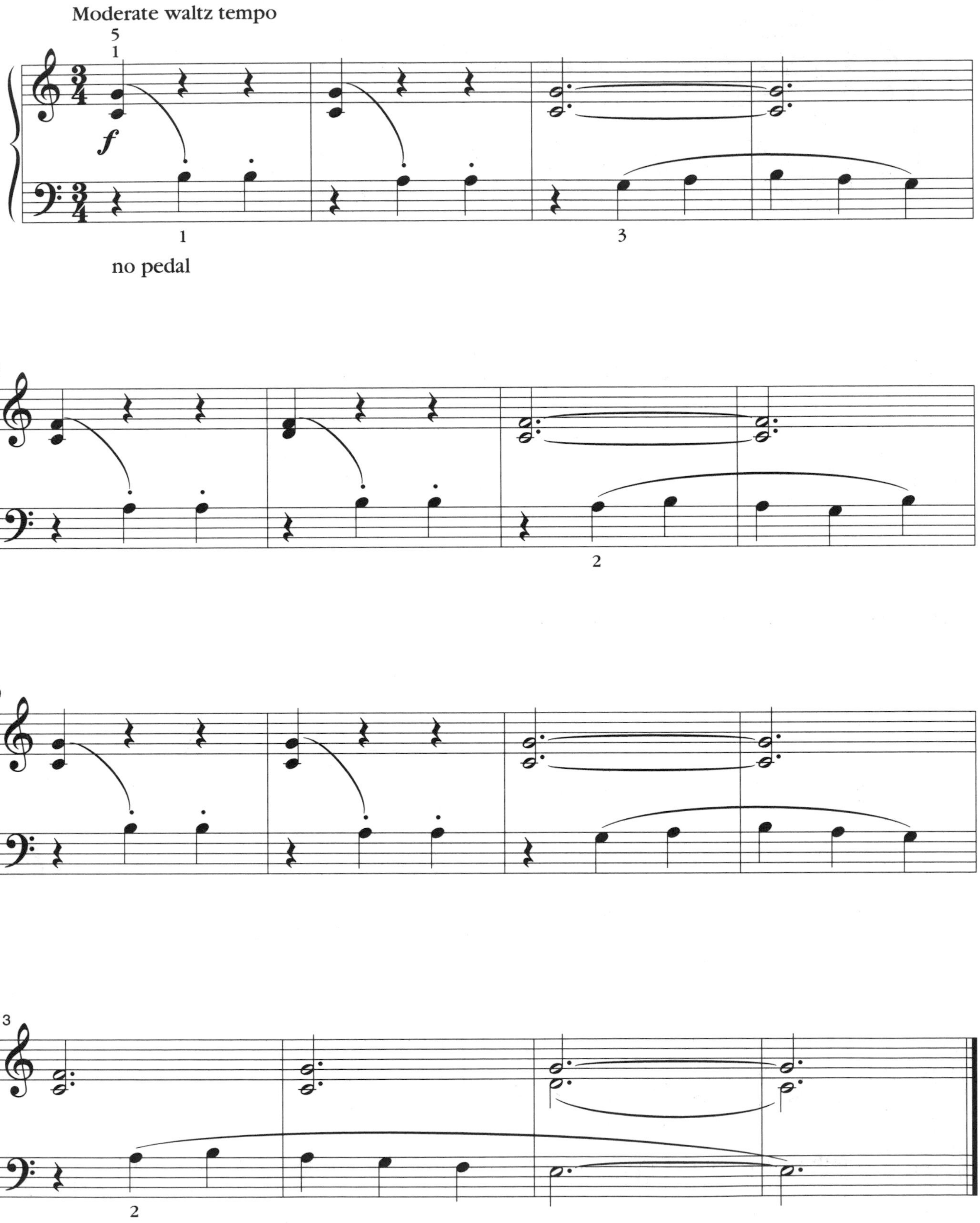

This piece is an example of "mirror composition," a popular 20th-century idiom. Notice that the LH is a mirror pattern of the RH; intervals in the RH are "mirrored" in the LH.

FIVE-FINGER PIECE

Halsey Stevens

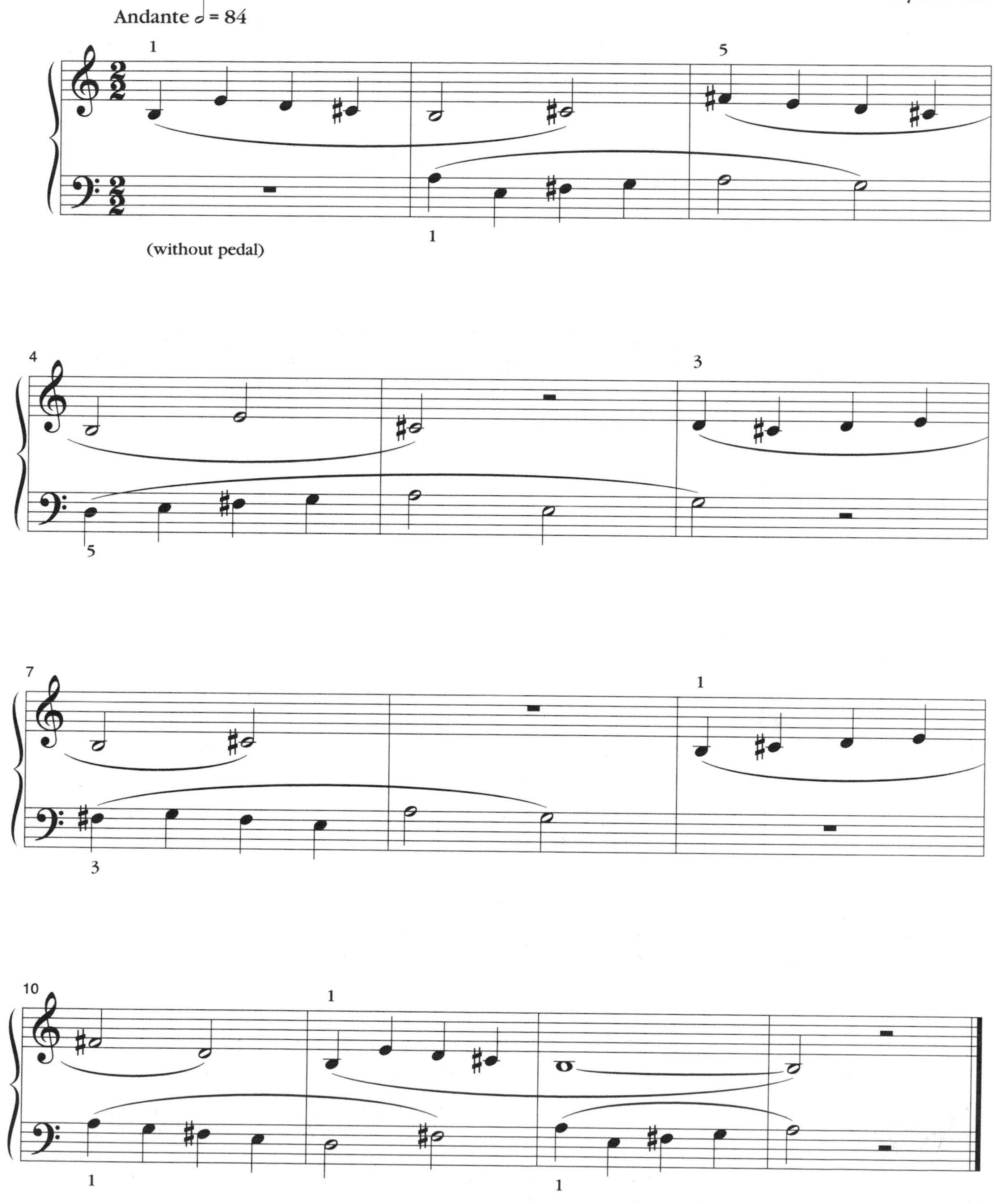

(Used by permission of Helias Music Edition.)

Practice Plan: Practice hands alone until a steady pulse is achieved. Isolate measure 13 striving for even eighth notes while holding the thumb note. Take note of the change of meter in measures 9–10.

FIVE FINGERS

Igor Stravinsky

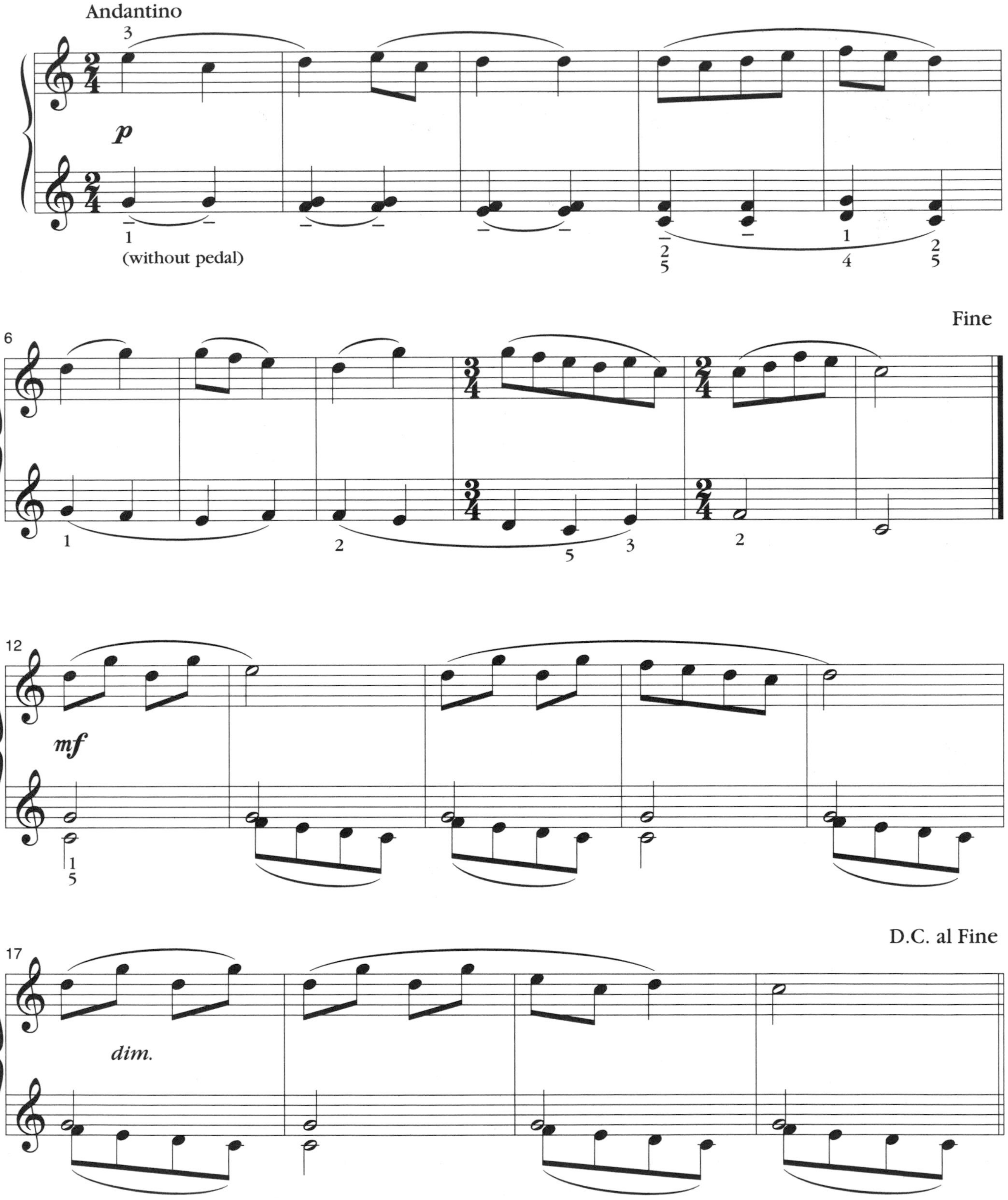

This "white key" piece has an austere sound due to the interval combinations of seconds, fourths and fifths. In the second section, practice the left hand alone until the thumb can hold its tone while the other voices move.

Practice Plan: Practice the LH alone until the moves from one fifth to another can be played with the eyes closed. At the same time, practice the pedal changes to avoid any blurring. Practice the RH final phrase (bars 13–16) until changing a finger on the same held note (G) becomes comfortable. Finally, combine the hands.

BELLS

Céline Bussières-Lessard

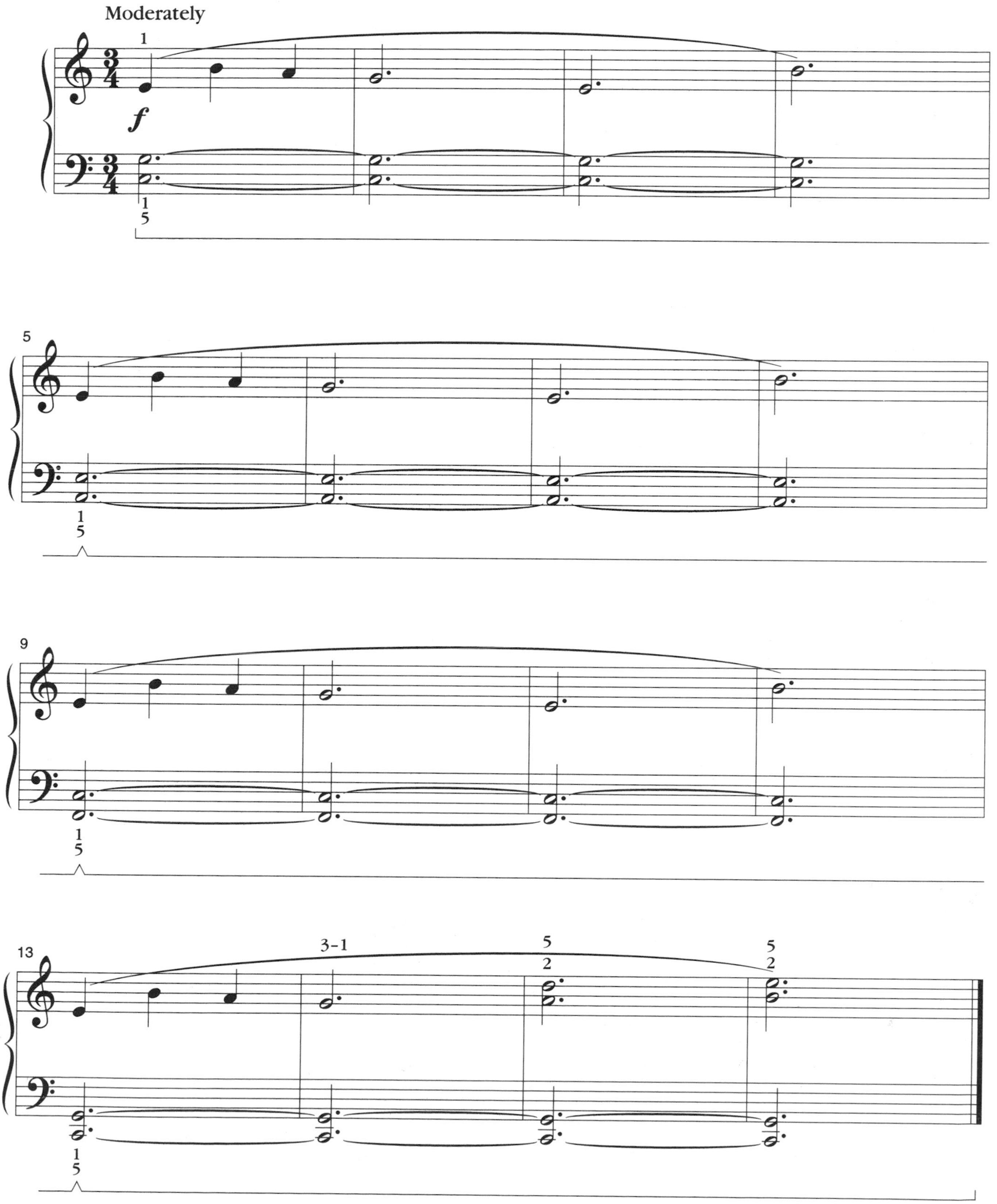

Practice Plan: Listen for clear, precise pedal changes. Take note of position shifts in measures 9–13. Block the triads.

SONORITIES

Tony Caramia

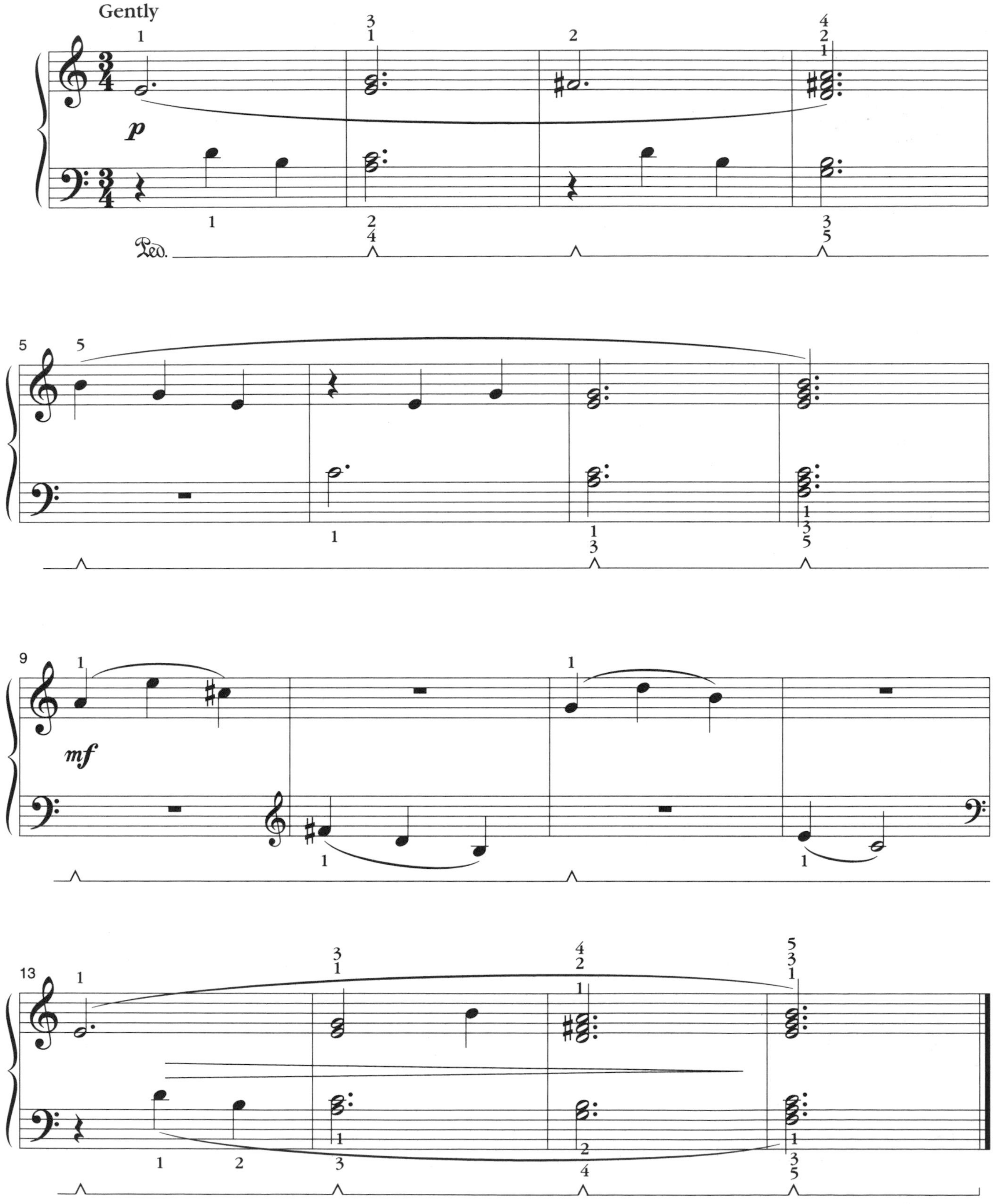

MUSICIANSHIP ACTIVITIES

Complete the following exercises which review various topics introduced in Chapter Two.

Major Pentachord Review

Build the major pentachords indicated below by drawing letters on the correct keys. Number one serves as an example. Then spell the major triad outlined by the 1st, 3rd, and 5th note of each pentachord.

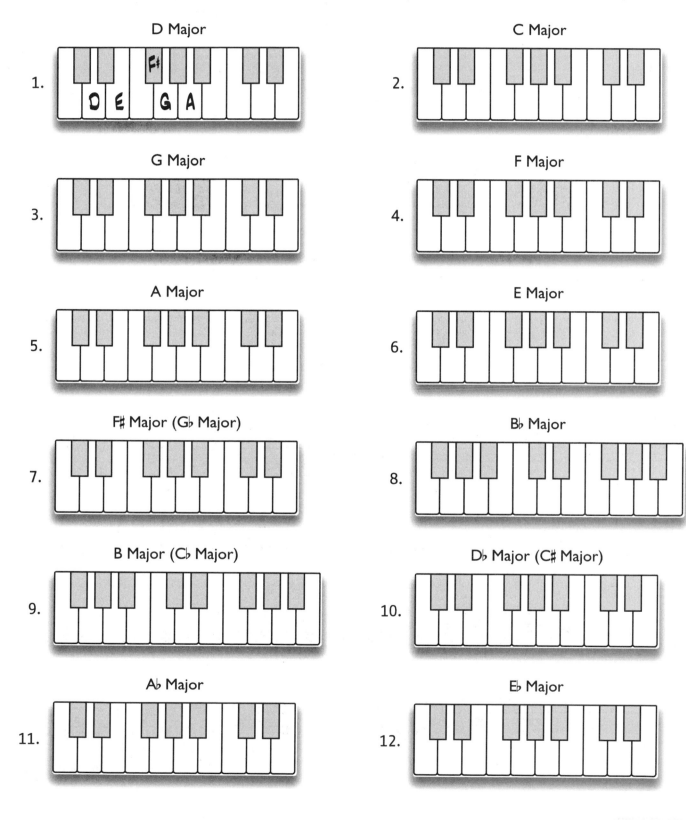

D Major

1. 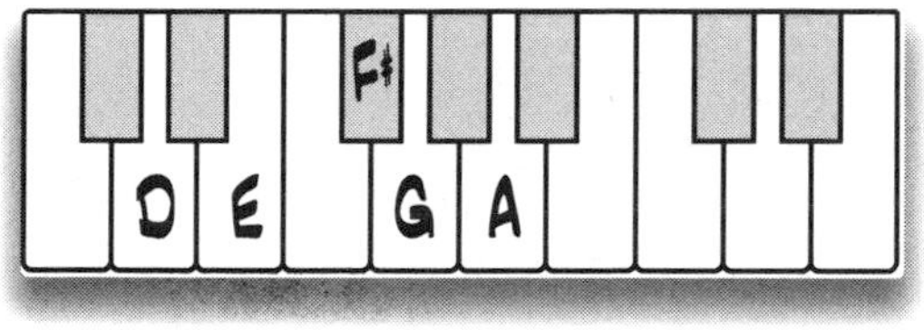

C Major

2. 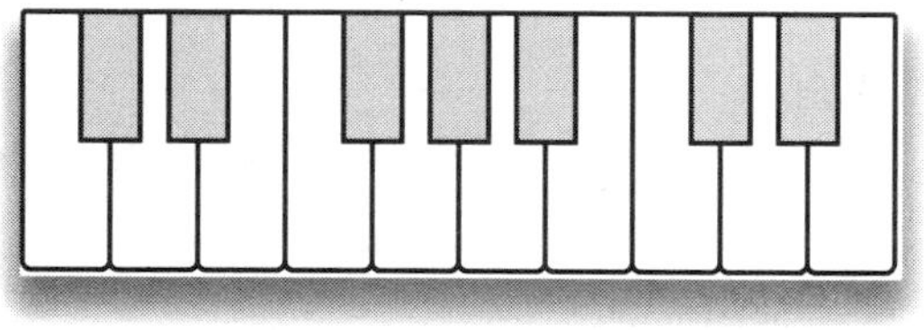

G Major

3. 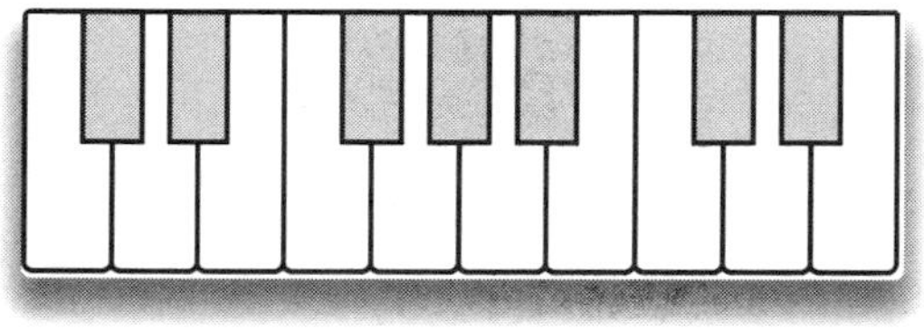

F Major

4. 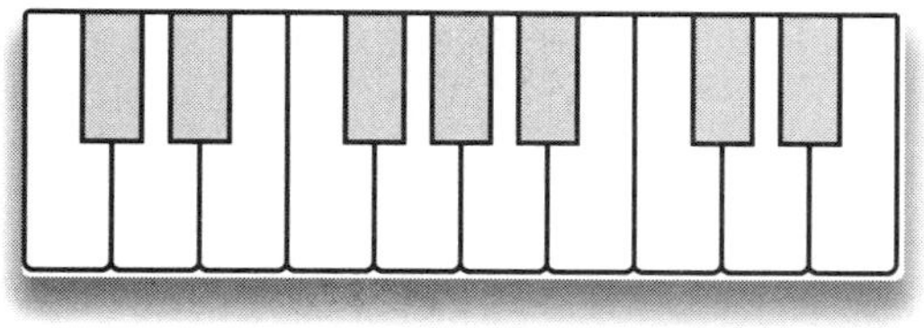

A Major

5. 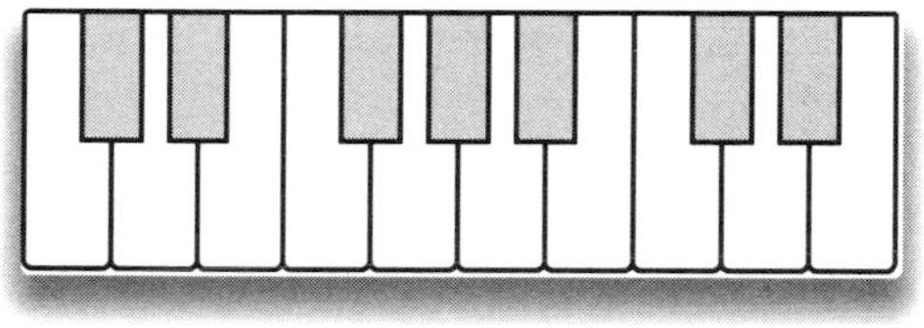

E Major

6. 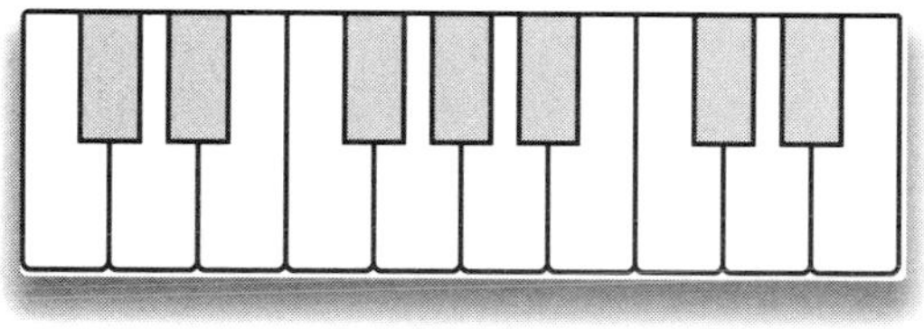

F♯ Major (G♭ Major)

7. 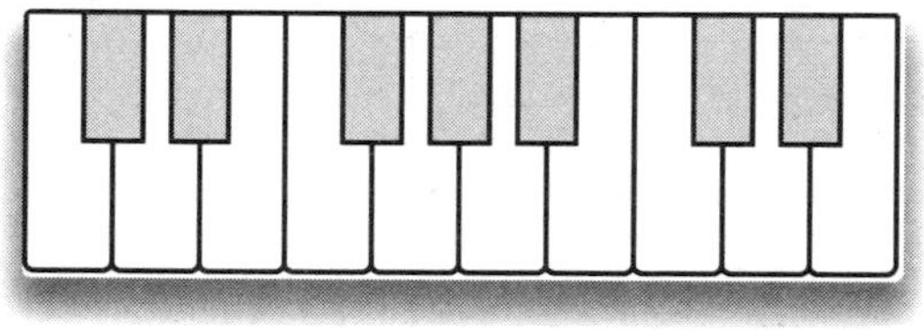

B♭ Major

8. 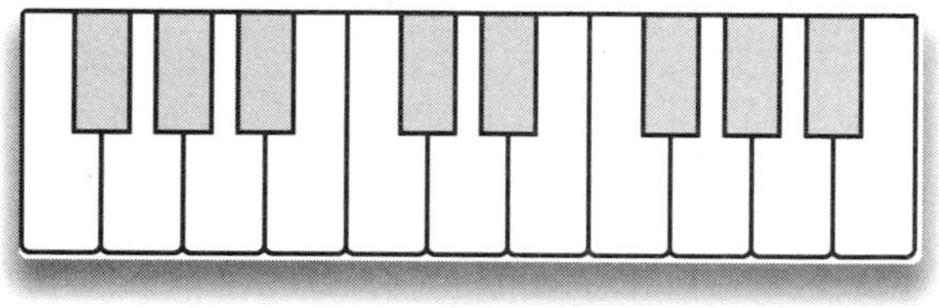

B Major (C♭ Major)

9. 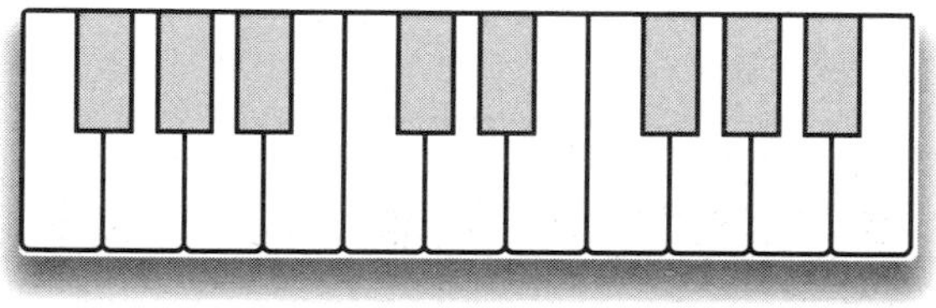

D♭ Major (C♯ Major)

10. 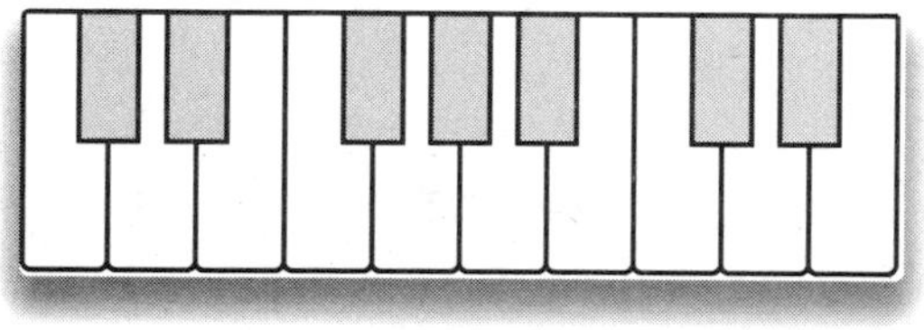

A♭ Major

11. 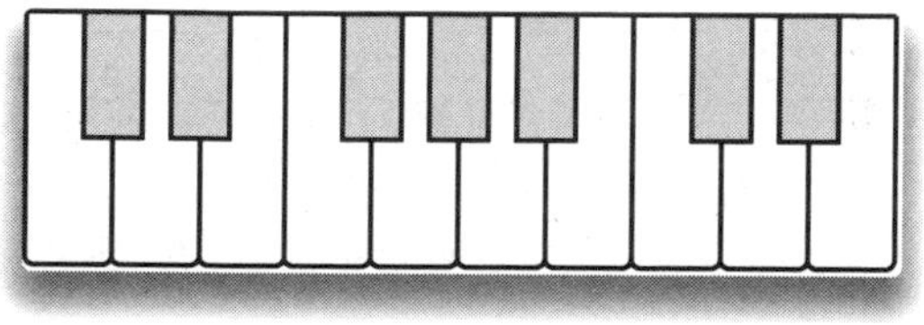

E♭ Major

12. 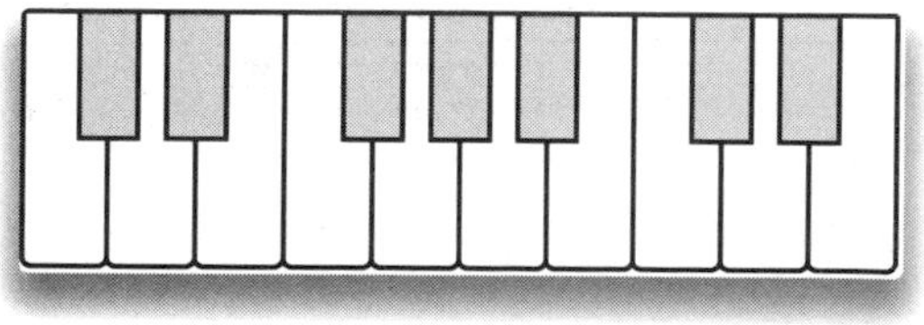

Technical Studies – Major Pentachord Exercise

Play the following major pentachords in sharp keys and flat keys. The top note of the triad becomes the bottom note of the new pattern. Remember the W W H W pattern.

Sharp Keys (C through C♯)

continue on to D, A, E, B, F♯ and C♯

Flat Keys (C♭ through C)

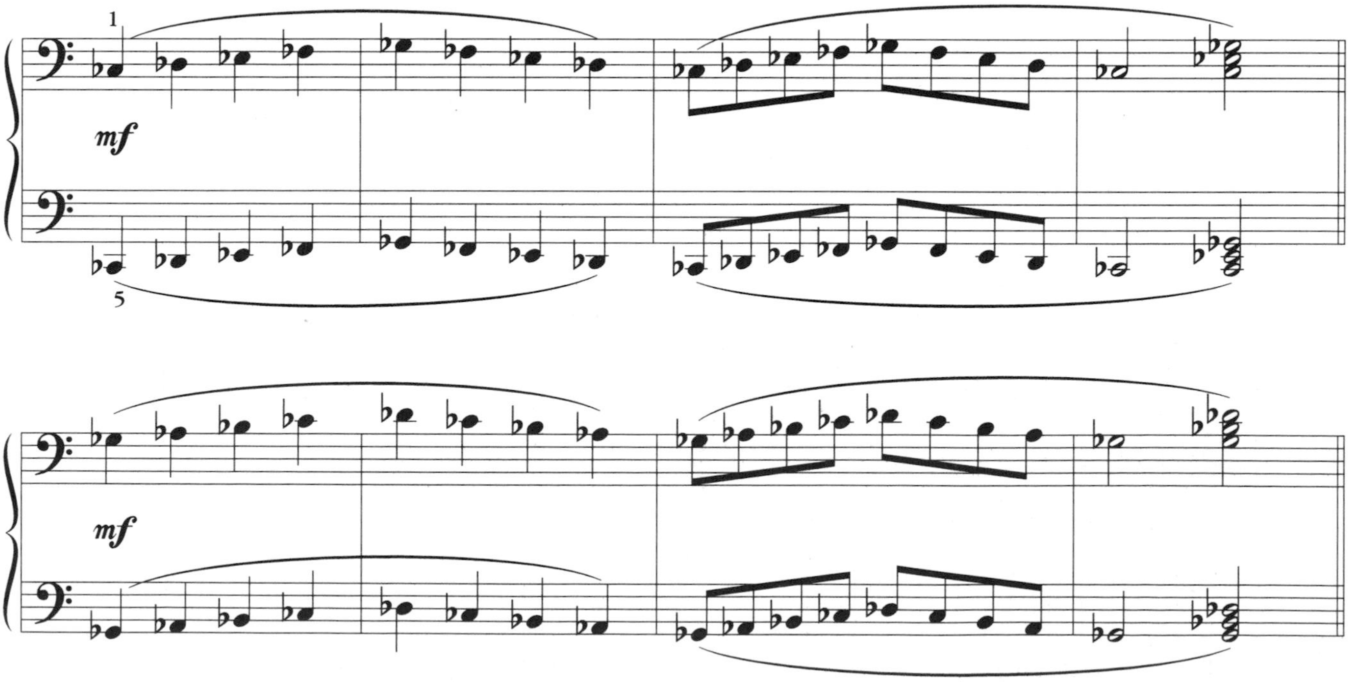

continue on to D♭, A♭, E♭, B♭, F and C

Major Pentachord Exercise

Play the following studies that make use of major triads in sharp keys and flat keys. The top note of the triad beomes the bottom note of the new pattern.

Sharp Keys

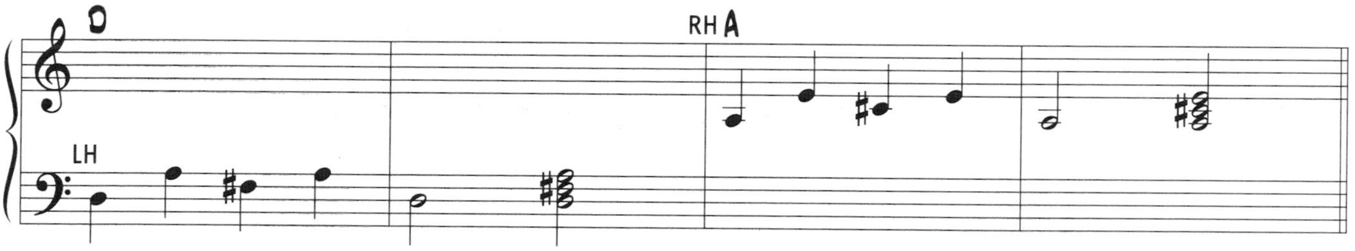

continue on to E, B, F♯ and C♯

Flat Keys

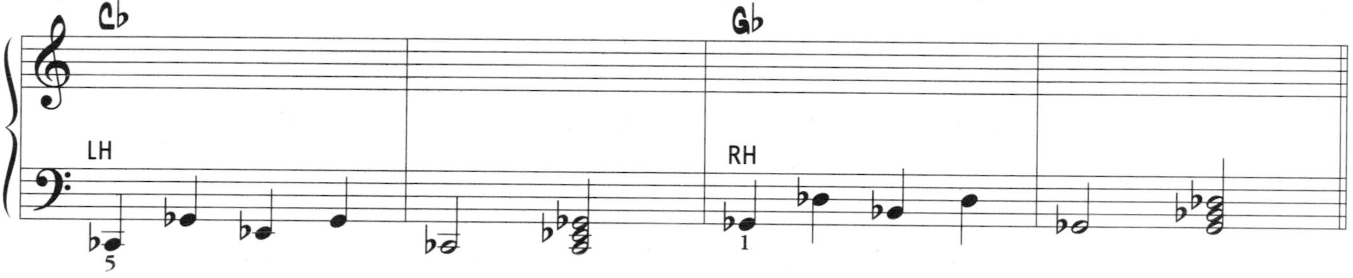

continue on to E♭, B♭, F and C

Two-Note Slur Exercises

Lift the wrist gently after each two-note group. Roll the wrist toward the fallboard.

Transpose to all white key pentachords.

SUGGESTED PLAYING EXAM TOPICS
CHAPTER TWO

1. Build and play major pentachords with keynotes beginning on any key. Use the example below in C. Then transpose to the other keynotes.

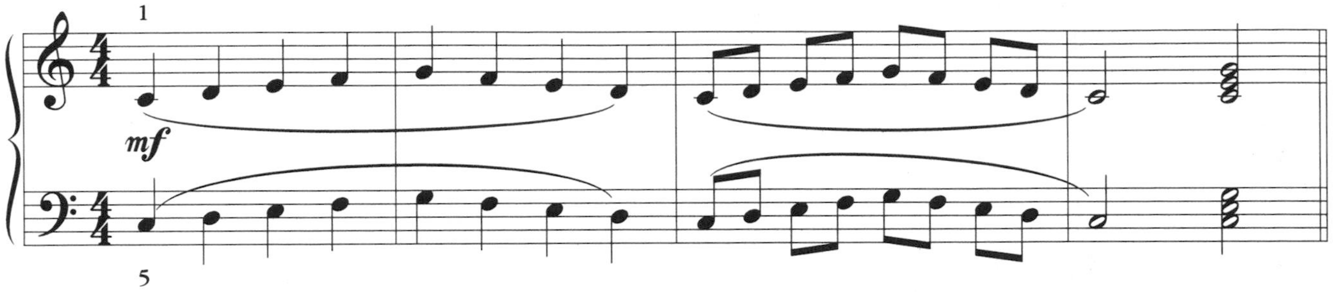

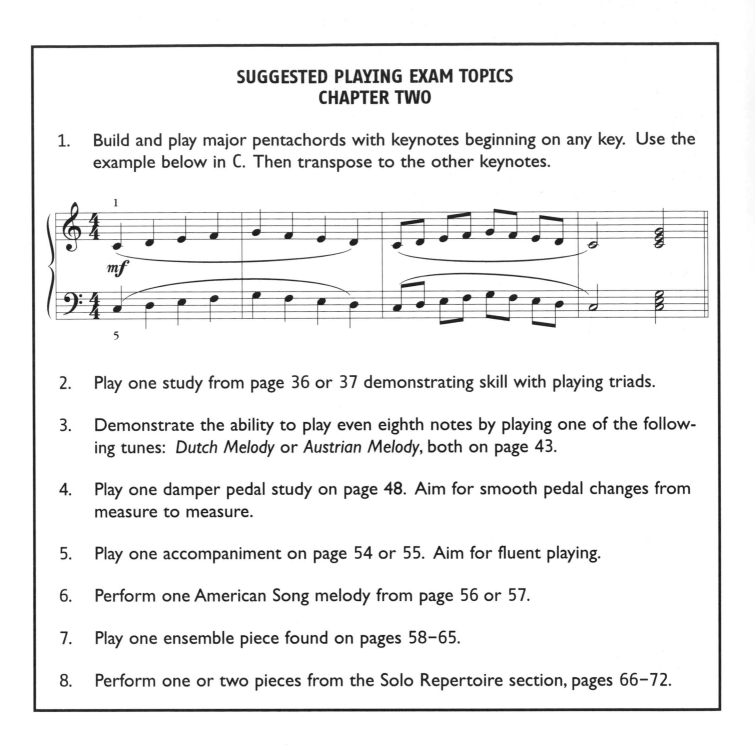

2. Play one study from page 36 or 37 demonstrating skill with playing triads.

3. Demonstrate the ability to play even eighth notes by playing one of the following tunes: *Dutch Melody* or *Austrian Melody*, both on page 43.

4. Play one damper pedal study on page 48. Aim for smooth pedal changes from measure to measure.

5. Play one accompaniment on page 54 or 55. Aim for fluent playing.

6. Perform one American Song melody from page 56 or 57.

7. Play one ensemble piece found on pages 58–65.

8. Perform one or two pieces from the Solo Repertoire section, pages 66–72.

3 chapter

Major Scales, Key Signatures, Dominant and Dominant 7th Chords, 6ths, 7ths and Octaves, Harmonization, Repertoire, Musicianship Activities, and Technical Studies

The Major Scale

Major Scale Song introduces a new time signature, $\frac{3}{8}$. Its RH melody uses the C major scale fingering. In a major scale, half steps occur between scale degrees 3-4 and 7-8.

MAJOR SCALE SONG

Traditional

Scale Fingering

Observe the descending RH scale and ascending LH scale below. Crossing over onto finger 3 enables each hand to play an additional three notes to complete the scale. Memorize the fingering in each hand. This same fingering is used for the scales of G, D, A and E.

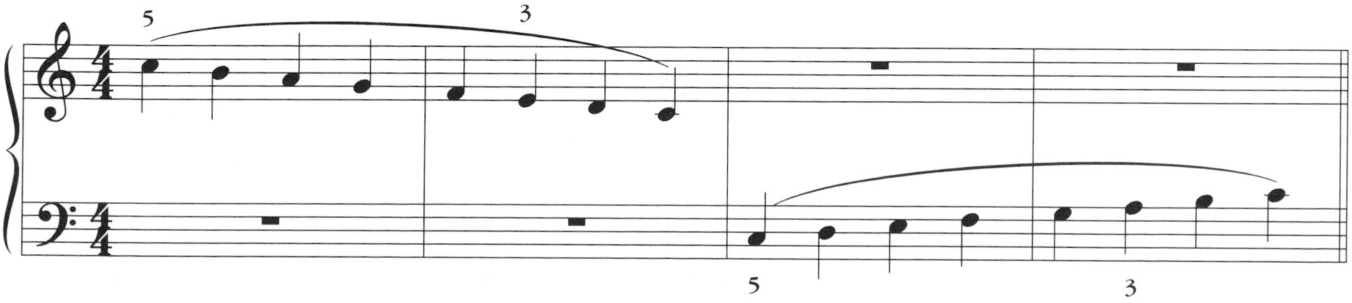

Transpose to the keys of G, D, A and E.

The major scale always contains half steps between scale degrees 3-4 and 7-8.

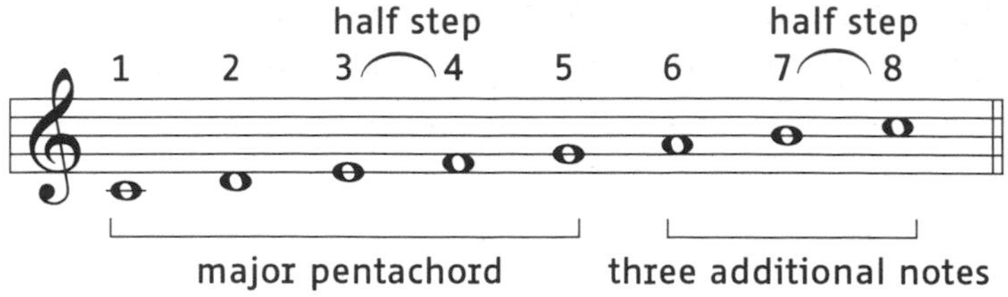

Key Signatures

If we try to build a major scale on other tones, the same whole step and half step arrangement (as in C major) must be maintained. Try playing the D major scale by ear. You will find that an F♯ and C♯ become necessary to maintain half steps between scale steps 3-4 and 7-8. The discovery of the step arrangement of the major scale brings us to the reason for *key signatures*.

In written or printed music, the sharps or flats required to build the various scales are assembled at the beginning of the staff, rather than appearing before the notes. This combination of sharps or flats indicates the key in which the piece of music is written and is called the *key signature*. It tells which notes are to be sharped or flatted throughout the piece in order to preserve the whole step and half step arrangement.

From the key signature it is possible to determine the *keynote* or first note in the scale. In sharp keys, count up one half step from the last sharp to the right to find the keynote. In flat keys the next to the last flat is the name of the keynote. Remember that the key of F major has only one flat.

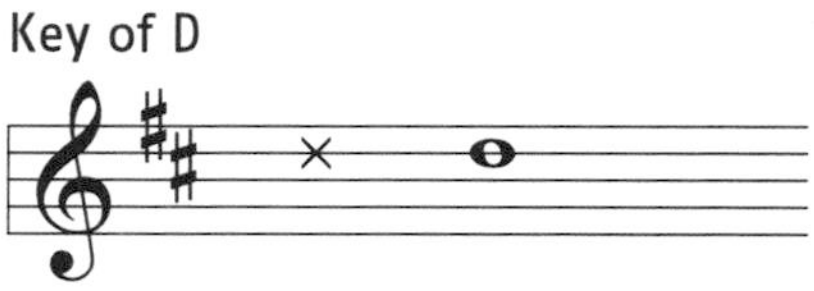

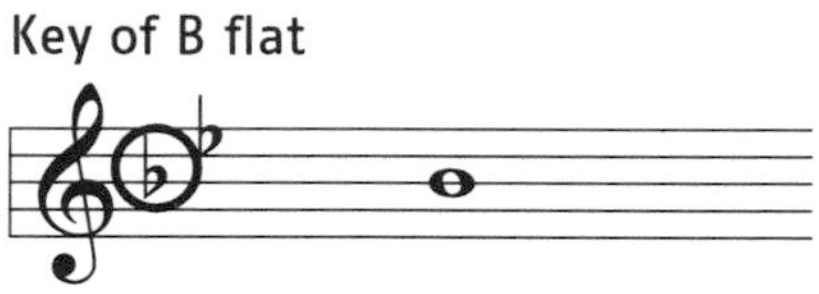

Identify the following major keys from the signature given.

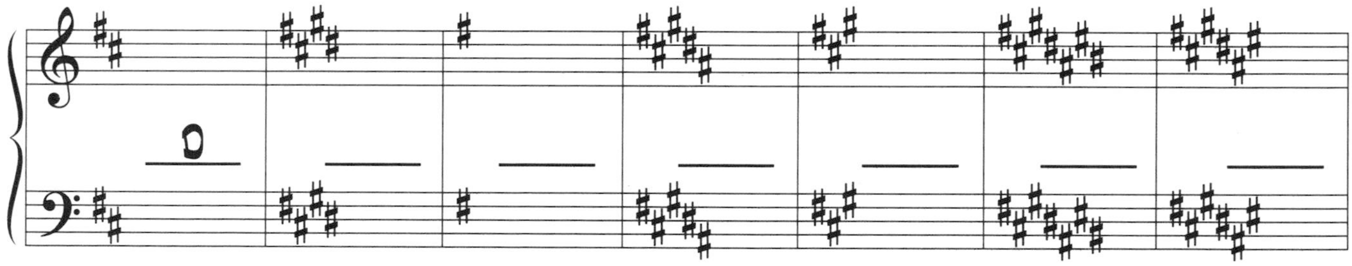

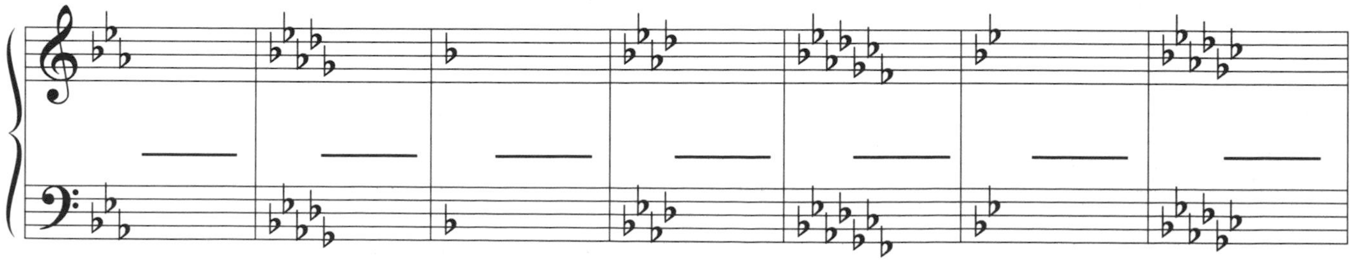

Forming Major Scales

If three more tones are added to the major pentachord (5 + 3), a major scale is formed. Added are two whole steps and a half step. Simply remember that half steps in the major scale occur between tones 3–4 and 7–8. Here are four major scales formed from the familiar C, G, D and A pentachords.

C Major Scale

G Major Scale

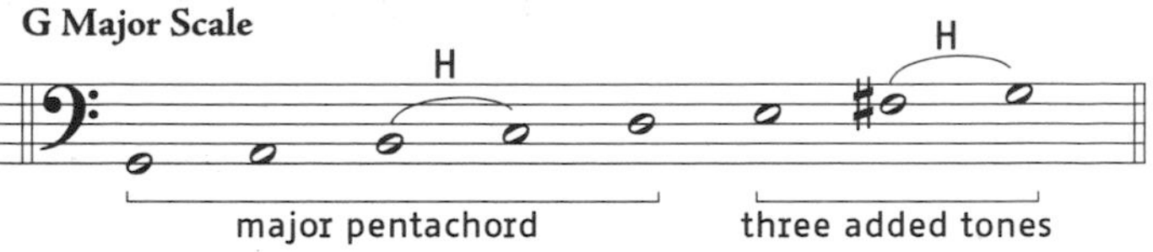

D Major Scale

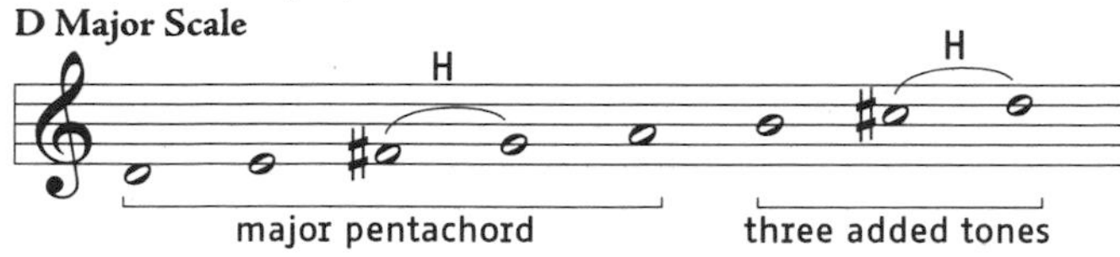

A Major Scale

Introduction to Scale Fingering

Study the following traditional fingerings for the scales of C, G, D and A (all use the same fingering). Play these scales hands alone ascending and descending using the given fingerings. Your instructor will point out *passing under* of the thumb and *crossing over* to the third finger. Scale study will have increasing importance throughout the text. Play each scale firmly and slowly. Memorize the fingering patterns. All major scales and fingerings may be found in Appendix B.

C Major Scale

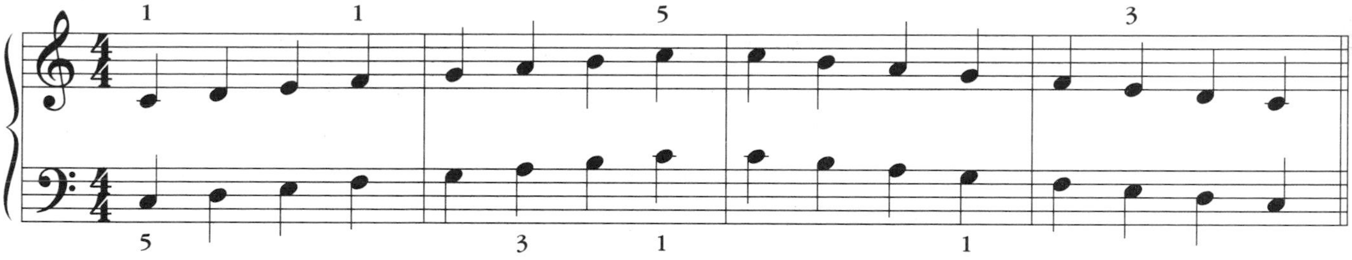

G Major Scale

D Major Scale

A Major Scale

Tetrachord Scales

Scales may be divided between the hands into two *tetrachords* (four-note patterns). There are two choices for fingerings. See the example below. Playing tetrachord scales in all keys appears at the end of this chapter as part of **Musicianship Activities**. Learn tetrachord scales in C and all sharp keys. Then learn them in all of the flat keys. An accompaniment is provided on the CD included with this book.

The A Major Scale Divided Into Tetrachords

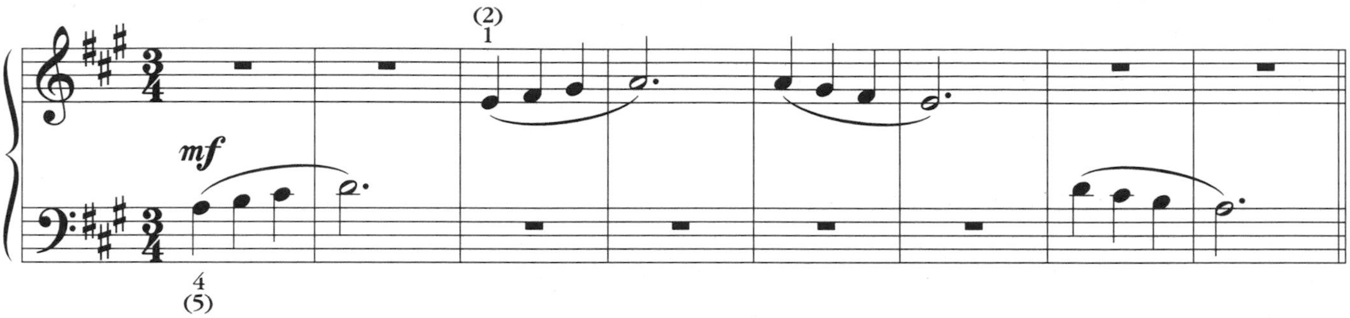

Playing Scale Melodies Divided Between the Hands in Tetrachords

Study and play the following scale melodies. The melodies are divided into tetrachords. Identify the major key and place your fingers in the tetrachord patterns indicated by the fingering. Some melodies will be in 𝄞 clef, some in 𝄢 clef and others will use both 𝄞 and 𝄢 clefs. Place your hands in the proper tetrachords according to the given fingerings.

BRITISH MELODY

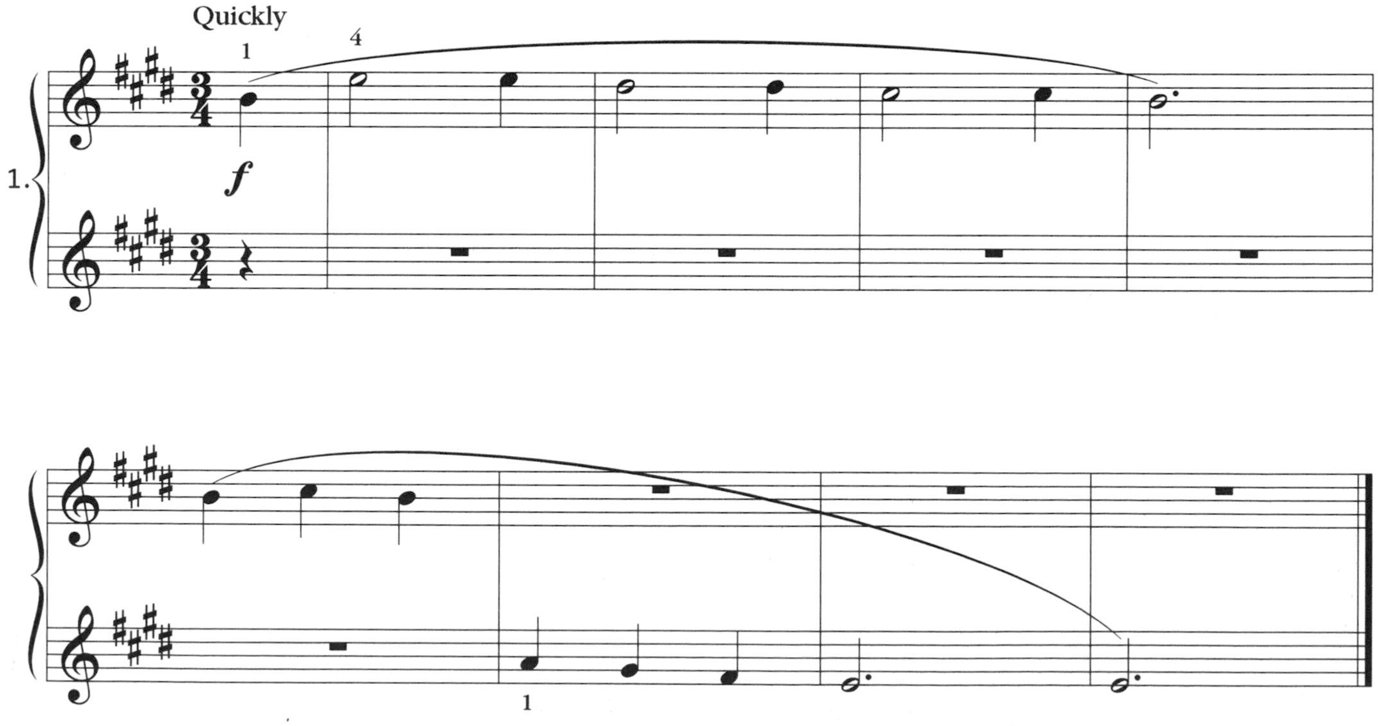

BRETON MELODY

FRENCH MELODY

BRITISH MELODY

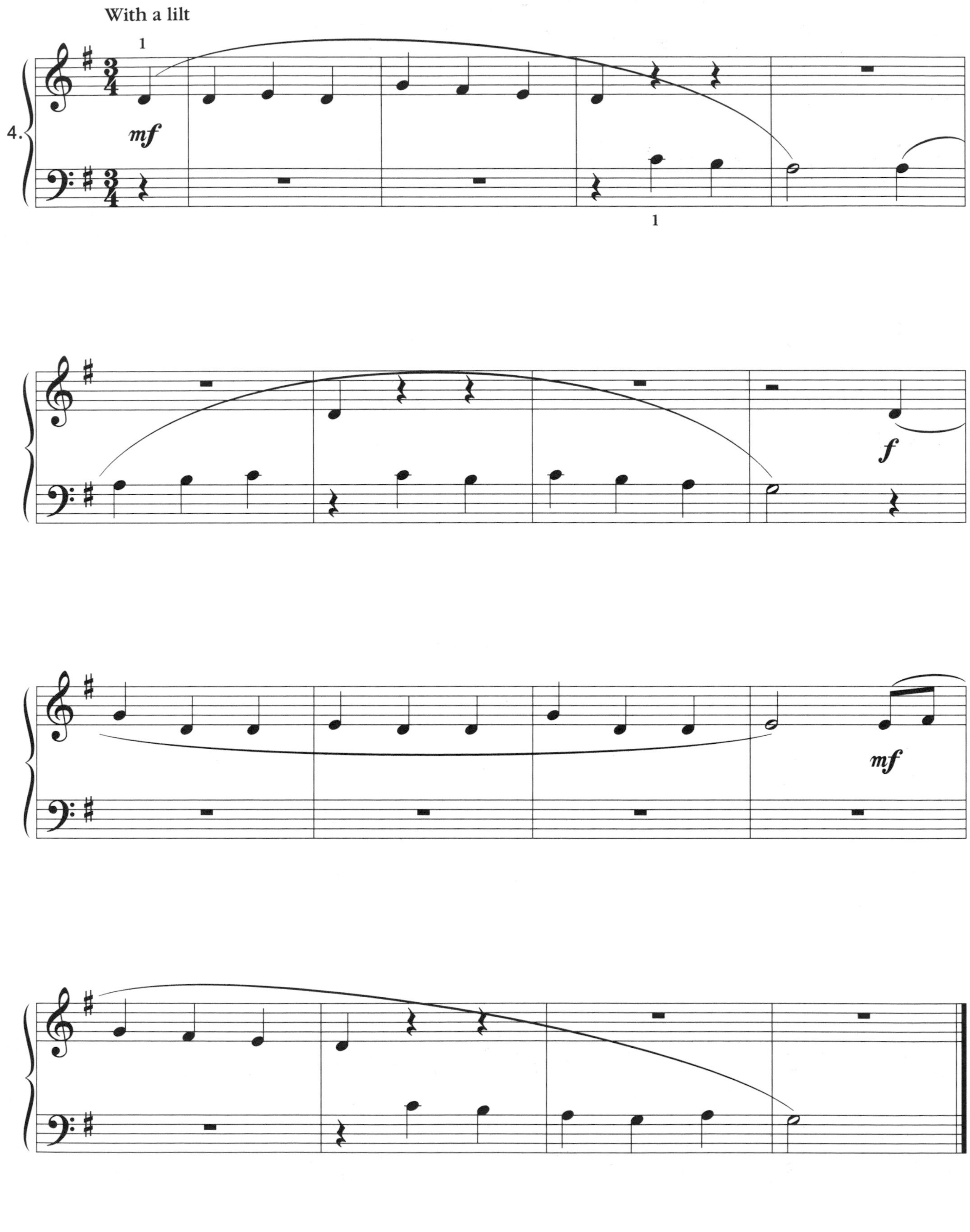

Dotted Quarter Note Followed by an Eighth Note

A dotted quarter note lasts as long as a quarter note tied to an eighth note (♩. = ♩‿♪). Tap the following rhythms found in *Ode To Joy*.

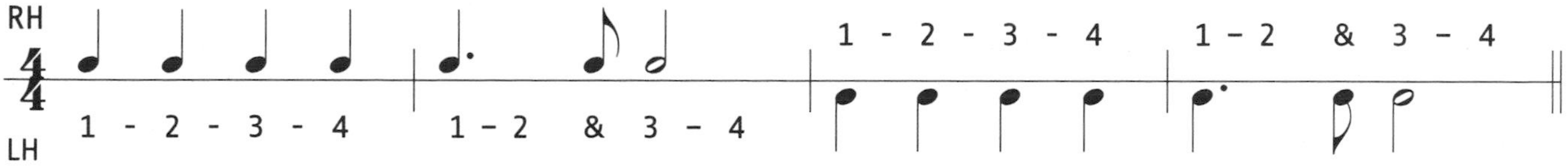

ODE TO JOY

Beethoven
arr. James Lyke

Maestoso

MICHAEL ROW YOUR BOAT ASHORE

U.S. Spiritual

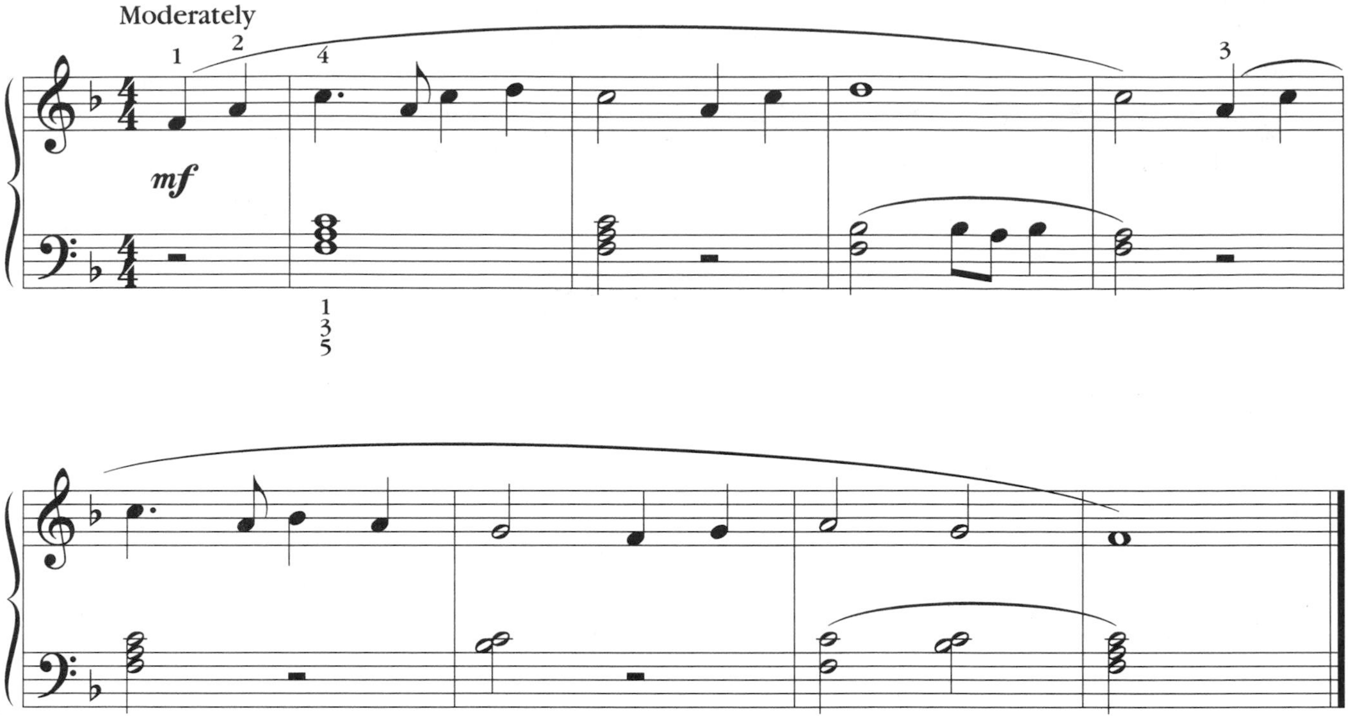

RISE UP SHEPHERD AN' FULLER

(Chorus)

U.S. Spiritual

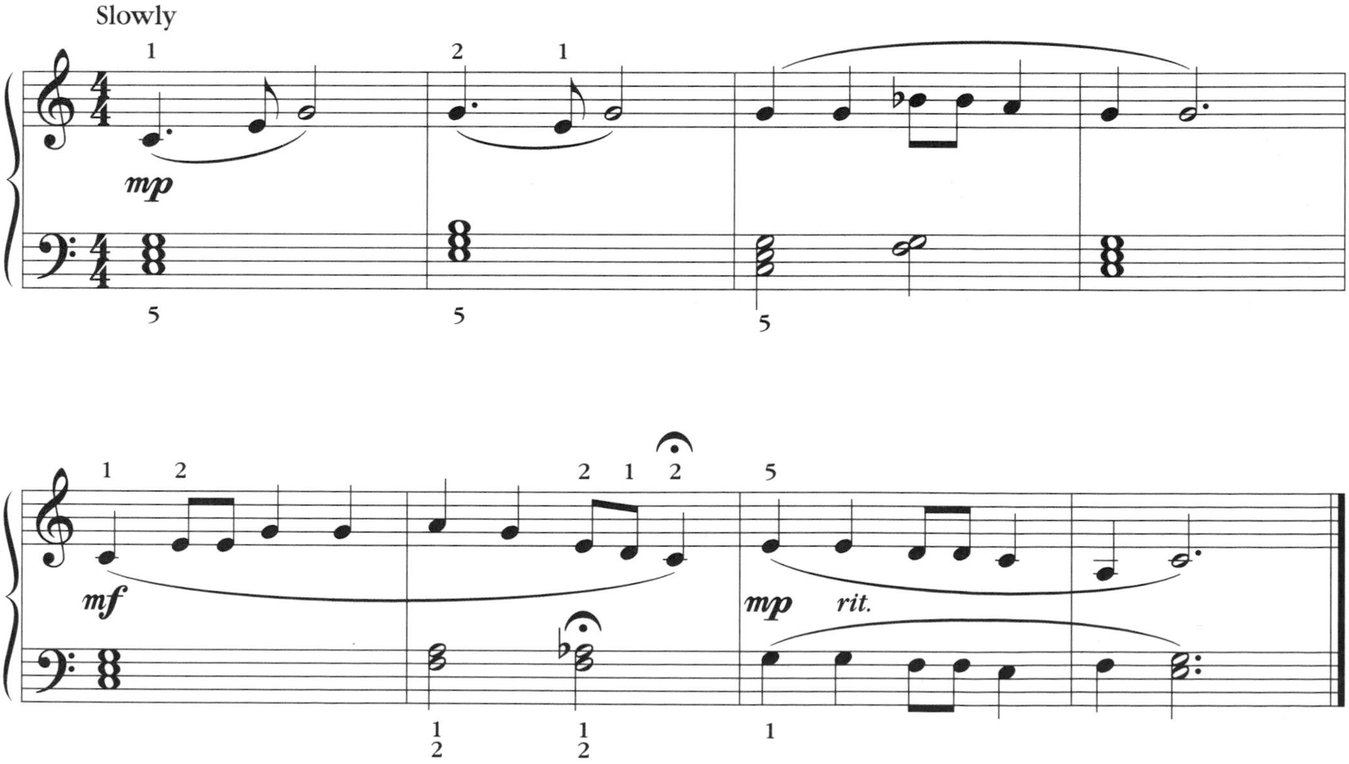

Four Dotted Quarter Note Studies

The following studies provide further experience with the ♩. ♪ rhythmic figure.

FRENCH MELODY

BRITISH MELODY

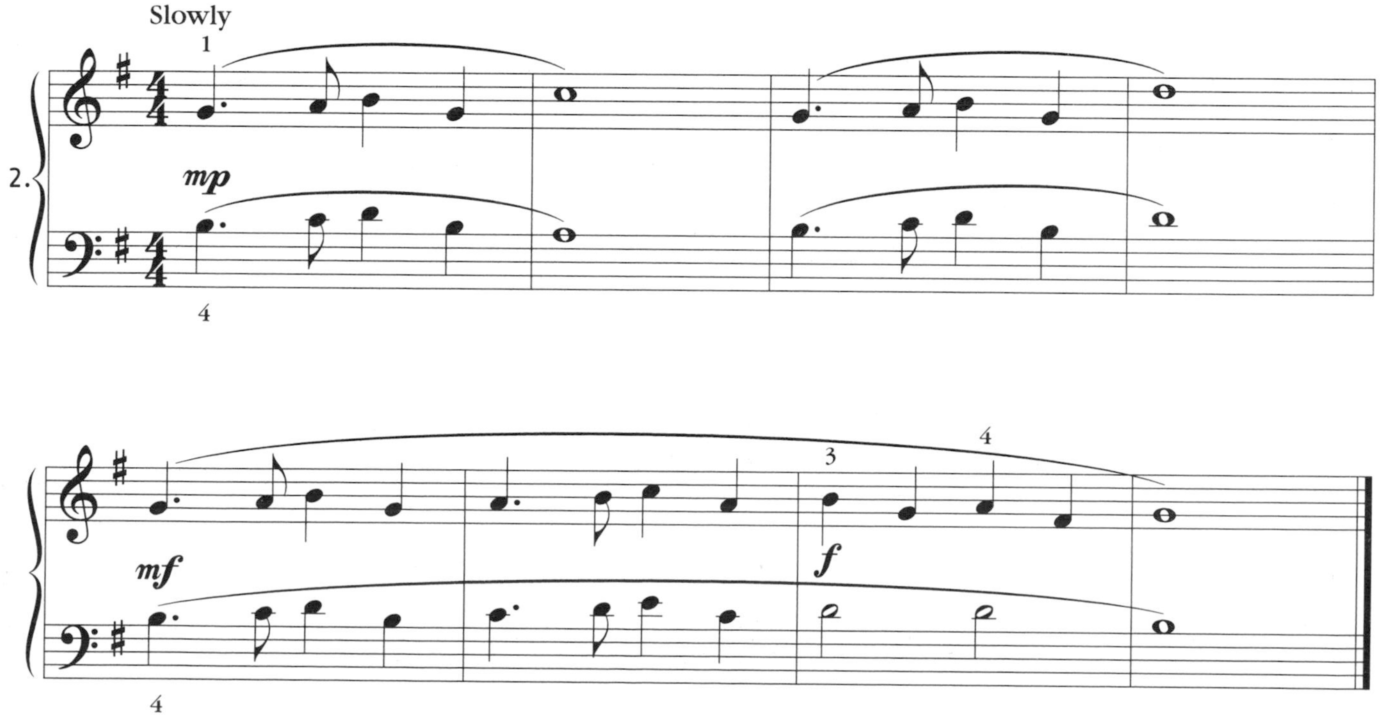

Note the use of scale fingering in the RH of *Flemish Melody.*

FLEMISH MELODY

BRITISH MELODY

Building 6ths, 7ths, and Octaves

Previously you blocked unisons, 2nds, 3rds, 4ths, and 5ths. Now that you've studied how a scale is formed, you need to block 6ths, 7ths, and octaves. Play the intervals shown below which start with a 5th and stretch to the octave. Then move from the octave back to the 5th in each hand.

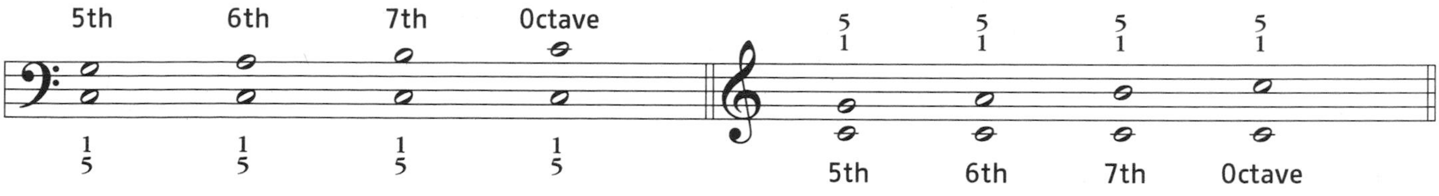

Play the following fragments from folk melodies. Identify the circled intervals. See the example.

1. 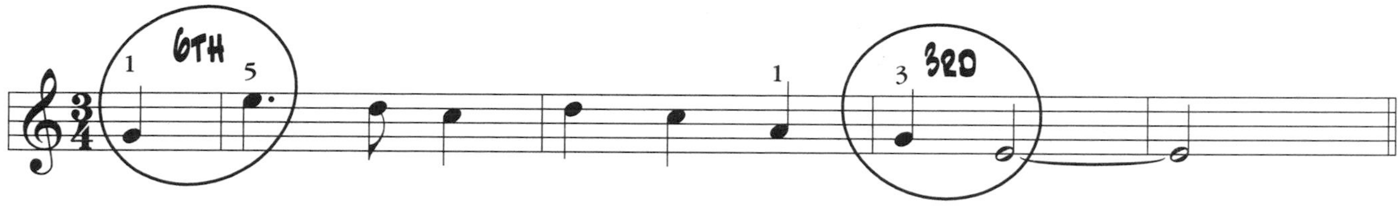

2. 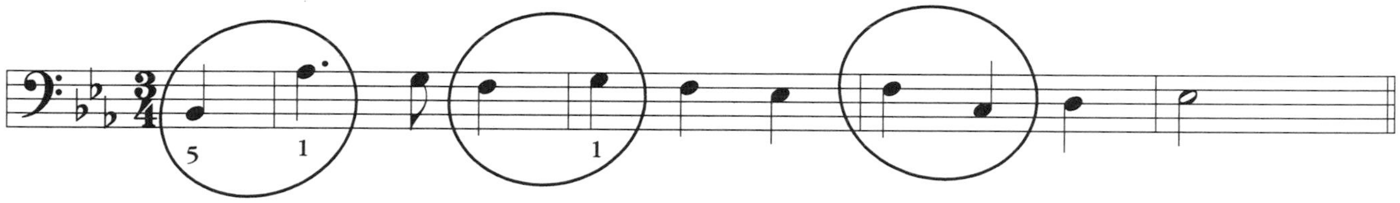

3. 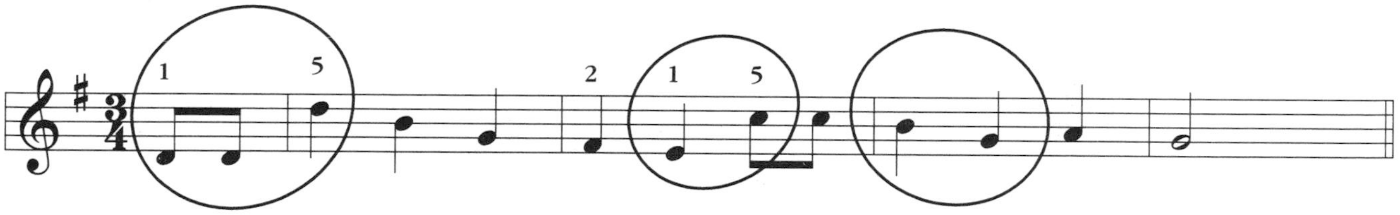

4. 

5. 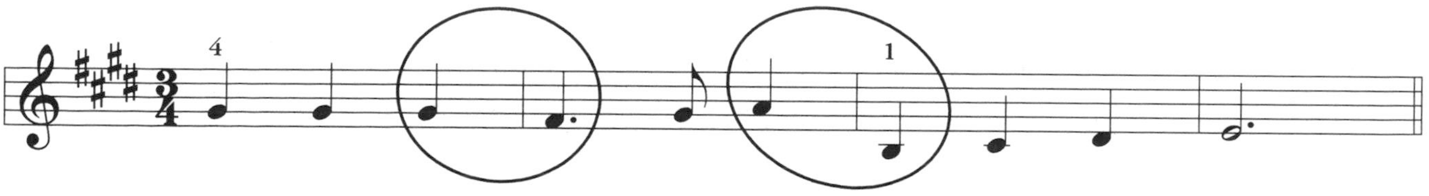

Interval Study

Study and play *Stretching* phrase by phrase. Analyze the intervals in each hand.

Practice Plan: Block the intervals in the LH, practice the move from the octave to a fifth (bars 8–9), and block intervals in the RH. Put hands together at a very slow tempo. Gradually increase to medium slow and medium speed. Drill the pedal changes.

STRETCHING

Denise Edwards

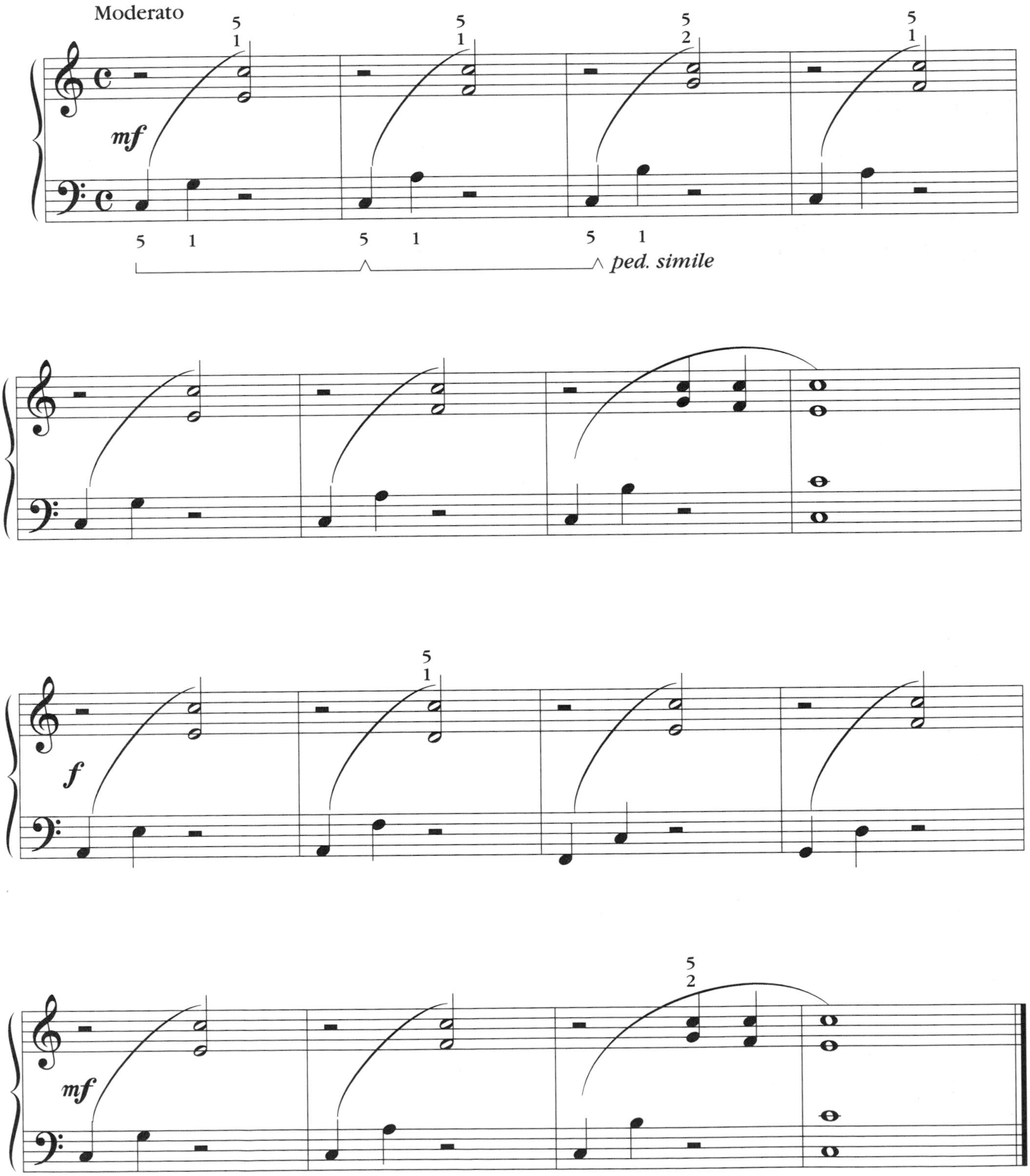

Tonic and Dominant Triads

A *tonic* triad is built on the first degree of a scale. A *dominant* triad is built on the fifth degree of the scale. The dominant triad, like the tonic, is often outlined in melodies. Study the following examples.

Ex. 1

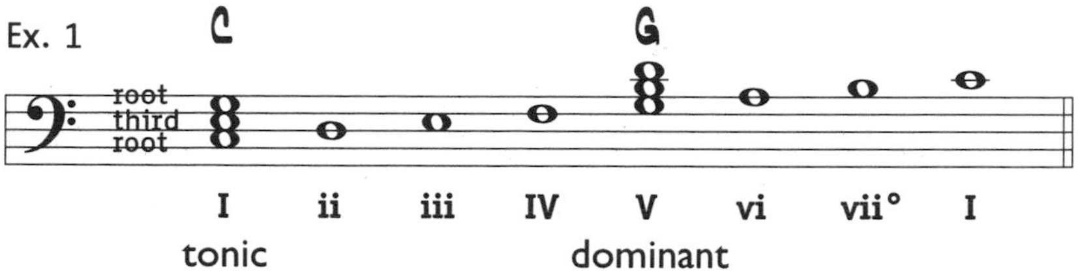

The dominant chord has a strong tendency to move to the tonic. You have already used tones of the dominant chord to harmonize non-tonic tones. Study the tonic and dominant outlines in the melody below.

Ex. 2

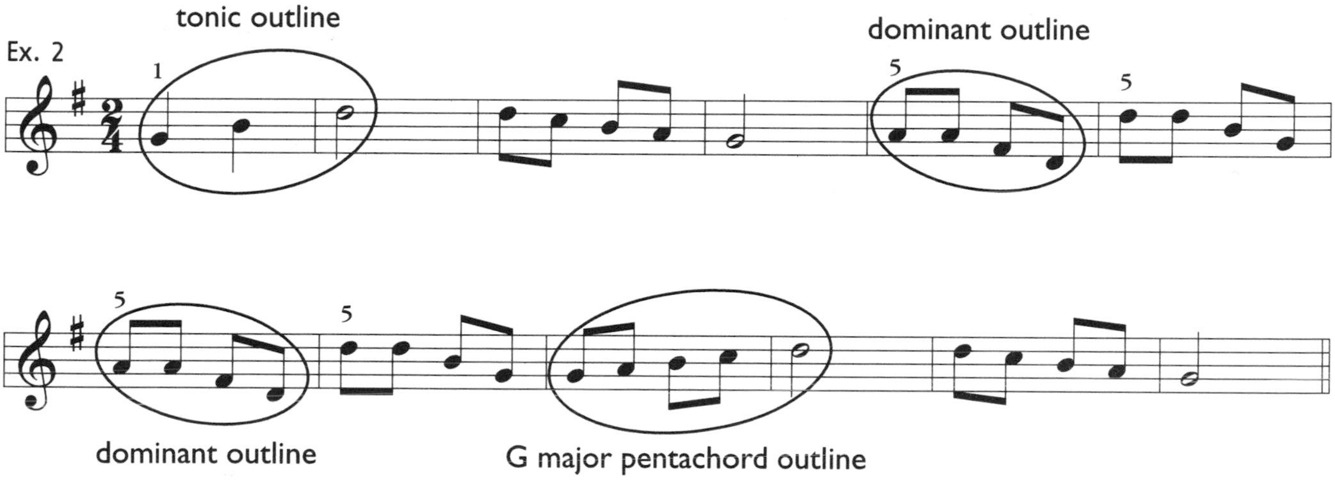

Study the harmonization below which uses the tonic and dominant chords. Capital letter names (G, D) indicate major chords. The capital letter refers to the root of each chord. (See Ex. 1 above.)

Folk Song

Ex. 3

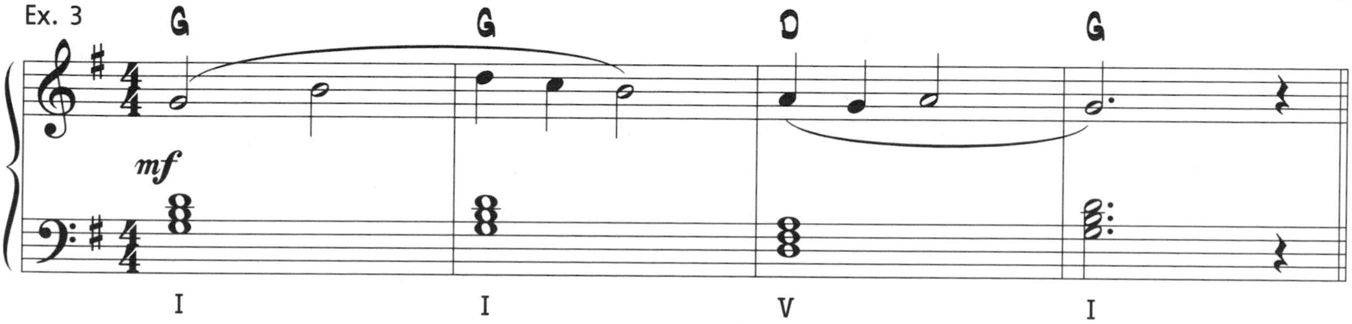

Transpose to F and A.

Harmonizing with Tonic and Dominant Chords

Harmonize the following melodies with tonic (I) and dominant (V) chords. The roots will be in the bass (lowest note). Later we will learn a smoother way to connect these chords. Notate the accompaniment in the blank LH measures.

American

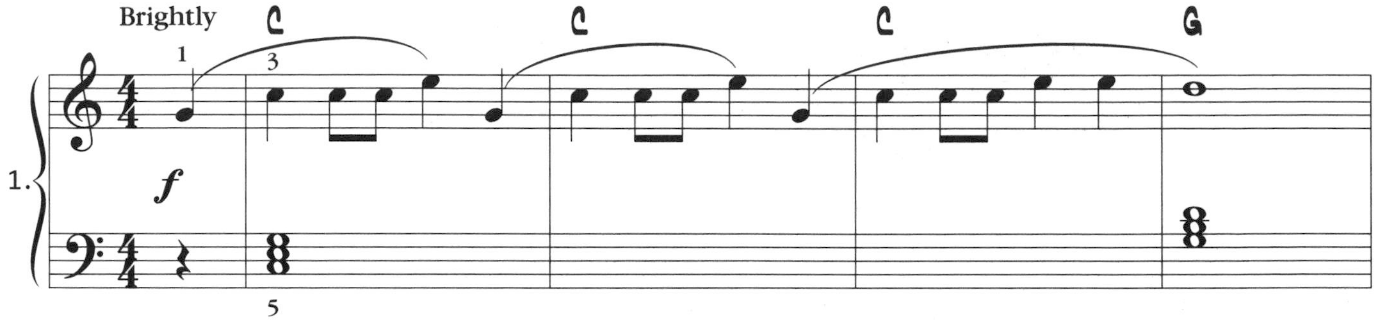

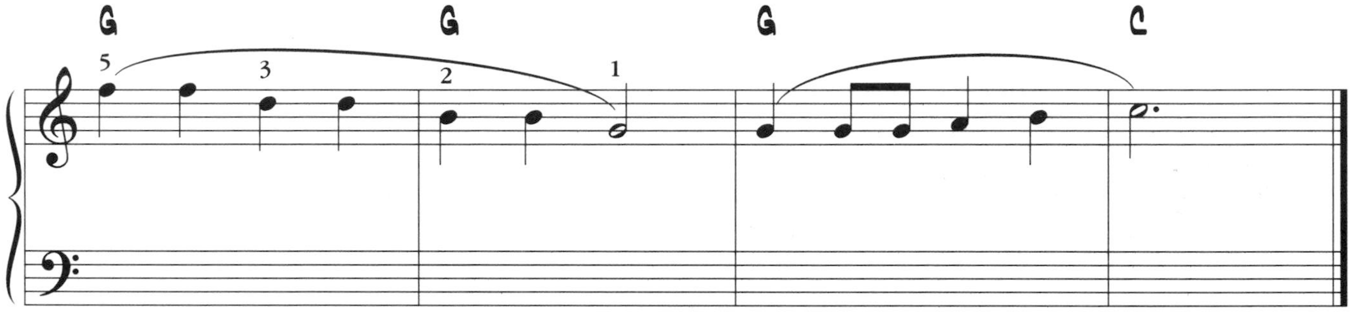

Transpose to B♭

French

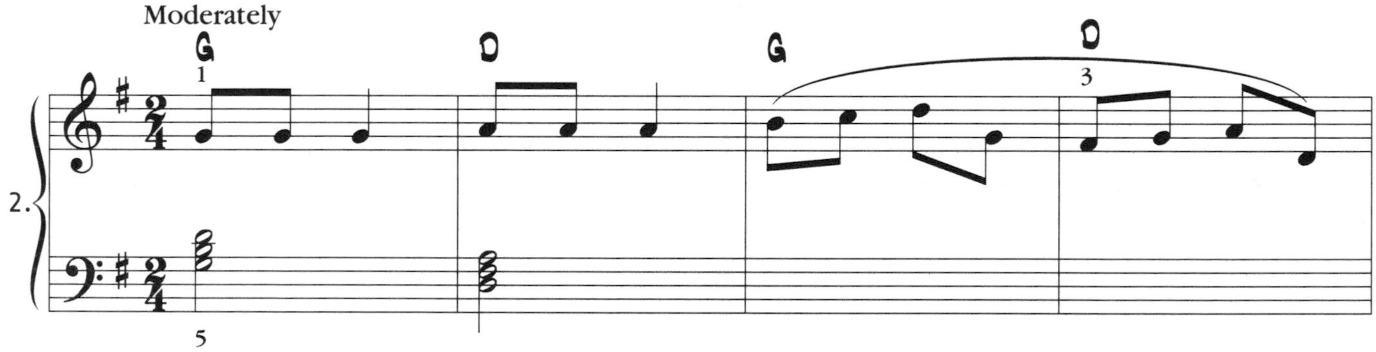

Transpose to F

The Dominant Seventh Chord: Root Position and First Inversion

Study the first four bars of the German folk song below. Note the four tones which are circled. Spelling from bottom to top (D, F♯, A, C), this four-note chord is called a *dominant 7th*. It is built on the 5th degree of the scale and adds one more third to the dominant triad. *Seventh chords* (there are many types) contain four notes built in 3rds. The essential tones of a seventh chord are the root, third, and seventh.

German

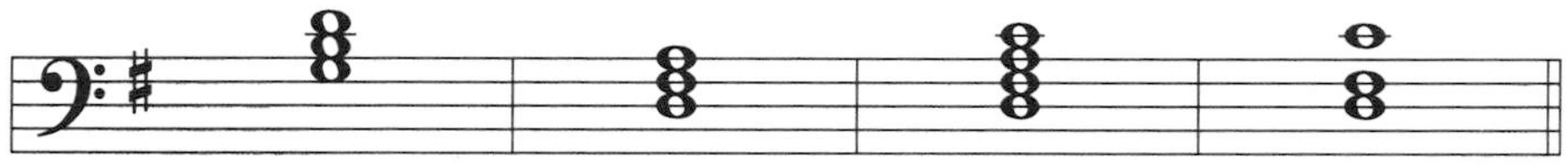

Tonic | Dominant | Dominant 7th | Dominant 7th (essential tones)

For ease in playing this chord, the essential tones may be rearranged, or inverted. For now, the first inversion will be useful.

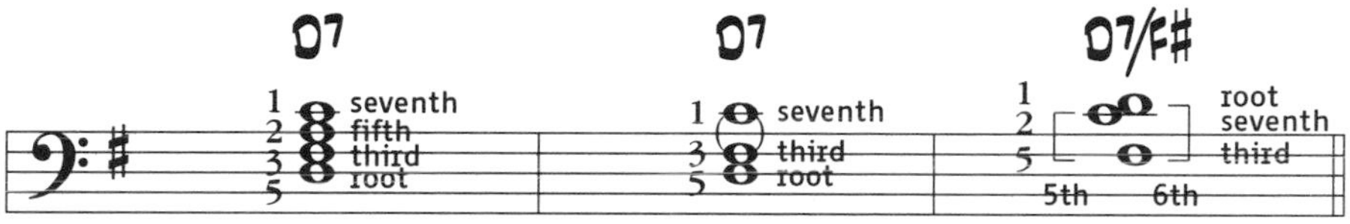

all tones | essential tones | first inversion (dominant $^6_5$)

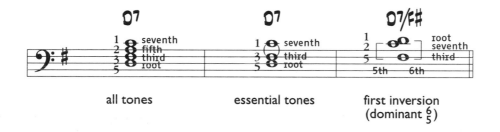

The "7" appearing after the capital letter D in the example above identifies this chord as a *dominant seventh*. There are many types of seventh chords which will be explored at a later time. The D⁷/F♯ chord means that F♯ is the lowest tone. Any letter following a slash normally indicates that tone as the lowest in the harmony.

Dominant Seventh Chord Drill

Write the letter name (e.g. chord symbol) in the box above each chord.

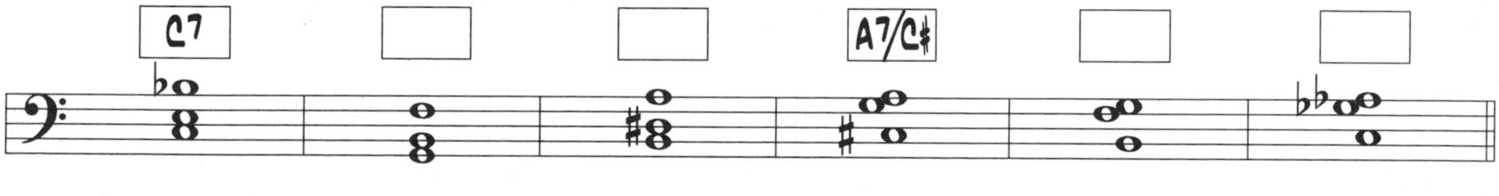

Harmonizing with Tonic and First Inversion Dominant 7th Chords

Harmonize melodies 1 and 2 using the familiar tonic chord and the first inversion of the dominant 7th chord (also known as dominant $^6_5$). Notate the LH chords. When no chord symbol appears above the melody, continue the previous harmony.

British

1.

French

2.

MENUET

Josef Haydn

3.

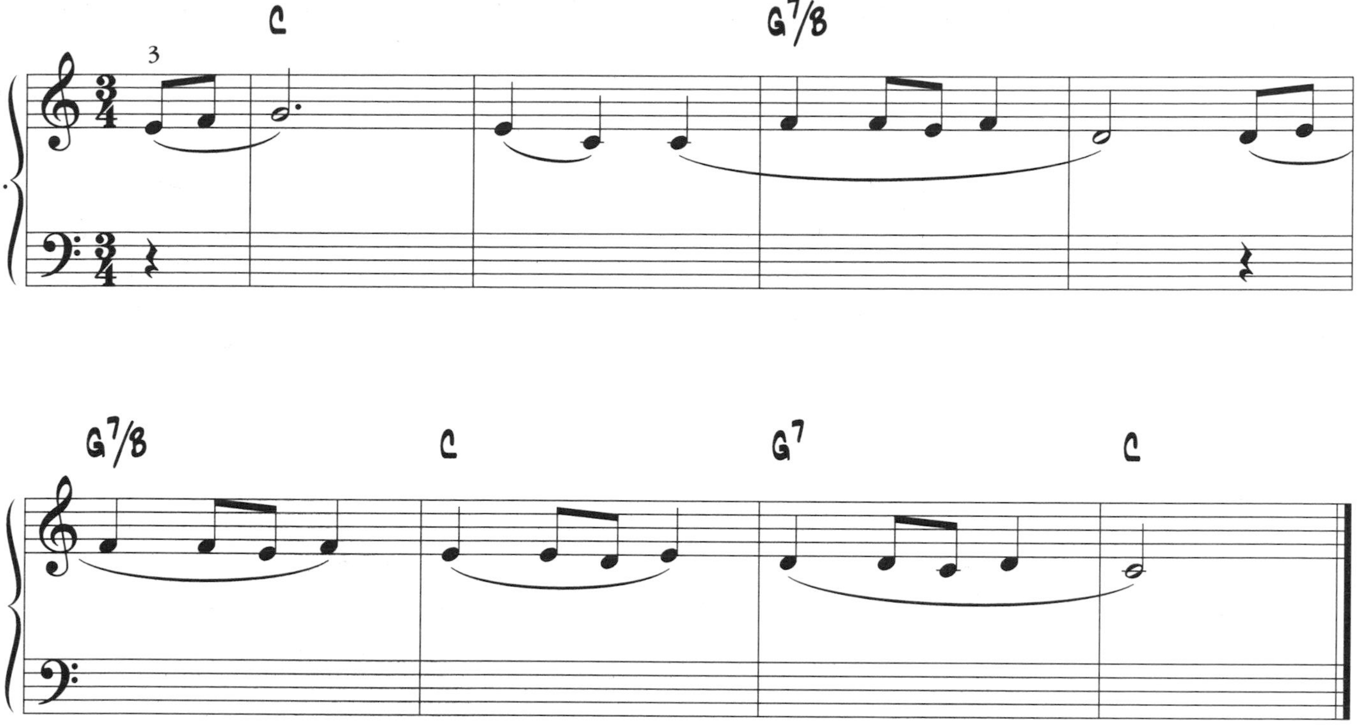

British

4.

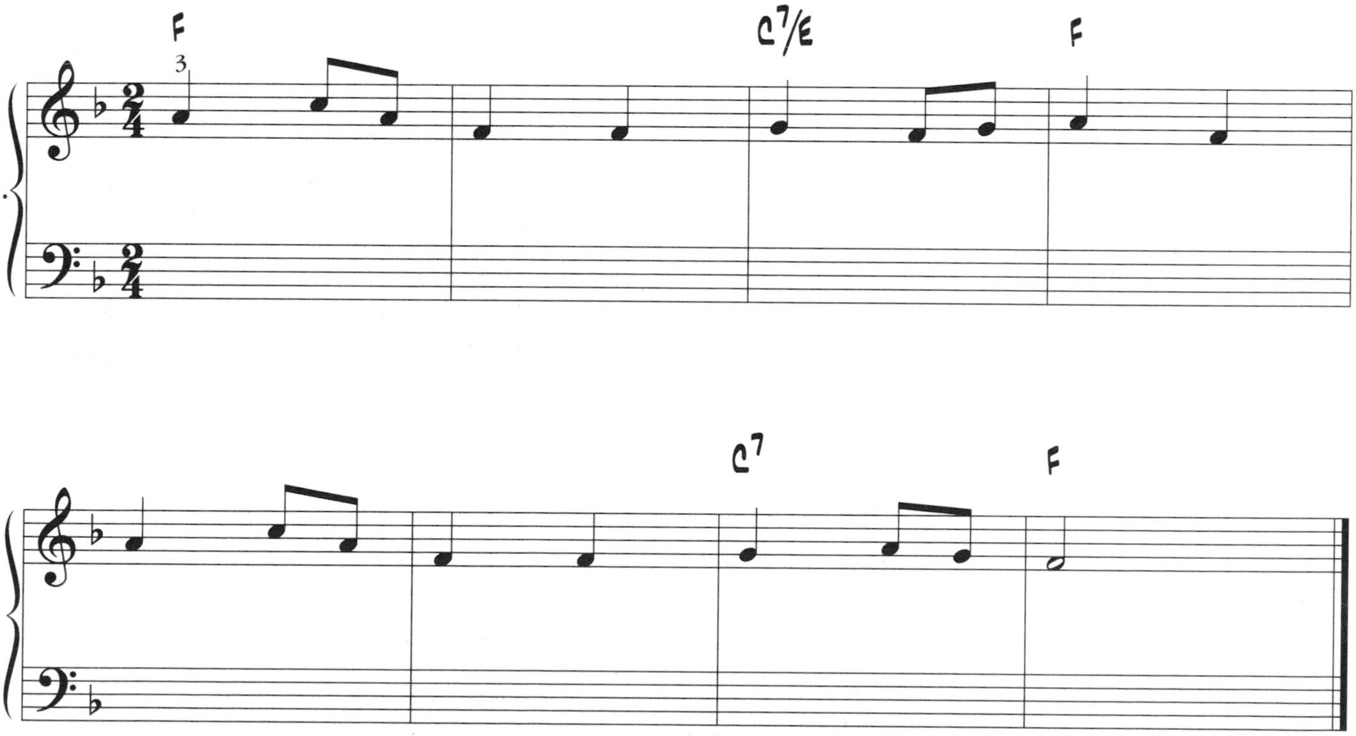

Music for Sight Reading and Transposing

Before sight reading the following studies, establish the habit of 1) identifying the key signature, 2) chanting and tapping the rhythms in each hand (or both hands together), 3) locating beginning pitches and fingerings, and 4) playing slowly to avoid halting at any point in the study. Analyze errors after the first reading. *Trust your hands.* Transpose selected studies to the keys indicated.

German

Joyfully ♩ = 84

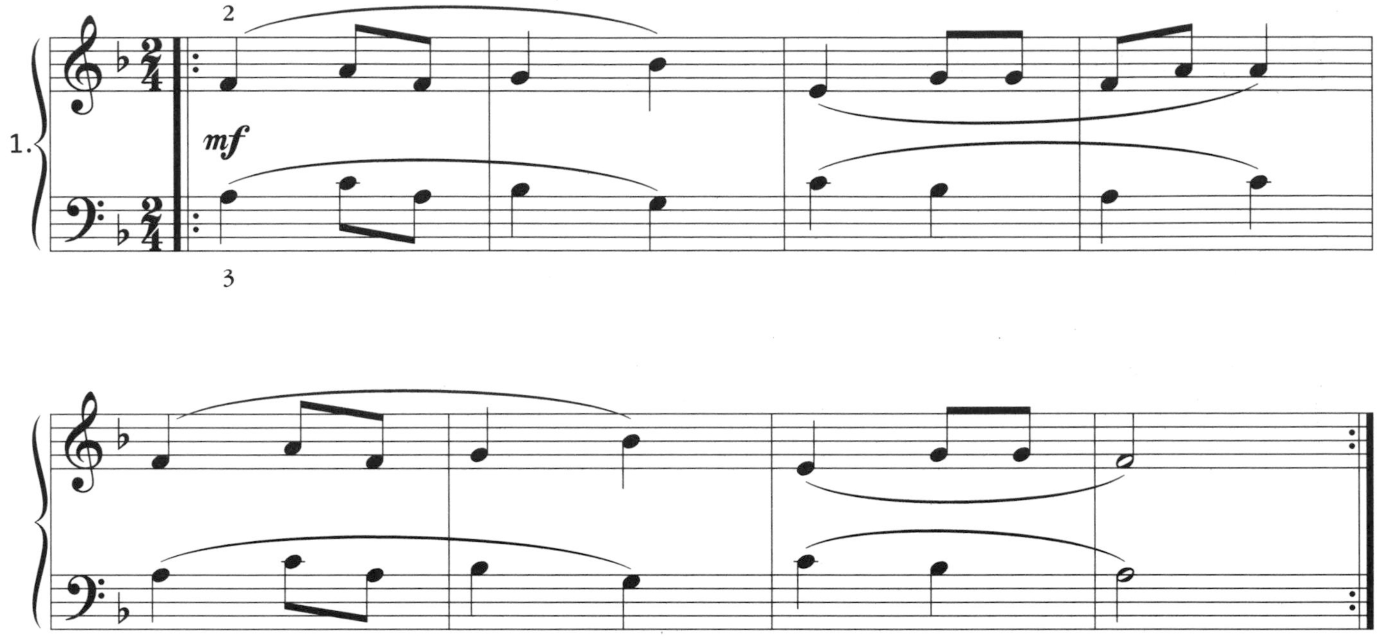

Transpose to A

A-TISKET A-TASKET

American Game Song

Leisurely

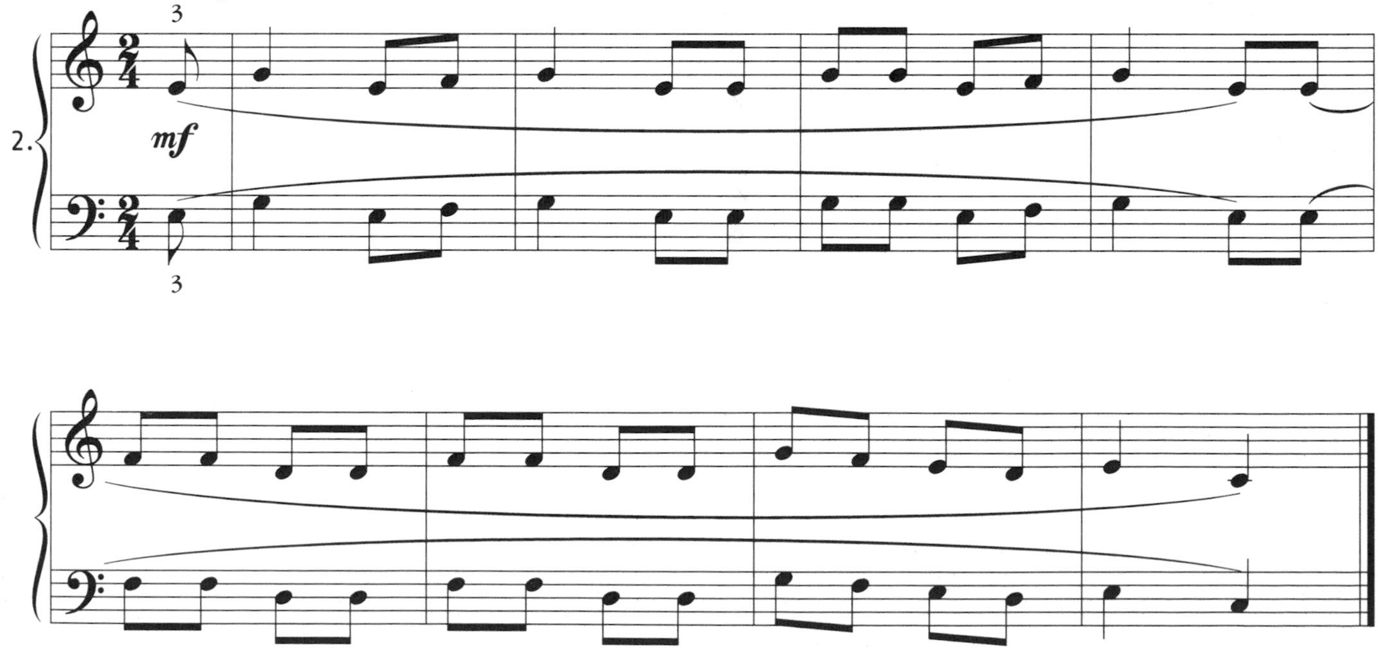

Transpose to D

SCOTLAND'S BURNING

English Round

Transpose to F

Hungarian

Transpose to E♭

WHAT TIME IS IT?

Dutch Folk Song

5.

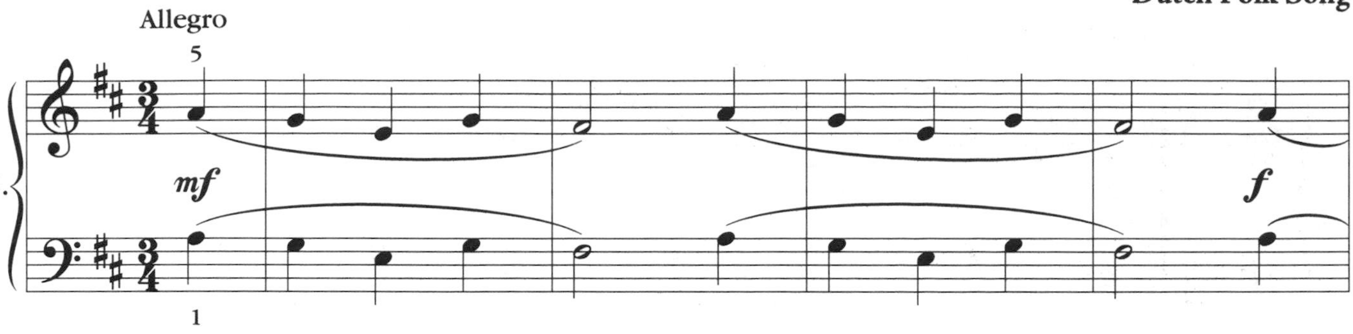

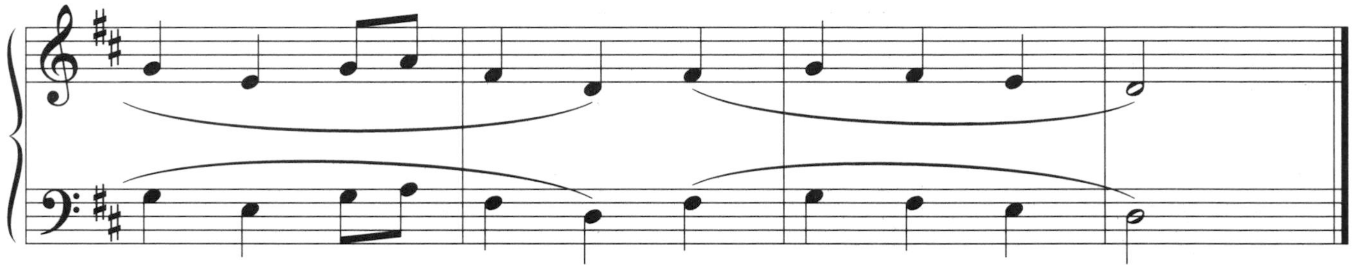

Transpose to C

Polish

6.

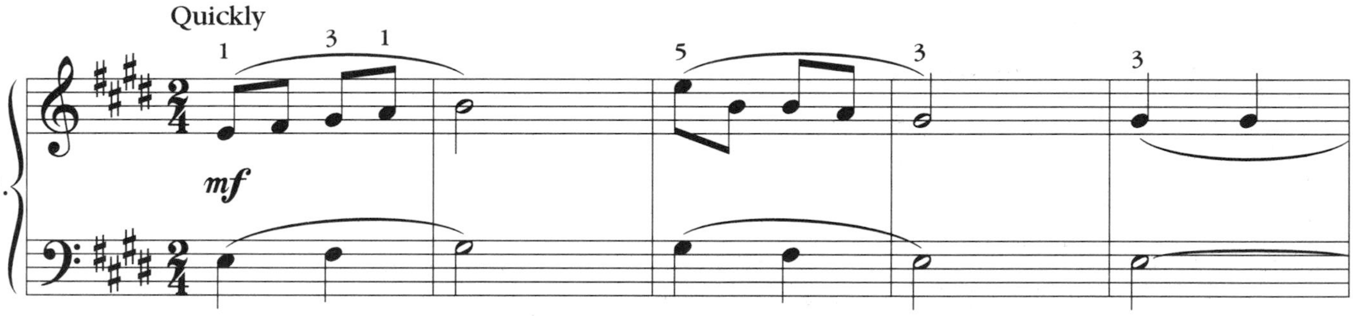

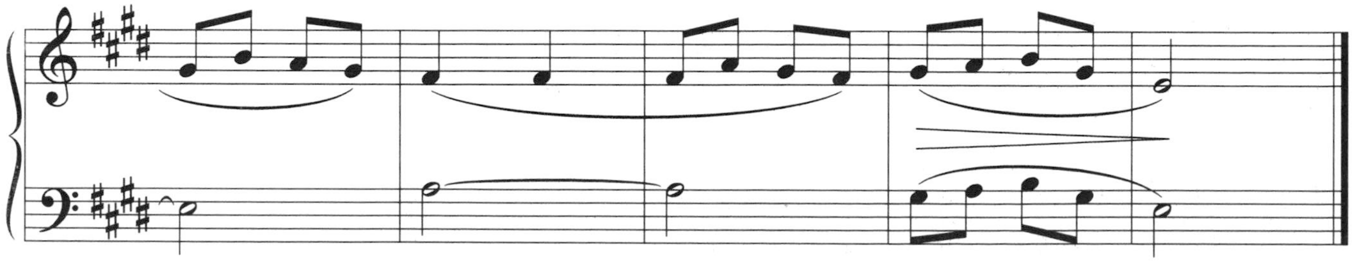

Transpose to D

British

With vigor

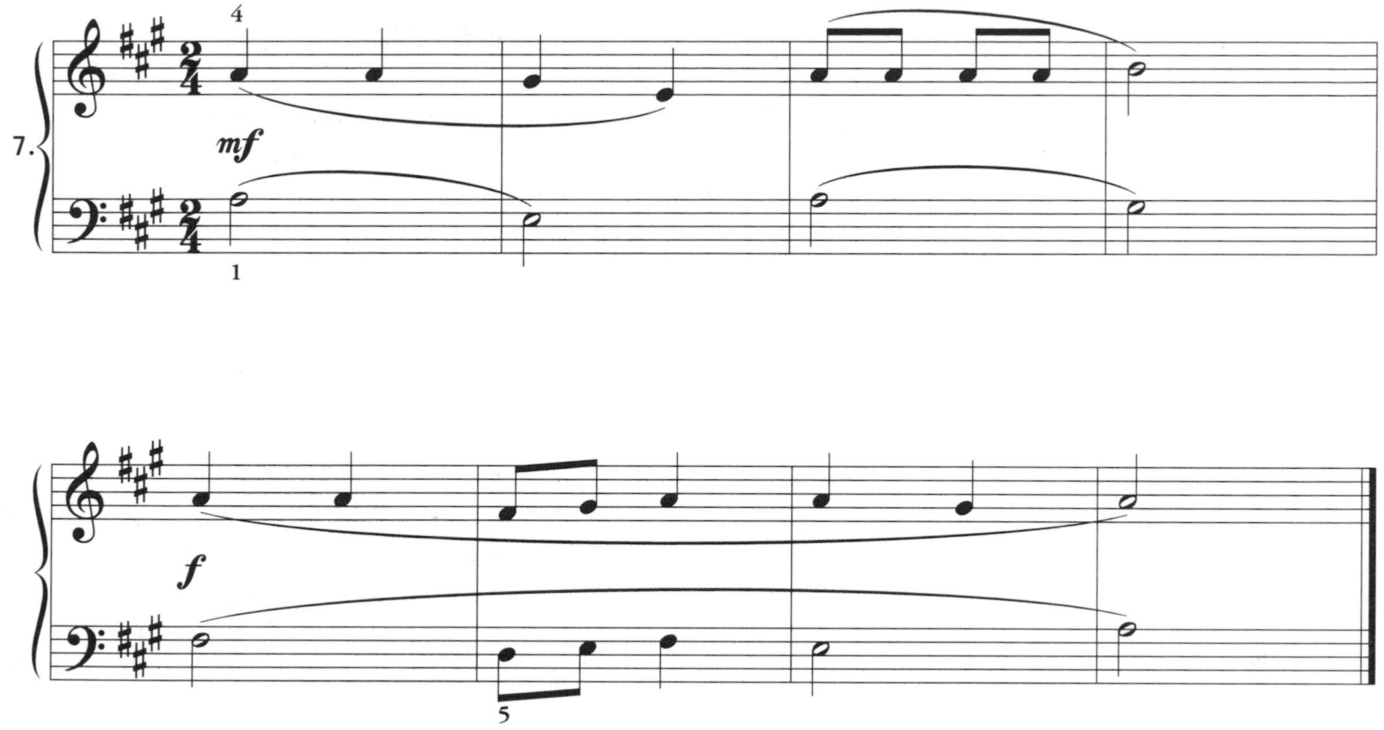

Transpose to G

Slovenian

Merrily ♩ = 80

no transposition

Czech

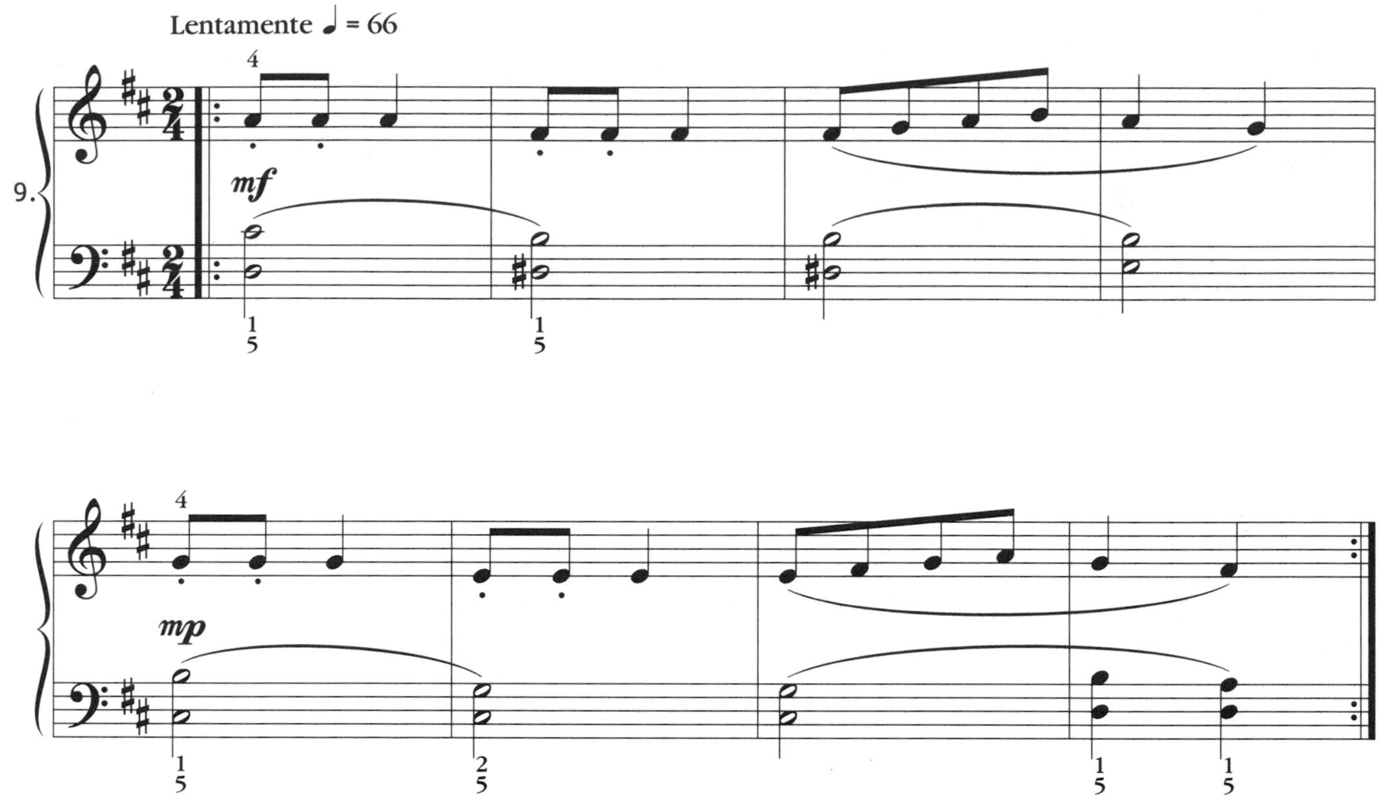

no transposition

Slovakian

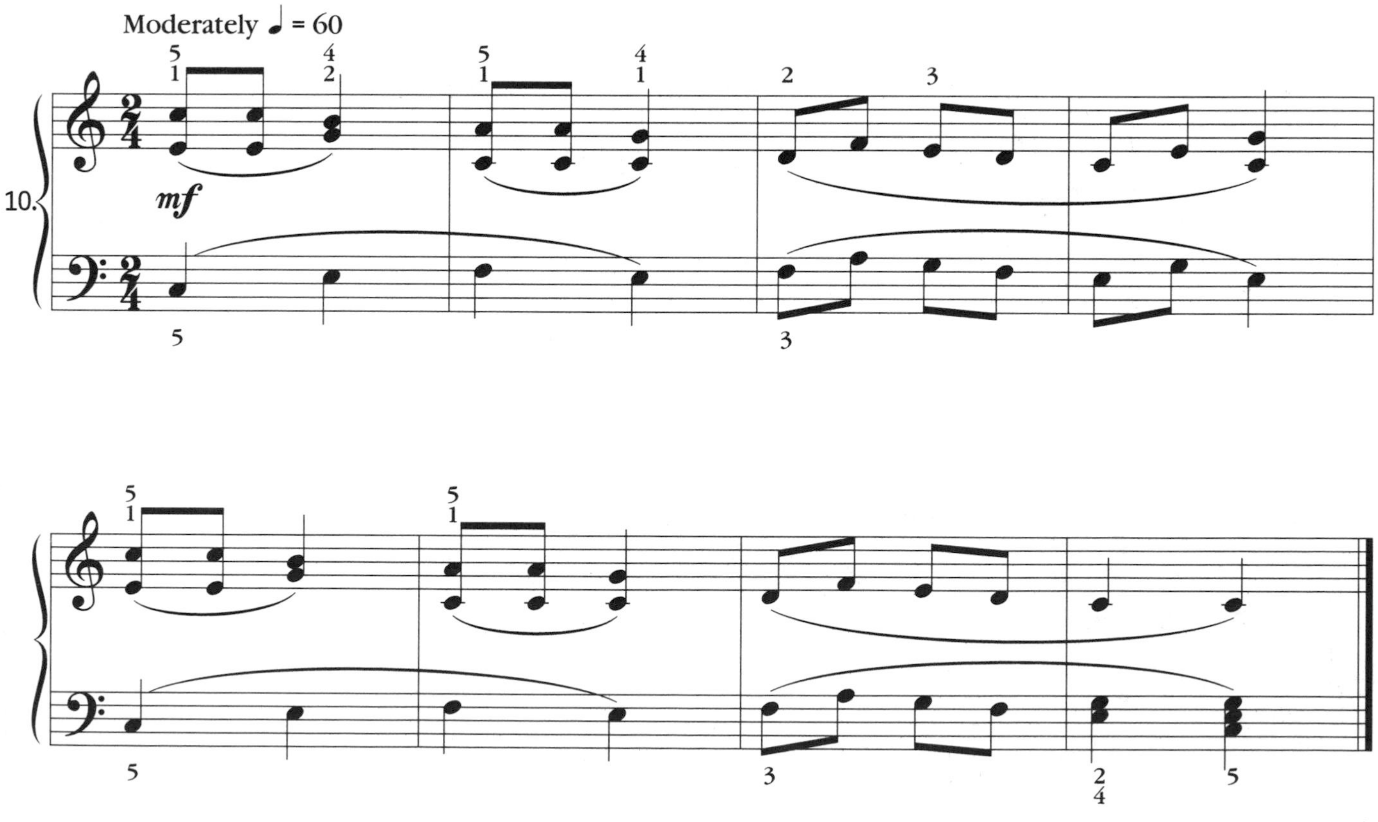

Transpose to B♭

ACCOMPANYING

Learn the student **(S)** or accompaniment part. Notice the easy LH pattern. The RH shifts between two intervals.

Teacher: Double the melody two octaves higher in *My Hat, Lone Star Trail,* and *Russian Song.*

11 CD

MY HAT

German
arr. **James Lyke**

Spirited

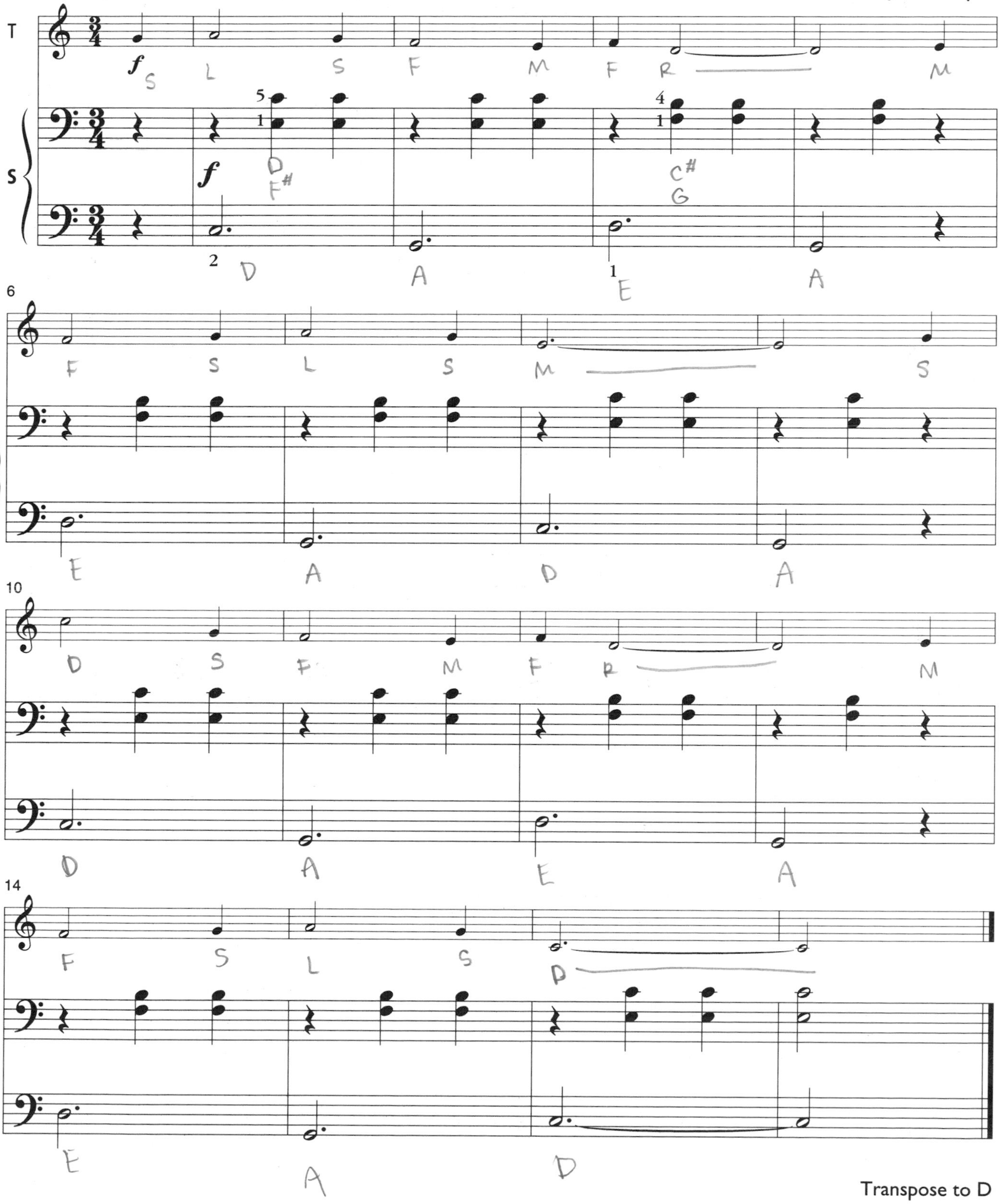

Transpose to D

12 CD

LONE STAR TRAIL

Cowboy Song
arr. James Lyke

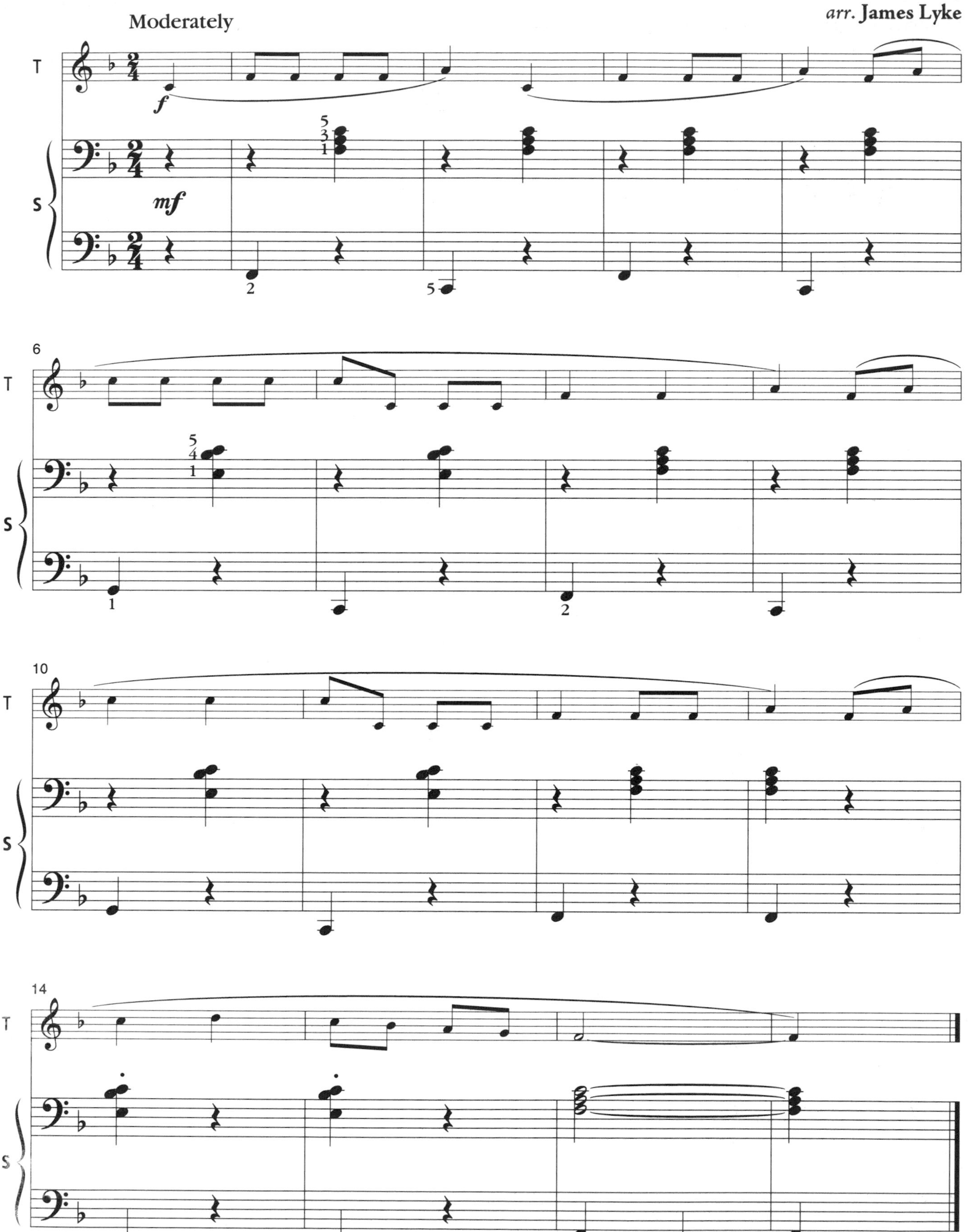

RUSSIAN FOLK SONG

arr. James Lyke

Moderato ♩ = 112

14 CD

WHEN I LOST YOU

music by **Irving Berlin**
arr. **James Lyke**

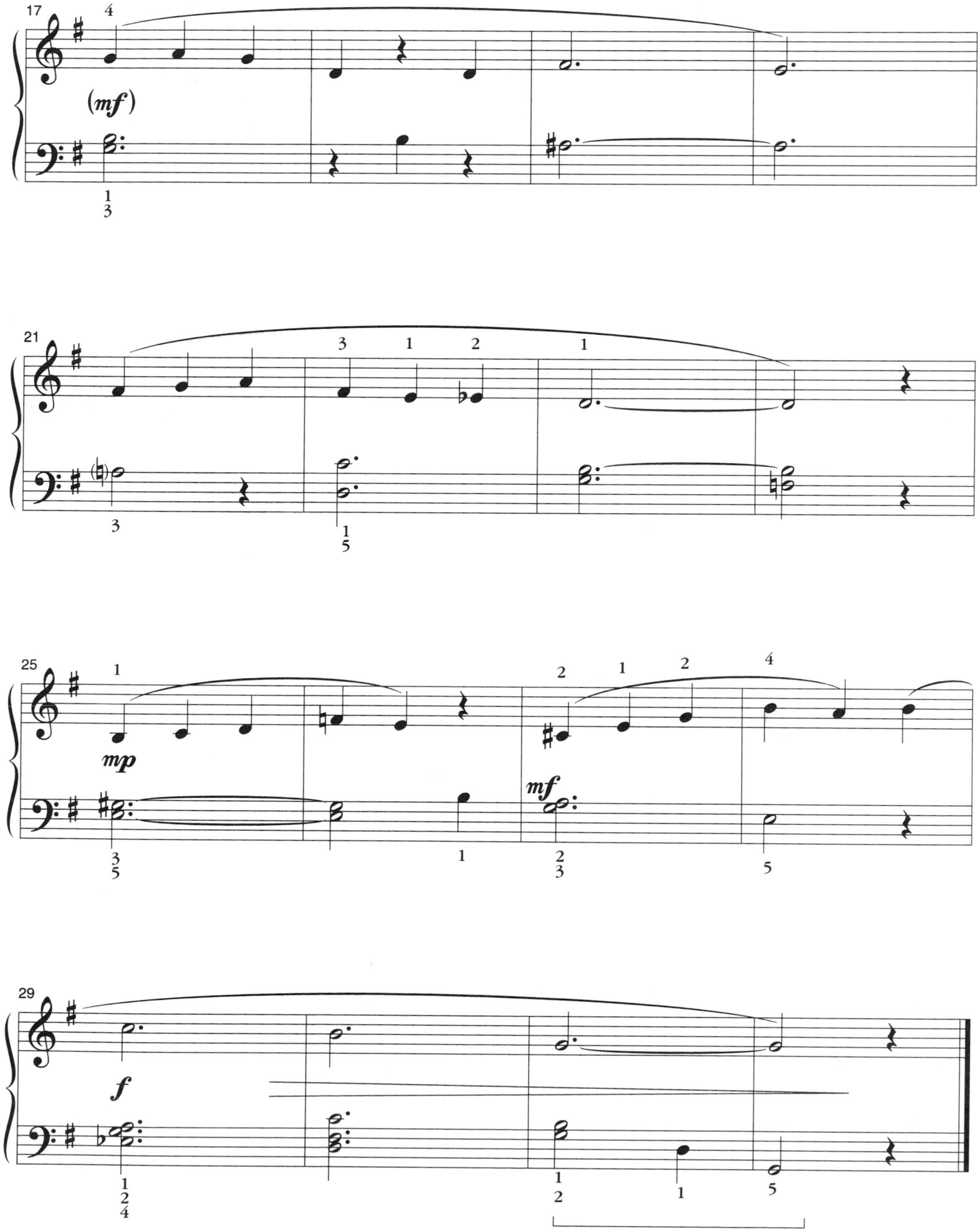
17
(mf)
21
25
mp
mf
29
f

THEY CALL IT DANCING

music by **Irving Berlin**
arr. **James Lyke**

17
21
25
29
33
f

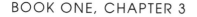

16 CD

RUMBA

Secondo – Teacher

James Lyke

16 CD

RUMBA

Primo – Student

James Lyke

THEME FROM POLOVETZIAN DANCES

Secondo – Teacher

Alexander Borodin
arr. **James Lyke**

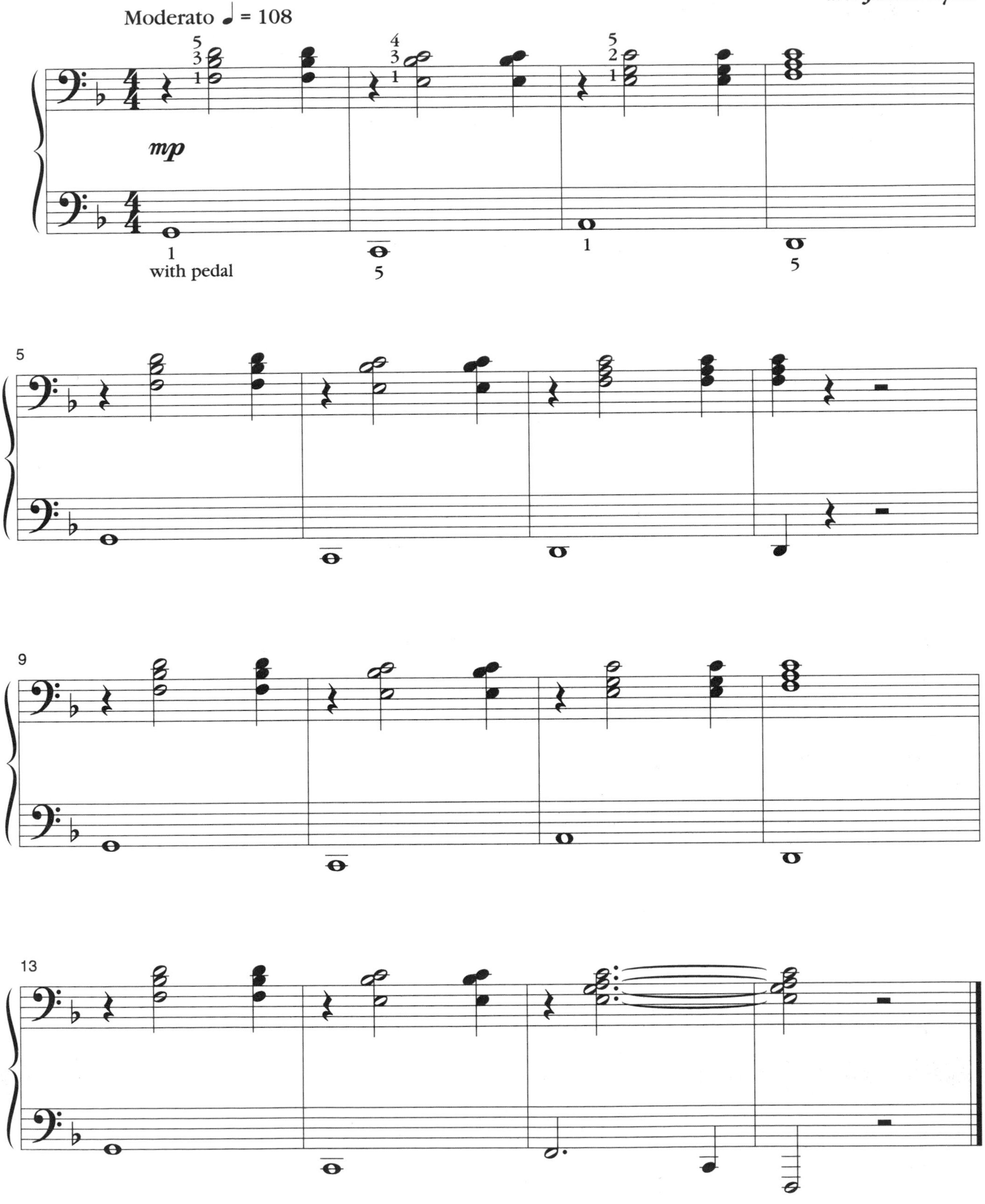

THEME FROM POLOVETZIAN DANCES

Primo – Student

Alexander Borodin
arr. **James Lyke**

Moderato ♩ = 108

Reminder: 8va ----- means to play the melody one octave higher than written.

Theme from Polovetzian Dances contains a recurring four chord pattern. Practice the following LH progression until it becomes fluent. Transpose the primo part one octave lower and you will have an effective solo! Add pedal.

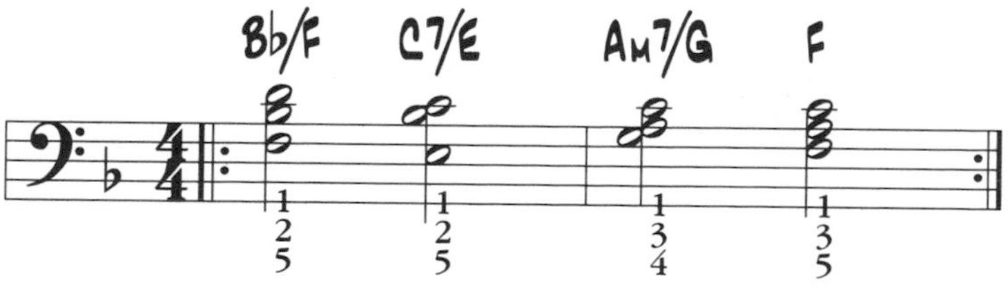

SOLO REPERTOIRE

From here through Chapter Eight look up all unfamiliar terms and signs in Appendix A.

Practice Plan: Practice hands alone and exaggerate two-note slurs and other phrase markings (RH). Keep eyes on the music and pay particular attention to shifts. D minor shares its key signature with F major. We will study minor keys extensively in Chapter Four.

BOURRÉE IN D MINOR

Christoph Graupner

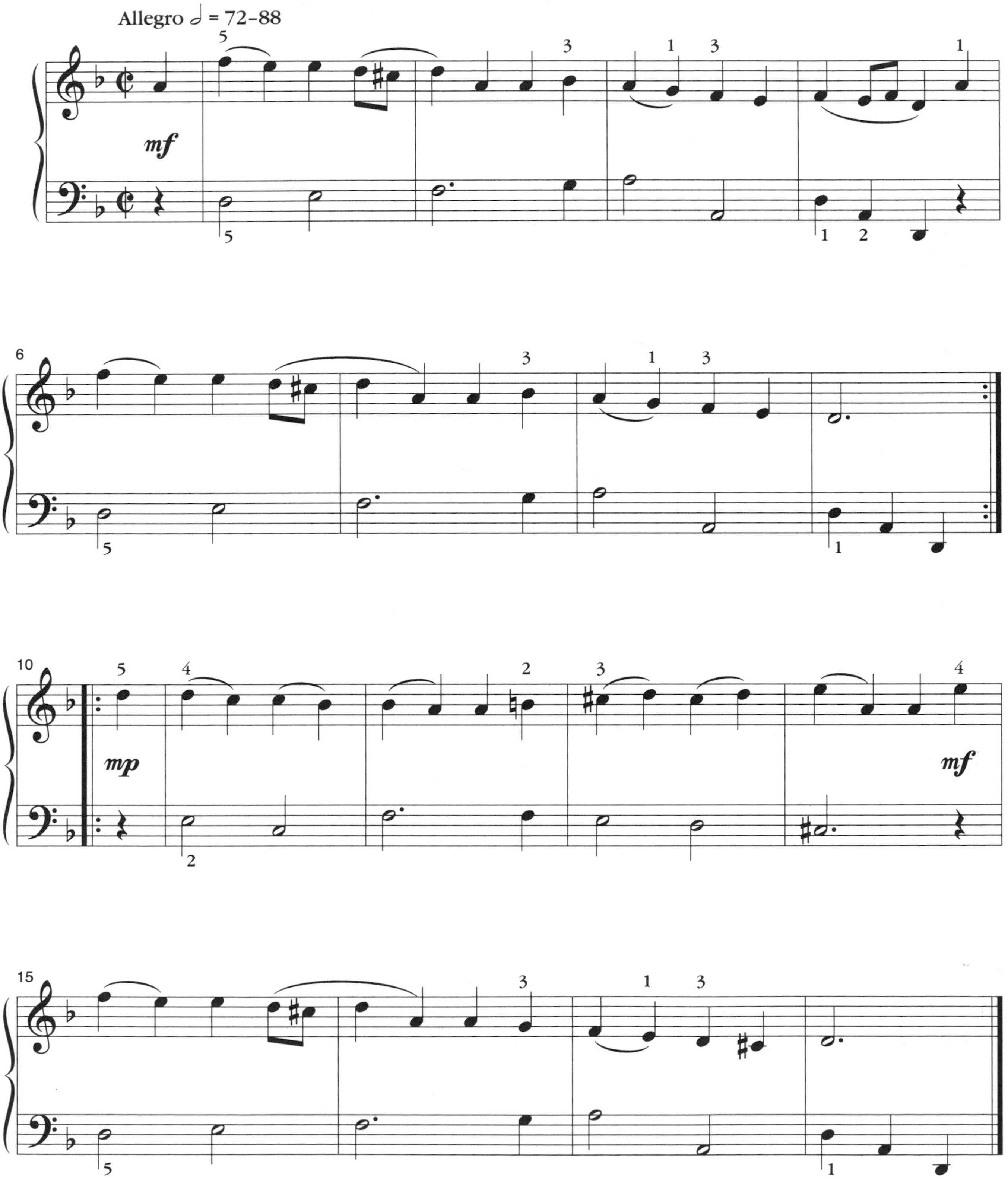

Practice Plan: Practice hands alone, as usual, to make fingering very secure. Perform cleanly with no pedal. Feel the shifts of position without looking at your hands.

TWO CLASSIC PIECES

Daniel Gottlob Türk

Andante

Daniel Gottlieb Türk

Allegro moderato

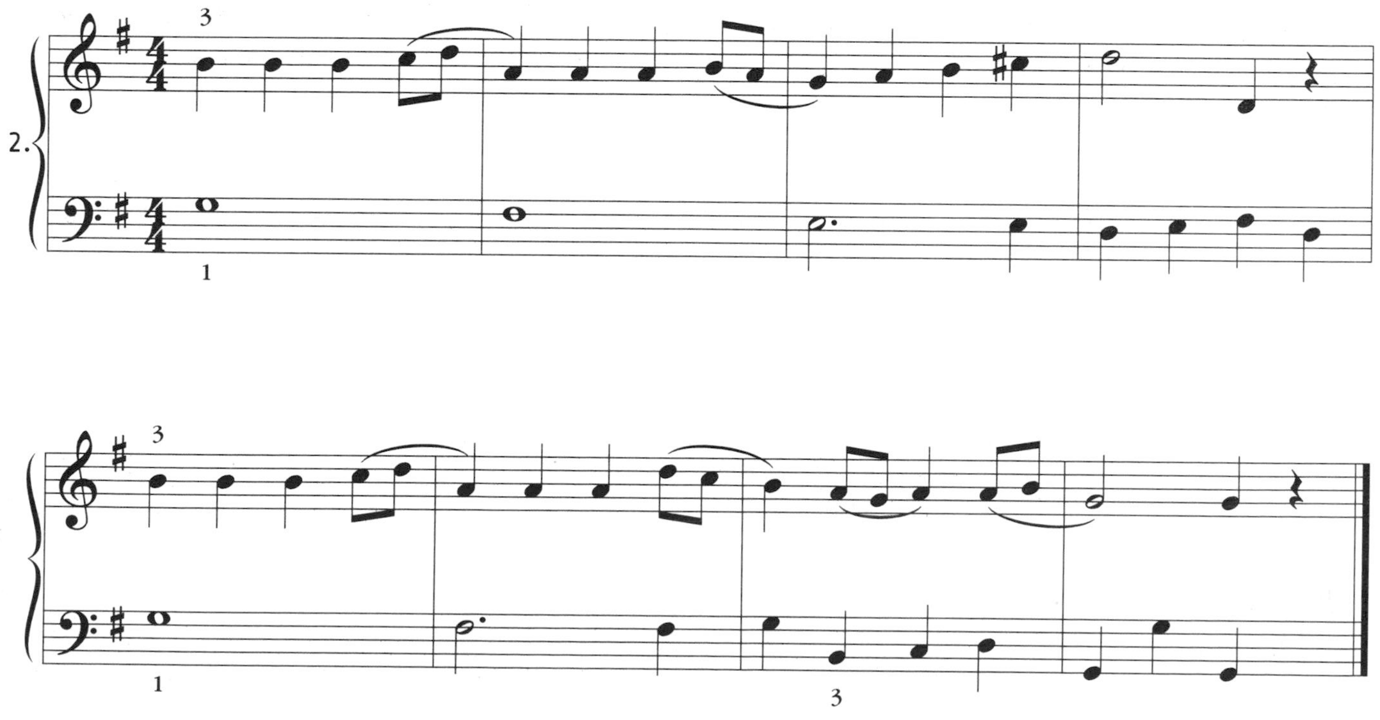

Practice Plan: Block each LH measure; all measures fall within the D major pentachord. To gain control of RH eighth notes, practice them detached (*staccato*). Drill RH bars 9–16 repeatedly. Look for an A^7/C♯ chord in the LH.

MUSIC BOX

Cornelius Gurlitt

Practice Plan: Practice hands alone and be attentive to touches (*legato, staccato*). Measures 9–16 require special work with changes of position and hand-over-hand arpeggiation. What patterns are suggested by the title?

PATTERNS

Tony Caramia

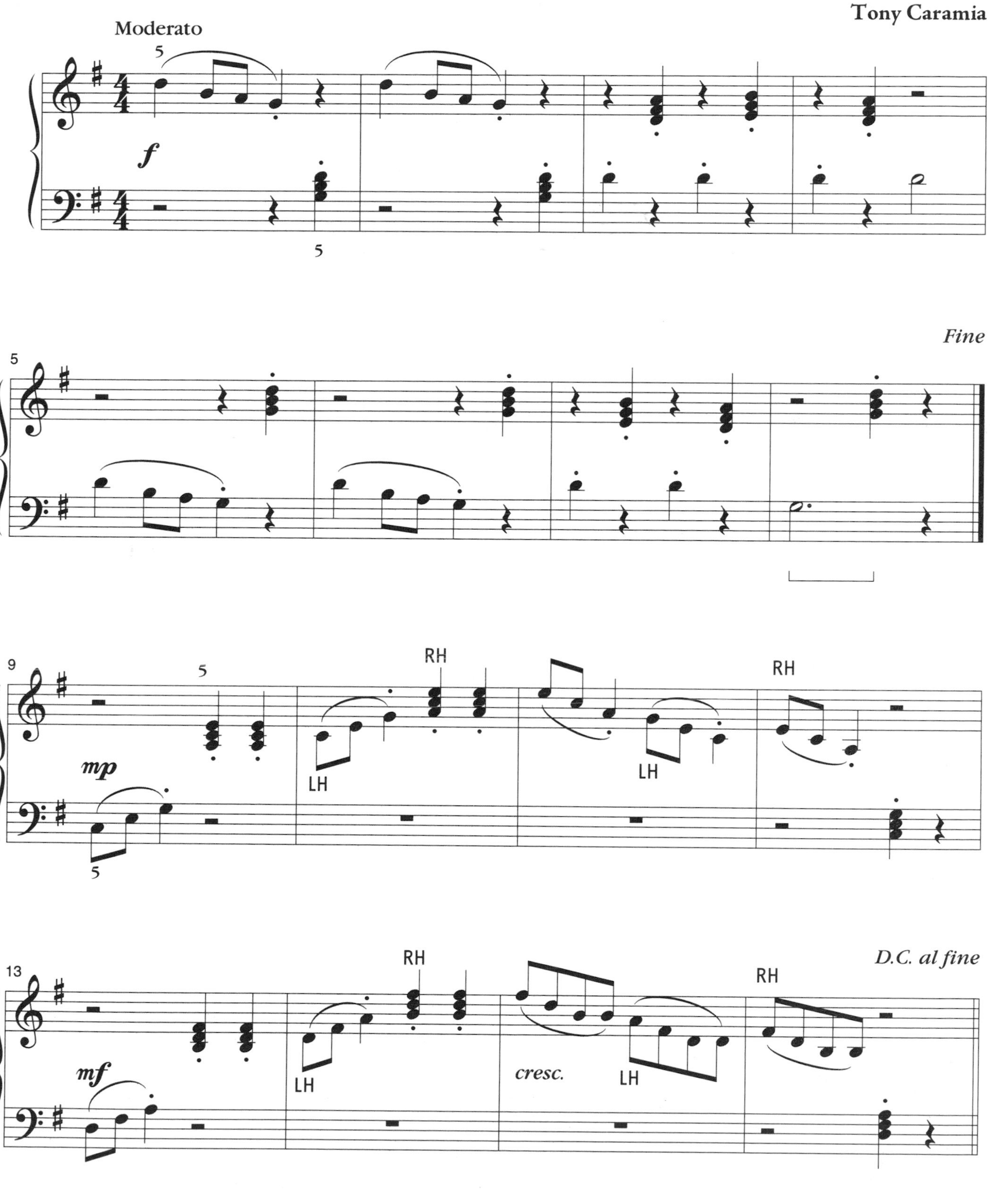

D.C. al fine means go back to the beginning and play to the place marked *fine*.

Practice Plan: Exaggerate the RH two-note slurs (drop ↓, lift ↑). Find examples of root position dominant seventh chords in the LH. In the second section, take note of the descending chromatic thirds. Isolate this passage for special practice.

MARIE DORT
(MARIE SLEEPS)

Darius Milhaud

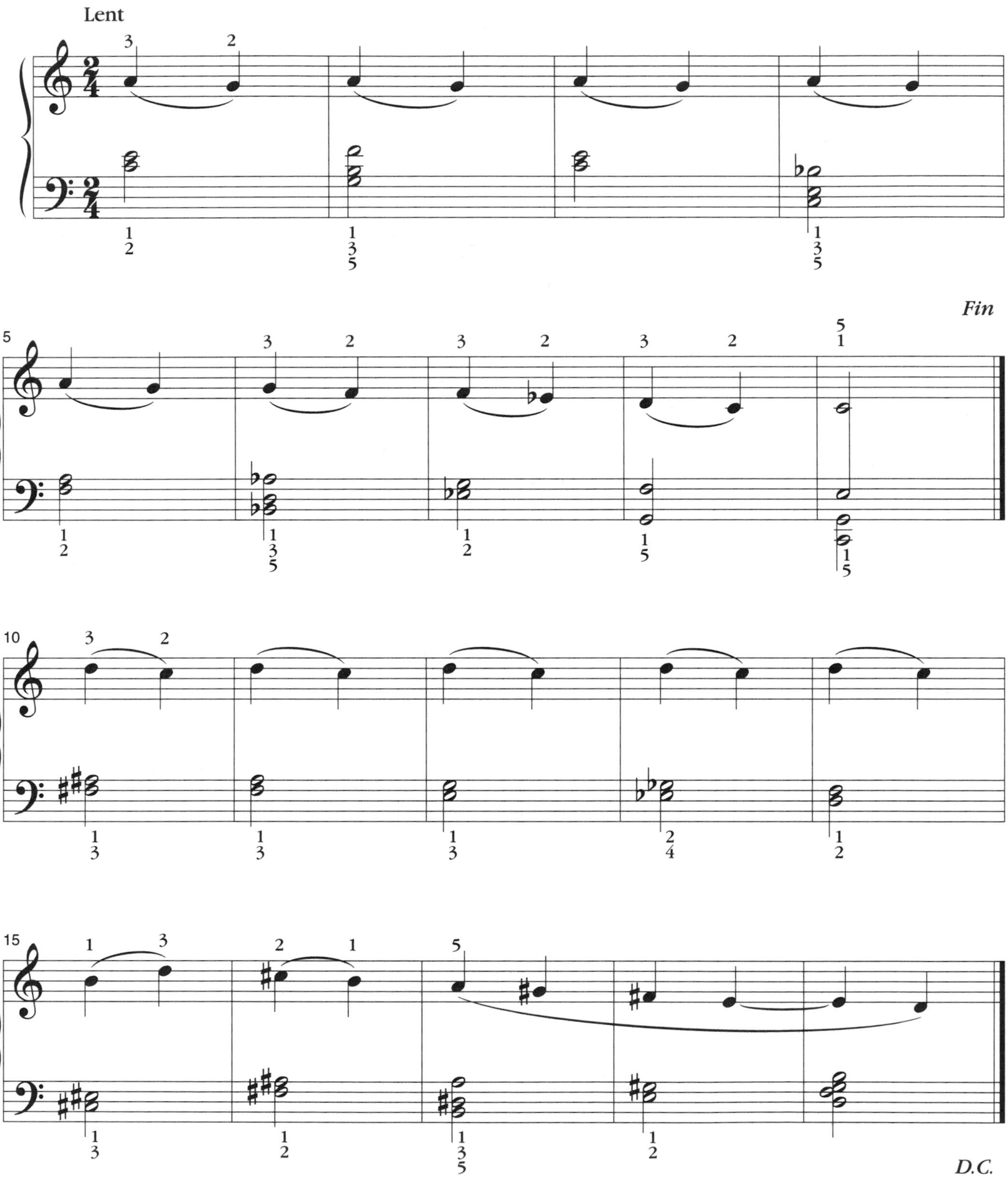

TAXIS

James Lyke

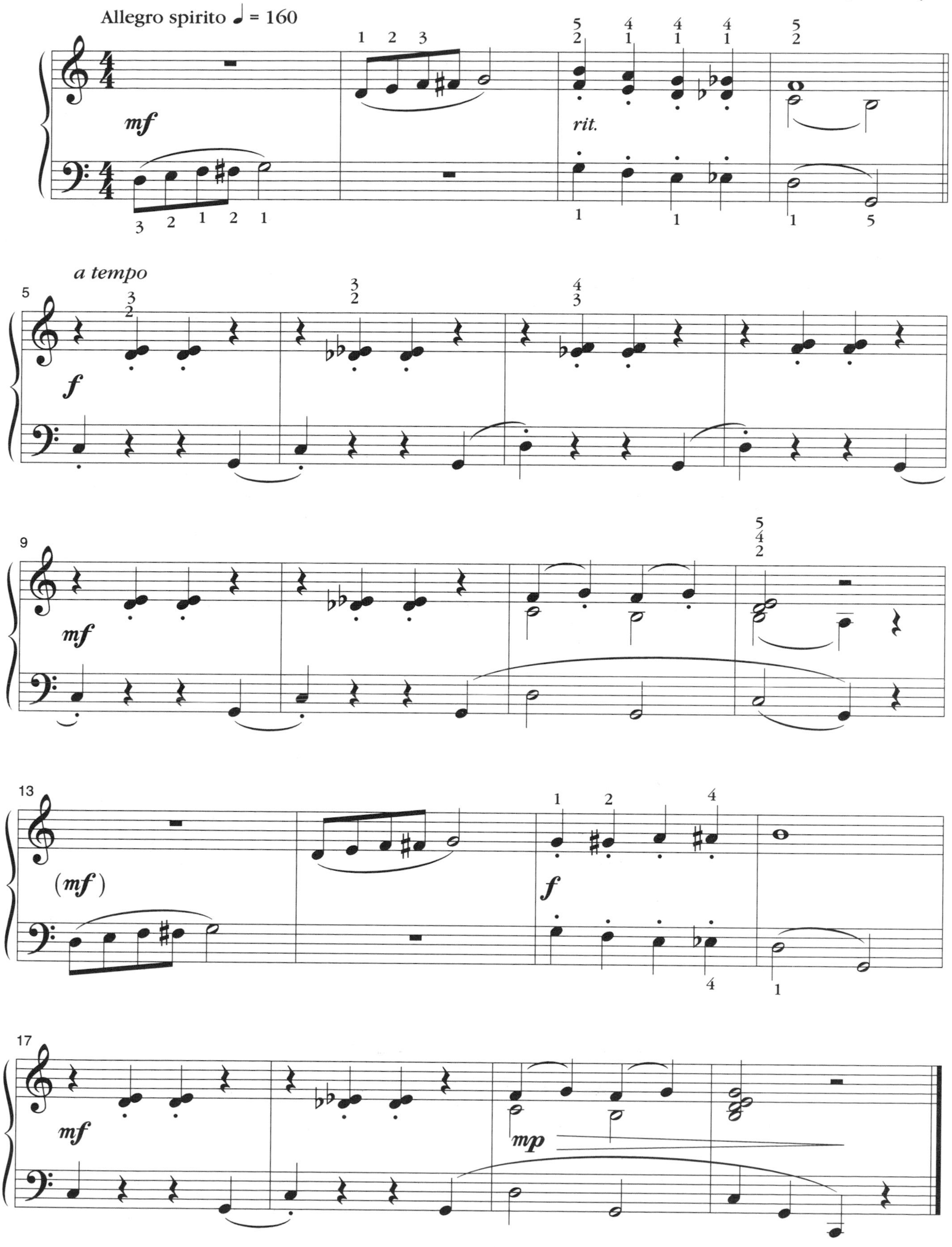

Practice Plan: This piece has rhythmic twists including the ♩. ♪ figure, counting rests, and holding ties. Notice the inverted figures in bars 6-8. The constant recurring LH figure A to E is an *ostinato* pattern. *Round Dance* is in the key of A minor and shares the same key signature as C major. More about minor keys in Chapter 4.

ROUND DANCE

Béla Bartók

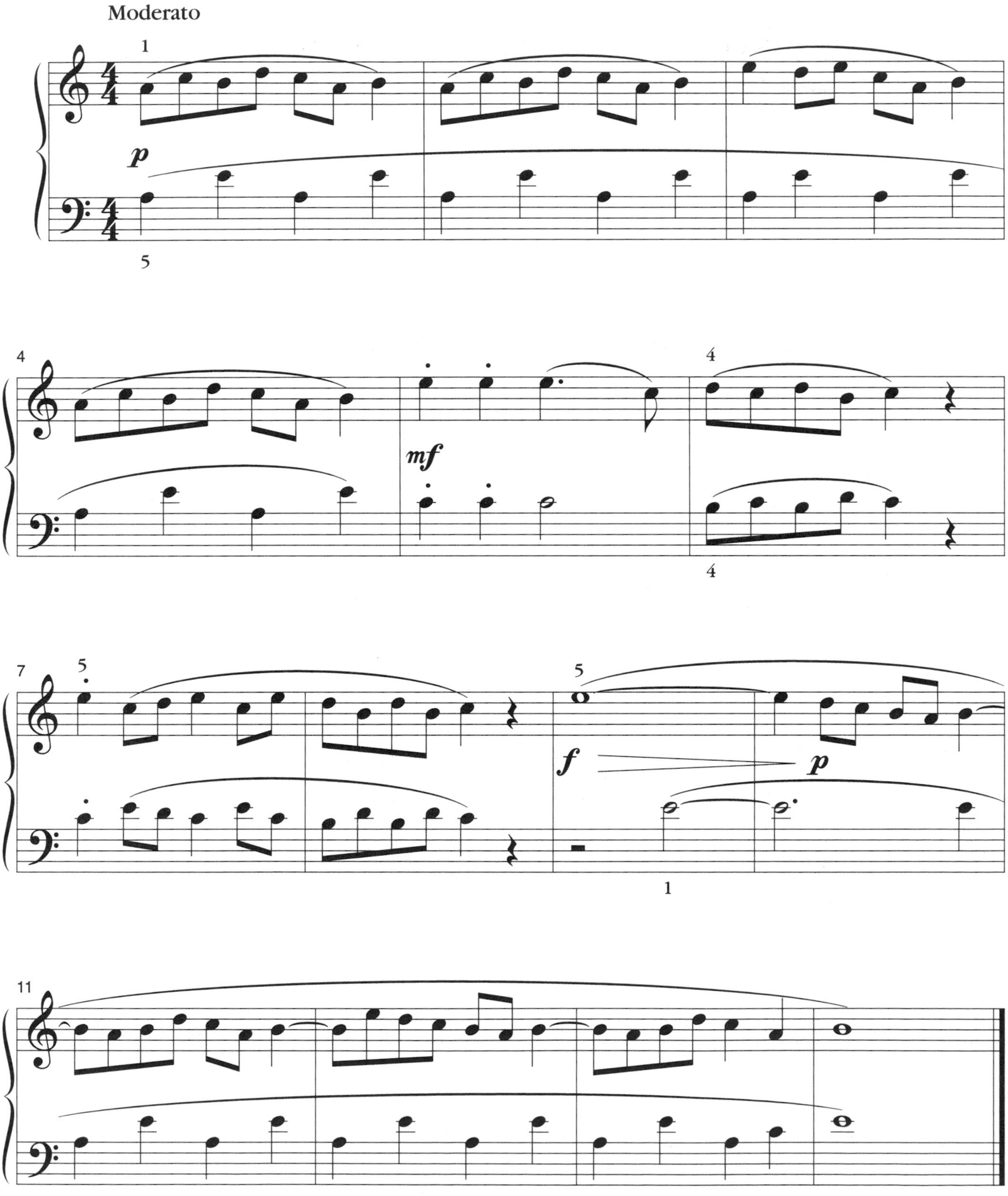

Practice Plan: Block intervals in both hands before performing as is. Take note of the *fermata* in bar 8 and the change of clef in measure 16, RH.

SEVENTH INNING STRETCH

Tony Caramia

MUSICIANSHIP ACTIVITIES

Tetrachord Scales: C and Sharp Keys via the Circle of 5ths

This study divides the scale of C (and the sharp keys that follow) into *tetrachords* (four-note scales in each hand). Each new scale starts a 5th above the previous scale. Follow the practice suggestions.

Practice Suggestions: (1) Shape each scale by making a *crescendo* to the top and *diminuendo* to the bottom, (2) vary the touch by playing one scale *legato* and the next *staccato*, and (3) vary the fingering by starting the LH on finger 4 and the RH on finger 1.

18 CD

Chant: C **No Sharps**

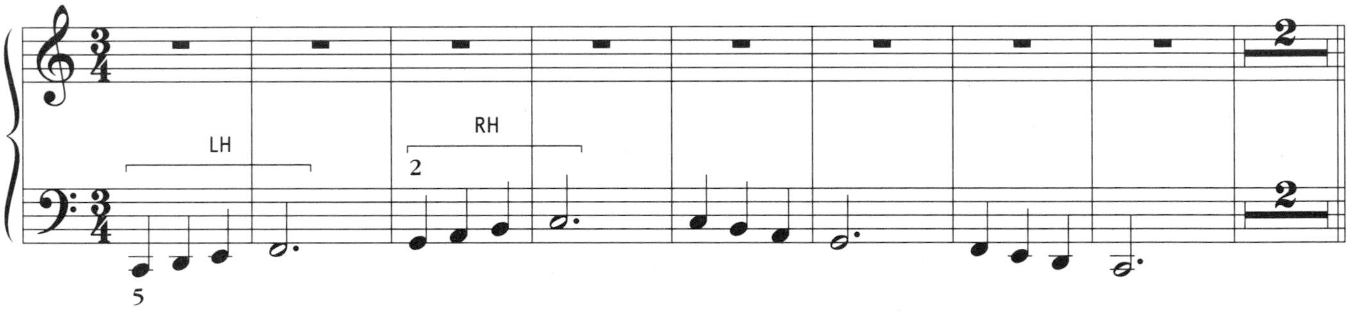

G **One Sharp**

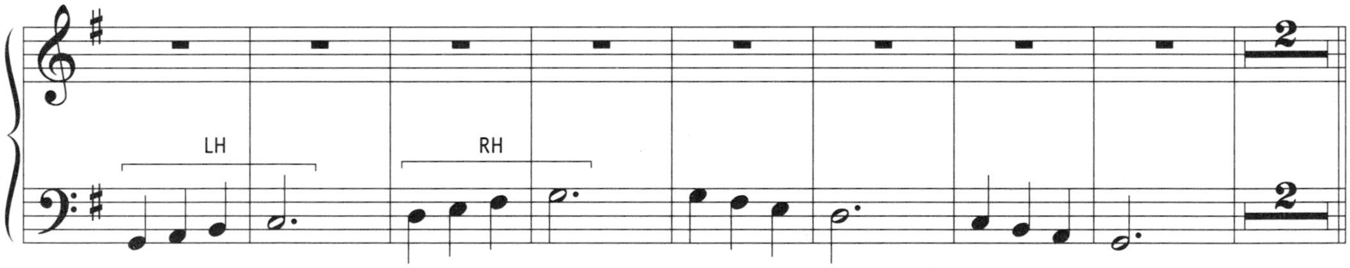

D **Two Sharps**

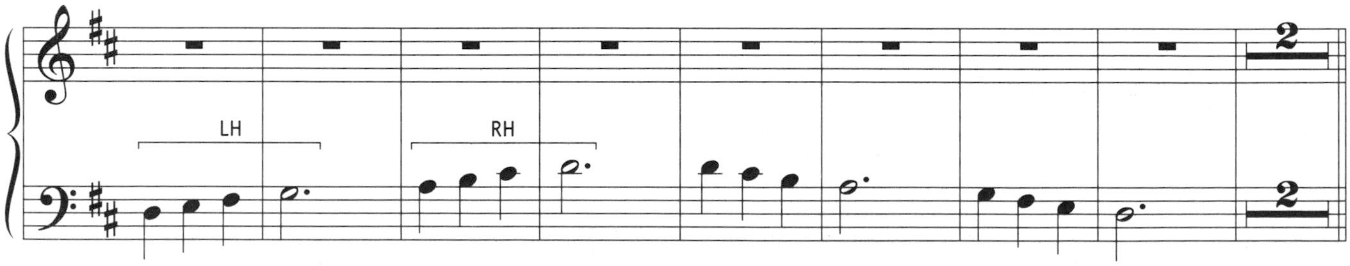

Chant: A **Three Sharps**

E **Four Sharps**

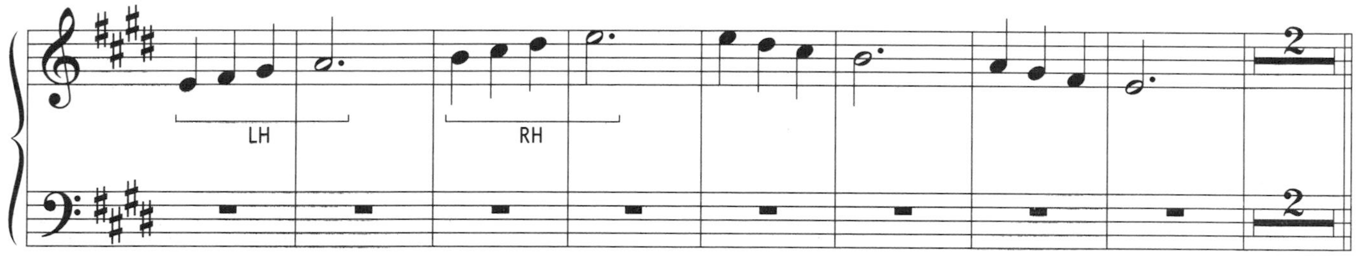

B **Five Sharps**

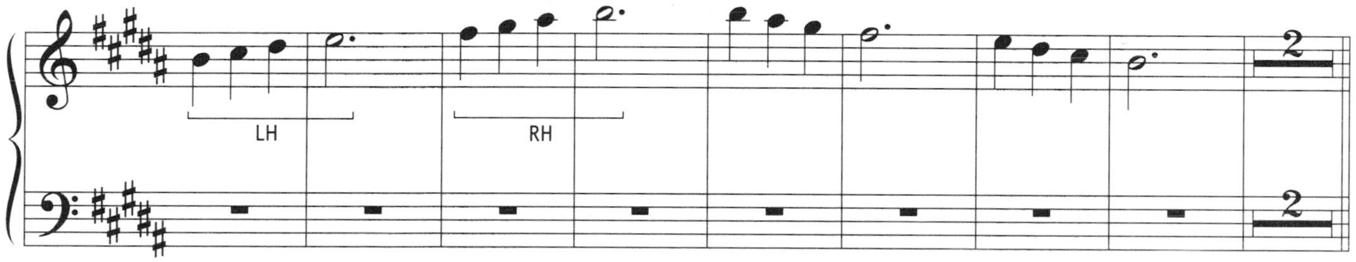

F♯ **Six Sharps**

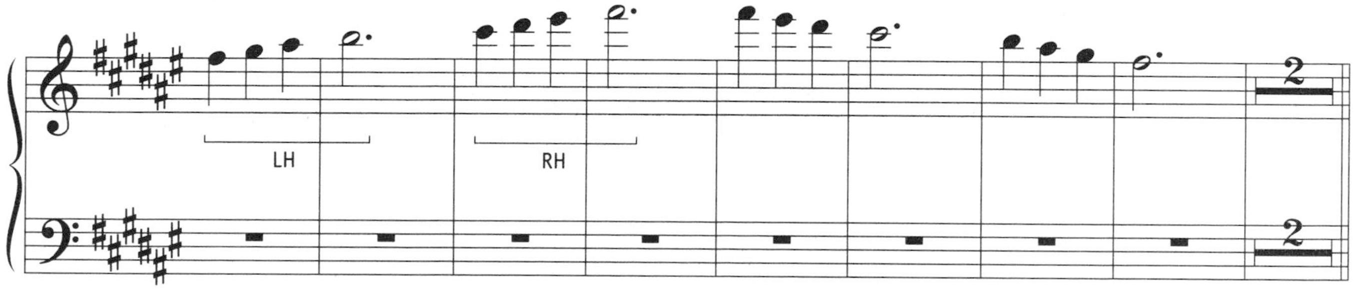

C♯ **Seven Sharps**

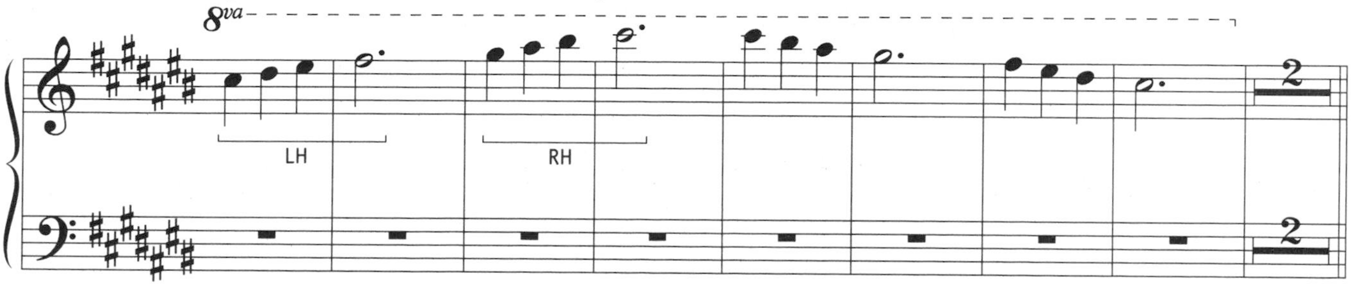

Tetrachord Scales: Flat Keys and C via the Circle of 5ths

This study divides the flat scales and C into *tetrachords* (four-note scales in each hand). The study begins with C♭ (7 flats) and progresses by 5ths to C (no flats). Follow the practice suggestions.

Practice Suggestions: (1) Shape each scale by making a *crescendo* to the top and *diminuendo* to the bottom, (2) vary the touch by playing one scale *legato* and the next *staccato*, and (3) vary the fingering by starting the LH on finger 4 and the RH on finger 1.

Chant: C♭ **Seven Flats**

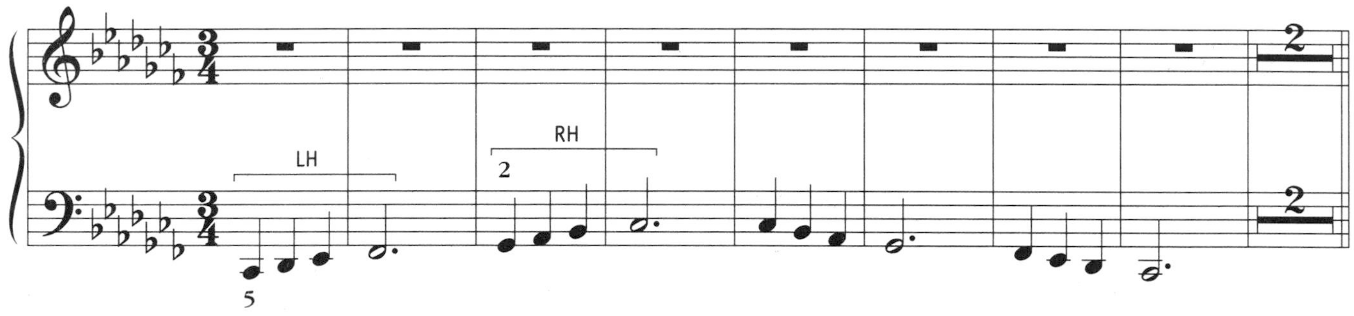

G♭ **Six Flats**

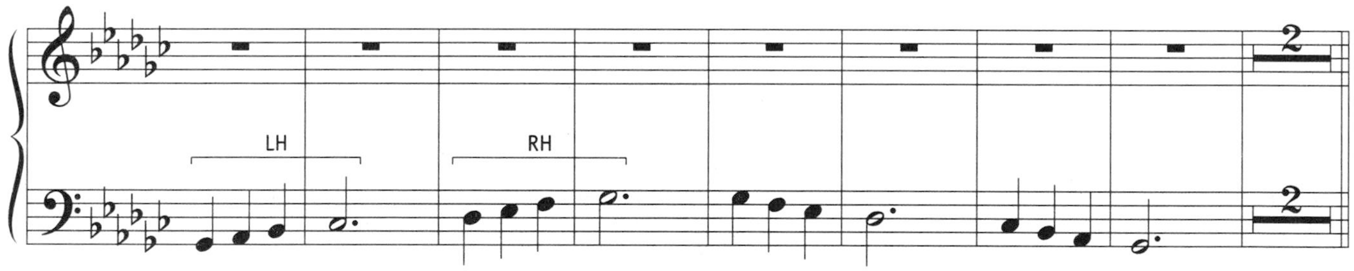

D♭ **Five Flats**

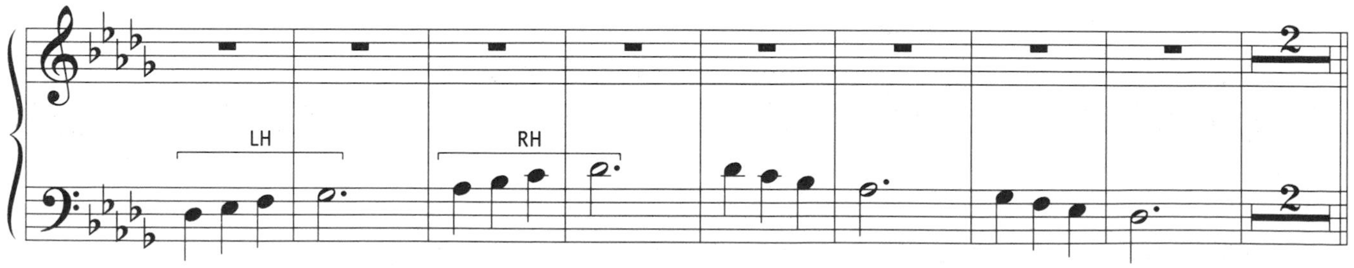

Chant: A♭ **Four Flats**

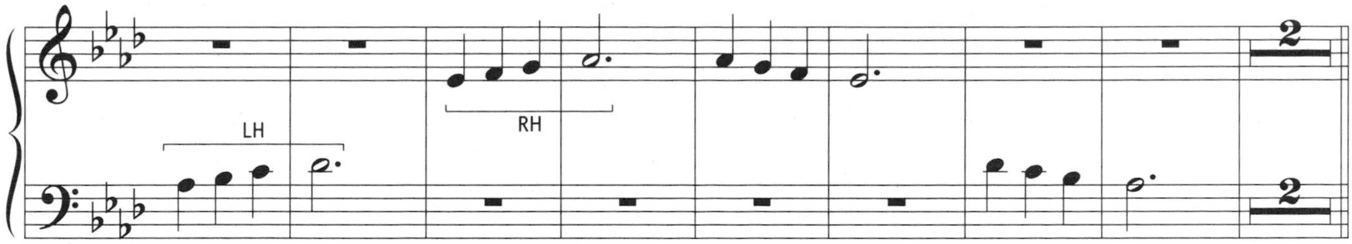

E♭ **Three Flats**

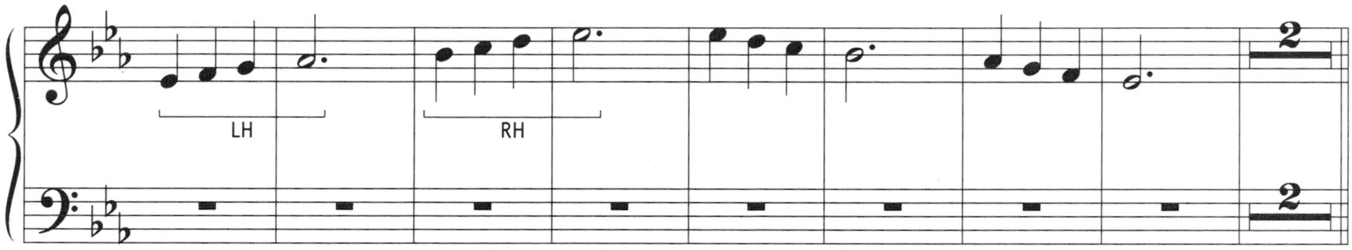

B♭ **Two Flats**

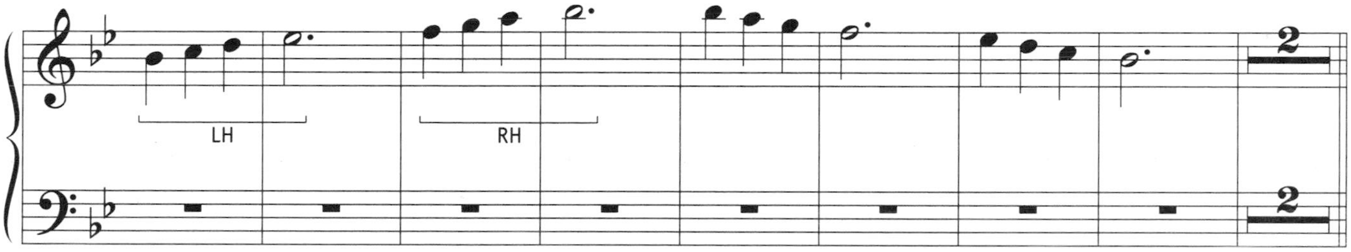

F **One Flat**

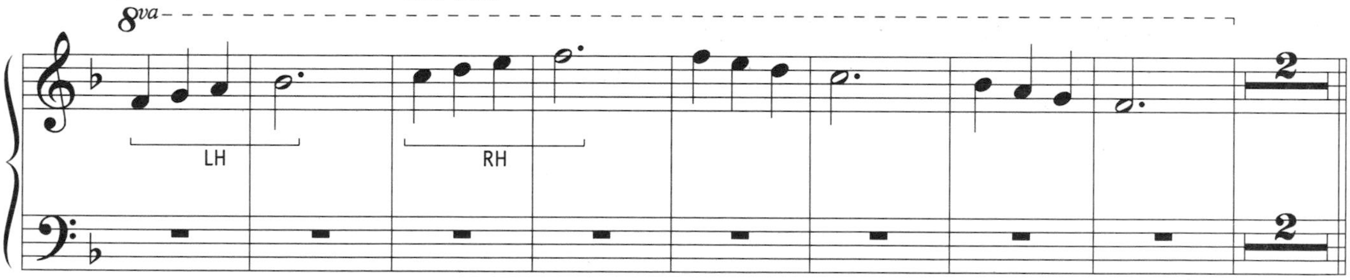

C **No Flats**

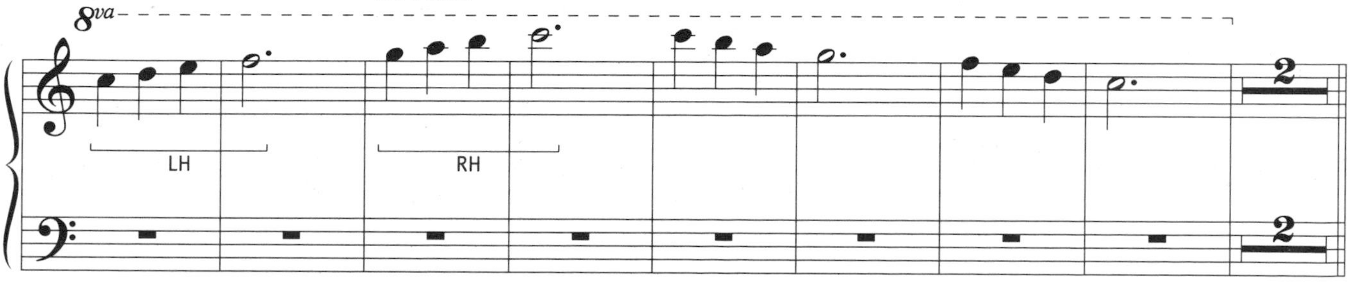

I-V^6_5-I and I-V^7-I Chord Progressions

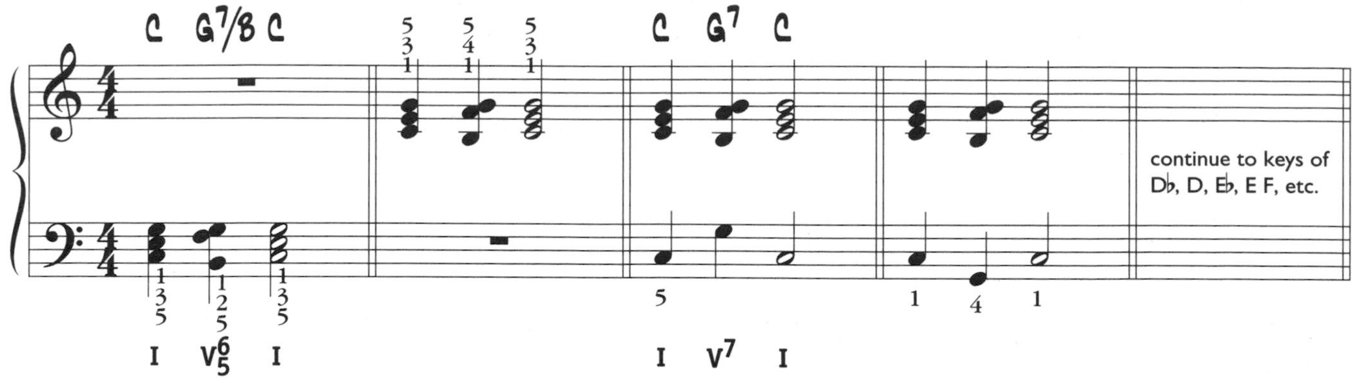

The opening measures of *When I Grow Too Old to Dream* by Oscar Hammerstein II (words) and Sigmund Romberg (music) serve as a perfect vehicle for transposition via the *circle of fifths*. Memorize these eight measures and gradually work through several keys as suggested by your instructor.

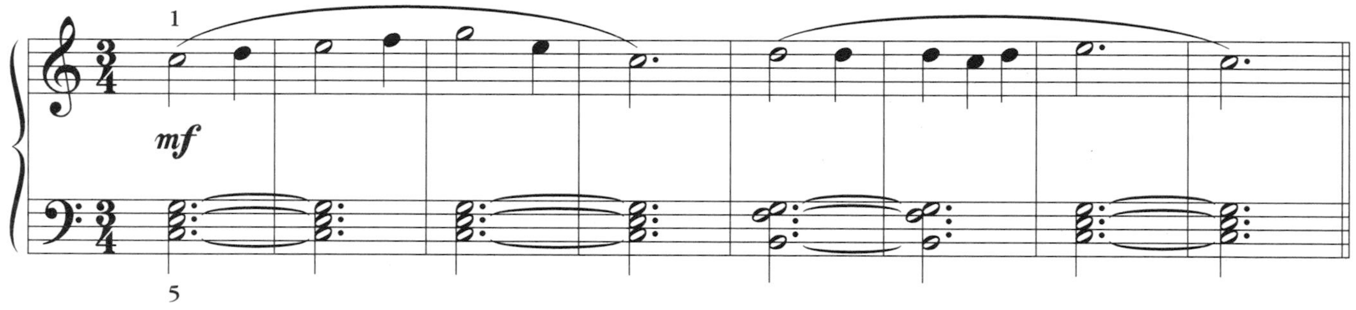

Dominant Seventh Chord Identification

Write the letter name (e.g. chord symbol) in the box above each chord.

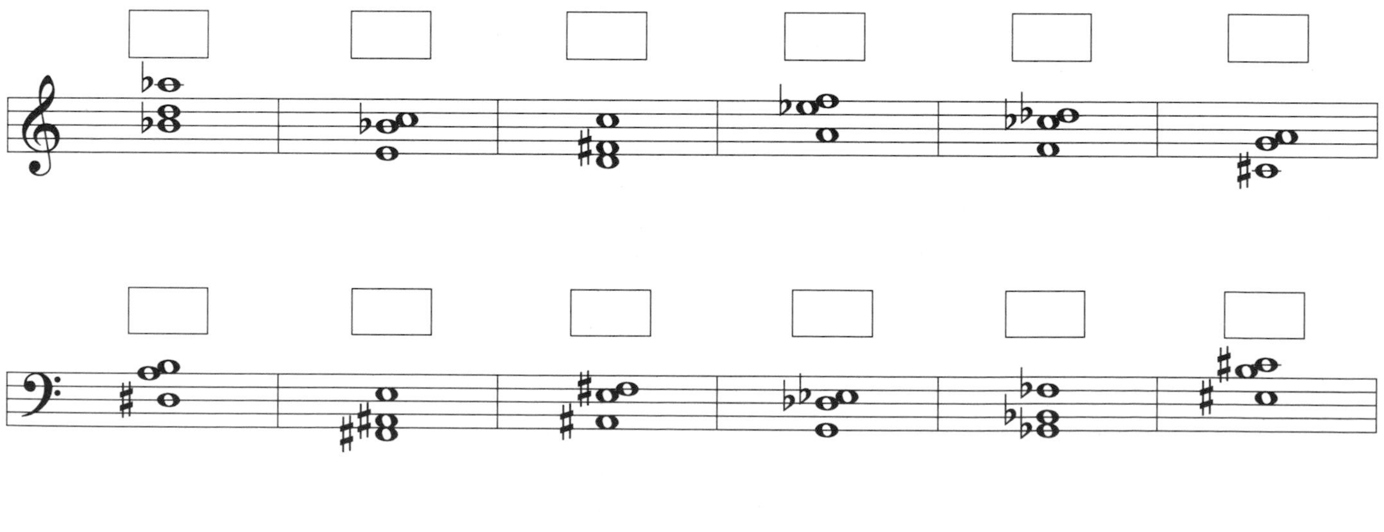

Begin Working on Major Scales: C, G, D, A, and E. Consult Appendix B.

Major Scales in Clusters and Single Notes

Practice blocking the RH scale clusters below. Notice the pattern of a group of three fingers (1 2 3) followed by a group of four fingers (1 2 3 4). Use the rest to prepare for the next fingering group.

RH Scale Clusters

1. 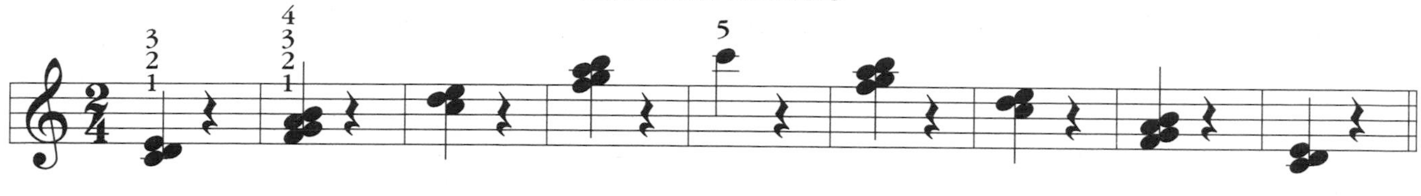

In the following exercise, practice sliding the thumb under the hand immediately after each 2-3 or 2-3-4 cluster is played.

2. 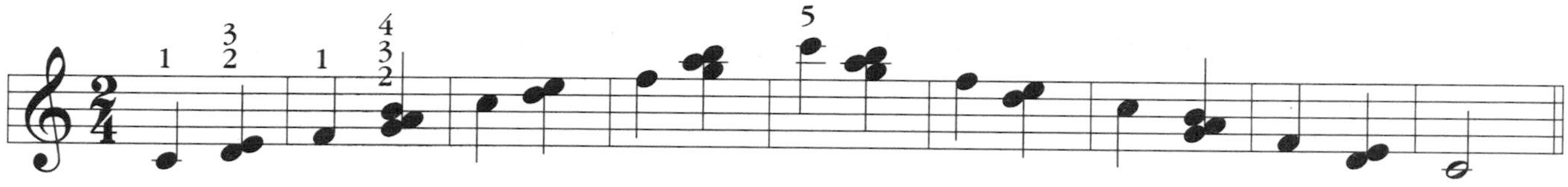

Practice *legato* and *staccato*, slow to fast. Transpose to G, D, A, and E major using the same fingering.

3. 

Practice blocking the following LH scale clusters as above. Then, in the second exercise, practice sliding the thumb under the hand immediately after each cluster is played

LH Scale Clusters

4. 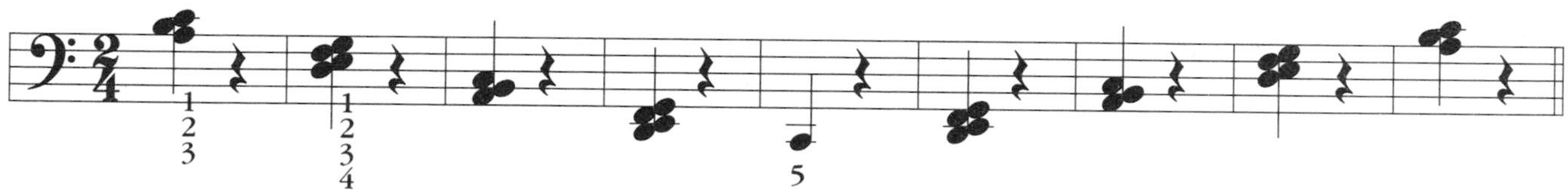

5. 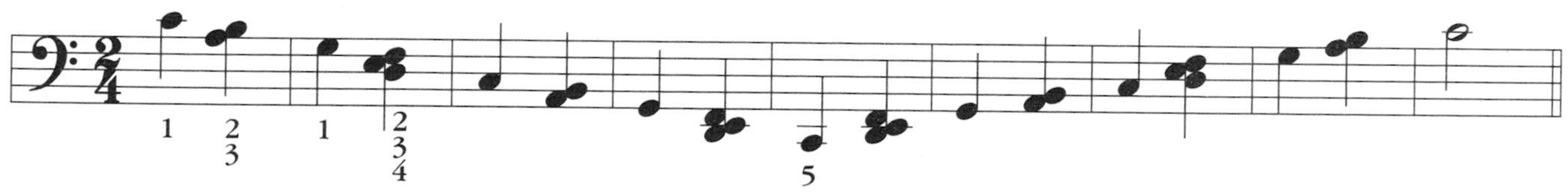

Practice *legato* and *staccato*, slow to fast. Transpose to G, D, A, and E major using the same fingering.

6. 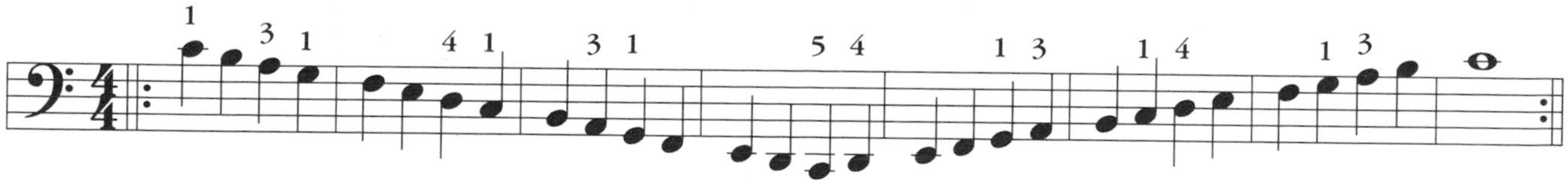

SUGGESTED PLAYING EXAM TOPICS
CHAPTER THREE

1. Play one of the harmonization studies on pages 92–93.
2. Play one of the accompaniments on pages 99–101 with fluency.
3. Perform one of the American Songs on pages 102-105.
4. Perform the primo part on page 107 or 109.
5. Perform one (or two) solos from the Solo Repertoire section, pages 110-117.
6. Play the tetrachord scale of any any key suggested by the instructor.
7. Transpose the excerpt from *When I Get Too Old to Dream* to any major key suggested by the instructor (or a classmate). See page 122.
8. Play the Scales C, G, D, A, and E, hands alone, two octaves as shown on page 123. Also consult Appendix B.

4 chapter — Minor Pentachords, Minor Triads, Subdominant Chord (IV), $\frac{6}{8}$ Meter, Sixteenth Notes, Harmonization, Repertoire, Musicianship, and Technical Studies

NOTE TO TEACHER: Now is a good time to begin working in Appendix C (Holiday Music).

Compare the C major scale with the most common form of the minor scale, the *harmonic minor.* Scale steps 3 and 6 are lowered one half step in this minor scale. All minor scales share a key signature with a major scale. The lowered third step of the minor scale is "borrowed" from the major scale which best fits its structure. Other forms of the minor scale are explored in a later chapter.

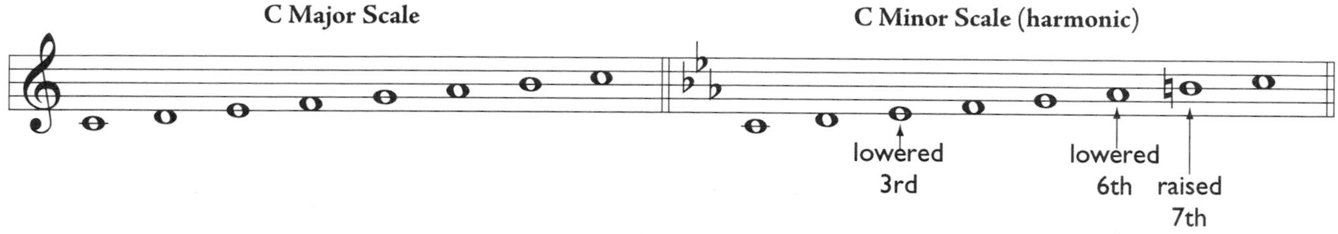

C Minor Spiritual Melody
(GO DOWN MOSES)

The Minor Pentachord (5-Finger Pattern)

We have learned the construction of the pentachord in major as: whole step, whole step, half step, whole step. This particular order of steps forms the first five notes of the major scale. *Major* is a quality and its sound is associated with brightness. The *minor* quality, by contrast, is associated with mournfulness or sadness. It differs from the major pattern in only one way: its third note is one half step lower.

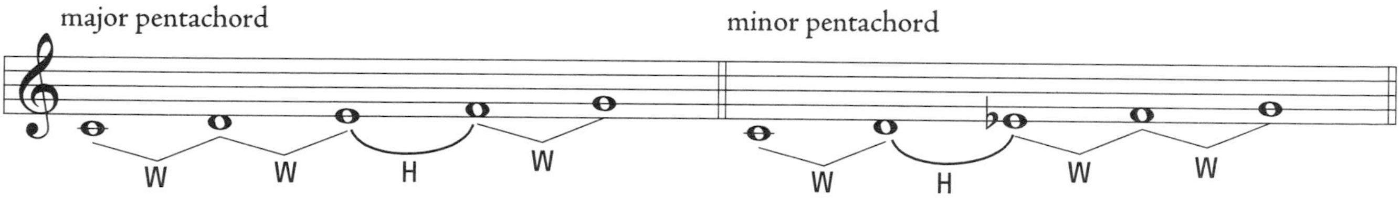

The Minor Triad

Play the major pentachord ascending and descending. Repeat it, but lower the 3rd tone by a half step. Then play the minor triad as shown.

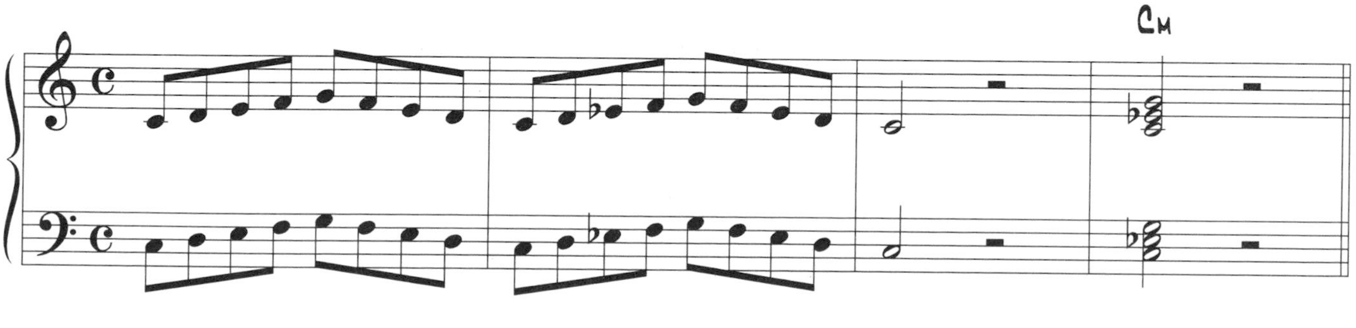

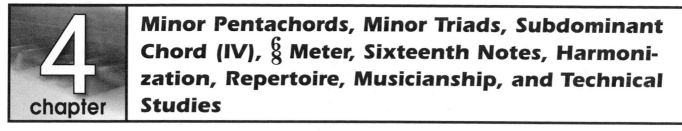

Transpose to all white keys, then to all black keys, then then play chromatically: C, D♭, D, E♭, etc.

Minor Melodies with Simple Harmonic Accompaniments

The following minor melodies stress accompaniment figures using 5ths, 6ths, 7ths, and the tonic minor triad. Before playing, practice the LH part. Remember that the minor key signature is determined by the middle note of the minor triad or by counting up one and a half steps from the keynote.

Example

Lettish

Moderato

Hungarian

Allegro

Transpose to F minor.

Russian

Polish

Minor 5-Finger Pattern Reading

Analyze and sight read the following melodies which lie within the minor pentachord in each hand. Be sure to establish the minor key by identifying the final note of the melody. Double check by counting down one and one half steps from the keynote of the *shared* major key. For example, number one has a G major key signature, but an analysis of the melody clearly establishes E minor (one and one half steps down from G). Follow the usual reading routine by playing the pattern in ascending and descending form, singing or saying letter names and chanting the rhythm if it poses a problem. Look for patterns which repeat. Observe touch and dynamic markings. Transpose the melodies to the suggested keys. The instructor should supply appropriate accompaniments according to the given chord symbols.

Russian

Transpose to D minor.

Bulgarian

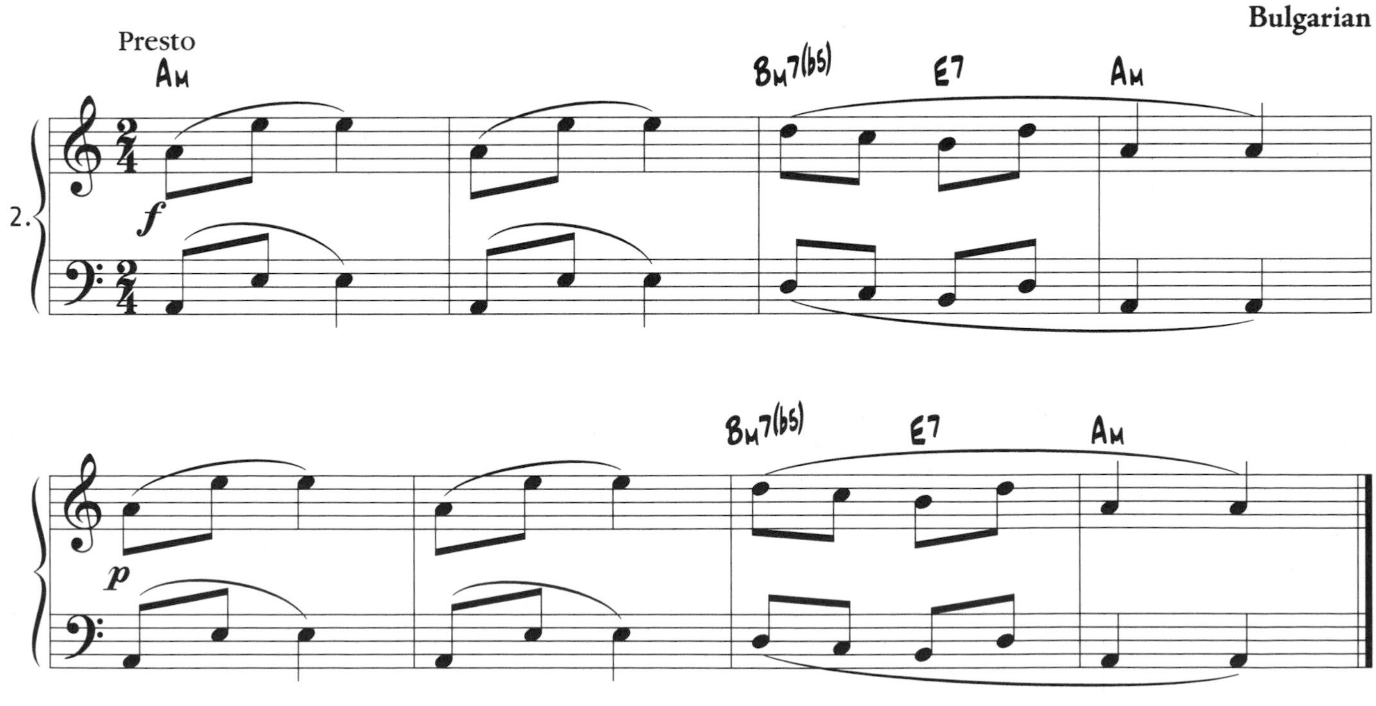

Transpose to G minor.

Latvian

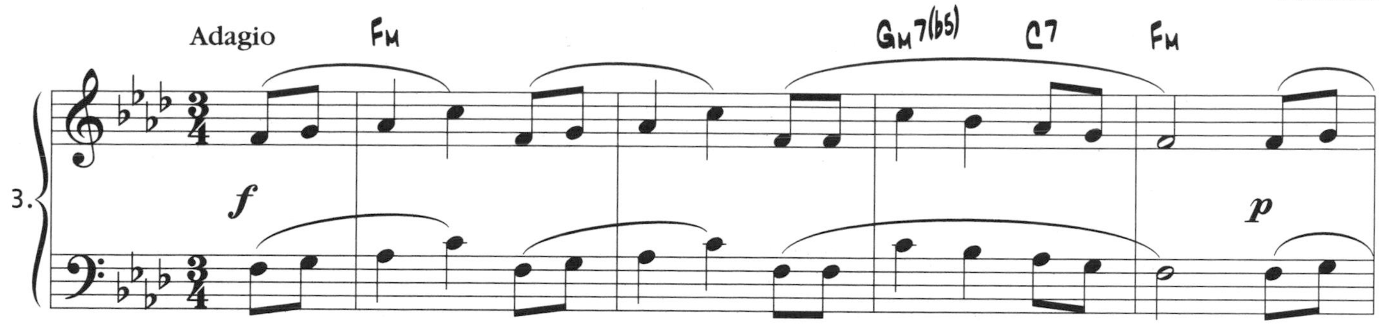

Transpose to G minor.

French

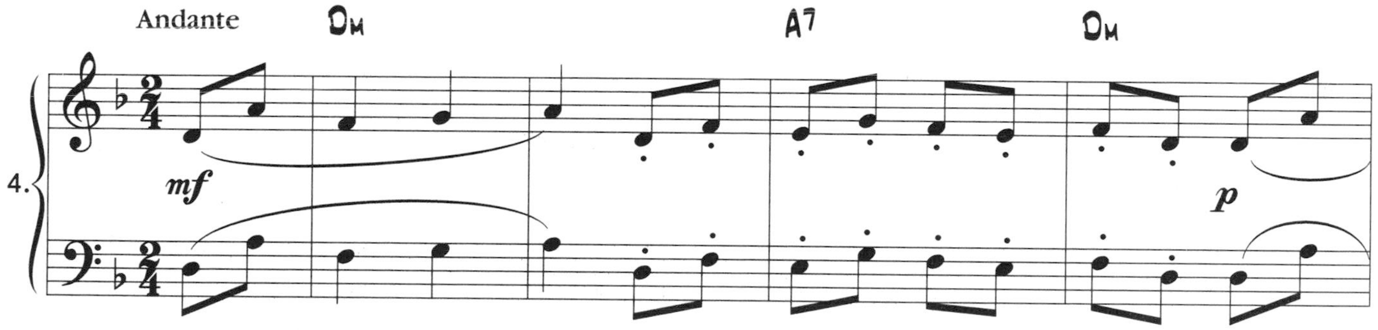

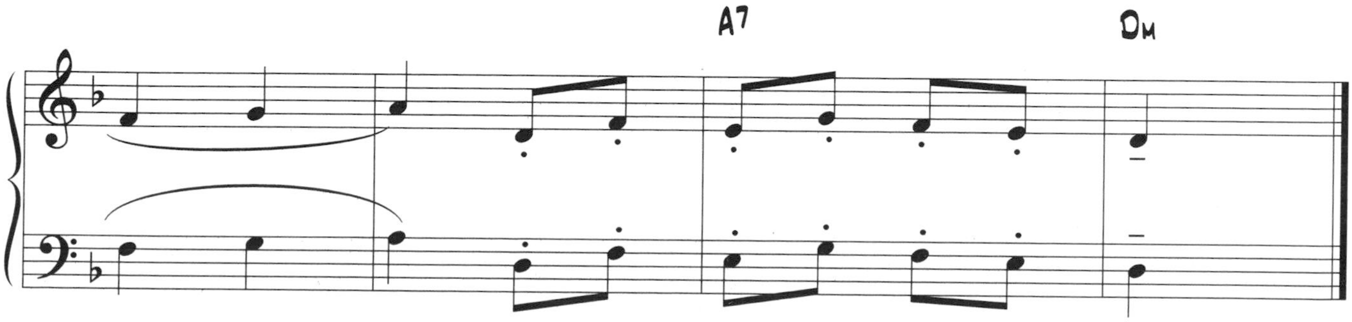

Transpose to C minor.

French

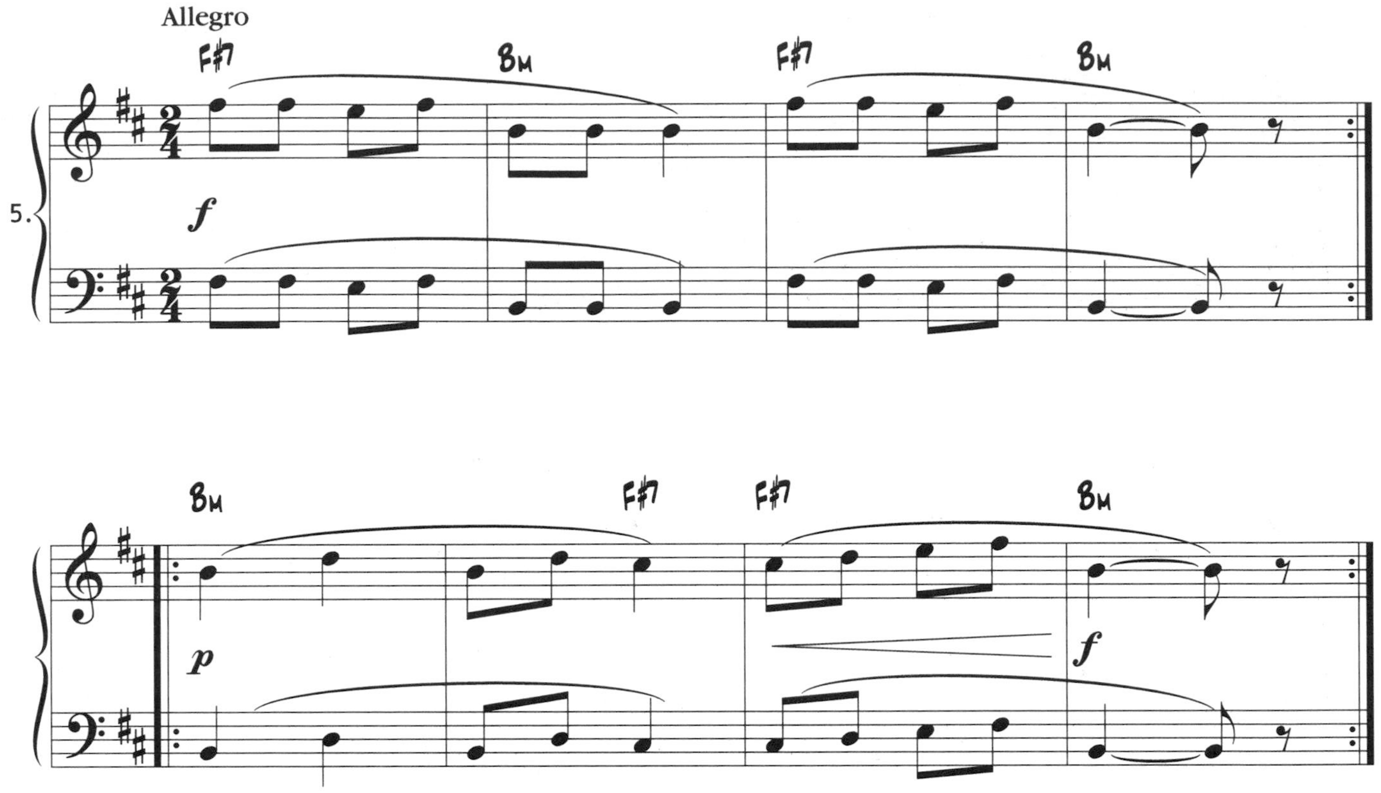

Transpose to A minor.

Russian

Transpose to F minor.

Harmonizing in Minor Keys with the Tonic and Dominant $^6_5$ Chords

Harmonize melodies 1–4 using the I, V^7 and V^6_5 chords. Complete the LH according to the examples given. Write the chord symbols in the boxes.

Russian

British

Czech

3.

Latvian

4.

The Tonic–Dominant $^6_5$–Tonic Progression: A Review

The dominant $^6_5$ chord was introduced in Chapter Three on page 91. Practice the tonic–dominant $^6_5$–tonic progression starting on all white keys. The $^6_5$ refers to the intervals measured from the bottom note to the two top notes. Remember that the LH thumb plays the dominant tone (or root of the chord), 2nd finger plays the seventh, and 5th finger plays the third of the chord.

Dominant $^6_5$ Intervals | Dominant $^6_5$ Tones | Dominant $^6_5$ Fingering

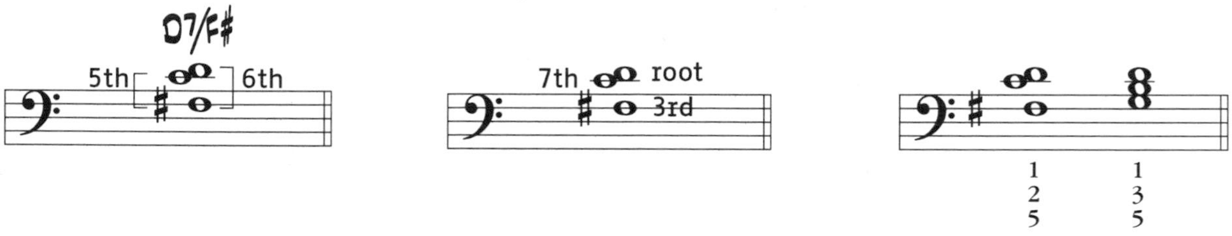

Left Hand
(pedal each chord)

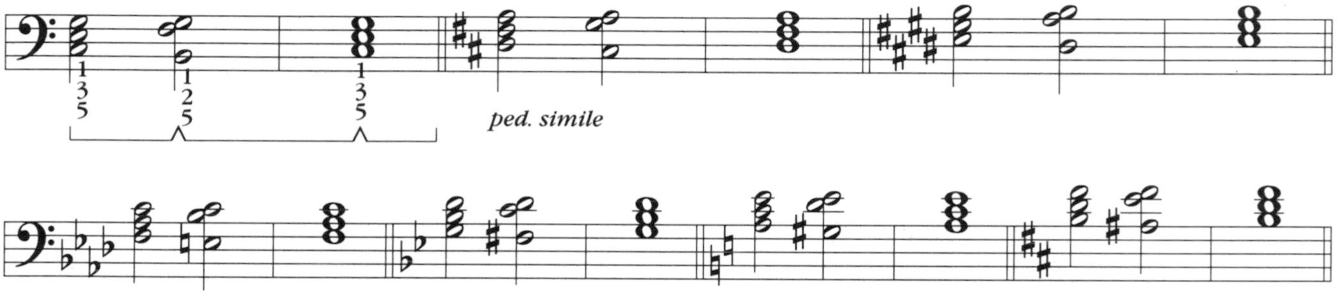

For accompanying and harmonizing purposes, it is necessary to put the chords in the RH, while LH bass notes supply fundamental tones and rhythm. Learn all the RH I–V$^6_5$–I patterns below.

Right Hand
(pedal each chord)

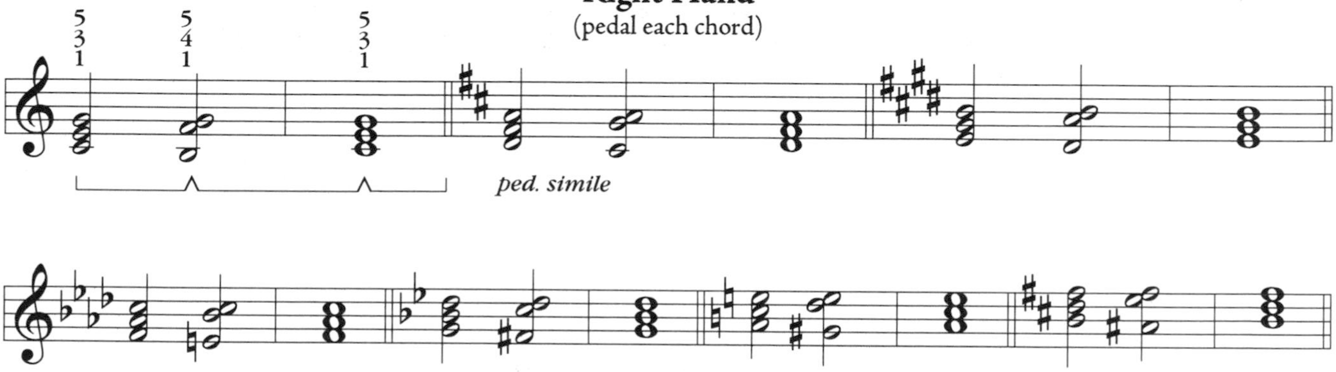

I–V^7–I: Four-Voice Texture in Major and Minor Keys

You have used the chords shown on the next page in various LH accompaniments. Now we will examine how these RH chords plus a bassnote form a *four-voice texture*. It is important to remember that the lowest tone (bass note in LH) determines how the chord is labeled. For example, a C$^6_5$ chord in the RH plus a bass note C would be labeled C^7. The four-voice texture becomes useful in chording an accompaniment. See the examples on page 134.

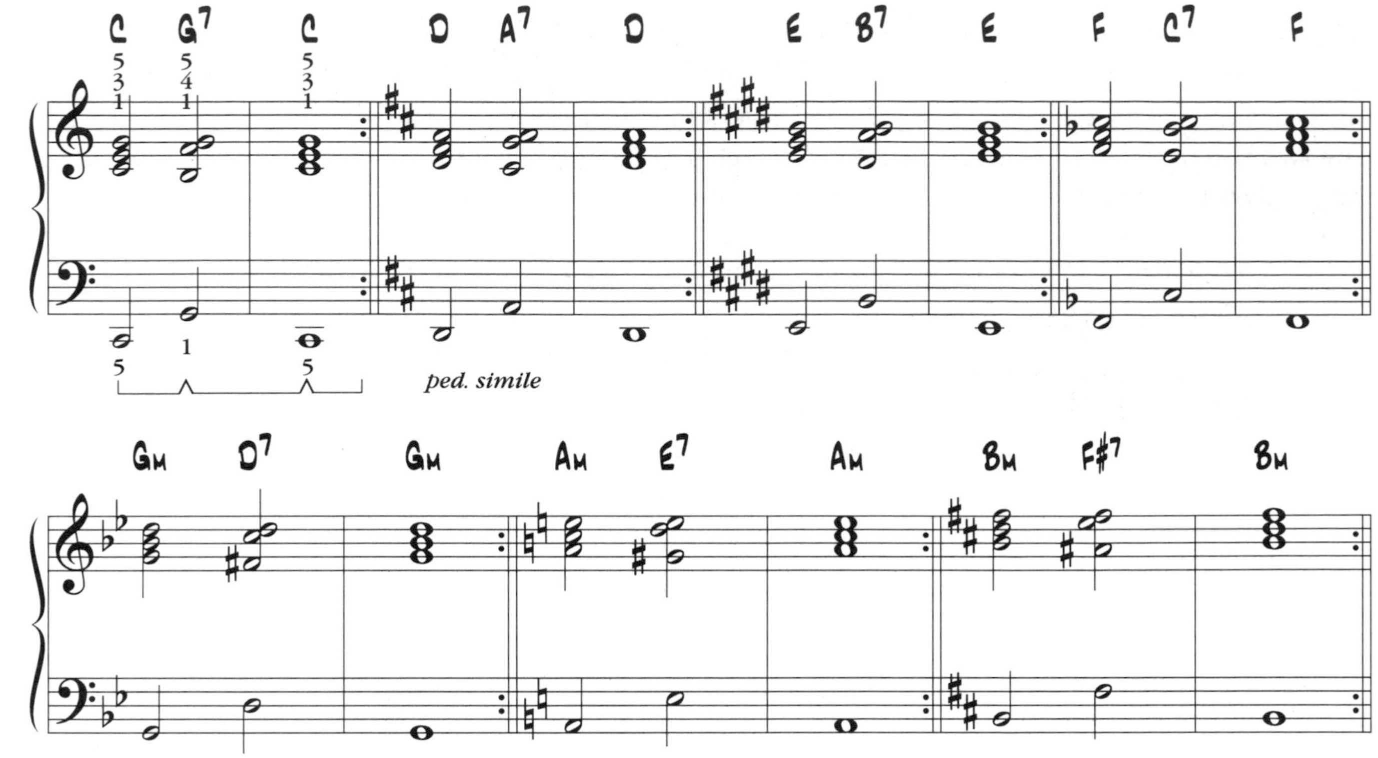

Chording An Accompaniment

There are various ways (styles) to create an accompaniment pattern. Example 1 shows a waltz pattern; Example 2, a march pattern. In the accompanying section in each chapter you will see various patterns employed. Examples 1 and 2 below are taken from the progression above.

Waltz

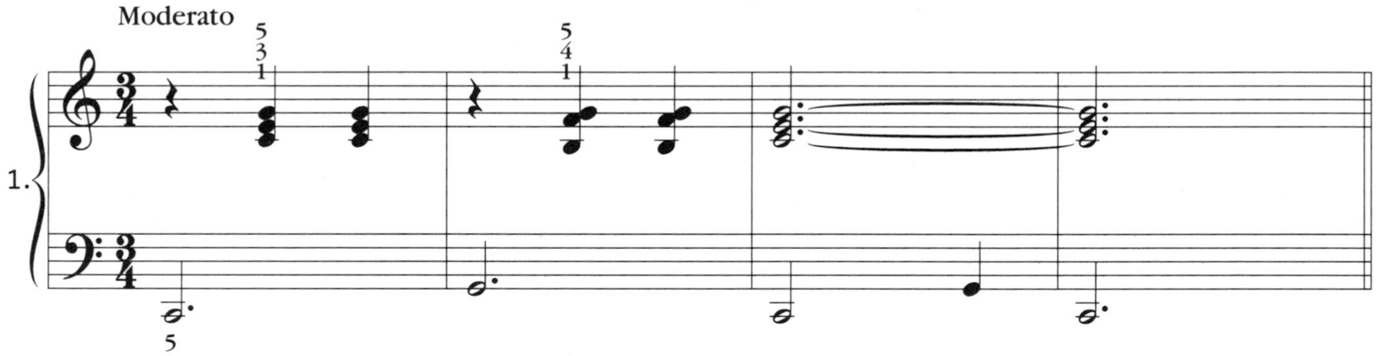

March (oom-pah)

Harmonizing with Chord Symbols in Major and Minor Keys

Harmonize the following four melodies according to the chord symbols. Only tonic triads and dominant $\substack{6\\5}$ chords are used. Notate the LH parts. *Take note of various LH styles of harmonization.*

LH: Block Style

Folk Song

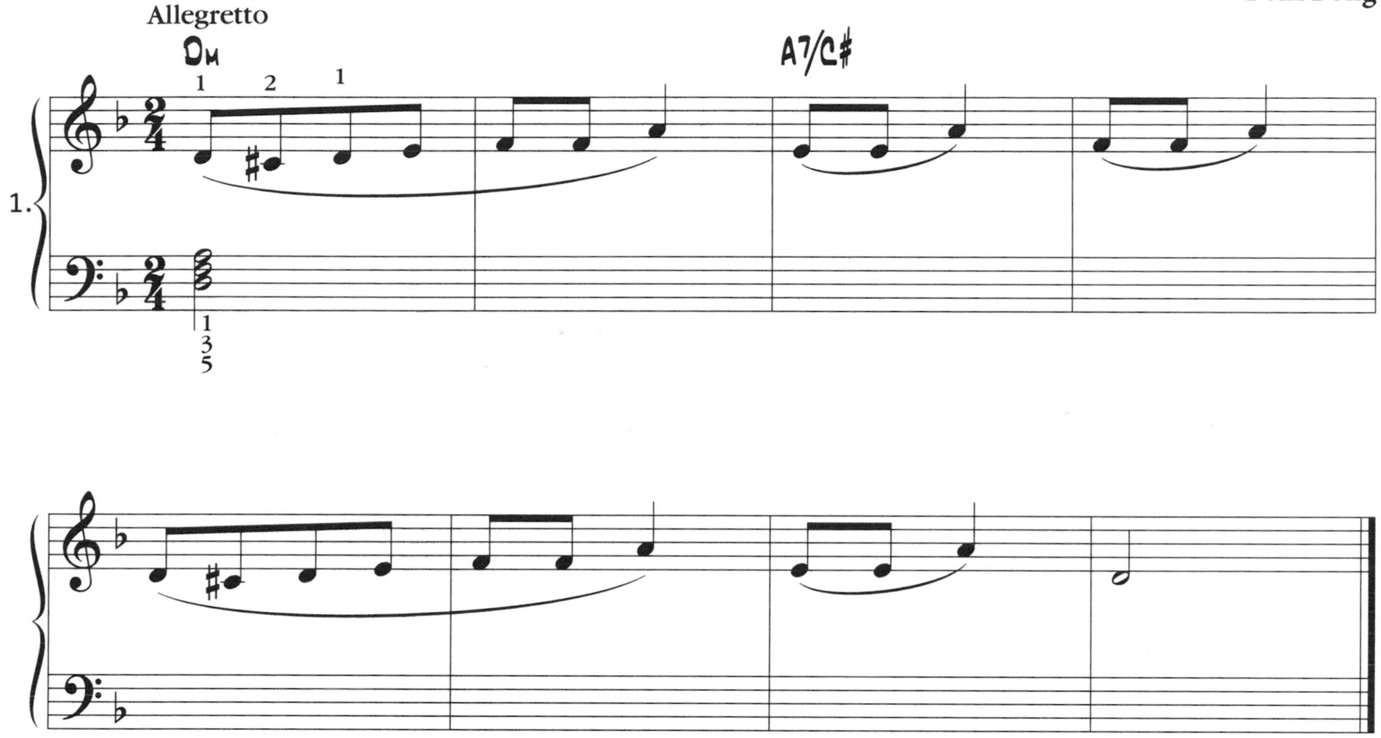

LH: Waltz Style

Bohemian

LH: Alberti Bass Style

Czech

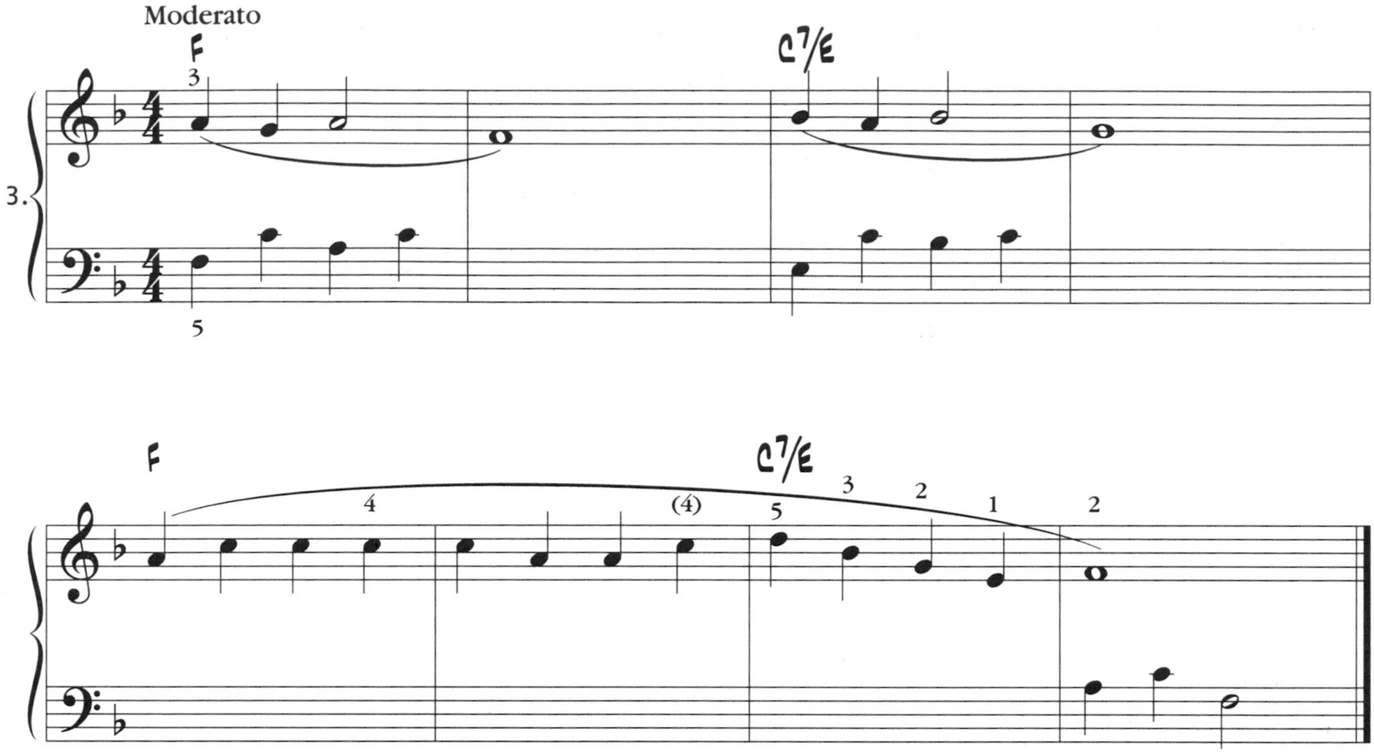

LH: Broken Chord Style

British

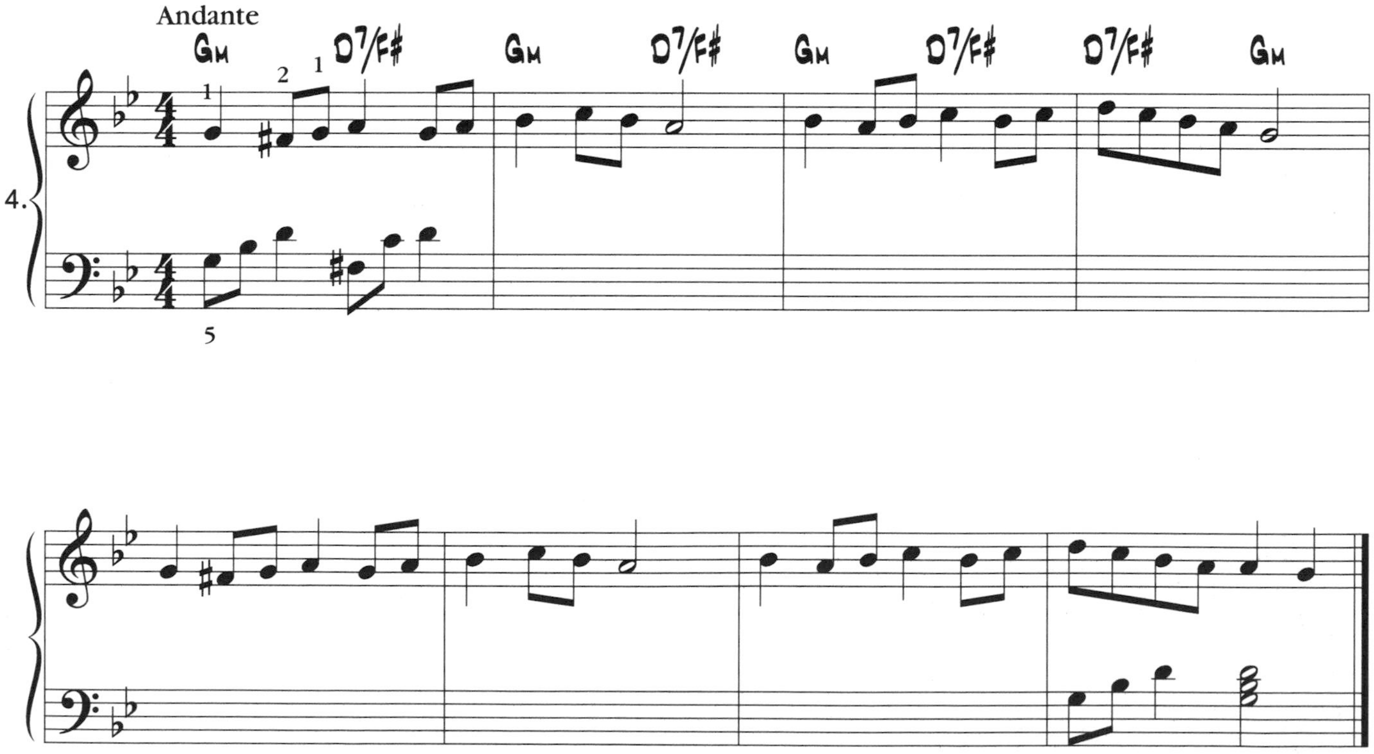

Harmonize *Melody No. 5* with tonic and dominant $^6_5$ chords, blocked style. Figure out the harmony from the melodic structure and from what sounds agreeable. Play one chord per measure. Notate the LH and put chord symbols above the melody.

Czech

Allegro

5.

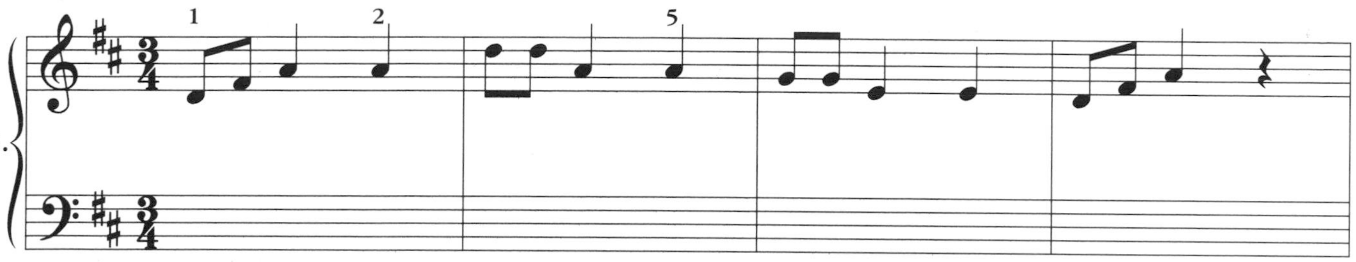

Harmonize *Melody No.* 6 with tonic and dominant $^6_5$ chords. Use a waltz style accompaniment (see page 135). Determine the harmony from a close examination of the melody. Non-tonic tones suggest the dominant $^6_5$. Notate the LH and write chord symbols above the melody.

Czech

Allegretto

6.

Sixteenth Notes

Four sixteenth notes are grouped to the beat in meters with 4 as the bottom number. Two sixteenth notes fill the time of one eighth note. Dotted eighth notes followed by a sixteenth note may be felt as an eighth note tied to the first of two sixteenth notes which follow. Study the example below.

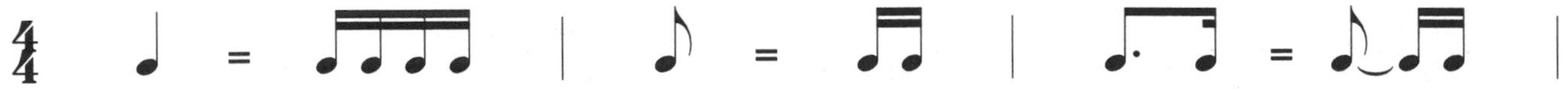

6/8 Meter

In 6/8 meter, the top number shows how many eighth notes are in a measure. In 6/8 meter it is important to feel the pulse as *two to the bar*. In other words, ♩. becomes the pulse. 6/8 is a *compound meter* because the subdivision of the pulse is three eighth notes. Other compound meters include 9/8 and 12/8. Tap and count the following rhythmic patterns.

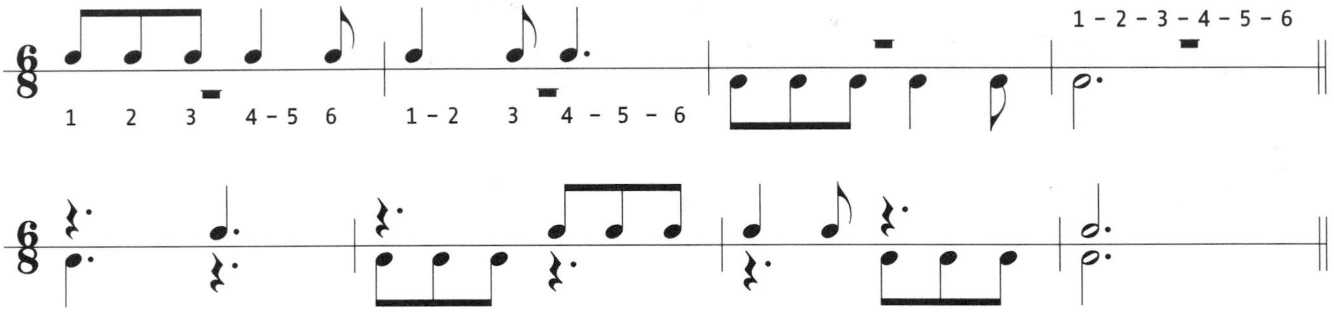

Rhythm Patterns to Tap

Tap the following rhythm patterns which involve sixteenth notes and 6/8 meter.

Folk Song Arrangements Incorporating 6/8 Meter and Sixteenth Notes

Study and play the following folk song arrangements highlighting the use of 6/8 meter and various combinations of sixteenth notes and 6/8 figures (♩.♪, ♪♬♪, etc.).

French

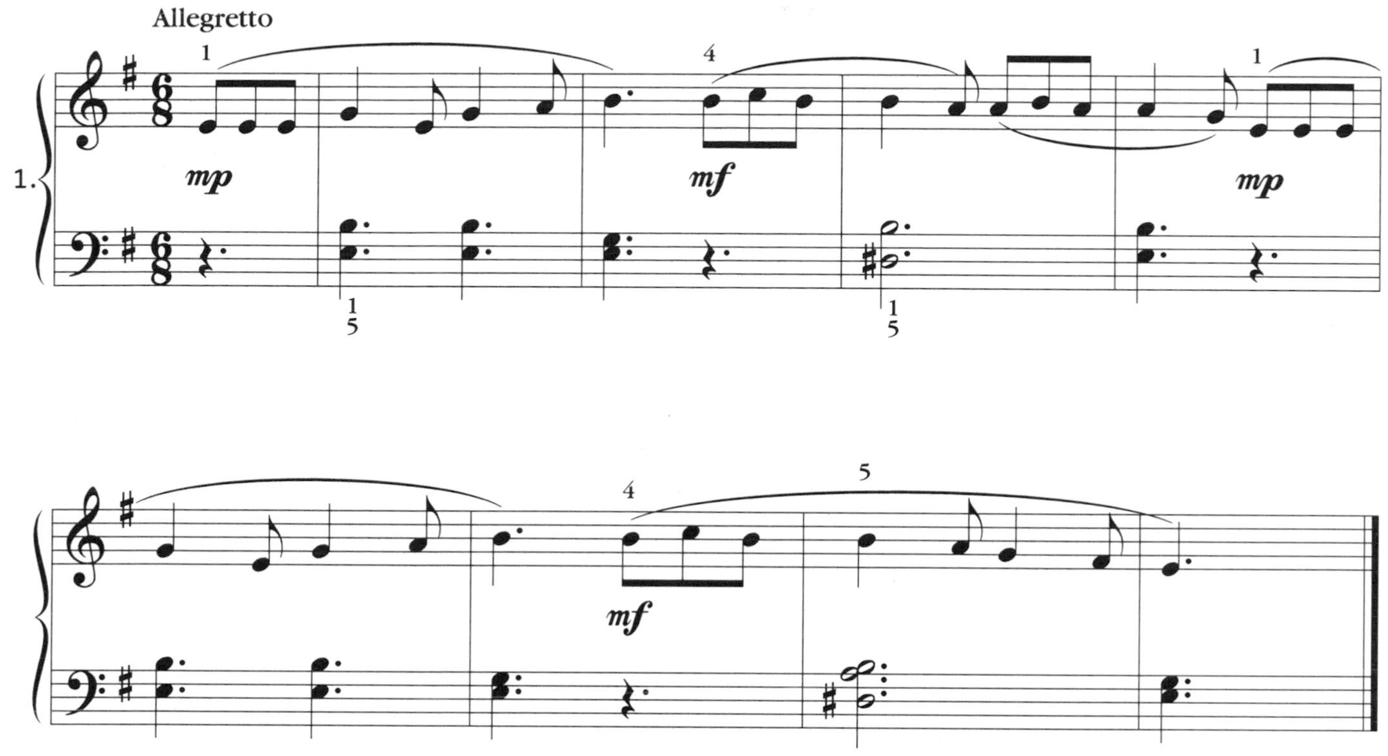

Italian

Dalmatian

Sprightly ♩. = 76

Spanish

Allegretto ♩ = 60

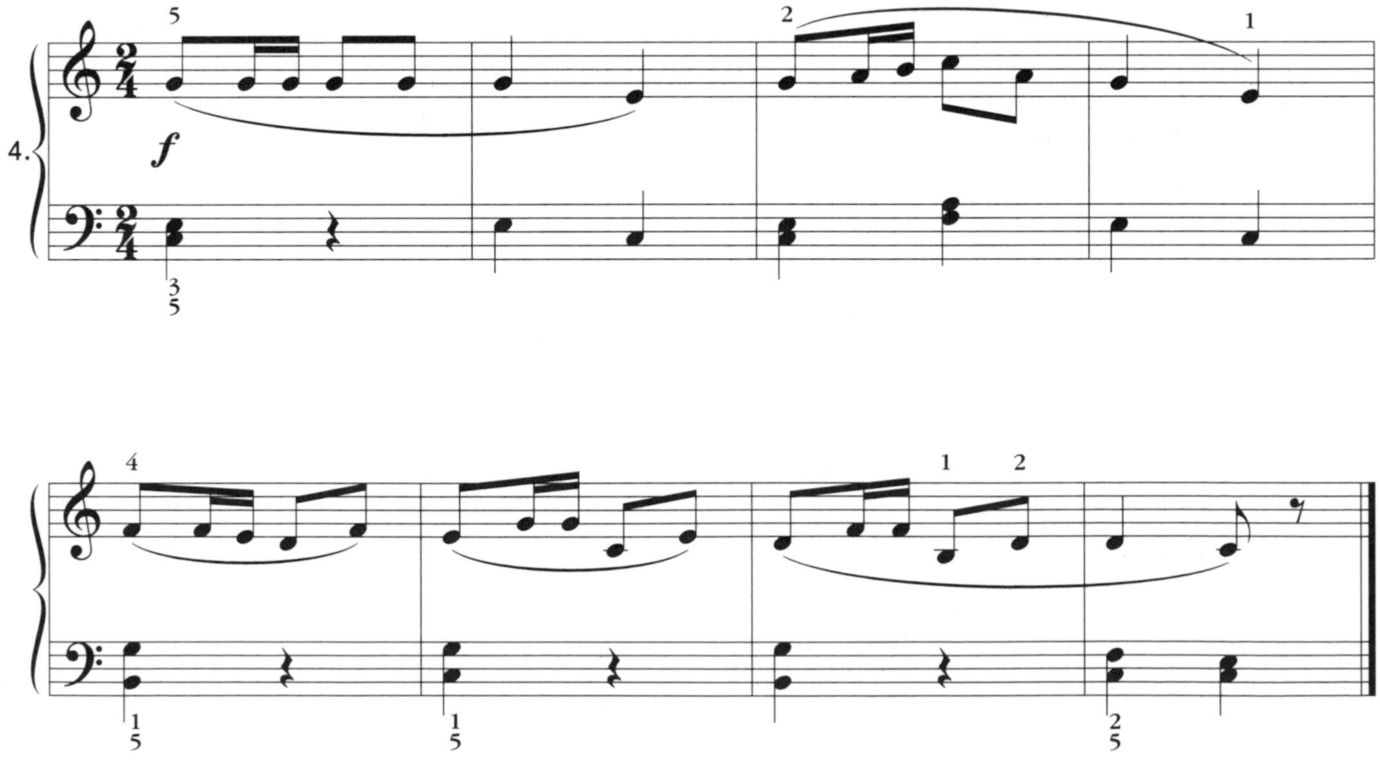

DONKEY RIDING

Sea Chantey

Jaunty ♩ = 72

5.

Croatian

Lento ♩ = 44

6.

The Subdominant (IV) Chord in Major Keys

In one measure of the *Norwegian Melody* below, the subdominant, or IV chord, is outlined.

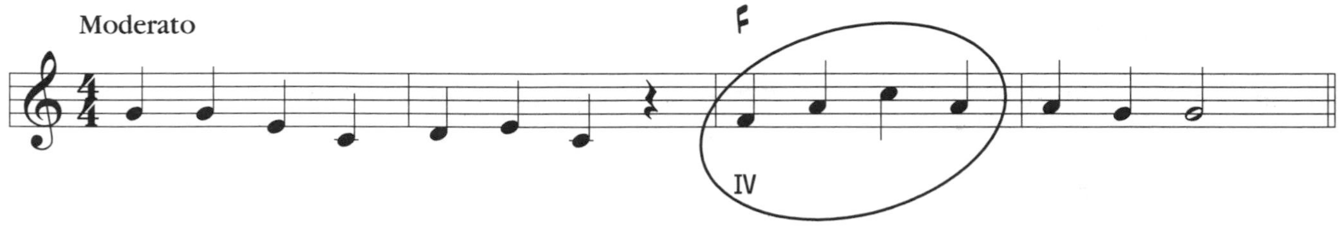

The subdominant chord is built on the 4th scale degree as shown below. It is major in quality and generally moves to V (dominant) or I (tonic).

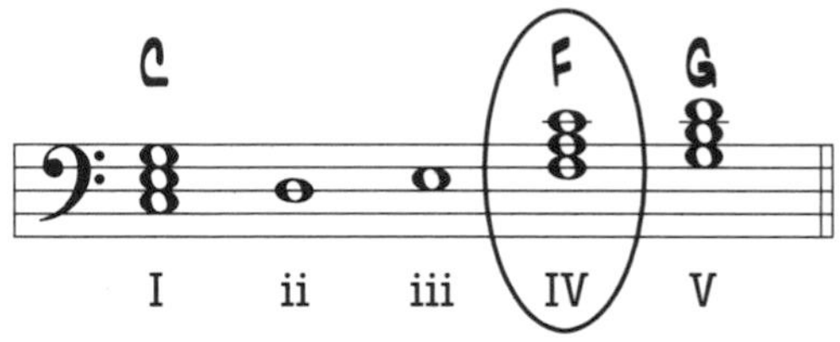

The three most common chords in music are the I, IV and V. These chords are known as *primary* chords. Chords built on other tones of the scale (ii, iii, vi, etc.) are called *secondary* chords.

As you learned when dealing with V^7 in root position as opposed to V^7 in first inversion (V^6_5), inversions help the hand assume a more comfortable position. In LH style harmonization, it is easy to move from I to V^6_5 and return to I. I–V^7–I is less smooth. The same holds true when I moves to IV or IV moves to I, or to V^6_5. Study the examples below.

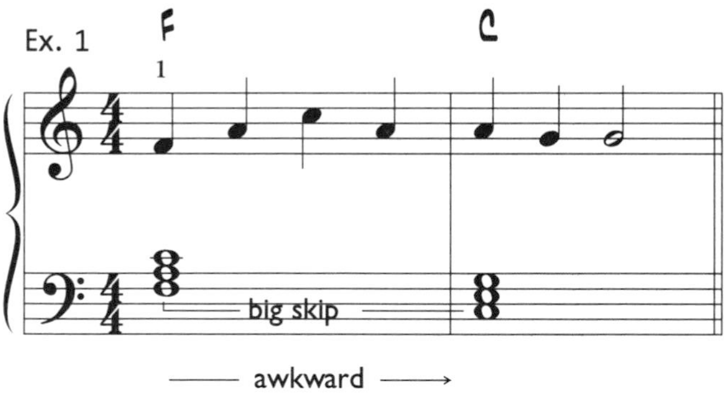

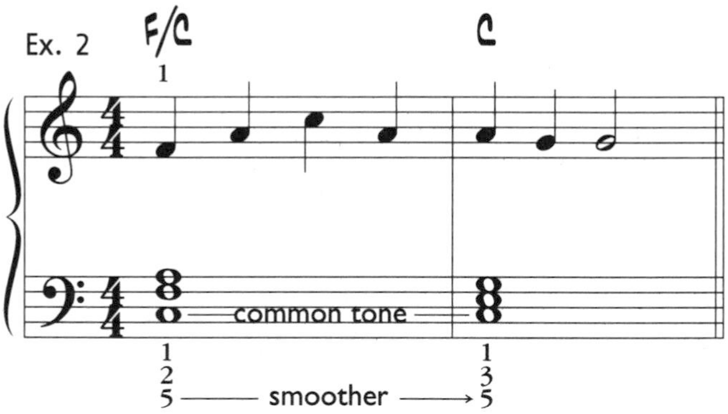

I–IV^6_4–I–V^6_5–I Chord Pattern

Practice the following chord pattern and transpose it to all white keys. Place letter name chord symbols above each chord as shown in the C major example. Pedal as indicated.

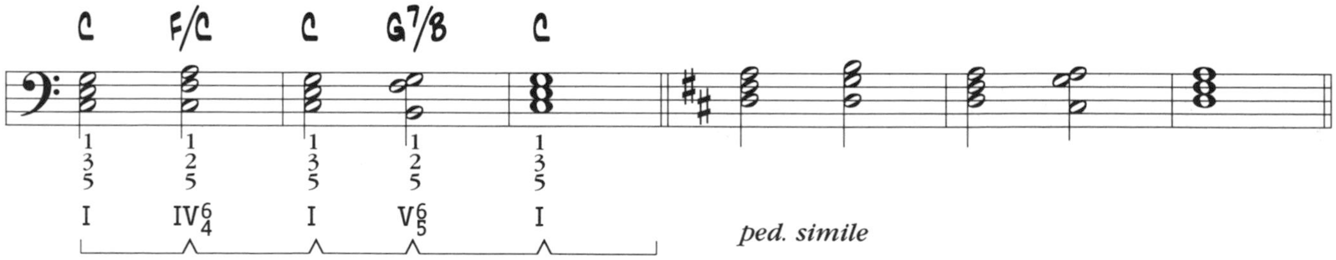

Harmonization Using I, IV_4^6, and V_5^6 in Major and Minor Keys

Harmonize the following melodies using the suggested LH style. The melody and chord symbols represent a lead line. Lead lines are used in jazz and popular music.

German

1.

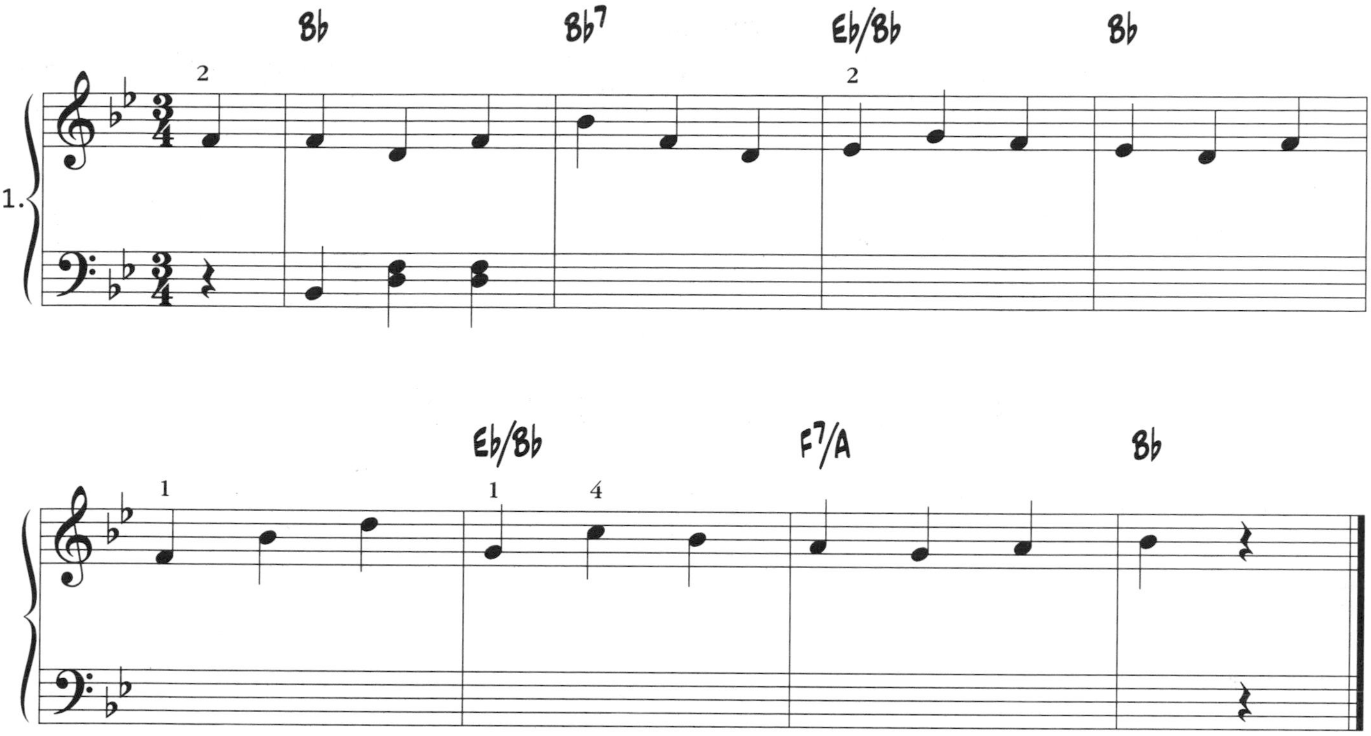

Polish

2.

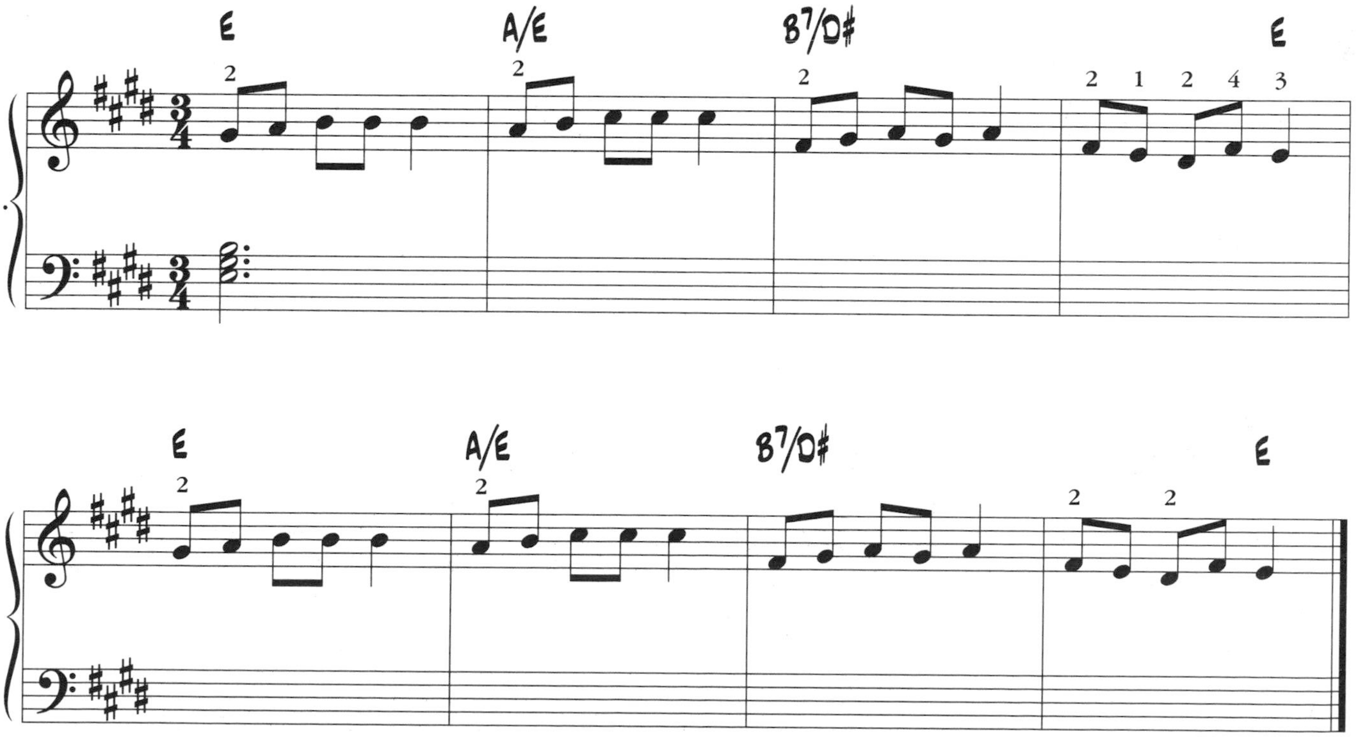

The subdominant chord in minor keys is minor in quality. The **iv** chord in minor generally moves to **V** (dominant) or **i** (tonic).

British

3.

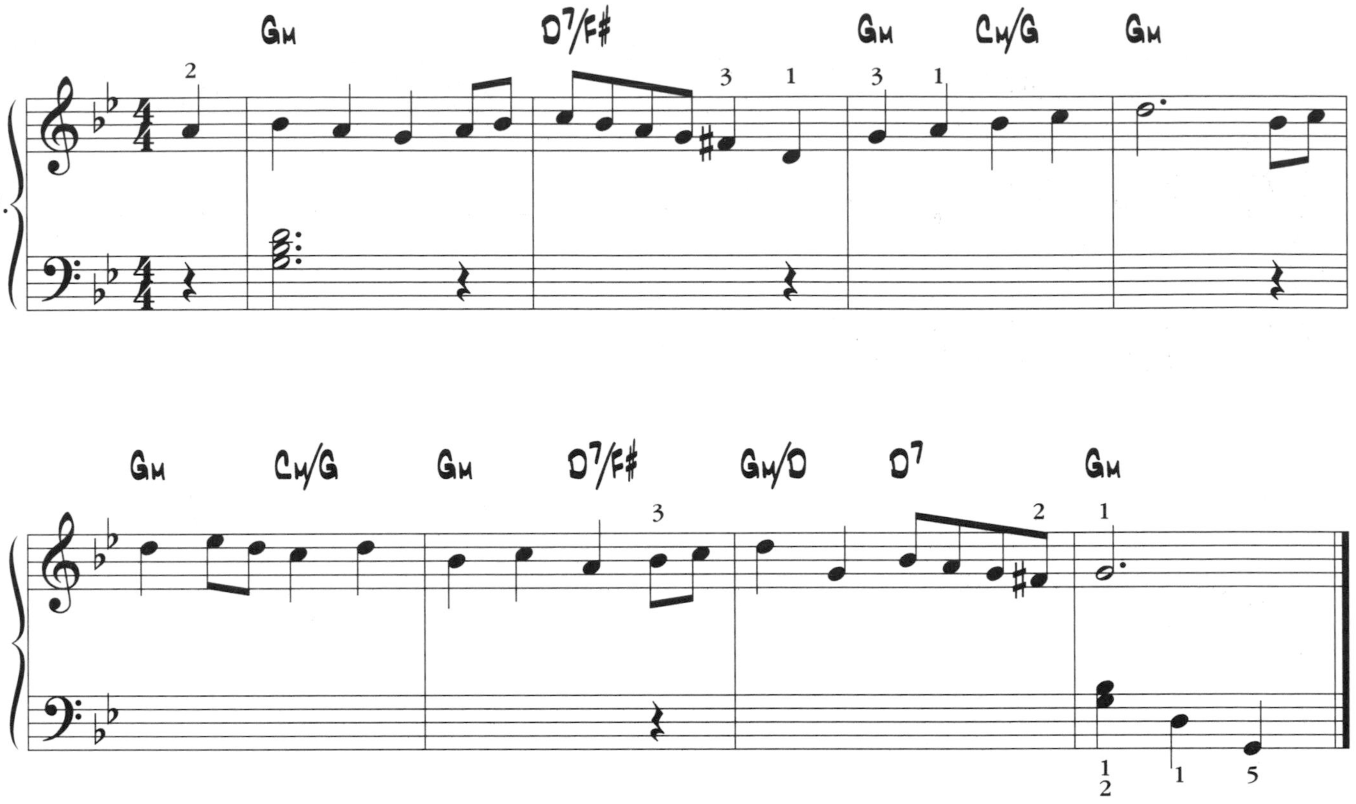

Spanish

4.

British

Russian

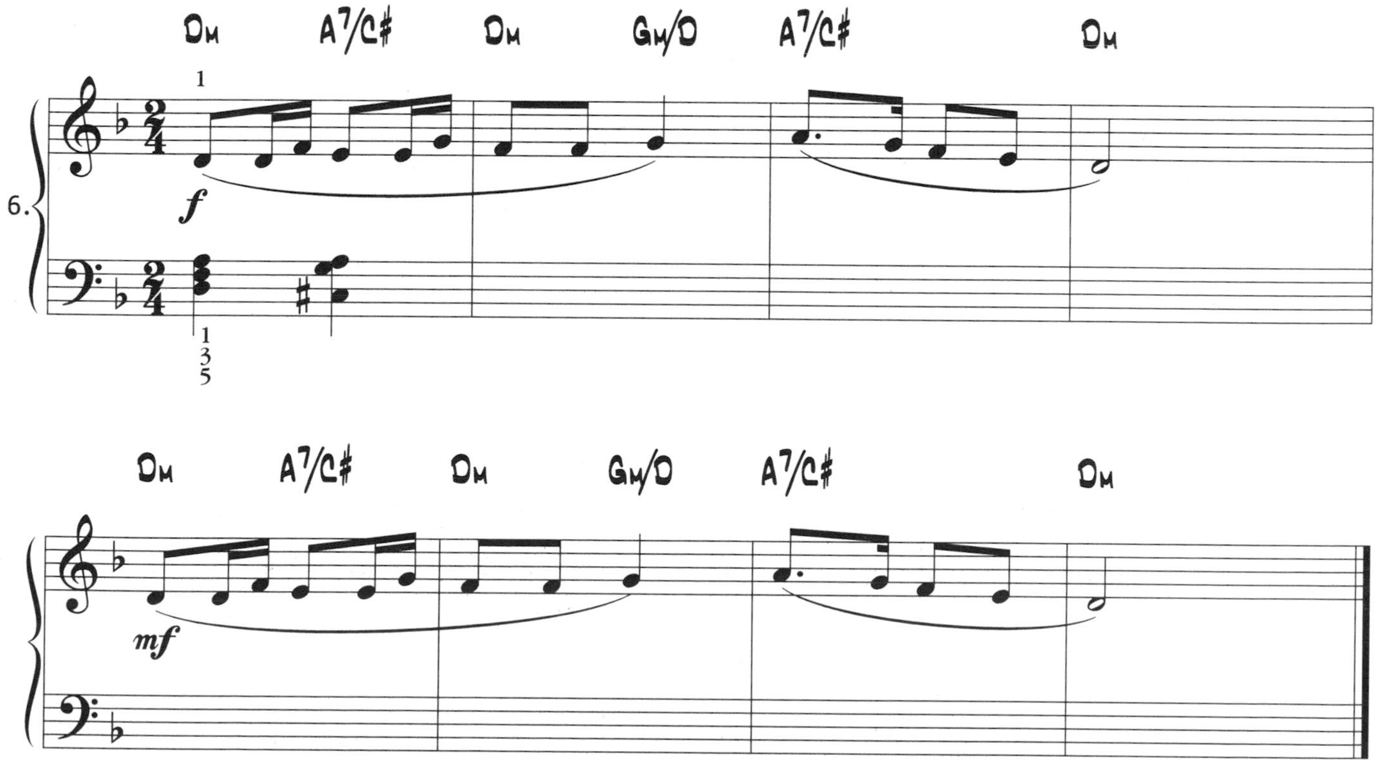

Music for Sight Reading and Transposing

Analyze the key of every reading example. As always, tap the rhythm of each hand before playing. Be certain your hands are placed in the proper register of the keyboard. Finally, follow the transposition suggestions. Elements contained in the reading studies include 1) minor mode, 2) $\frac{6}{8}$ meter, 3) sixteenth notes, and 4) tonic, subdominant and dominant harmonies and review material.

British

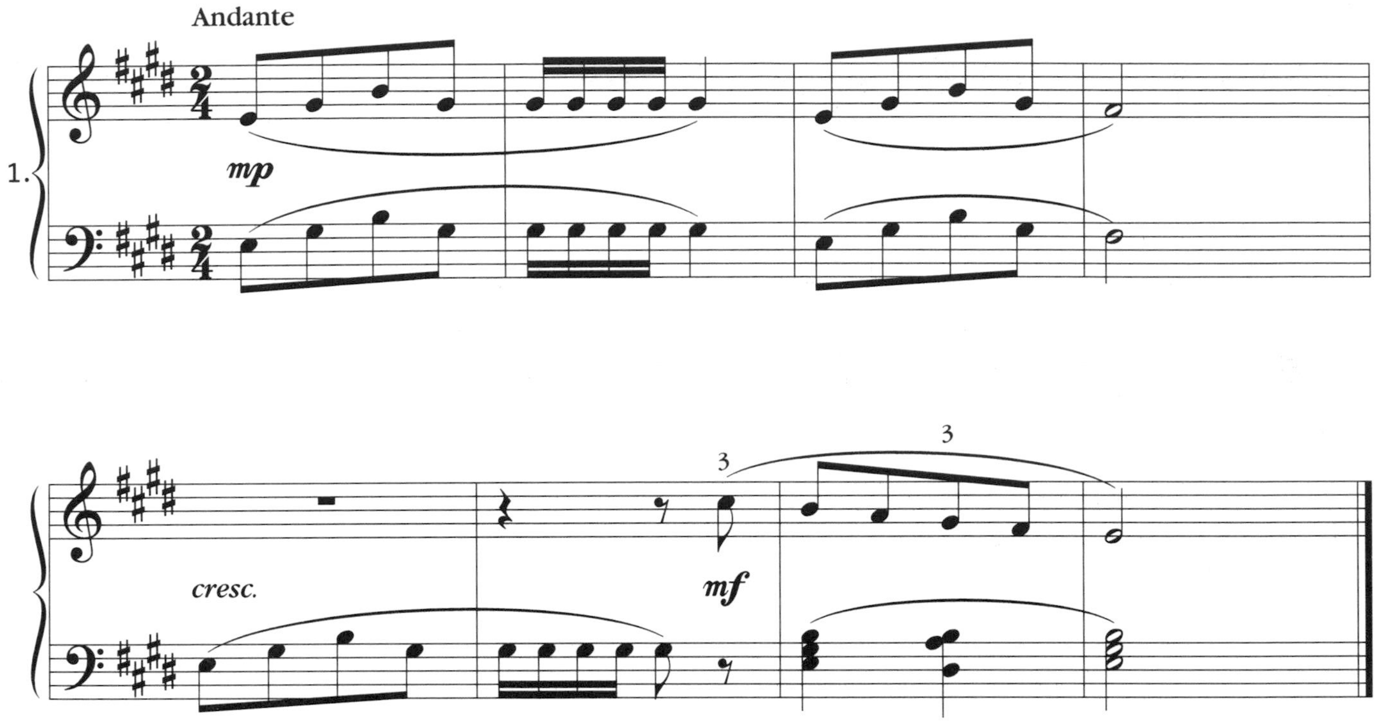

Transpose to D and F.

Dutch

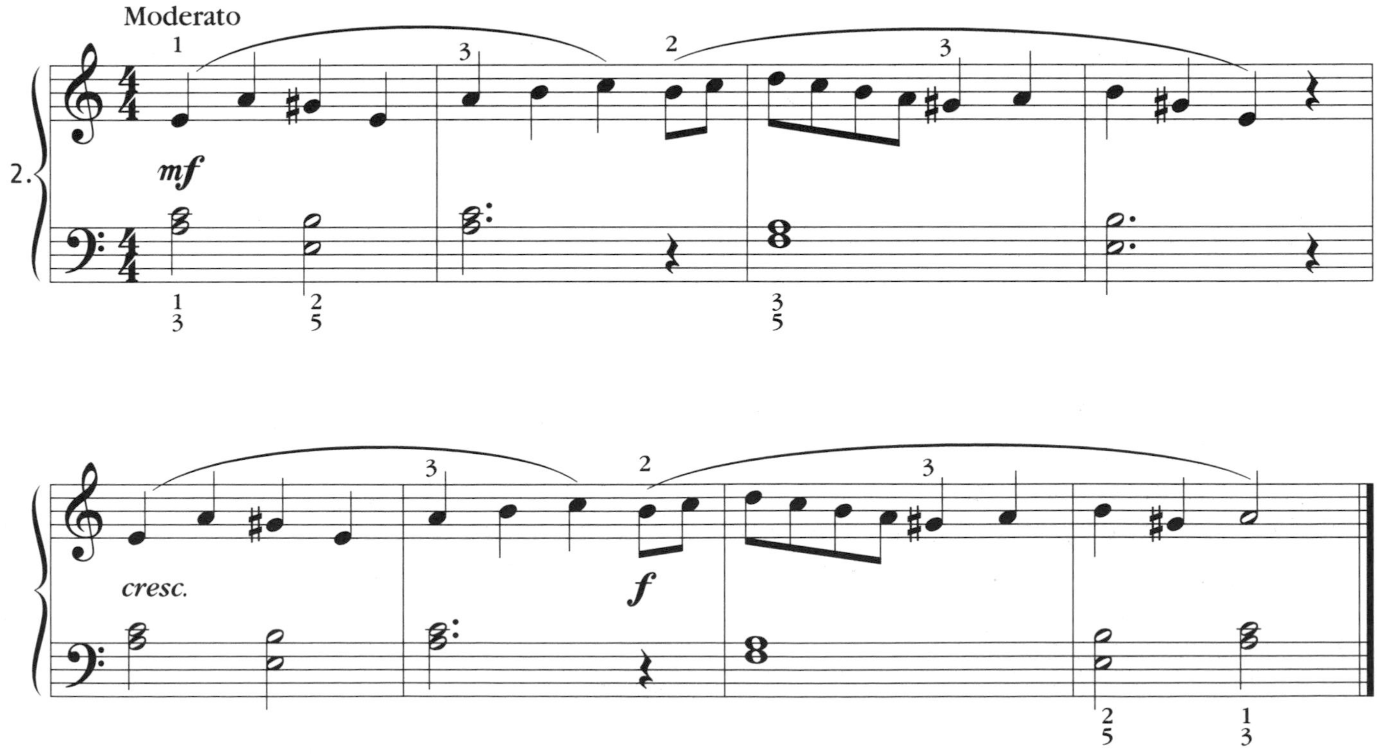

no transposition

Italian

Lento

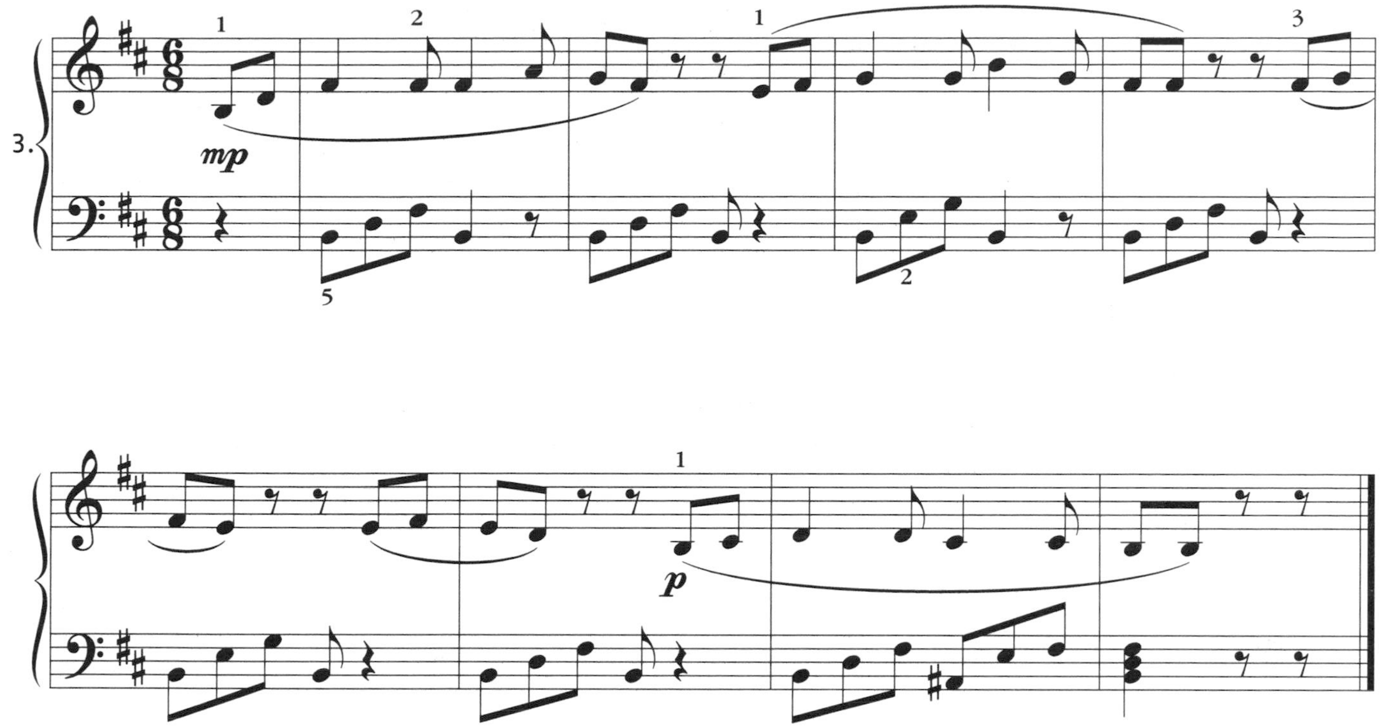

Transpose to C minor.

Old Folk Song

Moderately

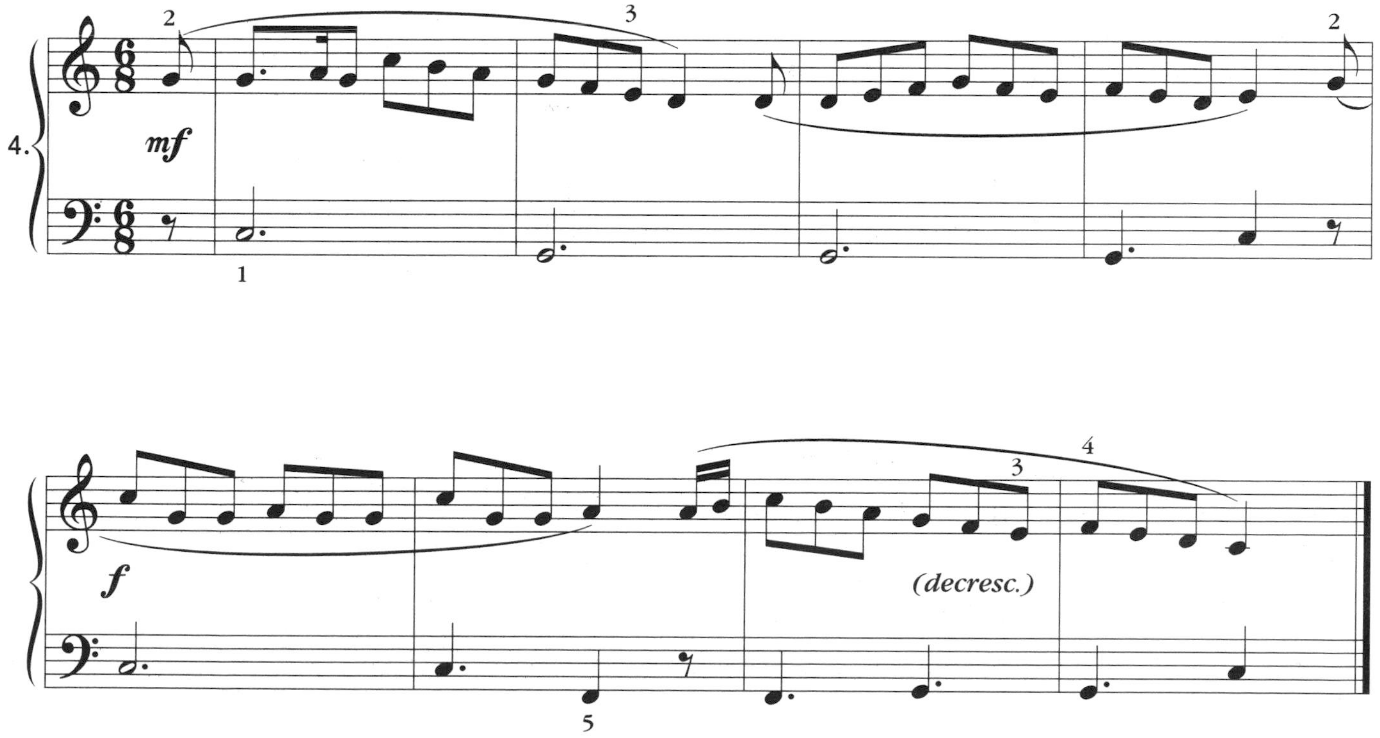

Transpose to D major.

French

Transpose to F major.

Polish

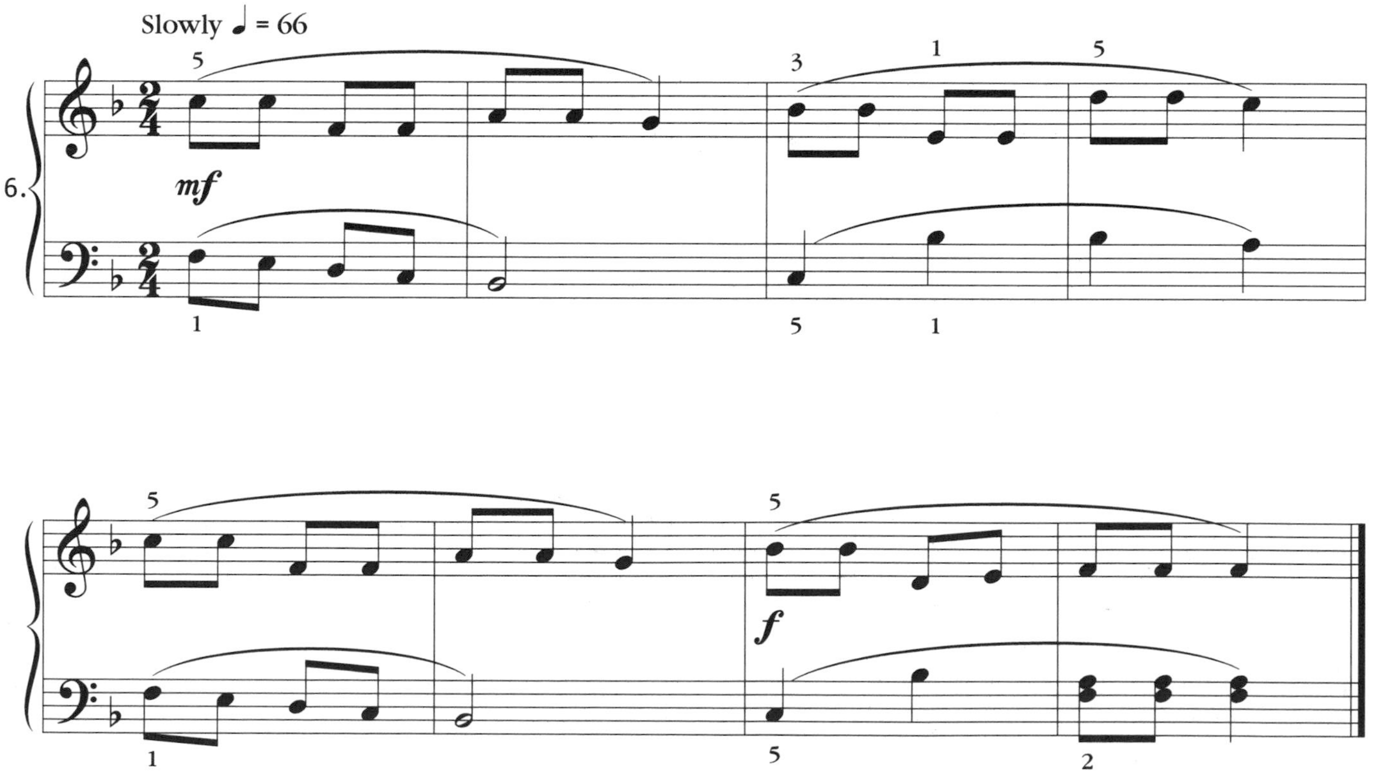

no transposition

Croatian

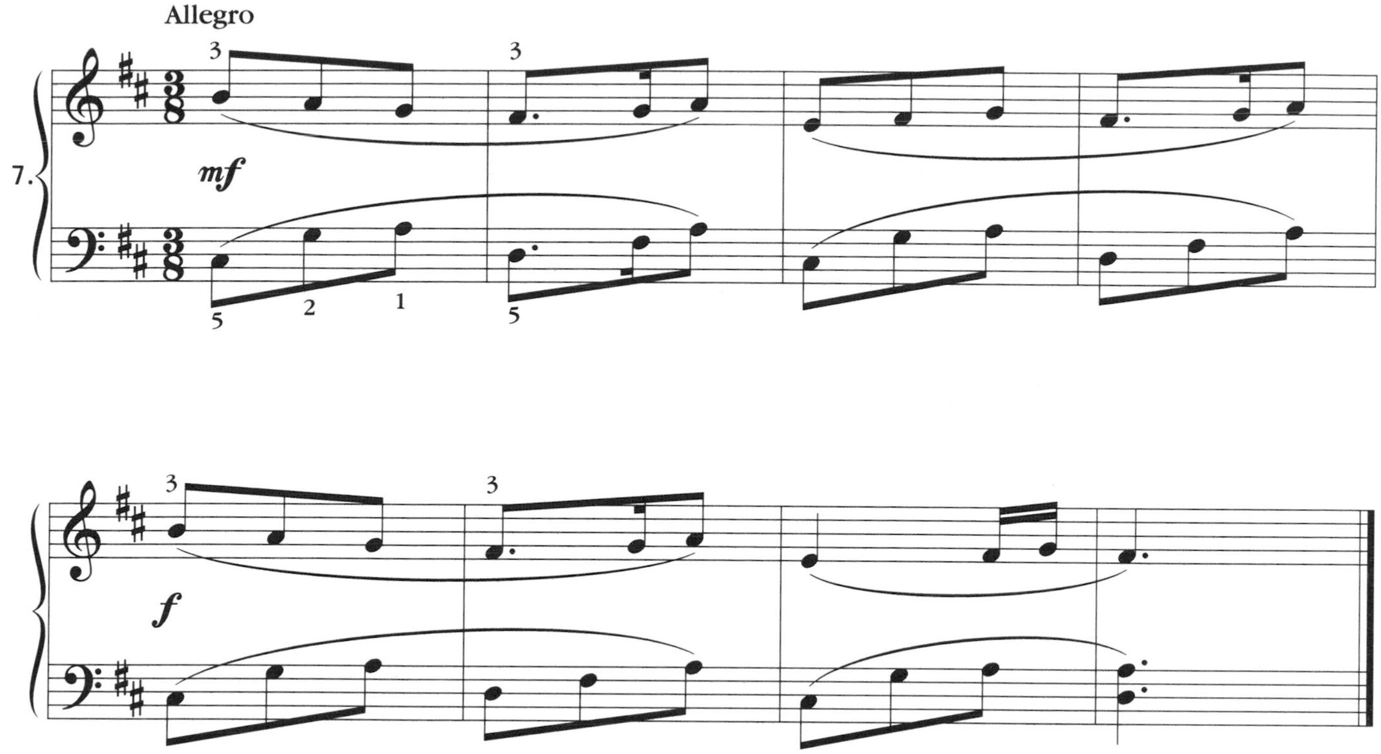

Transpose to C major.

Dutch

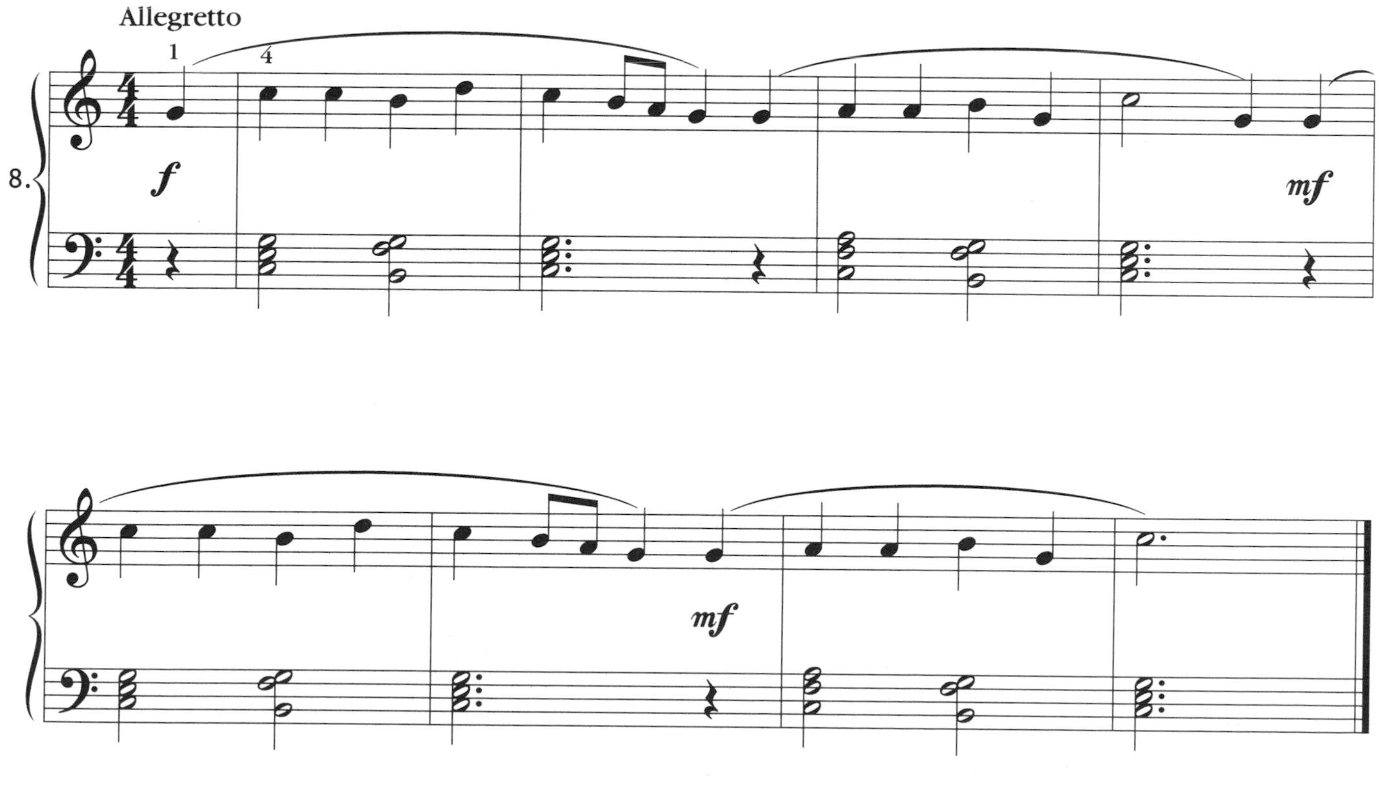

Transpose to B♭ major.

ACCOMPANYING

This accompaniment makes use of tonic, subdominant (IV), and dominant seventh chords. Only one chord is different. The first two beats of measure 3 is a Gm^7 (ii^7) which moves smoothly to C^7. Analyze all of the chords.

Teacher: Double the melody two octaves higher.

20 CD

FROM BEYOND THE ISLAND

Russian
arr. James Lyke

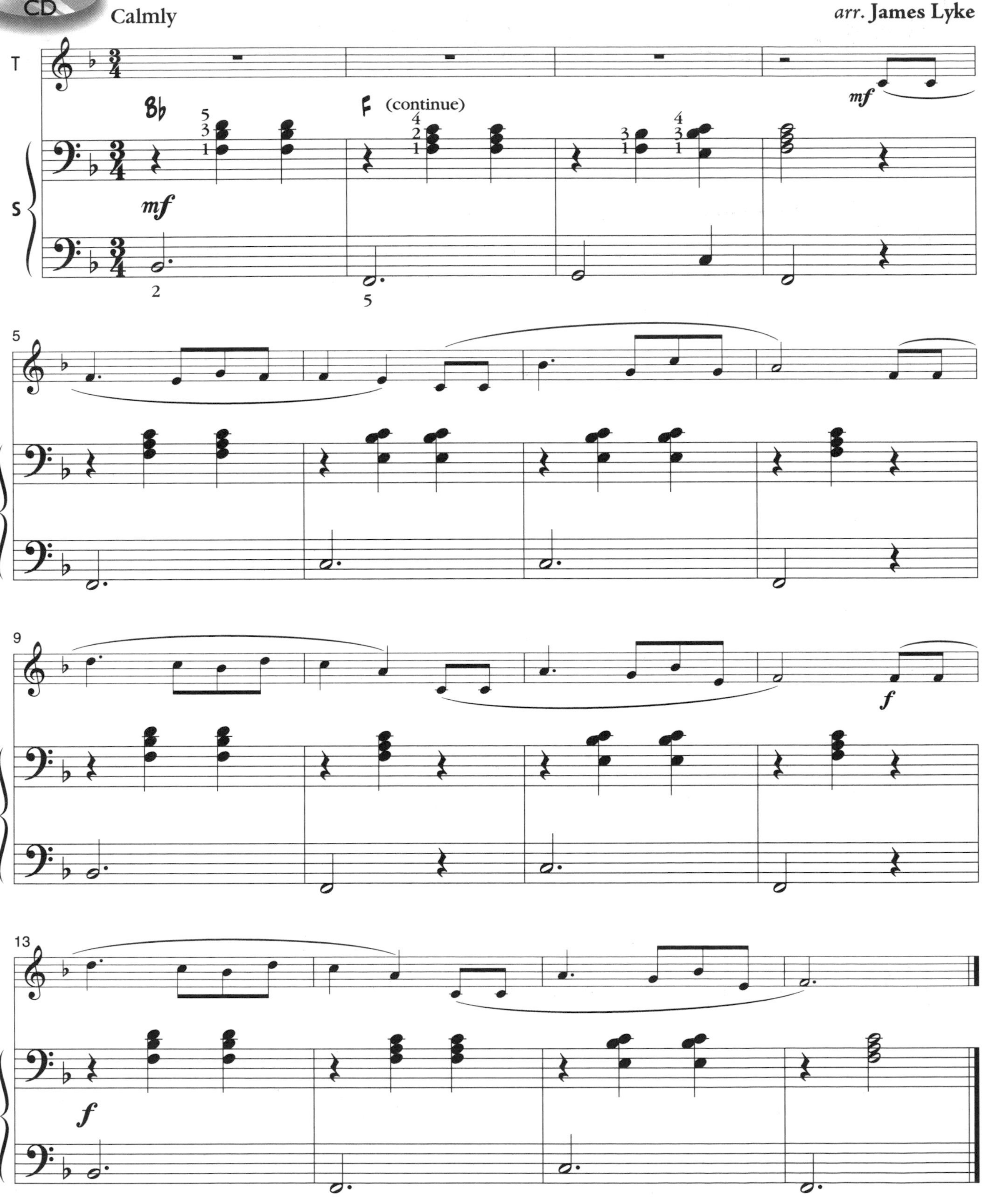

Learn the accompaniment for *The Slender Mountain Ash* by blocking the harmony in both hands. The LH is a snap (Em pentachord). The RH will take some practice, especially with fingering. Analyze the harmony with help from your instructor.

Teacher: Double the melody two octaves higher.

21 CD

THE SLENDER MOUNTAIN ASH

Russian
arr. **James Lyke**

22 CD

BY THE BEAUTIFUL SEA

music by **Harry Carroll**
arr. **James Lyke**

Moderately fast

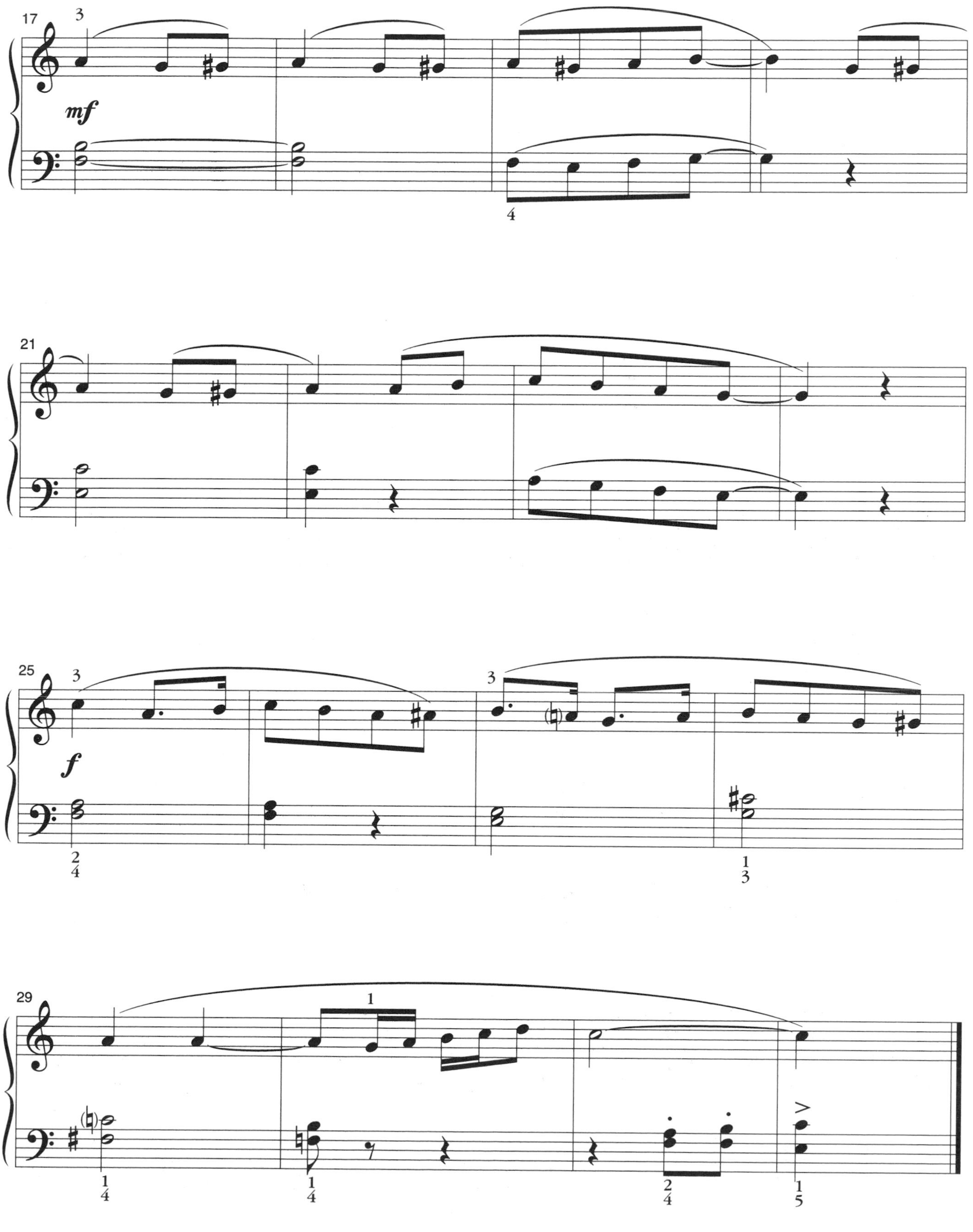
17
mf
21
25
f
29

CD 23

K-K-K KATY

music by **Geoffrey O'Hara**
arr. **James Lyke**

Briskly ♩. = 100

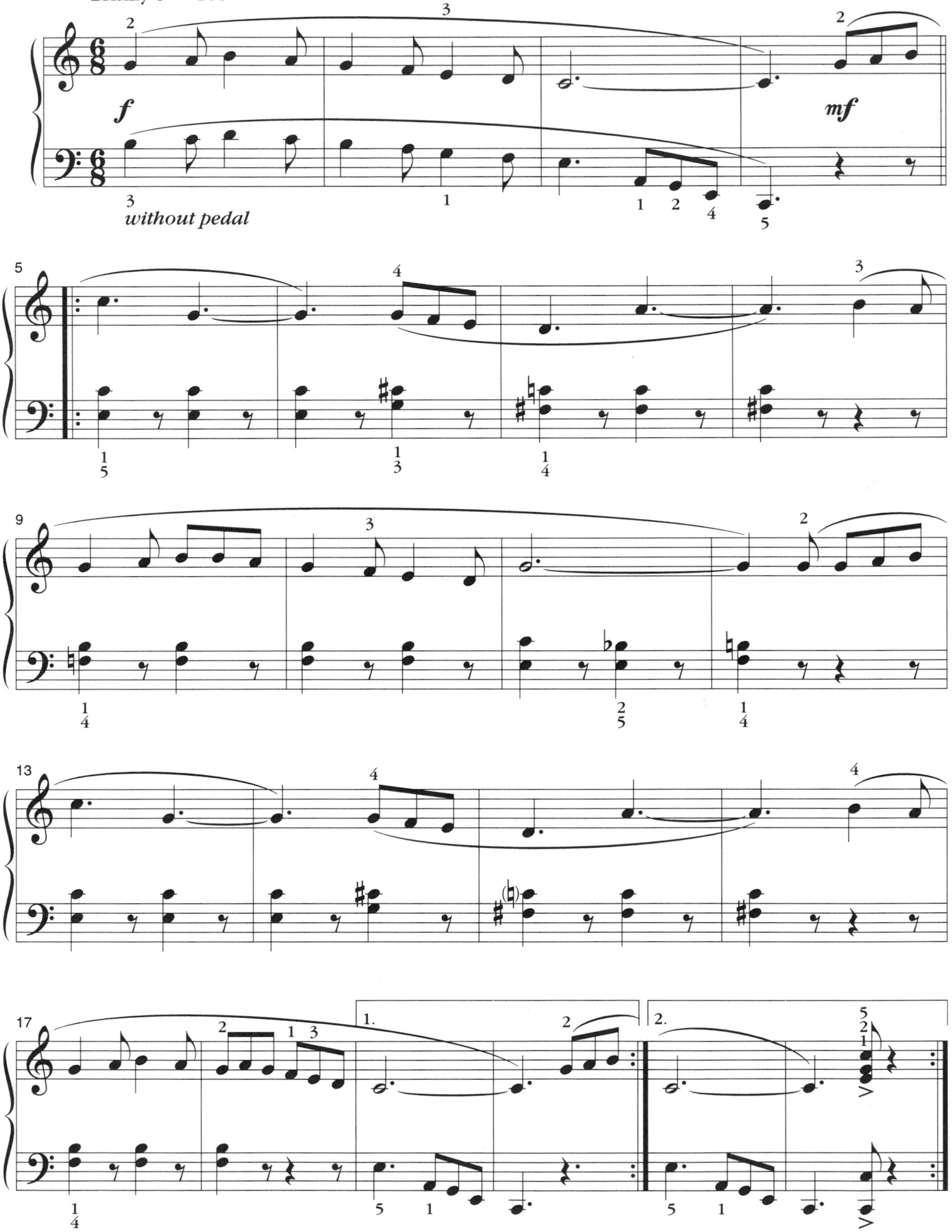

LH Chord Analysis

Label each chord in the LH where you see a box. Take note of the bass notes for "slash" chords (C^7/E, etc.). One student plays the RH while another student plays the LH. Then switch parts.

BEAUTIFUL BROWN EYES

Old American Song
arr. James Lyke

Moderato

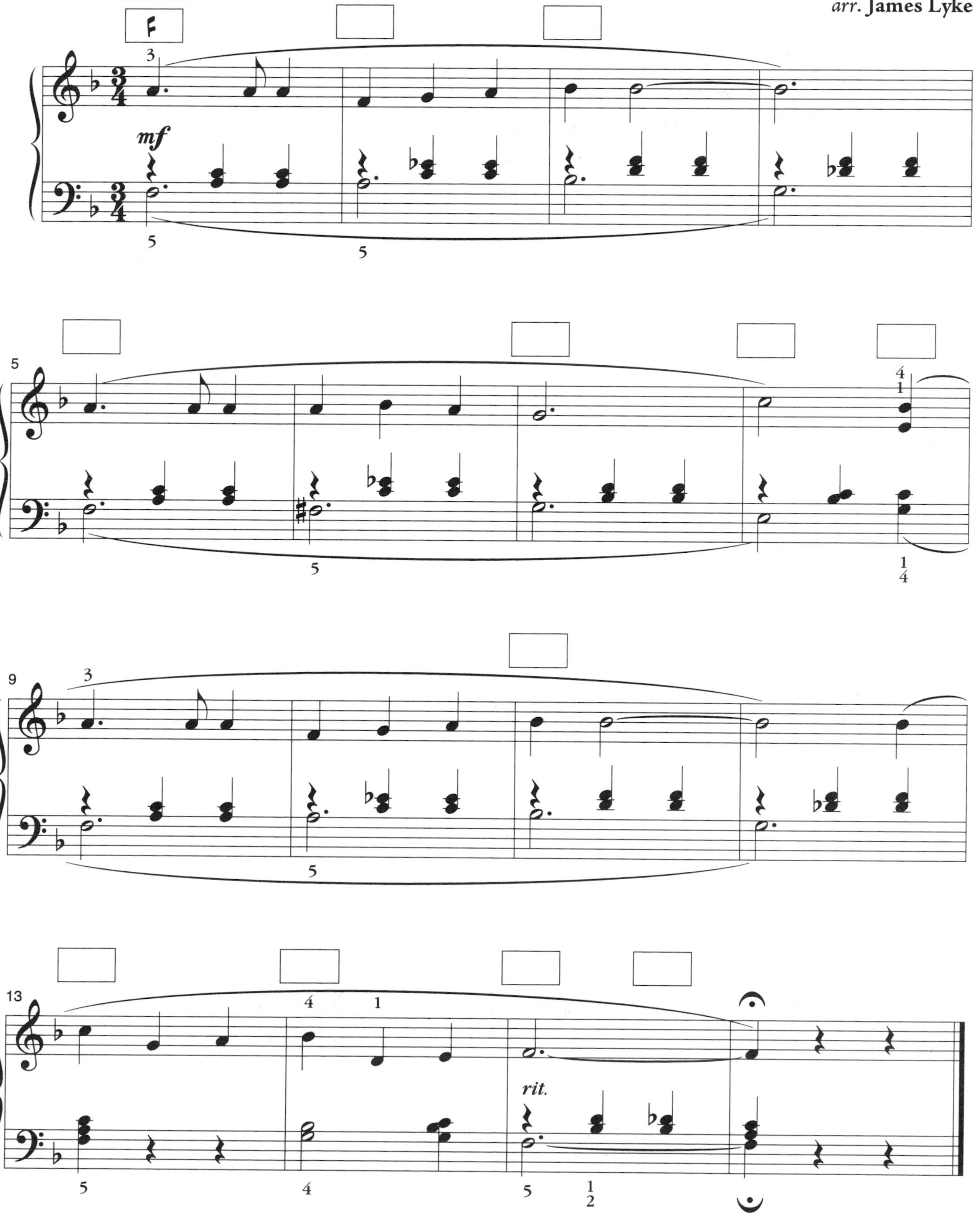

ENSEMBLE REPERTOIRE

24 CD

WHAT I'M LONGING TO SAY

Secondo – Teacher

music by **Jerome Kern**
arr. **James Lyke**

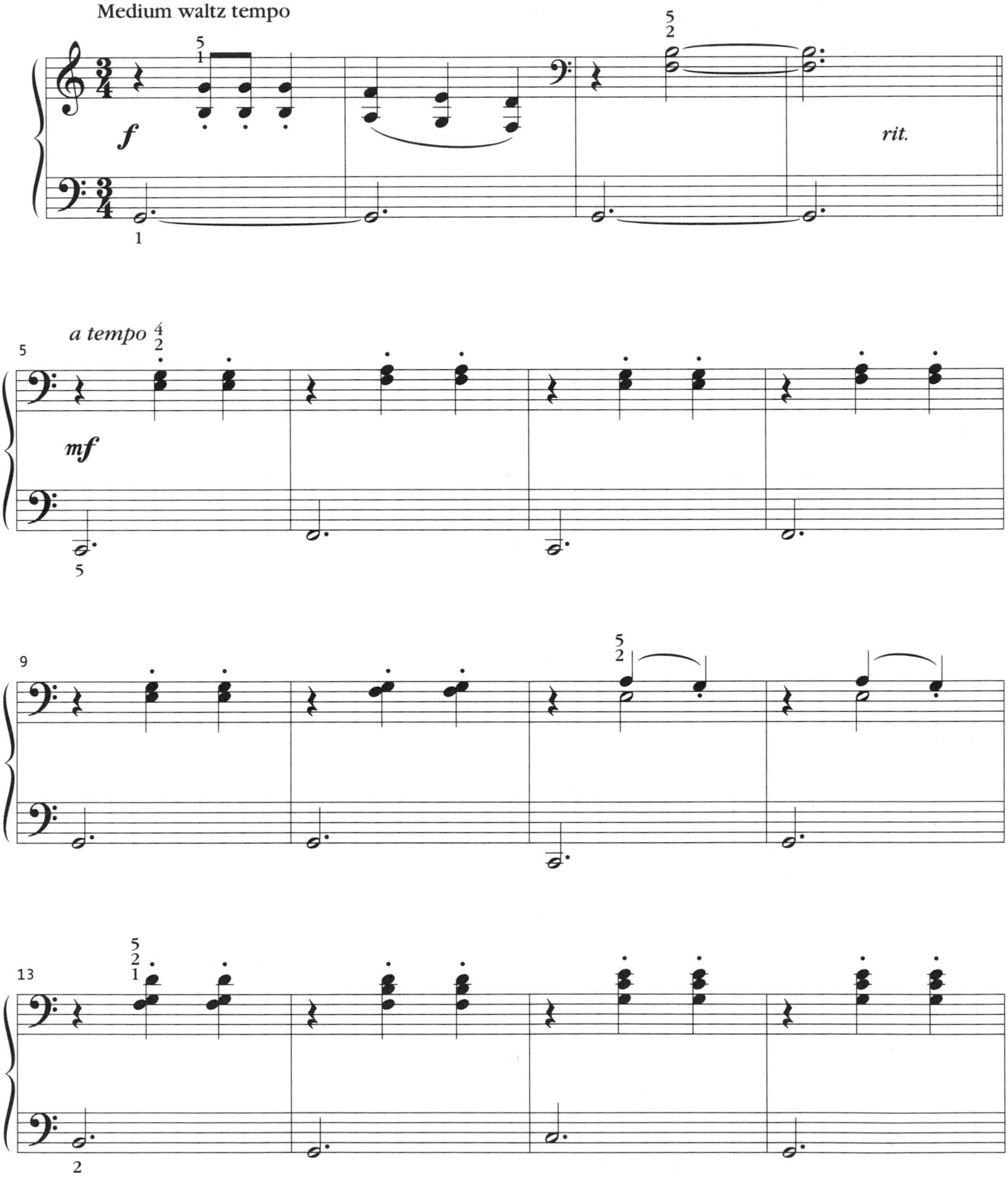

Practice Plan: 1) Practice each part slowly to learn the fingerings; 2) work on "here to here" (rapid shifts) such as bars 12 to 13, 14 to 15, and 16 to 17; and 3) observe the "stretches" (RH) in bars 21–22 and 25–26. *Legato* playing and attention to phrasing is very important.

24 CD

WHAT I'M LONGING TO SAY

Primo – Student

music by **Jerome Kern**
arr. **James Lyke**

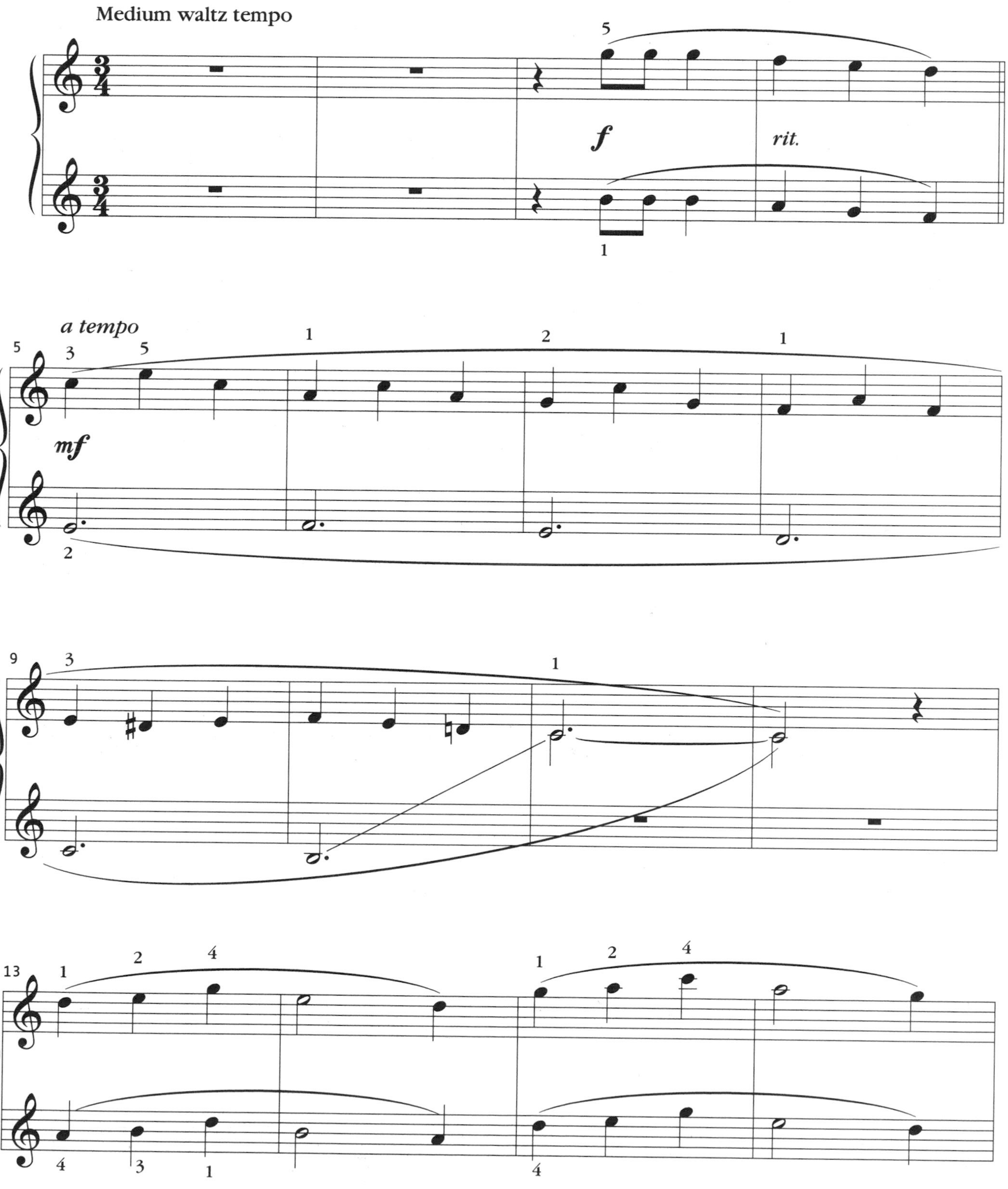

Secondo

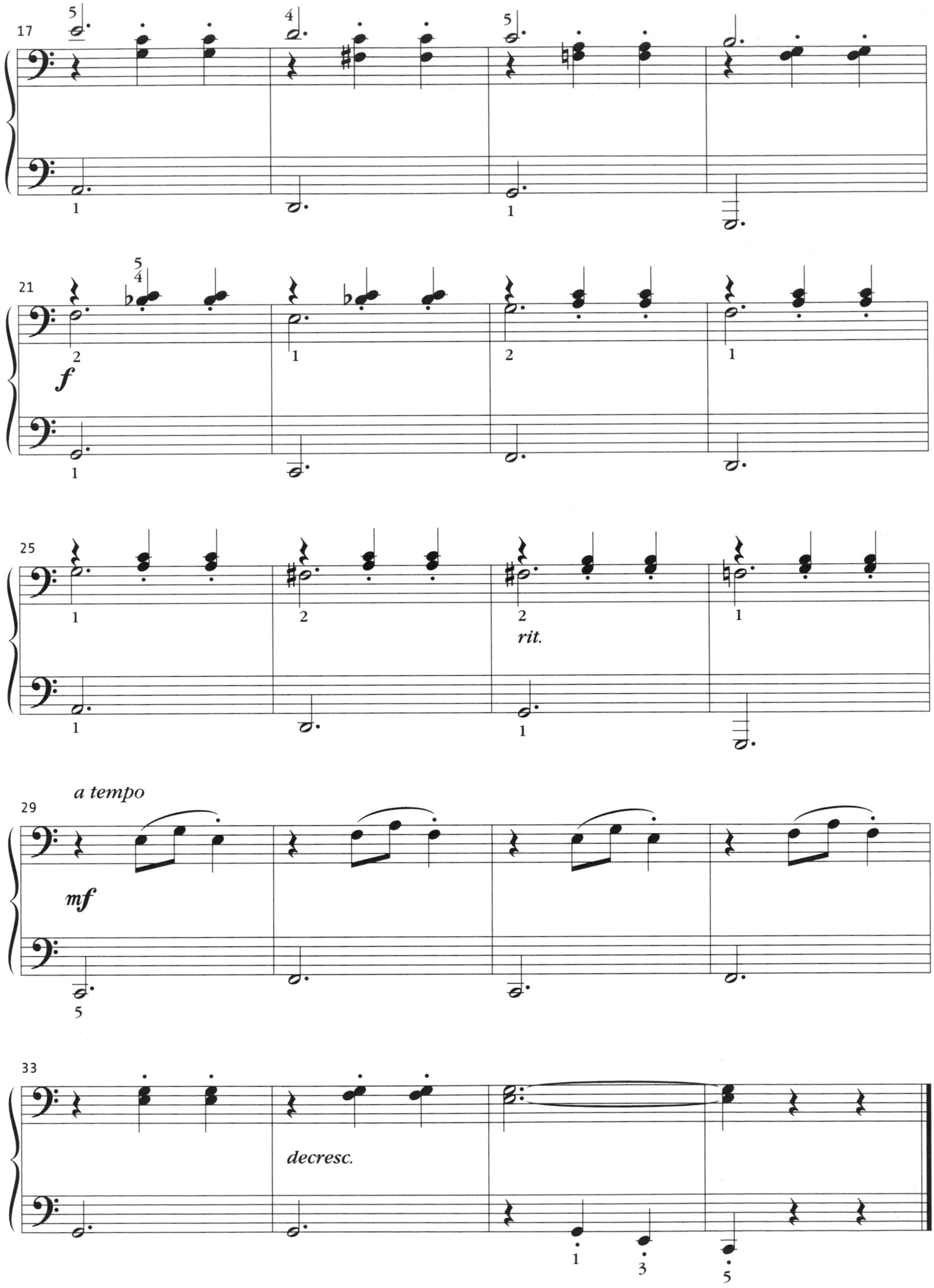

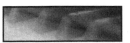

Primo

COUNTRY GARDENS

Secondo – Teacher

English Morris Dance
arr. **James Lyke**

25 CD

COUNTRY GARDENS

Primo – Student

English Morris Dance
arr. **James Lyke**

Allegro

SOLO REPERTOIRE

Practice Plan: Practice the LH alone until position changes become comfortable. Play all RH sixteenth-note figures *staccato* at first (slow tempo). Take care with touch differentiation in the RH. Practice the RH alone several times before putting the hands together.

THE FIFES

Jean François Dandrieu

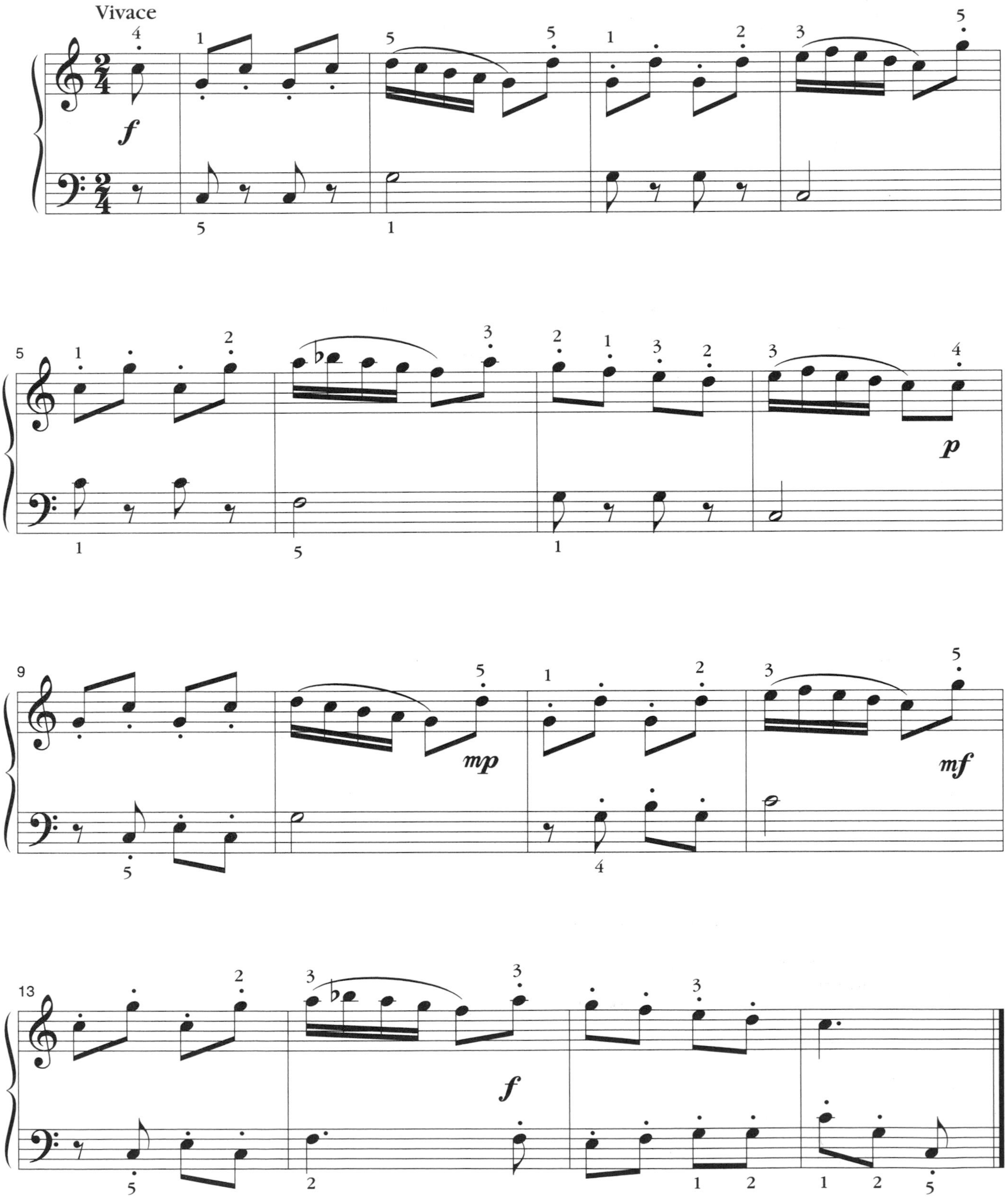

Practice Plan: Practice the LH alone until chords and single tones become easy. Practice shifts of position in the LH (bars 7–8, 8–9 and 12–13). In the RH, block all chord shapes as well as familiar patterns such as the major five-finger pattern (measures 6–8, 9–12). Put the hands together at an extremely slow tempo. Analyze the harmony and find the tonic, subdominant, and dominant chords. Label them with both Roman numerals (below the staff) and letter name symbols (above the staff).

MINUET

Leopold Mozart

Andantino grazioso

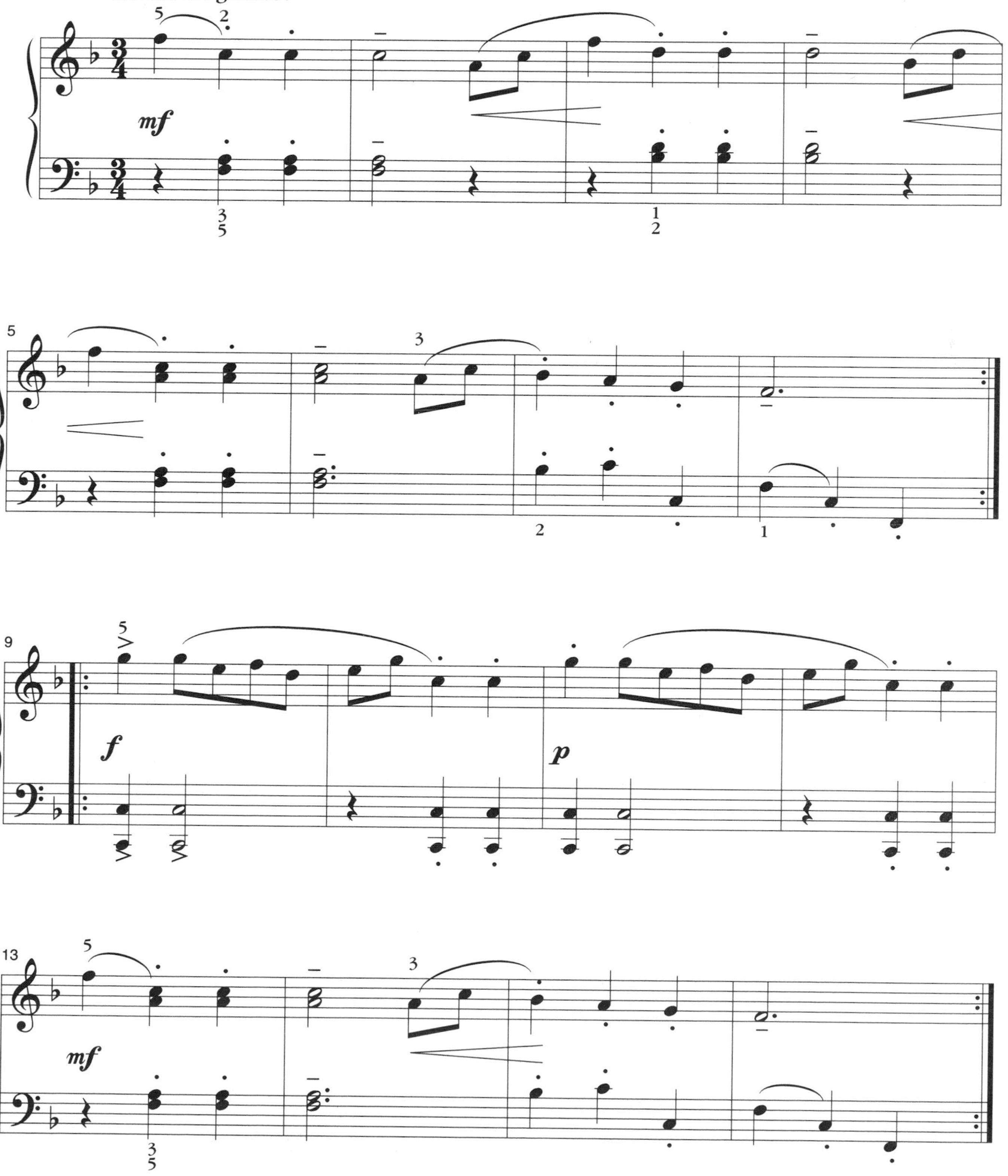

Practice Plan: Play hands alone and study the fingering. This $\frac{6}{8}$ piece should be played at a slow tempo. Practice two measures at a time with several repetitions before combining hands.

LAZY BLUES

Tony Caramia

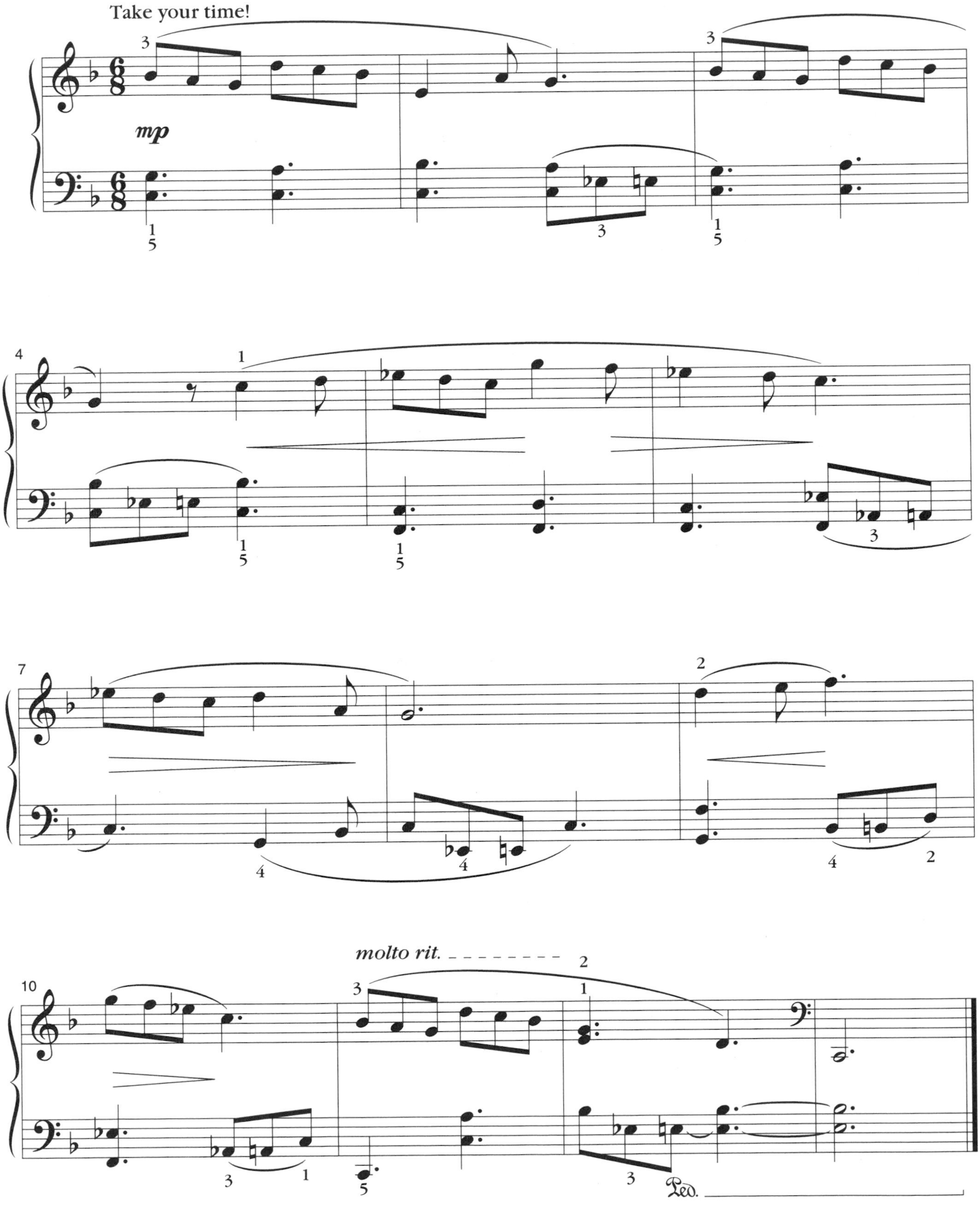

Practice Plan: Play LH alone several times and identify intervals. Practice RH alone until position shifts and fingering become solid. In the second section following the double bar, make sure the 3rds (RH) are smooth. Put hands together when these details have been mastered.

CHANSON TRISTE

Céline Bussières-Lessard

Adagio con espressione

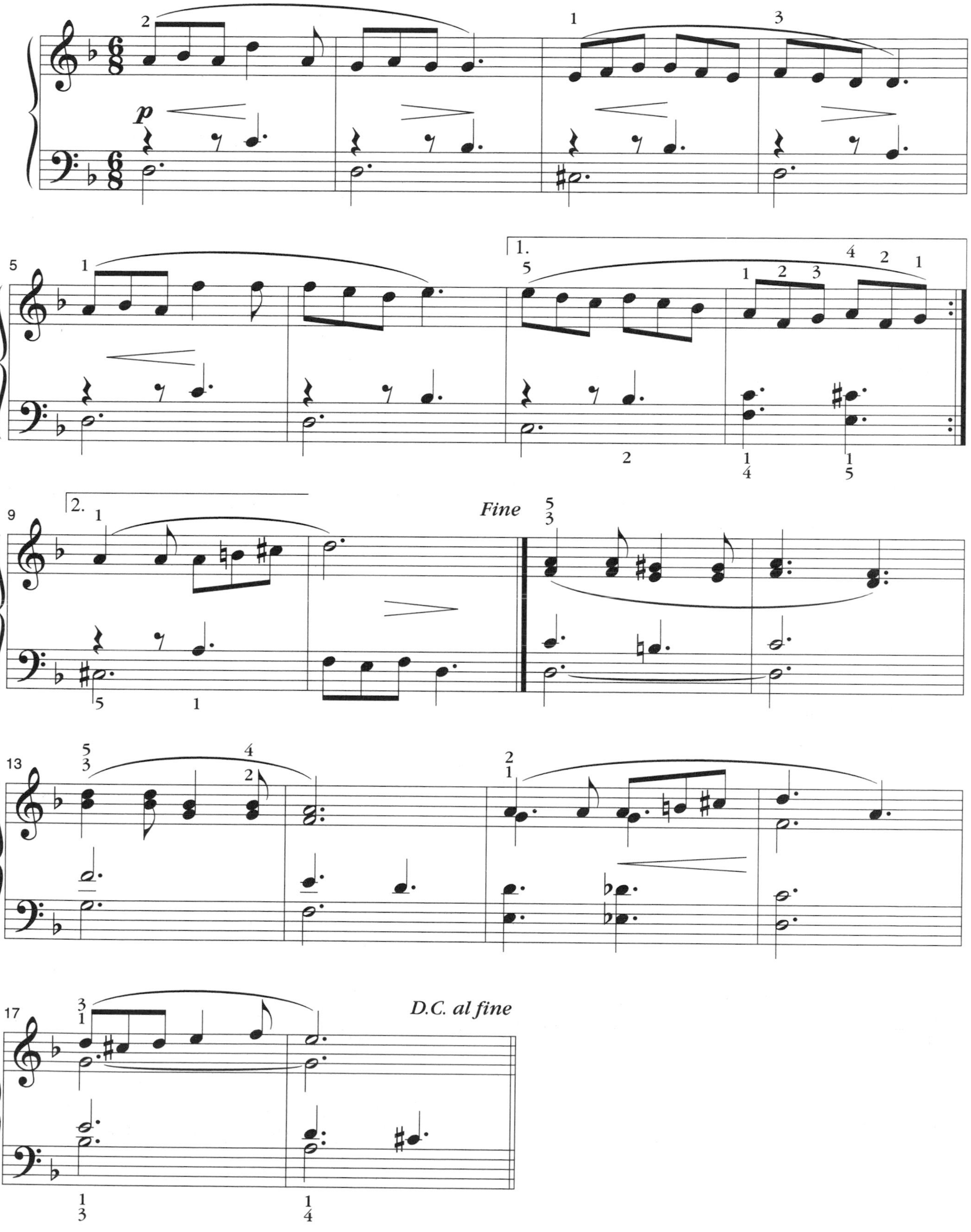

Practice Plan: Practice hands separately at a slow tempo. Listen for even sixteenths and take note of phrase markings and articulations. Careful fingering is needed.

A MINOR PIECE

Tony Caramia

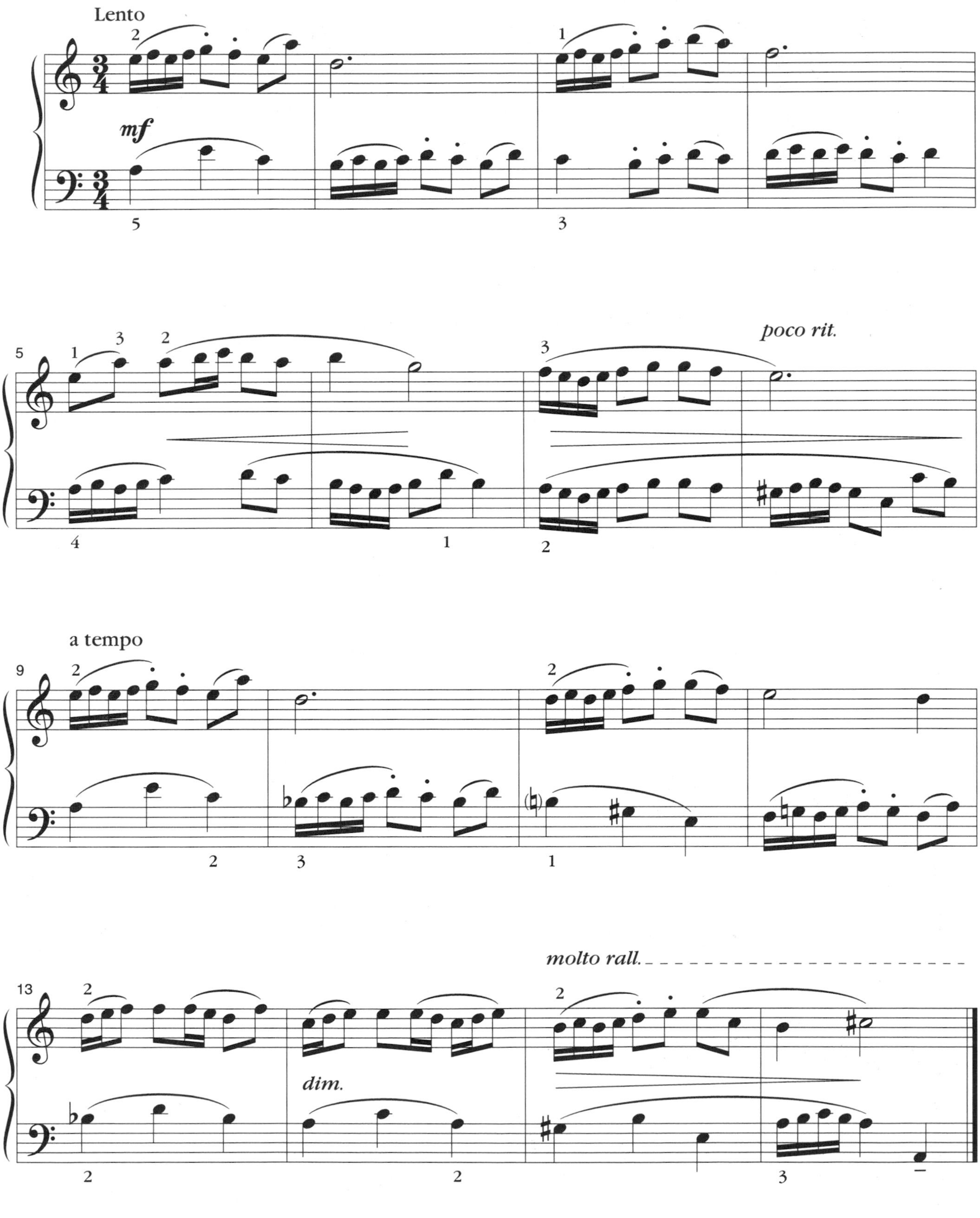

Practice Plan: Analyze all five-finger patterns which begin with sixteenth notes (RH bars 1–16 and LH bars 17–24). Practice bars 1–16 hands alone (LH then RH). Practice measures 17–24 hands together slowly. Notice that the thumb of the LH is adjacent to the thumb of the RH in the sixteenth-note figures. Combine hands slowly. Sixteenth-note figures must be crisp!

SCHERZO

Céline Bussières-Lessard

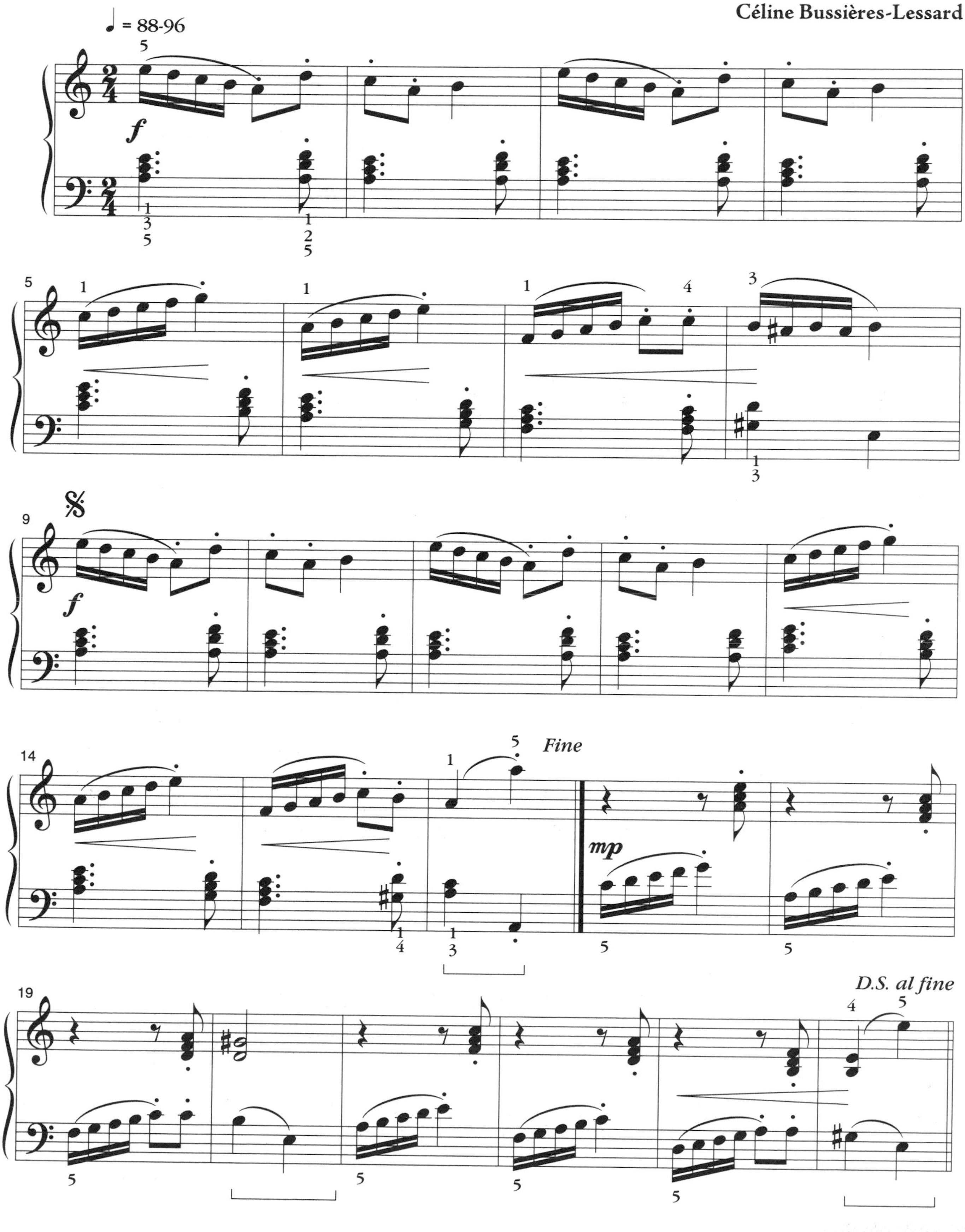

Practice Plan: Identify all the whole note triads (LH bars 1–8, RH bars 9–15). Play these triads first. Next play the melodic lines (RH measures 1–8, LH measures 9–15). Know the triads outlined. Then play hands together with a steady rhythm.

MAJOR–MINOR MIX-UP

Tony Caramia

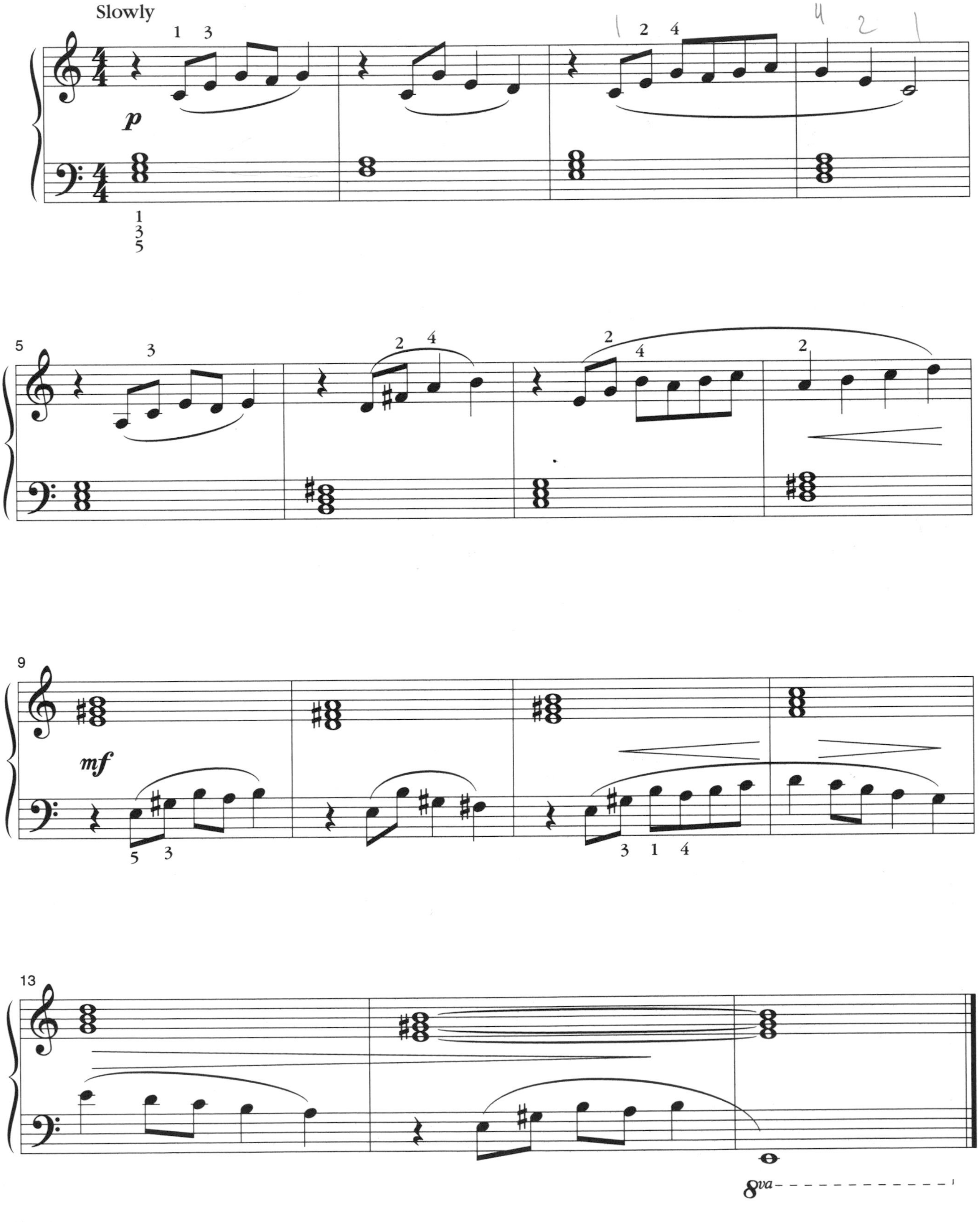

Practice Plan: Play LH alone at first. Focus on good rhythm and fingering. When trying the RH in beginning stages, tap the rhythm of the LH near the music rack of the keyboard. Analyze all chords and patterns in the RH. Combine hands at a slow and steady tempo. Gradually increase the speed.

LAMENT

Céline Bussières-Lessard

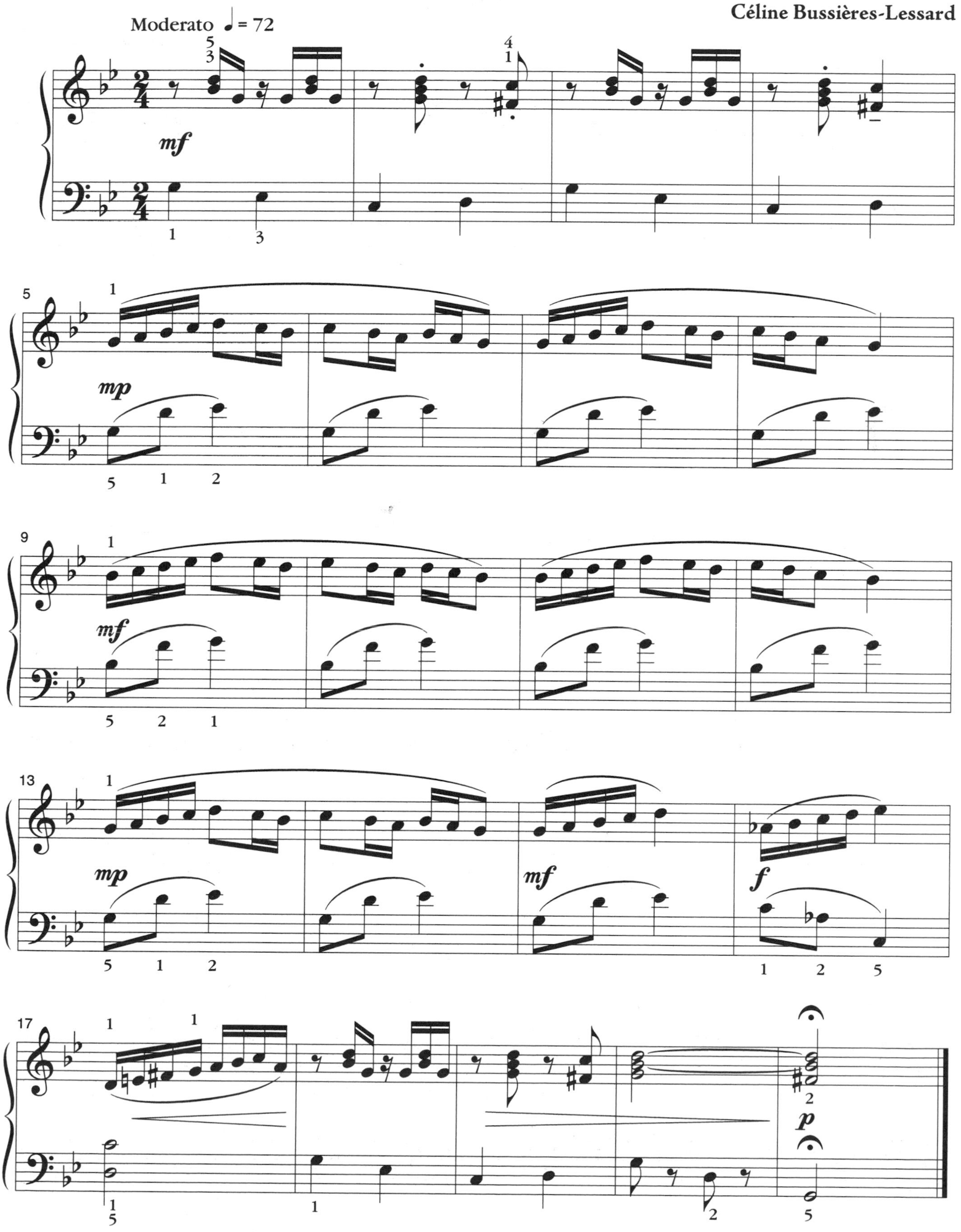

Practice Plan: At first, block the 5ths in each hand and choreograph the LH cross (over the RH). Measures 12–15 present special challenges in LH to RH playing. Next, play hands together slowly as written until all crosses are in place. Finally, add the pedal and enjoy the sonority it provides.

CROSSES

Céline Bussières-Lessard

MUSICIANSHIP ACTIVITIES

Complete the following exercises which review various topics introduced in Chapter Four.

Minor Pentachord Review

Build the minor pentachords indicated below. Draw letters on the correct keys, as shown in number one below.

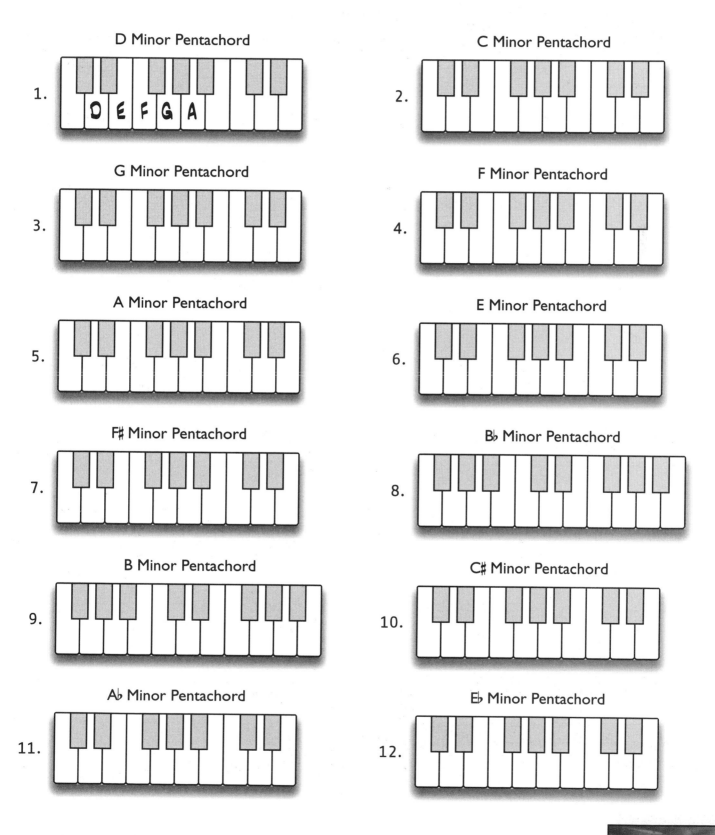

D Minor Pentachord

1. 

C Minor Pentachord

2. 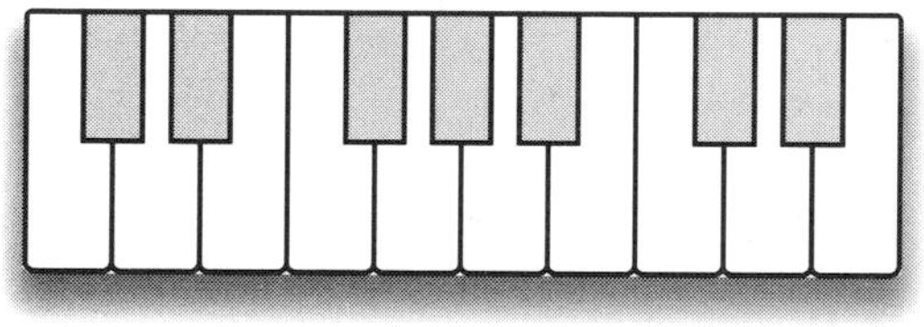

G Minor Pentachord

3. 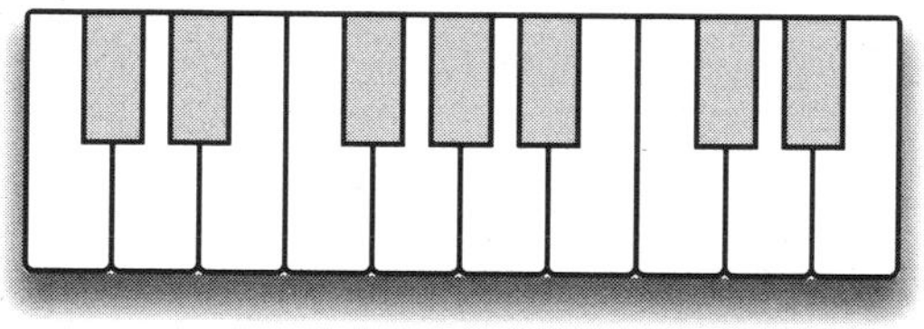

F Minor Pentachord

4. 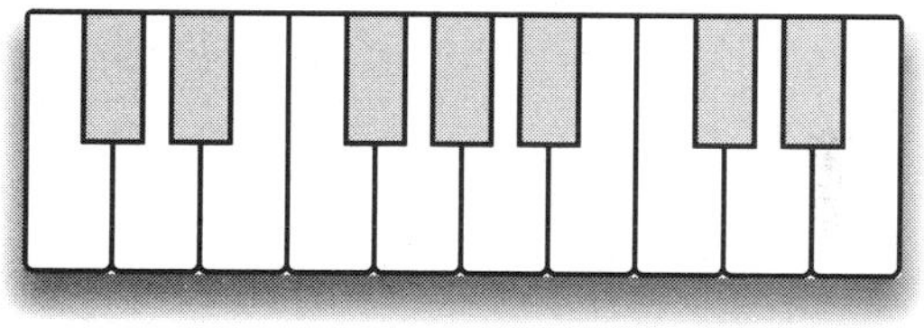

A Minor Pentachord

5. 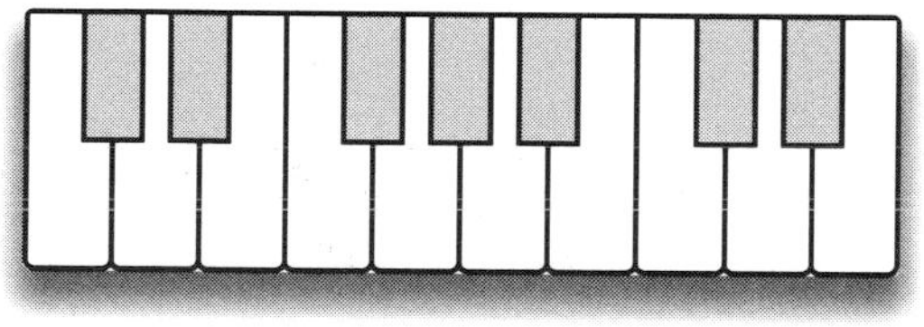

E Minor Pentachord

6. 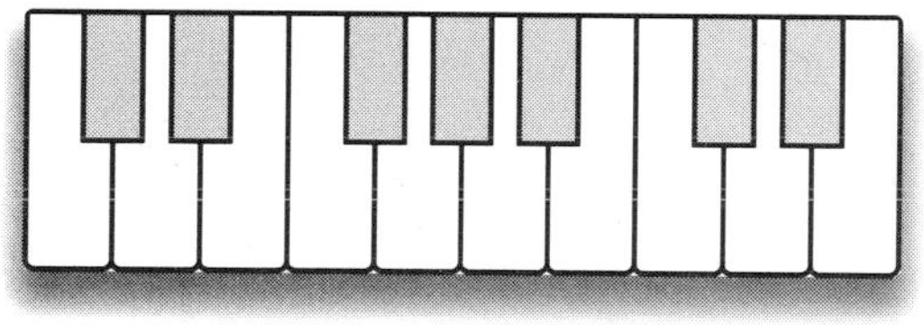

F♯ Minor Pentachord

7. 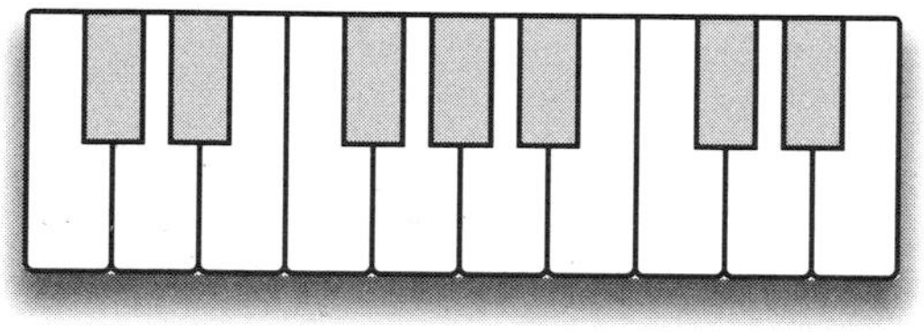

B♭ Minor Pentachord

8. 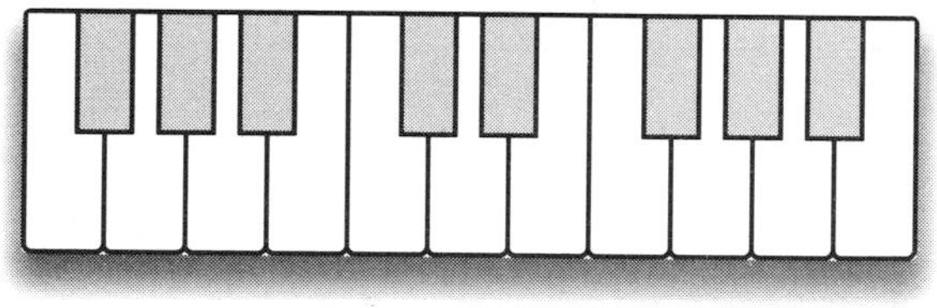

B Minor Pentachord

9. 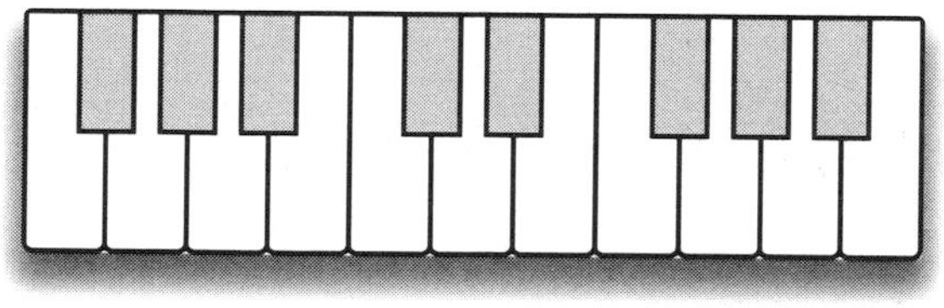

C♯ Minor Pentachord

10. 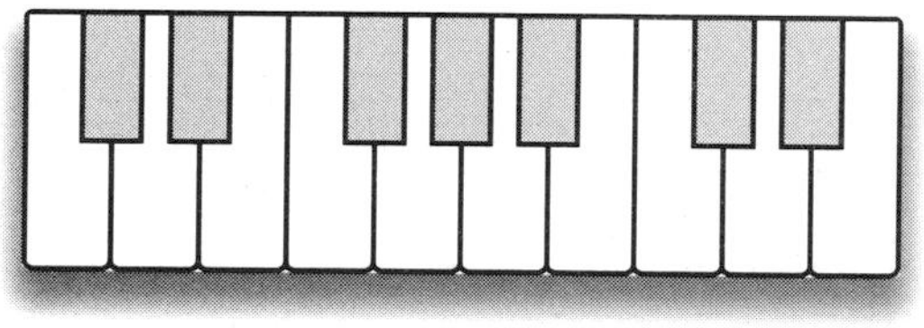

A♭ Minor Pentachord

11. 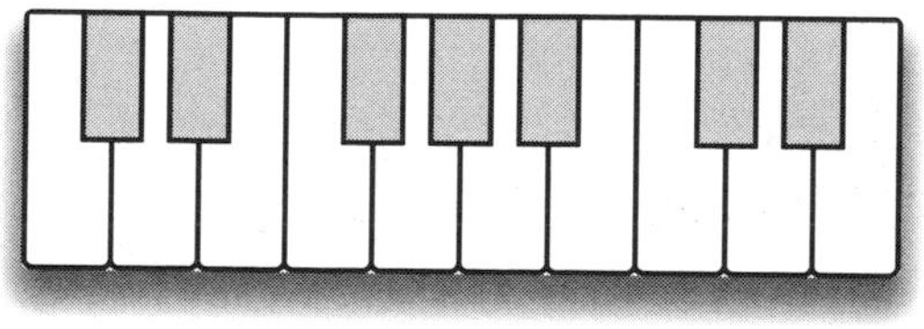

E♭ Minor Pentachord

12. 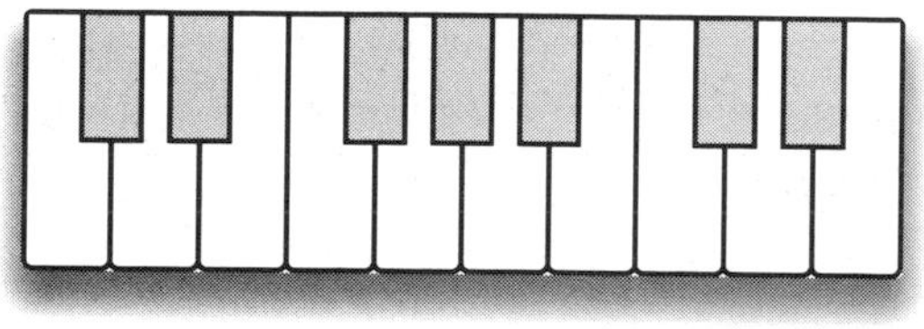

TECHNICAL STUDIES

Broken Chord Studies: Develop a feel for 1st and 2nd inversion triads. Practice using various major and minor triads.

1.
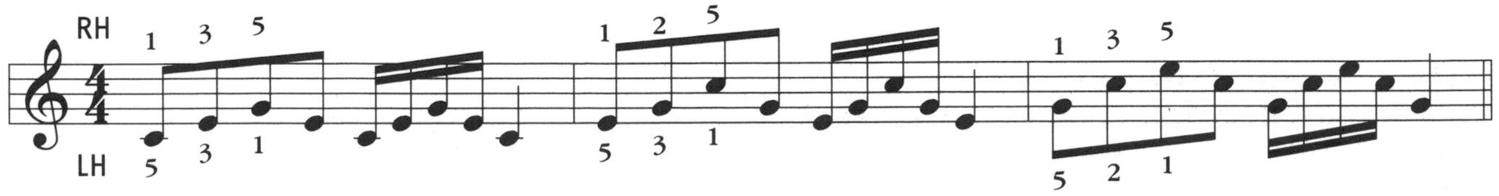

2.

Arpeggio Studies: Practice these studies using the following minor triads: Am, Bm, Cm, Dm, Em, Fm, F♯m, and B♭m.

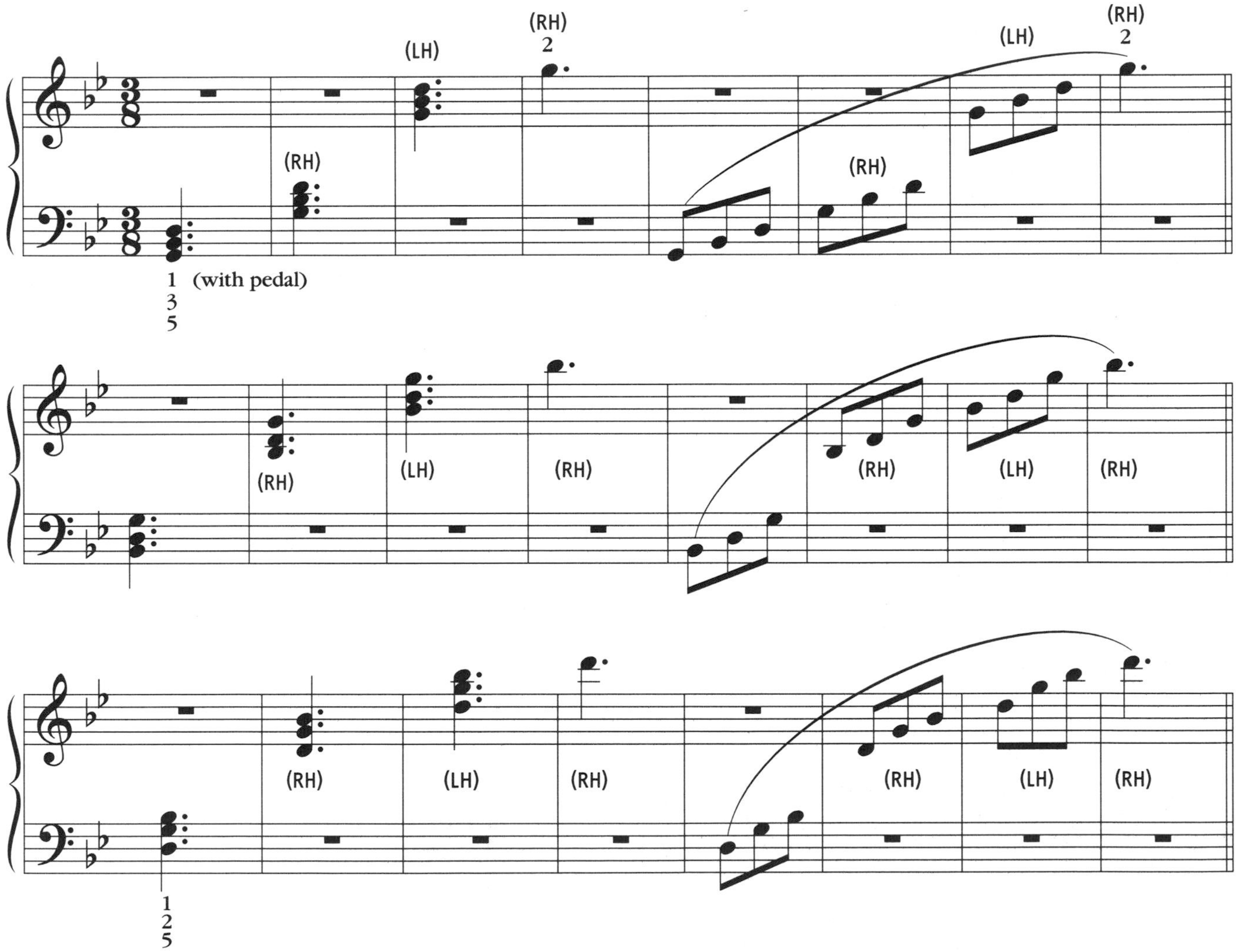

Major Scales: Perform the following major scales in two octaves, hands together.

Chapter 3 REVIEW SCALES: C, G, D, A, E
Chapter 4 NEW SCALES: G♭ (F♯), D♭ (C♯), C♭ (B)

Consult Appendix B for a thorough presentation of all scales and fingerings. The Scale Fingering Chart on page 215 may also be examined.

HARMONIZATION STUDIES

Harmonizing the Minor 5-Finger Pattern: Harmonize the following 5-finger patterns using only i, iv, and V⁷ chords. Try using various LH styles: Blocked, Alberti Bass, Broken Chord. Transpose to other keys.

1.

2.

3.

Harmonizing the Harmonic Minor Scale: Harmonize the harmonic minor scales below using only i, iv, and V⁷ chords. Transpose to other keys.

4.
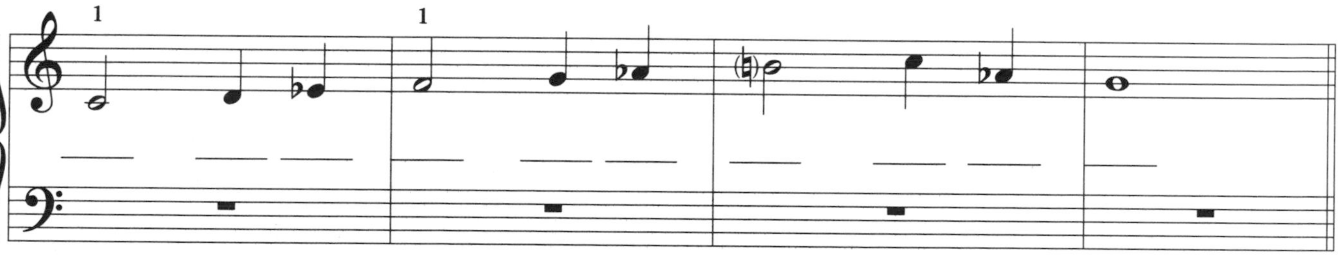

5.

SUGGESTED PLAYING EXAM TOPICS
CHAPTER FOUR

1. Play a harmonization example from pages 131–132.

2. Show fluency playing sixteenth note figures and $\frac{6}{8}$ meter by playing examples taken from pages 139–141.

3. Play the I–IV$^6_4$–I–V$^6_5$–I chord patterns (LH) in the keys of C, D, E, F, G, and A. See the bottom of page 142.

4. Play a harmonized example using I–IV–I–V$^6_5$–I from pages 143-145.

5. Perform one of the accompaniments from pages 150–151.

6. Play one of the American Song arrangements from pages 152-154.

7. Perform one Ensemble Repertoire piece from pages 156-161.

5. Perform one or two solos from the Solo Repertoire section, pages 162–170.

5 chapter

Chord Inversions, I–IV–I_4^6–V^7–I Progression (Four Voices), Expanding Keyboard Textures, Harmonization, Triplets, Syncopation, Repertoire, Musicianship Activities, and Technical Studies

Read the melody of *American Folk Song* and notice the chord outline of the tonic in bars 1 and 2. All of the tones of C major are present, but the lowest tone is G. Block this chord. The fifth is on the bottom, root in the middle, and third on top.

AMERICAN FOLK SONG

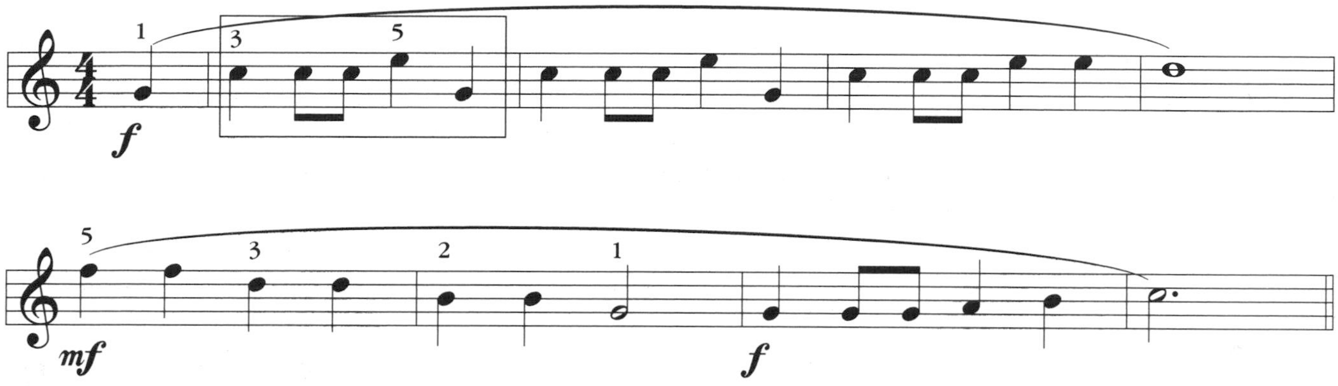

Chord Inversion

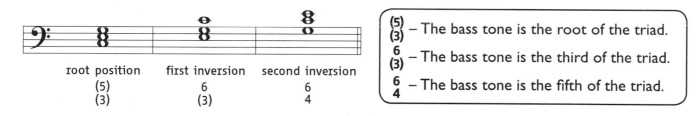

The rearrangement of chord tones results in a *chord inversion*. Study the following chord in root position, first inversion, and second inversion. Any triad may be inverted.

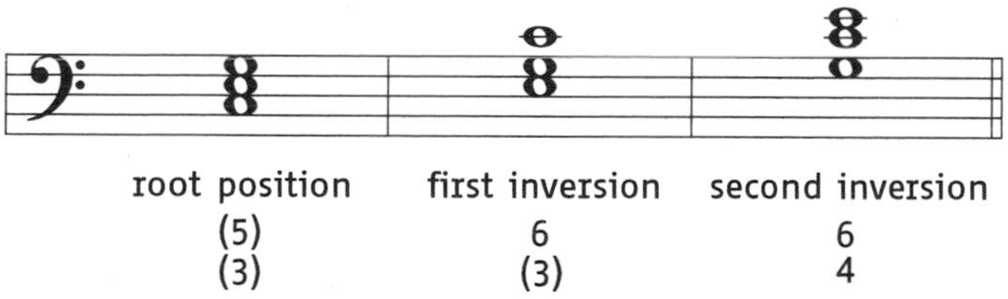

(5)
(3) – The bass tone is the root of the triad.

6
(3) – The bass tone is the third of the triad.

6
4 – The bass tone is the fifth of the triad.

A kind of musical shorthand known as *figured bass*, or *thorough bass*, flourished in the seventeenth and the first half of the eighteenth centuries. In this system, chords were represented by Arabic numerals that related the upper tones to the bass. These numbers delineated intervals above the bass tone, but not necessarily in any particular vertical order. In figured bass playing, the numbers in parentheses were taken for granted and not included. An absence of numerals meant the triad was in fundamental position (root in bass).

Pop Song and Jazz Chord Symbols

In folk and popular music, another system is used. The letter names of the chords appear above the melody line. Often letter names will appear with a slash mark. The letter following the slash tells what note should be in the bass (the lowest note).

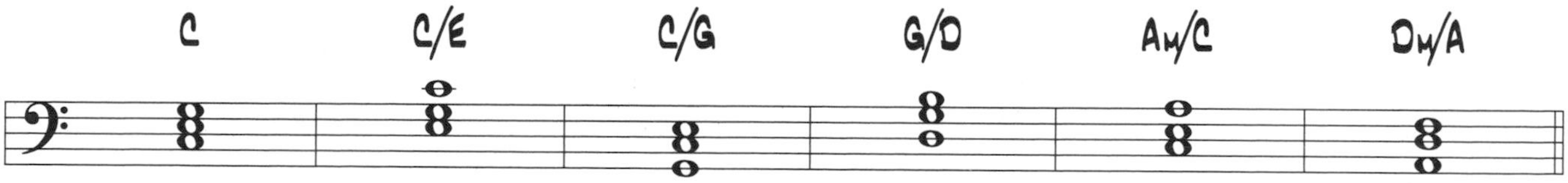

AMERICAN FOLK SONG

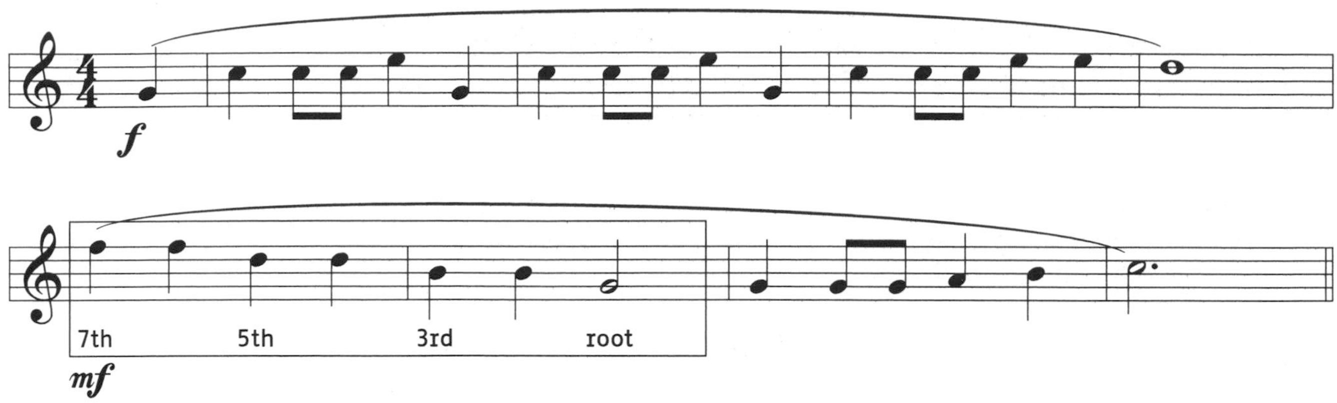

In the same song, study the chord outline in bars 5 and 6. Here, the dominant seventh chord is completely formed. You will recall from Chapter Four that seventh chords contain four tones, the most important being the root, third, and seventh. It is common to omit the 5th. Study the inversion of the dominant seventh chord in the key of C.

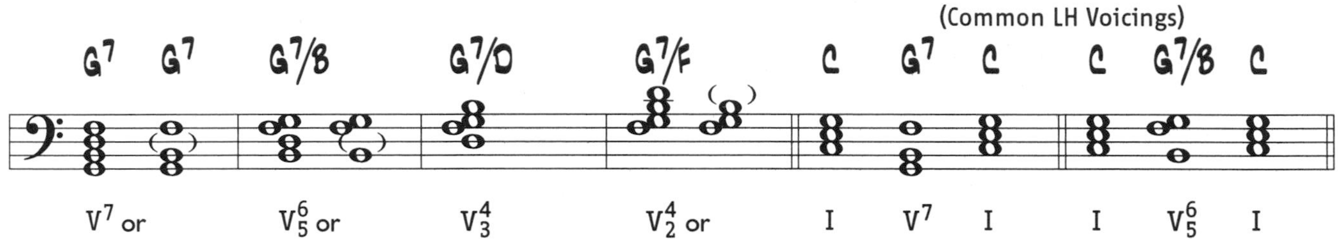

Voice Leading

To avoid awkward sounds (and awkward fingerings), it is important that tones of successive chords move to the nearest chord tones, or to common tones. Study the examples below to understand how inversions help chord voices move smoothly.

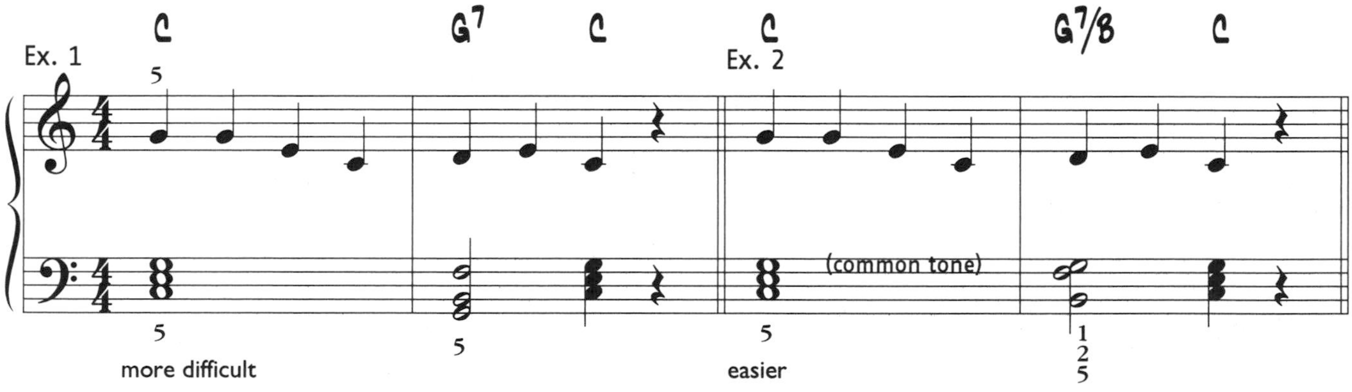

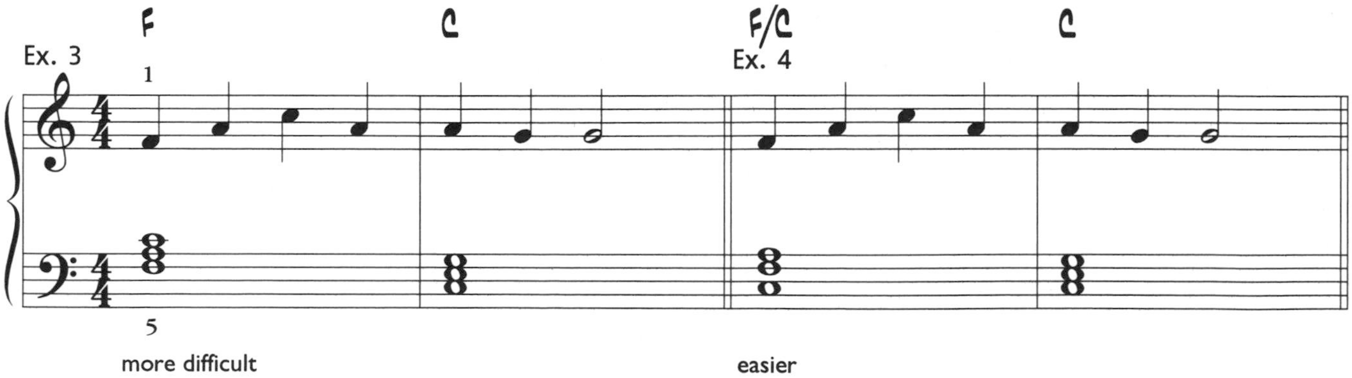

Two Styles of Harmonization

Compare the LH harmonization of *Skip to My Lou* to the harmonization of *German Carol. German Carol* puts the harmony in the RH with single bass notes (chord roots) in the LH creating a different texture.

SKIP TO MY LOU

In *German Carol*, put the harmony in the RH and single bass tones in the LH (chord roots).

GERMAN CAROL

Again, compare the LH chord harmonization of *Study No. 3* with the expanded harmonic treatment of *Study No. 4*.

Folk Song

Study and play *No. 4* which uses the same melody as *No. 3*. Here, the RH incorporates a two-voice texture and the LH plays bass notes approximately two octaves lower. This style is one we will work with in future harmonization exercises, one that is more pianistic and has a richer texture.

Italian

Completion Studies

Complete *Study No. 5* and *Study No. 6* following the suggested texture given in the first measure.

Study No. 5 continues with a RH two-voice texture and LH bass notes approximately two octaves lower. Notate the alto voice (mostly in 6ths with some 3rds) and the LH bass.

British

In *Study No. 6*, rely mostly on 3rds and 6ths in the RH.

Folk Song

Reviewing the Subdominant Chord (IV)

The IV chord was presented in Chapter 4 both in root position and inverted form IV^6_4. Observe both tonic chord (C) and subdominant chord (F) outlined in the melody of *My Home's in Montana.*

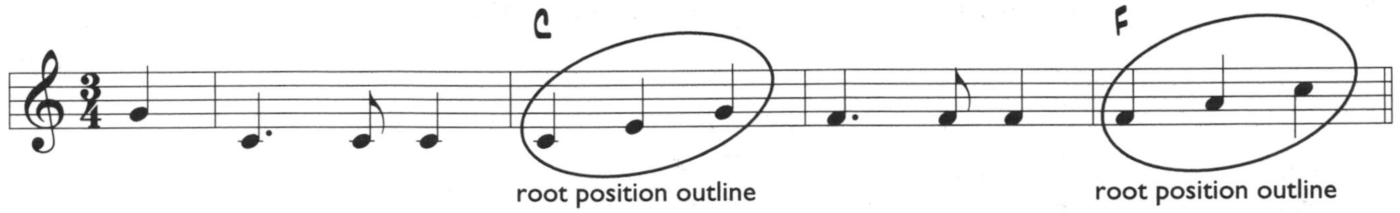

The subdominant chord is built on the 4th scale degree as shown below. It is major in quality and generally moves to V (dominant) or I (tonic).

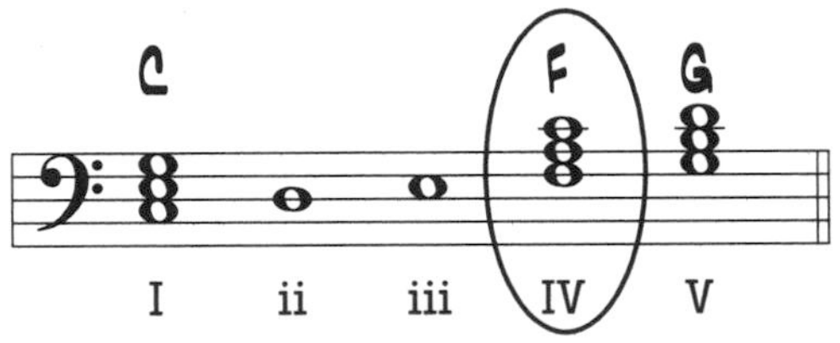

The three most used chords in music are the I, IV and V. These chords are known as *primary* chords. Chords built on other tones of the scale (ii, iii, vi, etc.) are called *secondary* chords.

I–IV^6_4–I Chord Pattern - LH

Practice the following chord pattern and transpose it to all white keys. Place letter name chord symbols above each chord as shown in the C major example. Also, place Roman numeral chord symbols below each chord as shown.

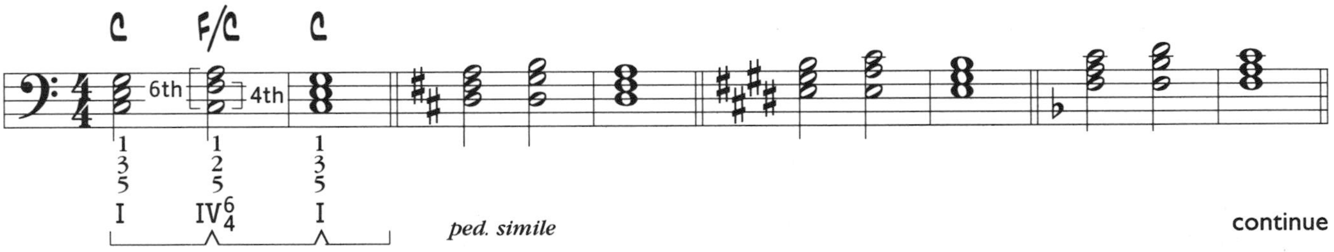

An Essential Chord Pattern: I–IV–I^6_4–V^7–I (Four Voices)

First, review playing the I–IV^6_4–I–V^6_5–I progression with each hand. Note the RH fingering on the tonic which simplifies the movement to the subdominant chord. Practice both of the two-handed style versions with LH playing roots of chords and RH playing the harmony.

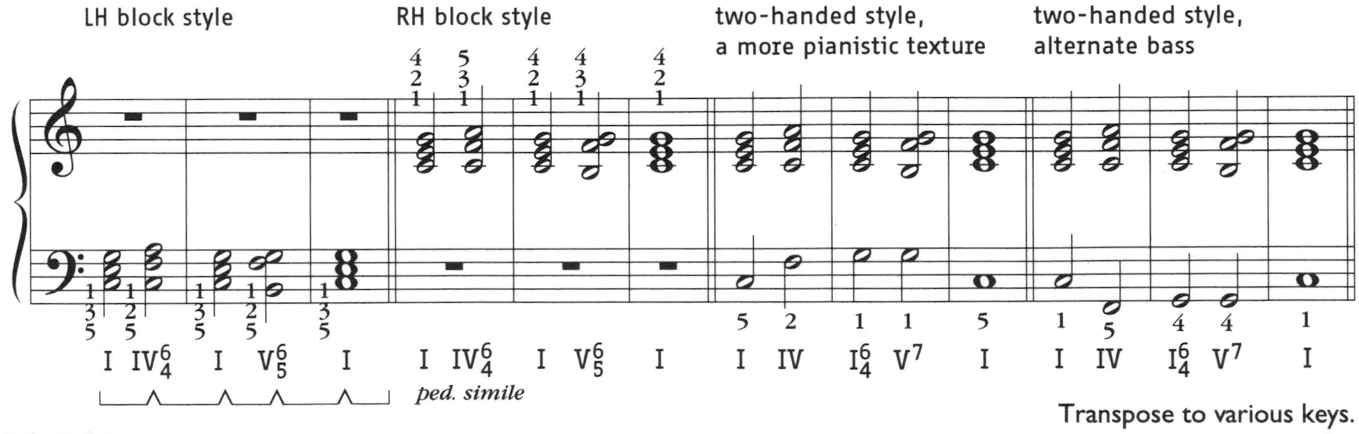

Transpose to various keys.

Triplets

An eighth note triplet (3) fills the time of one quarter note. Practice tapping and clapping the following rhythmic pattern.

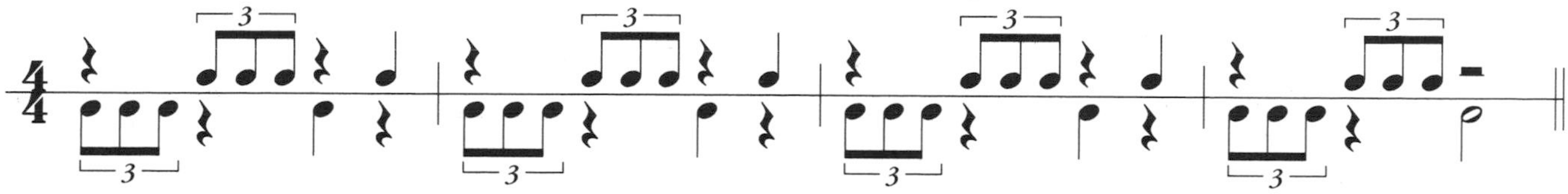

Triad Triplet Study

Practice the following study which outlines triads and the dominant $^6_5$ in triplet figures. Transpose this study to various major and minor keys suggested by your instructor.

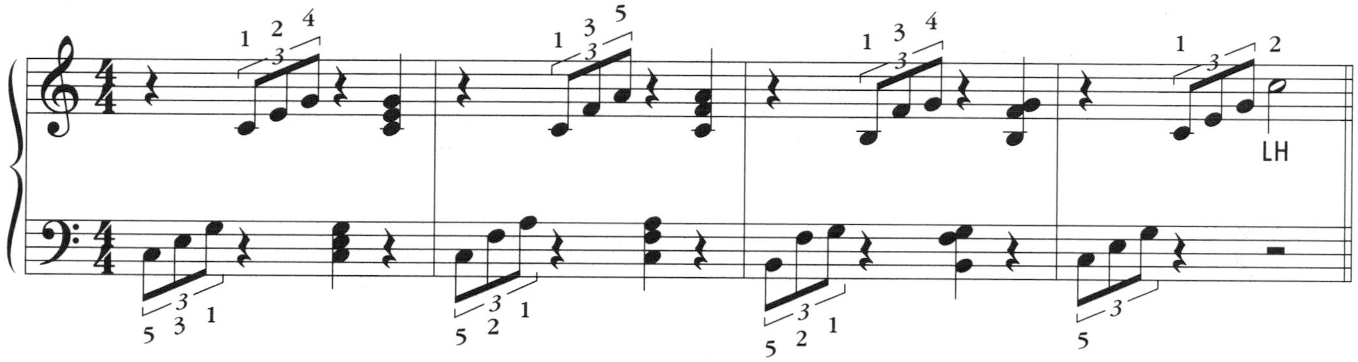

Song Arrangements That Include Triplets

Sometimes triplets are notated as (3) (without brackets). Study and play the following song arrangements.

SALLY GO ROUND THE SUNSHINE

South Carolina

POLISH FOLK SONG

Allegretto

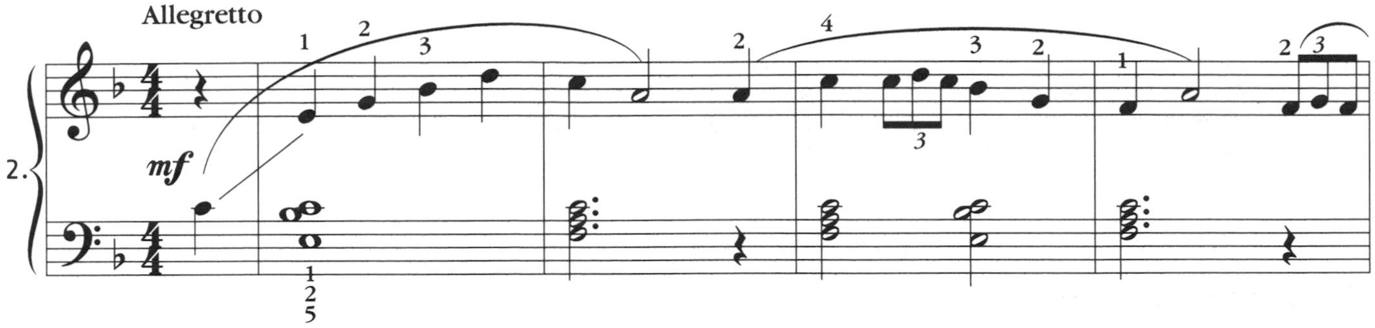

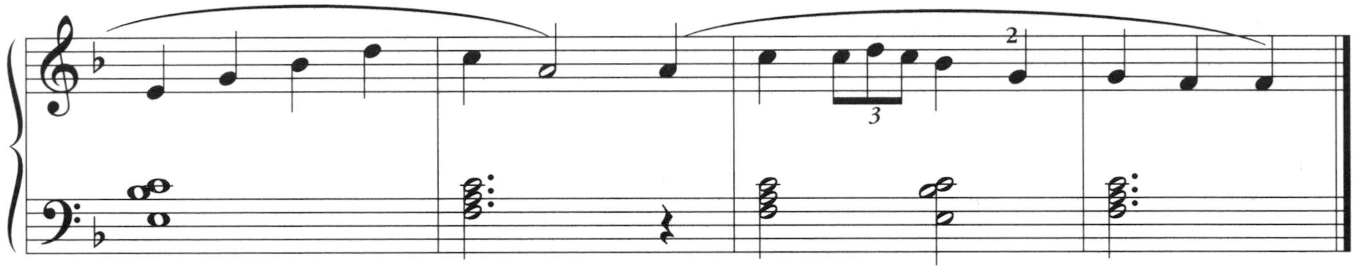

Dutch

Bouncy ♩. = 78

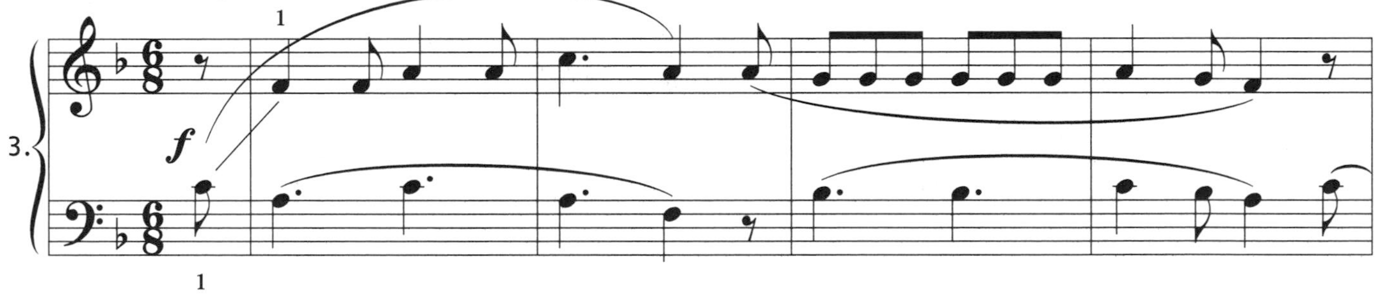

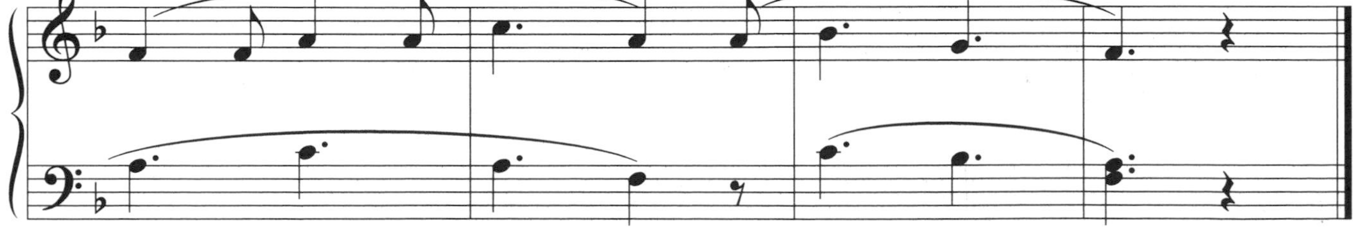

Syncopation

When a weak beat, or a weak part of a beat is stressed, *syncopation* occurs. Practice the rhythmic pattern before studying and playing *Hello Ma Baby*.

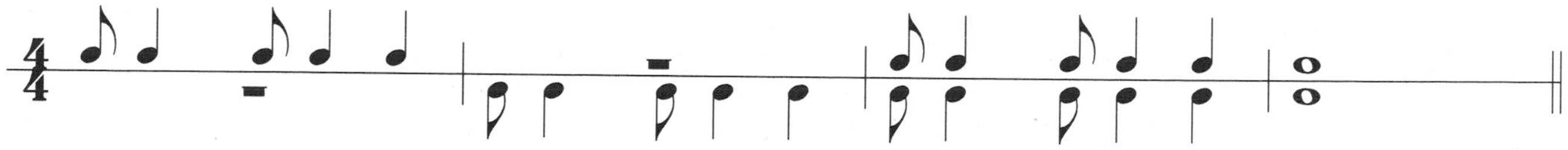

HELLO MA BABY

music by **Joe Howard**
arr. **James Lyke**

MR. BANJO

Louisiana Creole
arr. James Lyke

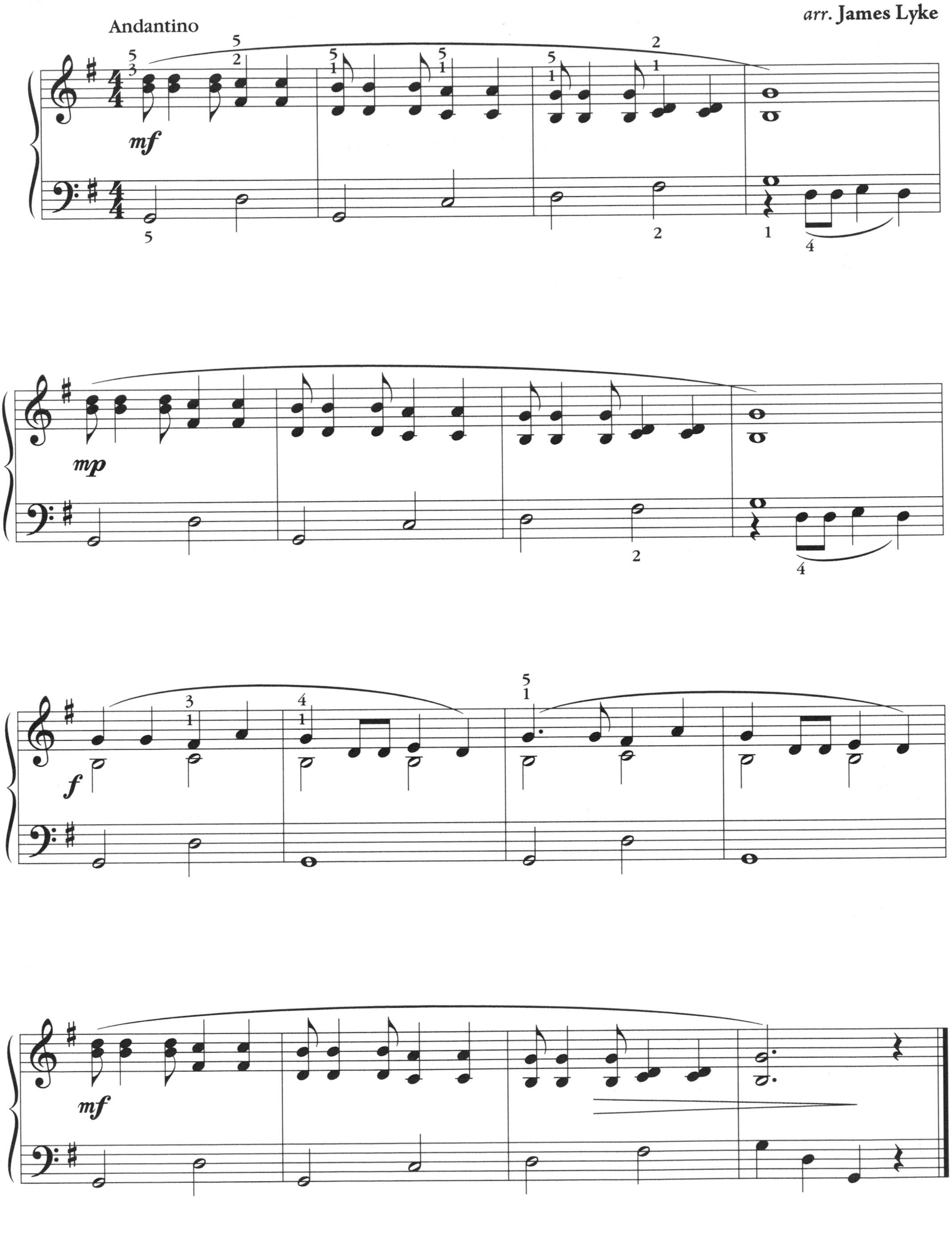

Music for Sight Reading and Transposing

Reading studies in Chapter Five include review material as well as new elements: chord inversion, voice leading, the subdominant chord, triplets, and syncopation. Continue the routine established earlier, e.g., tap rhythms, identify the tonality, find patterns such as chord outlines, and so on. In addition, pay attention to elements beyond notes and rhythm such as touch, dynamics, phrasing, tempi, and fingerings.

FOR HE'S A JOLLY GOOD FELLOW

Transpose to G major.

British

Transpose to A.

COTTON-EYED JOE

Tennessee Folk Song

Transpose to G♭ major.

RUSSIAN DANCE

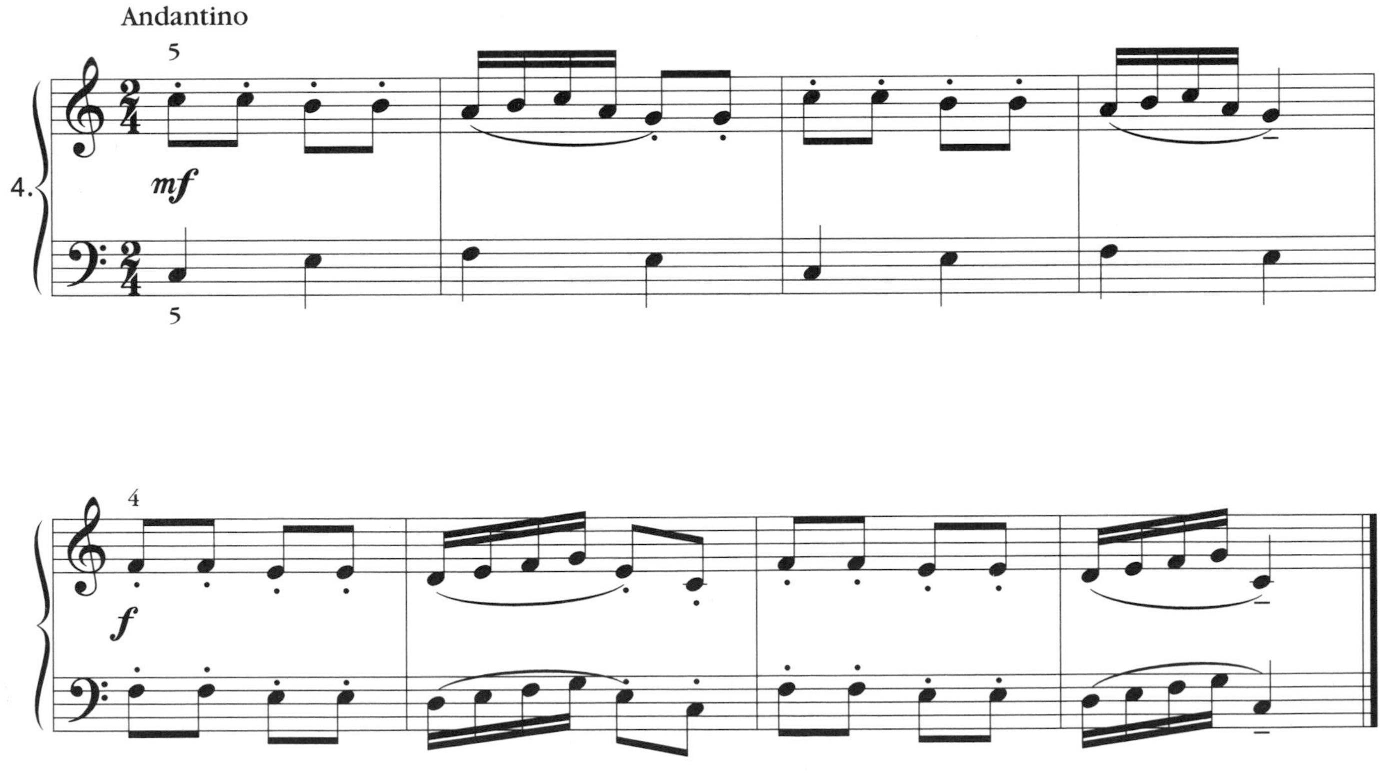

Transpose to B major.

Allegretto

5.

Transpose to A♭ major and G major.

Italian

Moderato ♩ = 110

6.

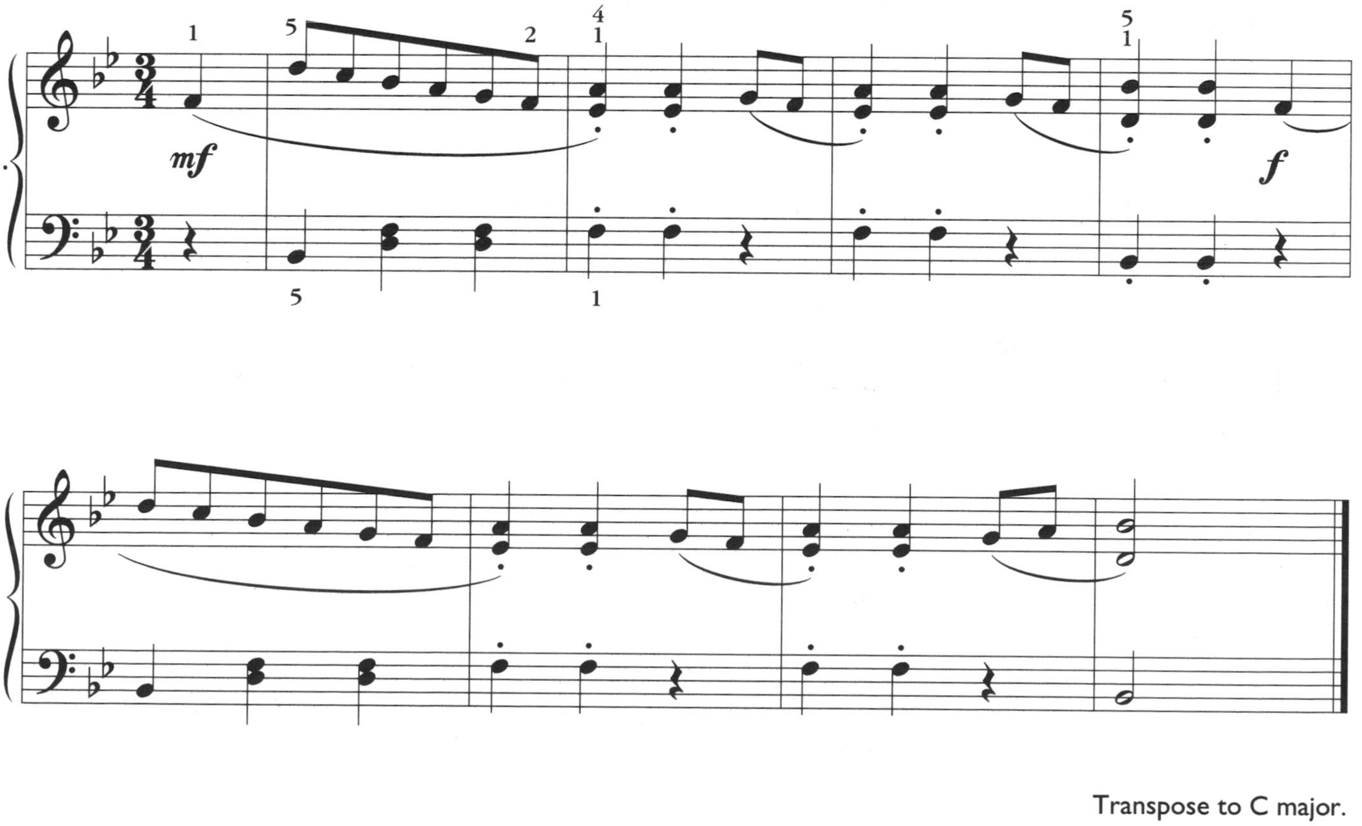

Transpose to C major.

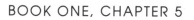

German

Transpose to D major.

Hungarian

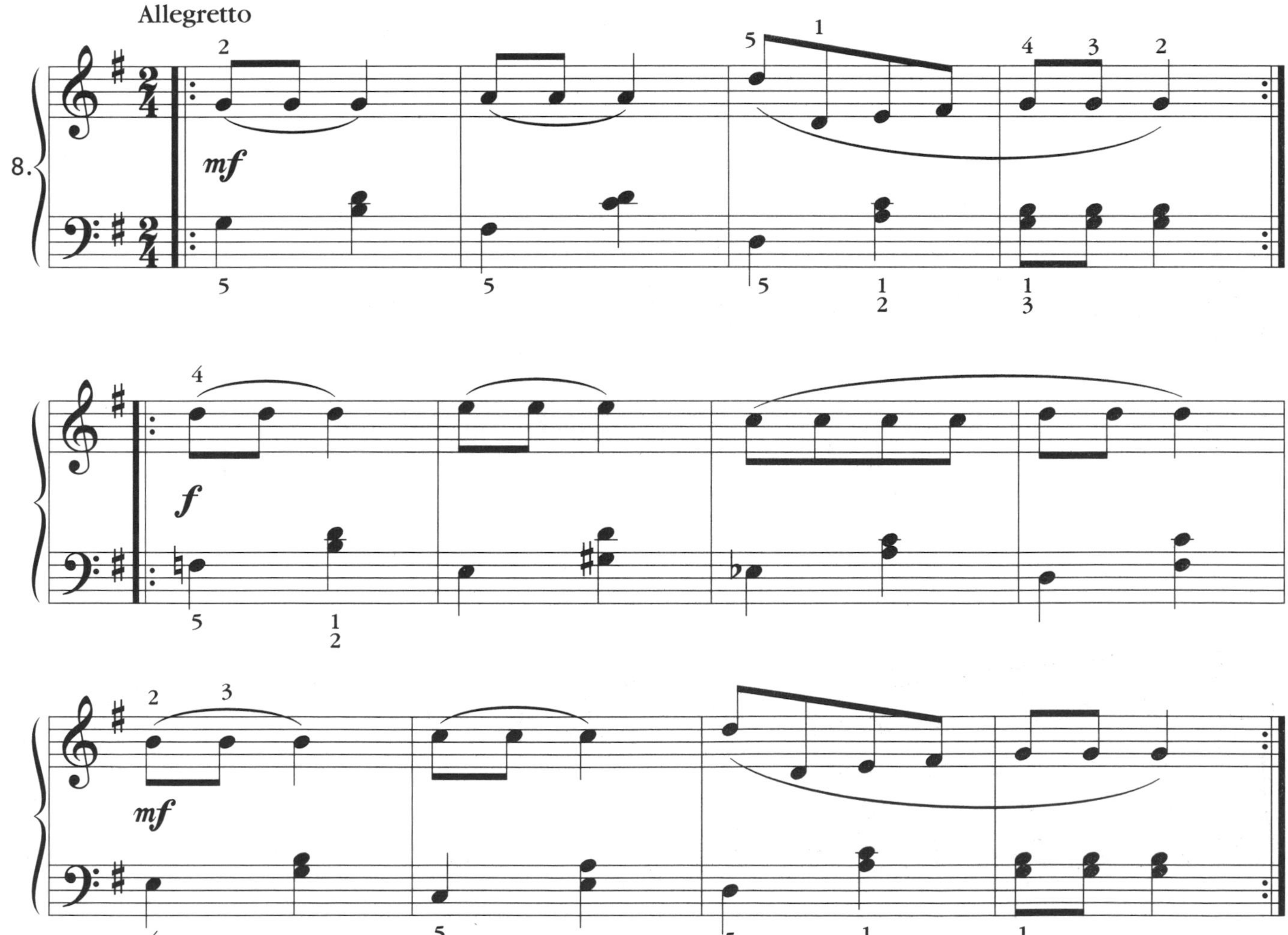

Transpose to F major.

RISE AND SHINE

Gospel Song

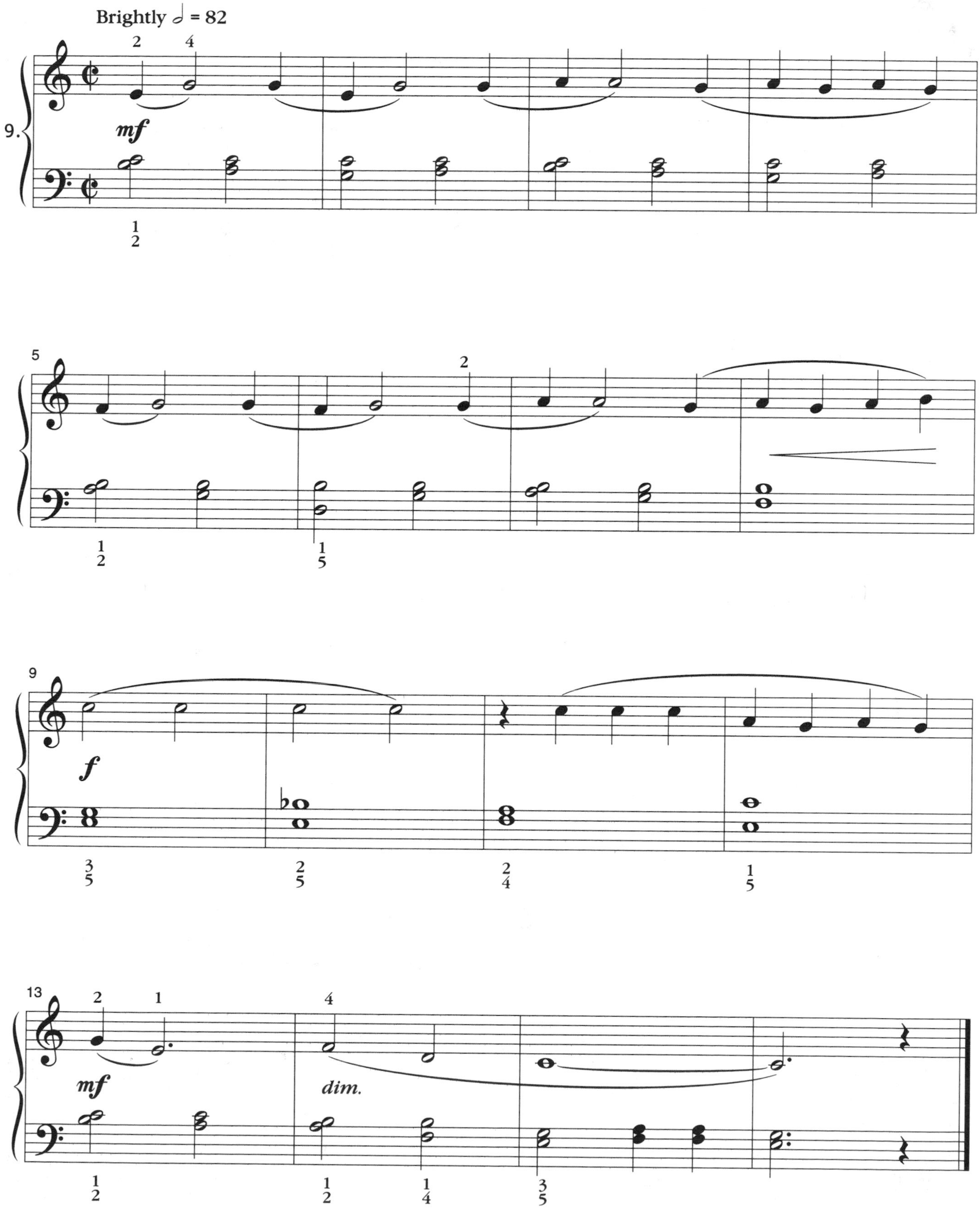

no transposition

ACCOMPANYING

Teacher: Double the melody two octaves higher.

26 CD

LONELY ACCORDIAN

B. Mokrousov
(Russian)
arr. James Lyke

T
S
dim.
8va

Before playing *Wearing of the Green* practice the following chord progression from slow to fast. Take note of the fingering.

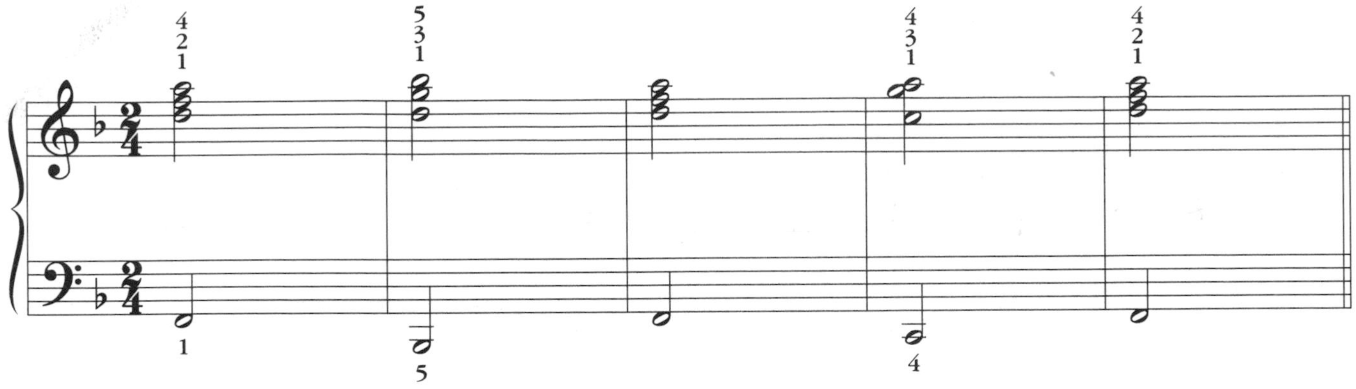

Teacher: Double the melody two octaves higher.

WEARING OF THE GREEN

Traditional
arr. **James Lyke**

Andante ♩ = 96

Teacher: Double the melody two octaves higher.

28 CD

IN THE VALLEY

Russian Folk Song
arr. James Lyke

YANKEE DOODLE BLUES

music by **George Gershwin**
arr. **James Lyke**

f
mf
f

KA-LU-A

music by **Jerome Kern**
arr. **James Lyke**

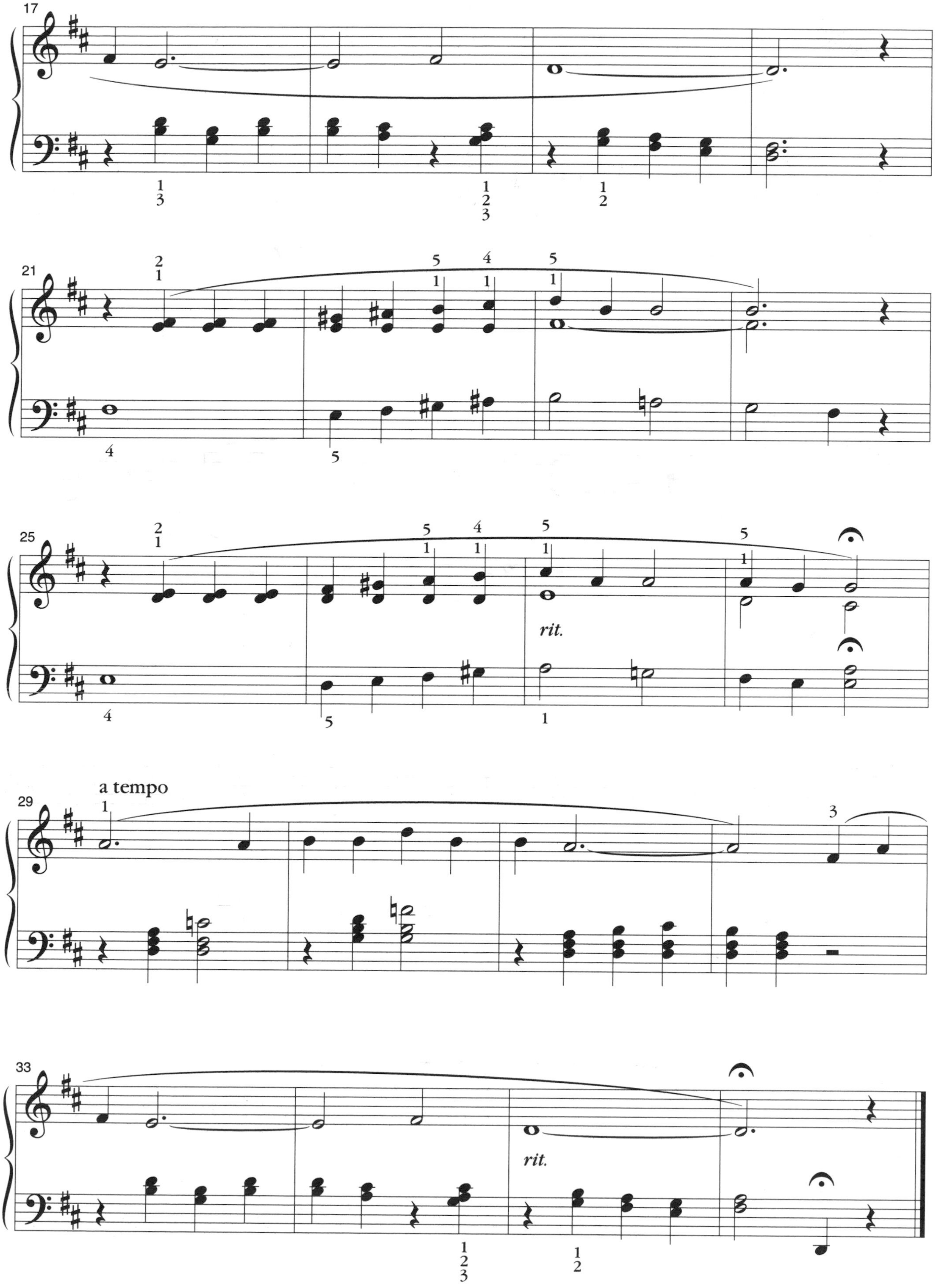
17
21
25
rit.
29
a tempo
33
rit.

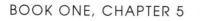

31 CD

EVERYBODY LOVES SATURDAY NIGHT

Secondo – Teacher

Nigerian Folk Song
arr. James Lyke

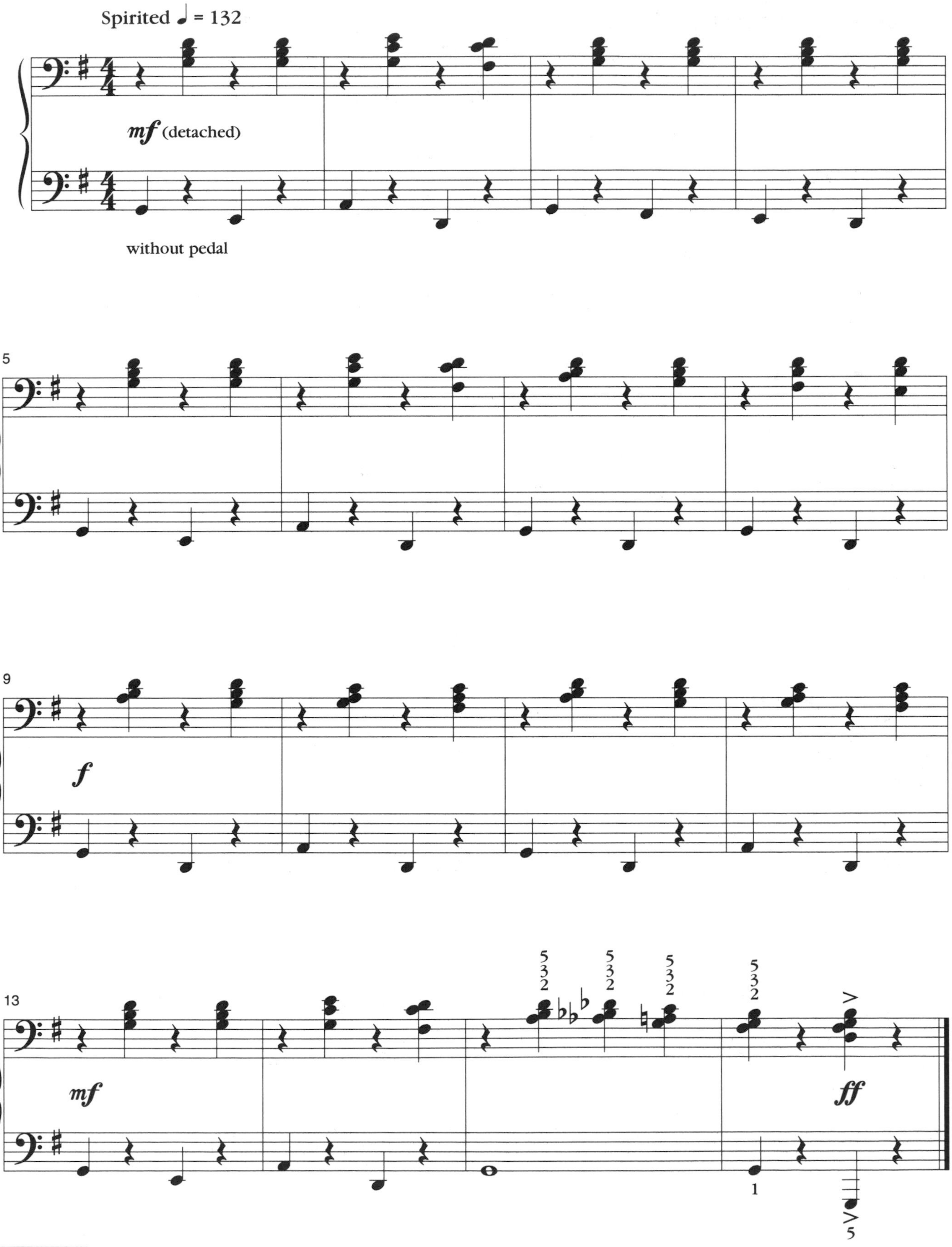

31 CD

EVERYBODY LOVES SATURDAY NIGHT

Primo – Student

Nigerian Folk Song
arr. **James Lyke**

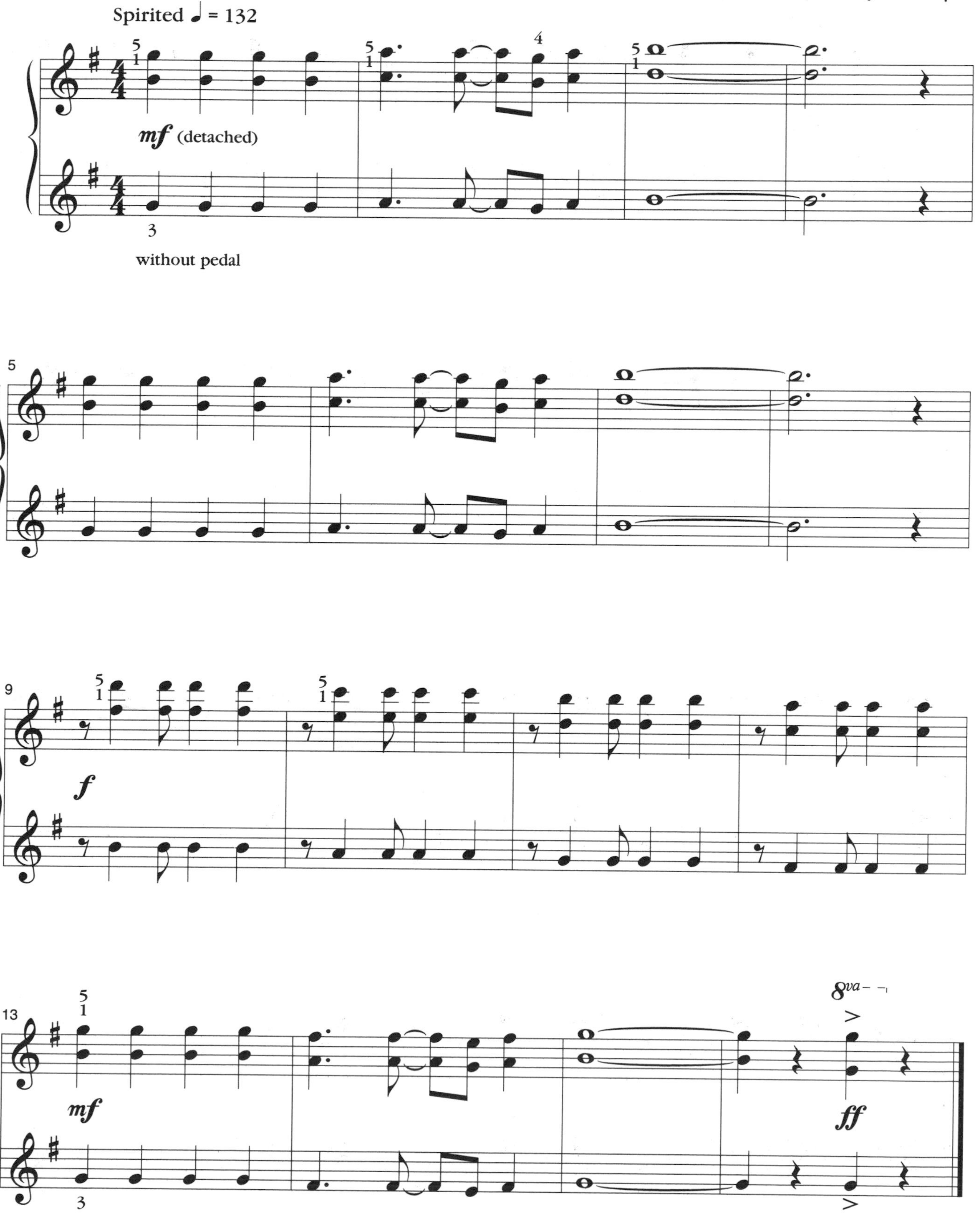

CIELITO LINDO

Secondo – Student (or teacher)

Mexican Popular Song
arr. James Lyke

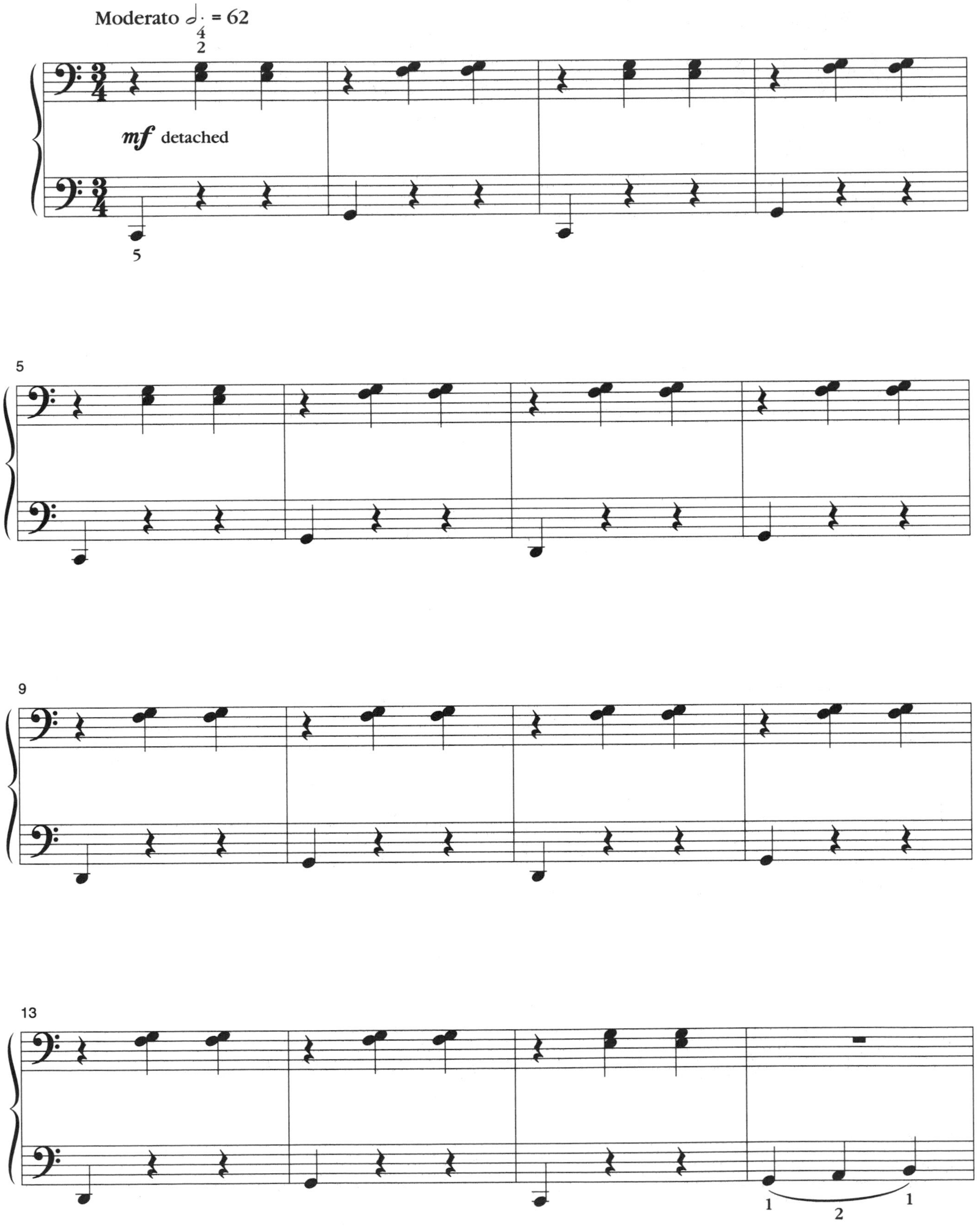

32 CD

CIELITO LINDO

Primo – Teacher (or student)

Mexican Popular Song
arr. **James Lyke**

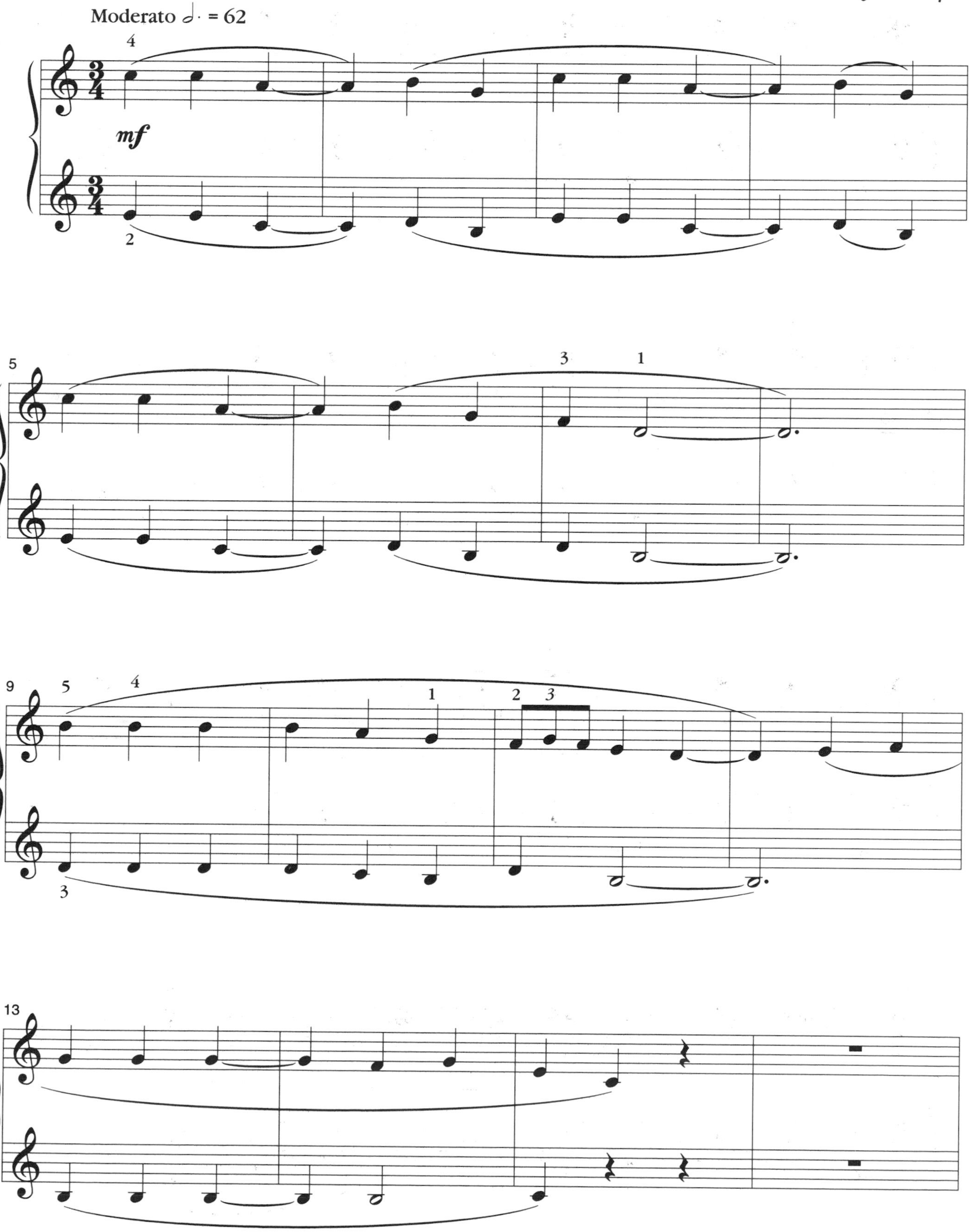

Secondo

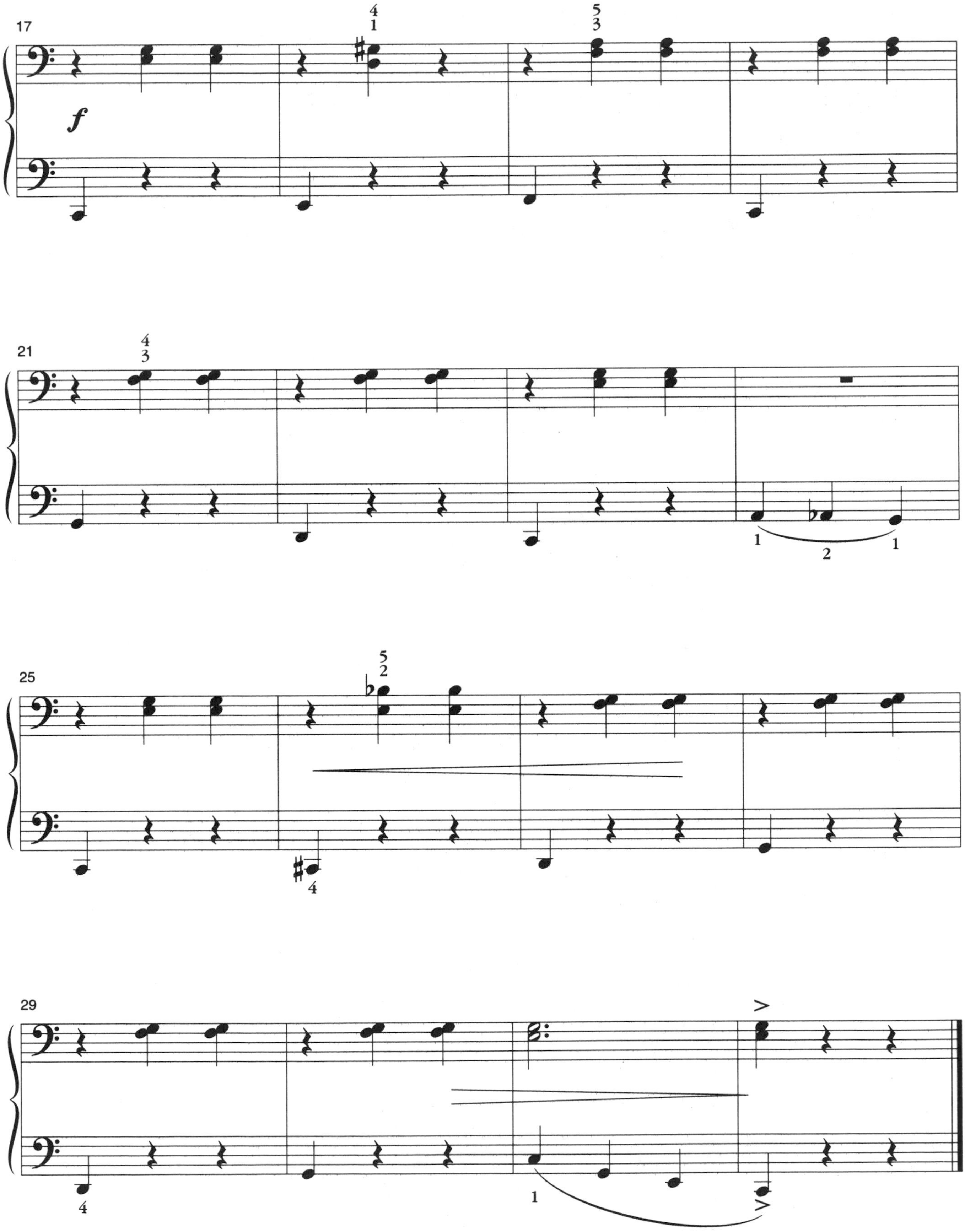

Primo

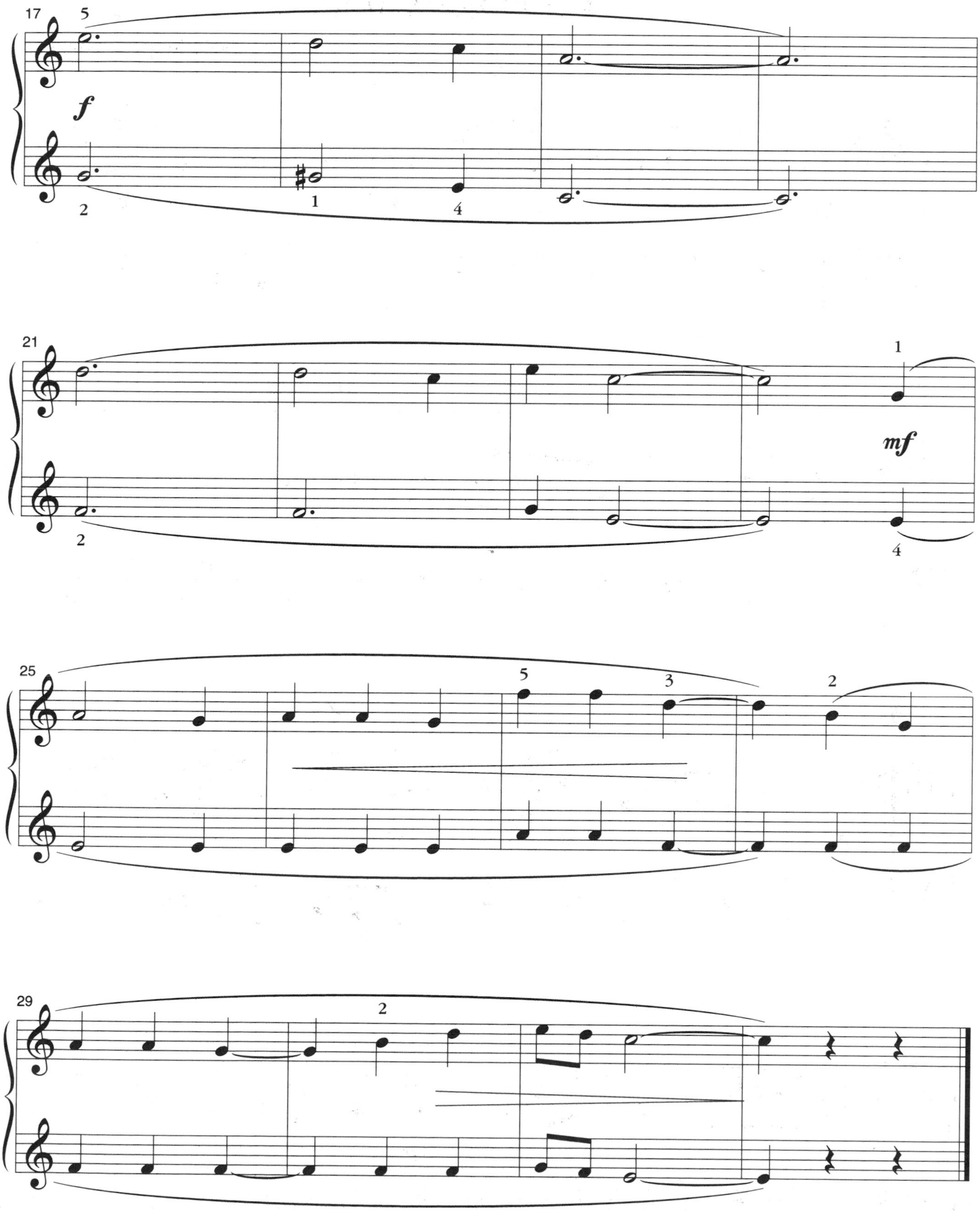

SOLO REPERTOIRE

Practice Plan: Practice hands alone, isolating shifts of position. Feel the octave stretches in the LH. Maintain proper fingering and precise rhythmic execution.

MENUET IN C MAJOR

Carl Philipp Emanuel Bach

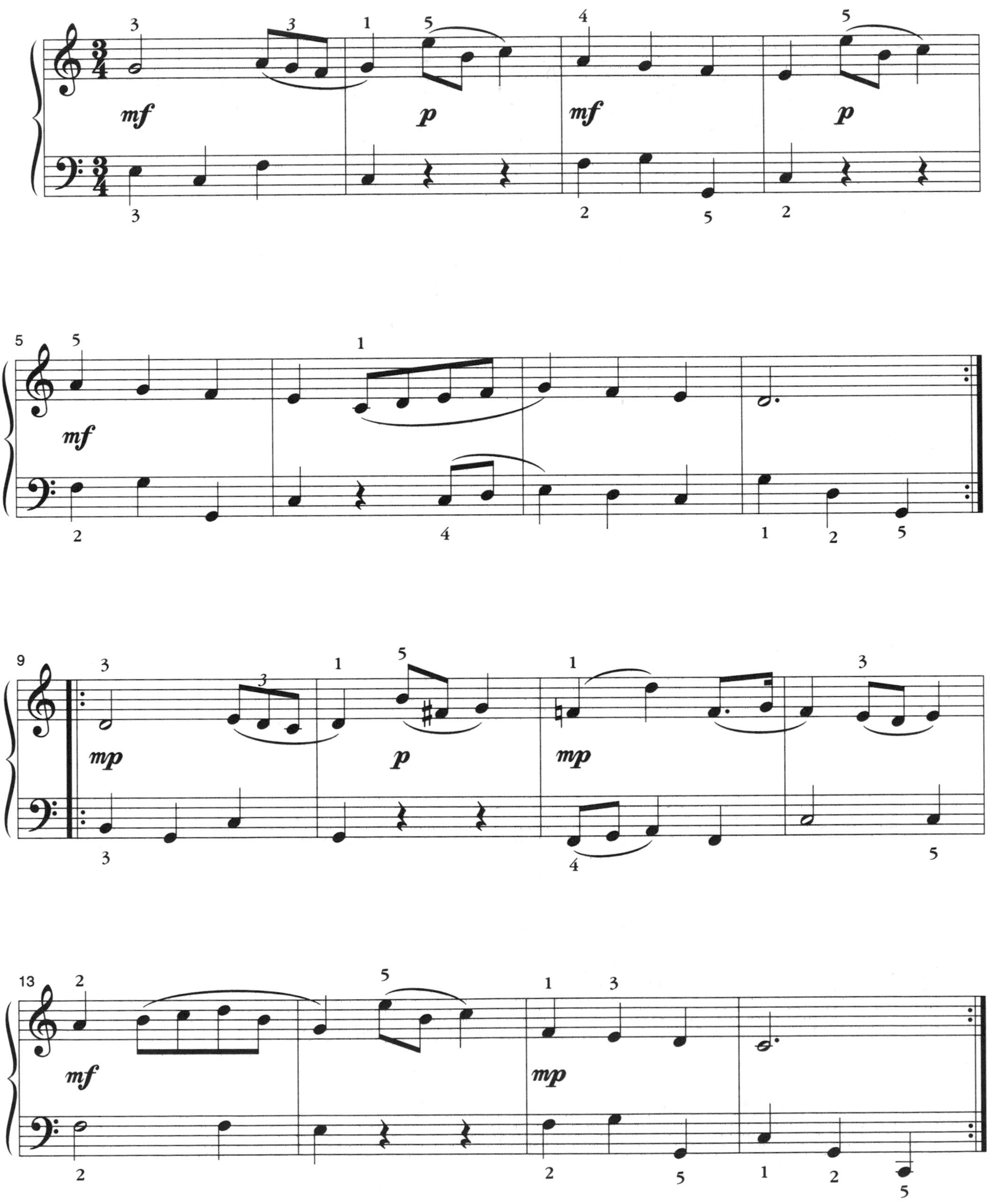

Practice Plan: Practice LH alone to attain good crosses and detached playing. Practice RH alone and find chord outlines. Master the mixture of *legato* and *staccato* touch. Combine the hands at a slow and steady tempo and gradually increase the speed.

MINUET IN G MAJOR

Franz Joseph Haydn

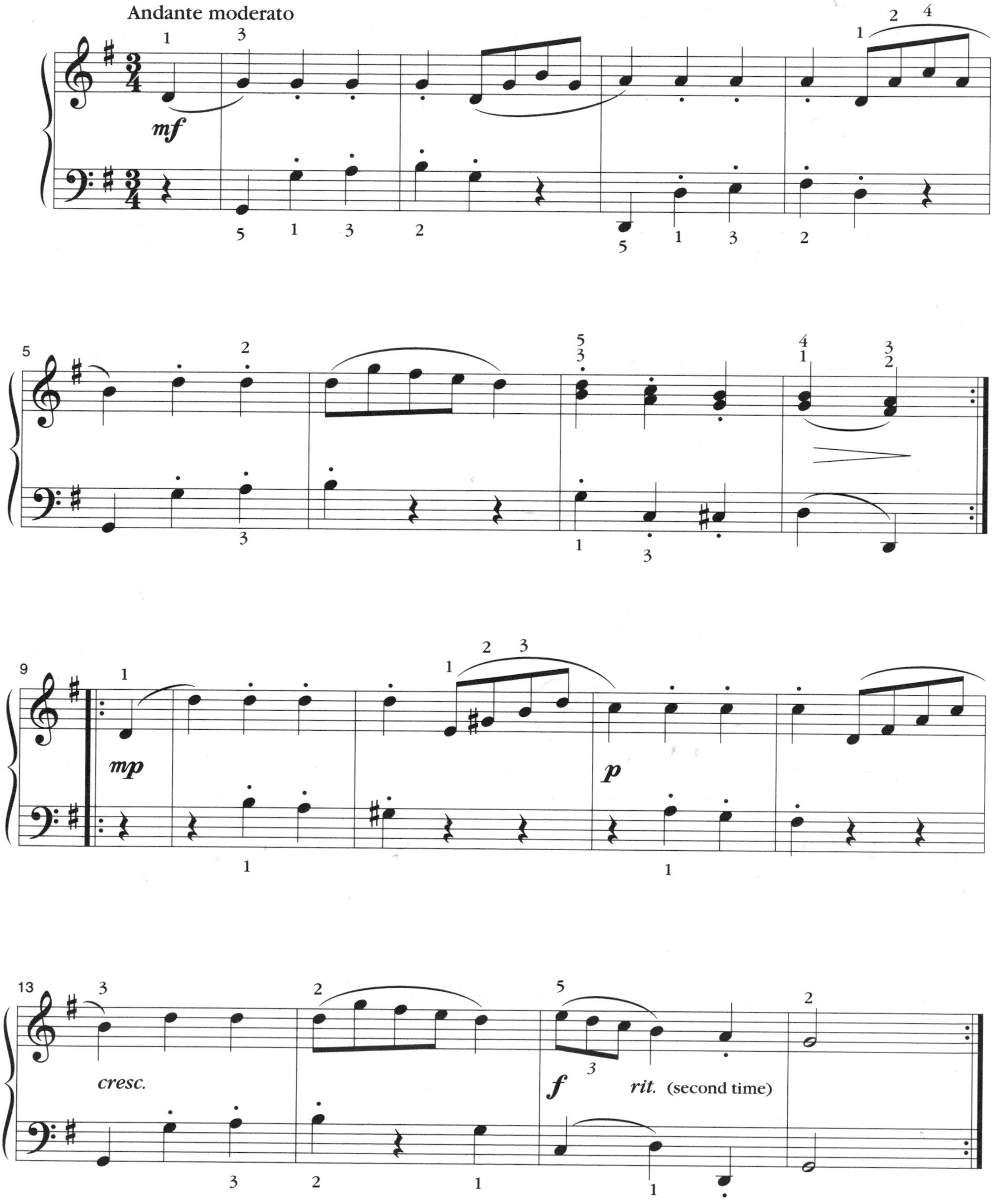

- pedal w/ left hand first
- cresc. / decresc. on phrasing
- repetition w/ both hands

Practice Plan: In *Romance*, locate subdominant harmonies. What inversion of the subdominant chord is used throughout? Practice hands alone to be certain of notes and fingering. Then, practice hands together without pedal. Add pedal when all is perfect.

ROMANCE

Céline Bussières-Lessard

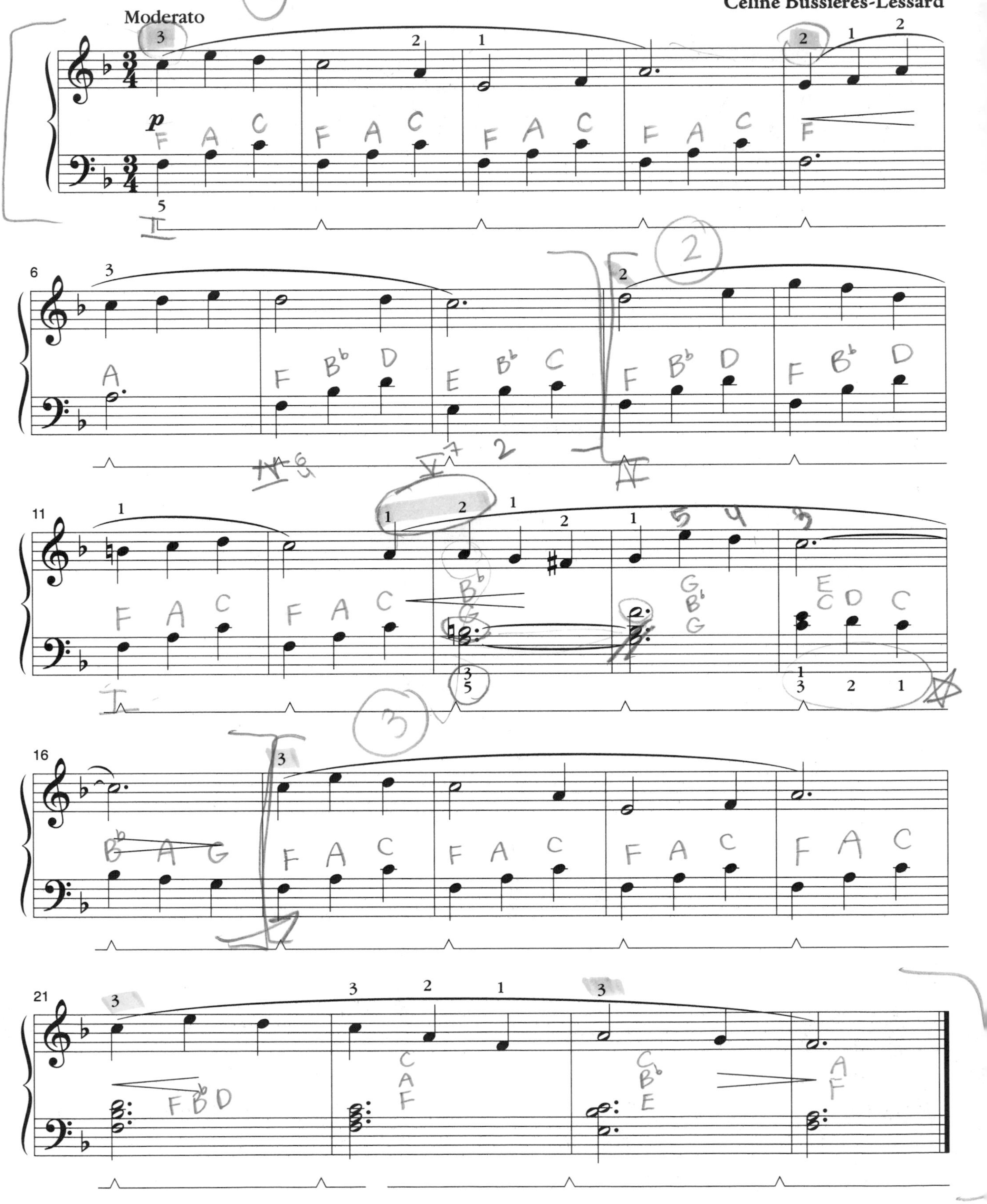

Practice Plan: *The Great Lawn* is based almost entirely on triads and inversions (RH), and octaves (LH). Careful fingering of the chords is necessary. Listen for clear, connected pedaling.

THE GREAT LAWN

James Lyke

Practice Plan: First, practice the LH part (easier than RH) and become familiar with all of the moves. Practice RH alone and be cautious with the fingering. Play very slowly hands together without pedal. When all is in place, add the pedal and listen carefully to the colors. Follow the pedal markings strictly.

ELEGY

Tony Caramia

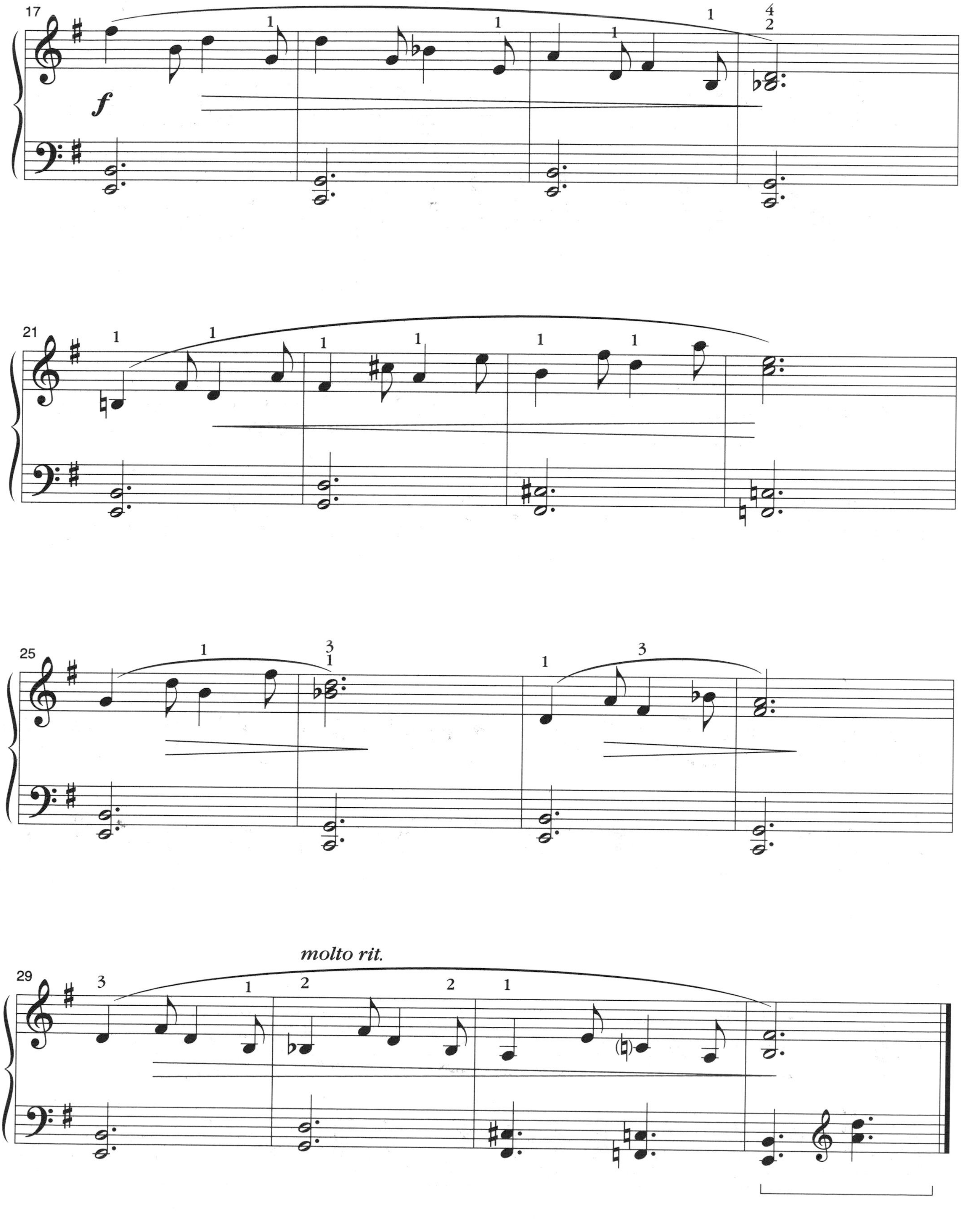
molto rit.

Practice Plan: The RH melody in *Serene Lagoon* should be heard over the LH accompaniment throughout. Shape the RH phrasing taking note of the dynamic markings.

SERENE LAGOON

Geoffrey Haydon

Practice Plan: *Easy Does It Rag* is a study in syncopation. Tap the rhythm of the RH throughout the piece. In the LH, note the use of the thumb to play two notes (bars 1, 5, 8, and 9). Isolate this figure for special drill. Once again, practicing hands separately will prove invaluable in the early stages of learning.

EASY DOES IT RAG

Geoffrey Haydon

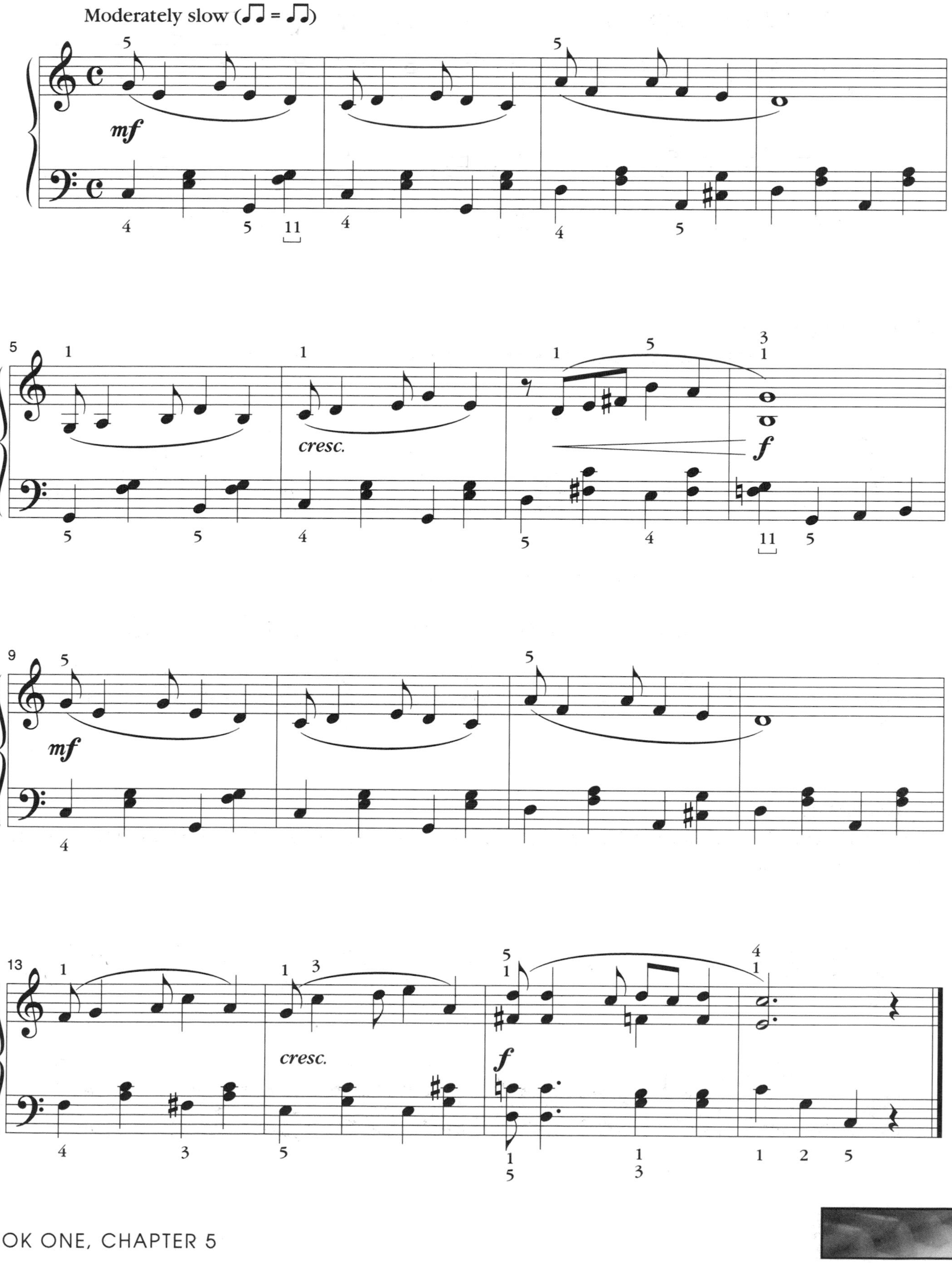

MUSICIANSHIP ACTIVITIES

Complete the following exercises which review various topics introduced in Chapter Five.

I–IV$^6_4$–I–V$^6_5$–I LH Progression

Notate this progression for the LH in the indicated keys. Follow the example.

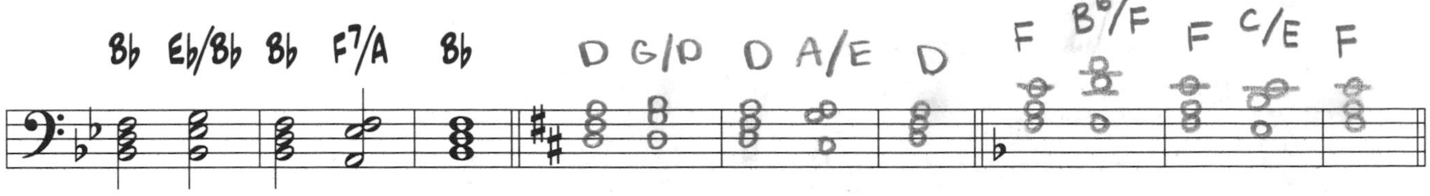

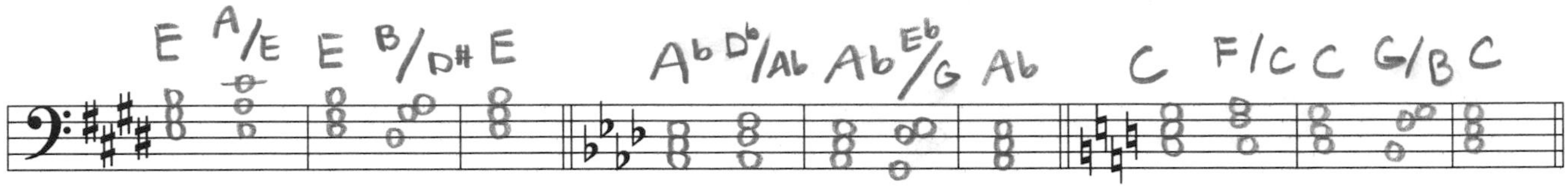

Chord Inversions

Use letter-name symbols to label the following root position and inverted triads.

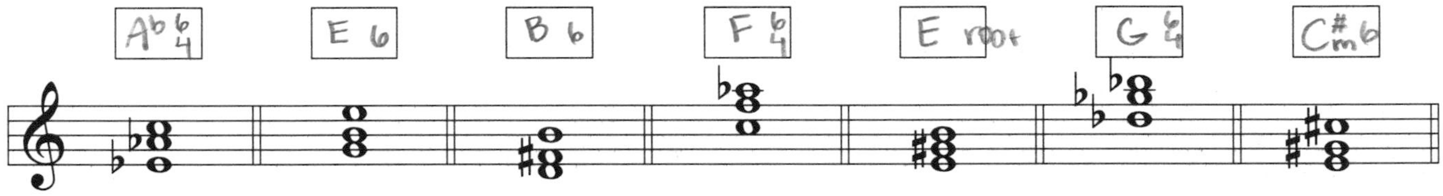

Notate the following chords on the staff. Be aware of the clef.

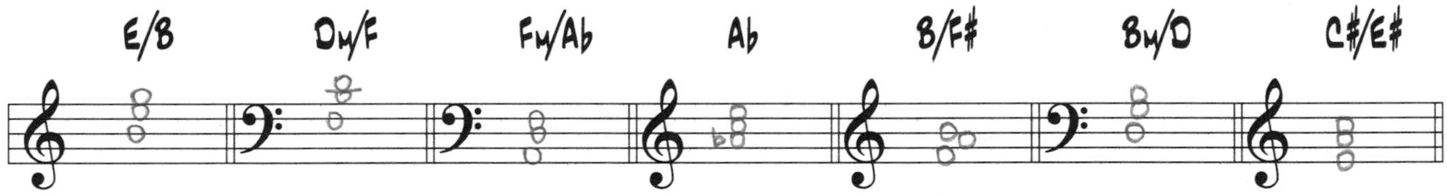

Improvising

Play the LH chord patterns while improvising RH melodies. Use tones of the respective major scales. Make use of sequences.

TECHNICAL STUDIES

Major Scale Review: C, G, D, A, E, G♭(F♯), D♭(C♯), C♭(B)

Two octaves. Hands together.

NEW Major Scale: F

RH	1	2	3	4	1	2	3	1	etc.
LH	5	4	3	2	1	3	2	1	etc.

Major Arpeggios: Up to this point, arpeggios have been performed within one octave, and hand-over-hand. Practice the following steps, first hands alone, then hands together. Transpose to F, G, D, E, A, B. **Consult Appendix B for a thorough presentation of all scales AND arpeggios.**

Step 1: BLOCKING Play the 3rd and 5th of the chord together.

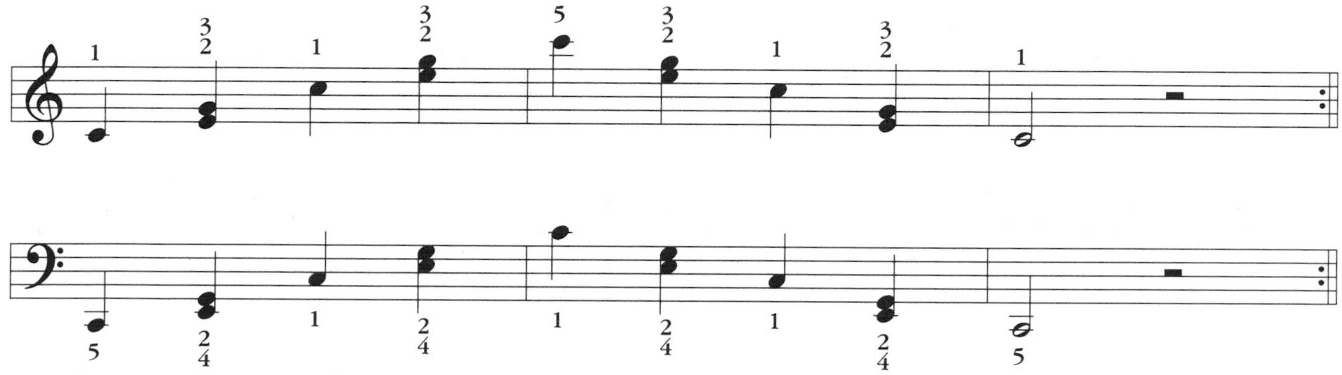

Step 2: THUMB TO THUMB Gently pass under and/or roll over with the thumb. Allow the thumb to be flexible and loose.

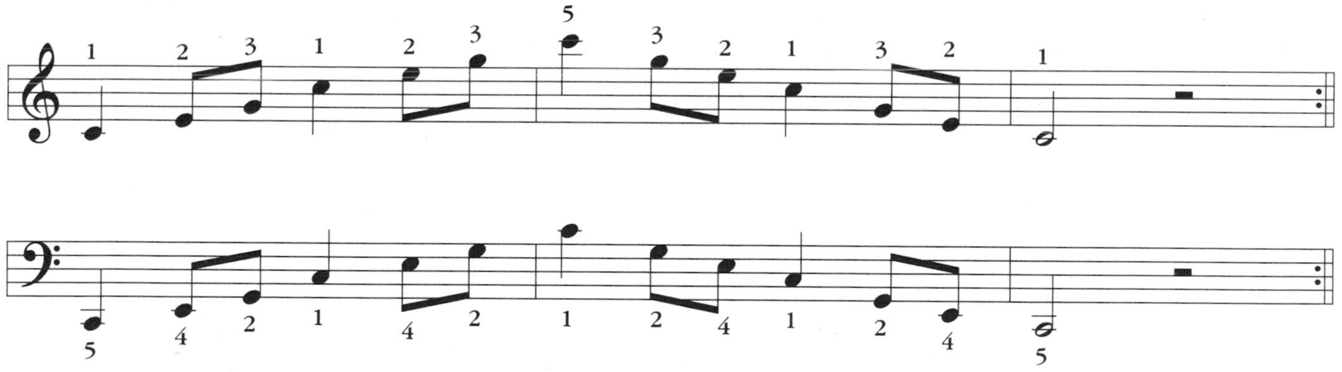

Step 3: TWO OCTAVE ARPEGGIO HANDS TOGETHER Strive to make all notes connected and even.

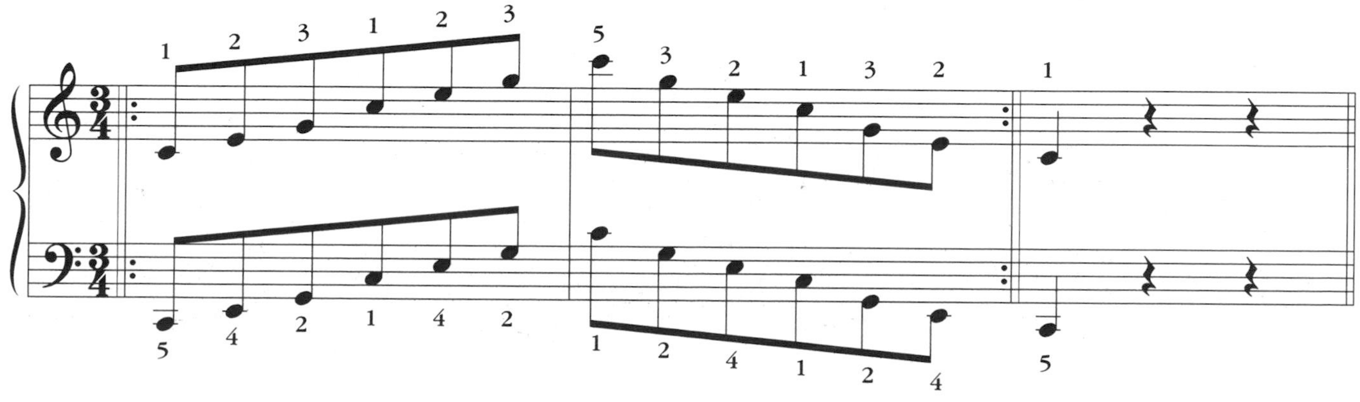

Broken Chords: Practice each pattern four times, twice slow and twice fast. Exaggerate the rotation to the outside of the hand. At the end of each repetition, lift the hand from the keyboard and let it hang loosely from the wrist.

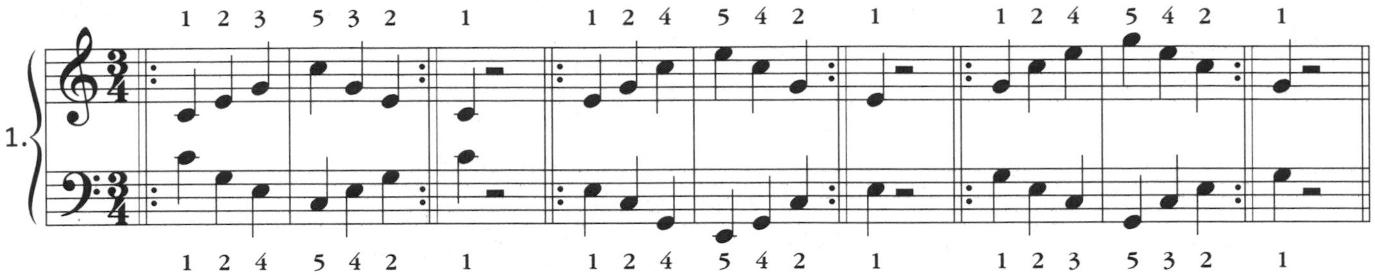

Black Key Arpeggio Preparation: Gently "roll over" your thumbs with either 2 or 4. Relax your thumbs. Hold the fermatas and take time preparing the next pattern.

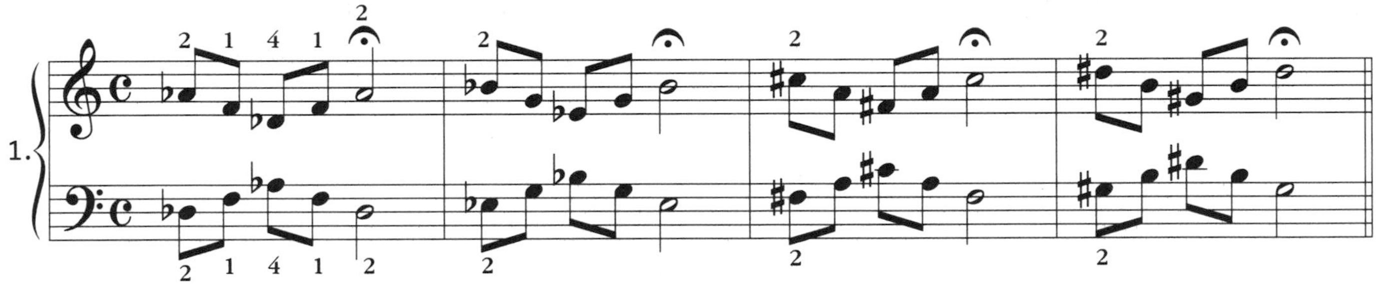

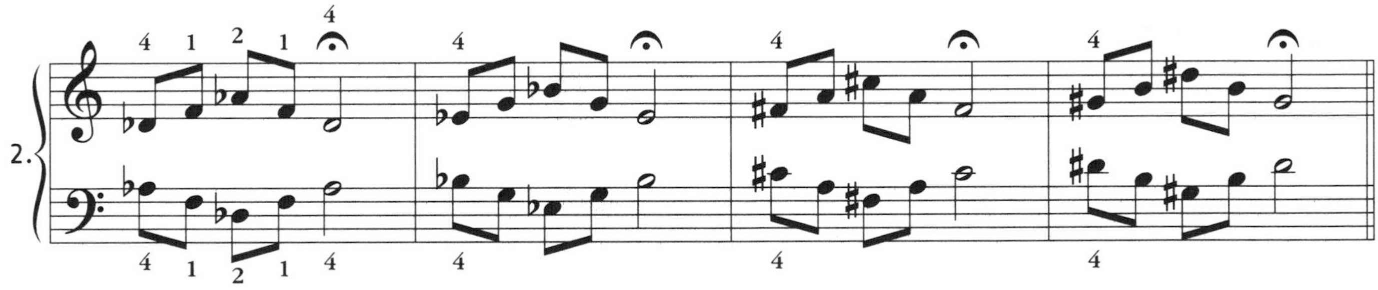

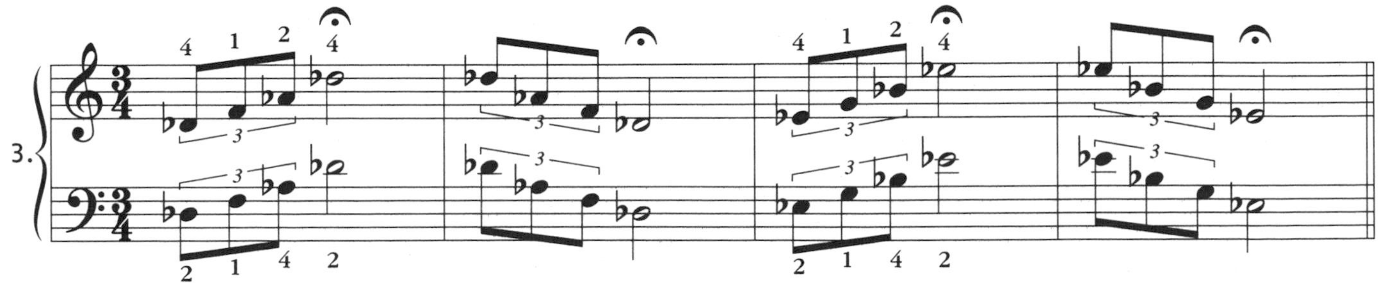

Fingering Concepts for Major Scales

The following chart outlines all fingering patterns for major and minor scales. Play scalar patterns by dividing each individual scale into its logical fingering clusters of three and four groups (123-1234). You've already worked on the major scales of C, G, D, A, E, B, F#, and C#. **Consult Appendix B for all major scale fingerings.**

SCALE FINGERING CHART

by Reid Alexander

MAJOR SCALE FINGERINGS (Two Octaves)	MINOR SCALE FINGERINGS (Harmonic Form, Two Octaves)
Right Hand White Note Scales C, D, E, G, A, B: 123-1234-123-1234-(5) F: 1234-123-1234-123-(4)	**Right Hand White Note Scales** Same as parallel major scale fingerings
Left Hand White Note Scales C, D, E, F, G, A: (5)-4321-321-4321-321 B: (4)-321-4321-321-4321	**Left Hand White Note Scales** Same as parallel major scale fingerings
Right Hand Black Note Scales D♭: (23)-1234-123-1234-1(2) E♭: (3)-1234-123-1234-123 G♭: 234-123-1234-123-1(2) A♭: 34-123-1234-123-123 B♭: (3)-123-1234-123-1234	**Right Hand Black Note Scales** E♭, G#, B♭: Same as parallel major scales C#: (34)-123-1234-123-123 F#: (34)-123-1234-123-123
Left Hand Black Note Scales D♭, E♭, A♭, B♭: 321-4321-321-4321-(3) G♭: 4321-321-4321-321-(3)	**Left Hand Black Note Scales** C#, F#, G#: Same as parallel Major scales E♭: (21)-4321-321-4321-32 B♭: (21)-321-4321-321-432

SUGGESTED PLAYING EXAM TOPICS
CHAPTER FIVE

1. Play An Essential Chord Pattern: I-IV-I_4^6-V^7-I (four voices), found at the bottom of page 180. Pedal the chord changes.

2. Perform two sight reading studies selected from pages 185-189.

3. Play a harmonization that requires RH harmony and LH single tones. Choose between *Completion Studies No. 5* and *No. 6* on page 179.

4. Play the accompaniment to *Lonely Accordian* (pages 190-191), *Wearing of the Green* (page 192), or *In the Valley* (page 193).

5. Play a selection from American Song Repertoire: Gershwin's *Yankee Doodle Blues* (pages 194-195) or Kern's *Ka-lu-a* (pages 196-197).

6. Play *Everybody Loves Saturday Night* (page 199) demonstrating a grasp of syncopated rhythms.

7. Perform one or two solos from the Solo Repertoire section (pages 204-211).

8. Play the *Broken Chords* studies on page 214 in the keys of B♭ and D.

6 chapter Secondary Chords, Augmented and Diminished Triads, New Scale Forms, Harmonization, Repertoire, Musicianship Activities and Technical Studies

Secondary Chords

Play the opening bars of Kern's *Look For The Silver Lining.* The harmony is spread between the hands in "piano style." Examine the harmony on the second beat of bar one (Dm) and the first beat of bar 2 (Gm) discounting the tied notes. These chords are known as secondary chords. Another way to label these chords is by Roman numeral. The Dm chord would be vi and the Gm chord ii – both of them minor chords in a major key. These chords are also known as *substitute chords*: vi substitutes for I and ii substitutes for IV. Dm shares two notes of the F major triad. Similarly, Gm shares two notes of the B♭ major triad.

LOOK FOR THE SILVER LINING

music by **Jerome Kern**

Slowly with expression

We have analyzed, played, and used the primary chords, I, IV, and V in various ways. Secondary chords, ii, iii, and vi, *substitute* for primary chords. Secondary chords are also known as *subordinate* triads. Study the bracketed secondary chords. All are minor in quality.

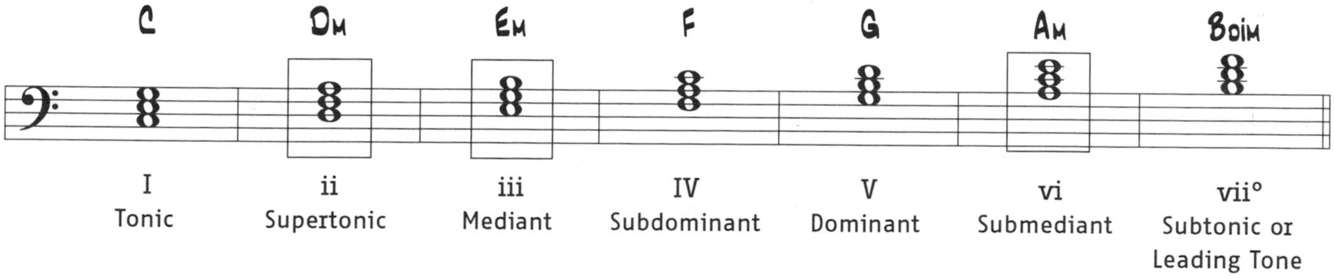

As *Look For The Silver Lining* continues, another important substitute (secondary) chord is used: Am or iii in the key of F major.

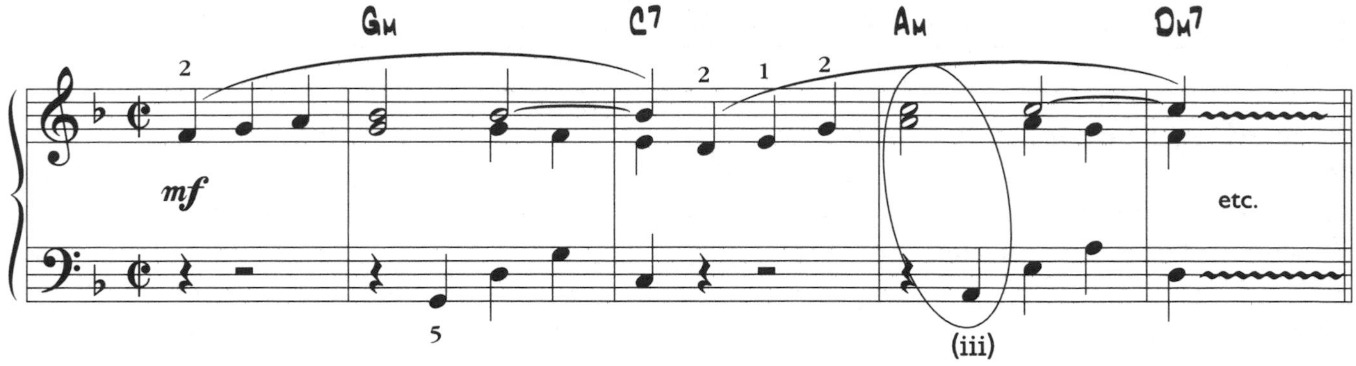

I–vi–IV–ii–I^6_4–V^7–I Chord Progression

This useful progression adds substitute chords to the familiar I–IV–V^7–I pattern. Gradually work toward mastering this progression in several keys. Play this progression and study the voice leading. Only one voice changes in the RH from I to vi and from IV to ii. Then a typical cadence (closing chords) of I^6_4–V^7–I ends the progression. Minor triads are symbolized with lower case Roman numerals.

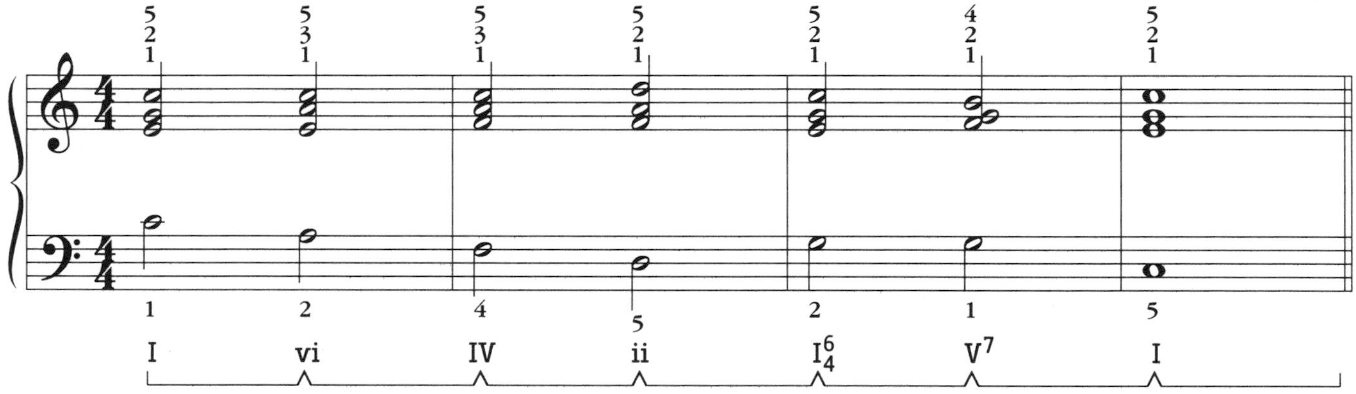

Transpose to several keys.

I–vi–ii(or ii^7)–V^7–I Chord Progression

This "formula" progression is often used in American popular music. The ii^7 chord, formed by adding another third to the ii chord, becomes important in our study of American popular songs. Work out this progression in several keys.

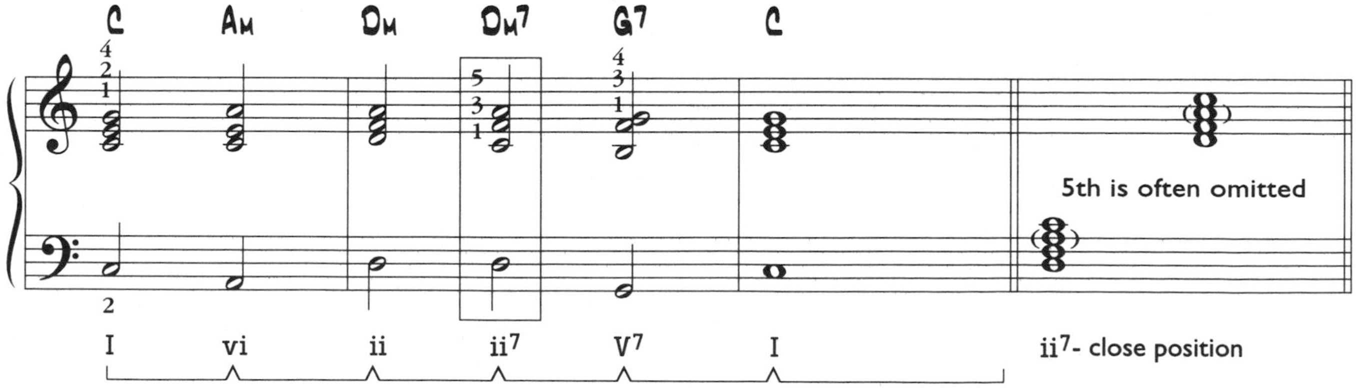

Folk Song Arrangements Using Substitute Chords ii, vi, and iii

Study and play the following folk song arrangements which contain substitute chords. Analyze each chord with a letter name symbol and Roman numeral symbol. Note that ii is frequently found in first inversion. Fill in the blank squares above selected chords with letter name symbols.

DANISH FOLK SONG I

DANISH FOLK SONG II

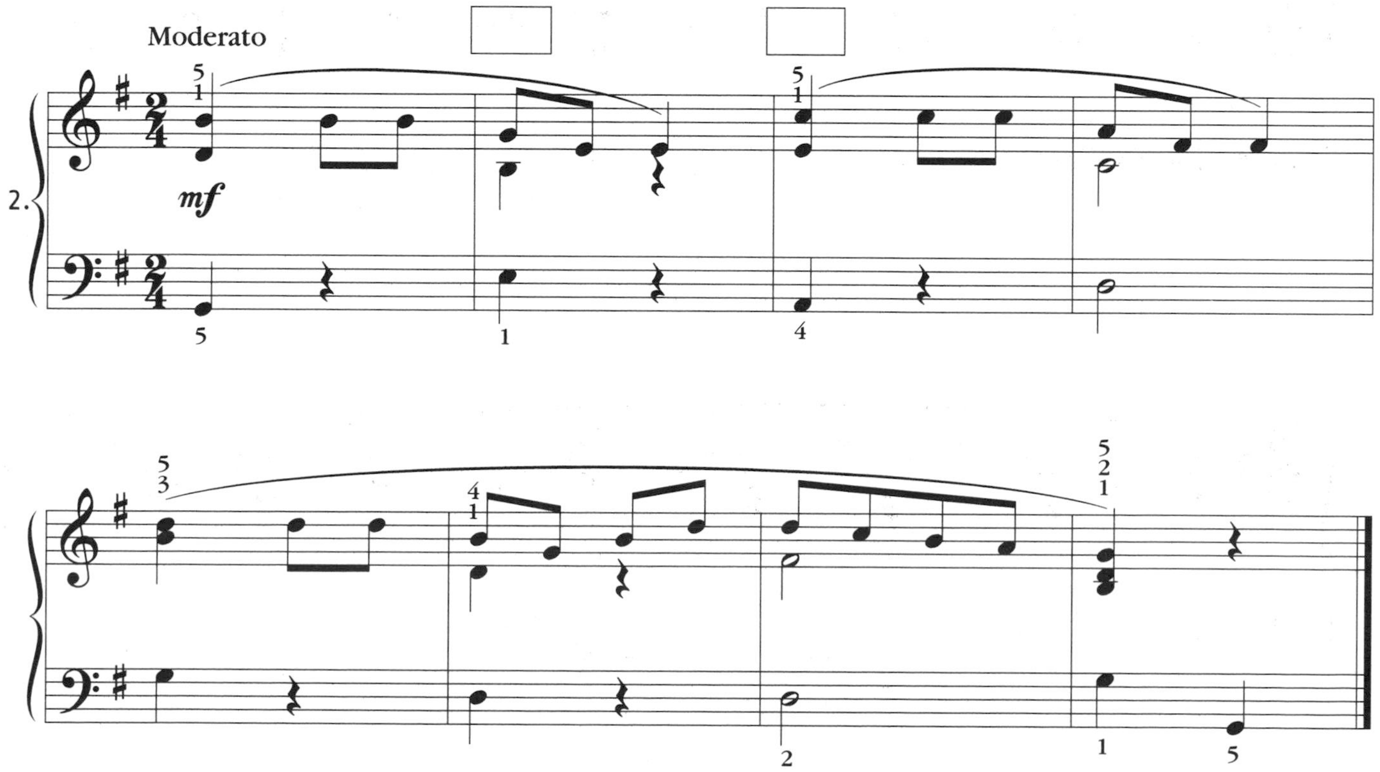

STOMPING DANCE

Czech

3.

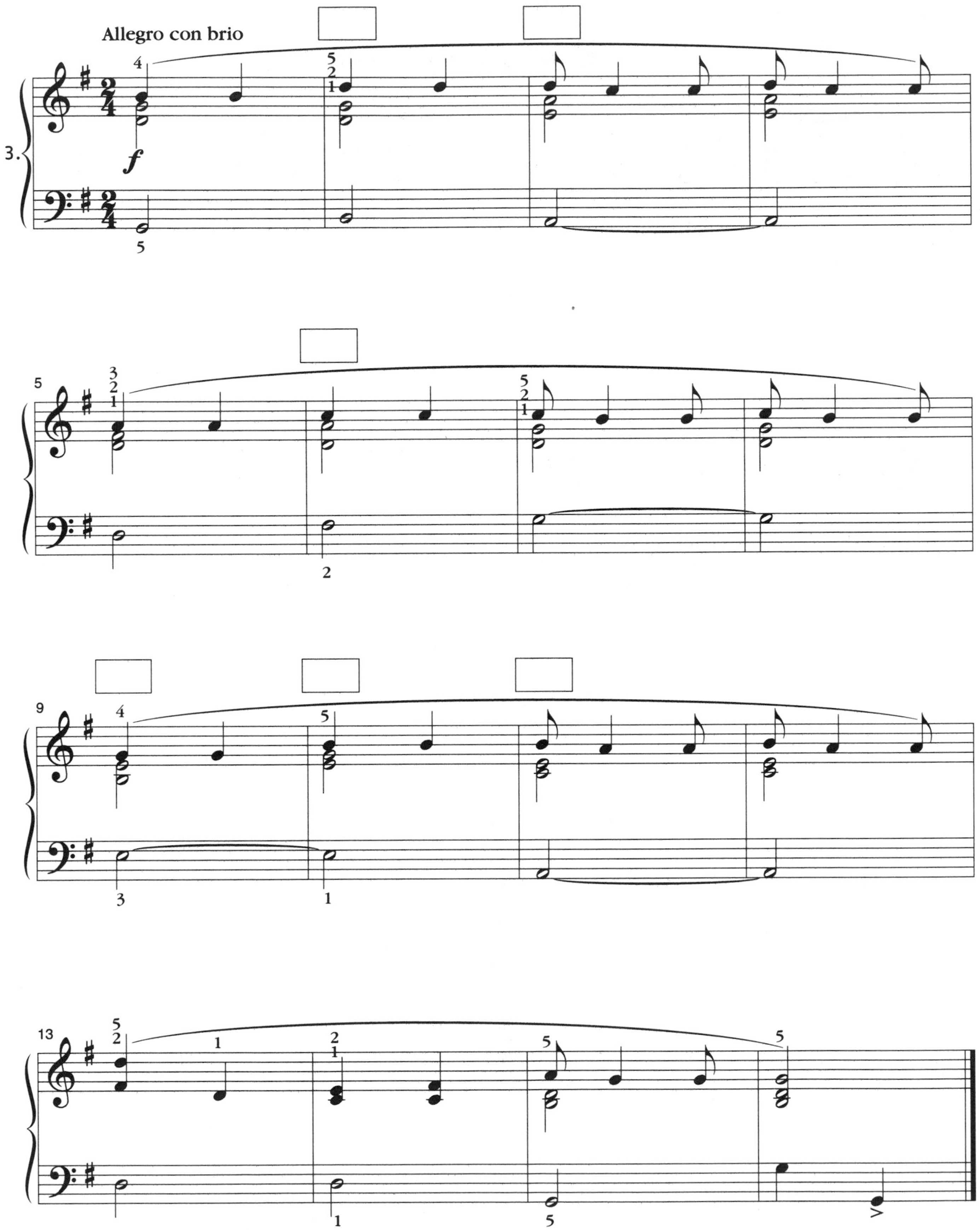

GERMAN FOLK SONG

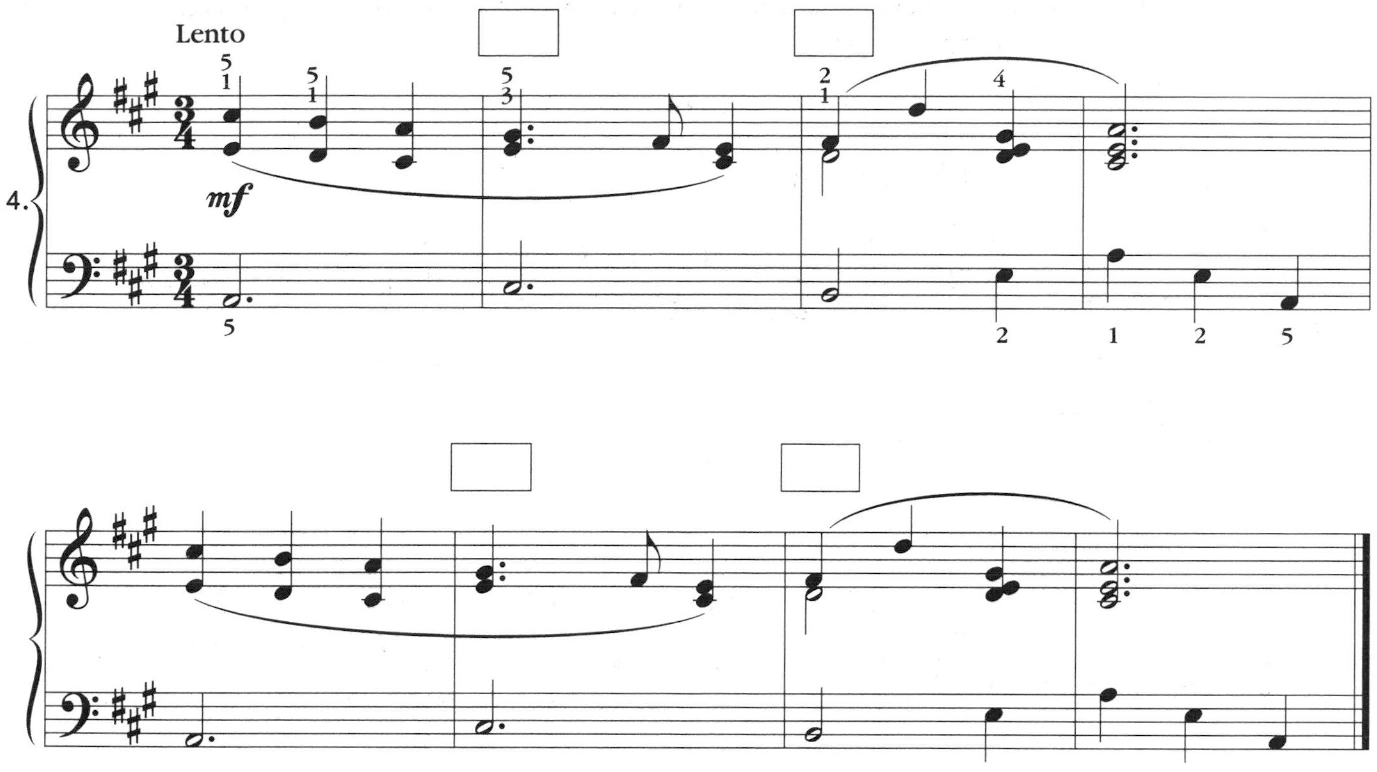

ENGLISH FOLK SONG

Harmonization Studies

The following melodies are textured such that the RH plays the melody and fills in harmony notes beneath the melody. The bass line plays roots and occasional inversions. Study the styles suggested in the first bar or two of the following examples.

MELODY

Giovanni Paisiello

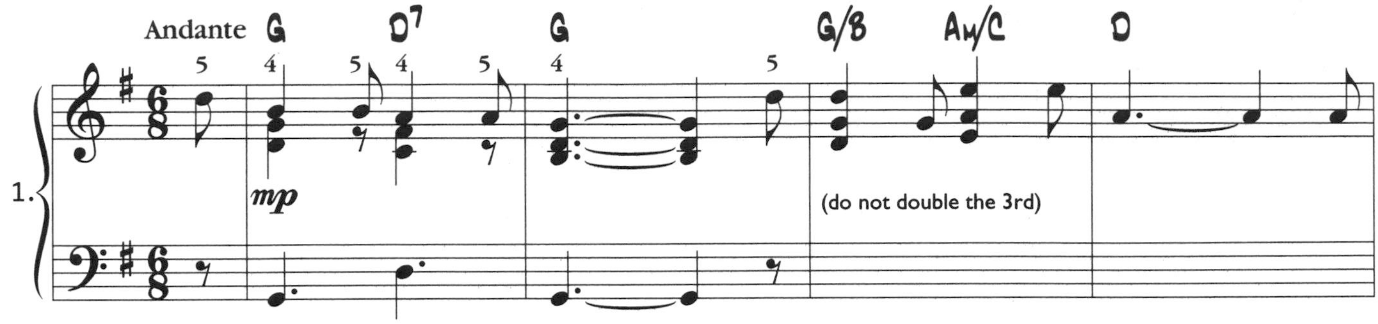

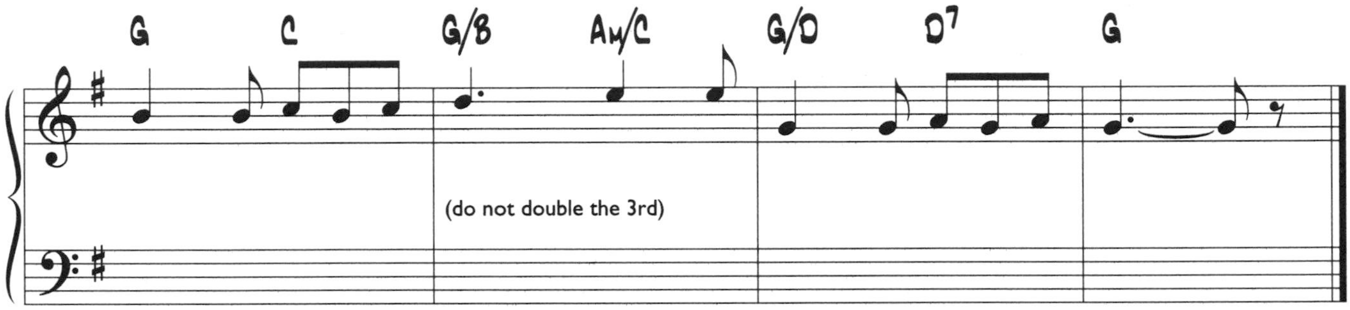

ITALIAN FOLK SONG

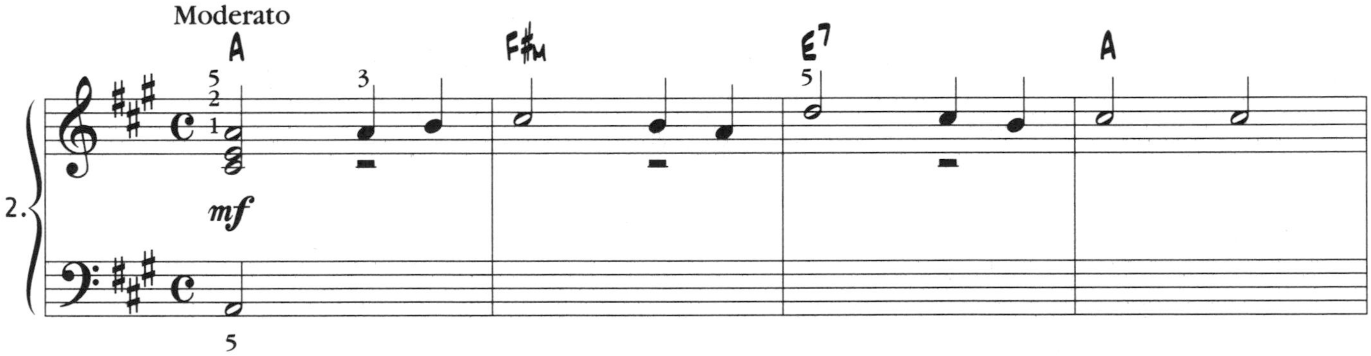

(add chord symbols)

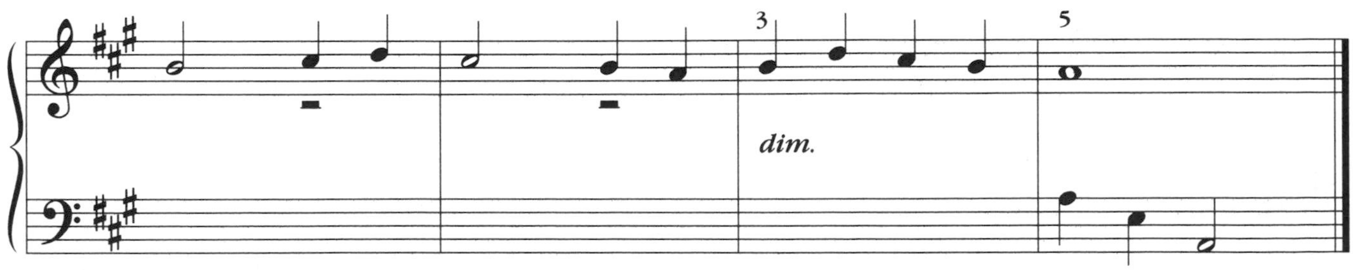

Note the three-voice texture of study no. 3.

FOLK SONG

United States

FOLK SONG

Traditional

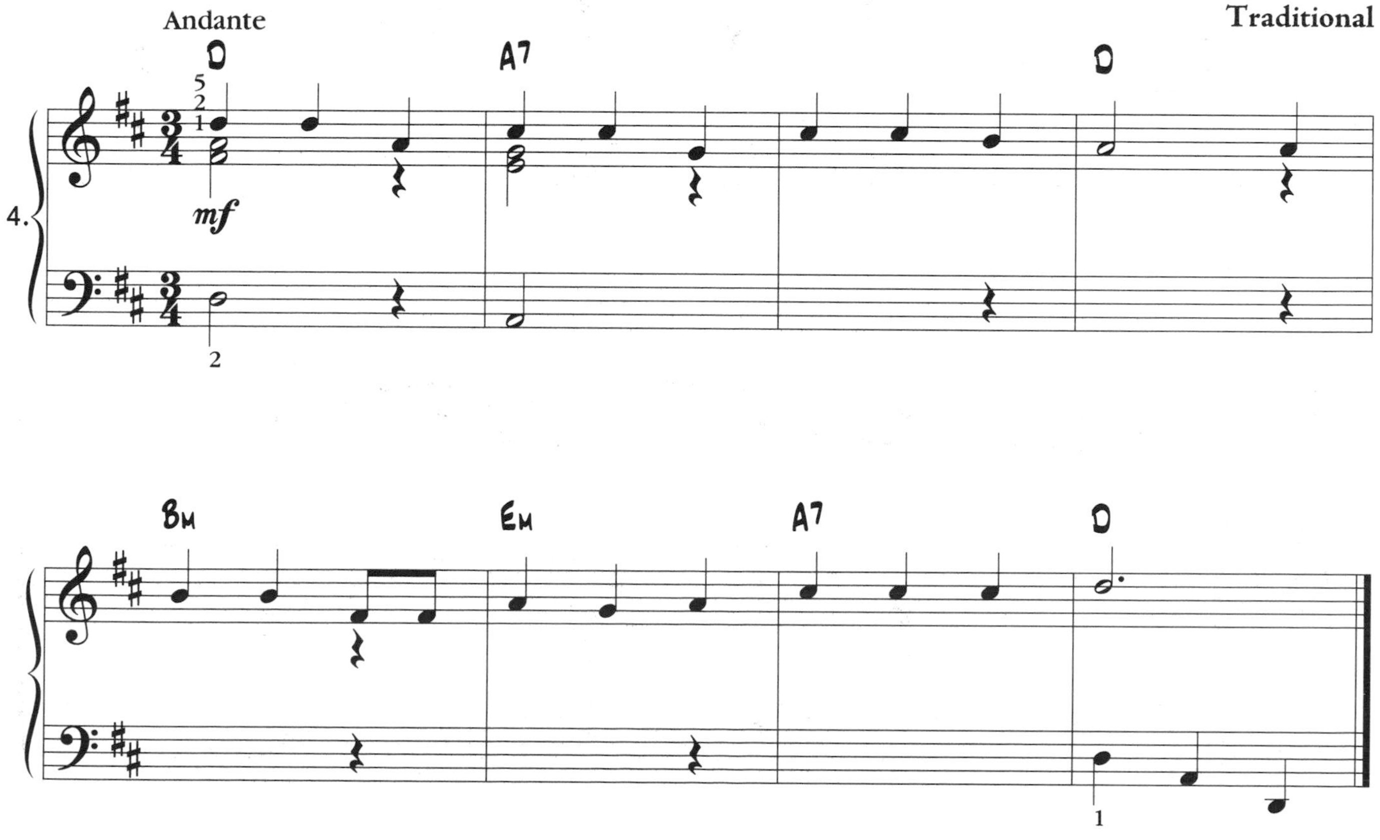

Using Substitute Chords in Accompaniment Patterns

Notice how effective the iii chord becomes when used to harmonize the 7th scale degree in a descending scale line (I–iii–IV–I). Generally, iii moves to a IV chord. Practice the chord pattern several times before attempting the accompaniment to Finnish Melody. Note also ii used in its first inversion. Avoid doubling the 3rd.

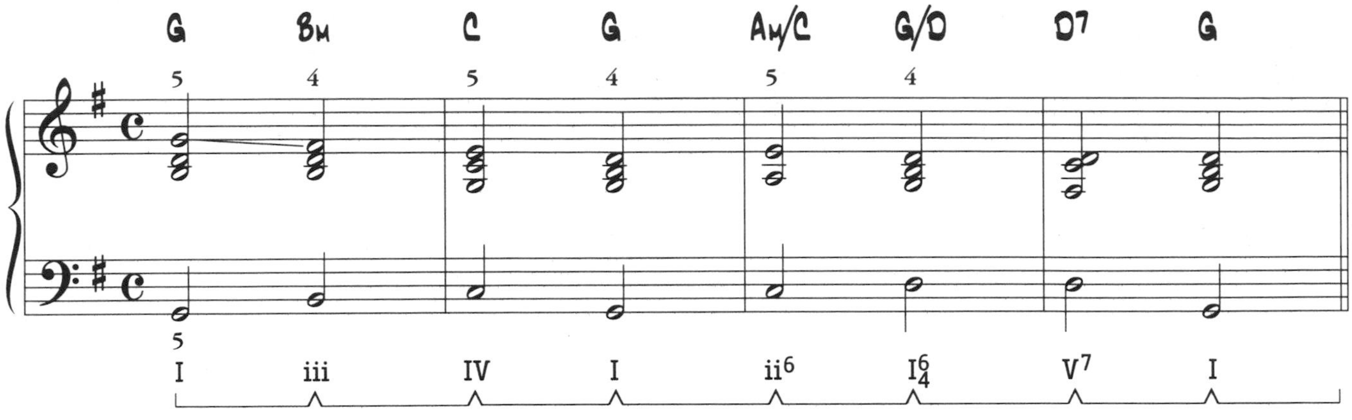

Teacher: Double the melody one octave higher.

FINNISH MELODY

Transpose to G♭ major.

Student: Analyze and label each chord with a letter name symbol. Note all inversions. These chords are used in the accompaniment to *Vive L'Amour*.

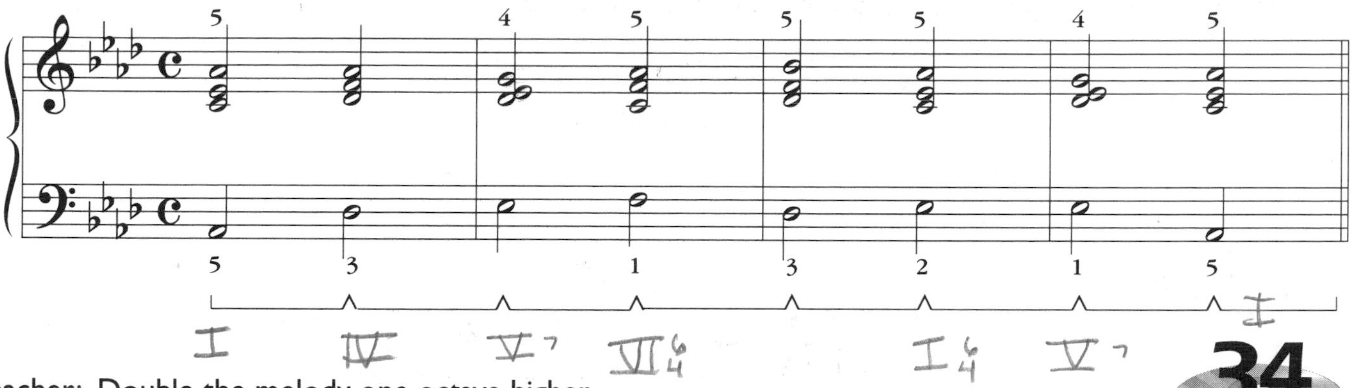

Teacher: Double the melody one octave higher.

34 CD

VIVE L'AMOUR

French

With spirit

Transpose to A major.

Study Piece – Substitute Chords

Austrian Carol contains two substitute chords (vi and ii). Study and play this arrangement. Notice the various inversions of chords. Label each chord where the squares appear: G, G/B, D, etc.

AUSTRIAN CAROL

(Study Piece)

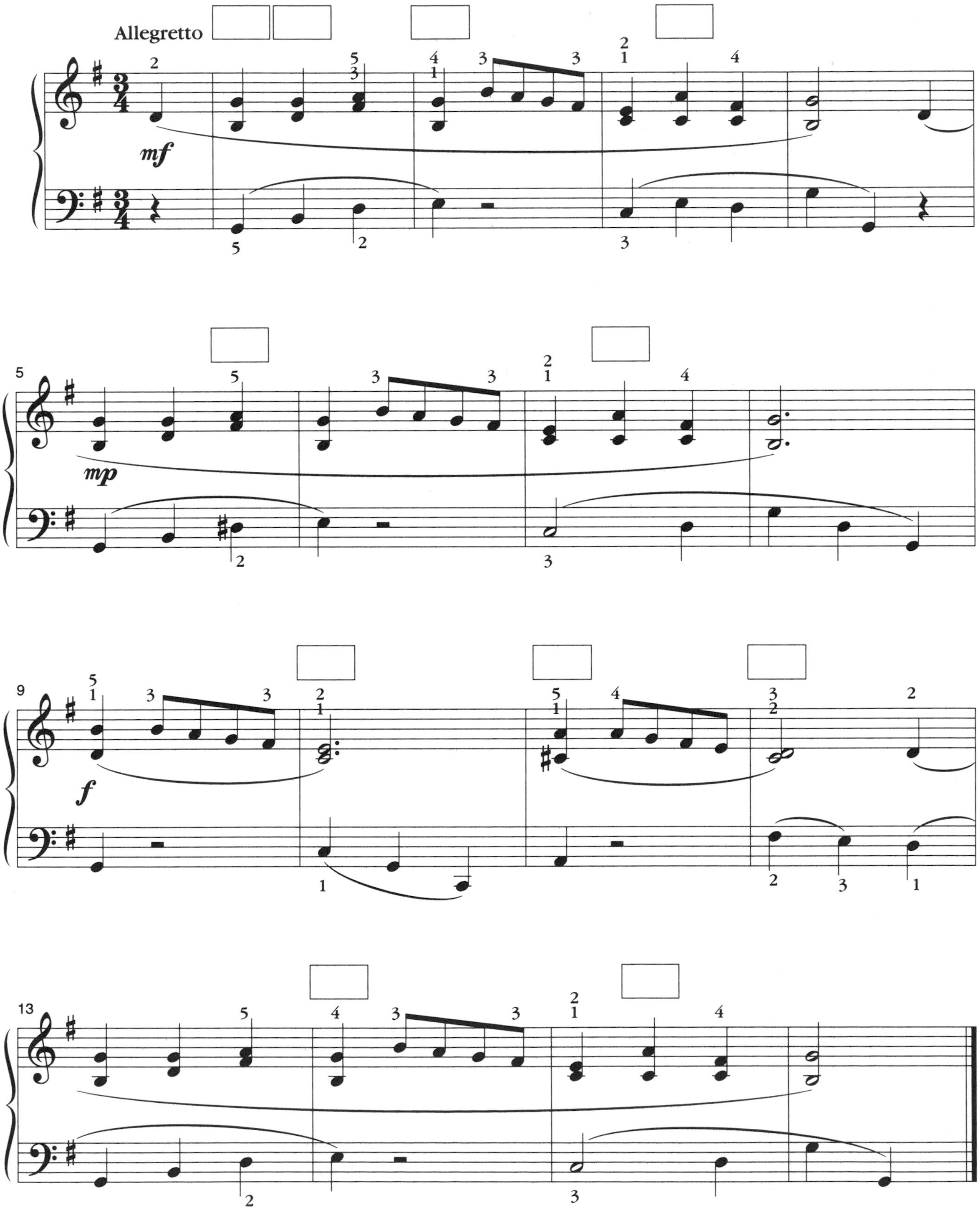

Altered Chords

Examine the circled triad in the first measure of *Deep River*. In root position the triad would be spelled C–E–G♯, similar to a C major triad but with a *raised fifth*. This *augmented* chord creates dissonance and calls for a resolution to a consonant sound. Find and circle three *secondary* chords which occur in succeeding bars. Label each of these substitute chords.

DEEP RIVER (excerpt)

Reverently

Spiritual

Augmented Triads

Complete the exercise below according to the example. Alter the major chord to create an augmented chord by raising the fifth. Augmented chords are symbolized by a + (C+), or aug (C aug).

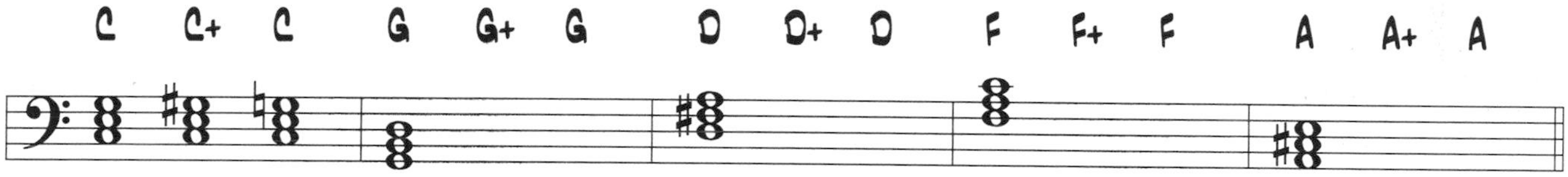

Study the circled triad in the fourth bar of *Melody in F*. This chord, spelled F♯–A–C, is similar to F♯ minor but with a *lowered fifth*. This *diminished* triad is very active and demands resolution to a more consonant chord. Analyze the other chords in this excerpt. Triads built on the 7th degree of a major scale are diminished (vii°).

MELODY IN F (excerpt)

Rubinstein

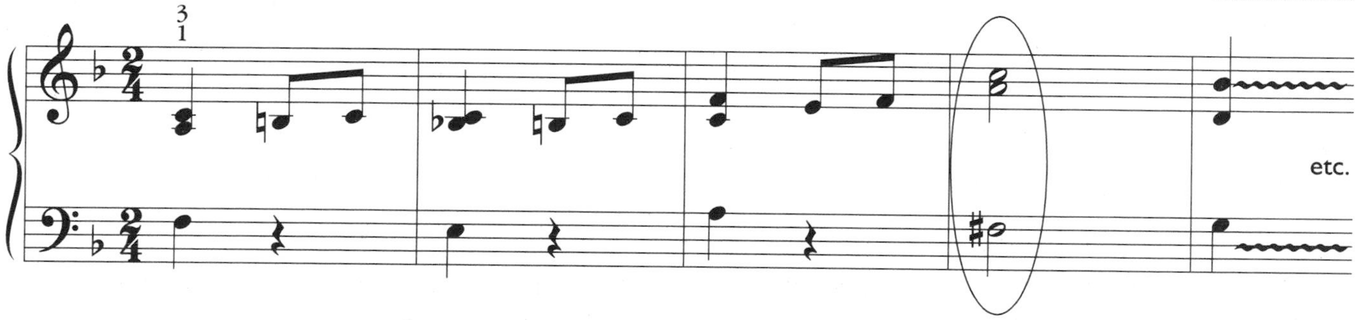

Diminished Triads

Complete the exercise below according to the example. Alter the minor chord to create a diminished chord by lowering the fifth. Diminished chords are symbolized by a ° (C°, vii°) or dim (C dim).

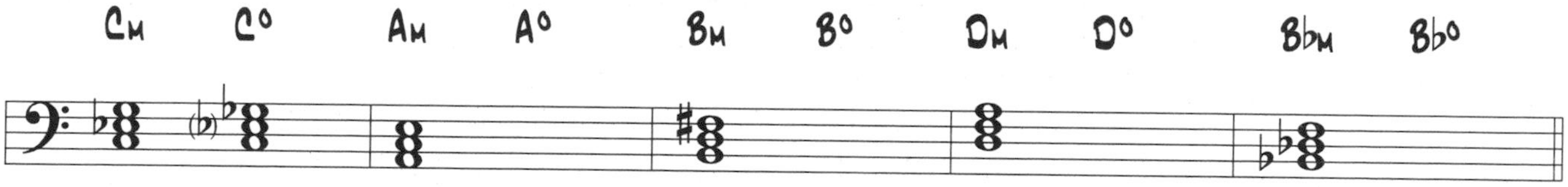

The Pentatonic Scale

Observe the keyboard diagram below which shows two patterns for the pentatonic scale. The pentatonic scale is a primitive scale consisting of five consecutive tones within the octave. The scale corresponds to the black keys on the keyboard. The pentatonic scale can begin on any black key.

Black Key Patterns
(RH)

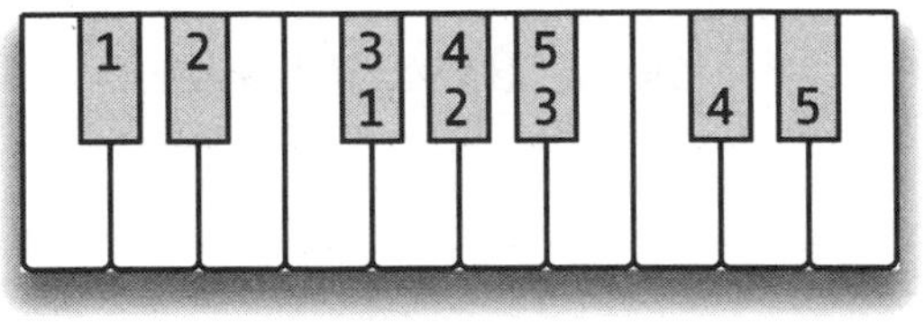

The pentatonic scale may be played on white keys also. Using the top numbers above, slide the hand right and play D E G A B. Using the lower numbers, slide the hand left and play F G A C D.

White Key Patterns
(RH)

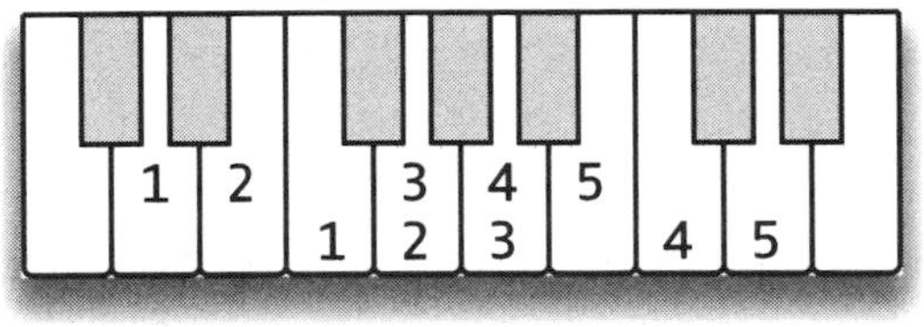

The Chromatic Scale

A *chromatic* (from chroma – color) scale consists of the twelve pitches within the octave, that is, the pitches of all the black and white keys. It is seldom used in its entirety. Examine the chromatic scale beginning on C.

The Whole Tone Scale

Another scale which twentieth-century composers, such as Debussy, have used in various ways is the whole tone scale. The *whole tone scale* is a six-note scale (hexatonic). Study the following diagram which shows the two possibilities for dividing the twelve tones into two patterns.

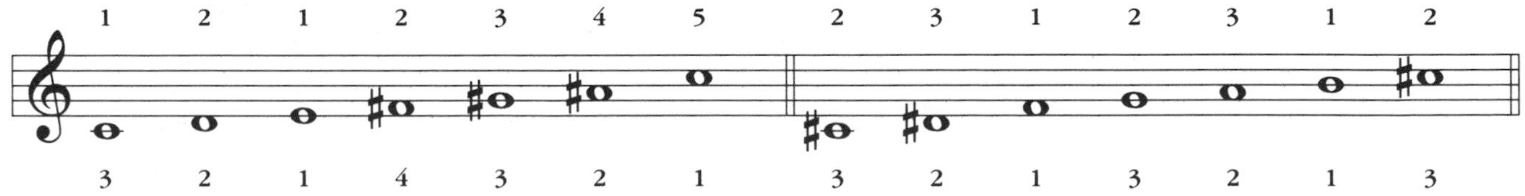

Use of the whole tone scale provides an atmospheric effect when the pedal is employed.

The Blues Scale

Any major scale can be turned into a blues scale by playing these tones: 1–♭3–4–♯4 (or ♭5)–5–♭7.

C BLUES SCALE

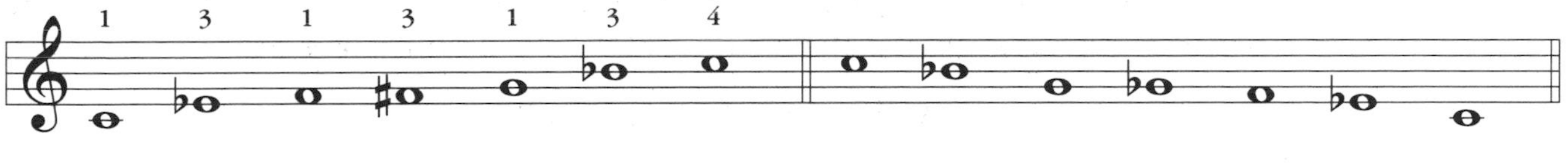

It is, of course, easier to build the blues scale from the natural minor form of the scale which already contains a ♭3 and ♭7. ♫ = ♩♪ (triplet) means that the eighths should be played thus: ♩♩♩ (triplet, first two tied). Divide ♩ values into triplet values, ♩ as ♩♩♩ (triplet), with the first 2 notes of the triplet tied (♩‿♩♩).

MOANIN' LOW BLUES

Geoffrey Haydon

Music for Sight Reading and Transposing

This section contains reading material which emphasizes secondary chords, pentatonic melodies, chromatic passages, and chromatic chords (augmented and diminished). It also contains review material. Follow the normal reading routine of tapping rhythm, pre-analysis of harmonies and patterns, etc. Some of the more challenging exercises might require one-handed reading (RH alone, LH alone, and then HT). Transpose each exercise as suggested. Write the letter name chord symbol in the boxes.

GERMAN FOLK SONG

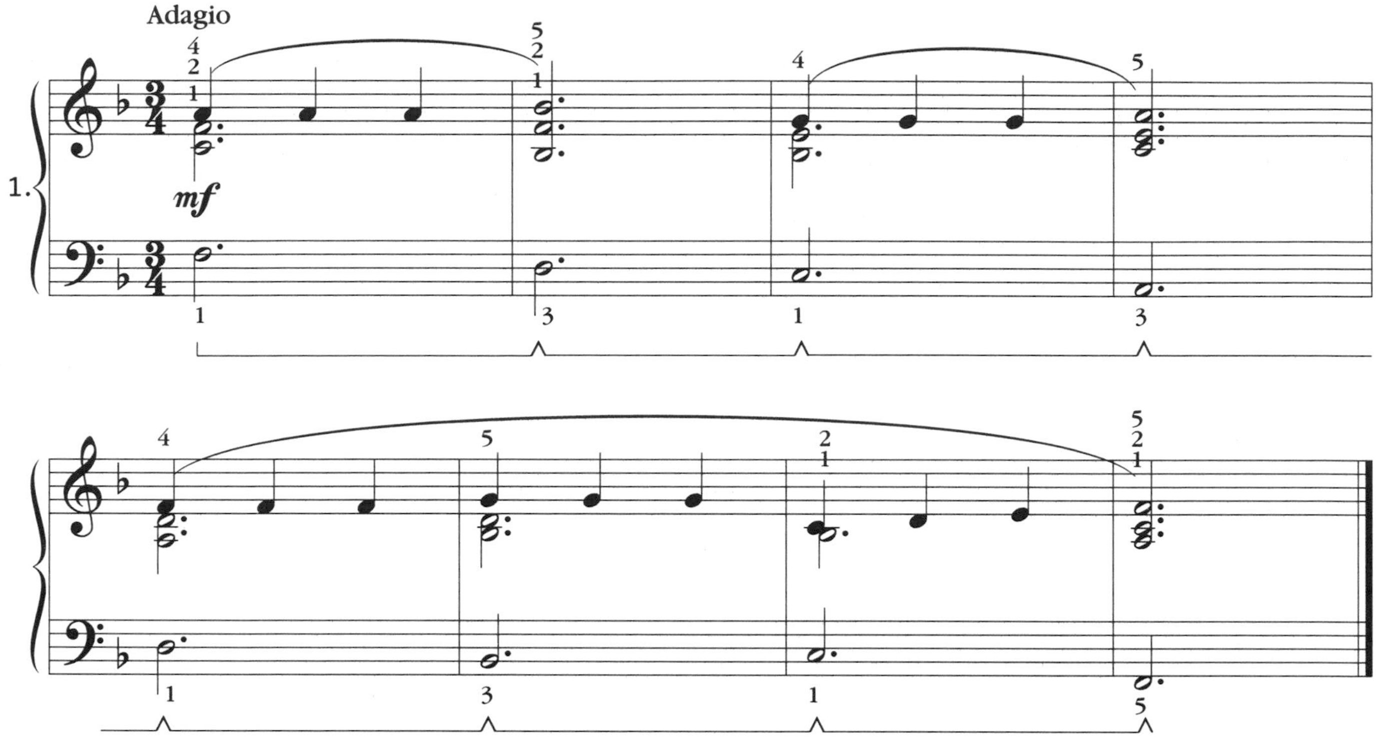

Transpose to G major.

FRENCH FOLK SONG

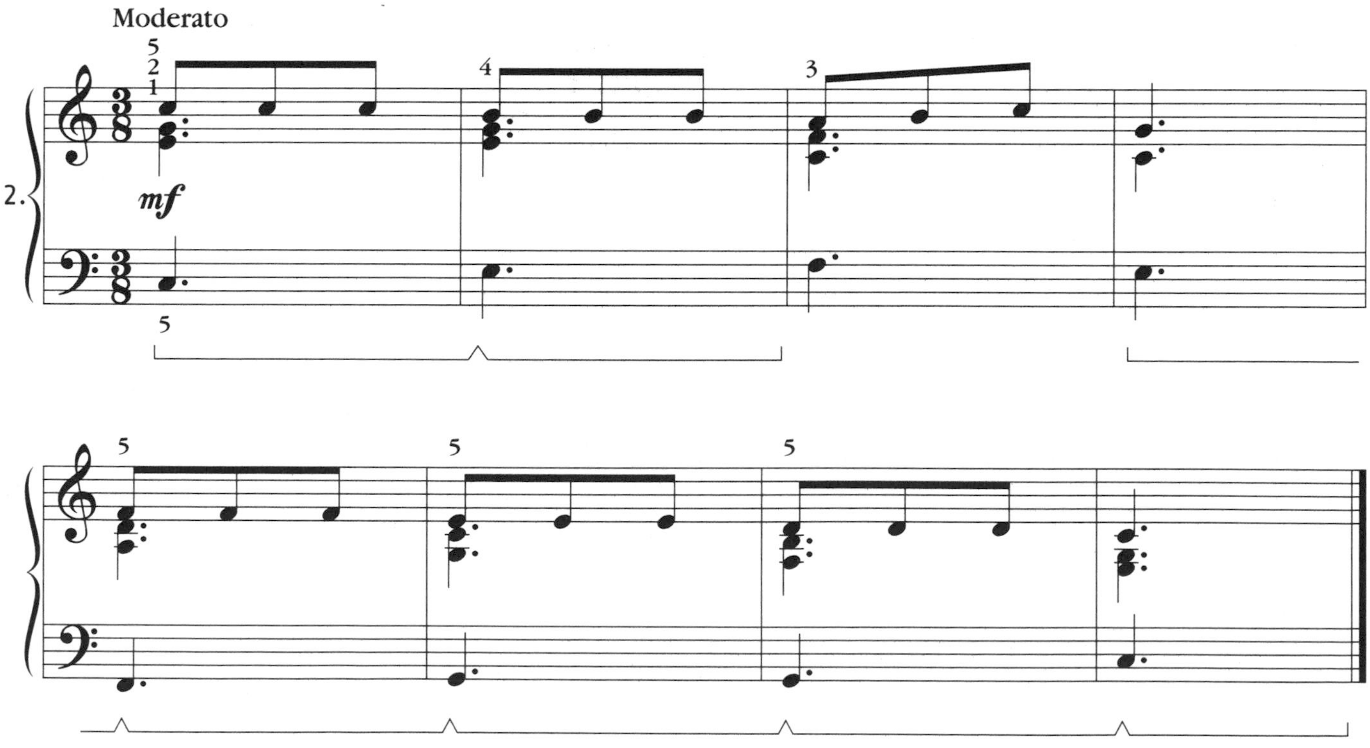

Transpose to D major.

ITALIAN FOLK SONG

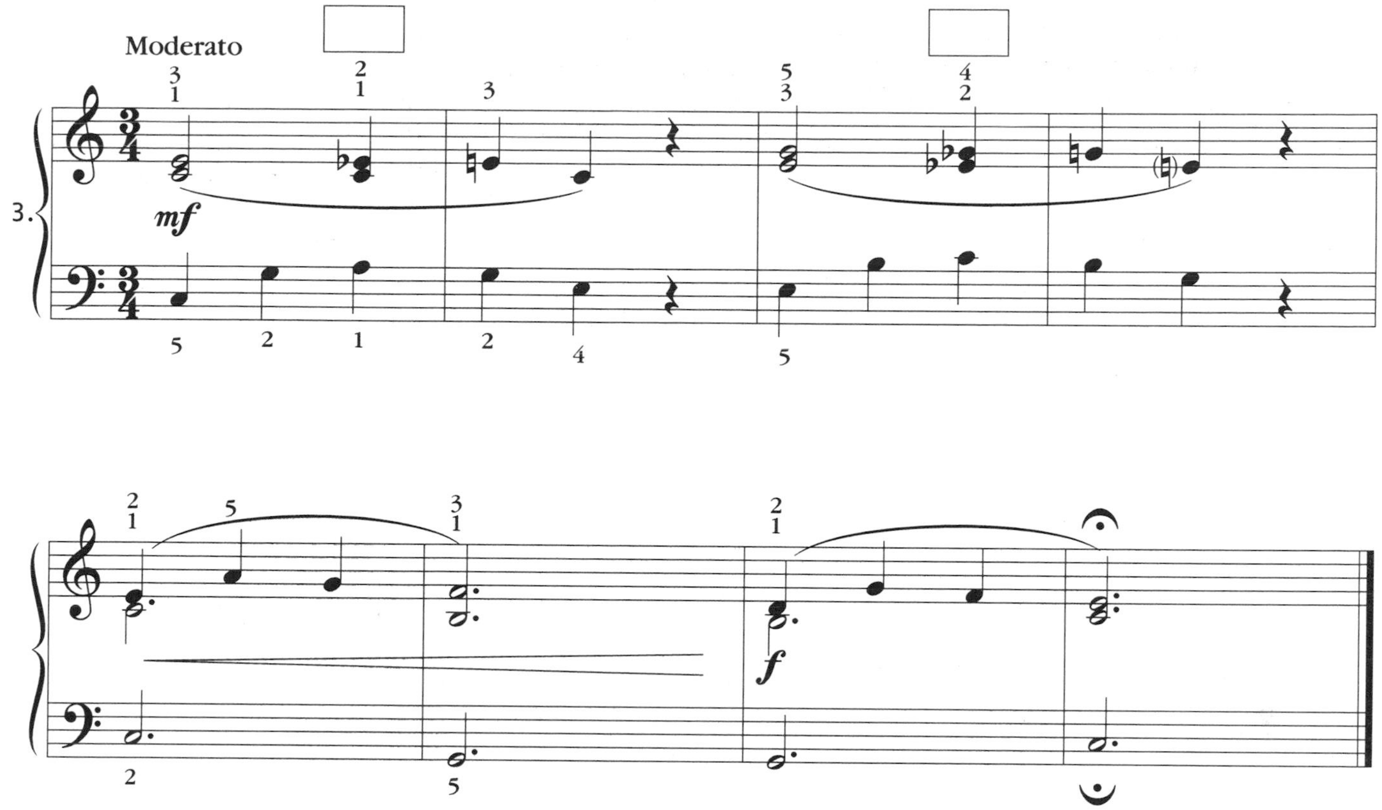

Transpose to B♭ major.

I'M TRAMPING

American

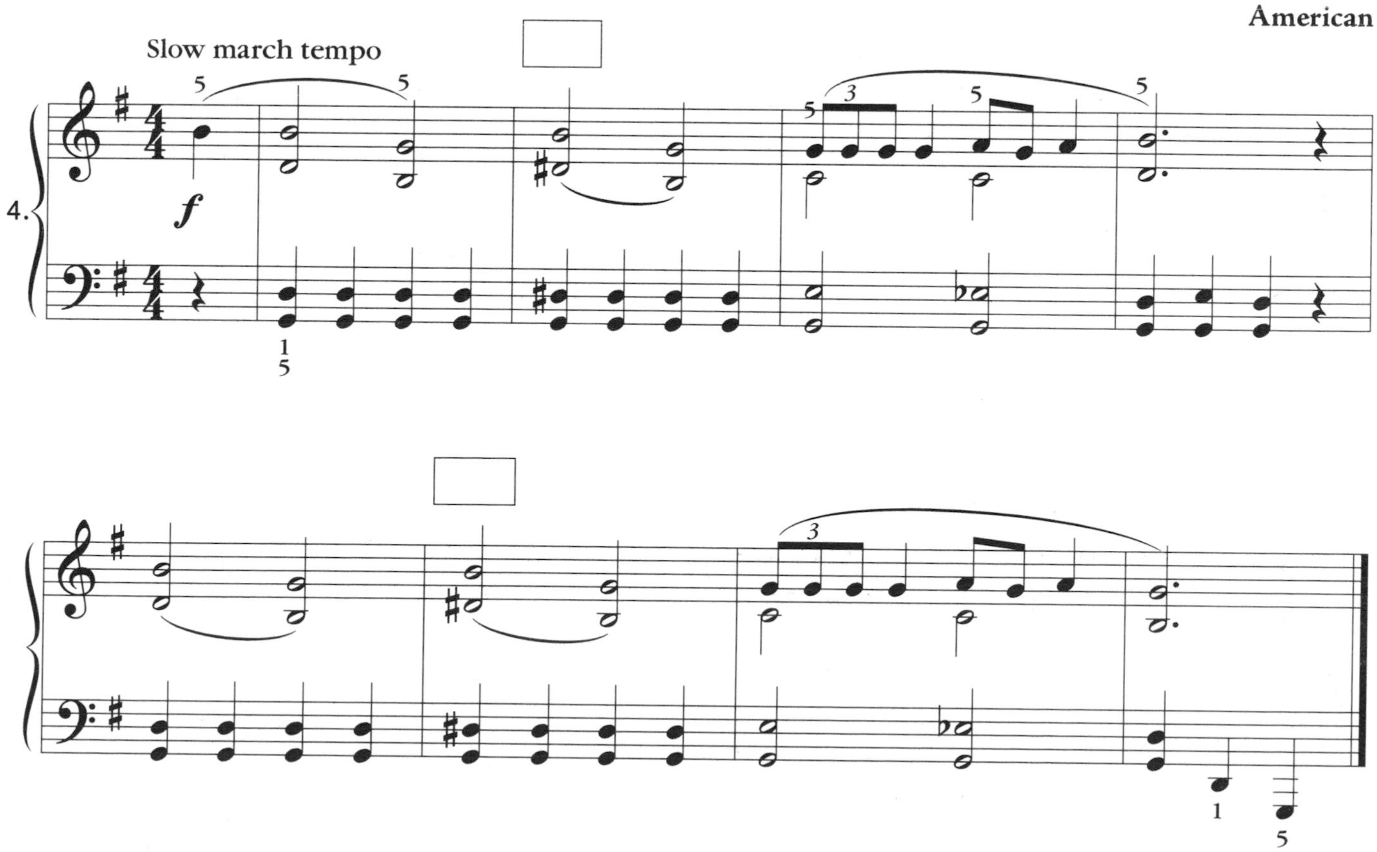

Transpose to F major.

IRISH SEA CHANTEY

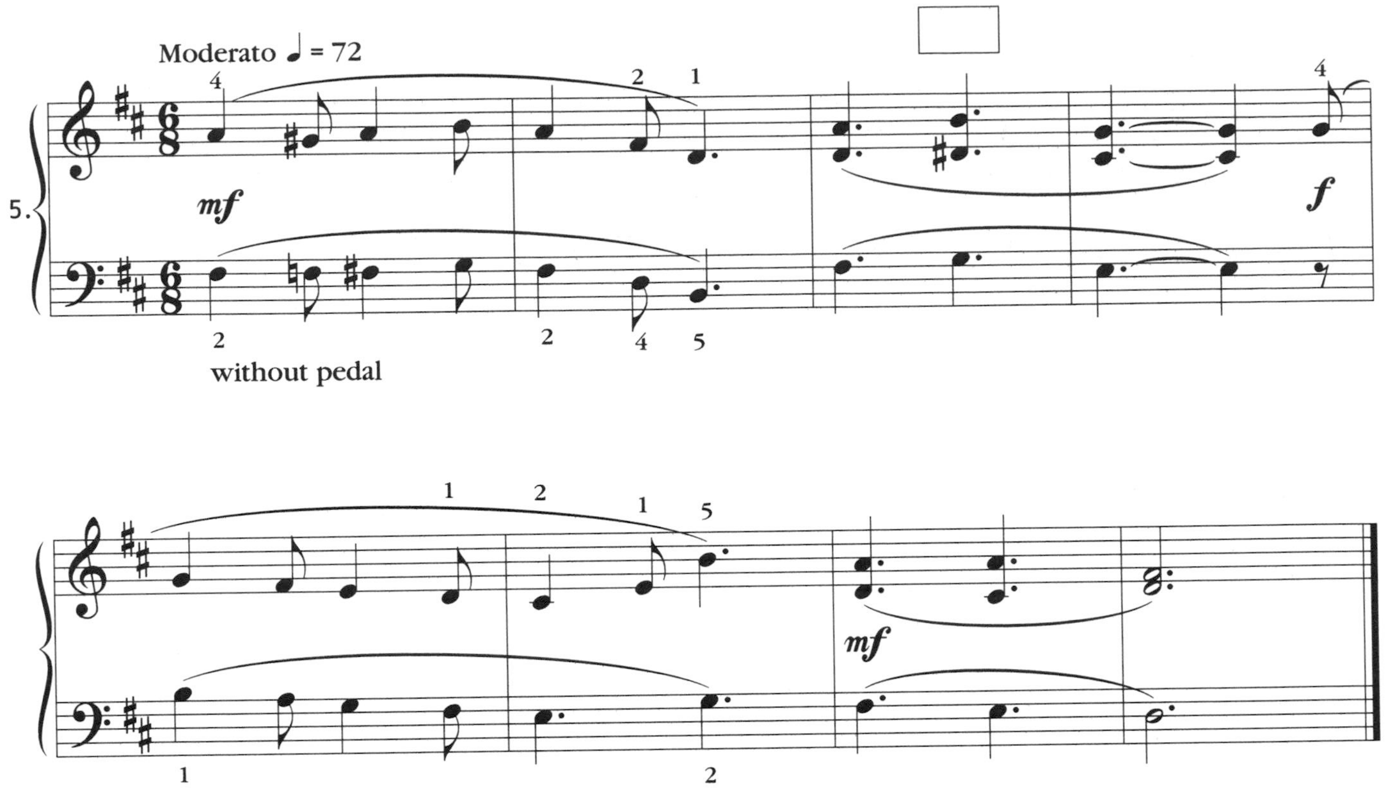

Transpose to C.

RUSSIAN FOLK SONG

Transpose to E and D♭.

In *The Mocking Bird Song*, what scale does the RH play?

THE MOCKING BIRD SONG

Southern U.S.

Andante

Transpose to G major.

Italian

Slowly

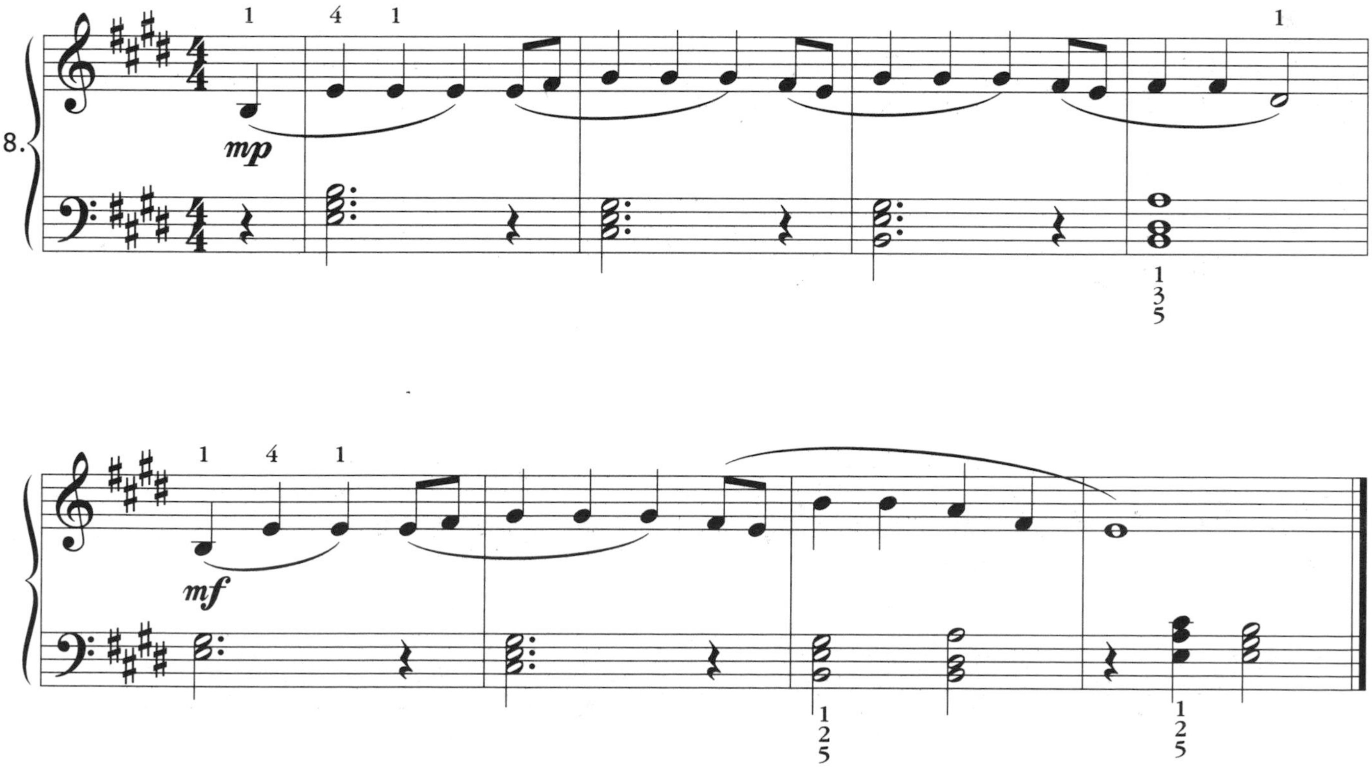

SONG TO THE EVENING STAR

Richard Wagner

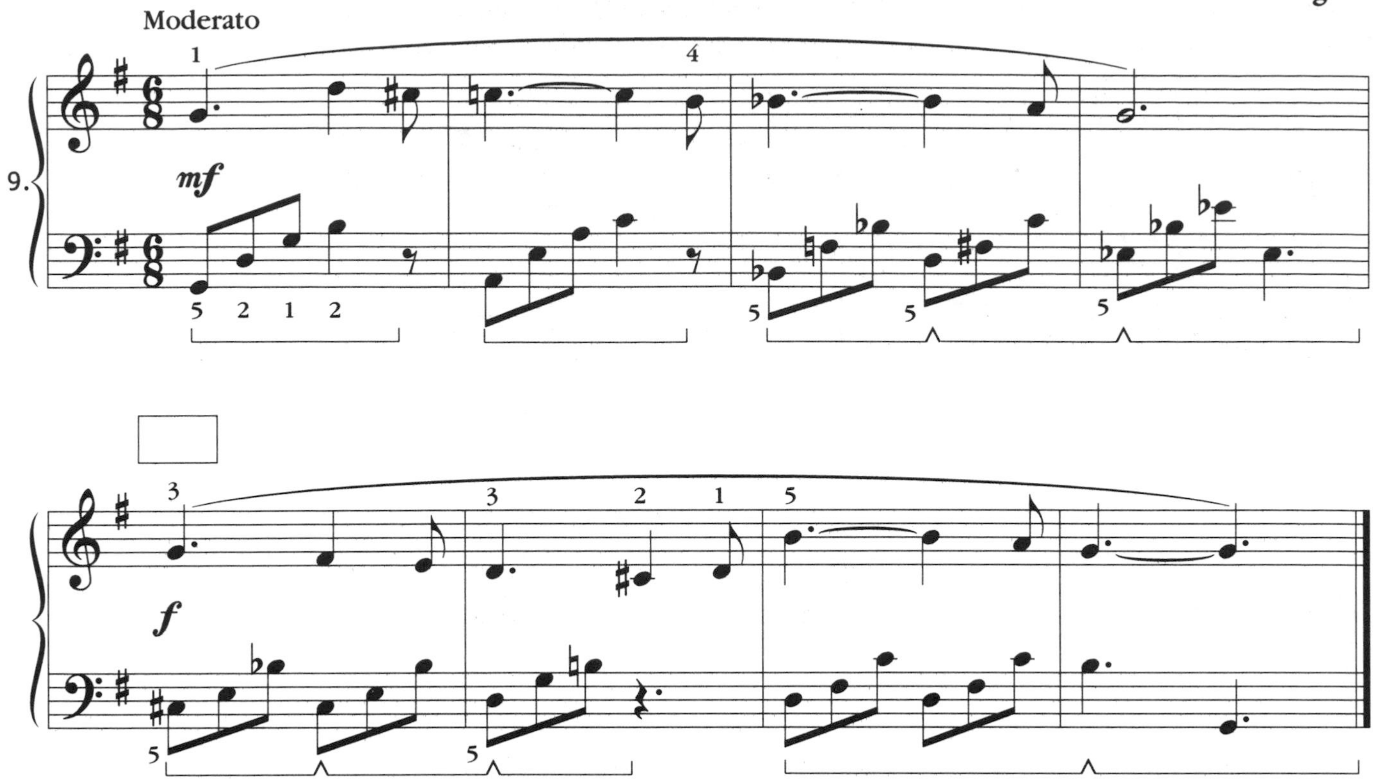

no transposition

LOTUS BLOSSOMS

Chinese

Transpose to F pentatonic.

Accompaniment Patterns

Before learning the accompaniments to *It's Delightful to Be Married* and *Draggy Rag* (pages 236, 237), some preliminary practice with essential chord patterns will be helpful. Practice these patterns until fluency is achieved at an acceptable tempo. Good fingering is essential. Label each chord with a letter name symbol.

It's Delightful to Be Married Patterns

1.

2.
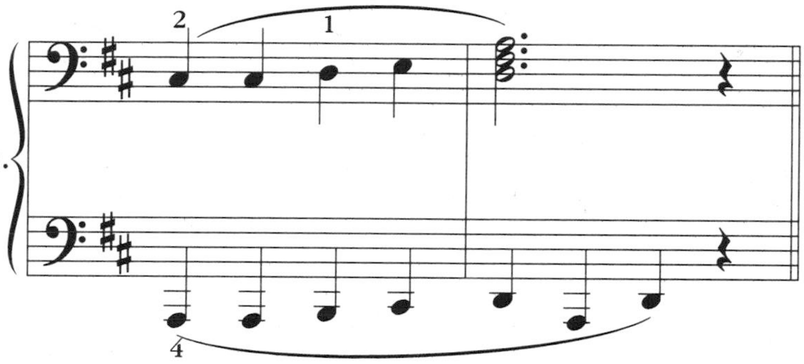

Play slow to fast.

Draggy Rag Patterns

1.
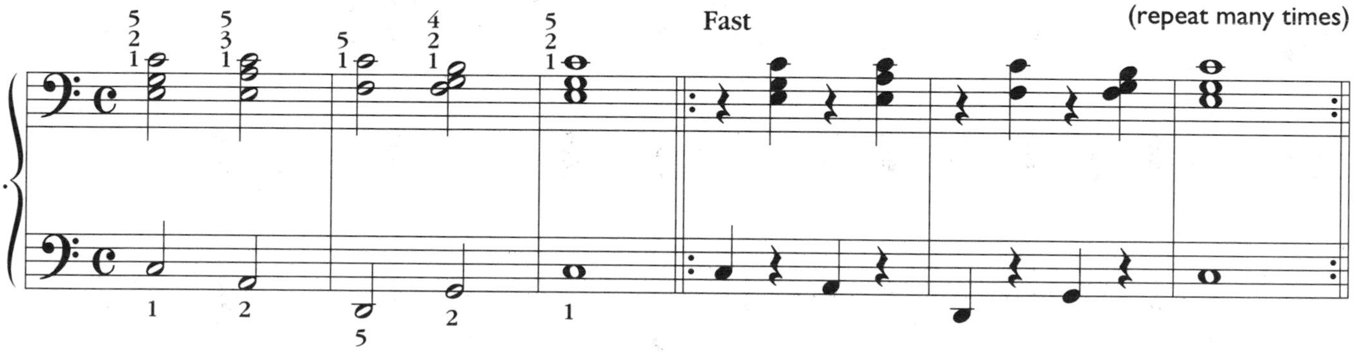

Same fingering as above, except for D^7.

2.

ACCOMPANYING

Teacher: Double the melody two octaves higher.

35 CD

IT'S DELIGHTFUL TO BE MARRIED

music by **V. Scotto**
arr. **James Lyke**

36 CD

Teacher: Double the melody two octaves higher.

DRAGGY RAG

music by **Irving Berlin**
arr. **James Lyke**

SWANEE

music by **George Gershwin**
arr. **James Lyke**

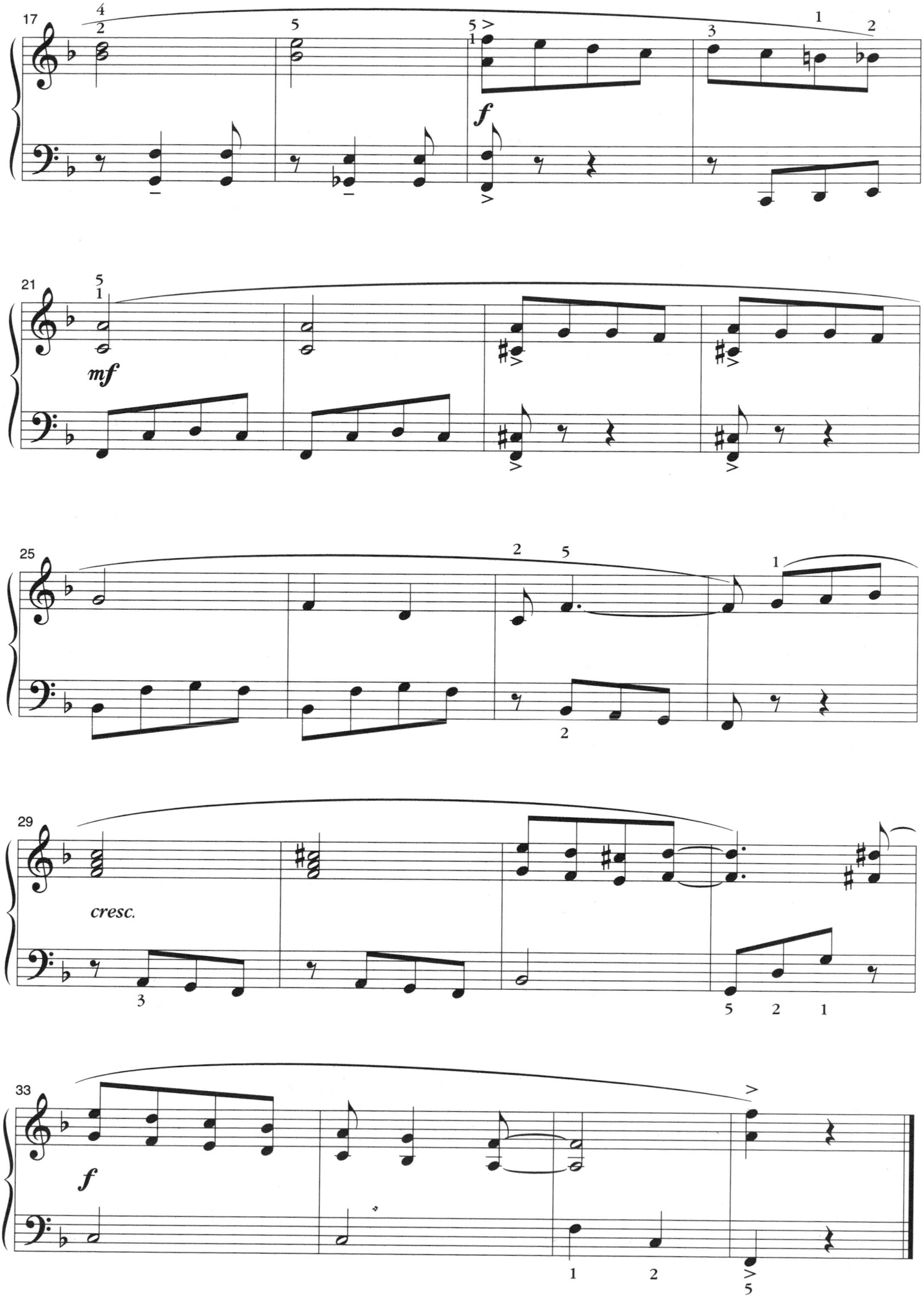
f
mf
cresc.
f

38 CD

ANY OLD PLACE WITH YOU

music by **Richard Rodgers**
arr. **James Lyke**

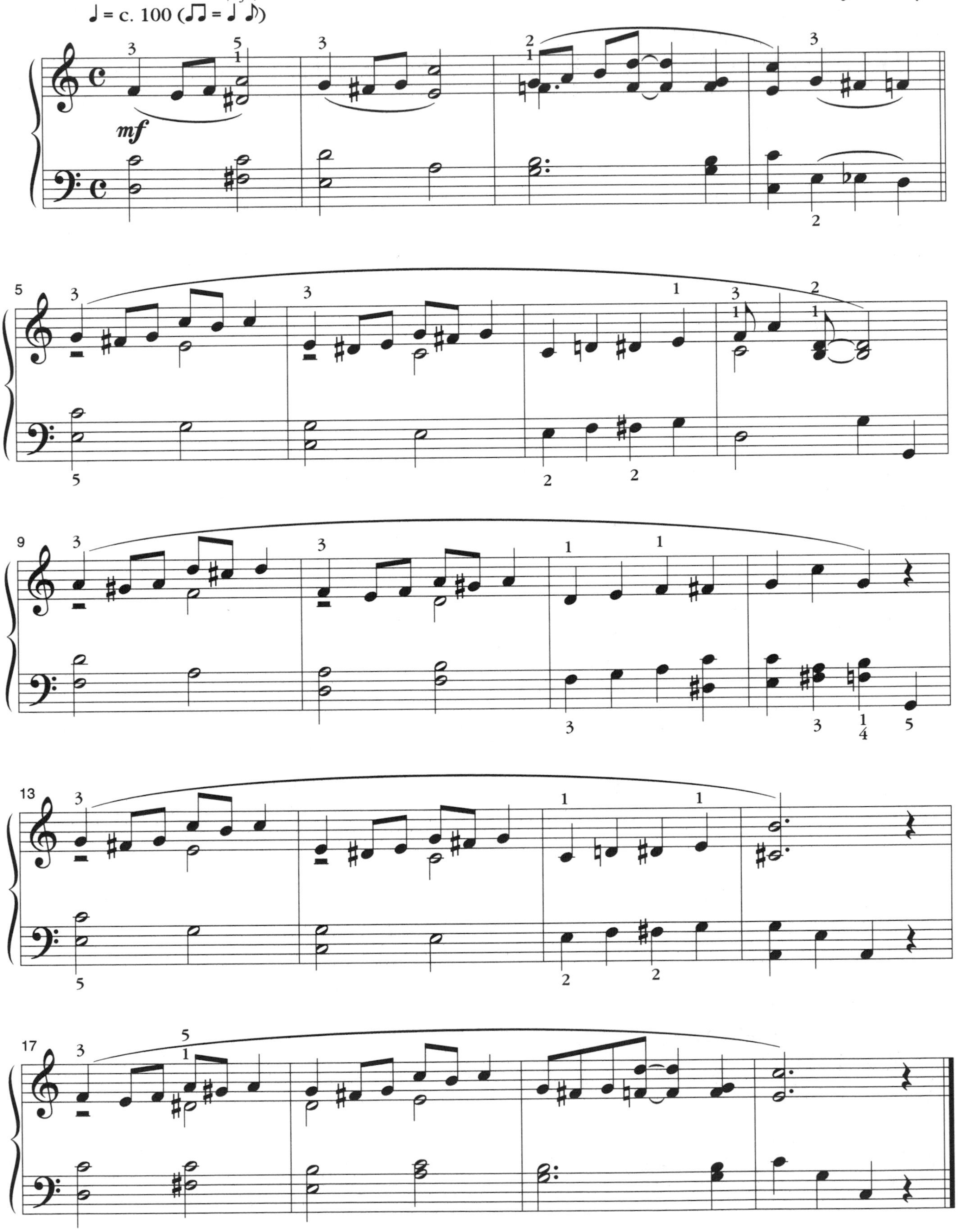

STOP, STOP, STOP

music by **Irving Berlin**
arr. **James Lyke**

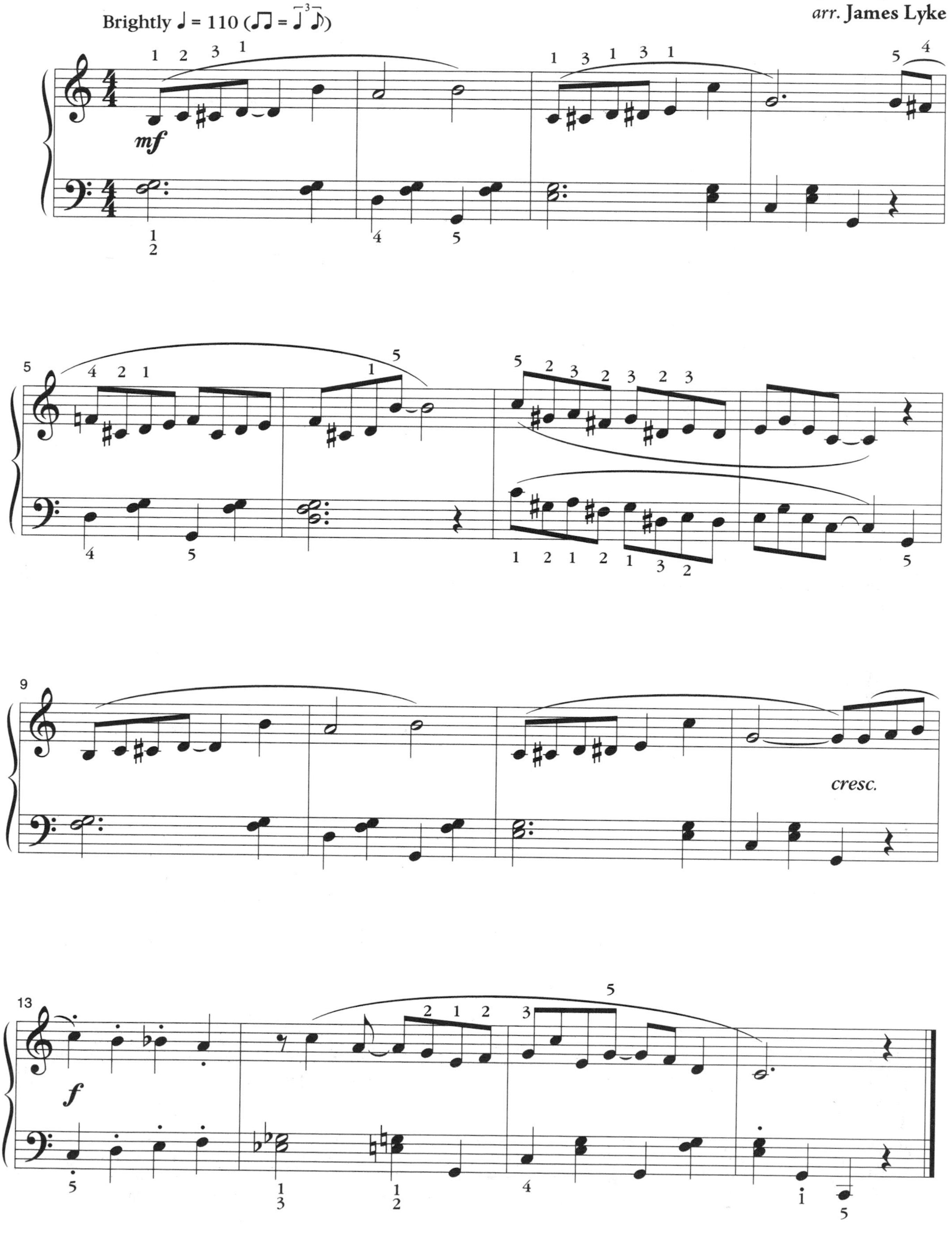

40 CD

EV'RY NIGHT WHEN THE SUN GOES DOWN

Secondo – Teacher or Student

U.S. Spiritual
arr. James Lyke

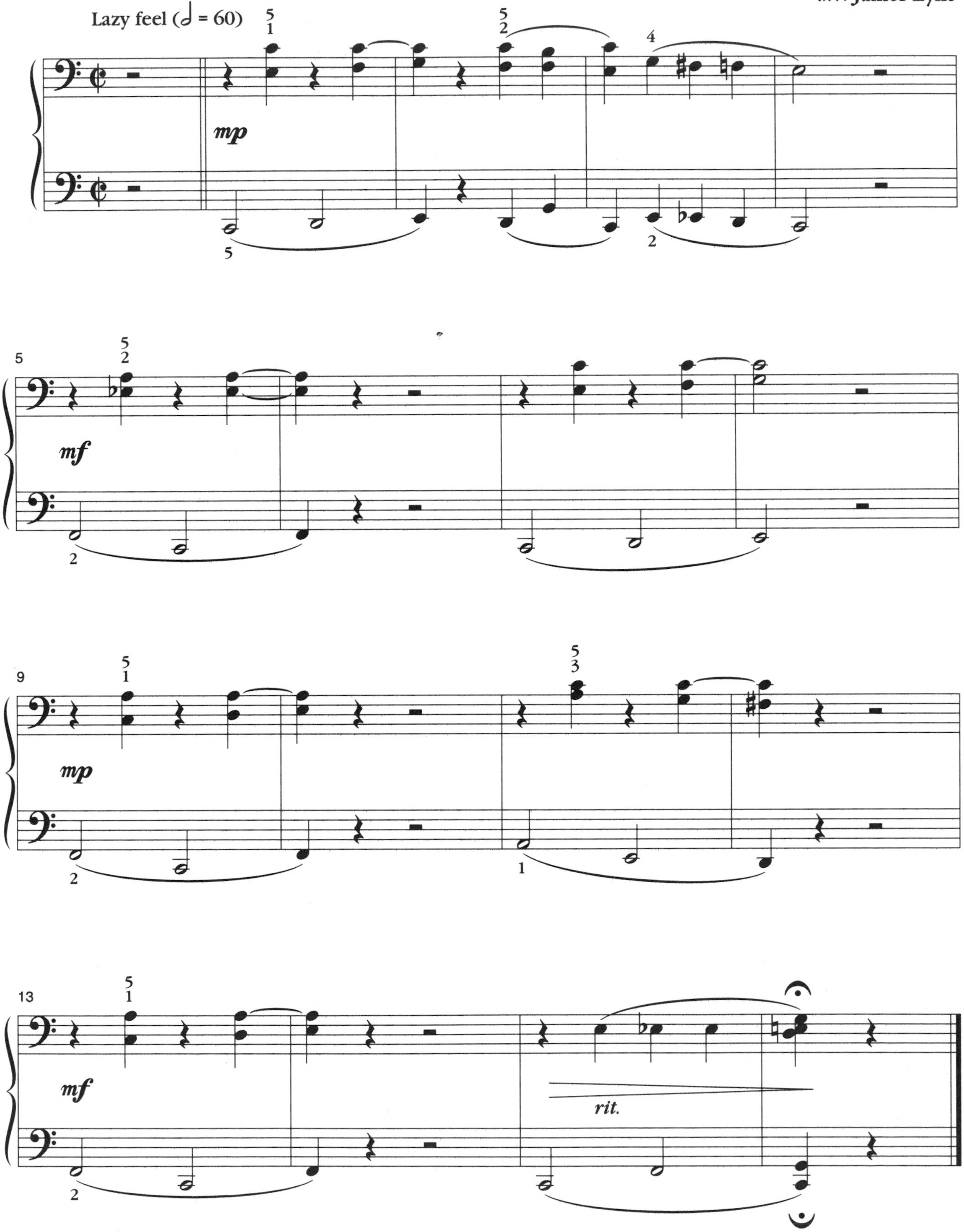

EV'RY NIGHT WHEN THE SUN GOES DOWN

Primo – Teacher or Student

U.S. Spiritual
arr. **James Lyke**

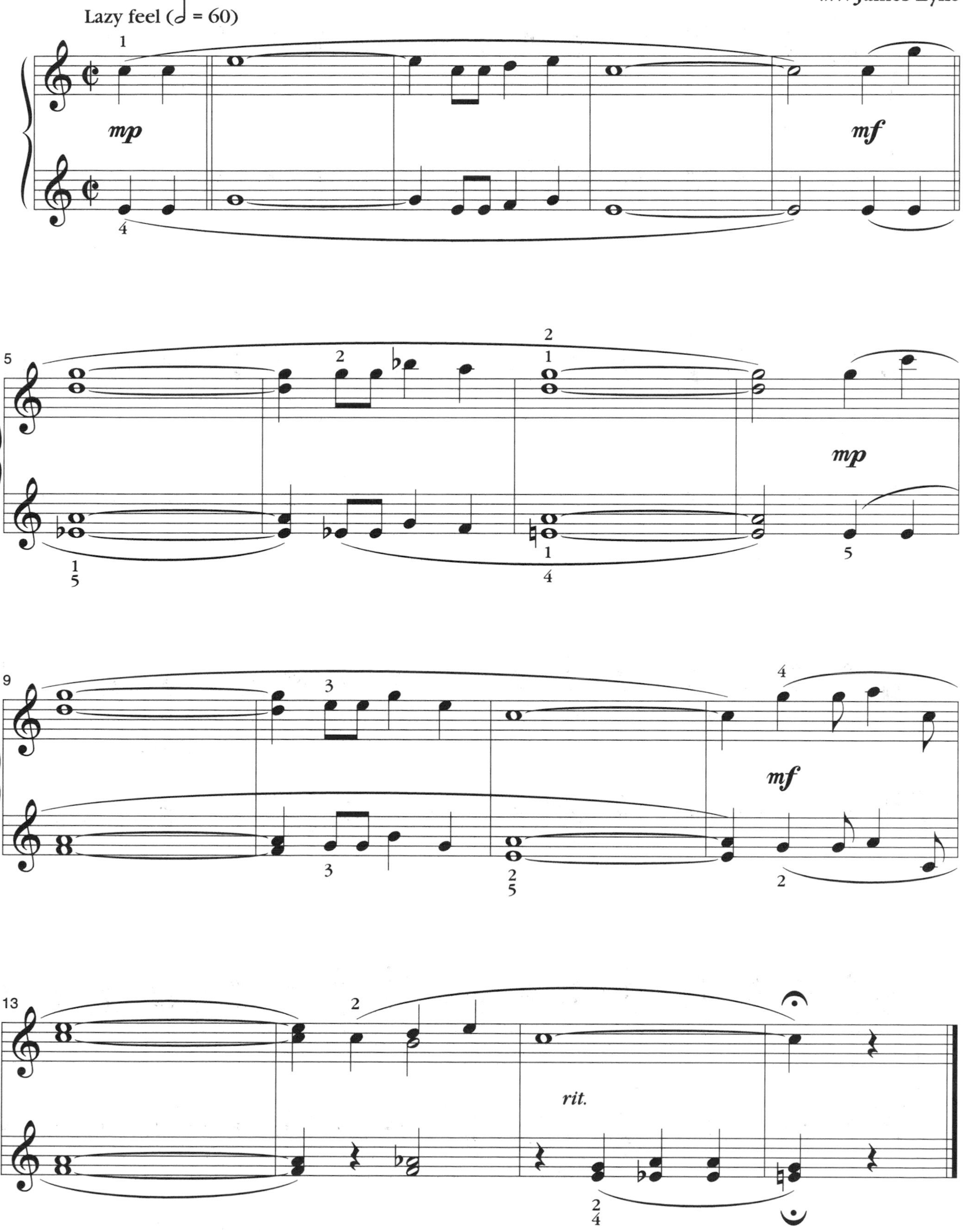

41 CD

TAP DANCE

(Secondo – Teacher)

James Lyke

Rhythmically 𝅗𝅥 = 92 (♩♪ = ♩♪)

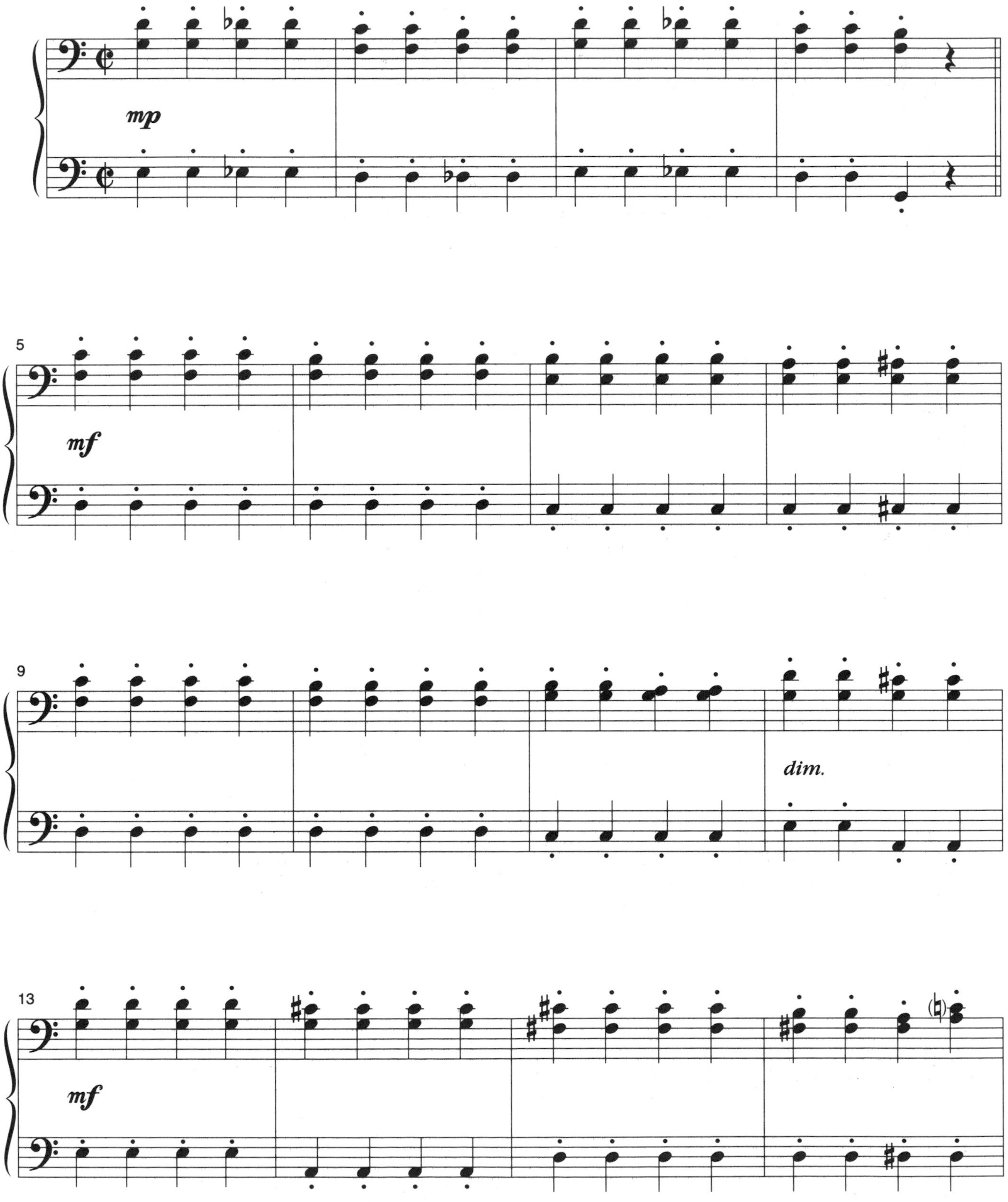

41 CD

TAP DANCE

Primo – Student

James Lyke

Rhythmically 𝅗𝅥 = 92 (♩♪ = ♩♪)

Secondo

Primo

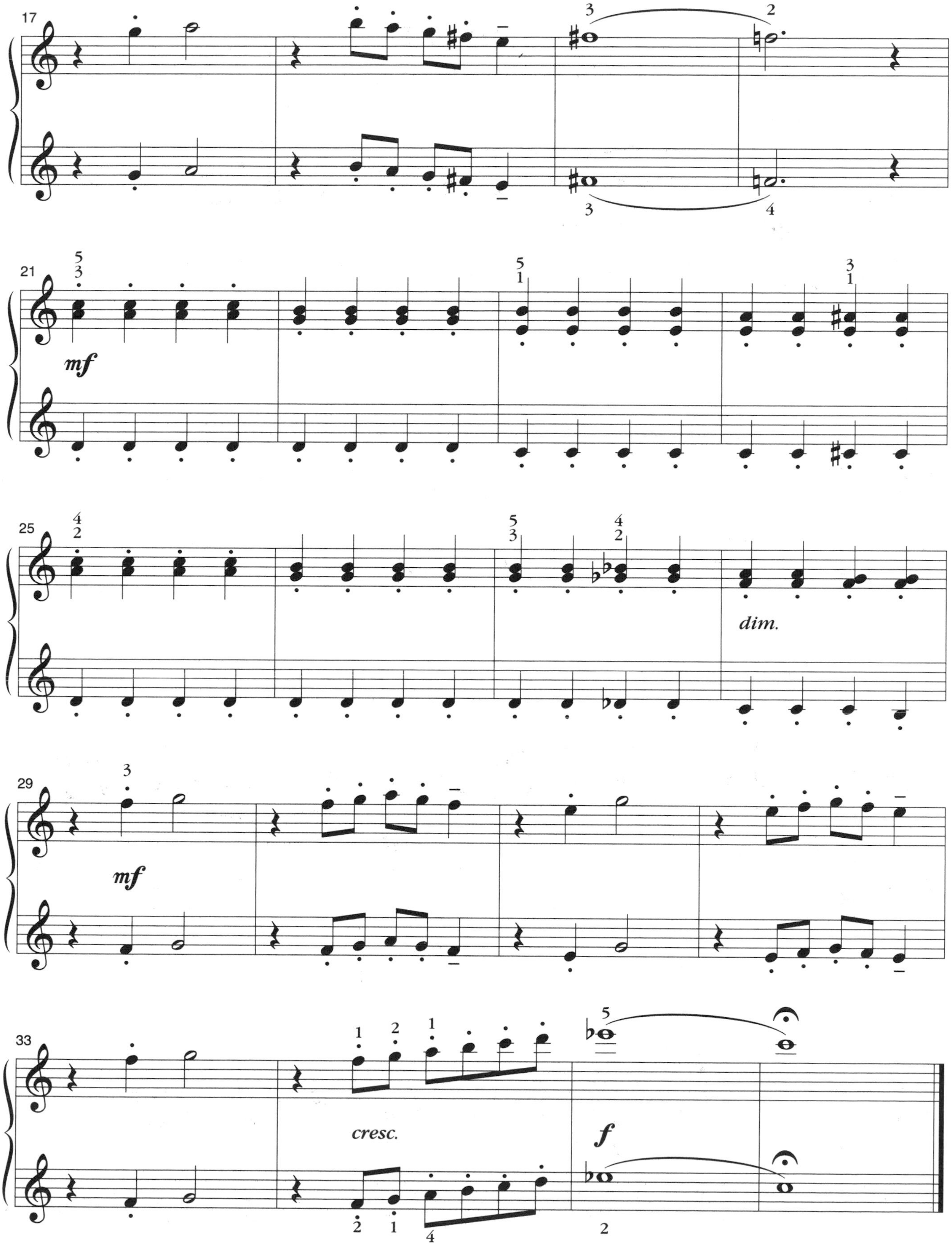

SOLO REPERTOIRE

Practice Plan: Strive for evenness of sound and touch when performing the triplet figure in measures 2, 4, 9, and 11. Pay special attention to two-note phrases, staccato notes, and legato phrases.

MINUET

George Phillip Telemann

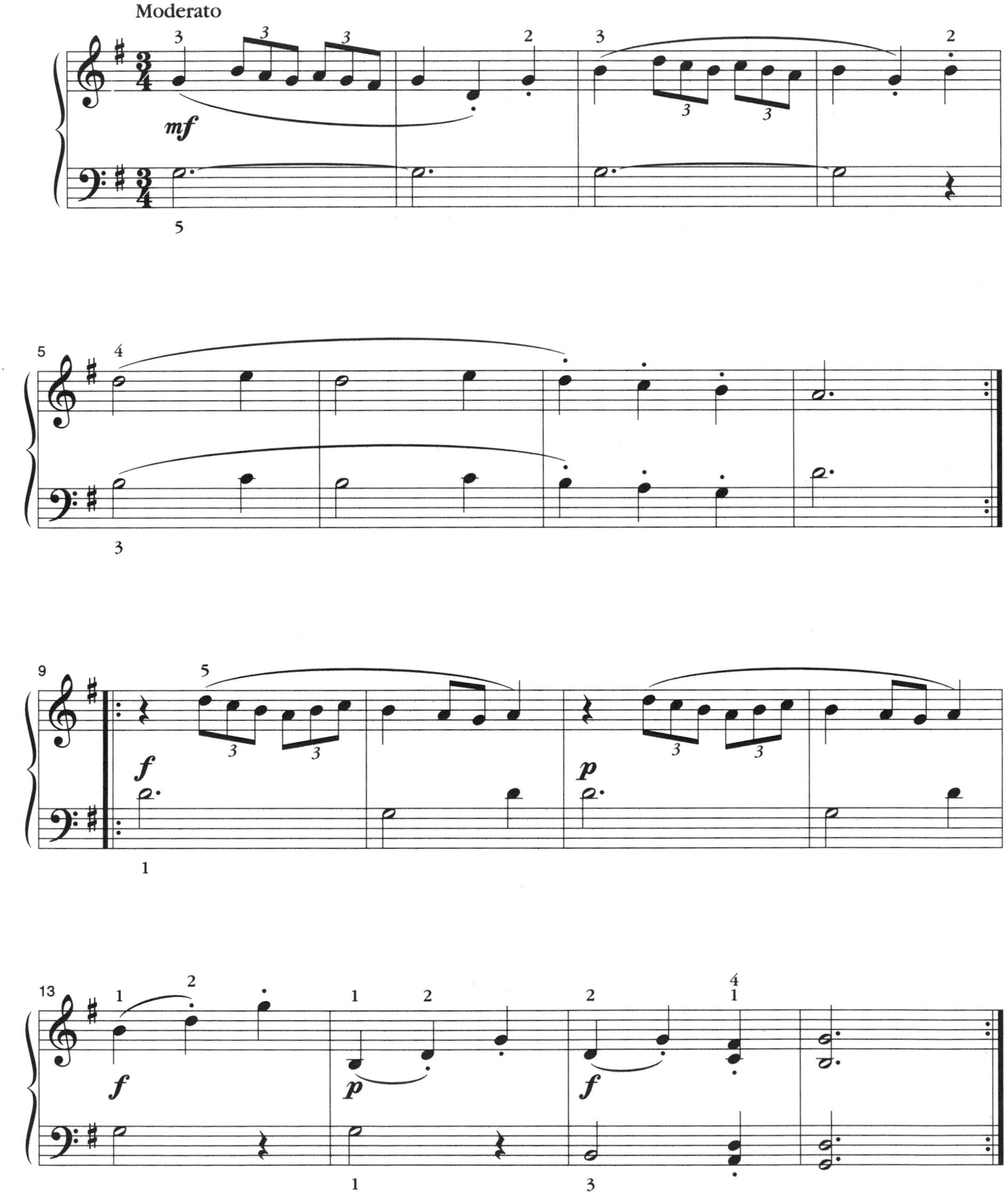

Fundamental Theory Patterns by Dr. Feezell

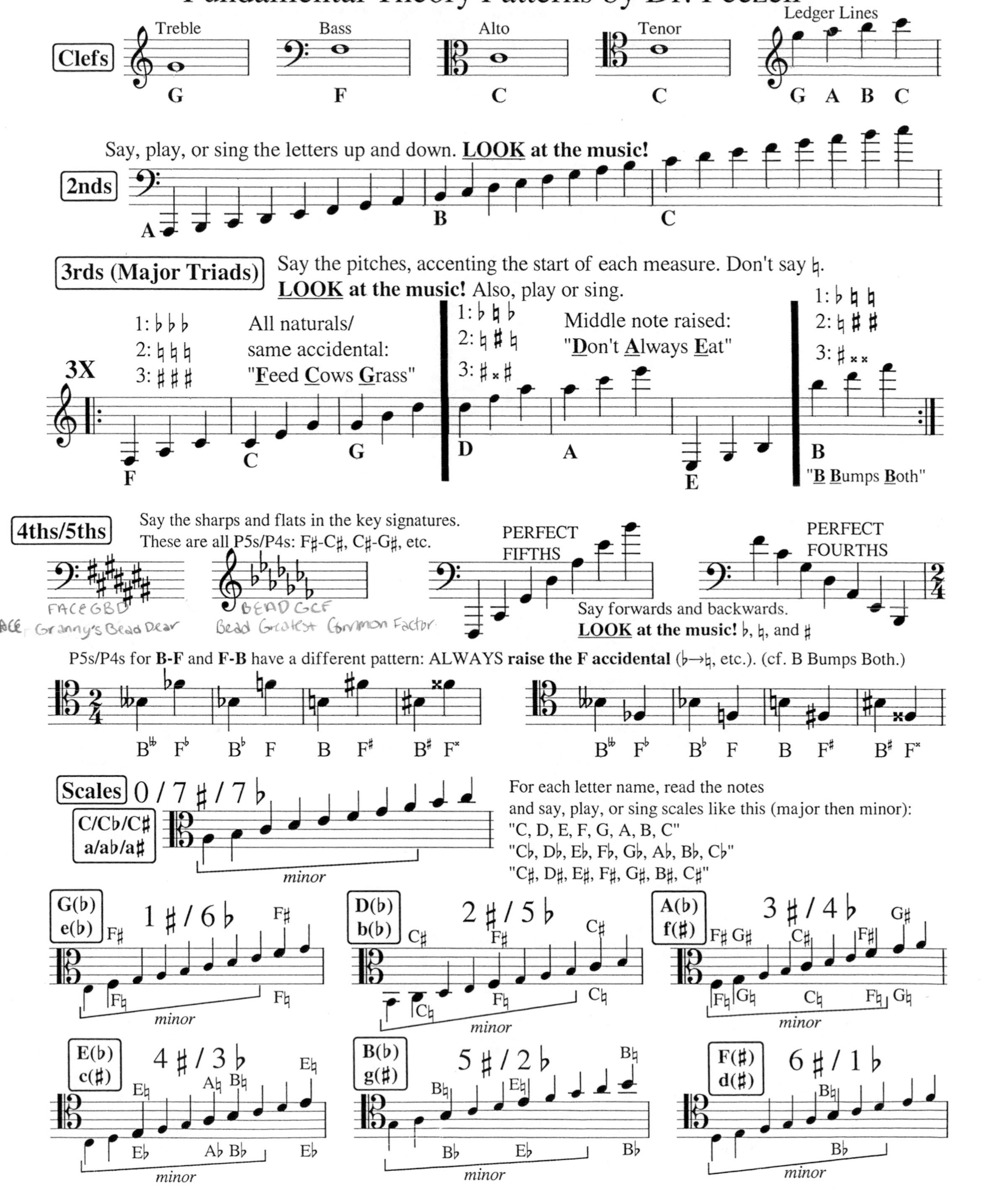

C/C#   Cmajor 0 sharps + C# major 7 = 7 accidentals

F/F#   Fmajor 1 flat + F# major 6 sharps = 7 accidentals

* always 7 total *

Practice Plan: Practice hands separately beginning with the LH. Pay attention to touch, fingering, and shifts of position. Be satisfied with slow work. Drill difficult spots when hands are put together.

GERMAN DANCE

Franz Joseph Haydn

Practice Plan: Block chord outlines in the RH and identify inversions. Down-up wrist movements in the RH should receive careful attention.

PRELUDE

Samuel Maykapar

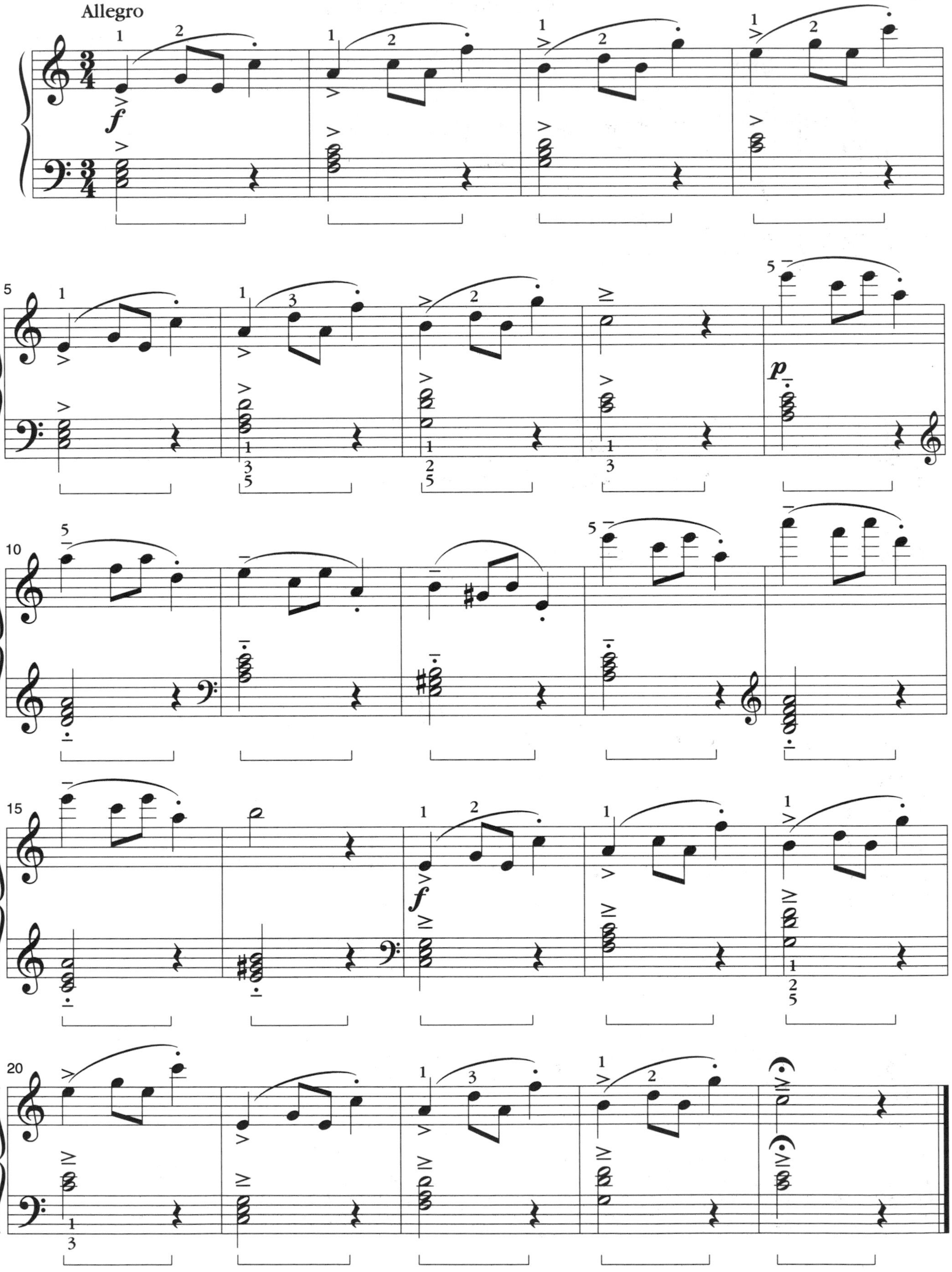

Practice Plan: Block the LH eighth notes creating harmonic intervals on beats 1, 2, 3, and 4 of every measure. Strive to bring the RH melody to the foreground, i.e., cantabile tone.

MELODY

Robert Schumann

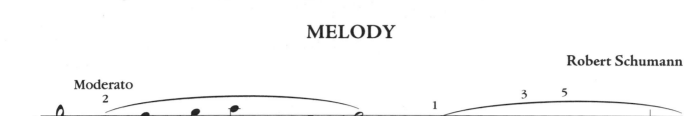

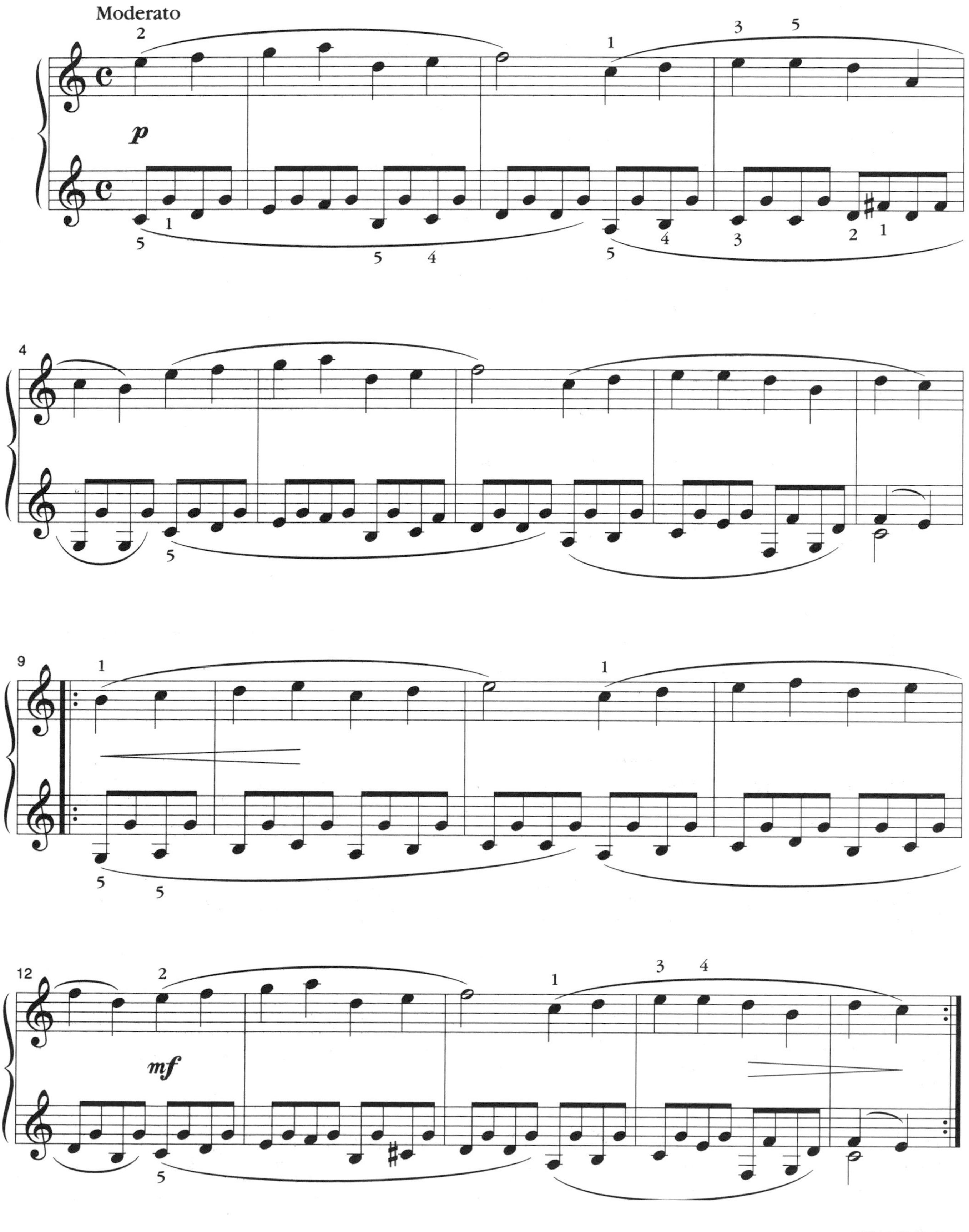

Practice Plan: *The Bear* is based entirely upon the whole-tone scale. Obviously, the LH ostinato figure will not be a problem. The RH (with assistance from the arm) should drop into the keys. Notice the tenuto (–) marks above single notes and thirds. What scale is used throughout in the RH?

THE BEAR

Vladimir Rebikov

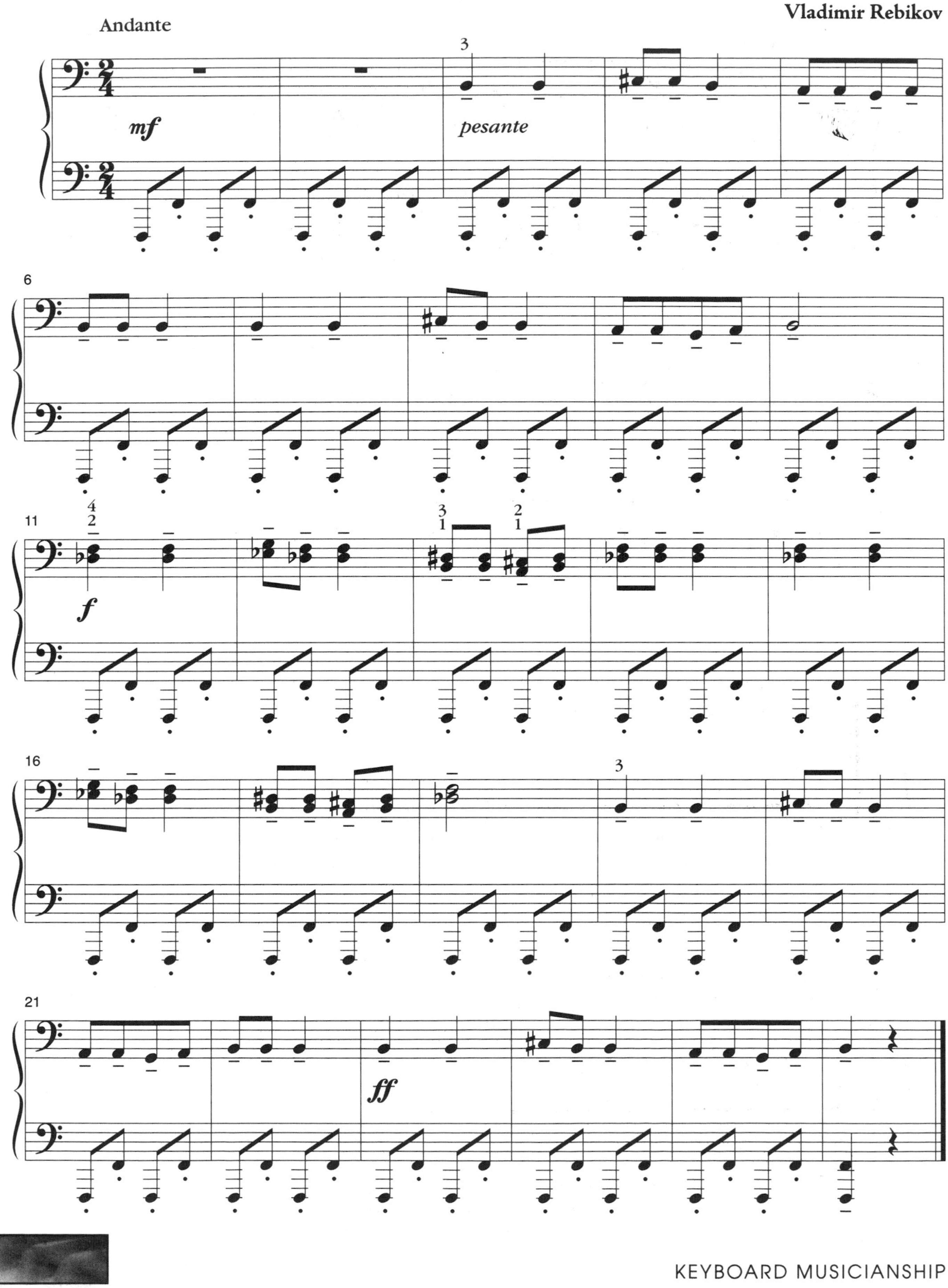

Practice Plan: *Sleepy Time* is composed using the pentatonic scale. Master the LH ostinato pattern at first. Take note of the time signature, $\frac{5}{4}$. The group of 5 beats may be throught of as either 2 + 3 , 3 + 2, or in groups of 5. Listen for a very legato RH.

SLEEPY TIME

Jean Eichelberger Ivey

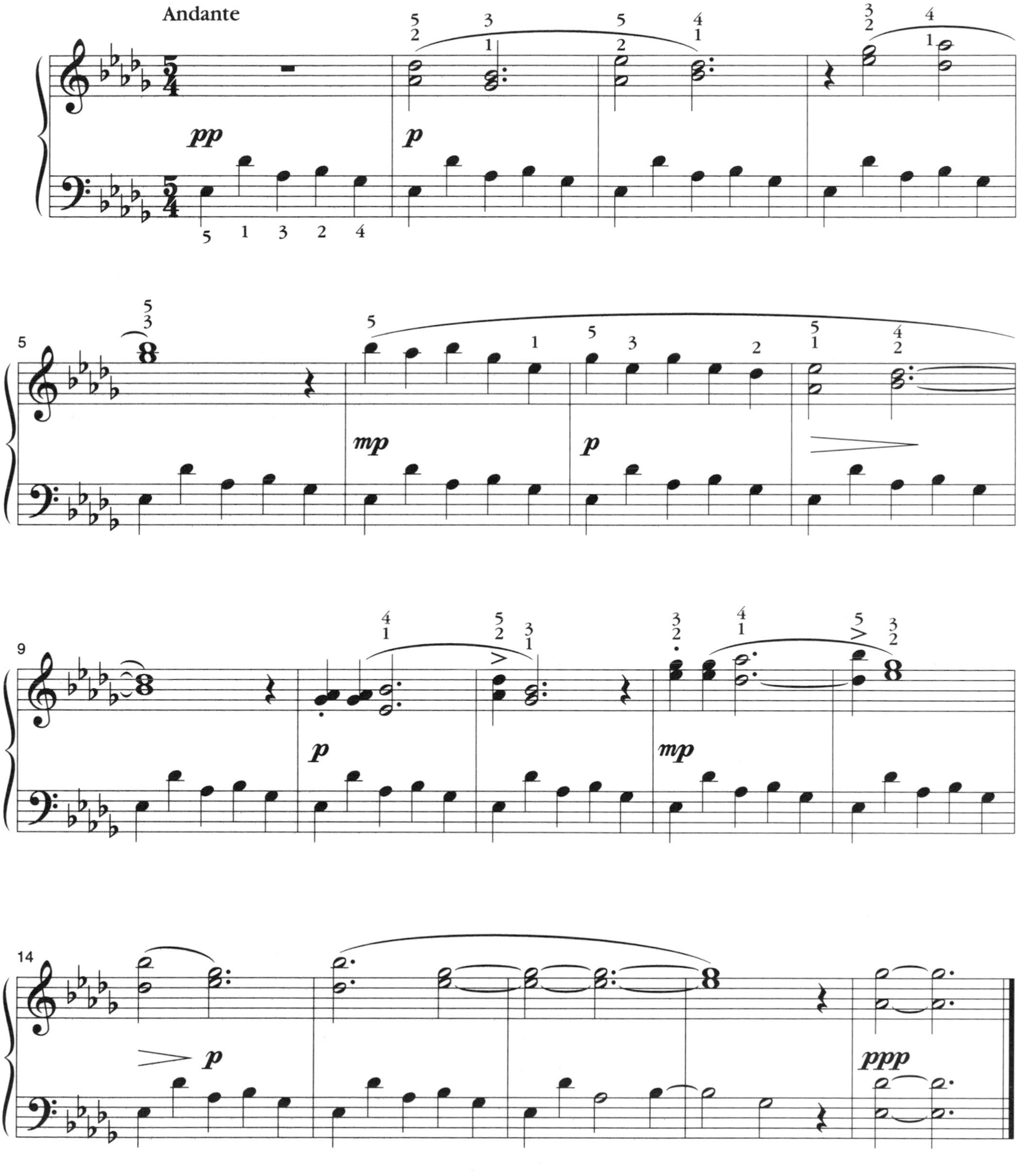

Practice Plan: Follow the fingering suggestions carefully. Take note of the hands together scale that occurs four bars from the end.

CHROMATIC BLUES

Tony Caramia

Not fast (can be swung or played with straight 8ths)

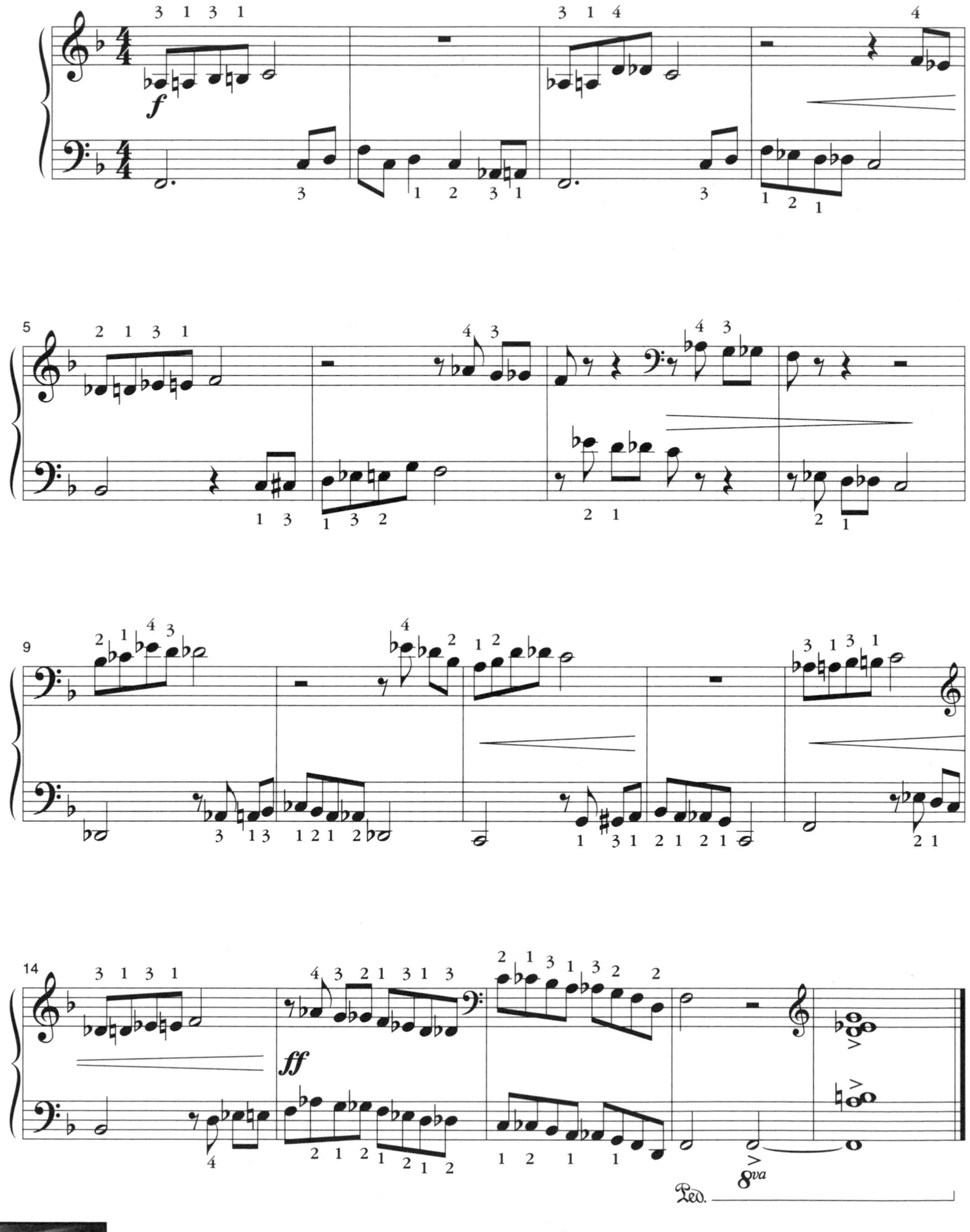

Practice Plan: With the RH follow the figure with your wrist and arm aiming for the long notes. Use the pedal where indicated.

BARCAROLLE

Céline Bussières-Lessard

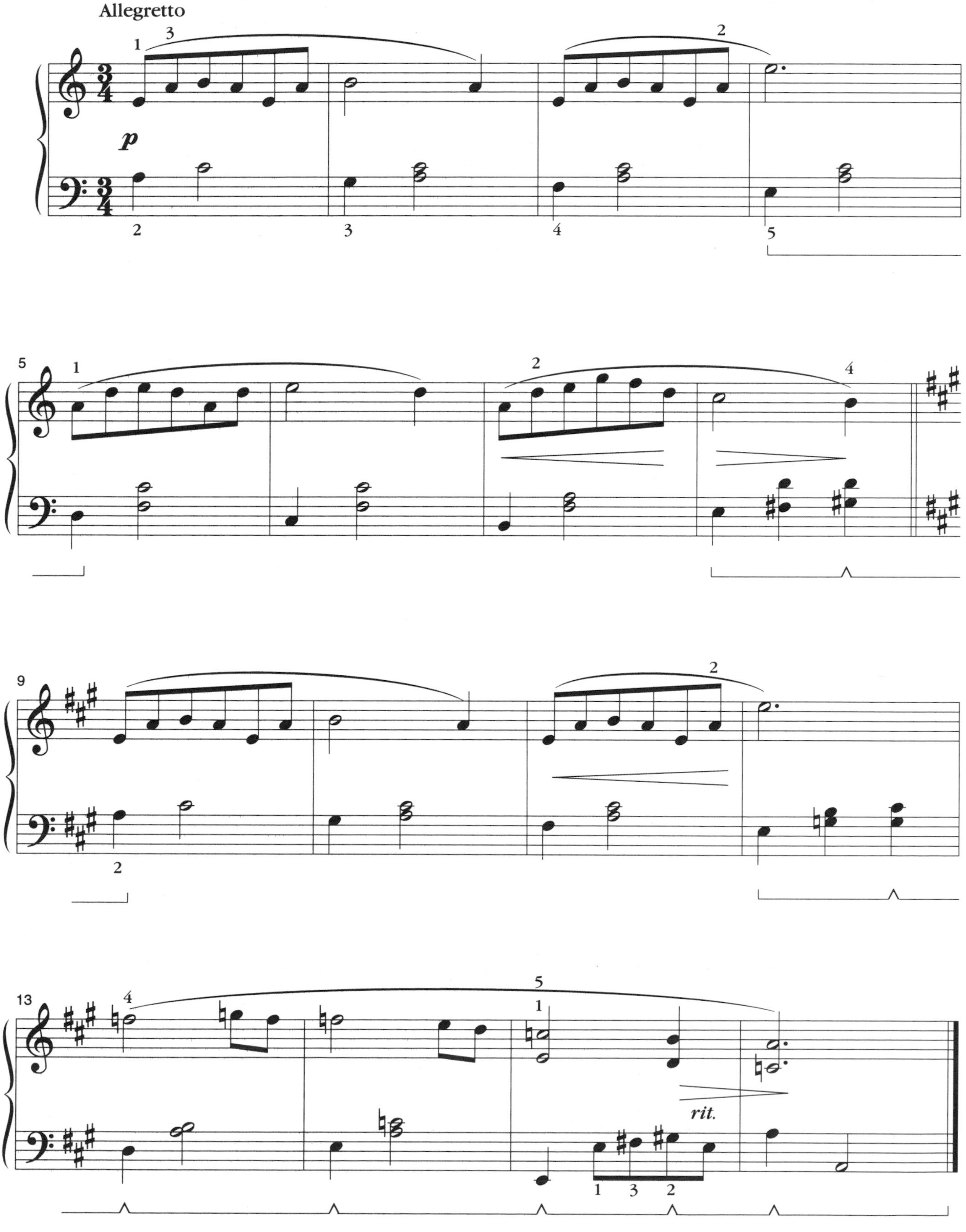

MUSICIANSHIP ACTIVITIES

Complete the following exercises which review various topics introduced in Chapter Six.

Secondary Chord Review

Build supertonic (ii) chords in the following keys. Notate root position and both inversions as shown in the example. Label each chord with Roman numerals (beneath) and letter names with appropriate slashes (above).

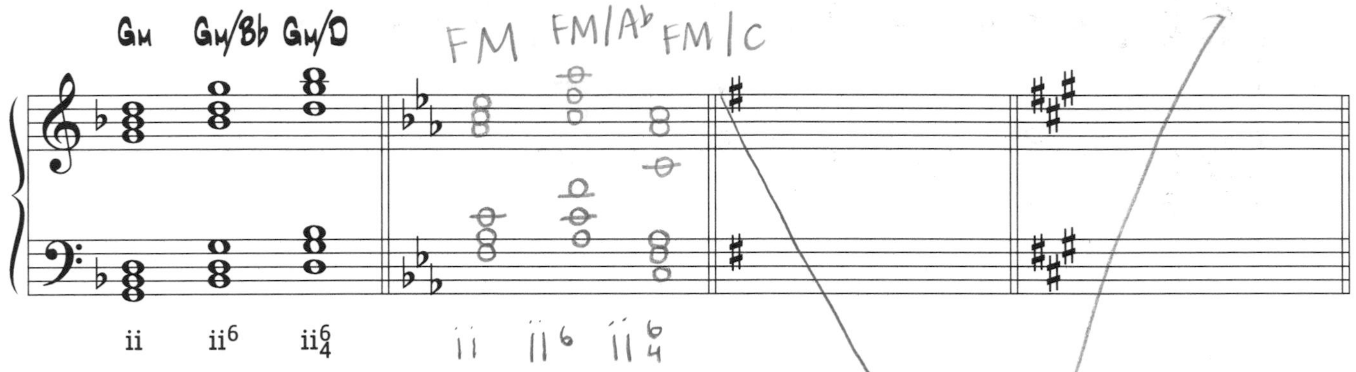

Follow the instructions above and notate submediant (vi) chords.

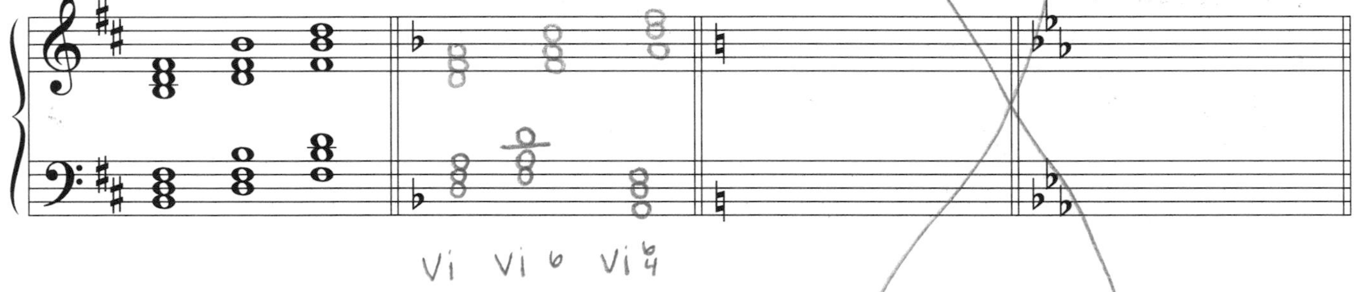

Follow the instructions above and notate mediant (iii) chords.

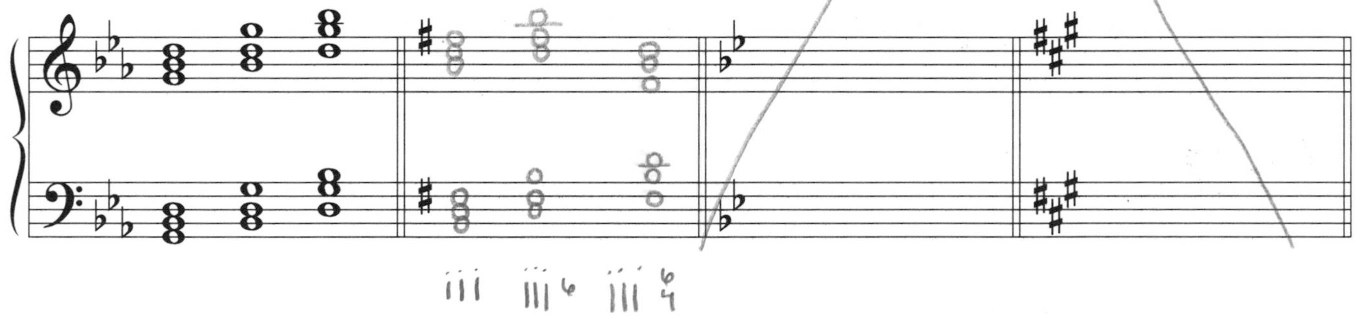

Fill in the RH missing notes for this familiar chord progression. Add letter name symbols.

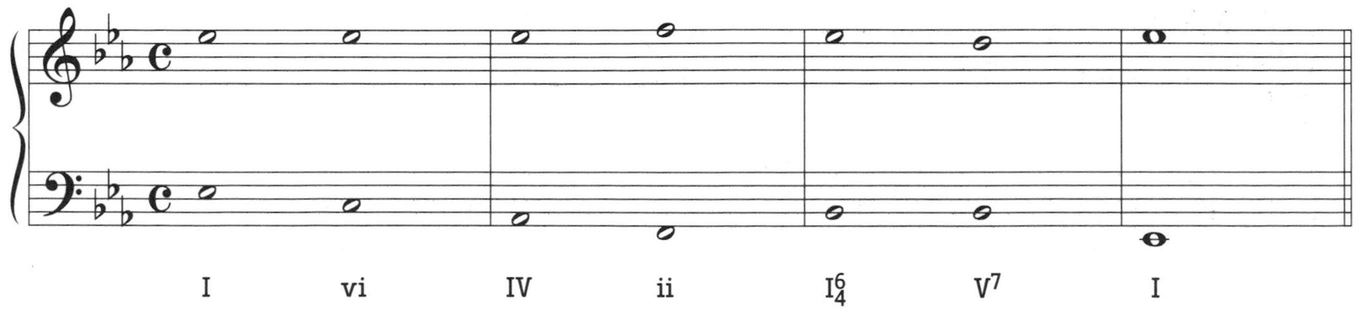

TECHNICAL STUDIES

NEW Major Scales: B♭, E♭, A♭

RH 4th finger is always on Bb, 3rd always on Eb. LH 3-2-1-4-3-2-1 (3). Consult the Scale Fingering Chart on page 168 for scale fingerings.

NEW Major Arpeggios: B♭, E♭, A♭, G♭

Consult Appendix B for a thorough presentation of all scales AND arpeggios.

Slowly practice scales and arpeggios hands together, two octaves.

Improvising

Using the beginnings of the following examples, expand each utilizing four-bar phrases. Maintain rhythmic unity and make use of melodic sequences.

White key pentatonic, LH ostinato

1.

Whole tone, LH ostinato

2.

Blues scale LH bass pattern

Expand to 12 measures using the normal progression (see page 233).

3.

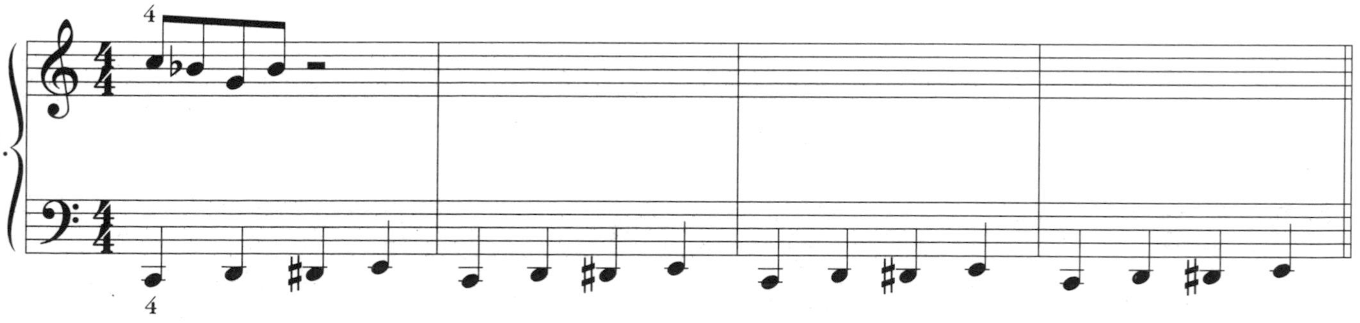

Chromatic Scale Exercise

The complete chromatic scale divides the octave into twelve half steps. Notice that by starting a third apart, and playing in contrary motion, the fingerings become mirrored and are, therefore, the same in each hand.

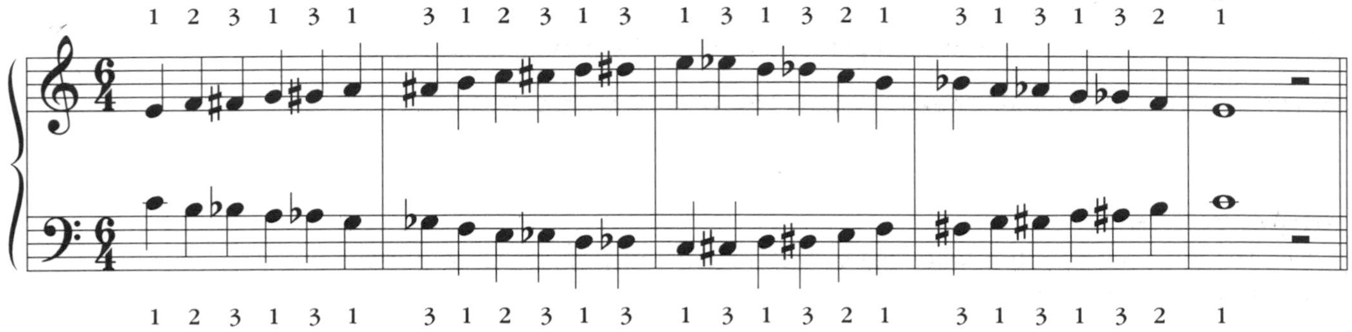

Triad Exercise

Practice the following exercise until all adjustments (maj to whole tone, whole tone to maj, etc.) are mastered. Transpose this exercise to all white major keys.

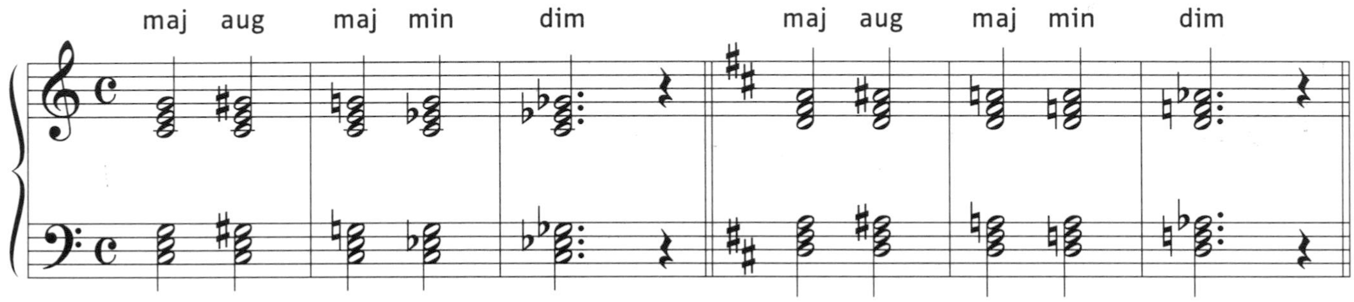

Five-Finger Exercise

Practice the following five-finger exercise until all adjustments to the various qualities (maj, min, aug, and dim) become automatic. Transpose this exercise to all the white major keys, e.g., D, E, F, etc.

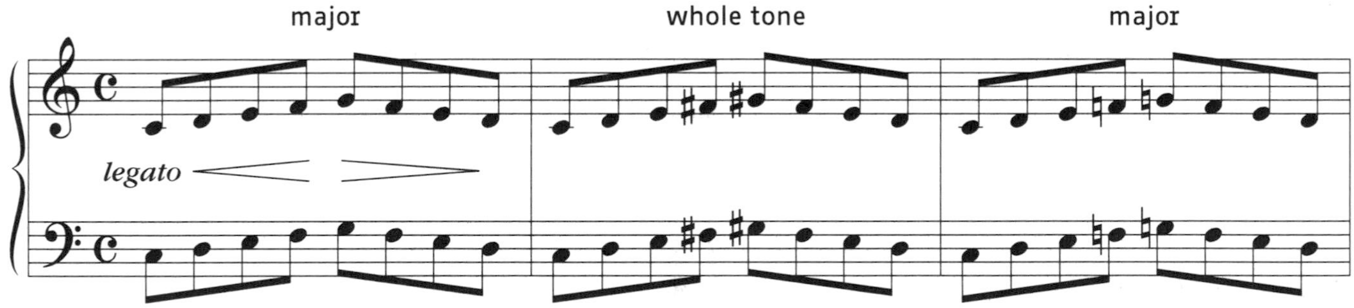

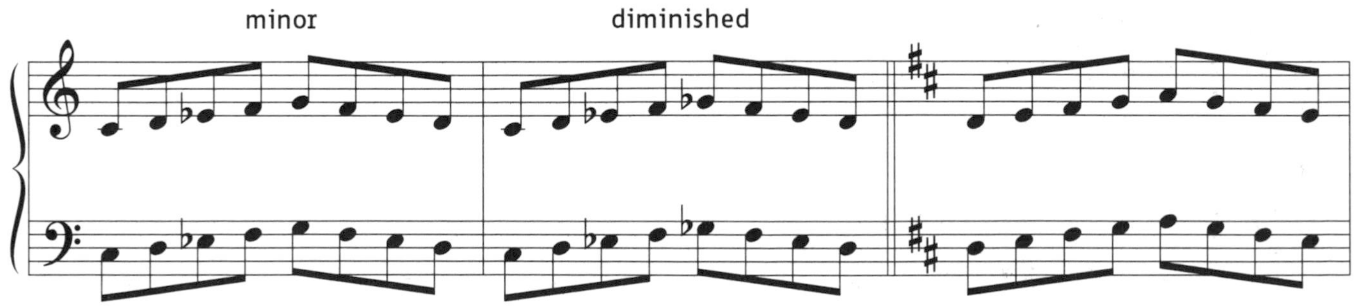

continue

The following *12 Bar Chromatic Blues* combines the 12-bar blues pattern and the chromatic scale. Practice hands separately, then combine. Special attention should be given to the RH chromatic scale fingering.

12 BAR CHROMATIC BLUES

James Lyke

SUGGESTED PLAYING EXAM TOPICS
CHAPTER SIX

1. Play the following chord progressions in keys suggested by your instructor:
   a) I–vi–IV–ii–I^6_4–V^7–I
   b) I–vi–ii^7–V^7–I
   (See page 218 to review these progressions.)

2. Play one of the harmonization melodies on pages 222–223 with chords in the RH and single bass tones in the LH.

3. Play one of the accompanying examples on pages 236–237.

4. Play all of the following scales:
   a) pentatonic (page 228)
   b) whole tone (page 228)
   c) chromatic (page 228)
   d) blues (page 229)

5. Play one arrangement from the American Song Repertoire section (pages 238–241).

6. Perform one piece from the Ensemble Repertoire section (pages 242–247).

7. Perform one (or two) pieces from the Solo Repertoire Section (pages 248–255).

8. Improvise a short piece using any of the three examples found on page 257.

7 chapter

Secondary Dominants, Minor Scale Review, Chord Progressions in Minor, Harmonization, Repertoire, Musicianship Activities, and Technical Studies

Study the D^7 chords in bars 2 and 6. This chord is not in the key of C, but embellishes the next chord V^7 (G) which is in the key. The D^7 chord has a root a fourth below or a fifth above G^7. In this key, the D^7 is termed the *dominant of the dominant* (V^7 of V or V^7 of V^7).

THAT'S WHERE MY MONEY GOES — American

Secondary Dominants

Any triad may be preceded by its own dominant or secondary dominant. These chromatic chords add color and enrich the harmony. The most common secondary dominant is $V^{(7)}$ of $V^{(7)}$. Study scale degree triads embellished by their respective dominants. The dominants are built a fourth below the root of each triad.

Chord Pattern: I–IV–V^7/V^7–V^7–I

Practice the familiar I-IV-V^7 chords with the added V^7 of V^7. Transpose to F, G and a few other keys.

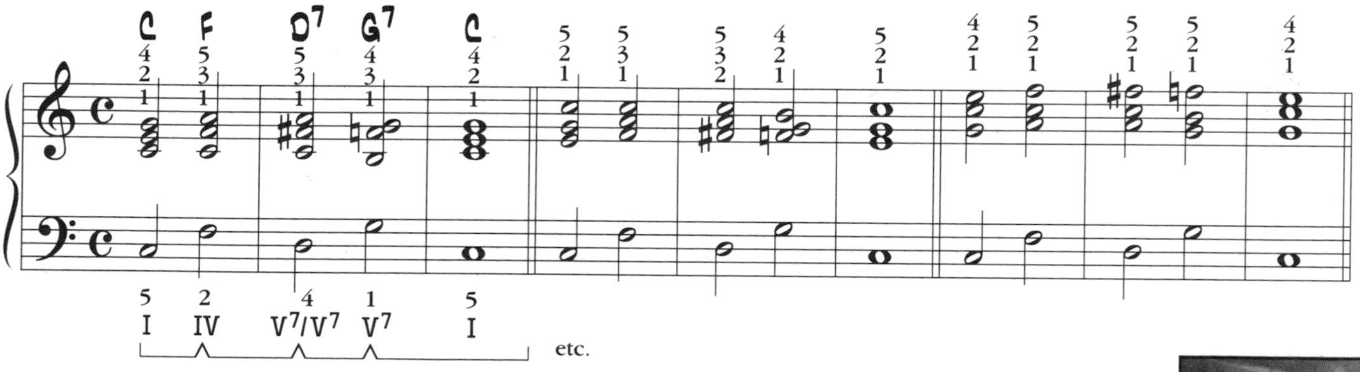

Building the Dominant of the Dominant

In any key, there is an easy way to figure out the dominant of the dominant. When LH finger 4 plays the second scale degree, mentally build a dominant seventh chord on that tone. Then rearrange the notes in the RH to conform to the spelling of the chord.

Practice with the $V^{(7)}$ of $V^{(7)}$ and Other Secondary Dominants

Study and play the following arrangements of folk songs which contain dominant of the dominant chords and other secondary dominant chords. Analyze each chord with a letter name symbol and Roman numeral.

FLOW GENTLY, SWEET AFTON

Alexander Hume
arr. James Lyke

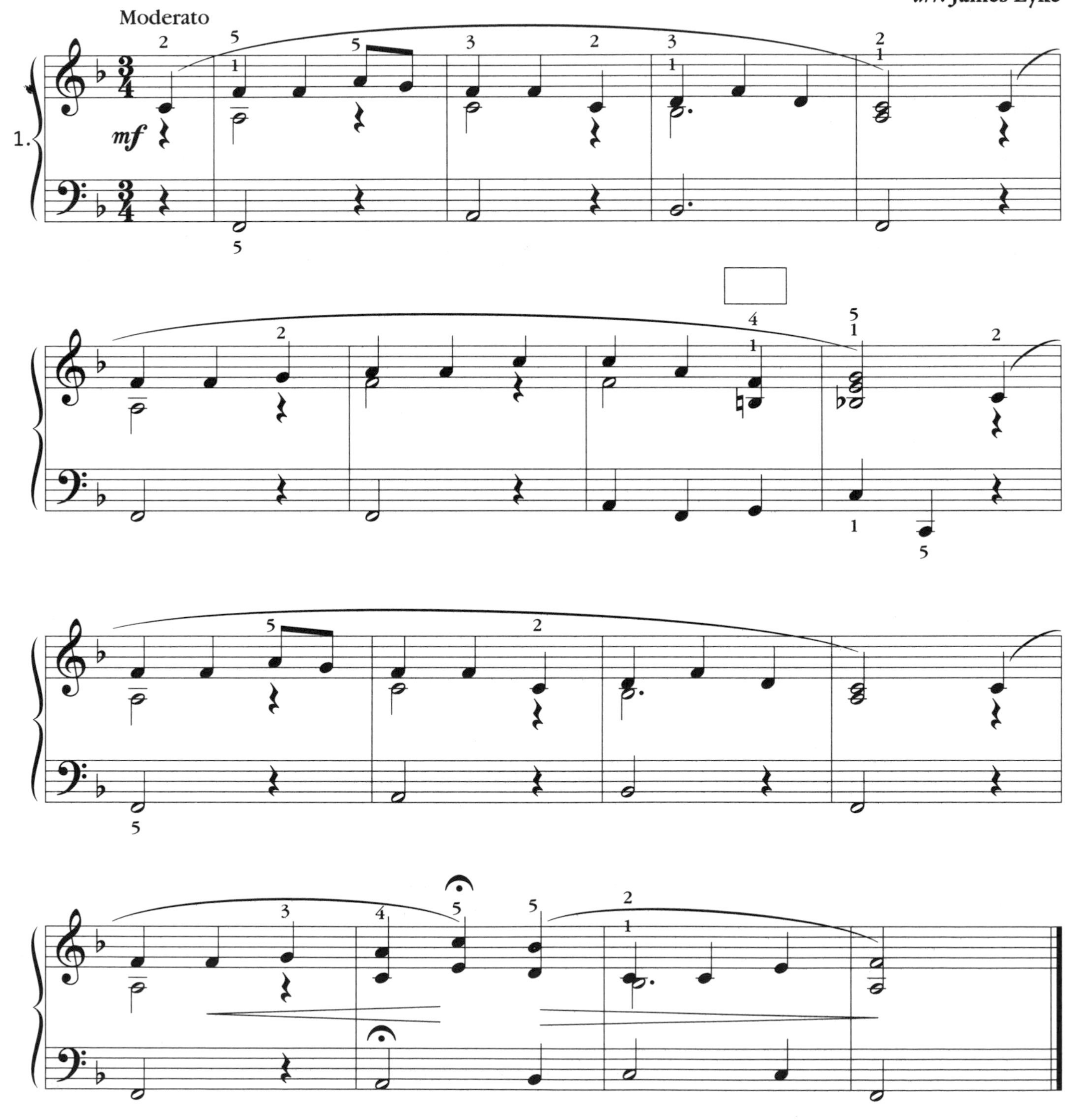

THE FOGGY, FOGGY DEW

British

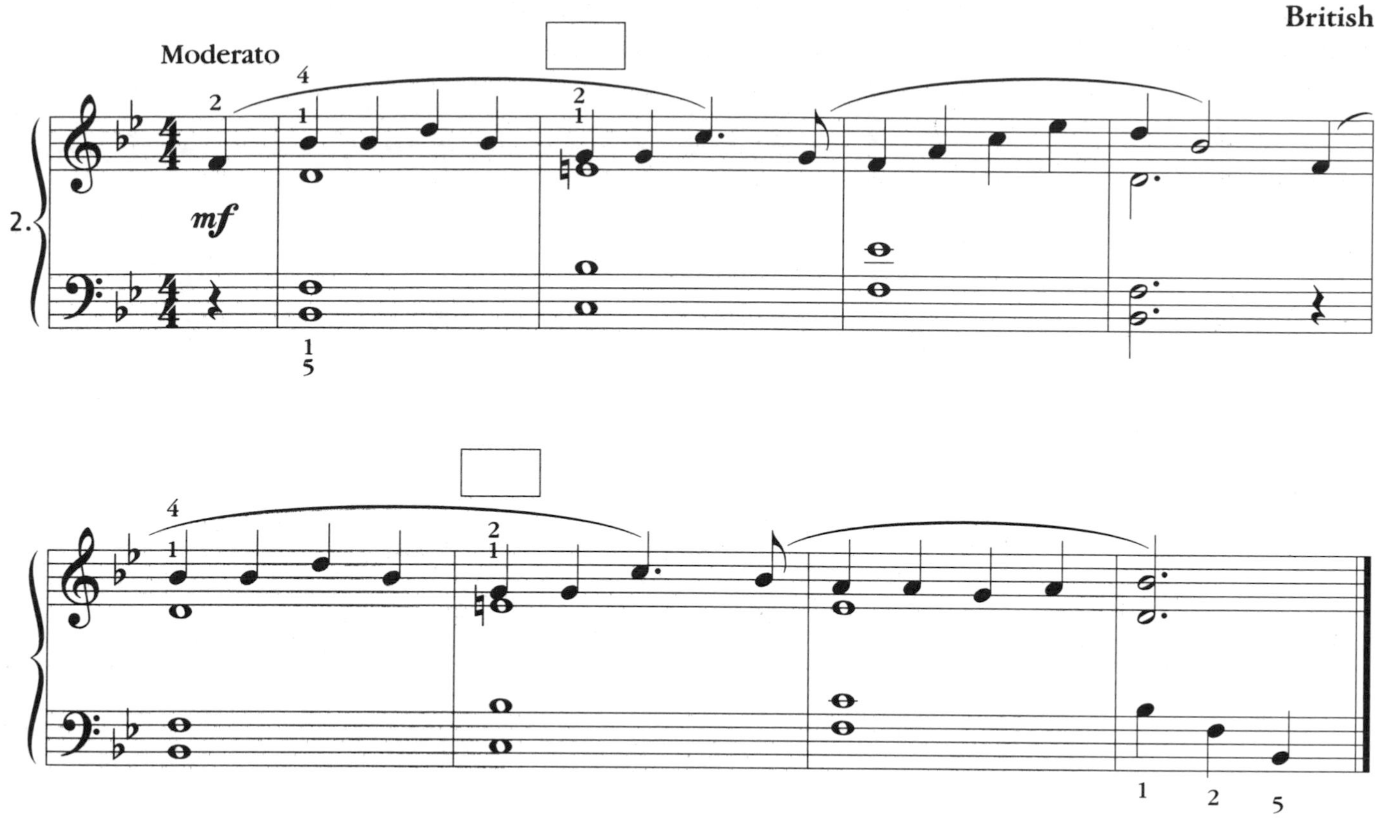

In *Home on the Range* find a V^7 of IV as well as a minor iv "borrowed" from the parallel minor key. (*Parallel* keys share the same keynote.)

HOME ON THE RANGE

(Chorus)

United States

DALMATIAN FOLK SONG

I'M GONNA SING WHEN THE SPIRIT SAYS SING

Spiritual

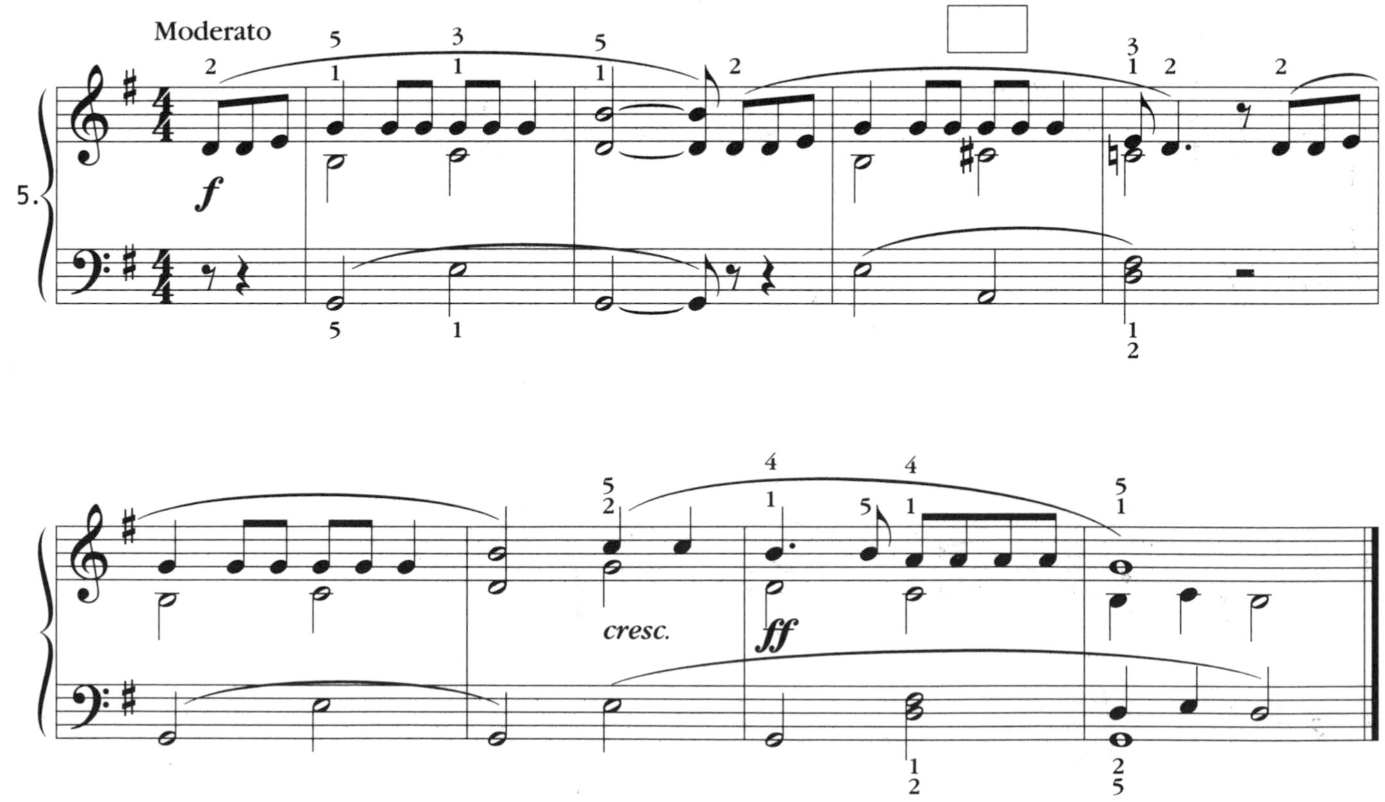

Harmonizing with $V^7/V^{(7)}$ and Other Secondary Dominants

Harmonize the following studies that make use of V^7 of $V^{(7)}$ and other secondary dominants such as V^7 of IV, V^7 of ii, etc. Continue in the suggested style. Notate your harmonization.

ALL THROUGH THE NIGHT

Wales

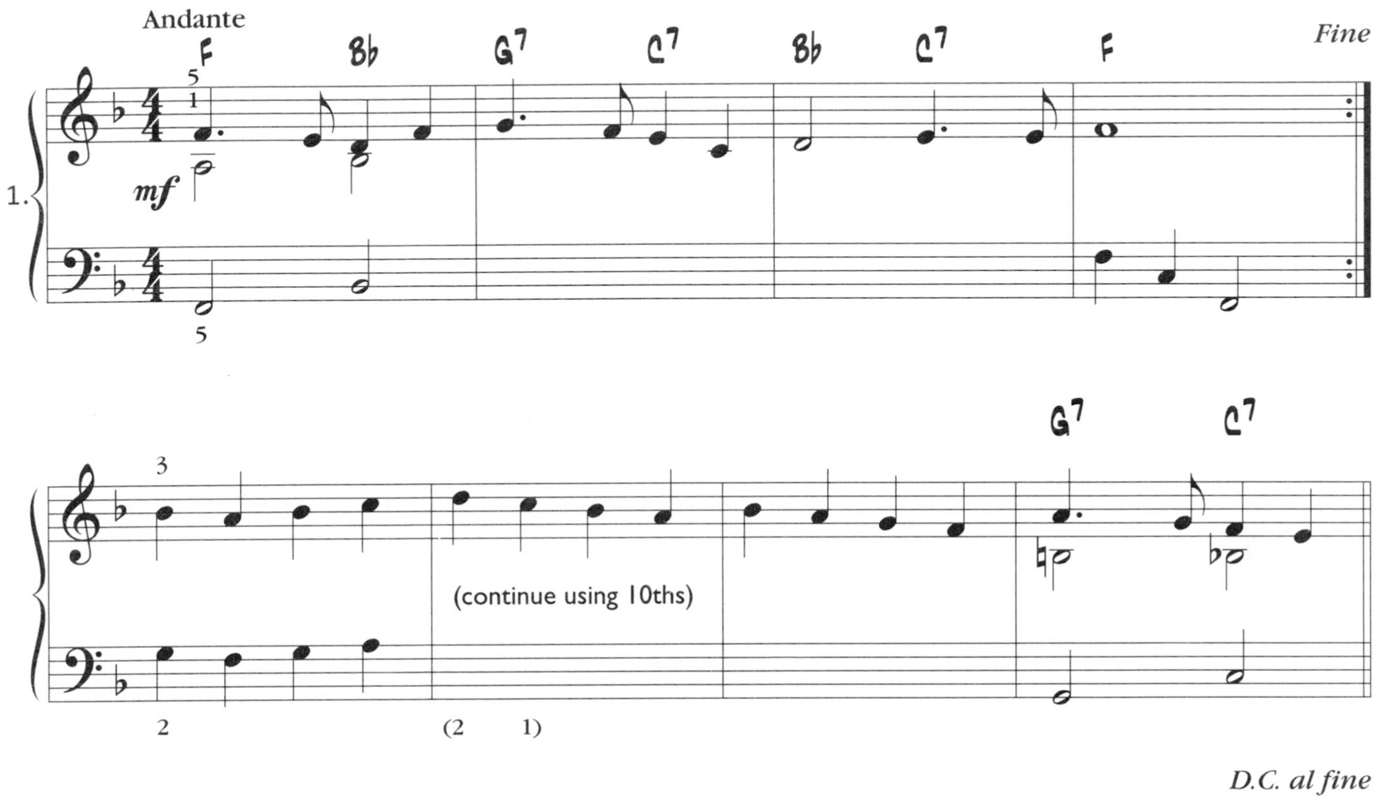

HUNGARIAN FOLK SONG

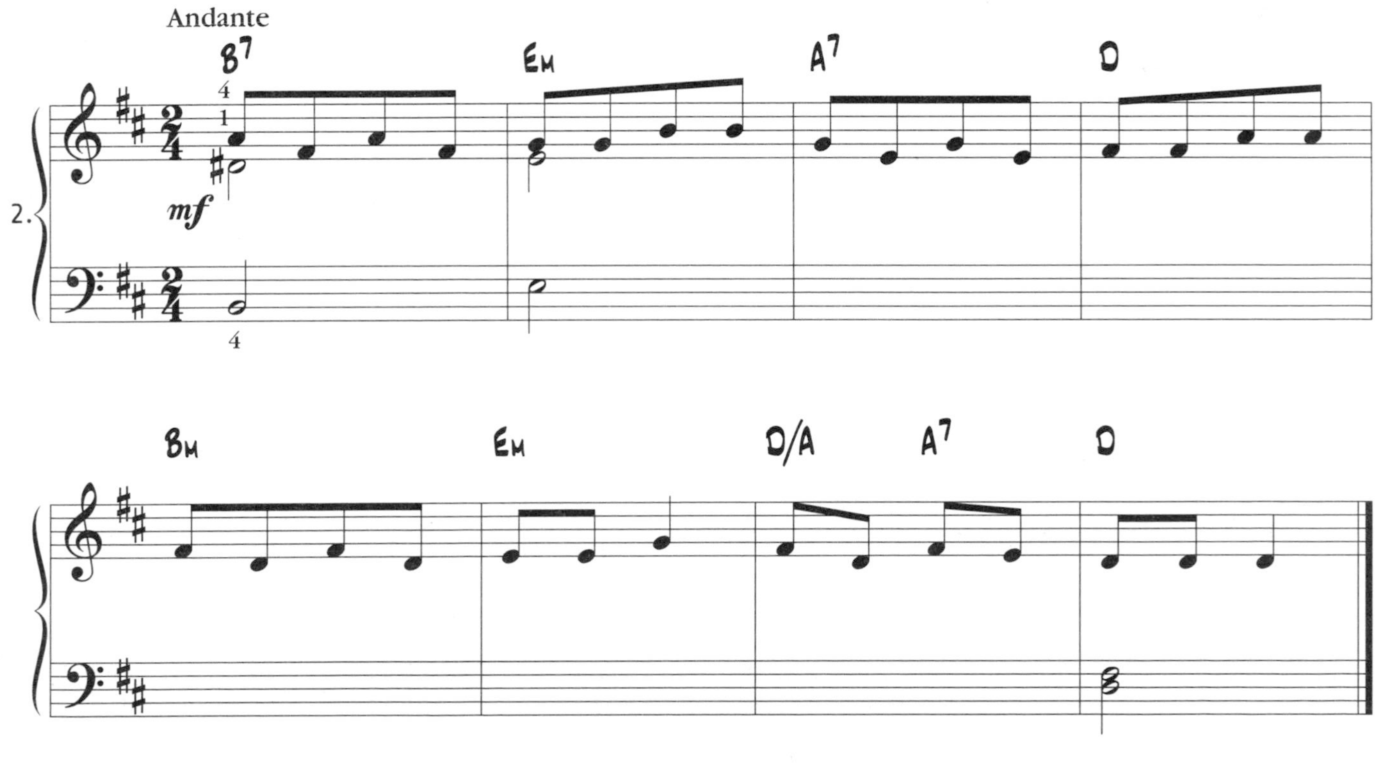

CZECH FOLK SONG

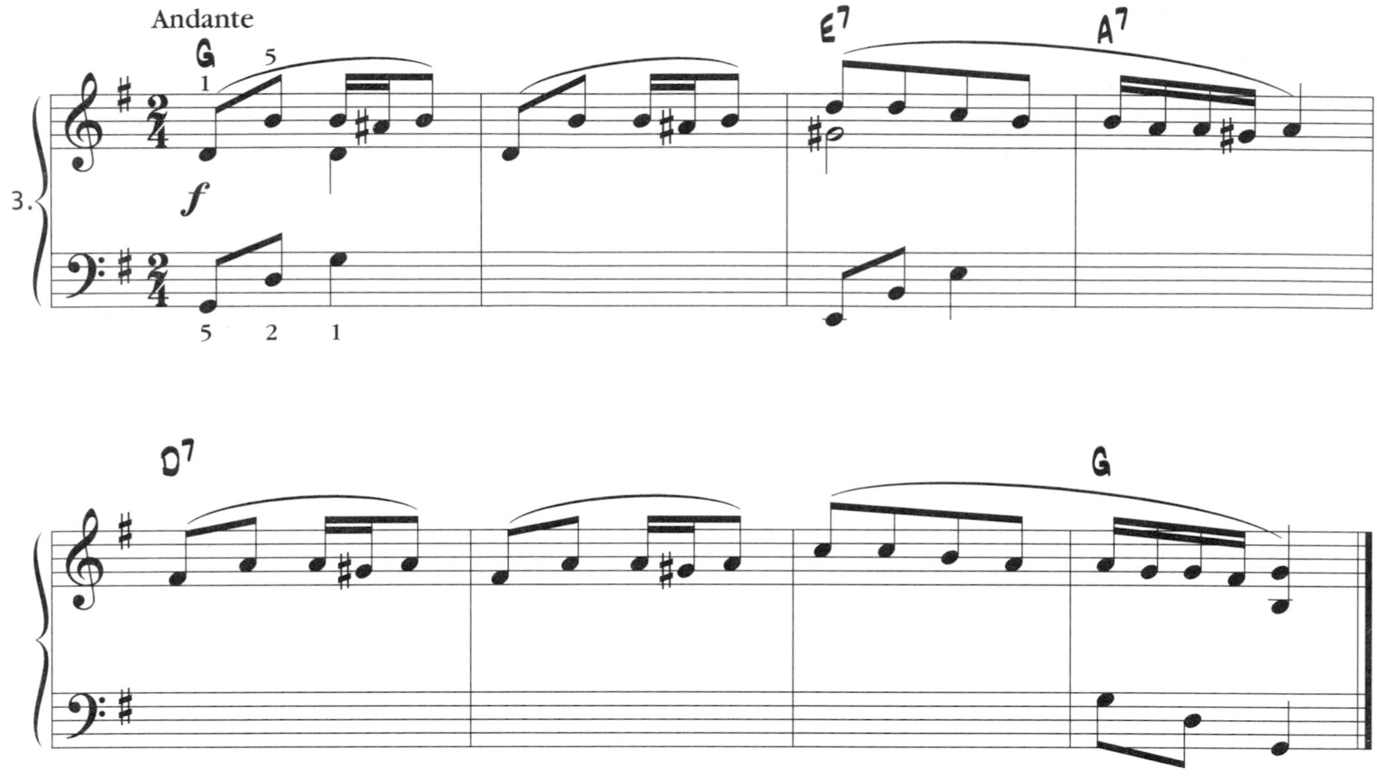

GERMAN FOLK SONG

Minor Scales – A Review

Minor scales have three forms: 1) *natural*, 2) *melodic*, and 3) *harmonic*. Study all three built on A.

A Natural Minor

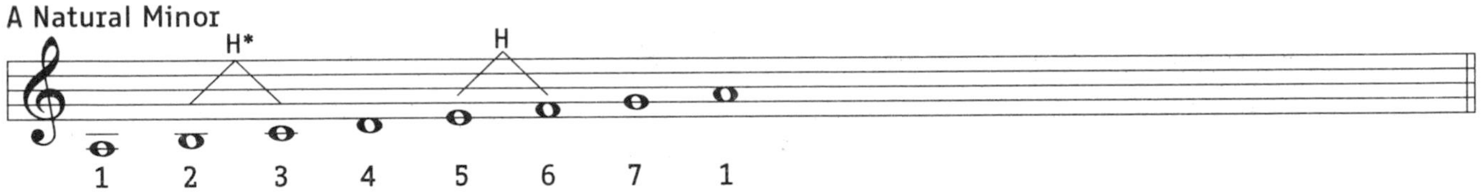

A Melodic Minor

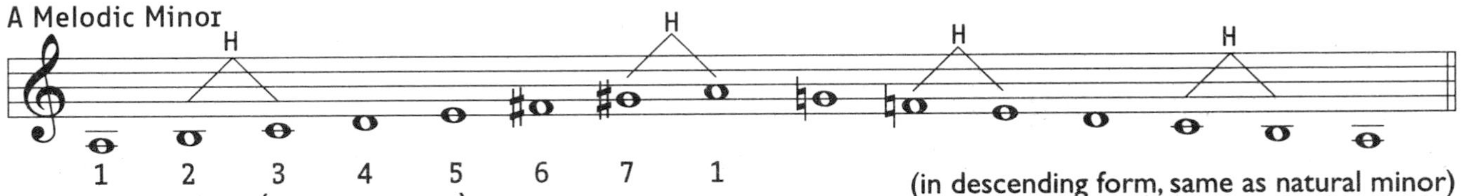

(in descending form, same as natural minor)

A Harmonic Minor (most common)

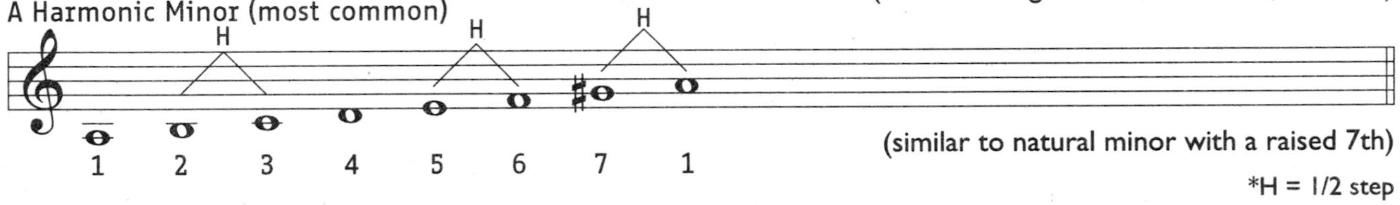

(similar to natural minor with a raised 7th)

*H = 1/2 step

Relative Minor Key Signatures

Minor scales share their key signatures with those of major scales. This key signature may be found by counting up three half steps from the minor keynote. C major is the *relative* major key of A minor. A minor is the *relative* minor of C major. To find the relative minor from the major scale keynote, count down three half steps. Study the whole step/half step arrangement of all three forms of the minor scales.

Parallel Keys and Scales

Keys such as A major and A minor share the same keynote. They are considered *parallel* keys. Play the A major scale that follows. Then play the A harmonic minor scale, contrasting it to the major scale. You will notice that in the harmonic minor scale, the 3rd and 6th degrees are lowered one half step. The 7th is the same as in A major.

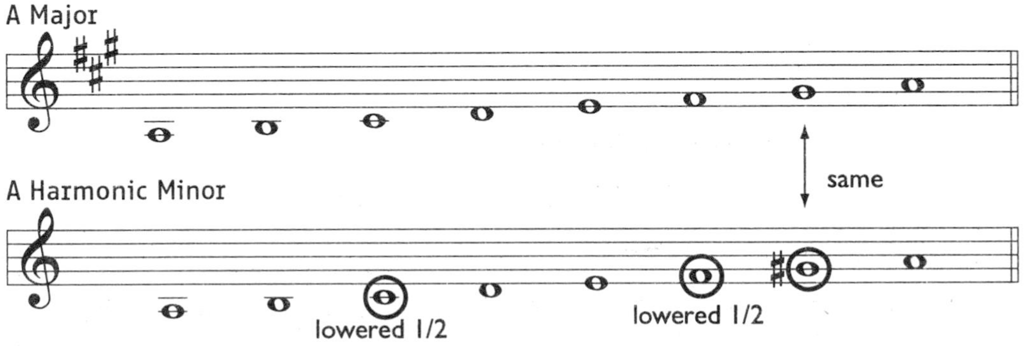

i-iv-i^6_4-V^7-i Chord Pattern in Minor

Practice this pattern in various minor keys.

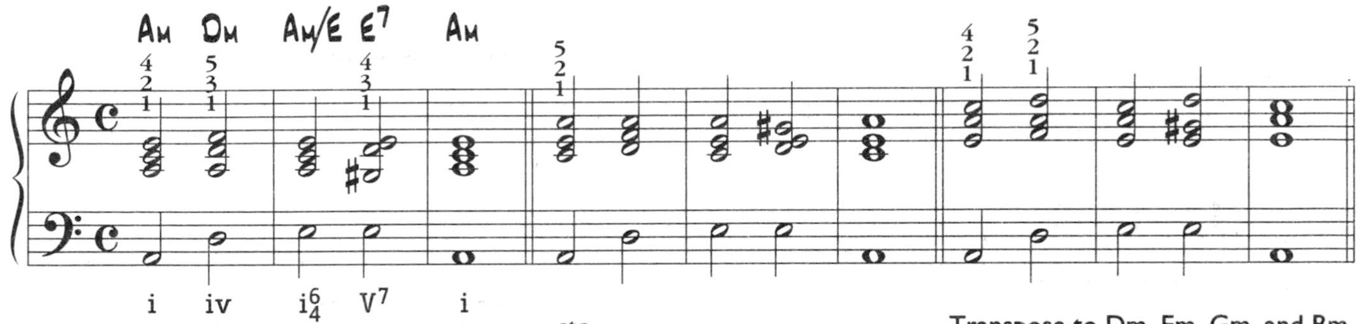

Transpose to Dm, Em, Gm, and Bm.

Chords Built on Scale Tones of the Minor Mode

In harmonic minor, chords built on scale steps i and iv are minor chords; the V chord is major (due to the raised seventh scale degree), as is the VI chord; ii° and vii° are diminished; and III+ is augmented.

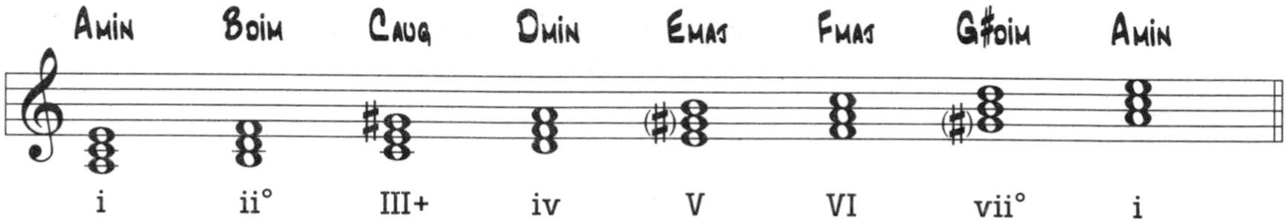

Two Study Pieces in Minor

Determine the minor key of *Two Guitars* (key of one flat, count down three half steps from the major keynote). The raised leading tone, C♯, tells us we are in harmonic minor. The tonic and subdominant chords in a minor key will be minor in quality. Analyze the chords and inversions.

TWO GUITARS

Moderately — **Slovakian**

Determine the key of *Russian Folk Song*. Analyze the harmony in each measure.

RUSSIAN FOLK SONG

Moderato — *arr.* **Beethoven**

Study Pieces: Folk Song Arrangements of Melodies in Minor Keys

Study and play the six arrangements that follow. Analyze each chord and add letter name symbols above the chords.

HUNGARIAN FOLK DANCE

PORTUGUESE FOLK SONG

LETTISH FOLK SONG

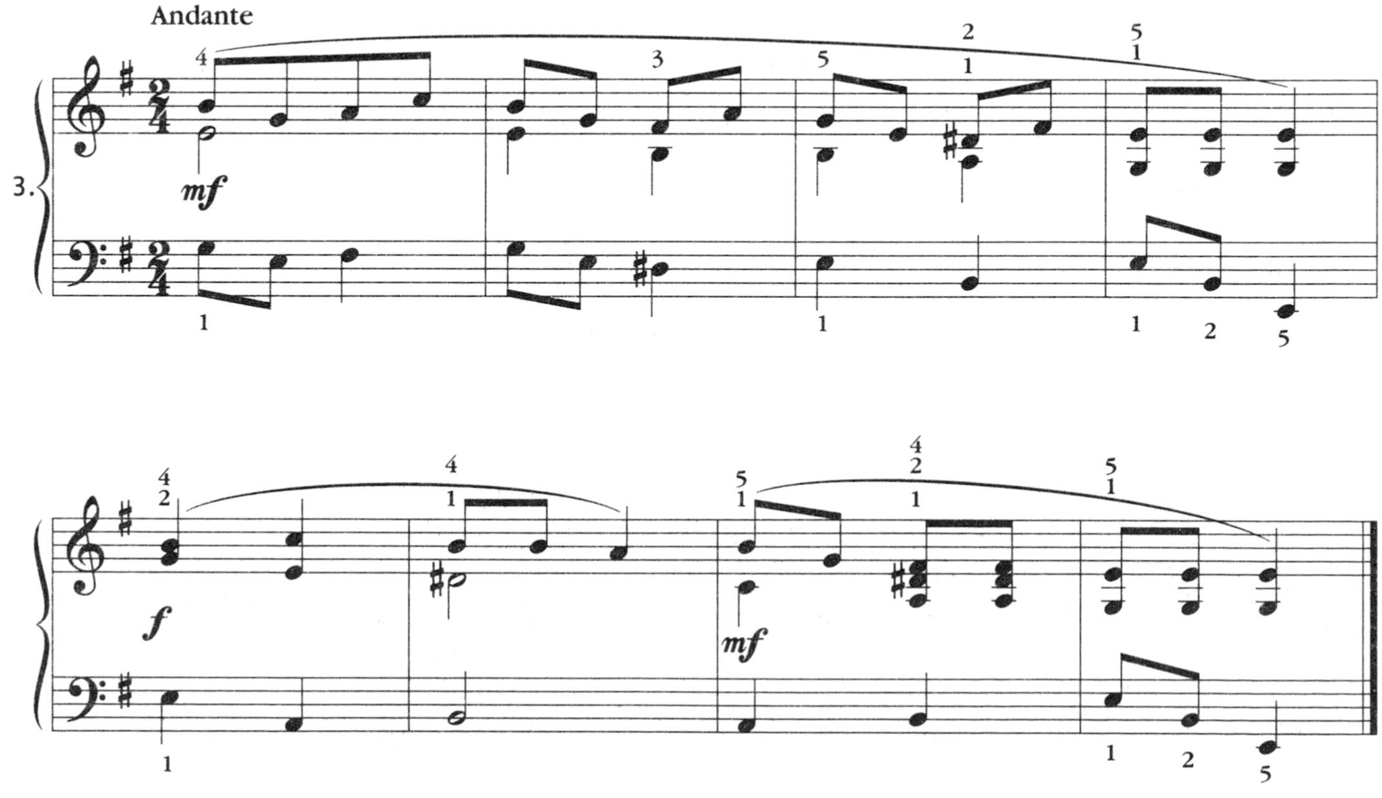

KALINKA

Russian

MEADOWLANDS

Russian

ALL THE PRETTY LITTLE HORSES

American Lullaby

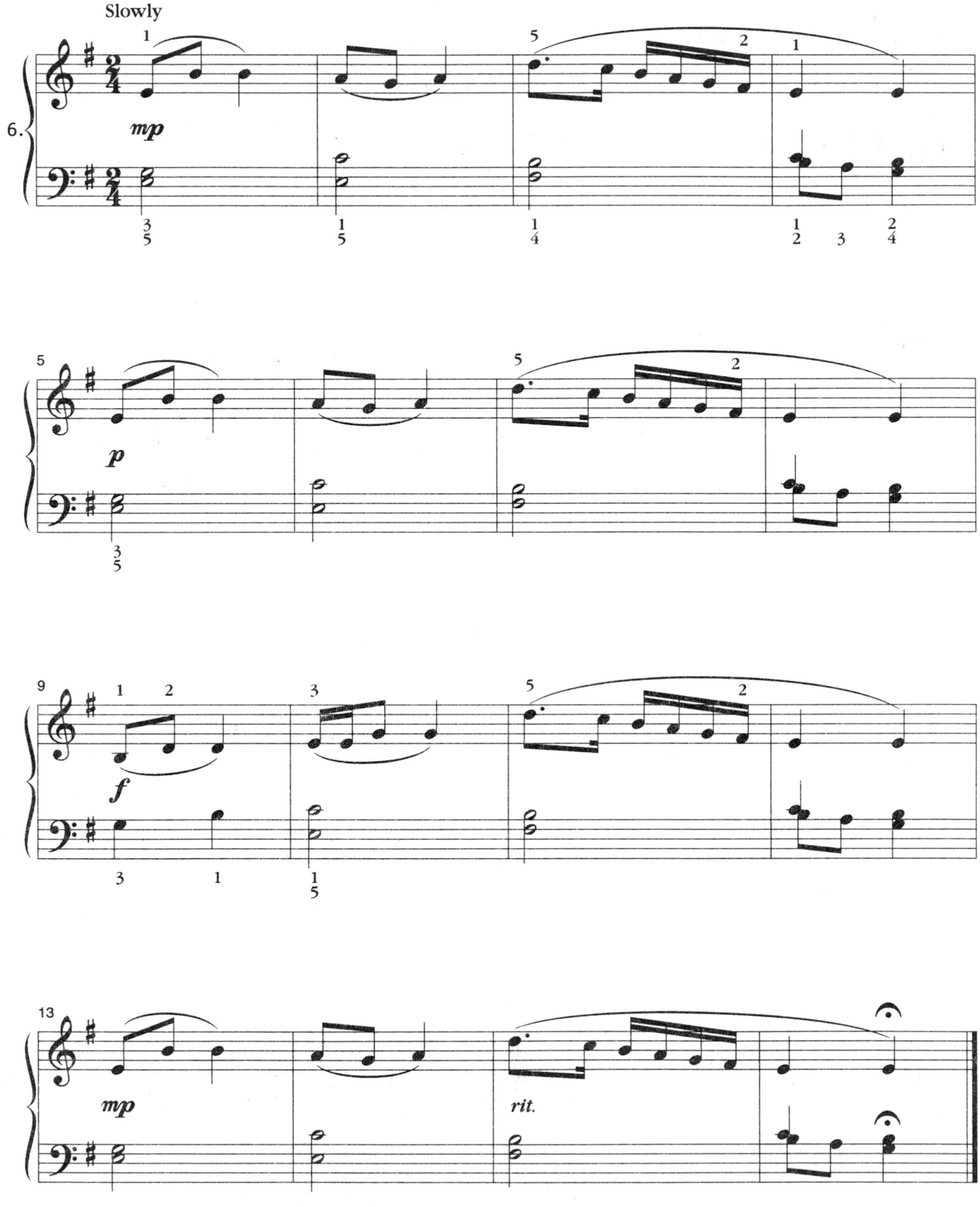

Harmonization of Melodies in Minor Keys

Harmonize the following minor key melodies. Use the suggested style as your guide. Notate your arrangements.

SPANISH FOLK SONG

Use your knowledge to harmonize *Italian Folk Song*.

ITALIAN FOLK SONG

Here is another harmonization without chords indicated. Use your knowledge to complete *Russian Folk Song* with your own chord choices.

RUSSIAN FOLK SONG

GO DOWN MOSES

Spiritual

In minor keys the ii^7 is a half-diminished seventh chord. In jazz harmony these chords are symbolized as either $ii^{ø7}$ or letter name $m^{7(\flat 5)}$. Notice the use of $Bm^{7(\flat 5)}$ in *Go Down Moses*.

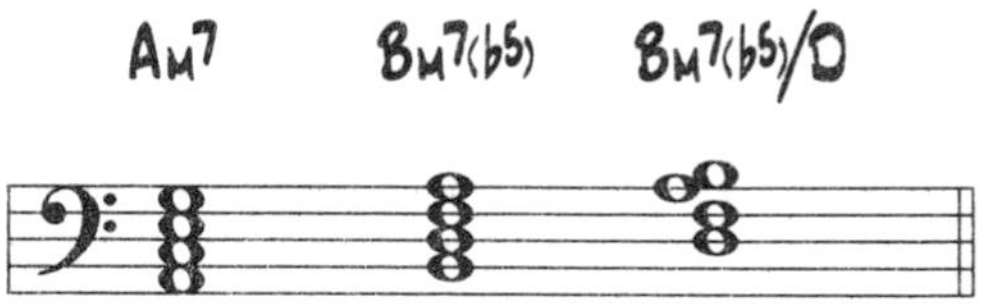

Music for Sight Reading and Transposing

This section contains reading material that emphasizes minor keys and secondary dominants. Follow the reading routine established earlier. Transpose these exercises as suggested.

Minor Harmonies

SPANISH FOLK SONG

Transpose to F minor.

RUSSIAN FOLK SONG

Transpose to G minor.

ITALIAN FOLK SONG

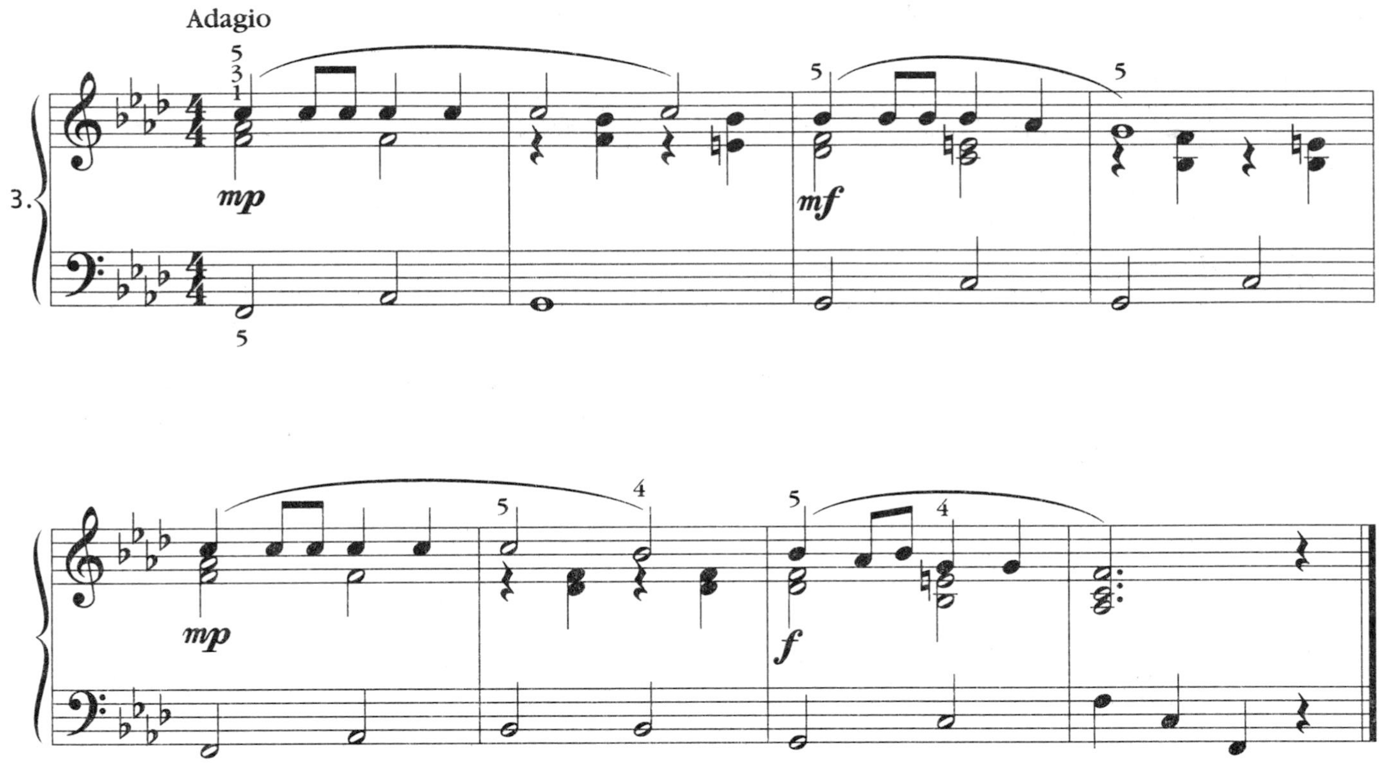

Transpose G minor.

BRITISH FOLK SONG

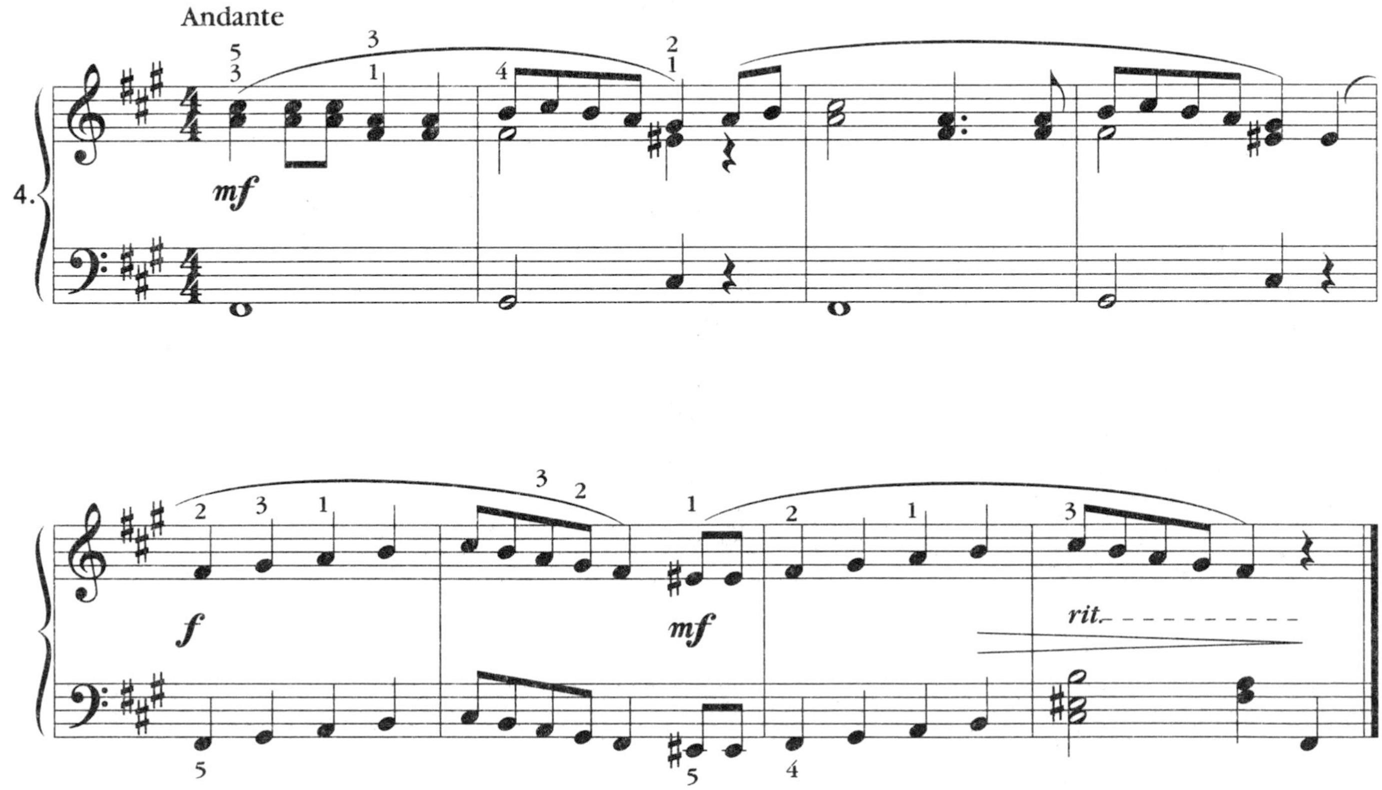

Transpose to F minor.

MEXICAN FOLK SONG

Transpose to D minor.

TROIKA RUSHING

Russian

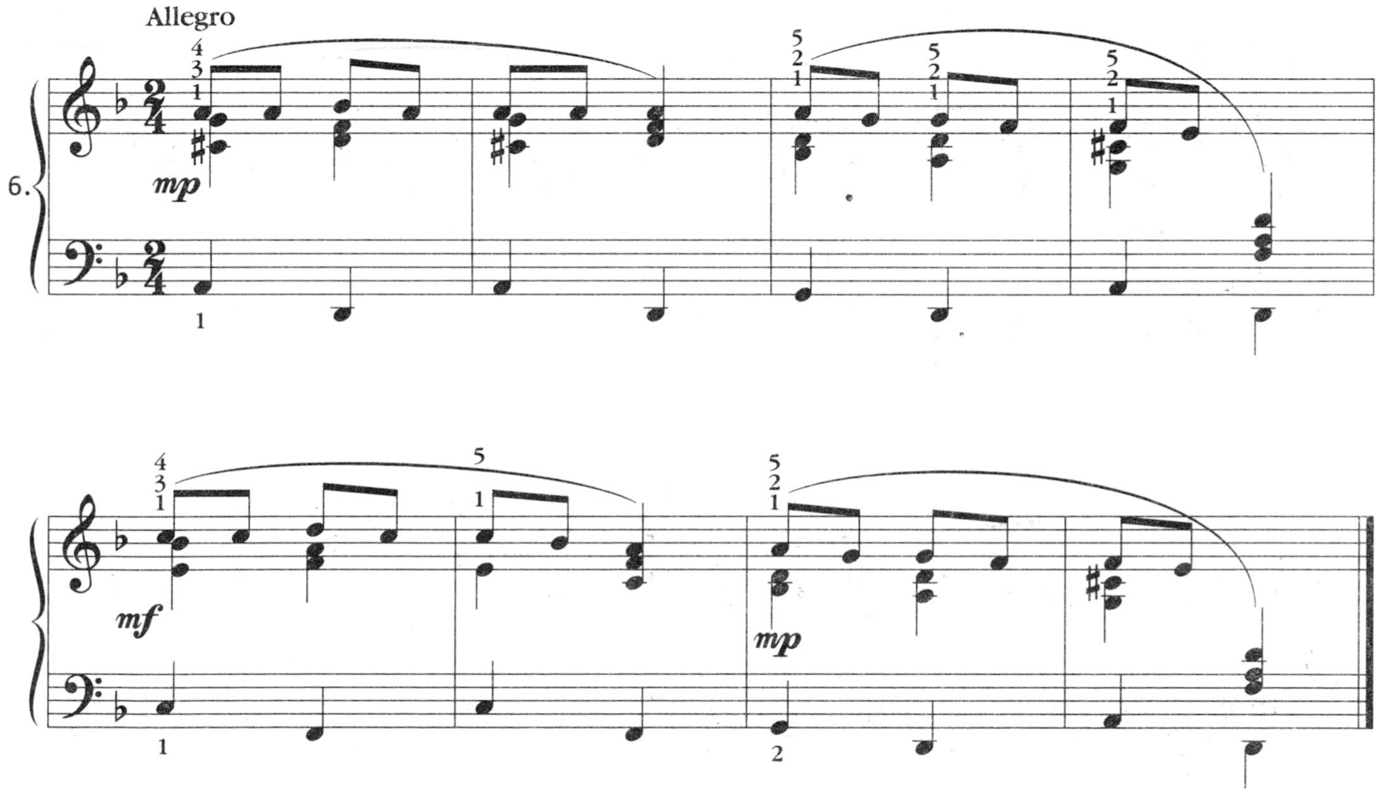

Transpose to E minor.

Harmonies with Occasional Secondary Dominants

Circle the secondary dominants and explain their function.

THE WHITE COCKADE

Scottish

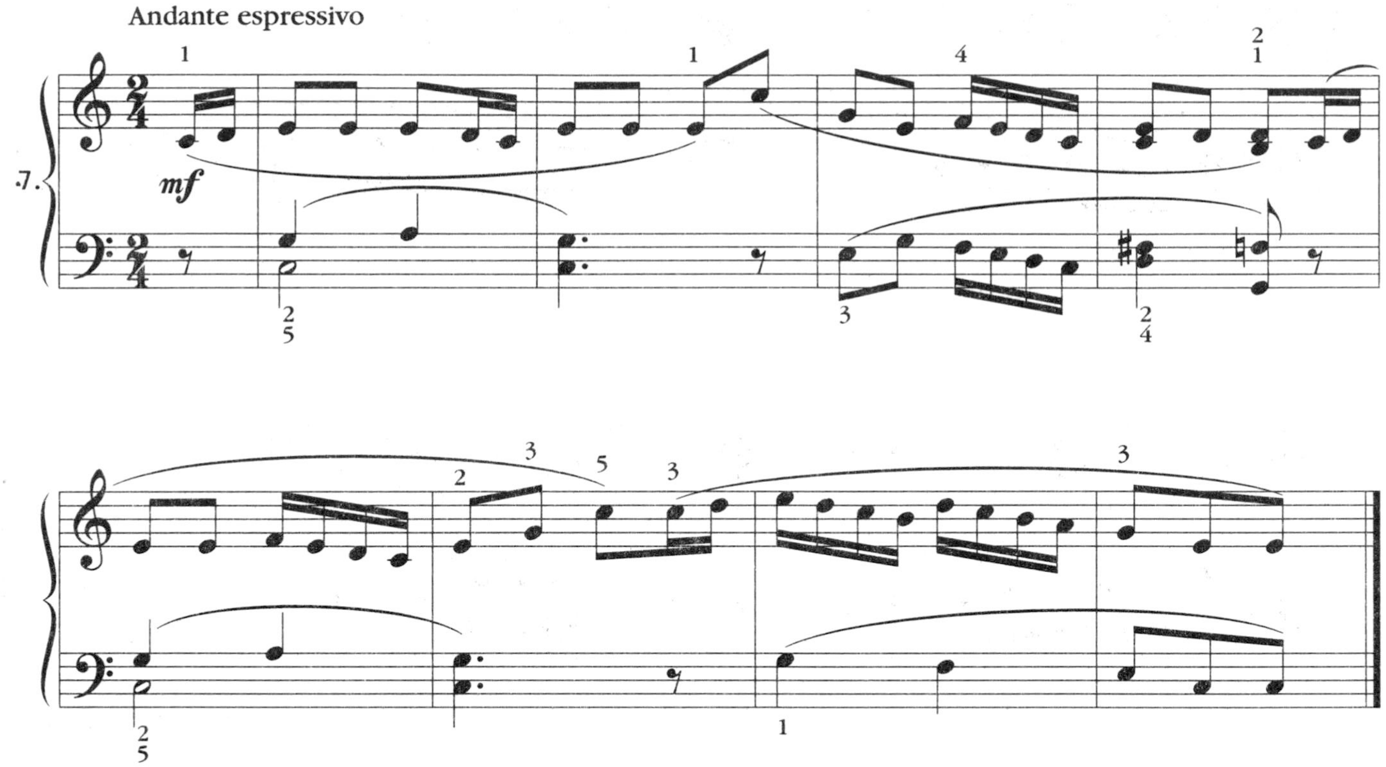

Transpose to D major.

OFT IN THE STILLY NIGHT

British

Transpose to F major.

BENDEMEER'S STREAM

England

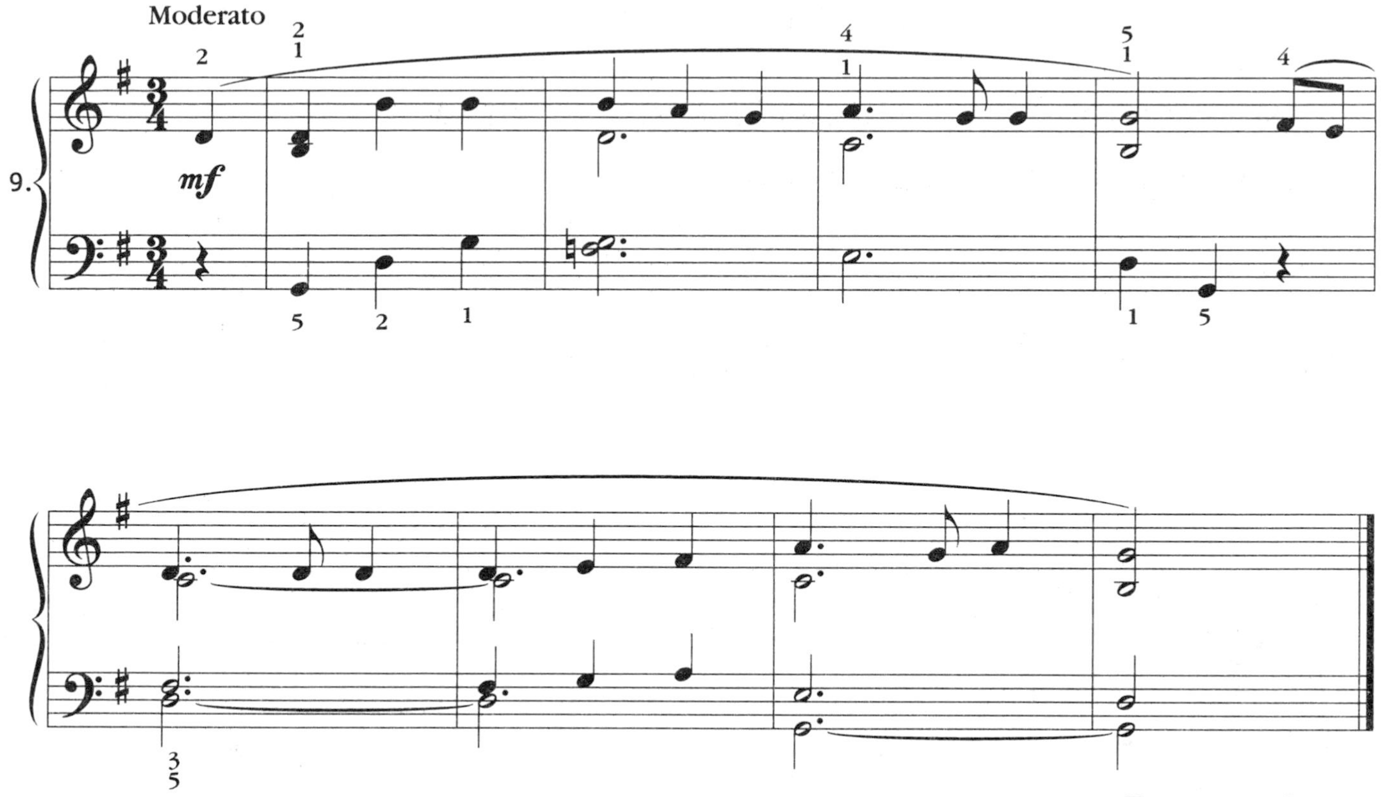

Transpose to F major.

WILL YE NO' COME BACK AGAIN?

Scottish

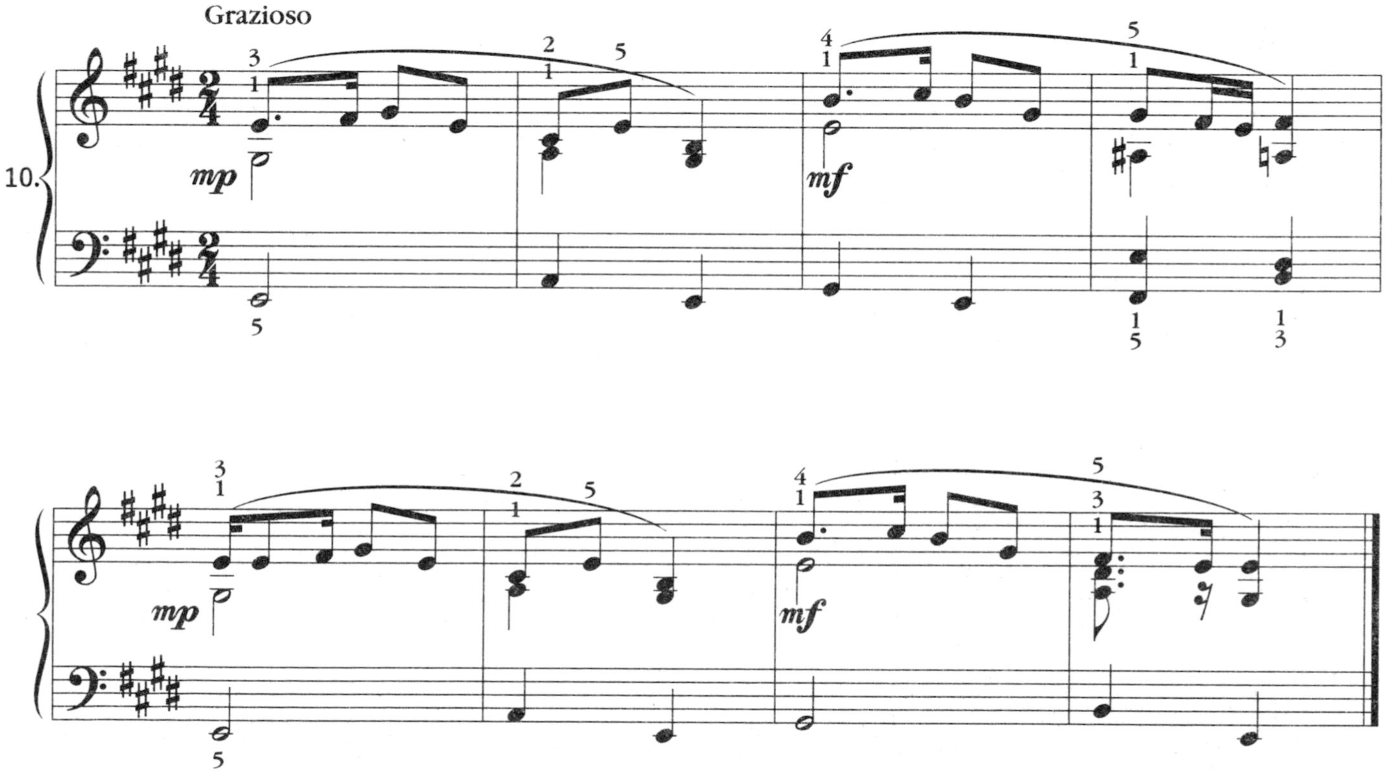

Transpose to E♭ major.

ACCOMPANYING

Practice the $\text{I-vi-V}^7/\text{V}^7\text{-V}^7\text{-I}$ progression located in bars 5–9 before learning the rest of the accompaniment. *Cockles and Mussels* includes secondary and dominant of the dominant chords.

Teacher: Double the melody one octave higher.

42 CD

COCKLES AND MUSSELS

Irish
arr. **James Lyke**

Lento

Transpose to G♭ major

In *Should the Volga Banks Be Flooded*, find instances of $ii^{\o 7}$ or $Em^{7(\flat 5)}$.

Teacher: Double the melody two octaves higher.

SHOULD THE VOLGA BANKS BE FLOODE

Transpose to D♭ major.

WHEN THE MIDNIGHT CHOO-CHOO LEAVES FOR ALABAM'

44 CD

music by **Irving Berlin**
arr. **James Lyke**

Moderato ♩ = 96

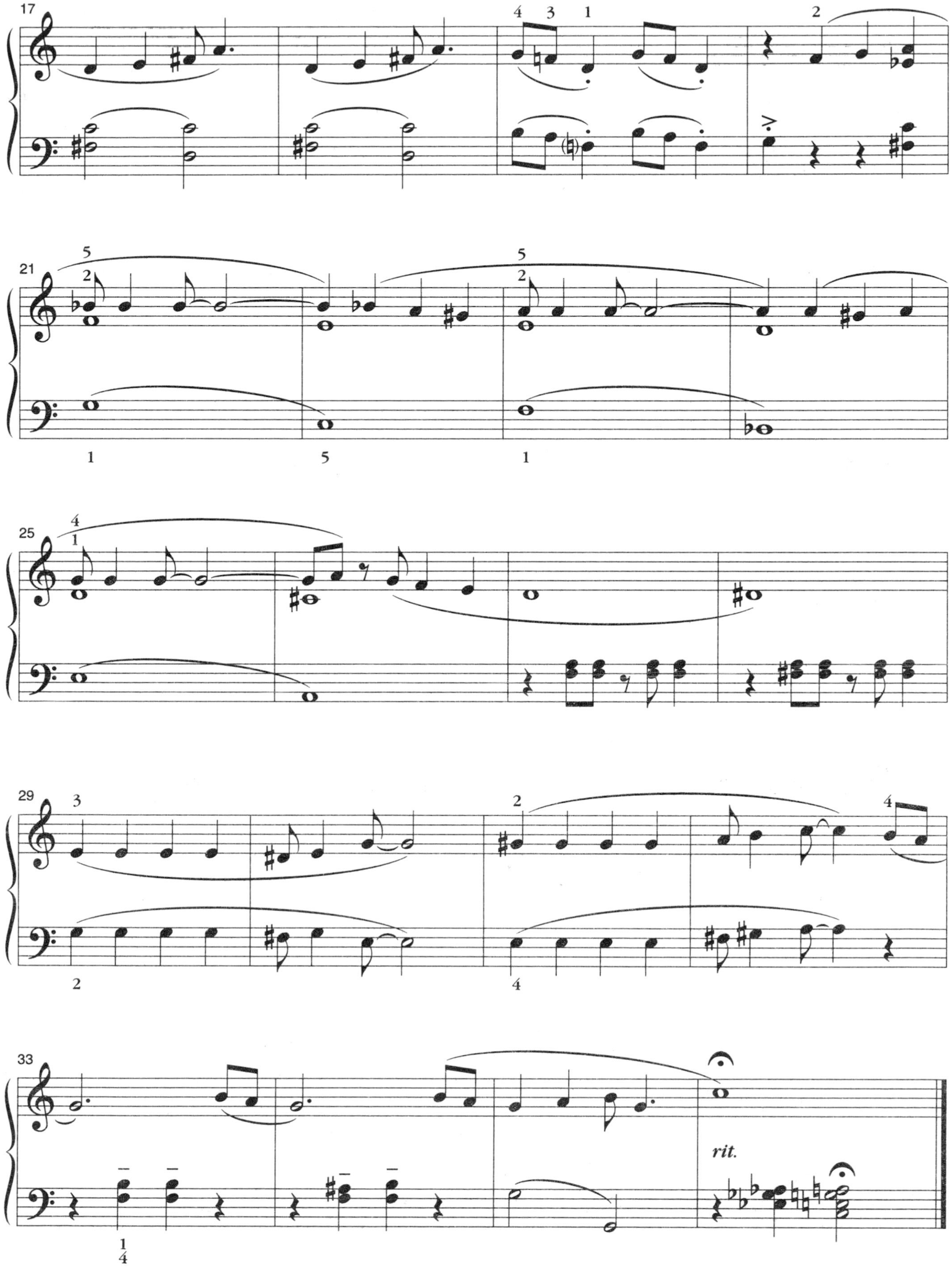
17
21
25
29
33
rit.

In *Ain't We Got Fun*, find ii–V–I chord progressions in F, B♭, and A minor. Also find a V^7 of vi.

AIN'T WE GOT FUN

music by **Richard Whiting**
arr. **James Lyke**

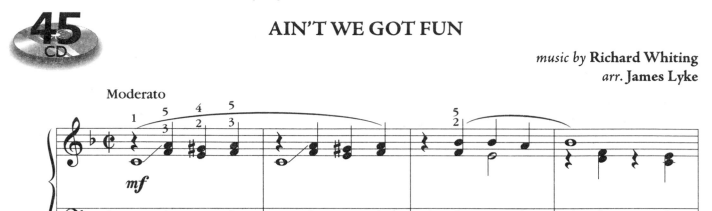

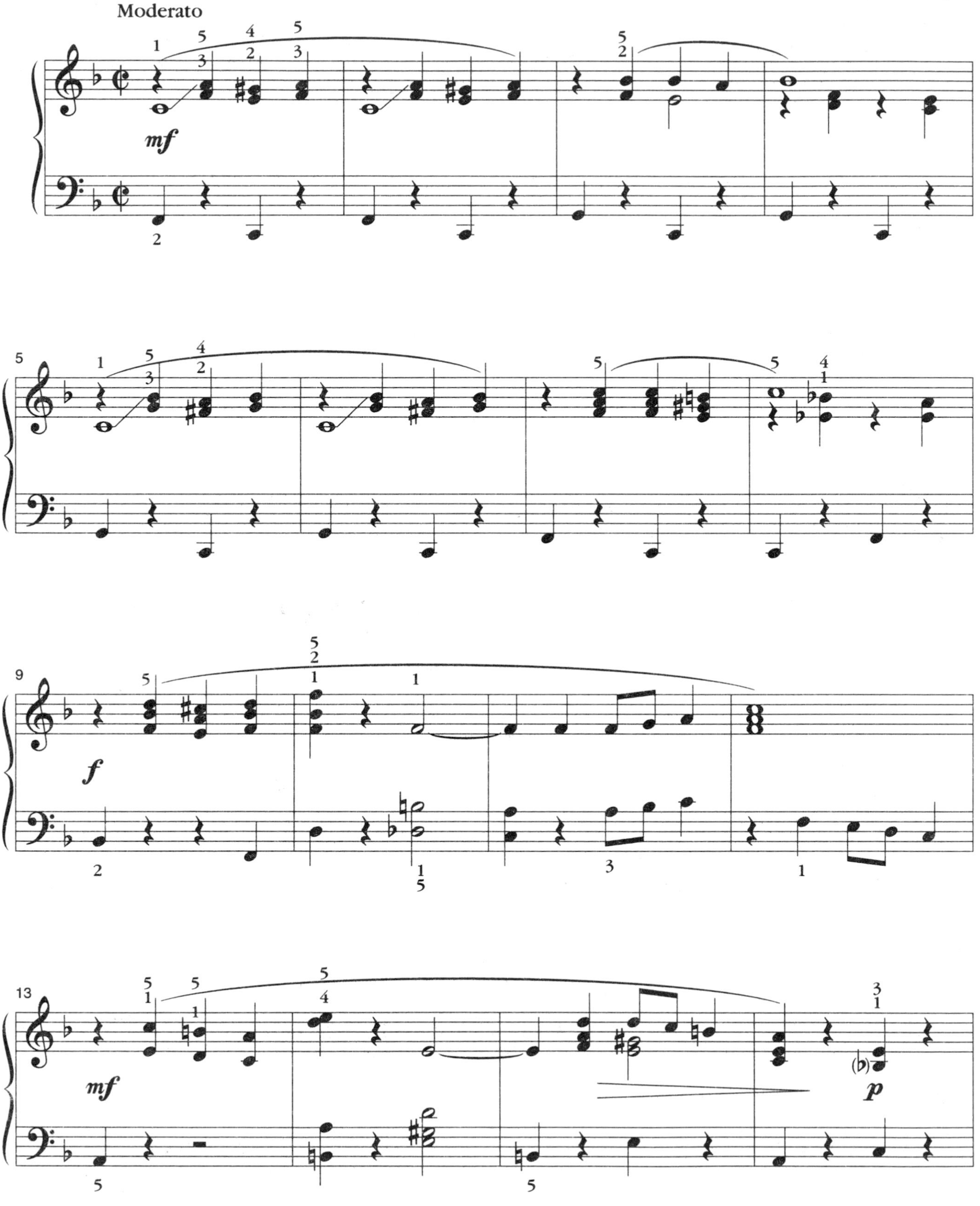

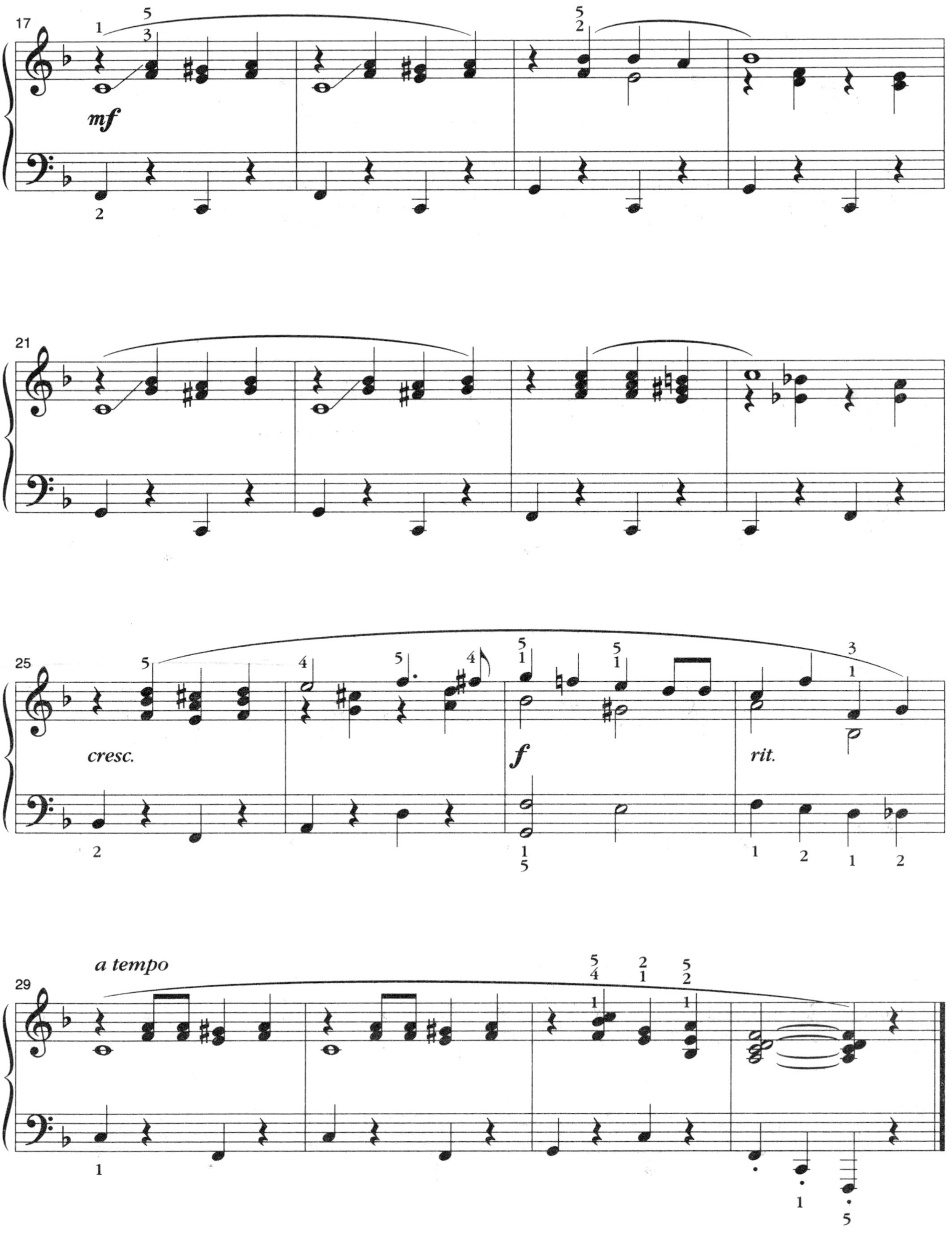
mf
cresc.
f
rit.
a tempo

ENSEMBLE REPERTOIRE

46 CD

ALL ABOARD FOR BROADWAY

Secondo – Teacher

music by **George M. Cohan**
arr. **James Lyke**

Spirited ♩ = 116

46 CD

ALL ABOARD FOR BROADWAY

Primo – Student

music by **George M. Cohan**
arr. **James Lyke**

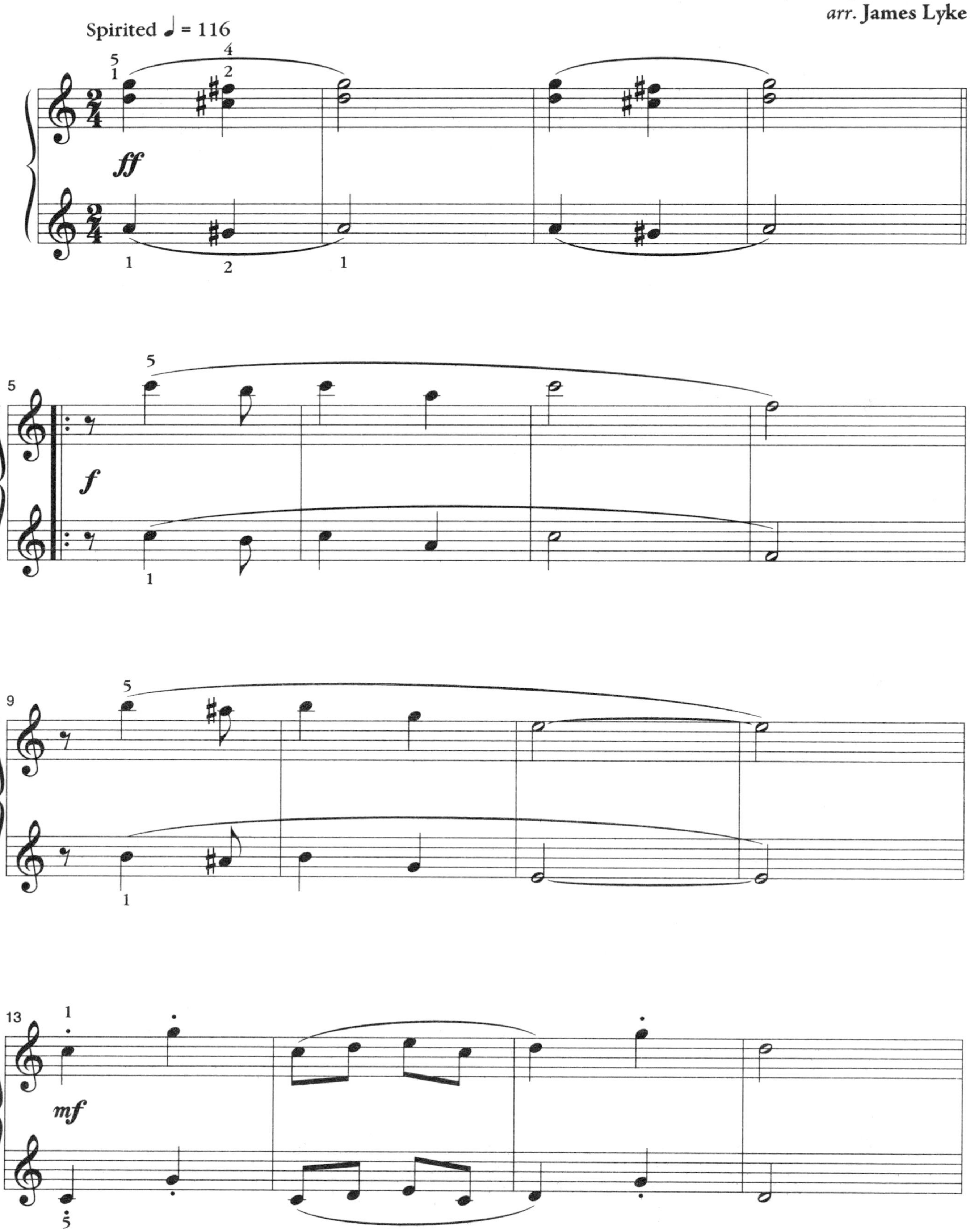

Secondo

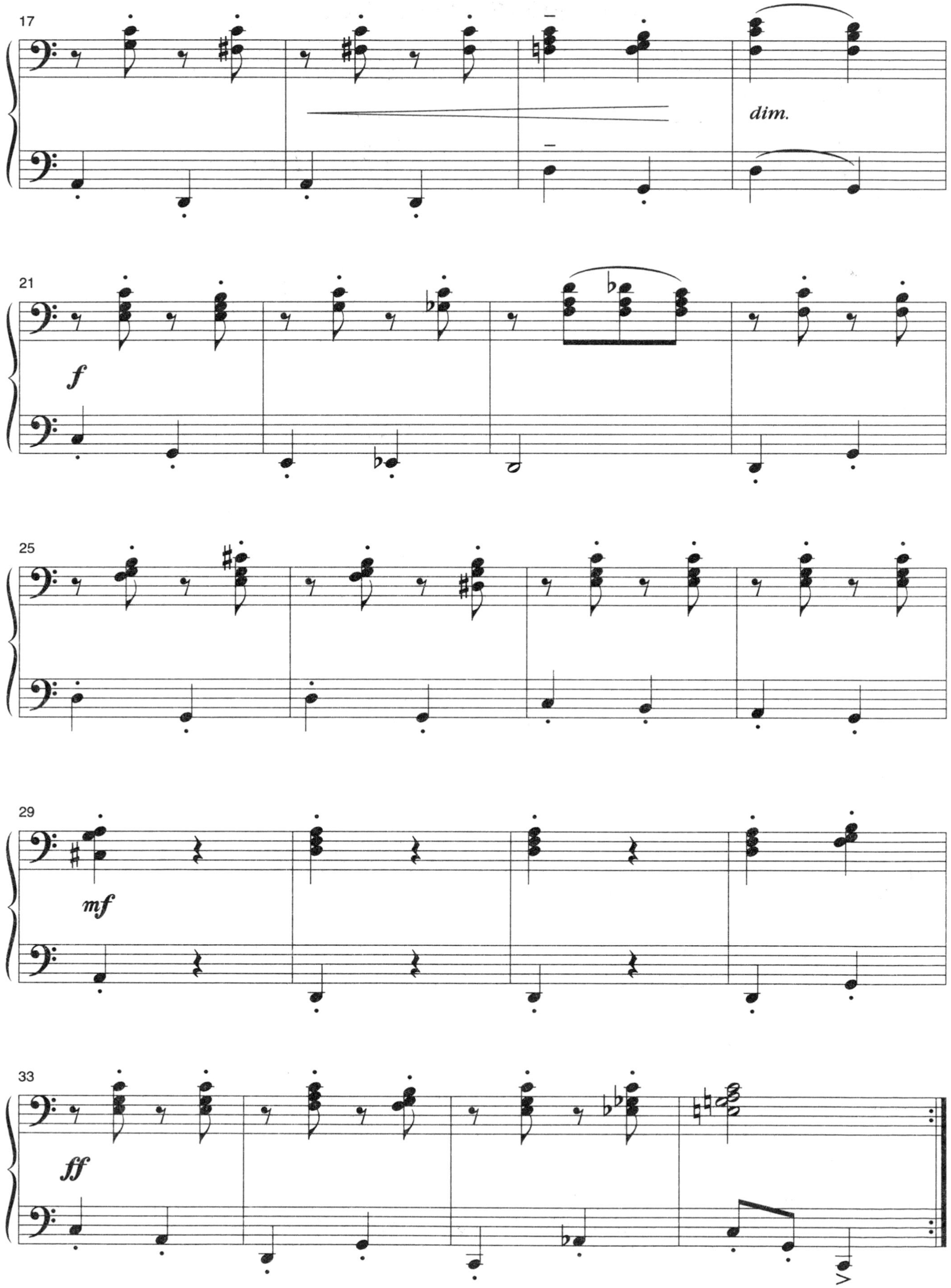

Primo

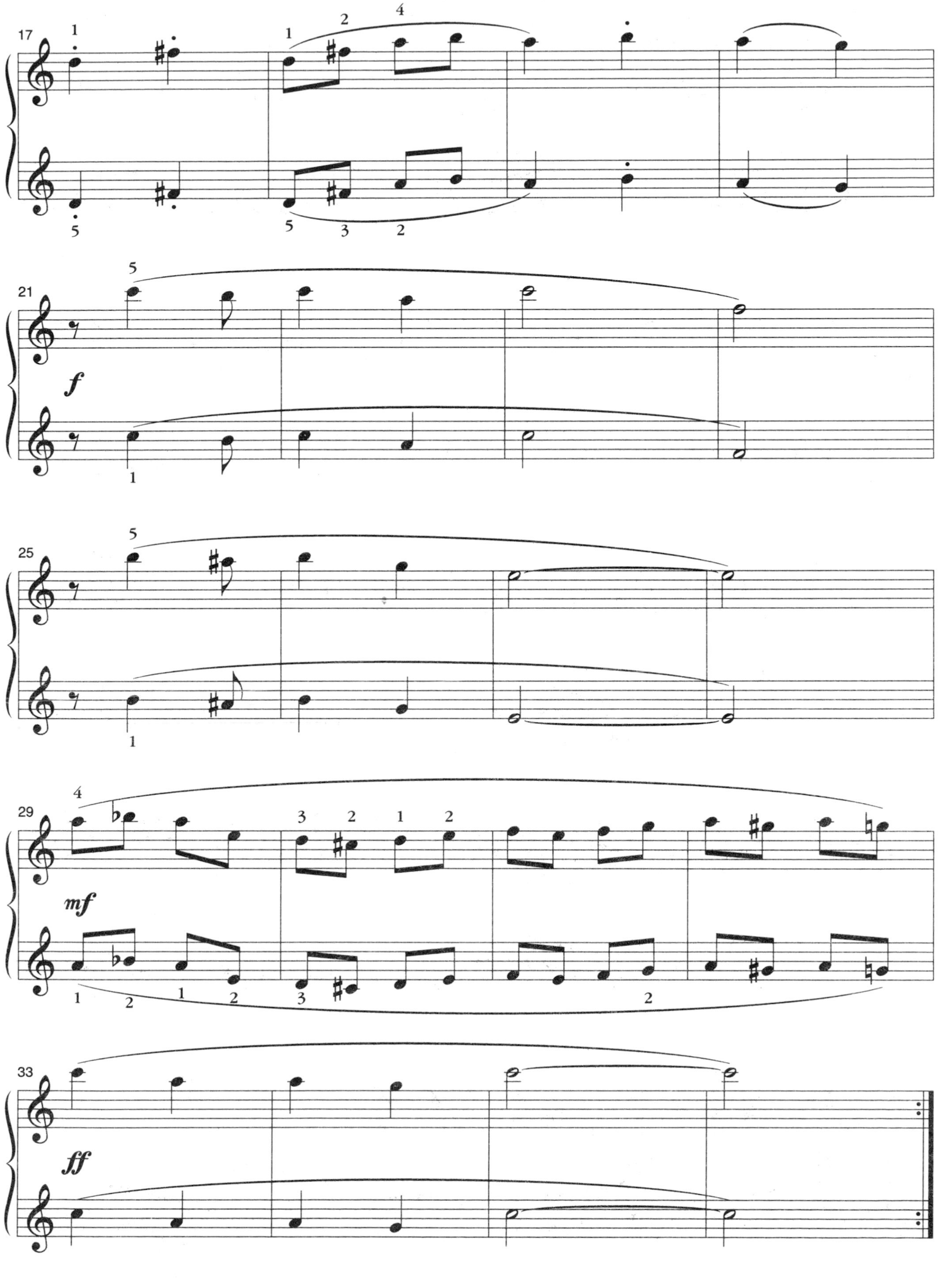

PARTNERS

Secondo – Teacher or Student

Tony Caramia

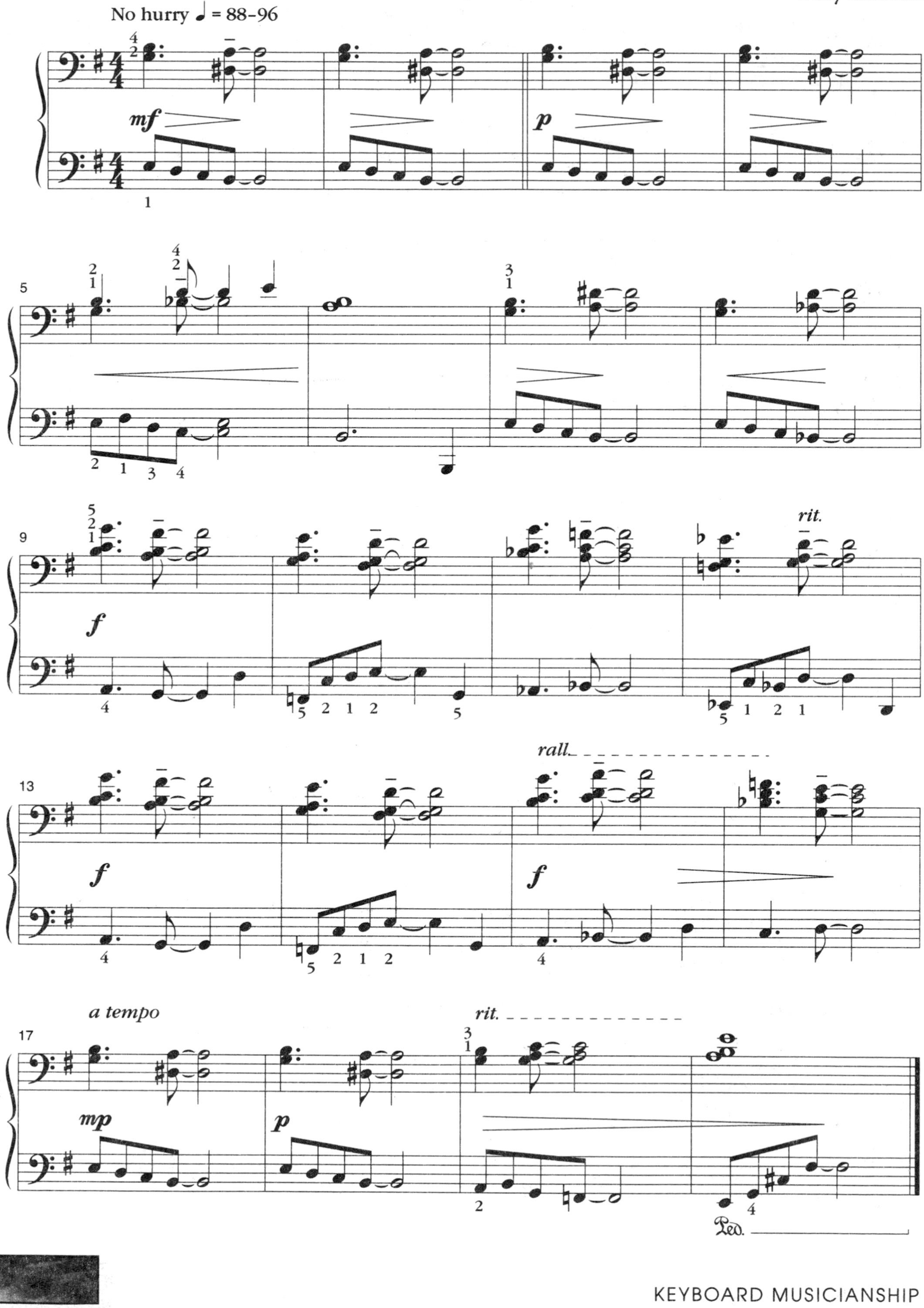

47 CD

PARTNERS

Primo – Student or Teacher

Tony Caramia

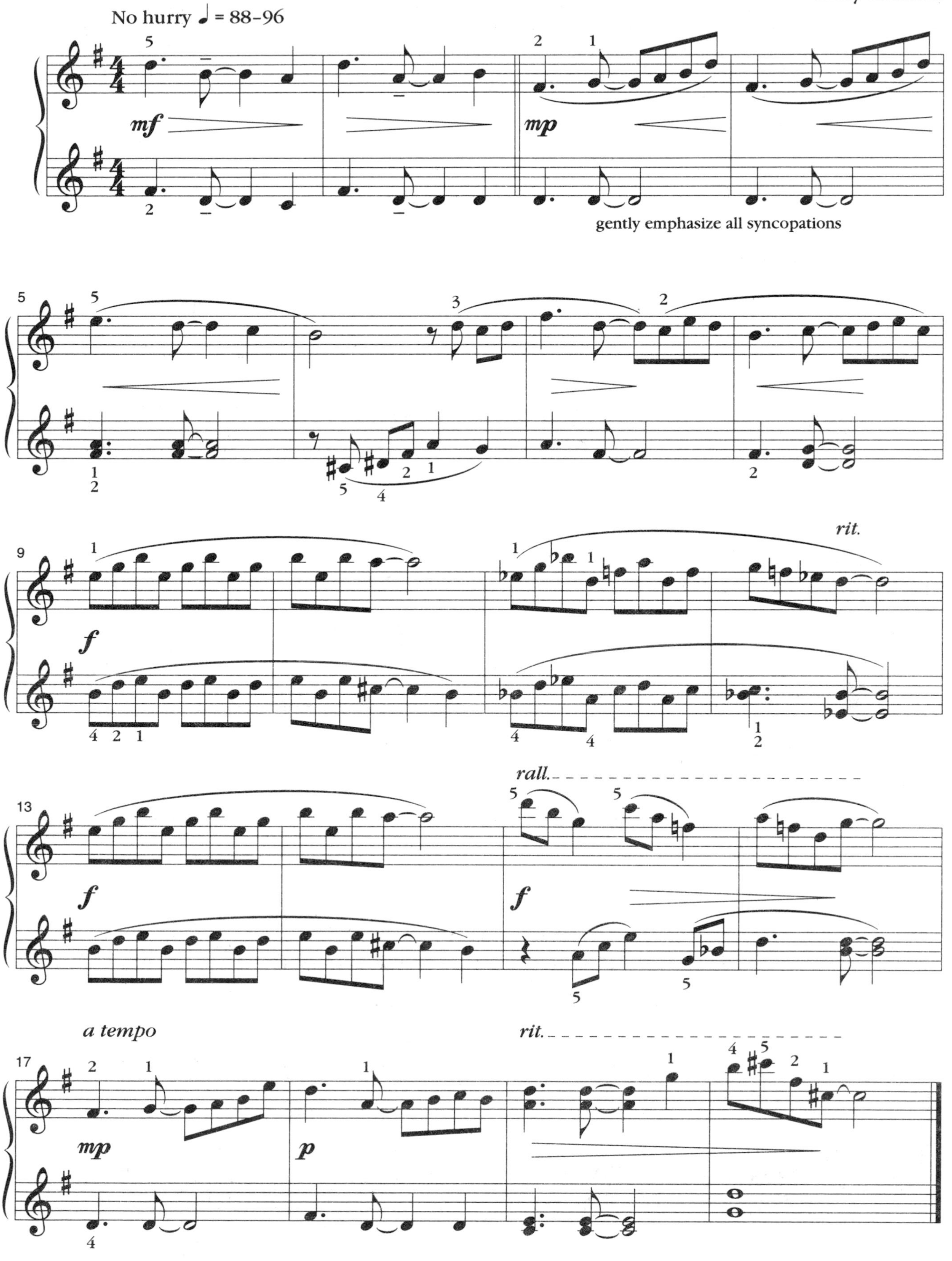

SOLO REPERTOIRE

Practice Plan: Block each RH triad which is outlined and identify it (Gmaj, Emin, etc.). Then play as written thinking about your moves. Block all LH triadic outlines and identify them by chord name. When beginning to put the hands together, play all eighth notes *staccato* (finger *staccato*). Then play as written.

PRELUDE

(Suite in G)

Henry Purcell

Practice Plan: Fingering is of utmost importance while playing this Telemann composition (see especially measure 8). What form of the minor scale does the F♯ suggest?

ANDANTE IN G MINOR

Georg Philipp Telemann

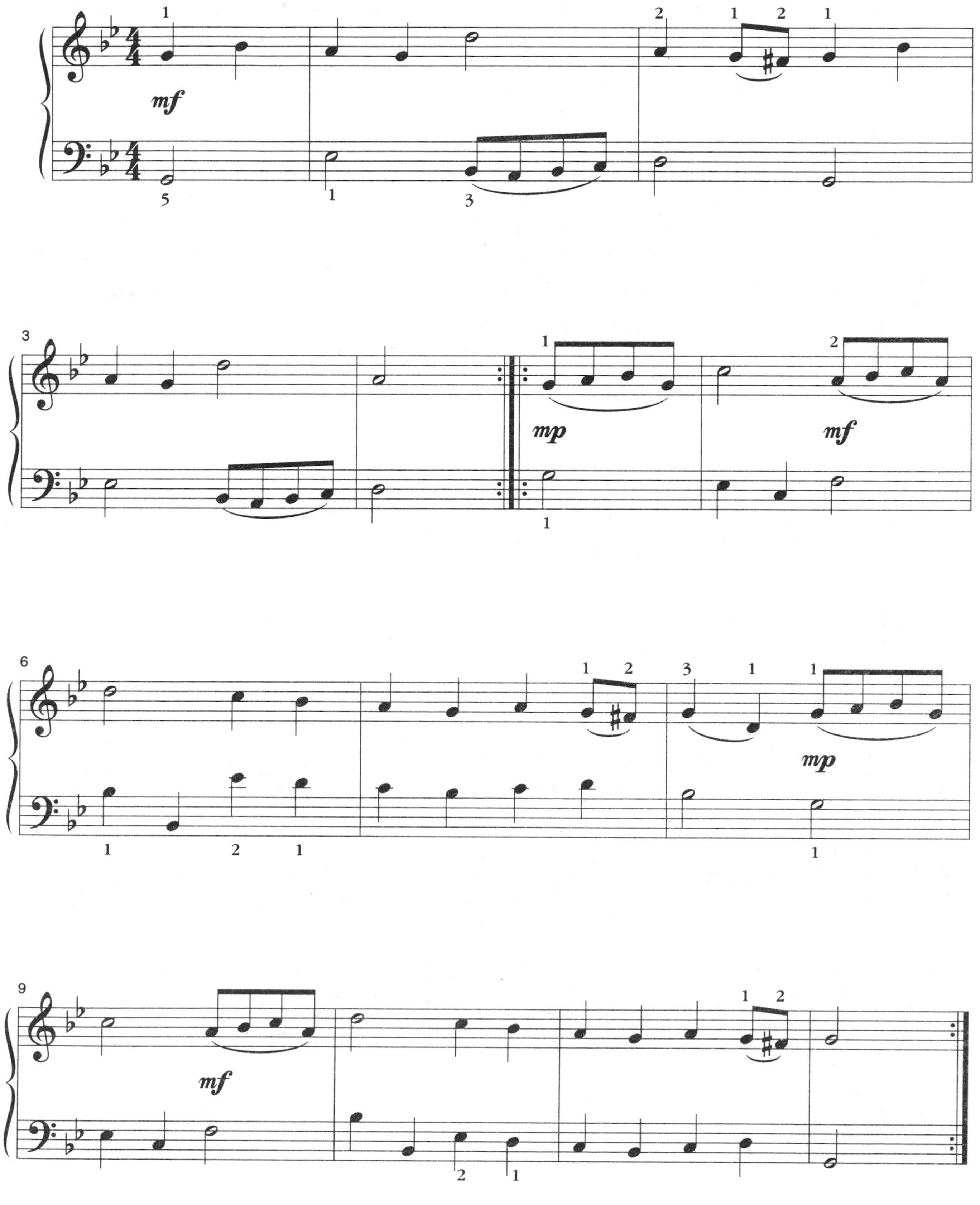

Practice Plan: Practice hands separately until secure fingering is achieved. Put hands together slowly at first. Measures 13-20 will require special attention.

MINUET IN D MINOR

attributed to **Leopold Mozart**

Practice Plan: Practice hands separately. Focus on performing a *legato* LH. Be mindful of the fingering. Strive to bring the RH melody to the foreground. Shape the RH melody as if singing it. Locate secondary dominants V^7/ii and V^7/IV.

SONATINA IN G MAJOR

(First Movement)

Carl Reinecke

Allegro moderato

Practice Plan: Block all LH chords and analyze them (E^7, Am/E, etc.). Then play LH as written. Play the RH alone giving an arc to each phrase (⌒). When playing hands together the first time, block the LH chords and "sing out" the melody. Finally, play as written and add pedal.

TIMID LITTLE HEART

Robert Fuchs

Somewhat agitated ♩ = 108

Practice Plan: *Leather Vest* requires careful counting. Subdivide all rhythms at first, paying special attention to the tied syncopation ♫♫♩ ♫♩♩. . Play with a full tone.

LEATHER VEST

Geoffrey Haydon

Practice Plan: In *Ragtime* good coordination is required to perform the rhythms correctly. Practice tapping certain measures hands together. Isolate measures 3 and 29-32 in order to practice the chromatic fingering. The 4ths in bars 13-18 need to sound together.

RAGTIME

James Lyke

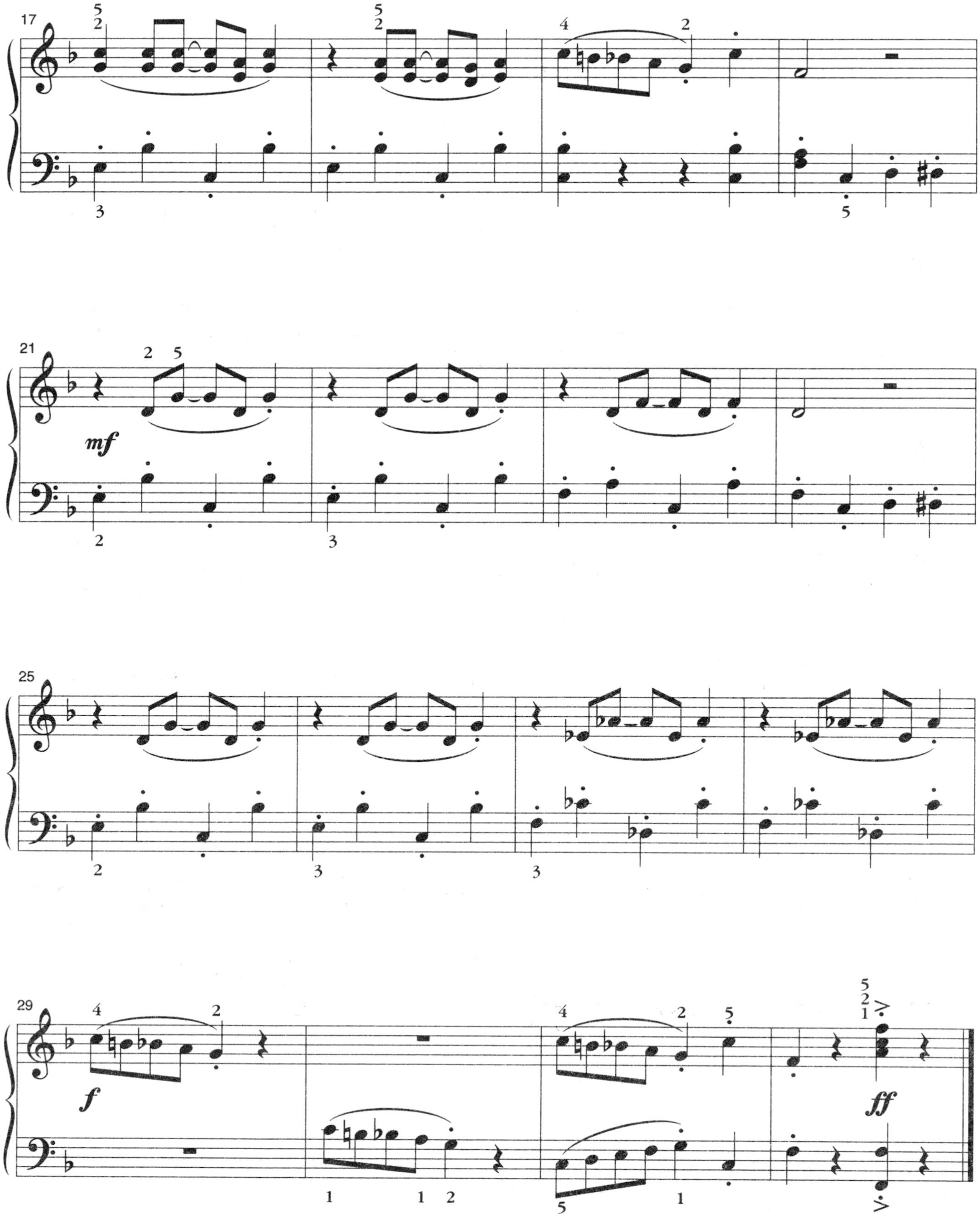
mf
f
ff

Practice Plan: Notice the *staccato* sixths that appear throughout *Morning March.* Practice bouncing with a light, detached touch. The sixteenth-note figures need to be even and crisp. Hold the ***tenuto*** notes full value.

MORNING MARCH

Tony Caramia

a tempo
mf
mp
p
pp
cresc.

MUSICIANSHIP ACTIVITIES

Complete the following exercises which review various topics introduced in Chapter Seven.

Chord Progressions in Minor

Fill in the missing tones in the following two progressions. Move to the closest voice.

Chord Progressions with V^7/V

Fill in the missing tones in the following two progressions. See page 265.

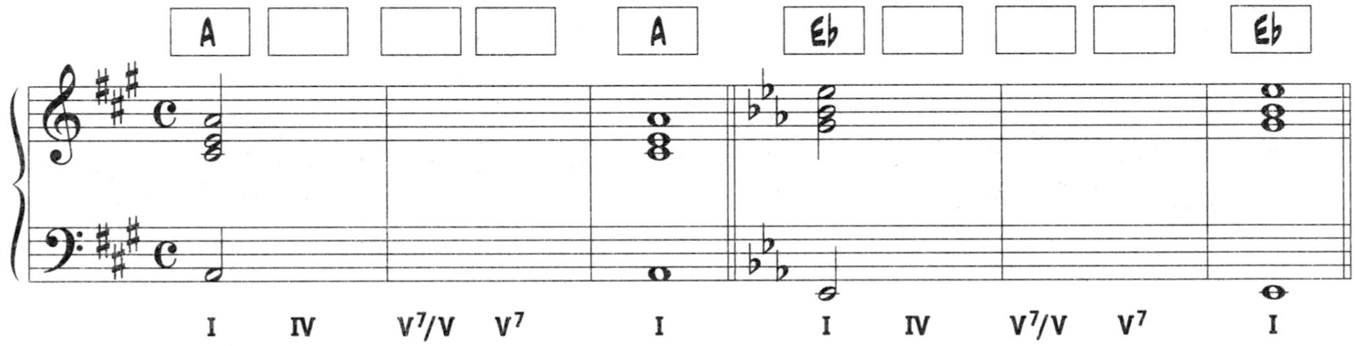

Improvising

While another class member (or the instructor) plays this salsa pattern, improvise a RH melody in E minor. Listen for the harmonic changes.

TECHNICAL STUDIES

Harmonic Minor Scales: c, g, d, a, e

Begin the study of harmonic minor scales. The fingerings are the same as the parallel major scales. Consult the Scale Fingering Chart on page 215 or Appendix B for a thorough presentation of all scales and arpeggios.

Minor Arpeggios: c, g, d, a, e

Begin the study of harmonic minor arpeggios. The fingerings are the same or similar to the major arpeggios. Consult Appendix B to check fingerings.

Example: Two Octave Minor Arpeggio, Hands Together (Play twice slow, twice fast.)

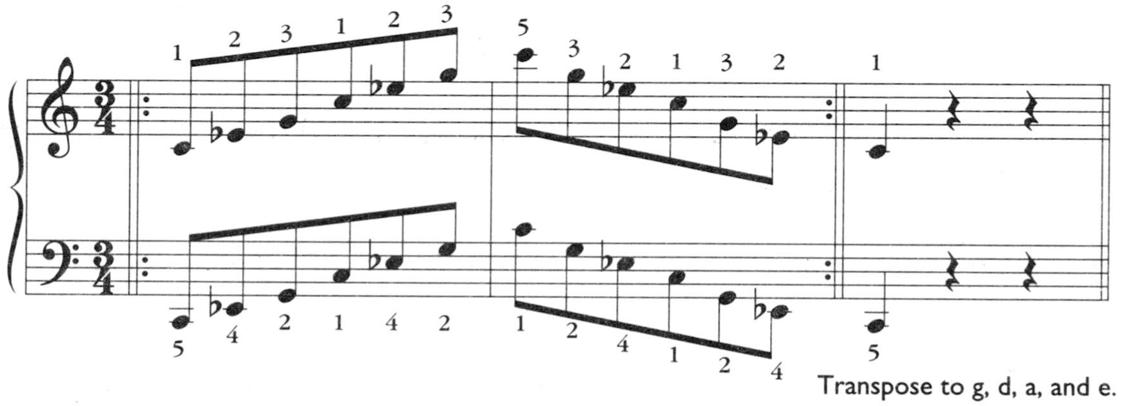

Transpose to g, d, a, and e.

Chromatic Scale Review: Play and learn the RH part of this excerpt from Köhler's *Polka.* This will serve as a review of chromatic scale fingering. The instructor (or another student) can play the LH part so that the focus remains on good fingering in the RH part.

Louis Köhler

SUGGESTED PLAYING EXAM TOPICS
CHAPTER SEVEN

1. Play the chord progression (from memory) i–iv–i^6_4–V^7–i in these minor keys: cm, dm, em, gm, am and bm. See page 267.

2. Play one harmonized melody that uses the dominant of the dominant on pages 265 and 266. Play one harmonized melody in minor from pages 273 and 274.

3. Play two sight reading studies from pages 275–279.

4. Accompany the melody to *Cockles and Mussels* (page 280) or *Should the Volga Banks be Flooded* (page 281).

5. Perform *When the Midnight Choo-Choo Leaves for Alabam'* (pages 282-283) or *Ain't We Got Fun* (page 284-285).

6. Perform either *All Aboard for Broadway* (pages 286-289) or *Partners* (pages 290-291) from the Ensemble Repertoire section.

7. Perform one or two pieces from the Solo Repertoire Section (pages 292–301).

8. Play the following white key minor scales hands together, two octaves, at metronome marking ♩ = 84: c, g, d, a, and e. Consult Appendix B.

8 chapter

Various Qualities of Seventh Chords, An Introduction to Modes, Harmonization, Repertoire, Musicianship Activities, and Technical Studies

In Chapter Six, Kern's *Look for the Silver Lining* was used to illustrate secondary chords (ii, iii, and vi). Review these seventh chords in the example below. Complete the analysis and practice slowly to savor the richness of the various 7ths and their qualities (maj., min., etc.).

LOOK FOR THE SILVER LINING

music by **Jerome Kern**

* Sometimes a 6th may be added to a major triad. 6th chords occur often in popular music (see bar 8).

Seventh Chord Qualities

Seventh chords can be built on major scale degrees I, ii, iii, etc. The resulting qualities, such as major and minor 7ths, need to be examined. The most common types of seventh chords appear below. Build these on various tones. Focus on the two types of diminished seventh chords.

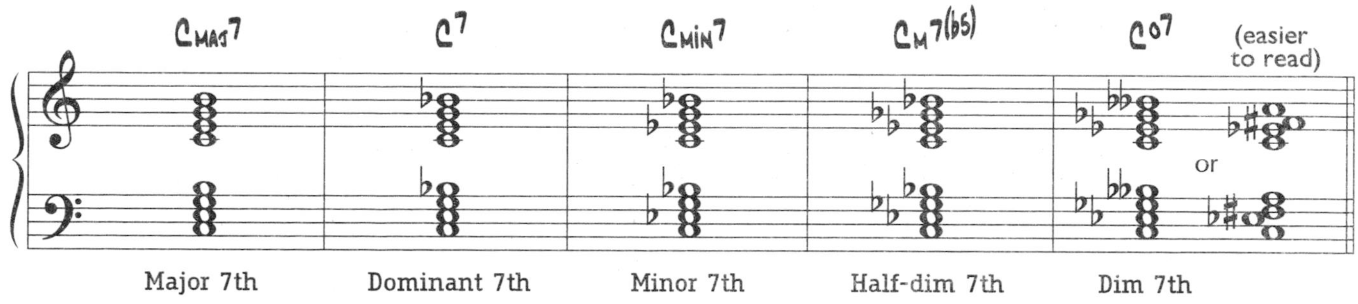

In the example from Kern's *Look For The Silver Lining*, these seventh chords are used: Dm^7 (vi^7), $Fmaj^7$ (I^7), and $B\flat maj^7$ (IV^7). These chords are in addition to the ii^7 chord which moves to the dominant. Study the various seventh chords built on each scale degree shown below. I^7 and IV^7 are major in quality; ii^7, iii^7, and vi^7 are minor in quality (secondary sevenths); and V^7 is dominant. The $vii^{ø7}$ is a special chord, half-diminished (diminished triad with a minor seventh.)

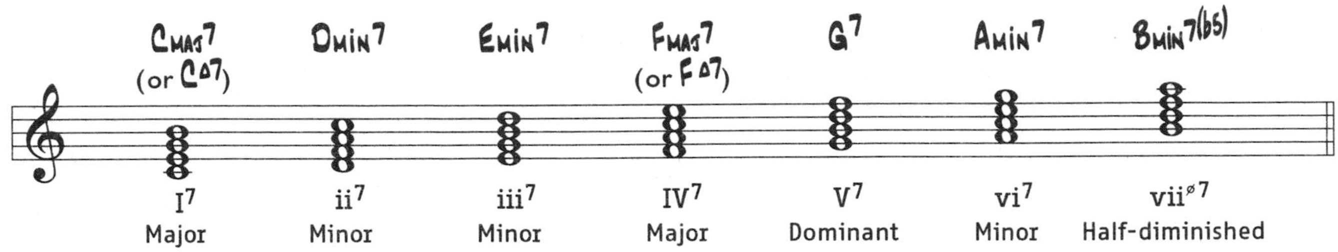

Study the quality of the various seventh chords built on degrees of the major scale above. Block seventh chords on scale degrees *in selected major keys* and identify the quality of each chord. Say the Roman numeral, letter name, and quality as you build each chord on scale degrees of each new key. Use both hands and play two octaves apart.

A Special Progression: ii–V–I

In jazz and popular music, the ii^7–V^7–I sequence is known as: "ii–V–I." Look back to the Kern song on page 305. Take note of Gm^7–C^7–F (bar 2 to bar 3), the "ii–V–I" progression. Learn this progression (very gradually) in the six keys shown below. Play each progression twice before moving on to the next. ($^{\Delta 7}$ = major seventh.)

Using vi^7

Another common minor seventh chord is vi^7. Learn this progression in F, C, and G. Later, you will use these harmonies in an accompaniment pattern.

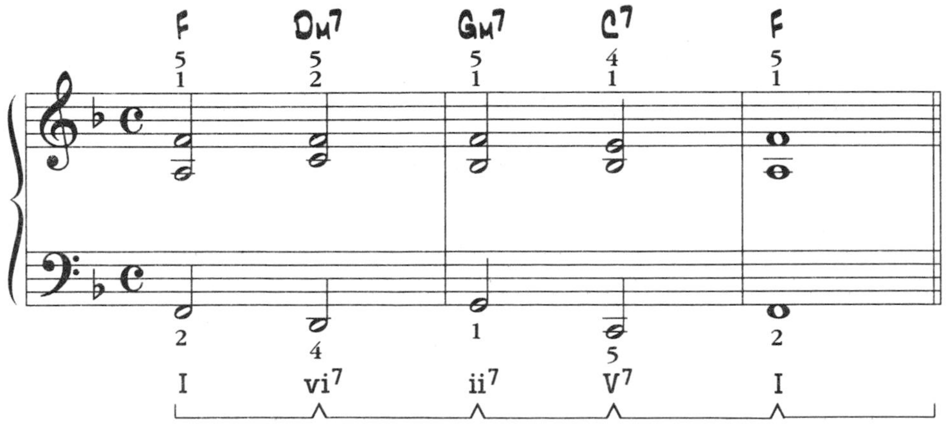

Study Pieces: Folk Song Arrangements Using Various Seventh Chords

Study and play the following four arrangements. Analyze the harmony and add letter name symbols above the chords. (Put chord symbols in the boxes.)

SOURWOOD MOUNTAIN

United States

1.

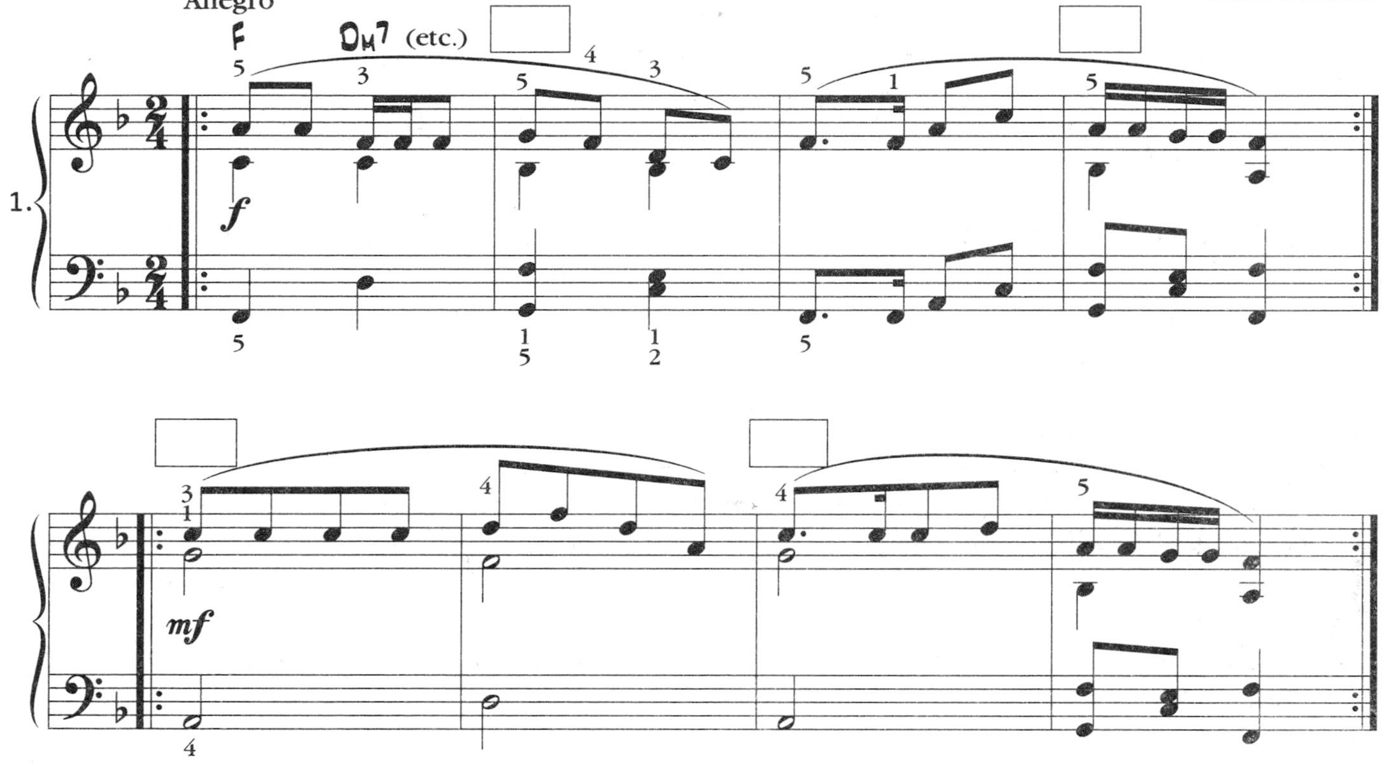

GERMAN FOLK SONG

2.

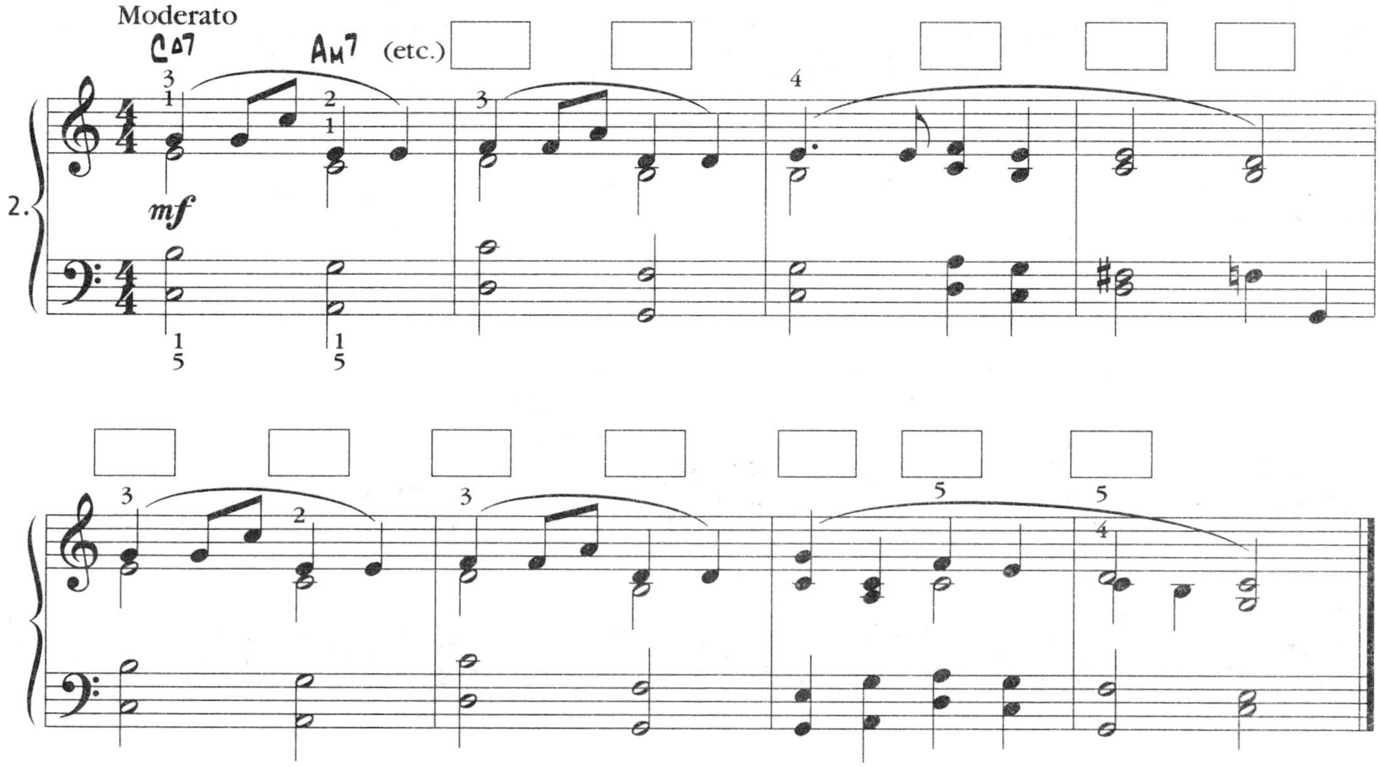

O COME, LITTLE CHILDREN

J.P.A. Schulz
arr. **James Lyke**

3.

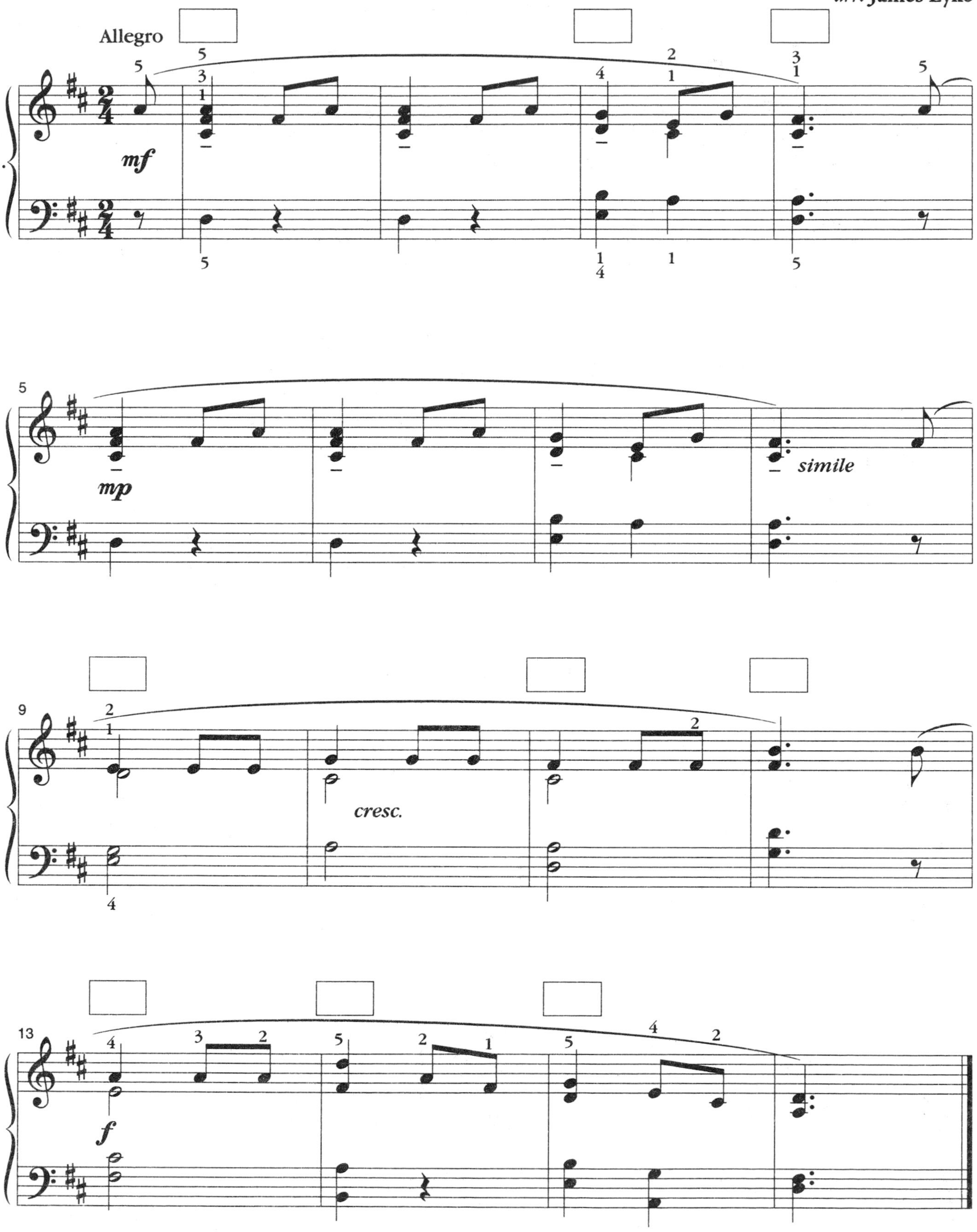

Jerome Kern's *Honeymoon Land* and *They Didn't Believe Me* illustrate various seventh chords. Fill in the boxes with the proper chord symbol as shown in the first measure of *Honeymoon Land*.

HONEYMOON LAND

music by **Jerome Kern**
arr. **James Lyke**

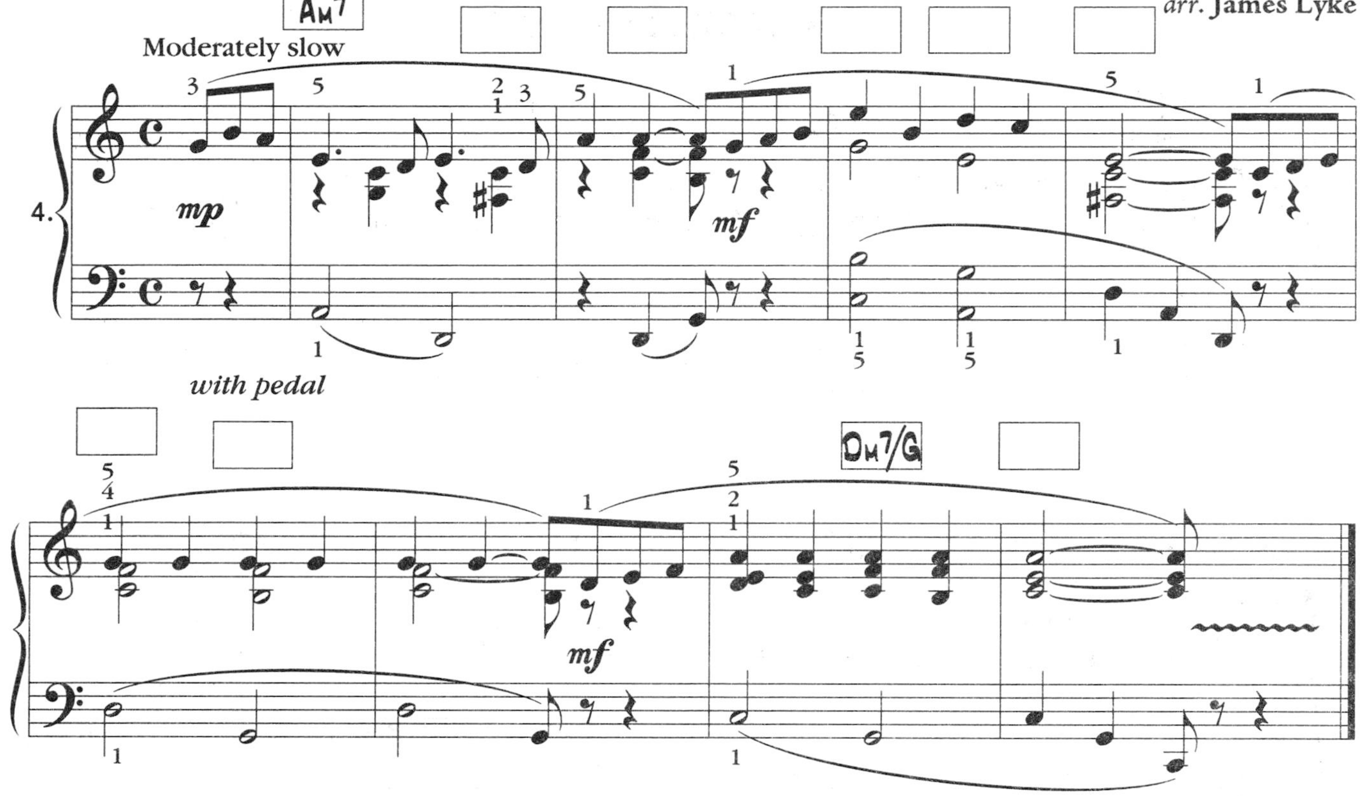

THEY DIDN'T BELIEVE ME

music by **Jerome Kern**
arr. **James Lyke**

Harmonization Using ii^7 and Other Secondary Seventh Chords

Harmonize the following melodies that occasionally call for secondary seventh chords. Follow the example at the beginning to attain a good keyboard texture. Notate and finger your arrangements. Keep the harmony limited to mostly three voices.

POLISH LULLABY

1.

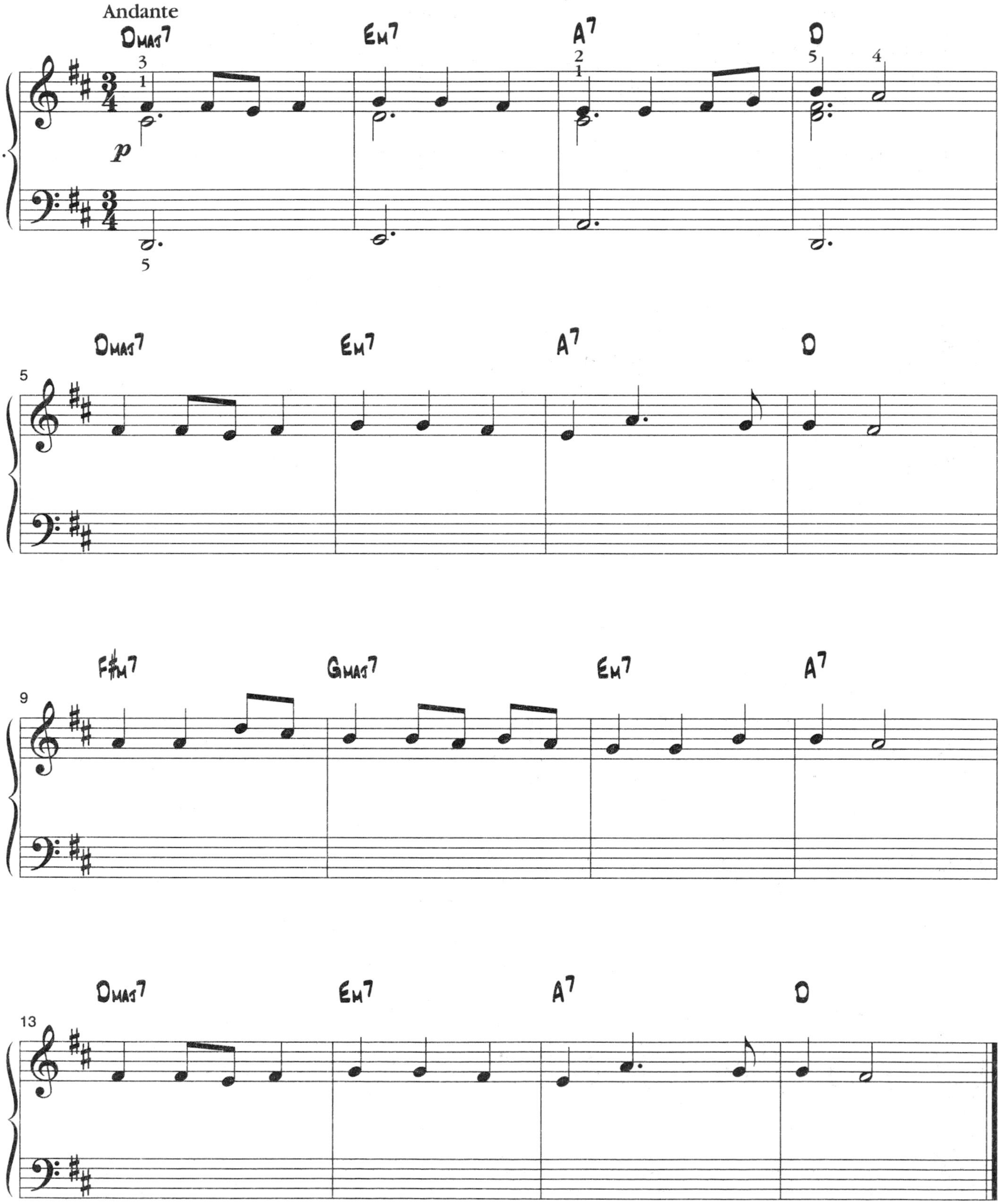

LAS MAÑANITAS

Mexico

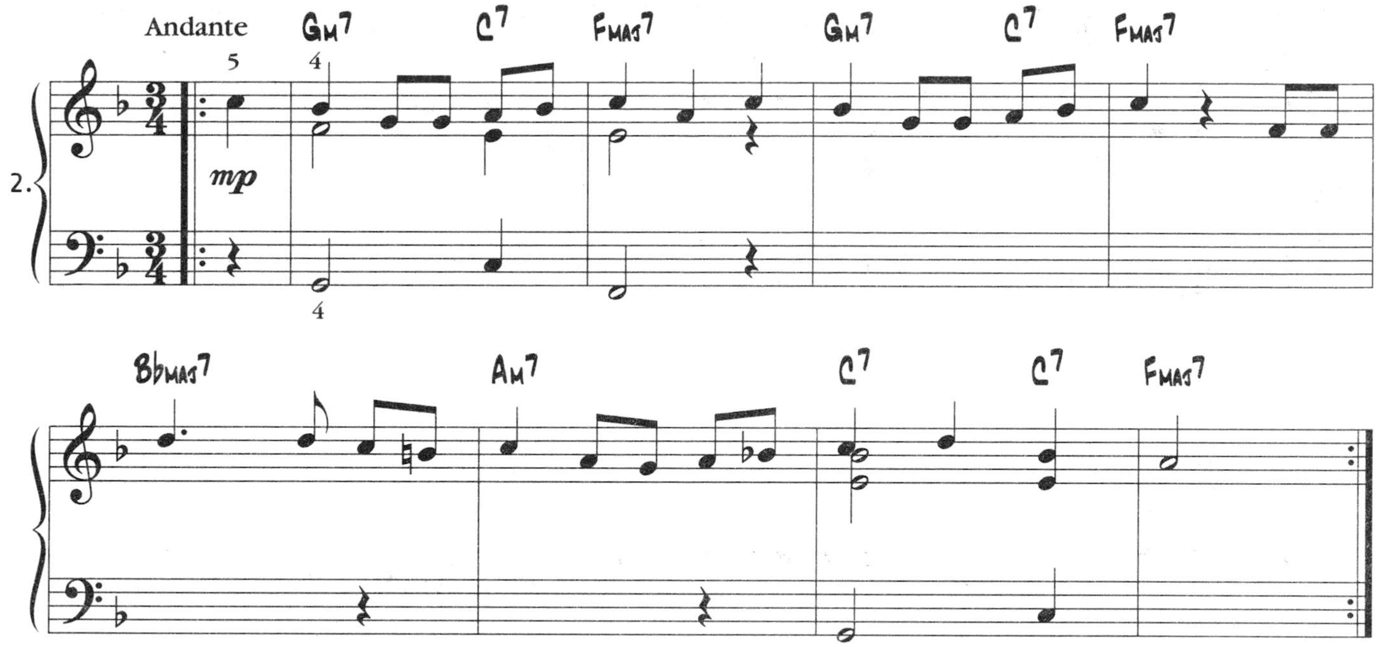

MUSIC ALONE SHALL LIVE

Germany

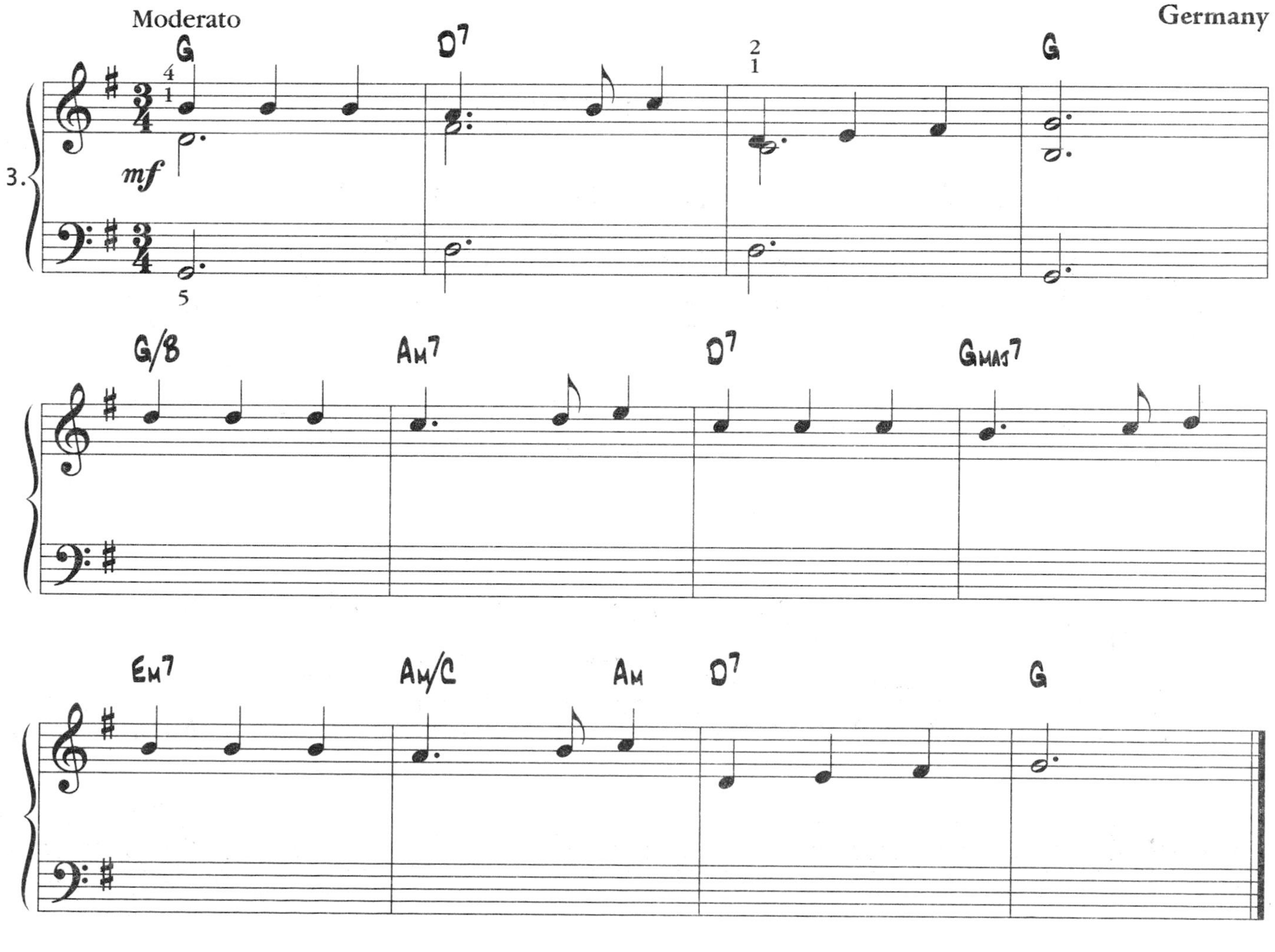

THE LITTLE SHOEMAKER

Janet Gaynor

EARLY ONE MORNING

British

Harmonic Review

Place chord symbols above each new harmony, then play the arrangement.

AMAZING GRACE

American
arr. James Lyke

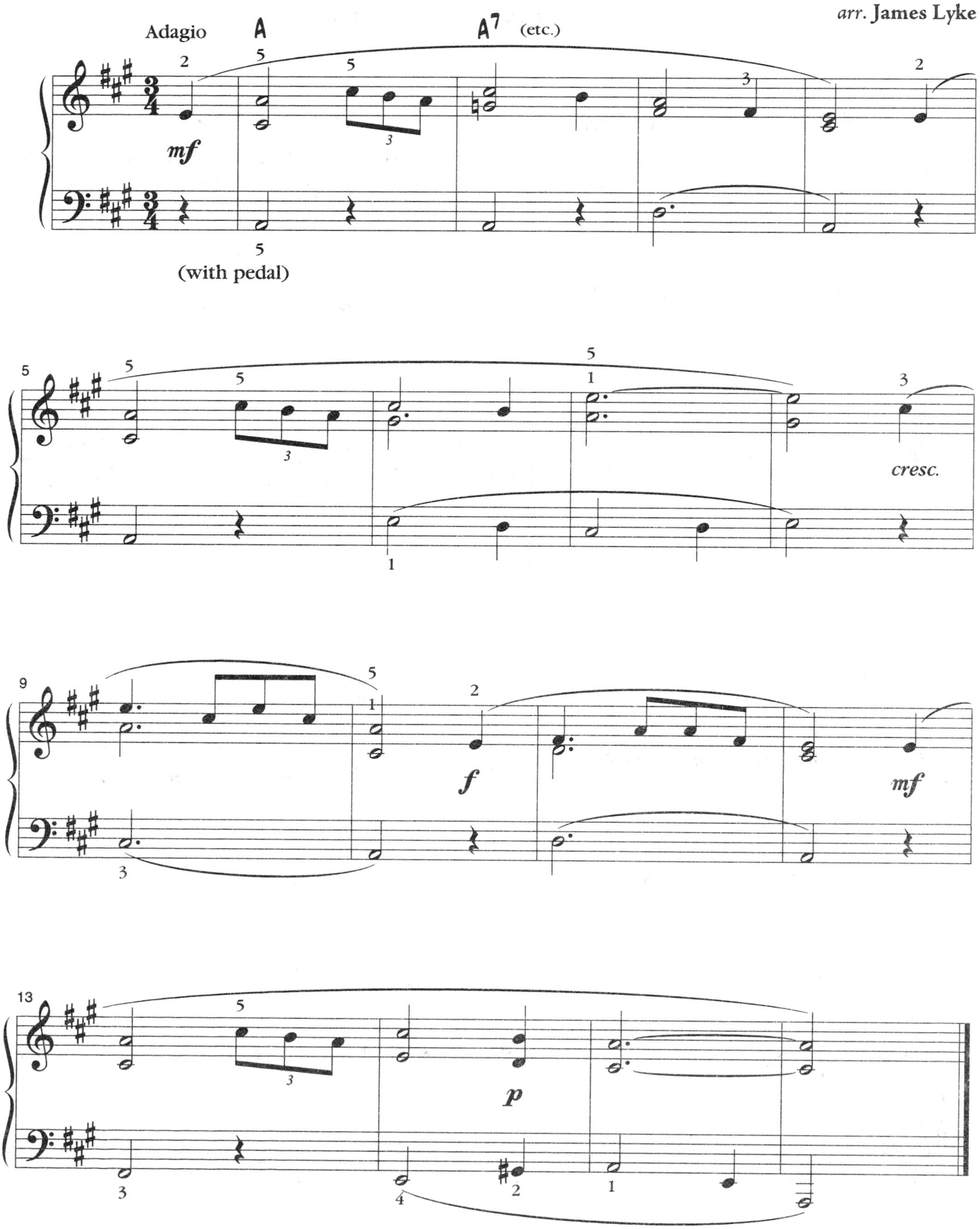

Lead Sheet Harmonization: Harmonizing Popular Songs with Various Types of Seventh Chords

The following two early American popular tunes make use of various types of seventh chords. Study the suggested styles given at the opening of each tune. Some students might find it helpful to notate certain passages (or even the entire arrangement).

YOU MADE ME LOVE YOU

James V. Monaco

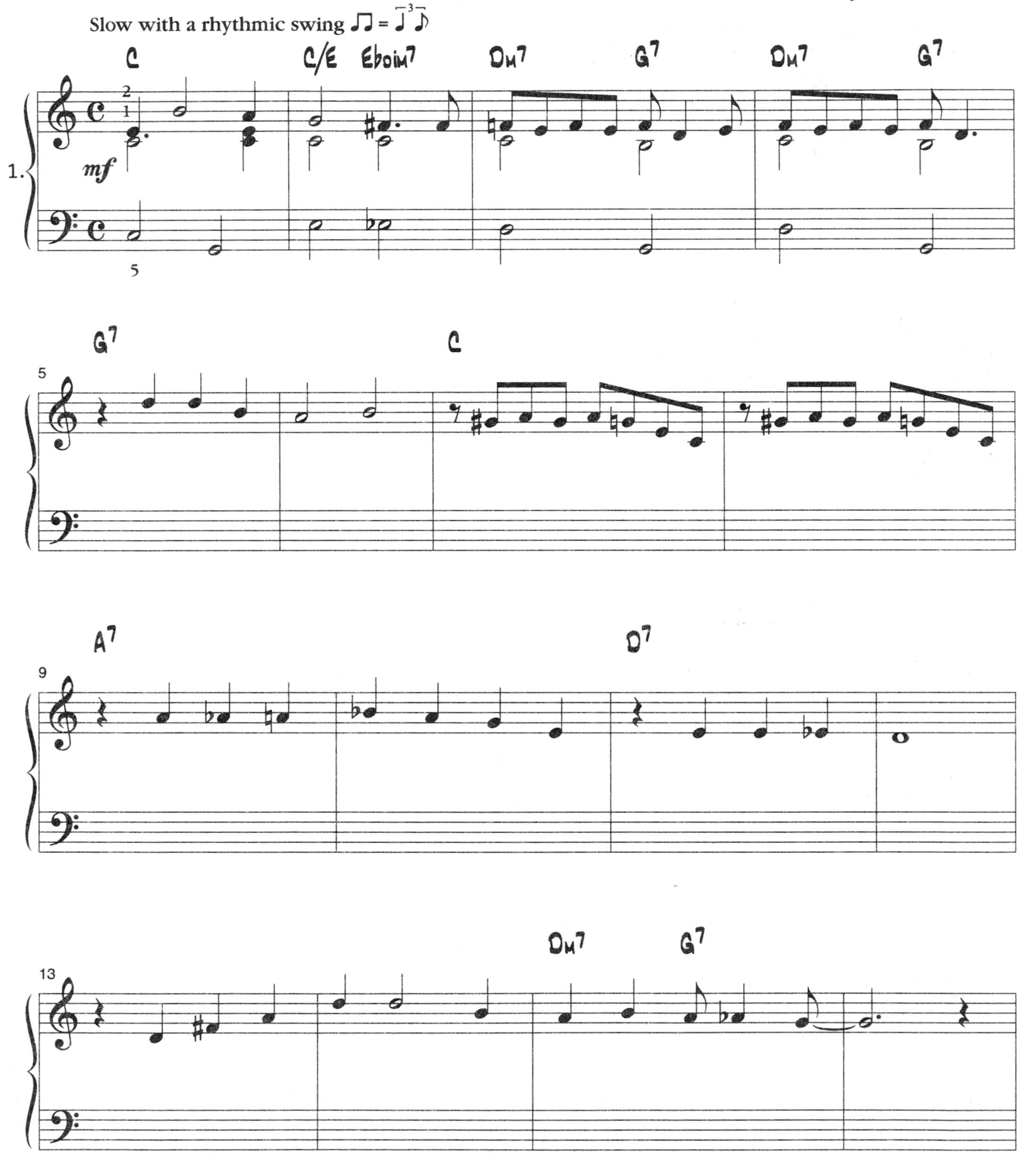

C C/E Ebdim7 Dm7 G7 Dm7 G7
17
G7 E7
21
A7 D7
25
C/G D7 G7 C
29

Gershwin's tune, *Sunday in London Town*, provides an opportunity to use both the diminished seventh and the half-diminished seventh chords ($m^{7(\flat 5)}$). Mostly, the harmonization requires 3 voices. Occasionally, four voices add richness, especially at the close of phrases.

SUNDAY IN LONDON TOWN

George Gershwin

17
C
Ebdim7
21
Dm7
G7
E7
A7
25
Dm7
Dm7(b5)
C/E
Am
29
Dm7
G7
C

Modes

We have already explored major and minor scales, or *modes.* And we have had experience with other modes such as the pentatonic and whole-tone. The Church modes are centuries old and have been used in folk song melody (particularly in Eastern Europe) and in plainsong (Gregorian chant). The untransposed modes can be played on the white keys of the piano with no accidentals. Two of the modes, Ionian and Aeolian, are constructed with the same half and whole step patterns as the major and natural minor scales. Twentieth century composers have used the church modes to get away from the traditional major and minor sound. Study the white key modes below. Play and listen to them. Analyze how each differs from the familiar major and minor scales.

UNTRANSPOSED MODES

Ionian mode – same as major.

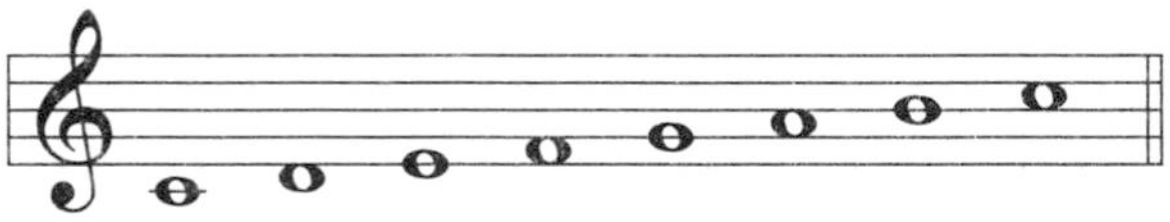

Lydian mode – resembles major except for the raised fourth.

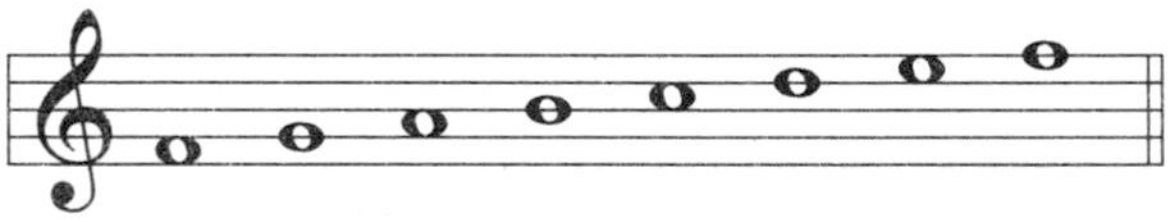

Dorian mode – resembles minor except for the raised sixth.

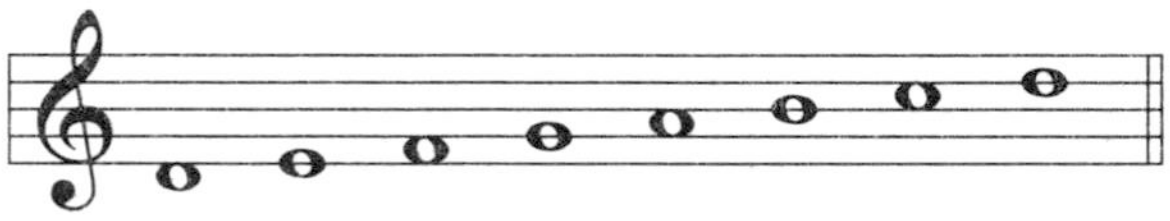

Mixolydian mode – resembles major except for the lowered seventh.

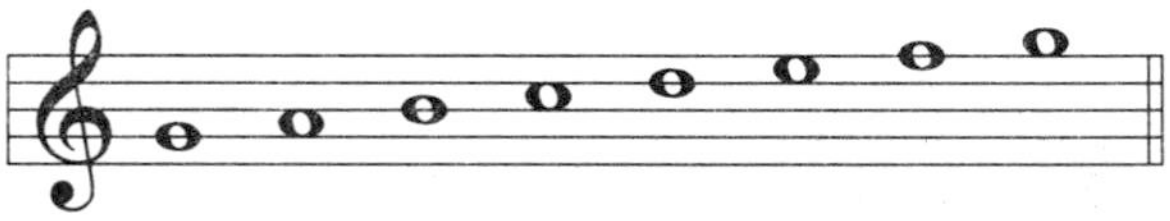

Phrygian mode – resembles natural minor except for the lowered second.

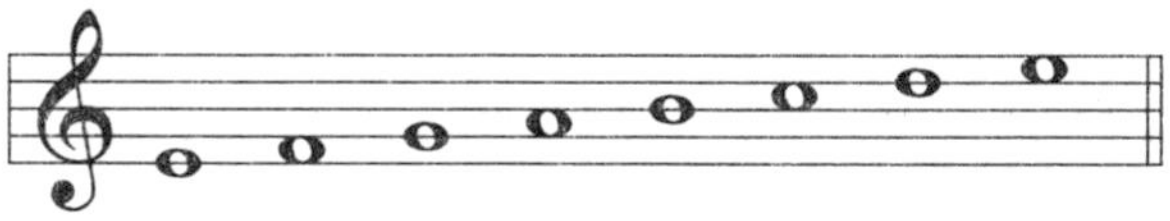

Aeolian mode – same as natural minor.

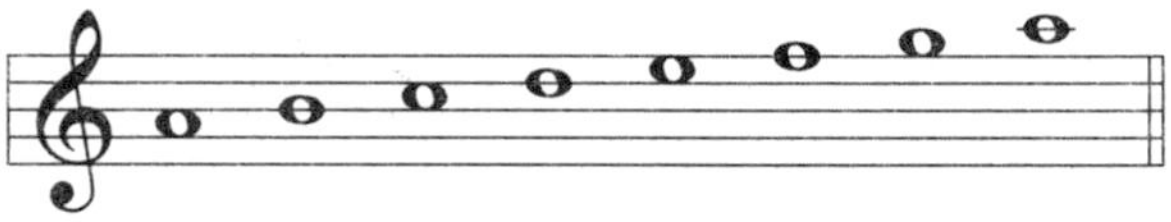

Locrian mode – a theoretic mode that is infrequently used.

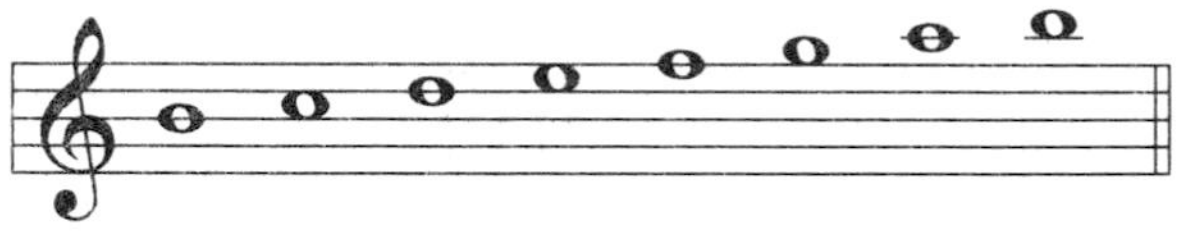

Transposing the Modes

The modes may be transposed to any key. Always think of the relationship the white key modes have with C major. For example, the Dorian mode on D takes the key signature of C major, which is a major second below D. Therefore, the Dorian mode beginning on E has the same key signature as the major scale located a major second below E—D major—and has two sharps. E Dorian is be spelled: E, F♯, G, A, B, C♯, D, and E. The interval relationship is always maintained. For Phrygian, use the major key signature a major third below the tonic; for Lydian, a fourth below; for Mixolydian, a fifth below (or fourth above); for Aeolian, a minor third above; and for Locrian, a half-step above.

When a piece appears to be modal, and the tonal center has been determined, the mode can be quickly analyzed. For example, if the tonal center appears to be F, and the key signature has five flats, the mode is Phrygian because D♭ is a major third below F.

Four Modal Folk Songs for Study

Study and play the following folk song arrangements that illustrate three different modes

CRADLE HYMN

(Aeolian)

Kentucky Folk Song
arr. James Lyke

Slowly ♩ = 90

1.

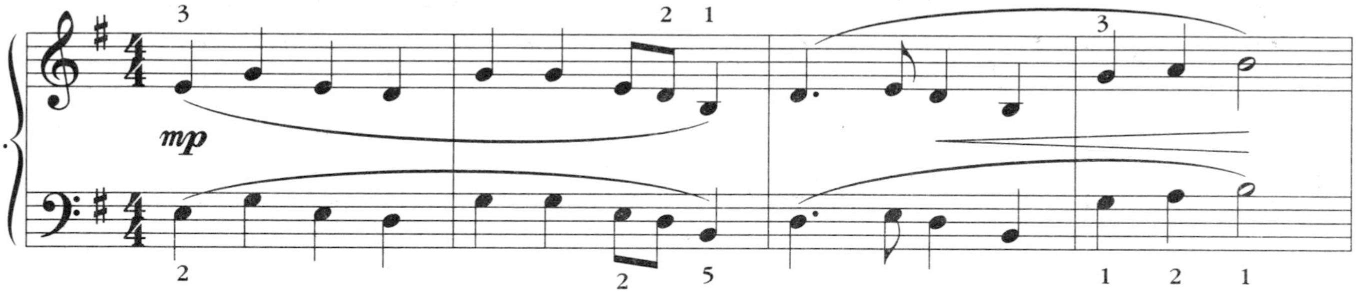

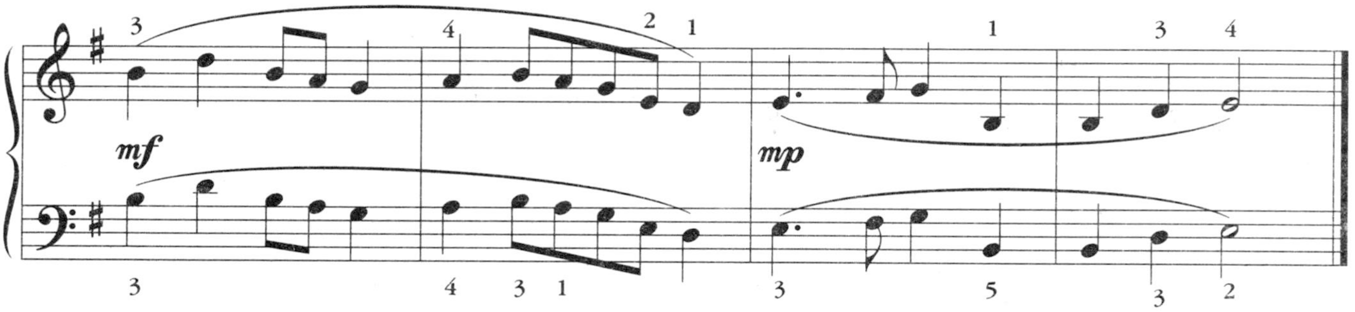

DOWN IN THAT VALLEY

(Phrygian)

Kentucky Folk Song
arr. James Lyke

Slowly ♩ = 60

2.

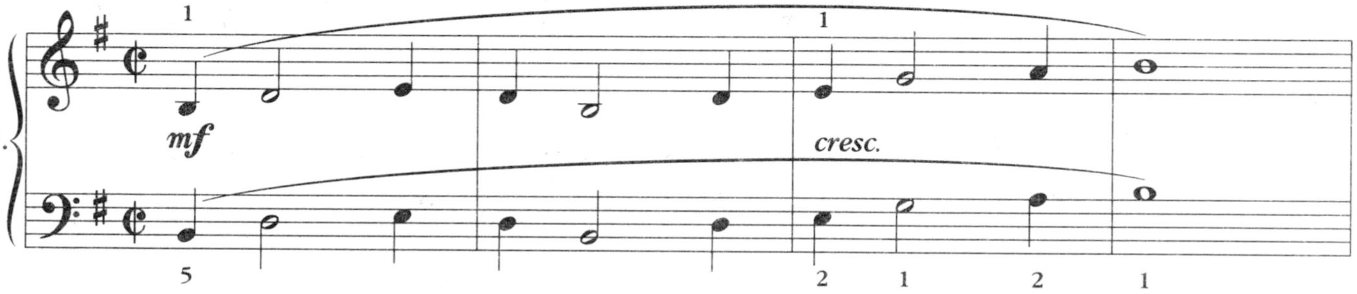

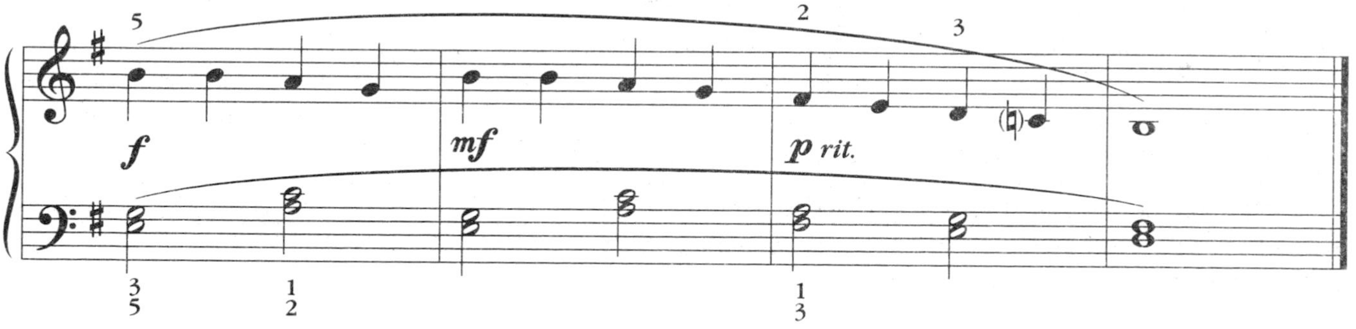

THE DRUNKEN SAILOR

(Dorian)

Chantey
arr. **James Lyke**

WHEN JOHNNY COMES MARCHING HOME

(Aeolian)

American
arr. James Lyke

Allegretto

4.

Two Original Modal Pieces for Study and Performance

Study and play *Phrygian Fever* and *Mixolydian Capers* to gain additional experience with modal writing. Both are white key (untransposed) compositions.

PHRYGIAN FEVER

Céline Bussières-Lessard

MIXOLYDIAN CAPERS

Céline Bussières-Lessard

Four Modal Melodies to Harmonize

Harmonize the following melodies according to the suggested style.

SCARBOROUGH FAIR

(Dorian)

British

JOHNNY HAS GONE FOR A SOLDIER

(Aeolian)

Irish

IROQUOIS SONG

(Dorian)

French Canadian

LULLABY

(Aeolian)

Japanese

Music for Sight Reading and Transposing

Analyze all seventh chords (Fmaj^7 or F$^{\Delta 7}$, Dm^7, etc.) before proceeding with reading.

Diatonic Sevenths

DANISH FOLK SONG

Transpose to G major.

LEAVE HER JOHNNY

Chanty

Transpose to F major.

CALYPSO SONG

Caribbean Islands

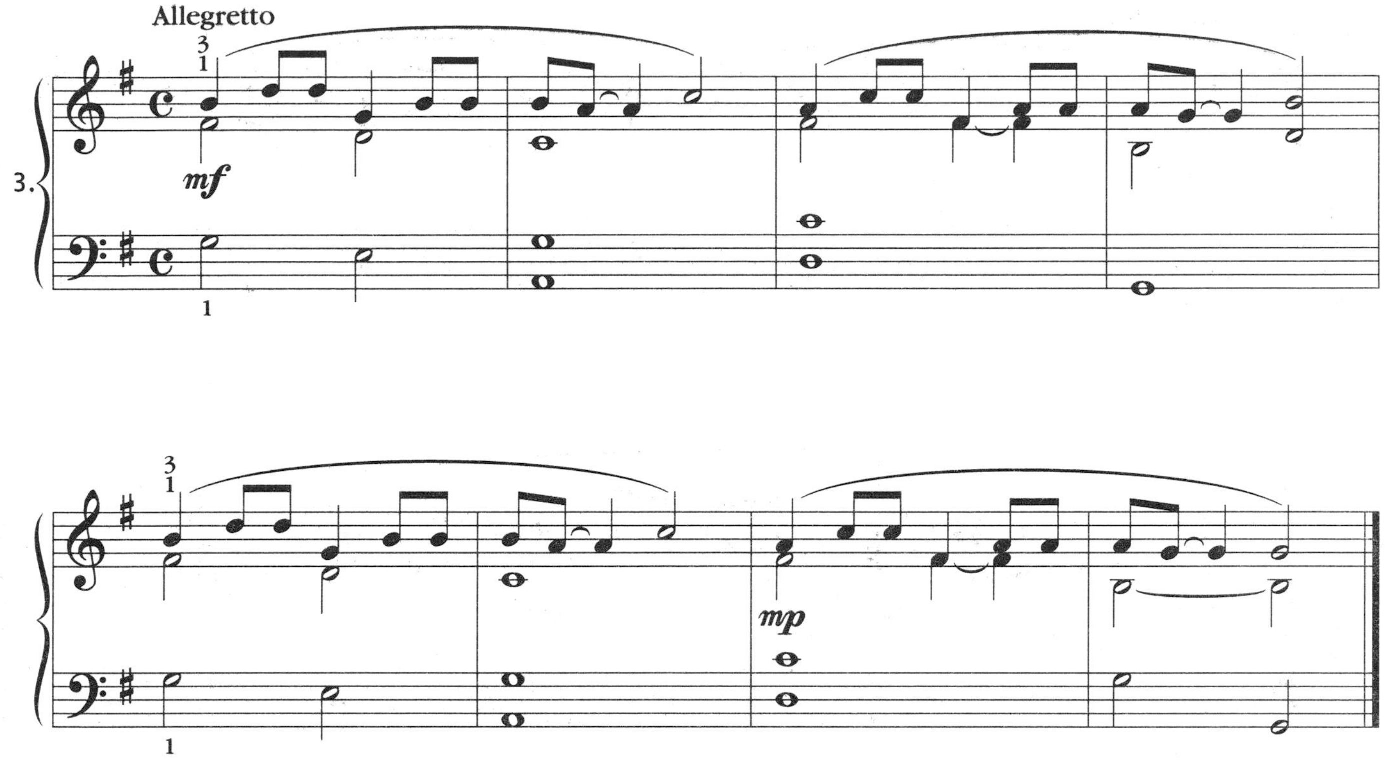

Transpose to F major.

BOBBY SHAFTO

British

Transpose to G major.

MEXICAN FOLK SONG

Moderato

Transpose to G major.

HEY, BETTY MARTIN

United States

Allegro

Transpose to F major.

Minor and Modal

KATIUSHA

Russian

Allegretto

Transpose to G minor.

IN THE VALLEY

Russian

Maestoso

Transpose to A minor.

THE TAILOR AND THE MOUSE

Allegretto

British

9.

Transpose to B aeolian.

THE OAK AND THE ASH

Andante con moto

British

10.

FOLK TUNE

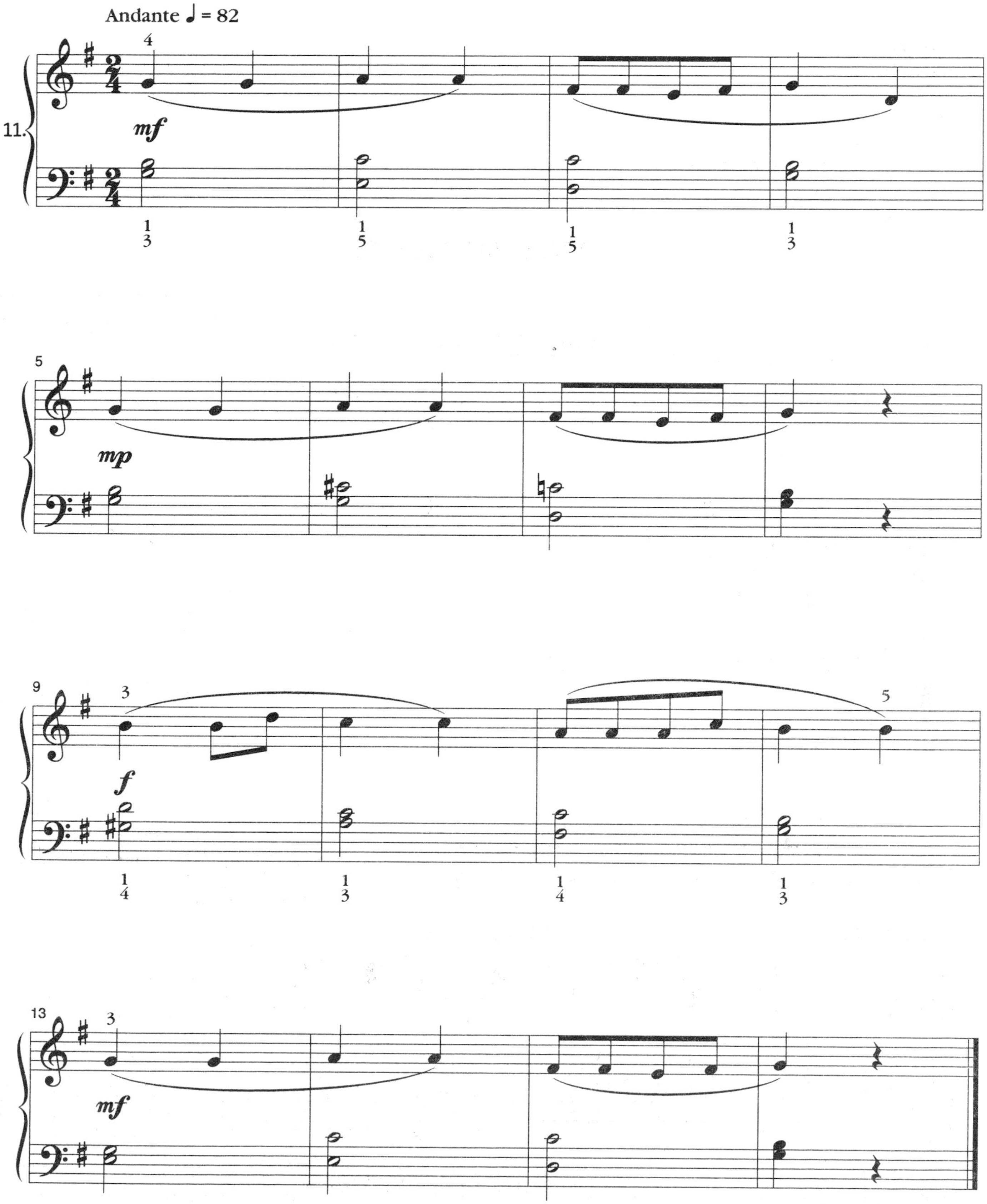

Transpose to F and A.

ACCOMPANYING

Before learning the accompaniment to *Peg O' My Heart*, block each chord in half notes (LH and RH). Analyze each chord and place letter name symbols above the accompaniment part. Then play as written.

48 CD

Teacher: Double the melody two octaves higher.

PEG O' MY HEART

music by **Fred Fisher**
arr. **James Lyke**

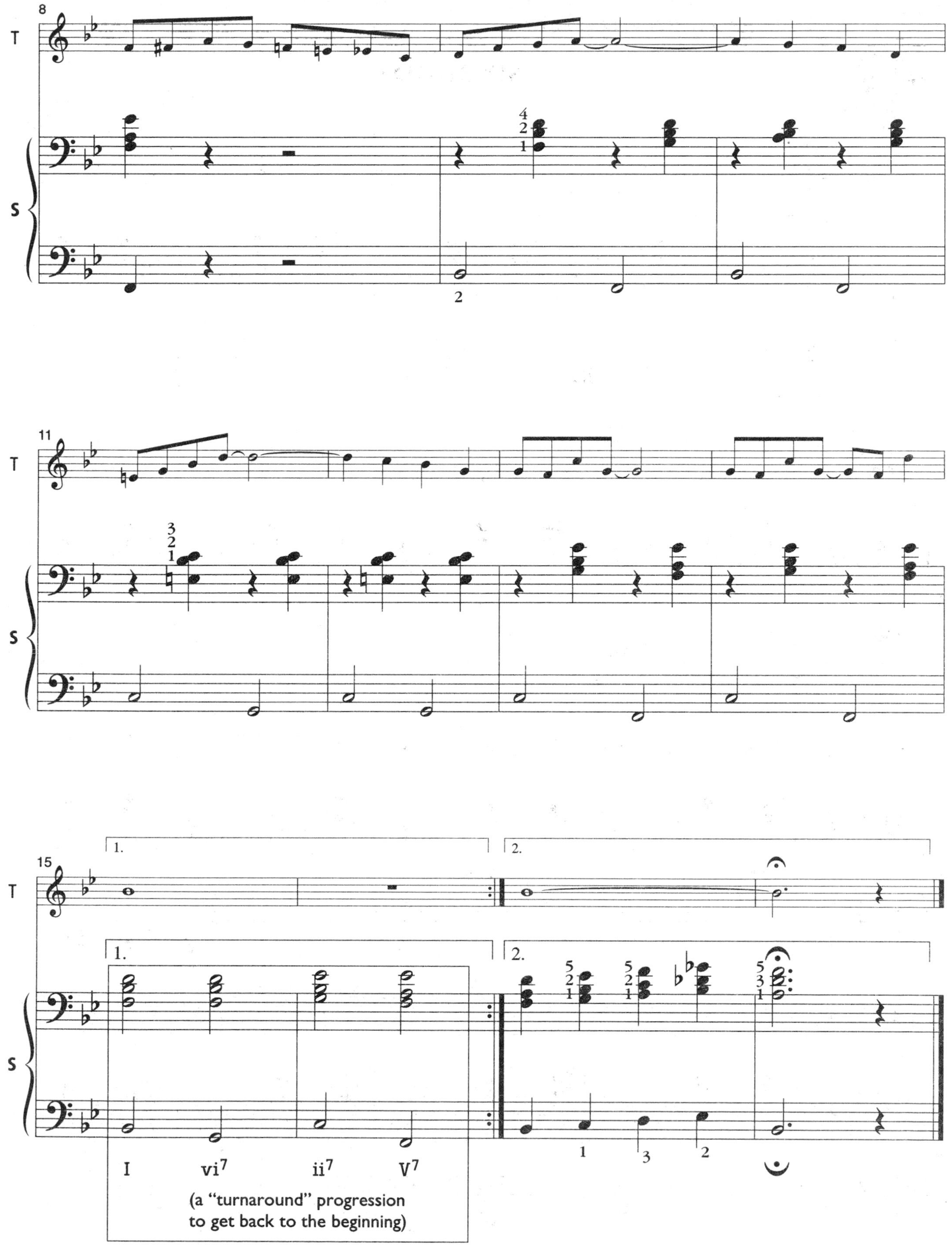
8
T
S
11
T
S
15
1.
2.
T
S
I
vi7
ii7
V7
(a "turnaround" progression
to get back to the beginning)

My Buddy uses diminished seventh chords very effectively. Find an example of an augmented dominant. Label all harmonies in the usual way.

Teacher: Double the melody two octaves higher.

49 CD

MY BUDDY

music by **Walter Donaldson**
arr. **James Lyke**

17
T
S
21
T
S
25
T
S
29
T
S

AMERICAN SONG REPERTOIRE

Cole Porter (composer of *Night and Day, Begin the Beguine*) ranks as one of America's greatest songwriters.

50 CD

OLD-FASHIONED GARDEN

music by **Cole Porter**
arr. **Geoffrey Haydon** *and* **James Lyke**

Moderately (♫ = ♫ straight eighths)

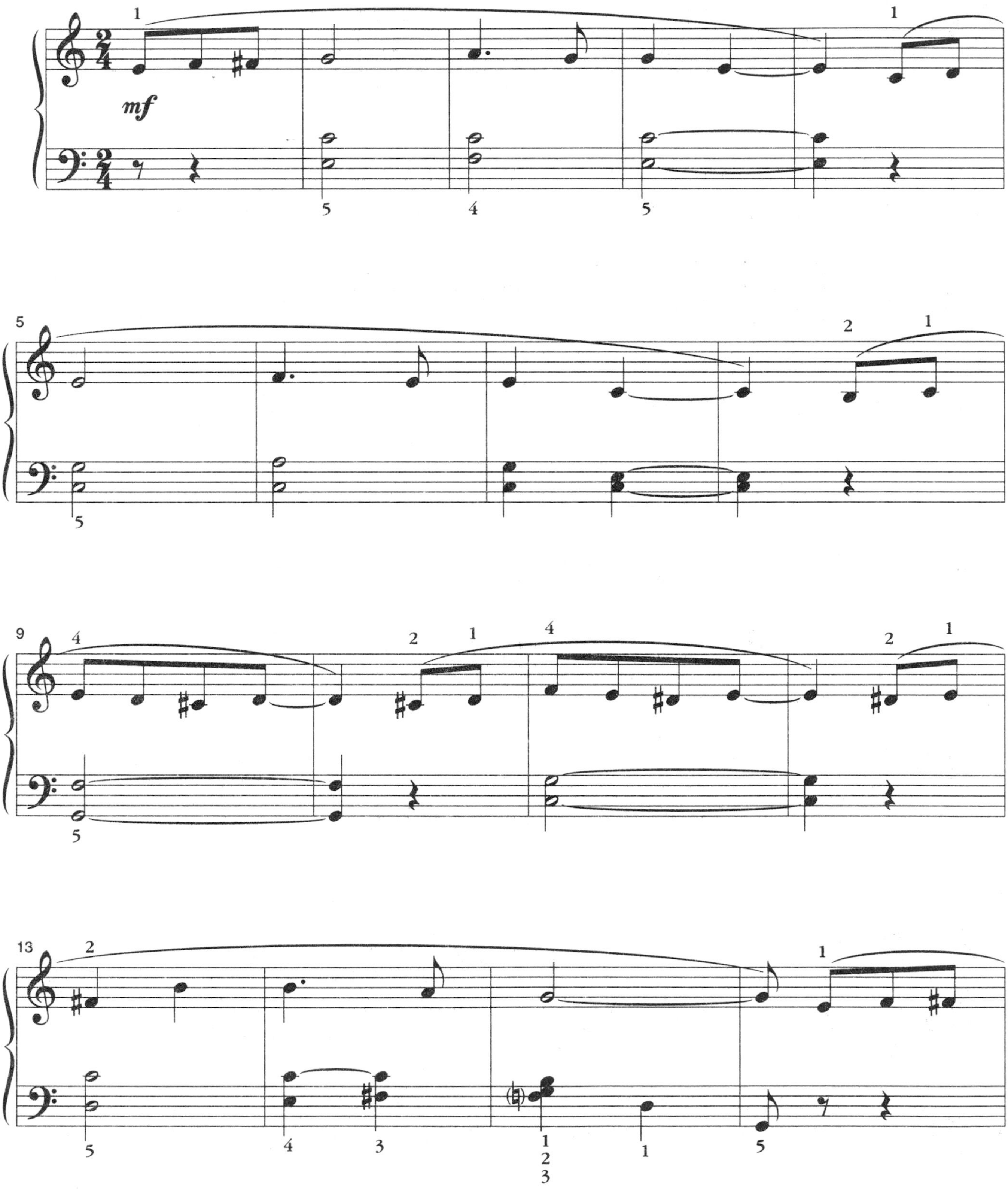

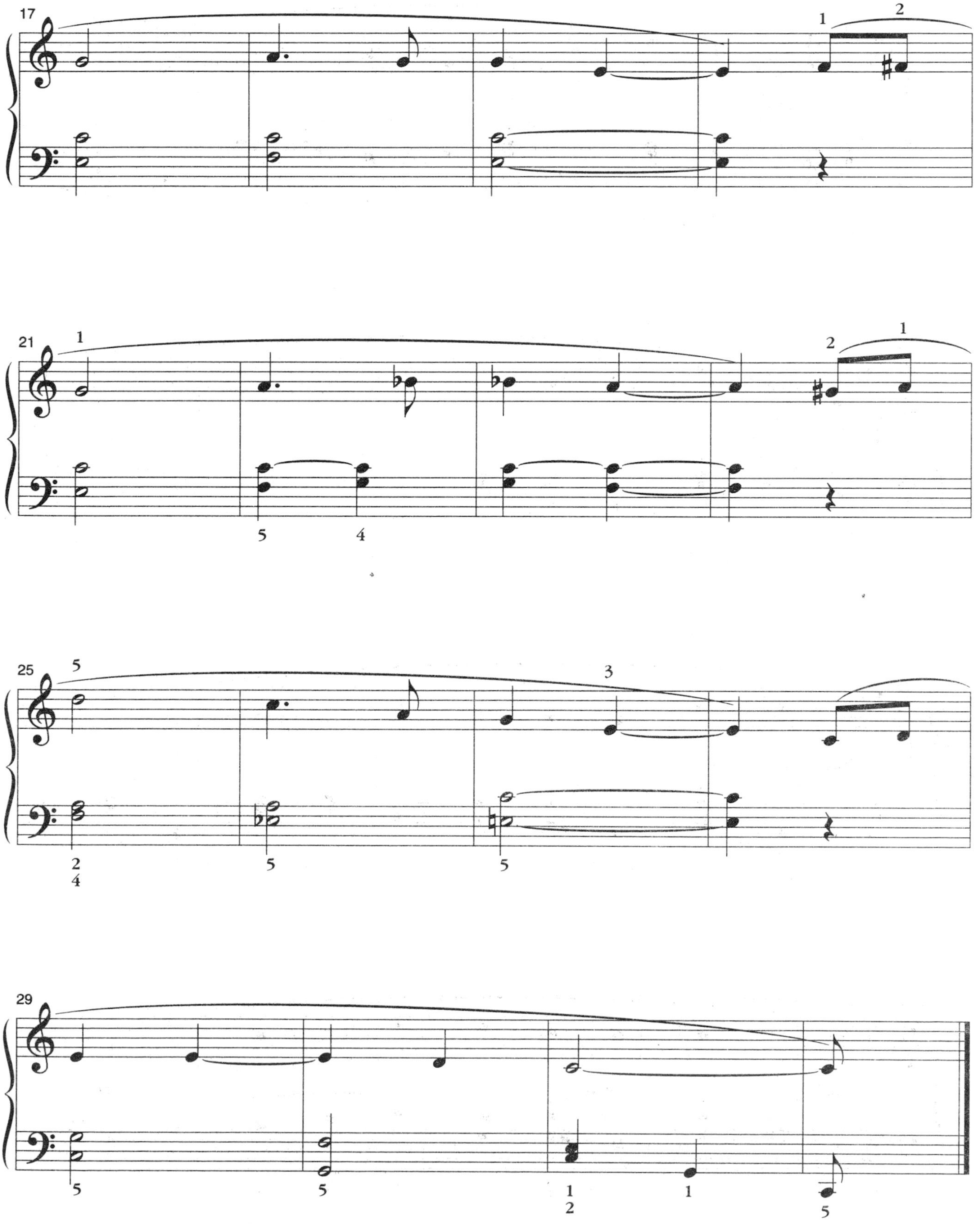

51 CD

TAKE ME OUT TO THE BALL GAME

music by **Albert von Tilzer**
arr. **James Lyke**

Presto ♩ = 130

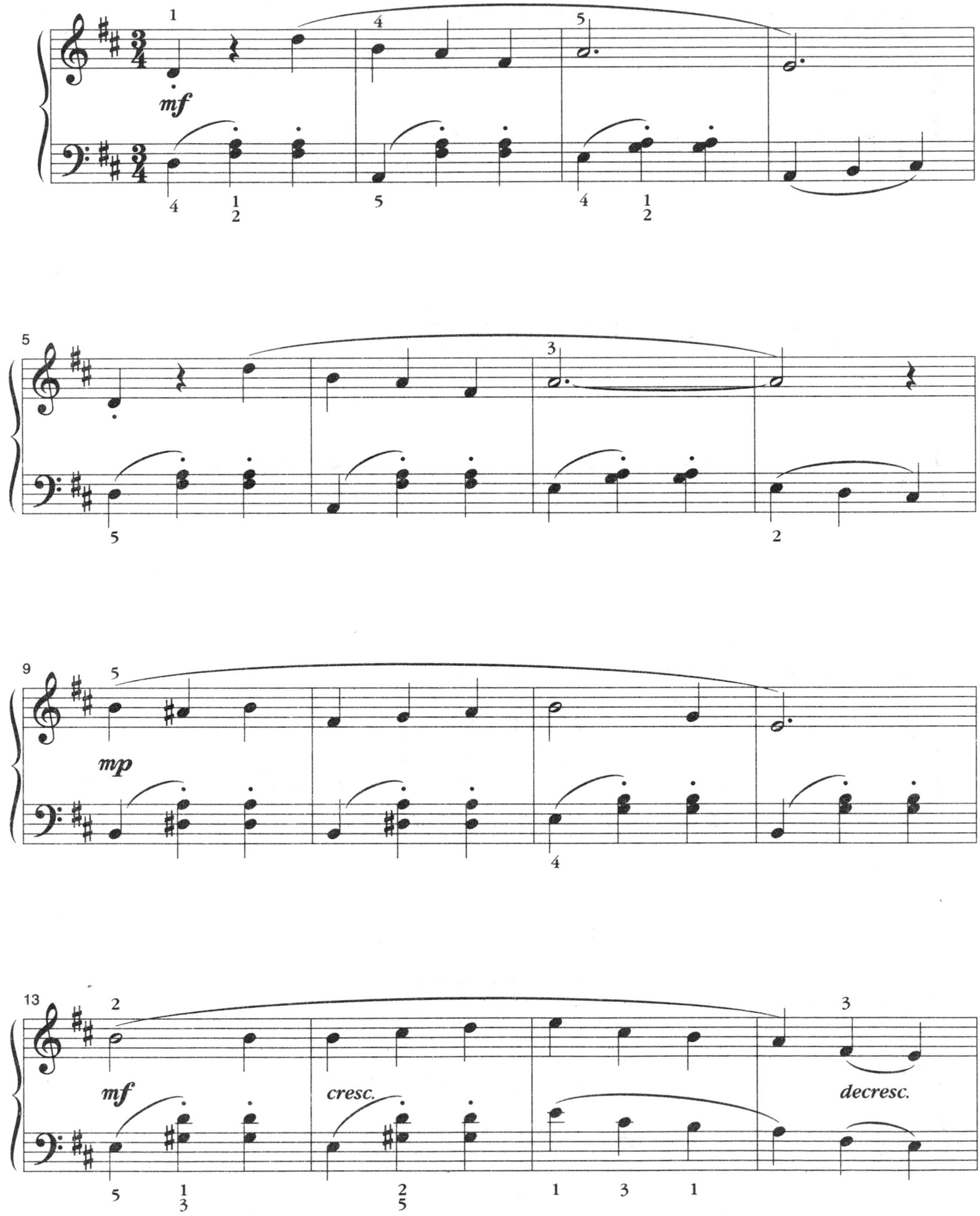

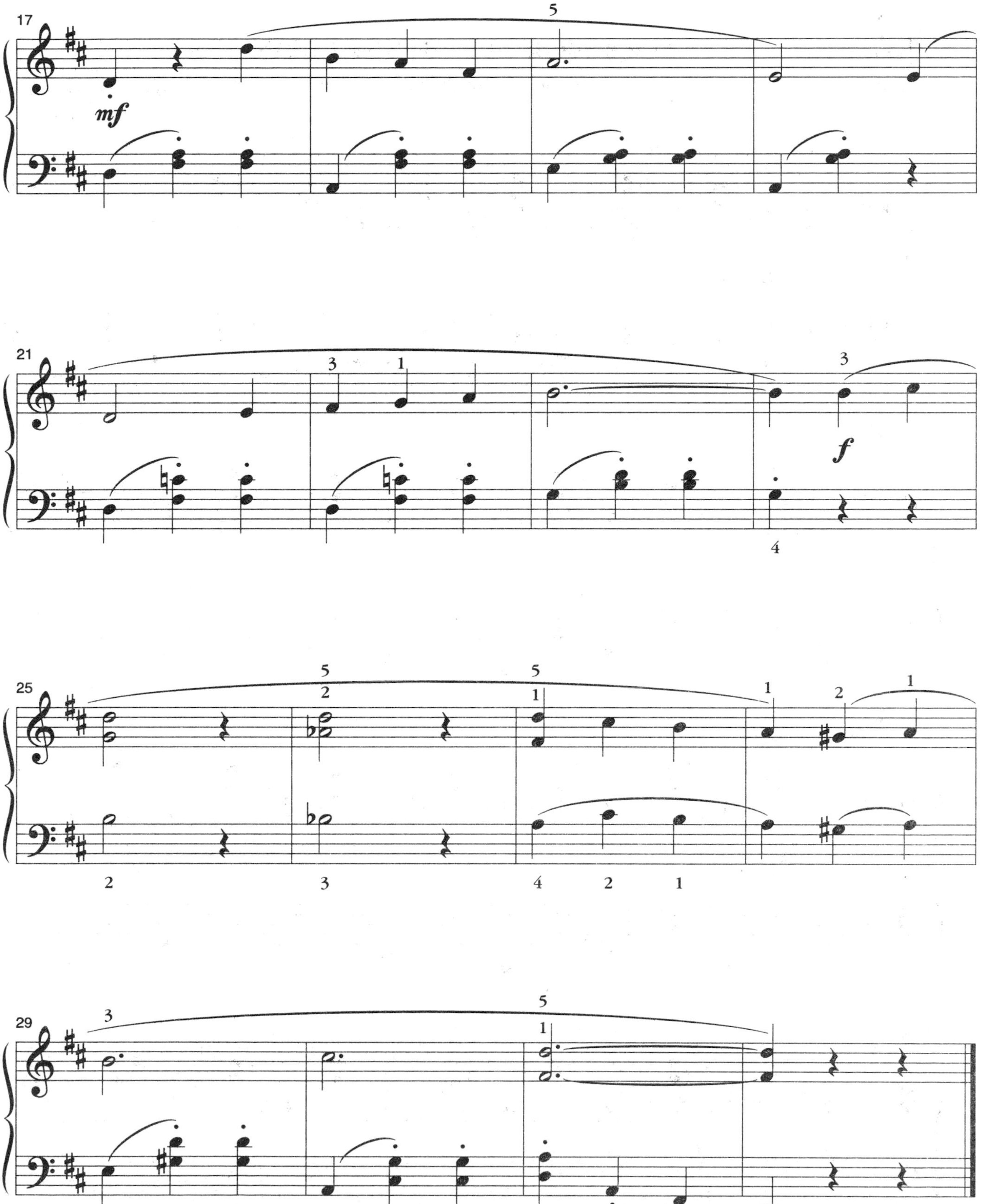
mf
f

ENSEMBLE REPERTOIRE

The secondo part of *Look for the Silver Lining* provides an opportunity to work with various types of seventh chords. Analyze the chords and work through the fingering. The tempo should allow fluency with the chord changes. This part is highly recommended for the student.

52 CD

LOOK FOR THE SILVER LINING

Secondo – Student or Teacher

music by **Jerome Kern**
arr. **James Lyke**

52 CD

LOOK FOR THE SILVER LINING

Primo – Teacher or Student

music by **Jerome Kern**
arr. **James Lyke**

Secondo

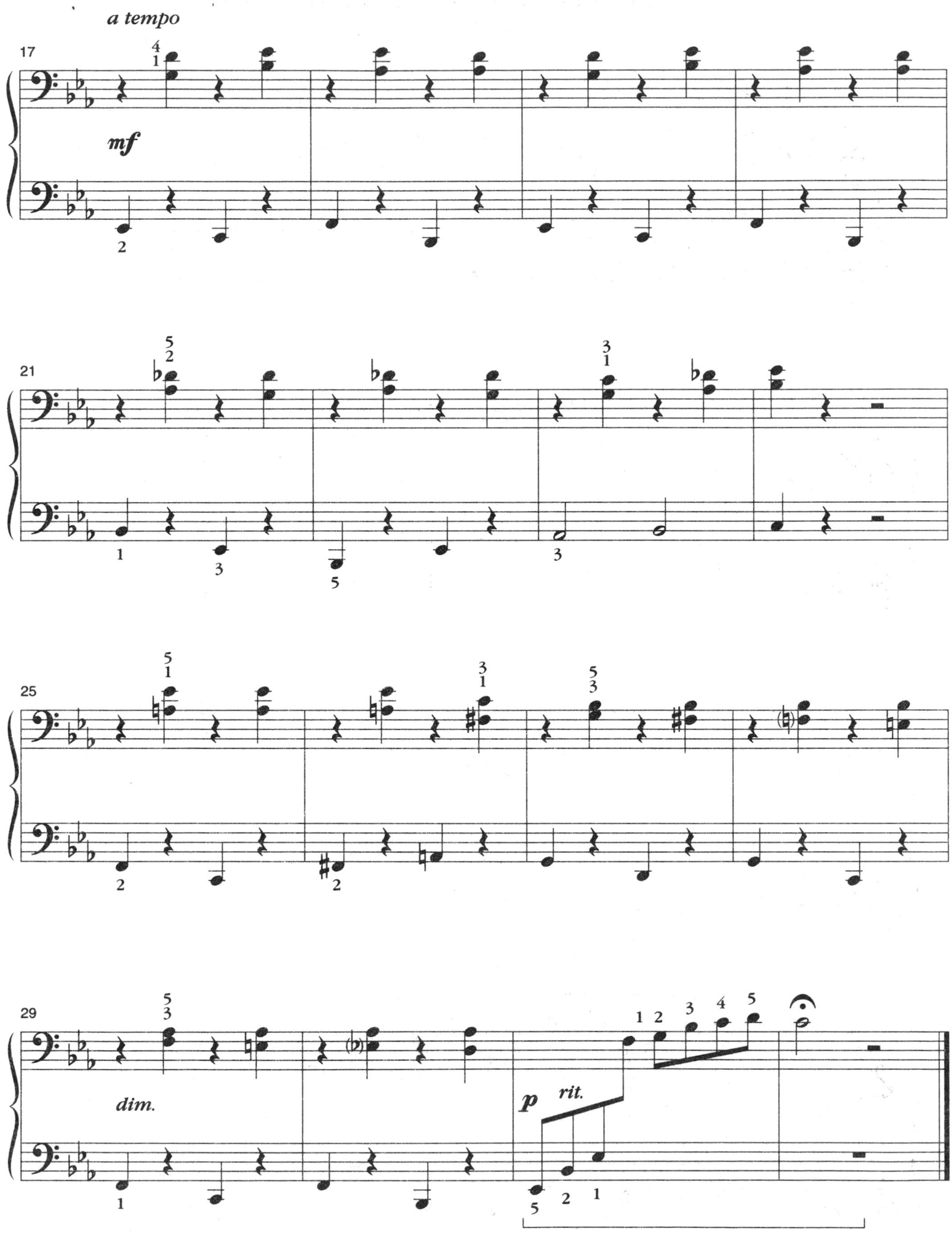

Primo

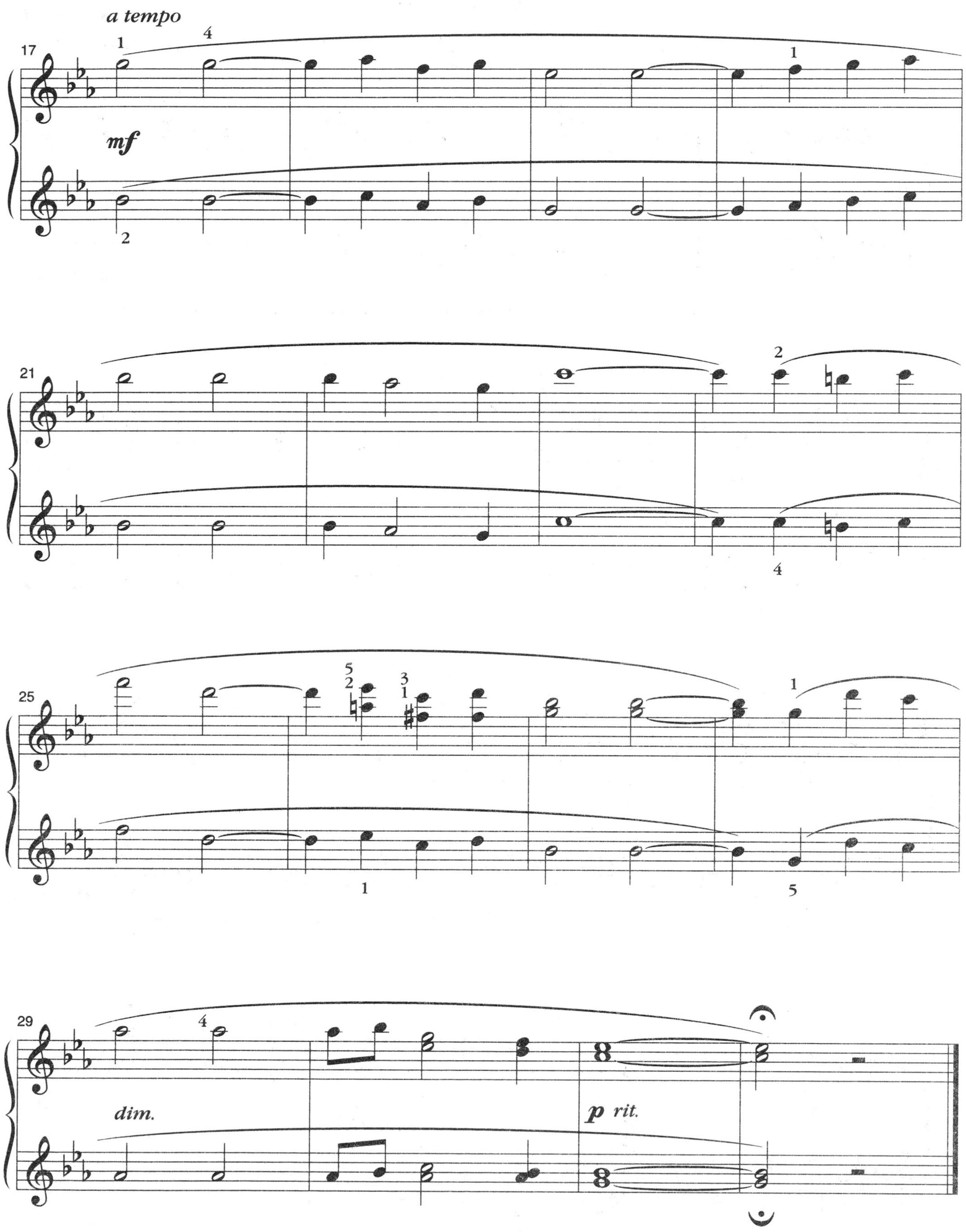

53 CD

EMPTY BED BLUES

Secondo – Teacher

Southern U.S.
arr. James Lyke

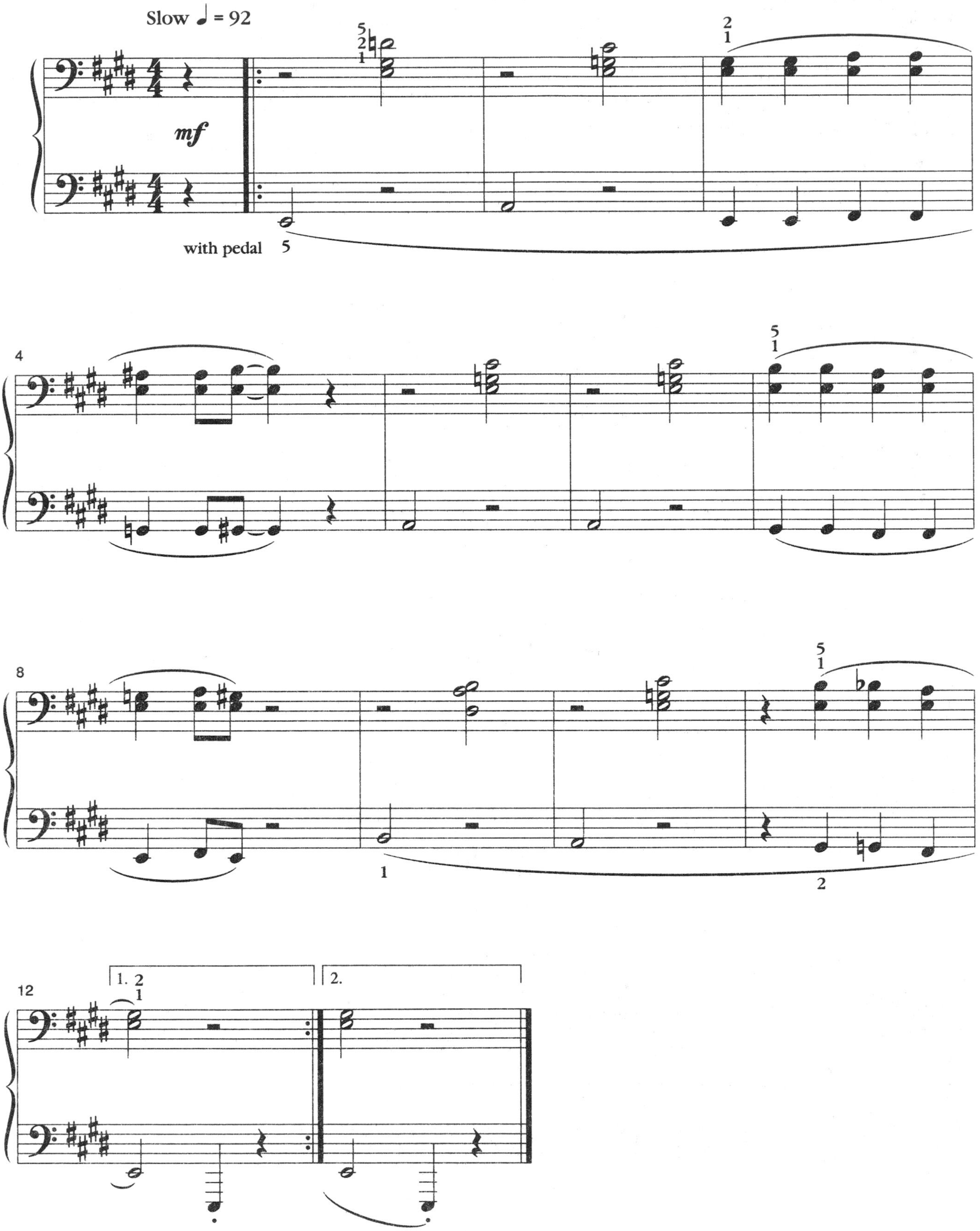

EMPTY BED BLUES

Primo – Student

Southern U.S.
arr. **James Lyke**

SOLO REPERTOIRE

Practice Plan: Slightly detach quarter notes. Be attentive to the phrase markings in each hand. Give rests full value.

MINUET

BWV 820

J.S. Bach

Tempo di minuet

Practice Plan: Practice hands separately with given fingerings. Perform proper 2-note slurs, keep firm finger tips and utilize a down – up wrist motion. Slowly play hands together.

ALLEGRO IN B FLAT, K. 3

W.A. Mozart

Practice Plan: Use a deeper touch on thumb notes and use circular motions to complete the RH triplet figure. The thumb note is the melody. Ask your instructor for guidance with pedaling.

THE LIMPID STREAM

Op. 100, no. 7

Friedrich Burgmüller

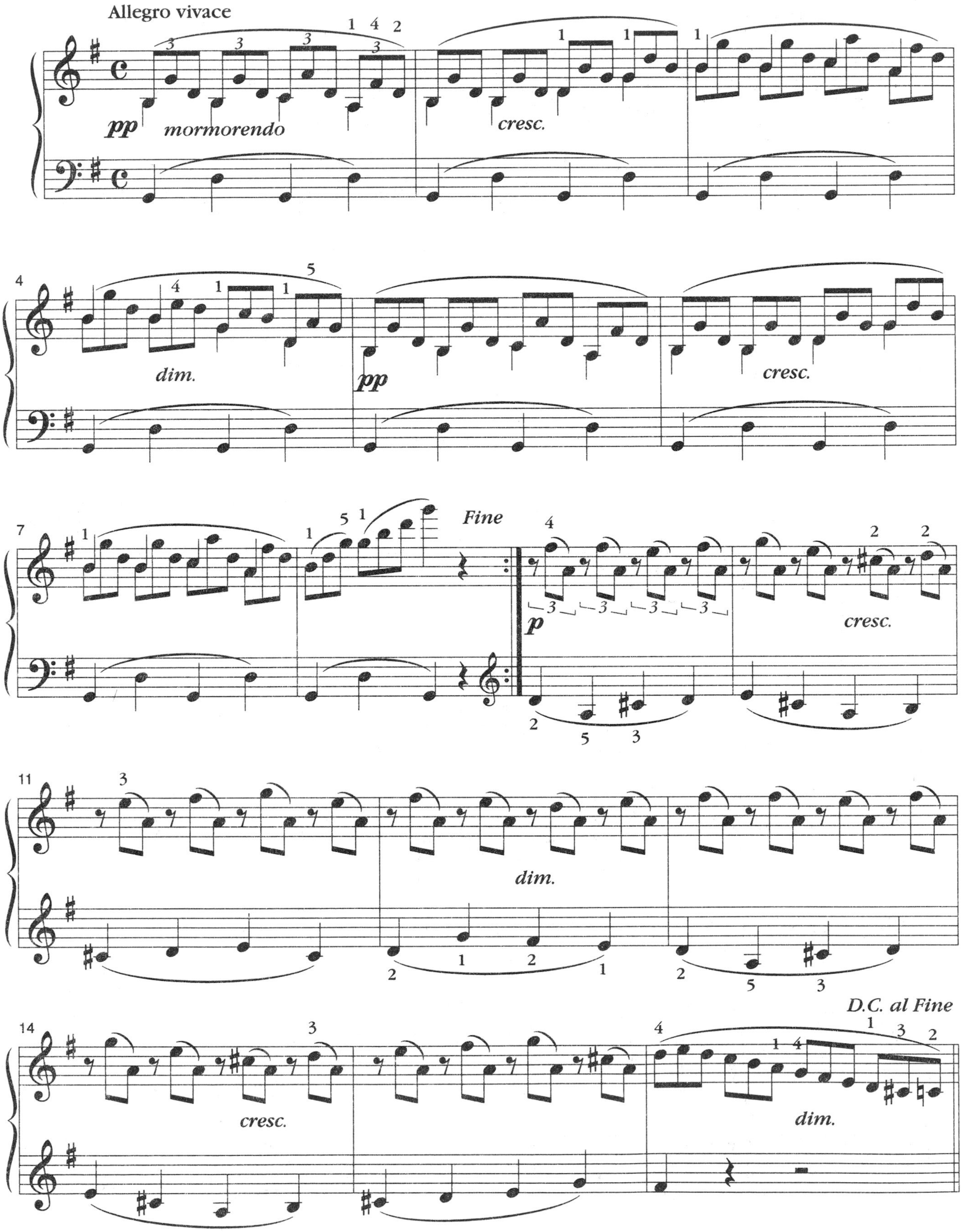

Practice Plan: Practice the LH alone, paying special attention to the shifts. Play the RH stronger than the LH. Observe pedal indications.

TANGO

Céline Bussières-Lessard

Practice Plan: Block the LH intervals at first. Isolate measures 1-4, 17-20, and 34-36 to practice quick shifts. Strive to bring the melody to the foreground (RH or LH). Careful pedaling is required.

ALONG THE SEINE

James Lyke

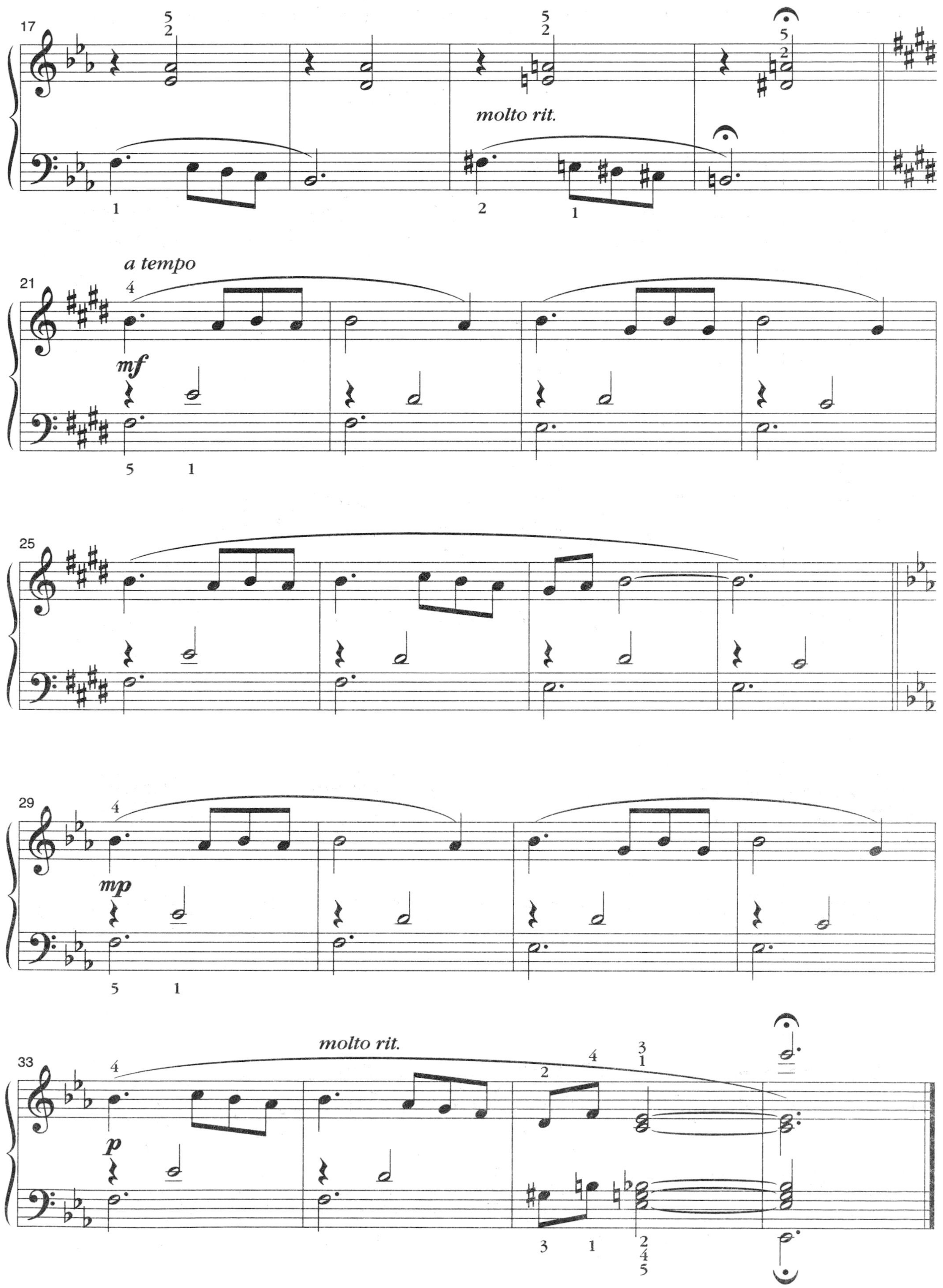
molto rit.
a tempo
mf
mp
molto rit.
p

Practice Plan: *Swing Street* has some sophisticated harmonies which bear careful scrutiny. You will find some instances of dominant sevenths sliding to a major seventh from a half step above. Analyze this composition and add chord symbols. Practice in the usual way (LH alone, RH alone, HT very slowly with a steady beat).

SWING STREET

Geoffrey Haydon

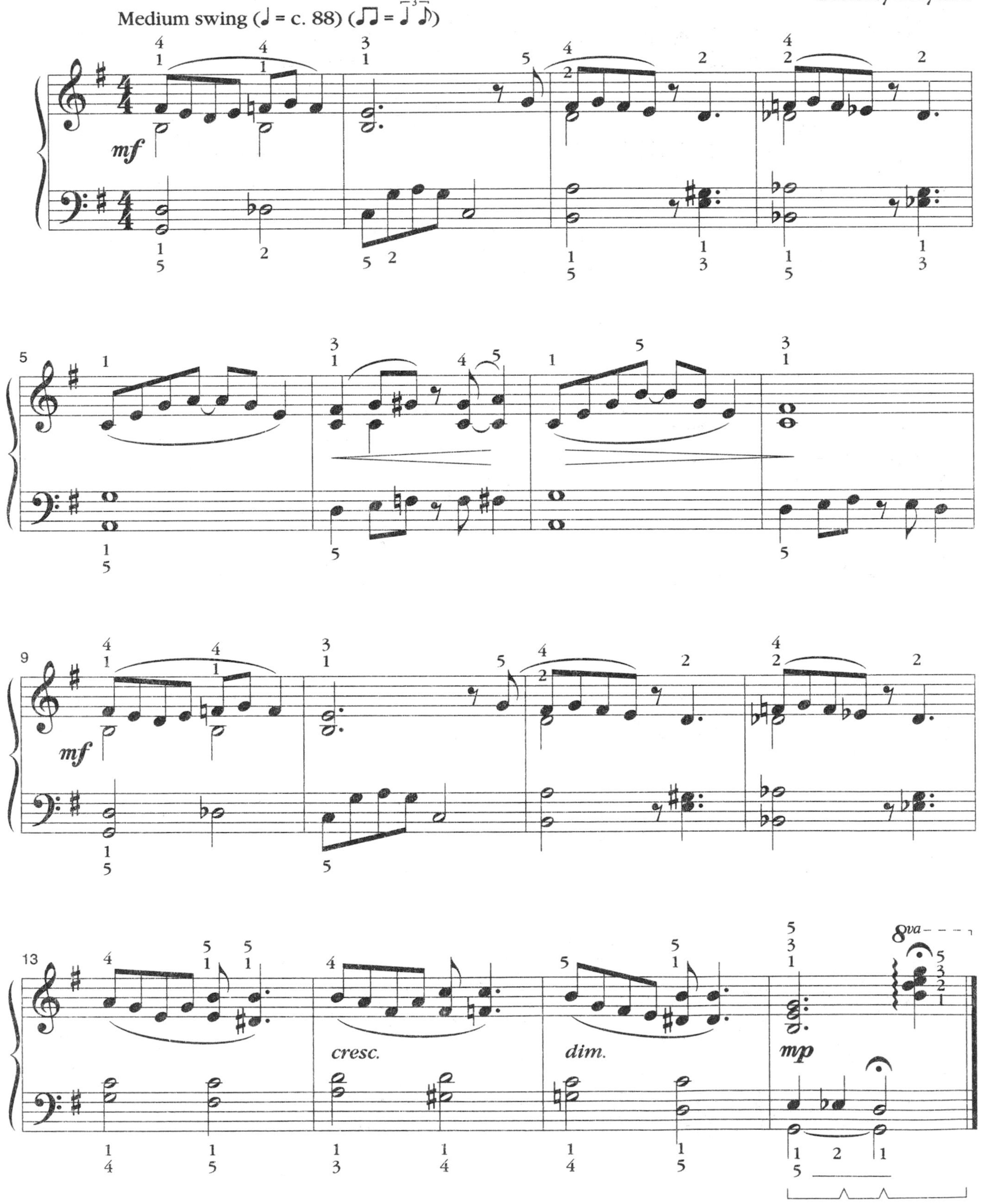

Practice Plan: LH will require much practice to shift from one chord to another. Play the RH alone many times with "swing" rhythm. Combine hands at a slow tempo and maintain swing eighths in the RH. The CD track supplies a jazz trio accompaniment for this selection.

In *Chromatic Promenade*, the LH mostly plays two- or three-note seventh chords which rarely contain roots. These LH voicings can be combined with an upright bass player's line in the context of a jazz duo.

54 CD

CHROMATIC PROMENADE

Geoffrey Haydon

MUSICIANSHIP ACTIVITIES

Complete the following exercises that review topics introduced in Chapter 8.

In both treble and bass clefts, build close position seventh chords on the various tones given below. Double-check the chord quality before notatng each chord.

1.

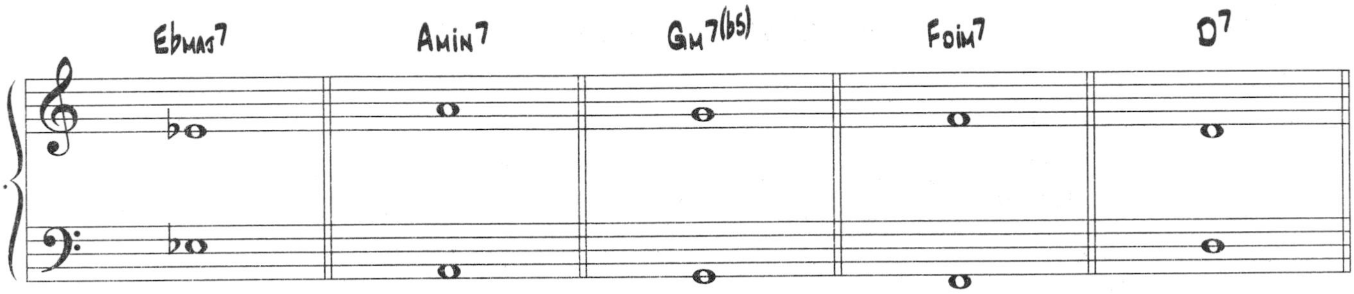

Analyze and label the following chords by letter name.

2.

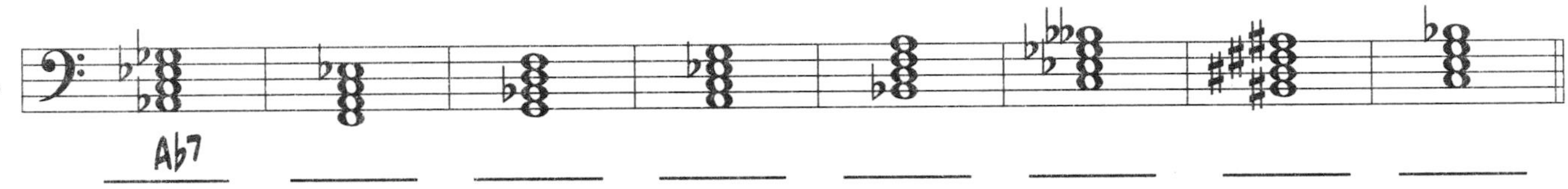

Build the following three modes from the given starting note.

G Lydian mode

3.

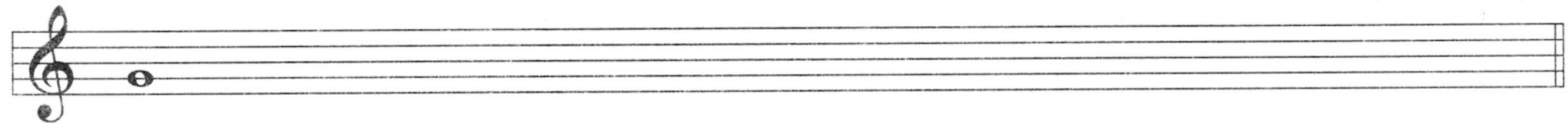

E Dorian mode

F Mixolydian mode

Modal Improvisation

Using the LH ostinato tango figure, improvise RH melodies in the Phrygian mode on white keys. Repeat several times until a satisfactory cadence is reached.

4.

Complete the following progression by providing the missing seventh of each chord. Label each chord. Play the progression.

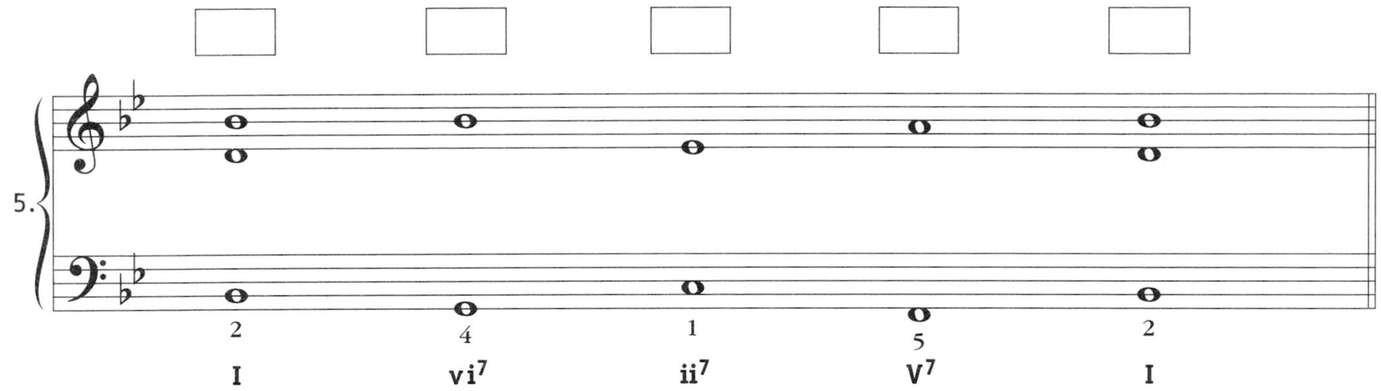

Complete the following progression by providing the missing third of each chord. Label each chord. Play the progression.

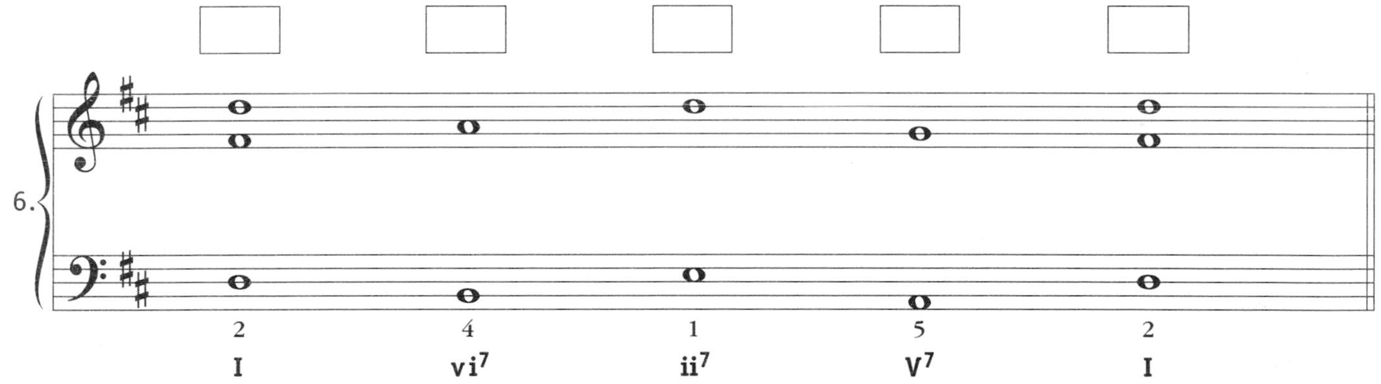

TECHNICAL STUDIES

Harmonic Minor Scales: f and b

Continue the study of harmonic minor scales. The fingerings of the f and b harmonic minor scales are the same as their parallel major scales. Consult the *Scale Fingering Chart* on page 215, or Appendix B for a thorough presentation of all scales and arpeggios.

Minor Arpeggios: f and b

Continue the study of minor arpeggios. The fingerings of the f and b minor arpeggios are the same or similar to the major arpeggios. Consult Appendix B to check fingerings.

SUGGESTED PLAYING EXAM TOPICS
CHAPTER EIGHT

1. Play the chord progression ii^7–V^7–I^7 in six keys suggested by your instructor. Play the chord progression I–vi^7–ii^7–V^7–I in the keys of G, D, F, and B♭. See page 306.

2. Play a harmonized example of *You Made Me Love You* (pages 314-315), or *Sunday in London Town* (pages 316-317).

3. Build and play modes built on white keys. Identify each mode and be able to transpose them (see page 318). Perform one arrangement of a modal folk song from pages 319-321.

4. Play two of the sight reaing studies on pages 326-331. Harmonize one of the modal studies from pages 324-325.

5. Play an accompaniment selected from pages 332–335.

6. Perform one of the American Song Repertoire solos from pages 336–339.

7. Perform an ensemble selection from pages 340–345.

8. Perform one (or two) pieces from the Solo Repertoire section found on pages 346-353.

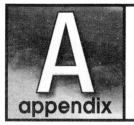

A appendix Glossary of Musical Terms and Signs

Musical Terms

Accelerando (accel.)	gradually increasing the speed or tempo.
Accidental	sharp, flat, natural, double sharp, double flat used separately from those in key signatures.
Adagio	slow, but quicker than Largo and Lento.
Agitato	agitated; restless.
Allegretto	lively; slower than Allegro.
Allegro	quick; lively; rapid.
Andante	moderately slow, but flowing easily (walking tempo).
Andantino	a little faster than Andante.
Animato (Animando)	lively; animated.
Arpeggio	playing the notes of a chord consecutively (harp style).
Assez vif (vite)	rather quickly.
A tempo	in time. A return to the original tempo after a ritard or accelerando.
Blues	slow style of music employing jazz rhythms.
Cadence	a close in melody or harmony. The end of a phrase.
Calma	calm, quiet.
Calypso	folk song from the Caribbean region with syncopated rhythms.
Cantabile	in singing style.
Cesura (//)	a complete separation.
Chorale	old form of psalm or hymn tune of the early German Protestant Church.
Coda	a passage added to the end of a composition.
Con	with.
Con anima	with animation; life.
Con brio	with fire; spirit.
Con fuoco	with fire.
Con moto	with motion.
Con Spirito (spiritoso)	with spirit.
Crescendo (cresc.)	gradually becoming louder.
Da Capo (D.C.)	from the beginning.
Dal Segno (D.S.)	repeat from the sign.
Decrescendo (decresc.)	gradually becoming softer.
Diminuendo (dim.)	gradually softer.
Dolce	sweetly; softly.
Ecossaise	a lively Scottish dance.
Espressione	expression, deep feeling.
Espressivo	expressive.
Fermata	a pause or hold.
Fine	the end.
Forte (*f*)	loud.
Fortissimo (*ff*)	very loud.
German Dance	a dance related to the Minuet in $\frac{3}{4}$ time.
Giocoso	happy; playful; mirthful.
Glissando	rapid sliding movement upward or downward across white or black keys using one or more fingers.
Grave	slow; solemn.
Grazioso	gracefully; elegantly.
Handset	placement of hands over a "set" pattern of notes.
Inversion	regrouping of the notes in an interval or chord. For example, a triad (3-note chord) can have two inversions in addition to its root position.
Largo	slow; stately.
Legato	smooth; connected; bound together. The reverse of staccato.
Leggeramente	lightly.
Leggiero	light; rapid; delicate.
Lento (Lent, Fr.)	slow, between Largo and Adagio.
Loco	play as written.
Maestoso	majestic; dignified.
Marcato	marked; emphasized.
March	music intended for marching (as in a parade).
Marcia	march.
Meno	less.
Menuet (Minuet)	a slow, stately dance in $\frac{3}{4}$ time.
Metronome	device to determine tempo (speed) in music; measured in beats per minute, ex. ♩ = 72.
Mezzo	half.
Mezzo Forte (*mf*)	half or moderately loud.
Mezzo Piano (*mp*)	half or moderately soft.
Minuet	dignified dance in triple meter.
Moderato	moderate.
Molto	very much; exceedingly.
Mosso	motion; movement.
Nocturne	night piece, sentimental or poetic character.
Ostinato	recurring figure, usually in the bass.
Pastoral (Pastorale)	portraying a rustic or rural scene.
Pensieroso	thoughtfully; pensively.

Musical Terms *(cont.)*

Pesante	heavy.
Piano (*p*)	soft.
Pianissimo (*pp*)	very soft.
Piu	more.
Poco	a little, rather.
Poco a poco	little by little; by degrees.
Portato	disconnected; neither staccato nor legato.
Presto	fast.
Primo	the first (upper part) of a piano duet.
Quadrille	a dance in five sections derived from an old French folk dance.
Rag	syncopated piano piece, forerunner of jazz.
Rallentando (rall.)	gradually becoming slower.
Religioso	in a religious manner.
Ritardando (rit.)	retarding; getting slower and slower.
Rubato	robbed; stolen. The rhythmic flow is interrupted by dwelling slightly on some melodic notes and slightly hurrying others.
Scherzo	light, humorous piece of music.
Secondo	the second (lower part) of a piano duet.
Sempre	always; continually.
Sforzando (*sfz* or *sf*)	forced; a strong accent.
Simile	the same.
Sonatina	a short sonata with two to three (sometimes four) movements. The first movement generally has two themes (exposition) followed by a development section and a recapitulation section.
Sostenuto	sustained; unhurried.
Spirito	animation, spirit.
Staccato	detached; separated.
Subito	suddenly.
Syncopation	accent on a weak beat commonly used in ragtime, jazz, and popular music.
Tranquillo	tranquil; calm.
Transposition	playing of music from one key to another.
Troppo	too much.
Upbeat	pickup note(s).
Vivace	animated; lively.
Vivo	lively; briskly.
Waltz	popular dance (slow to moderately fast) in triple meter ($\frac{3}{4}$).

Musical Signs

sharp	♯
flat	♭
natural	♮
double sharp	𝄪
double flat	𝄫
fermata	𝄐 or 𝄑
repeat sign	𝄆 𝄇
tie	
slur	
staccato	
portato (see Glossary)	
accent and sustain	
break or breath mark	’
rolled or "strummed" chord	
tenuto mark – sustain	
triplet	3
accent	>
endings	1. 2.
pedal	Ped. ✻
acciaccatura	
ottava	8va
swing (♫)	♫ = 3 ♩ ♪

B
appendix

Part 1: Major Scales and Arpeggios

Major Scales – Two Octaves

C Major

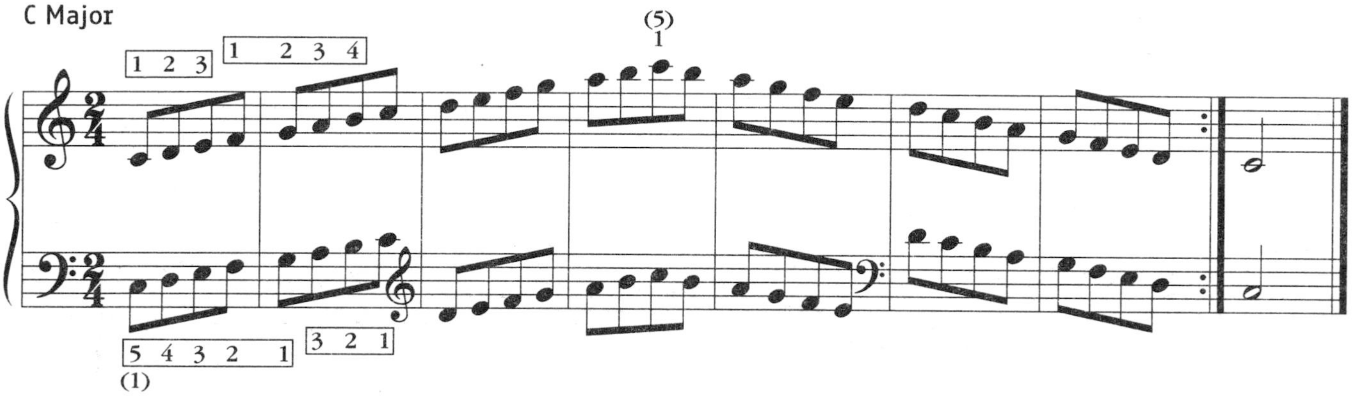

When putting hands together, notice that thumbs fall on the tonic, and the third fingers play together on the third and sixth scale degrees. This will hold true for the scales of C, G, D, A, and E.

G Major

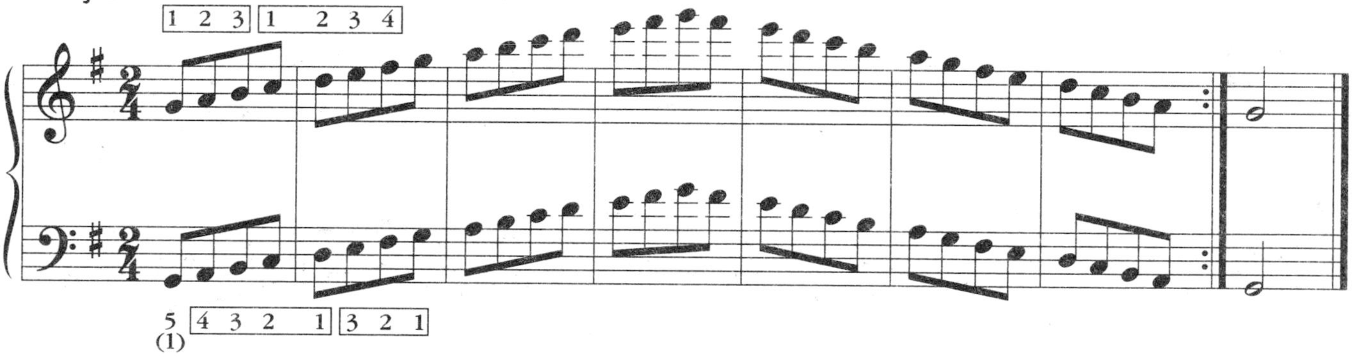

D Major

A Major

E Major

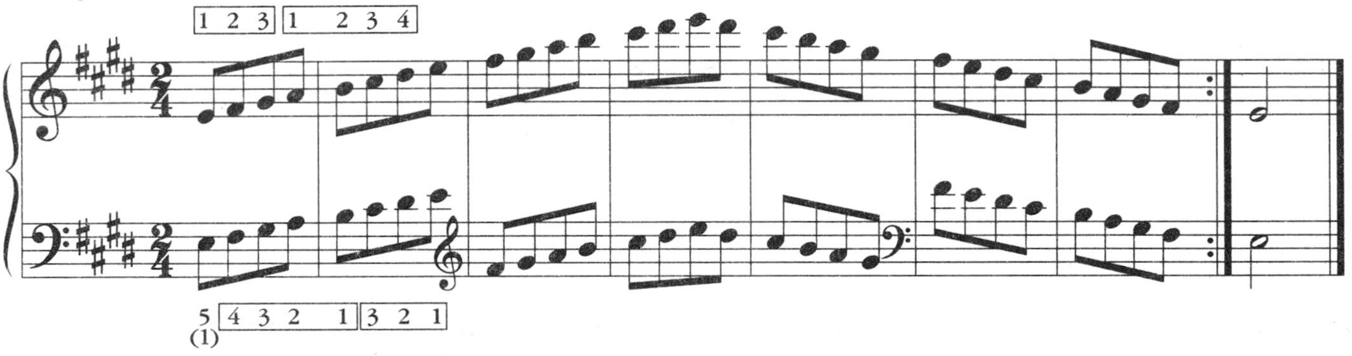

B Major

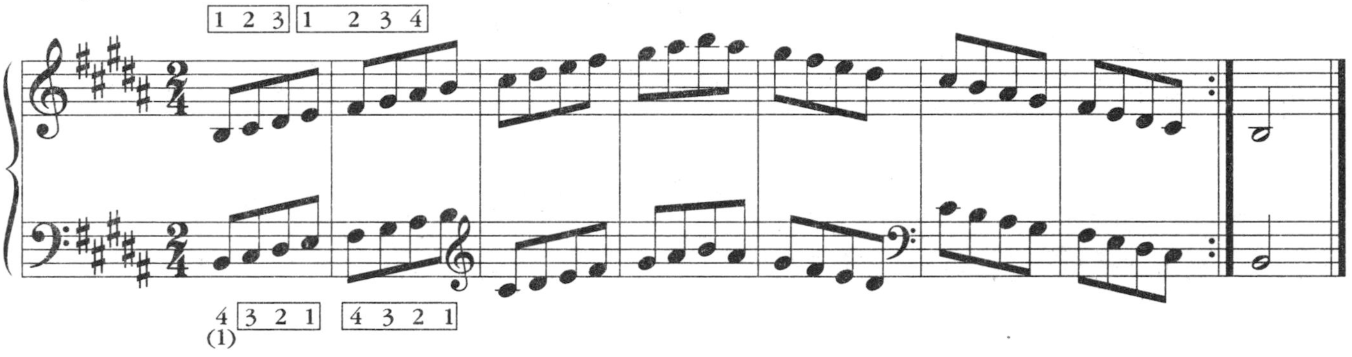

F Sharp Major

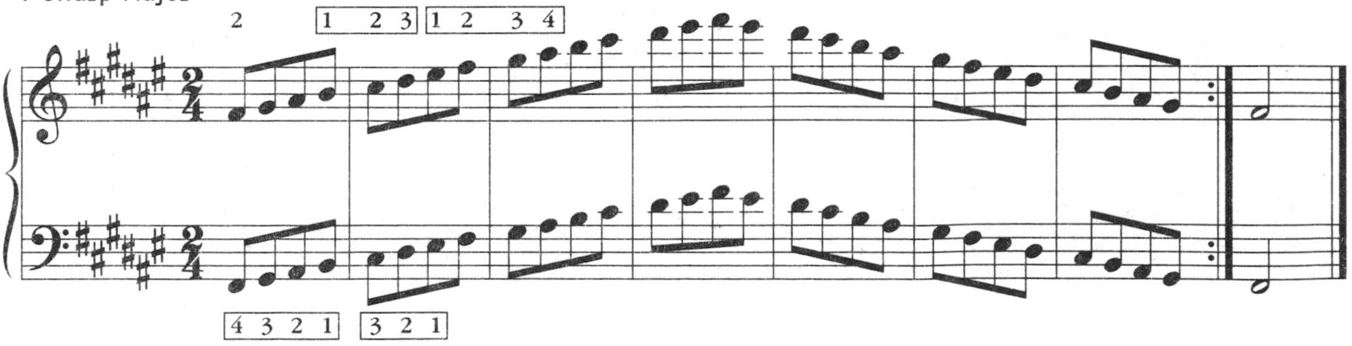

C Sharp Major

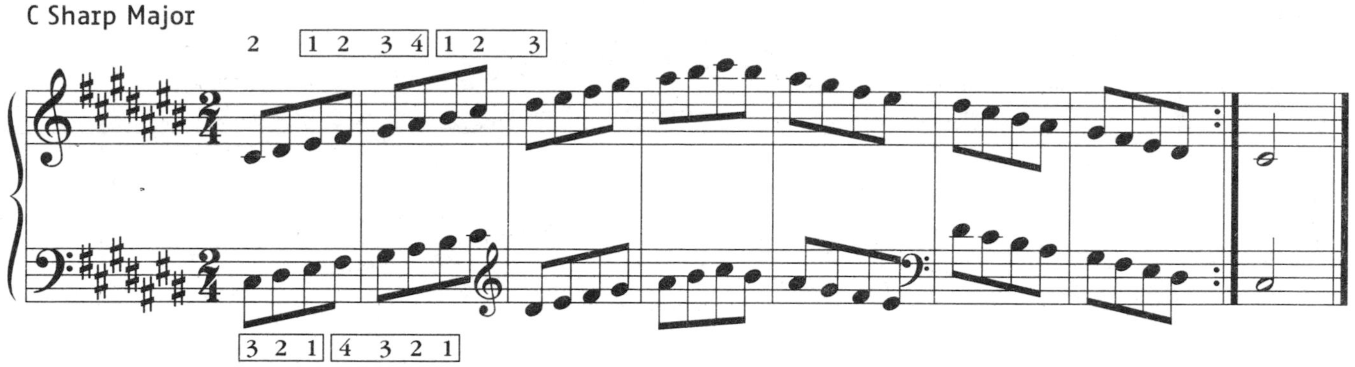

Flat Scale Fingerings

Study the following principles which apply to fingering flat scales. (1) The fourth finger of the right hand will always play B flat. Knowing this makes it possible to figure out any right hand flat scale fingering. In any flat key, simply place the right hand fourth finger on B flat and let the other fingers fall on adjacent scale tones in the key. Determine the groups of three and four. (2) The fingering pattern in the left hand for the keys of B flat, E flat, A flat and D flat is [3 2 1] [4 3 2 1]. This fingering may also be used for the F scale, but the traditional fingering for the left hand is like C major [(5) 4 3 2 1] [3 2 1]. The fourth finger of the left hand always adds a new flat for each new key, when using the [3 2 1] [4 3 2 1] pattern. The order of the scales below begins with F and proceeds through the circle of fourths, e.g., F, B flat, E flat and so on. Learn these scales gradually and be guided by your teacher as to various ways to practice the scales.

F Major

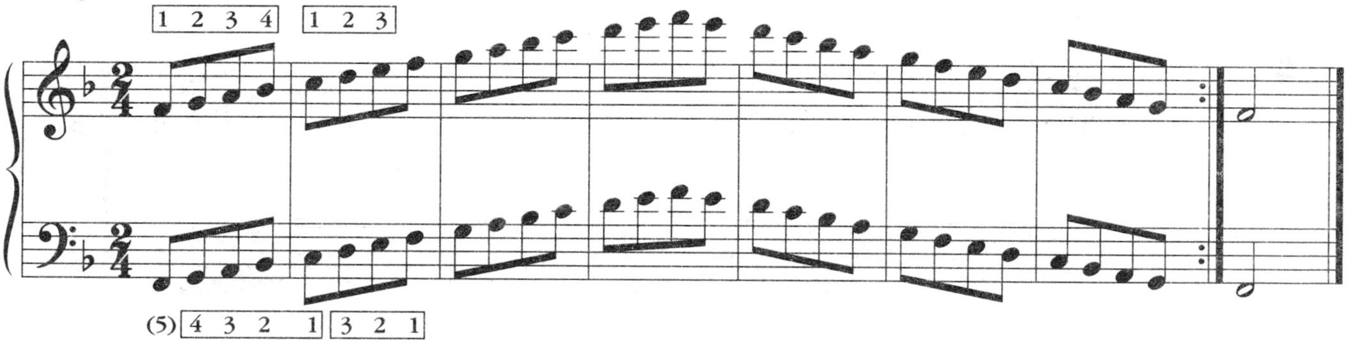

B Flat Major

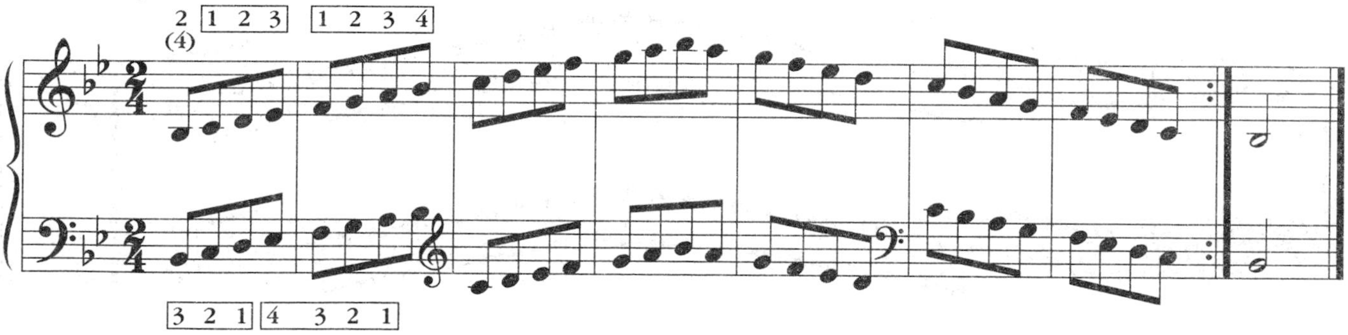

E Flat Major

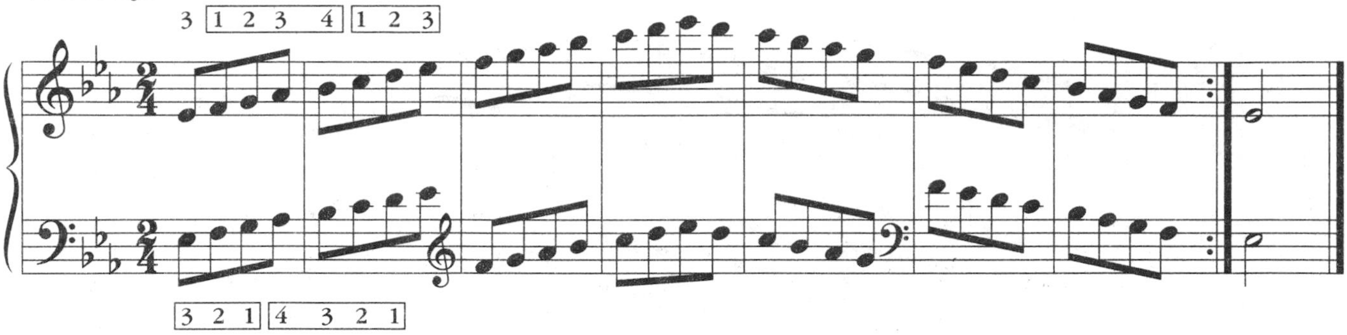

A Flat Major

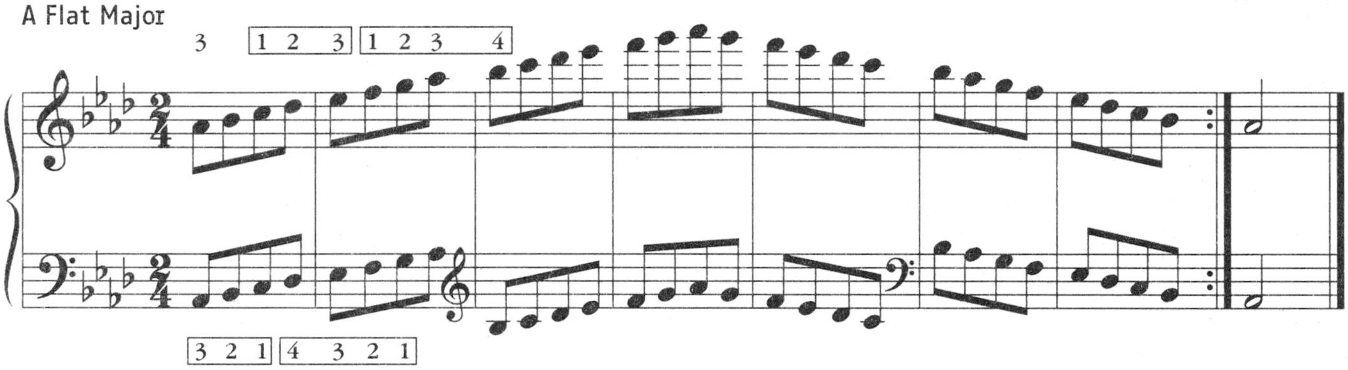

D Flat Major (enharmonic with C Sharp Major)

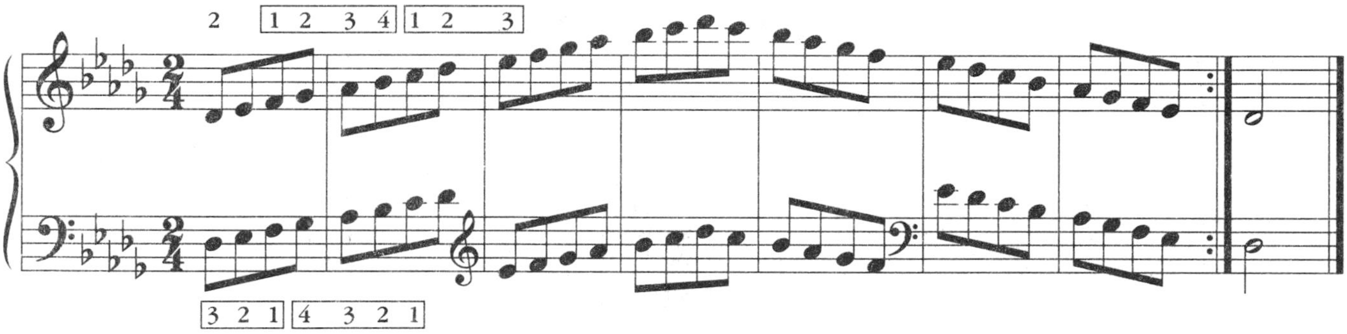

G Flat Major (enharmonic with F Sharp Major)

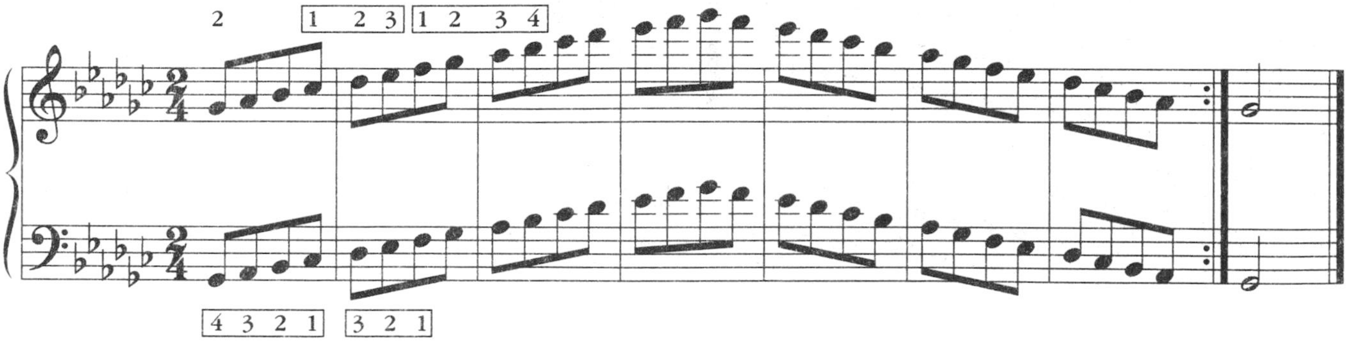

C Flat Major (enharmonic with B Major)

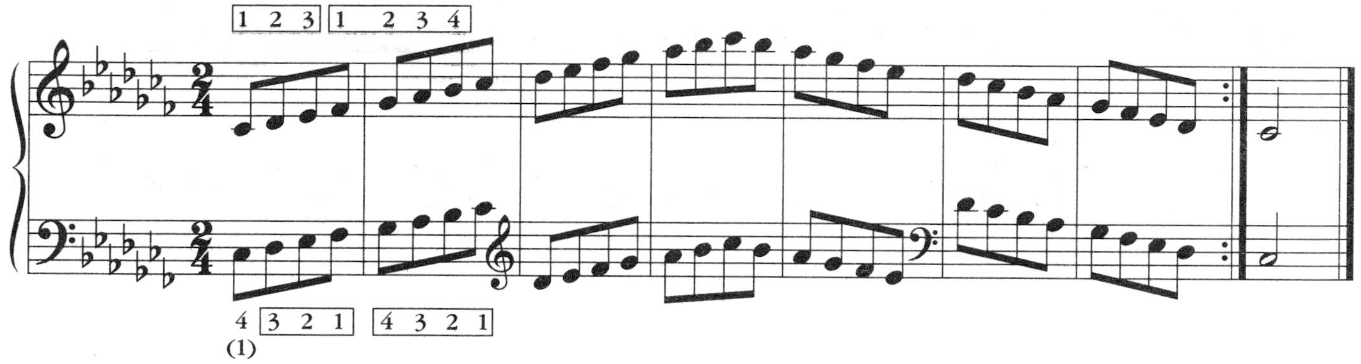

Major Arpeggios – Two Octaves

Add arpeggio practice immediately following scale practice. Learn the fingerings carefully. Slide the thumb under quickly.

C Major G Major

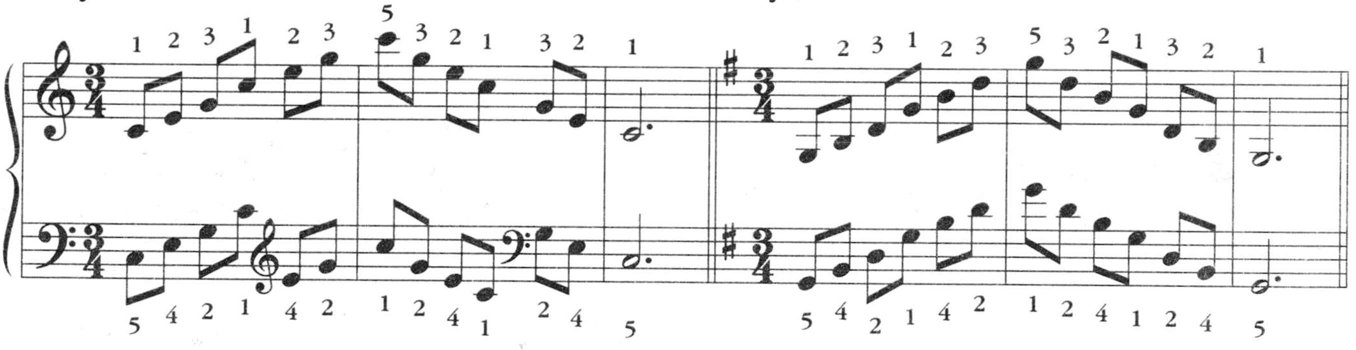

D Major A Major

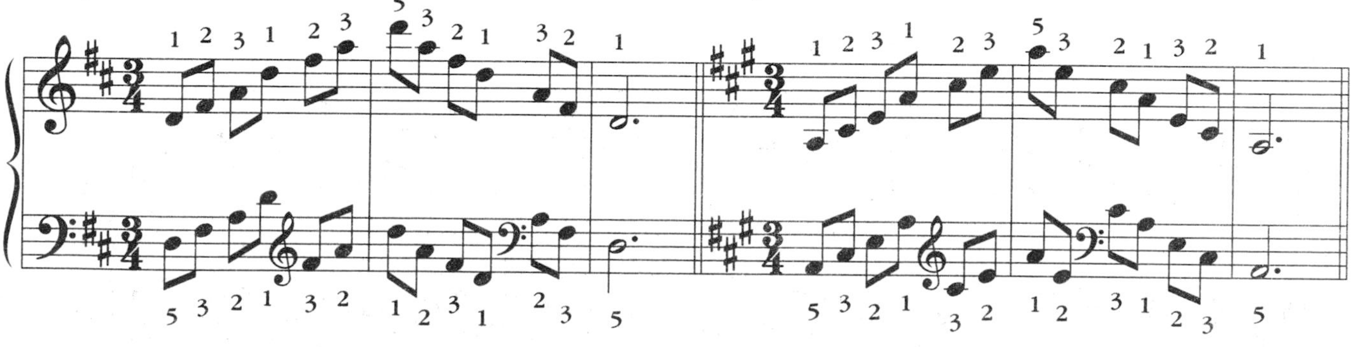

E Major

B Major

F Sharp Major
(G Flat Major)

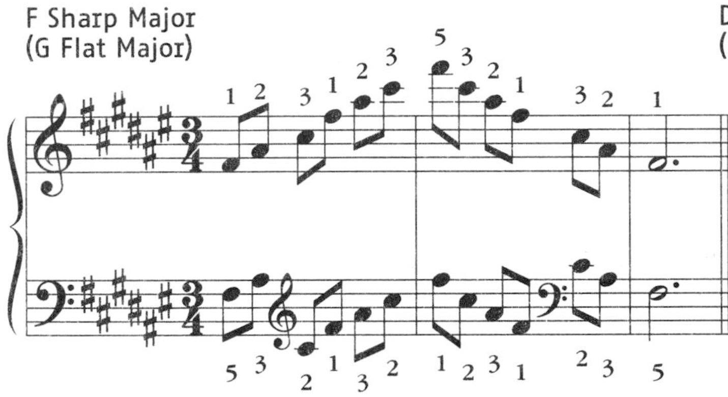

D Flat Major
(C Sharp Major)

A Flat Major

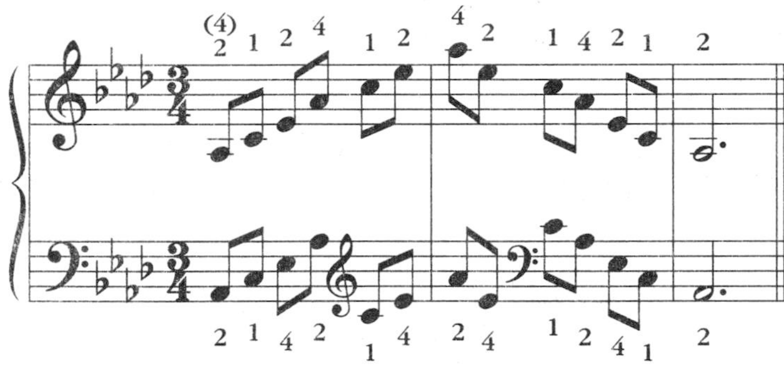

E Flat Major

B Flat Major

F Major

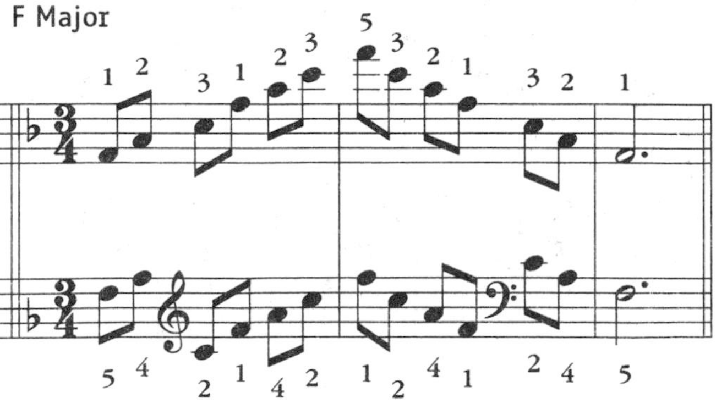

B appendix

Part 2: White Key Minor Scales and Arpeggios

C Harmonic Minor Scale

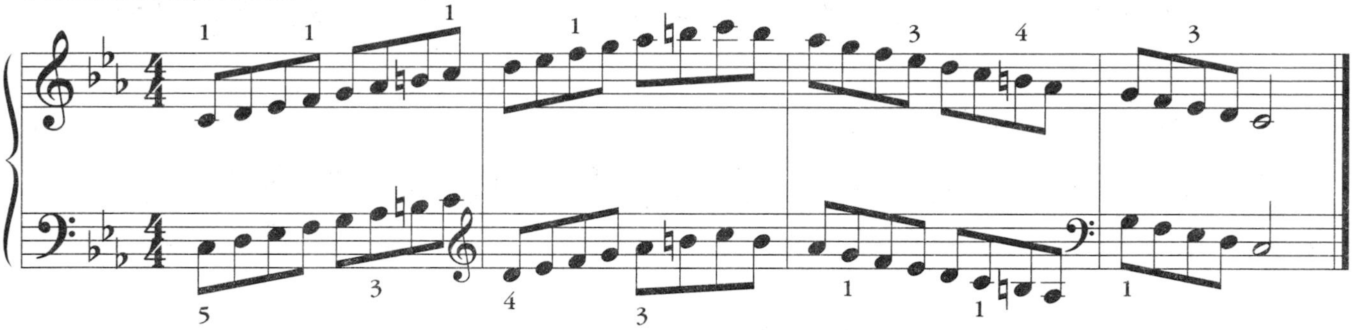

C Minor Arpeggio

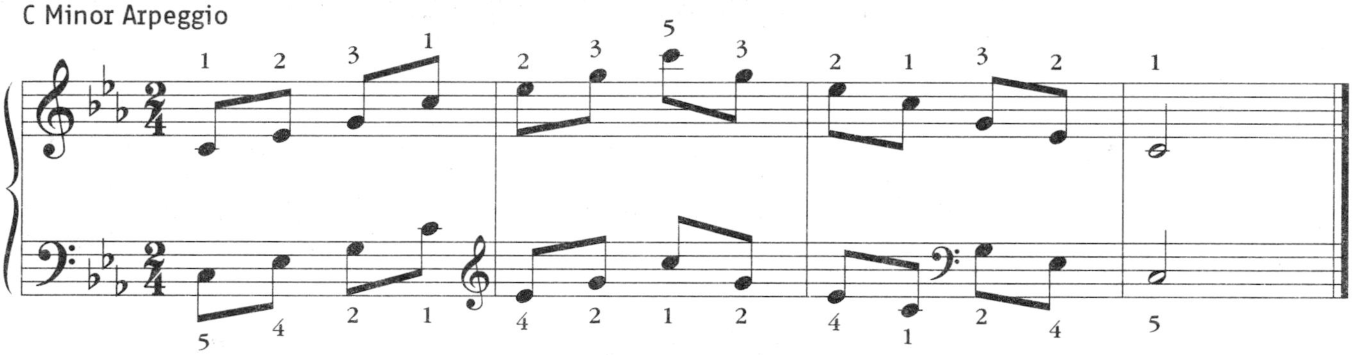

D Harmonic Minor Scale

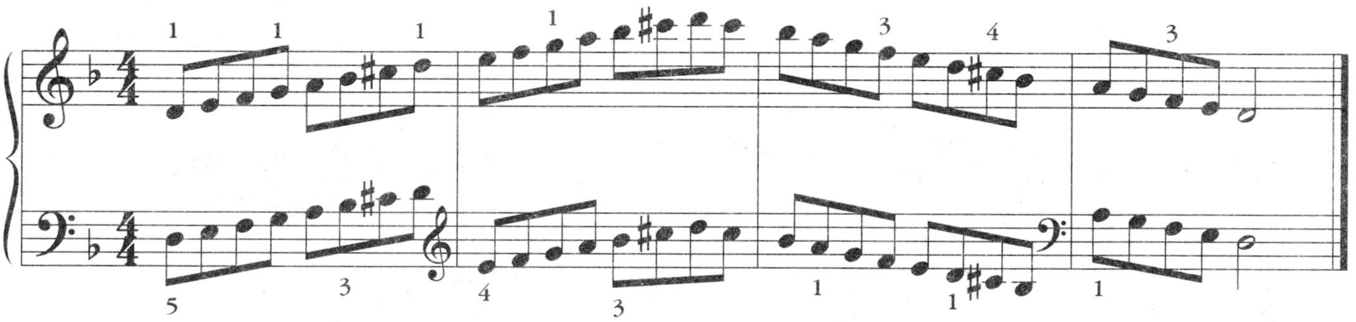

D Minor Arpeggio

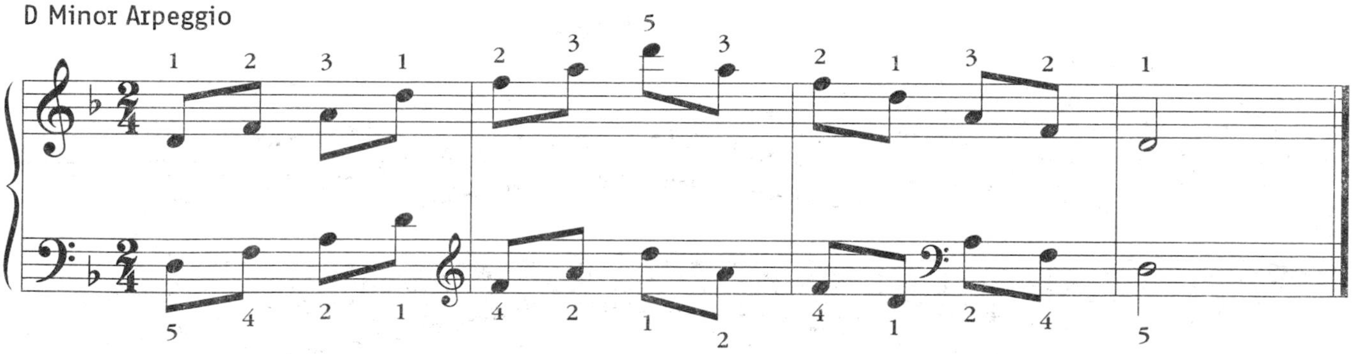

E Harmonic Minor Scale

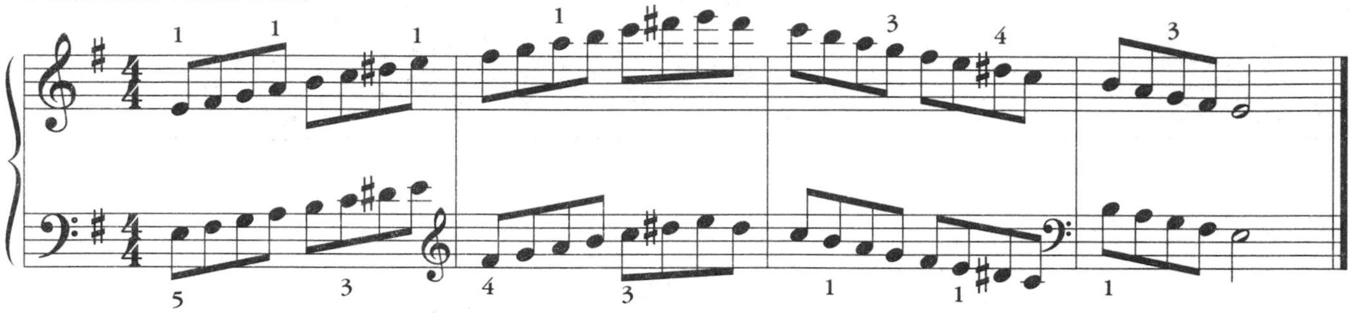

E Minor Arpeggio

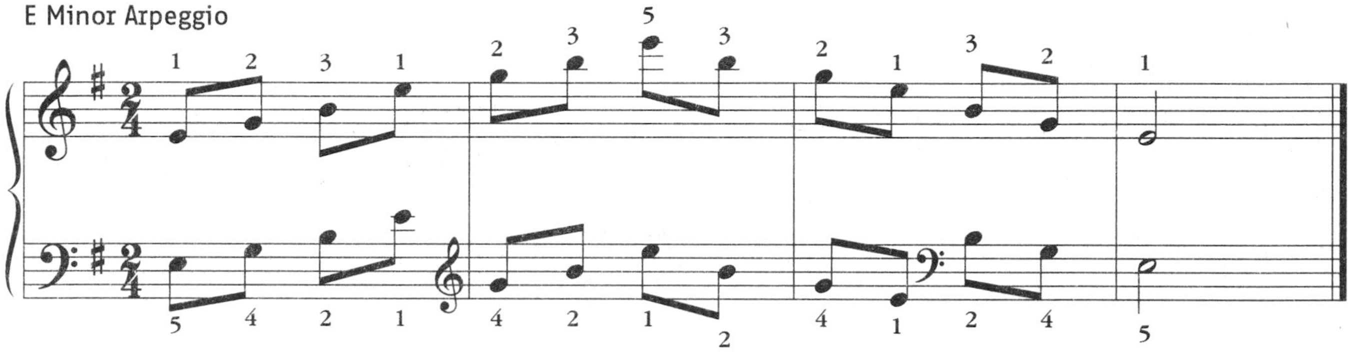

F Harmonic Minor Scale

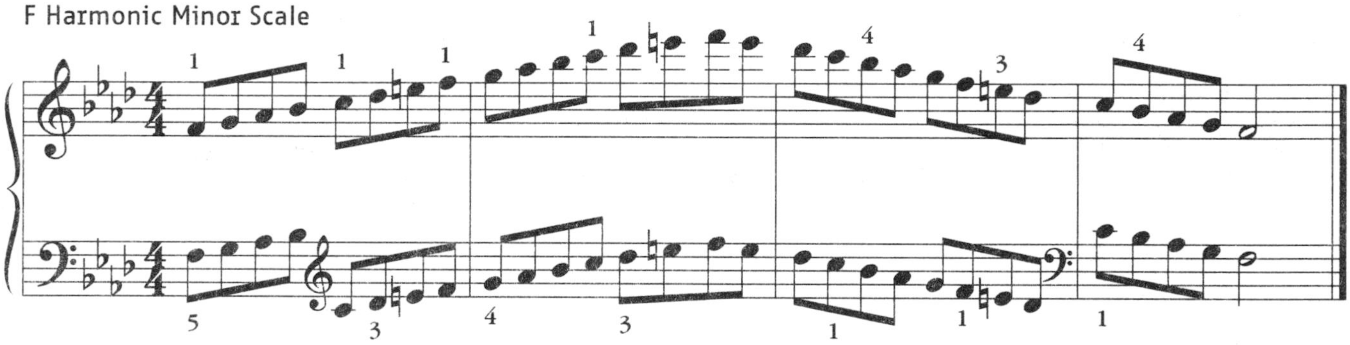

F Minor Arpeggio

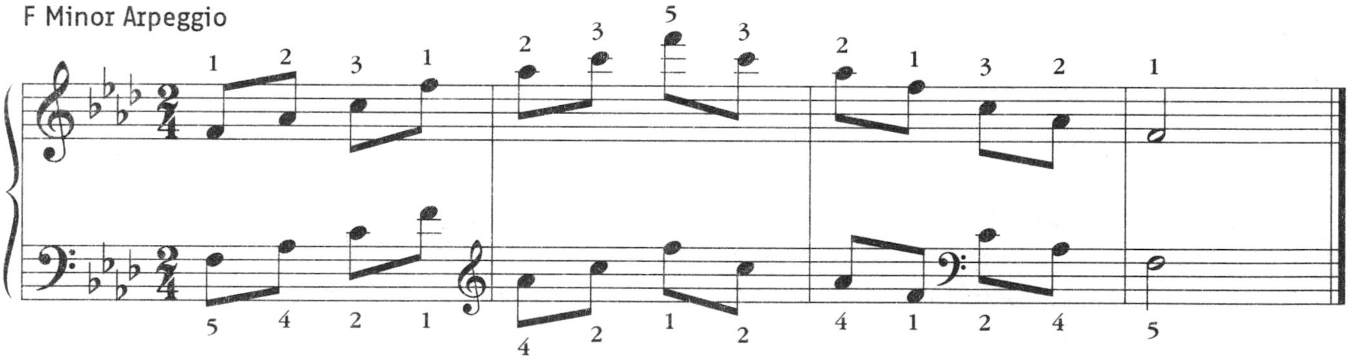

G Harmonic Minor Scale

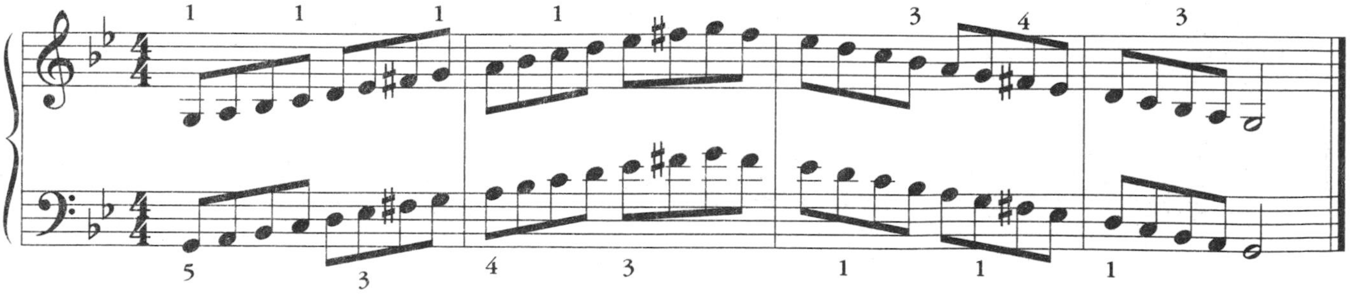

G Minor Arpeggio

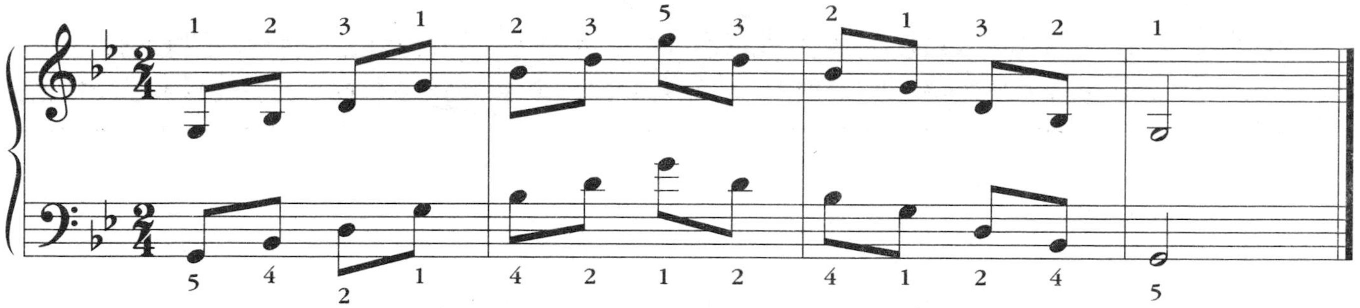

A Harmonic Minor Scale

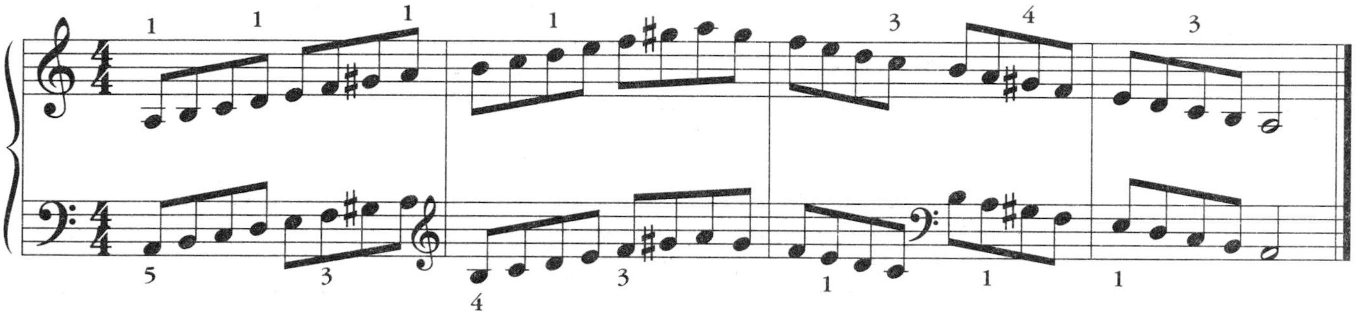

A Minor Arpeggio

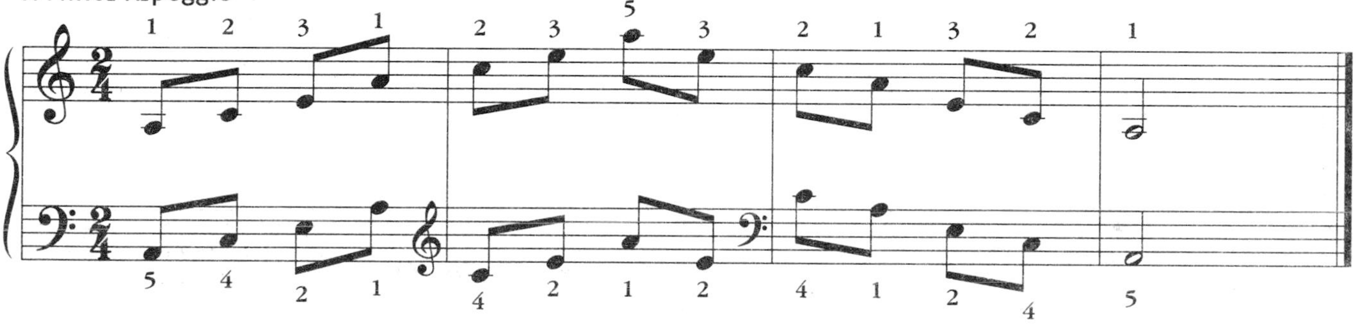

B Harmonic Minor Scale

B Minor Arpeggio

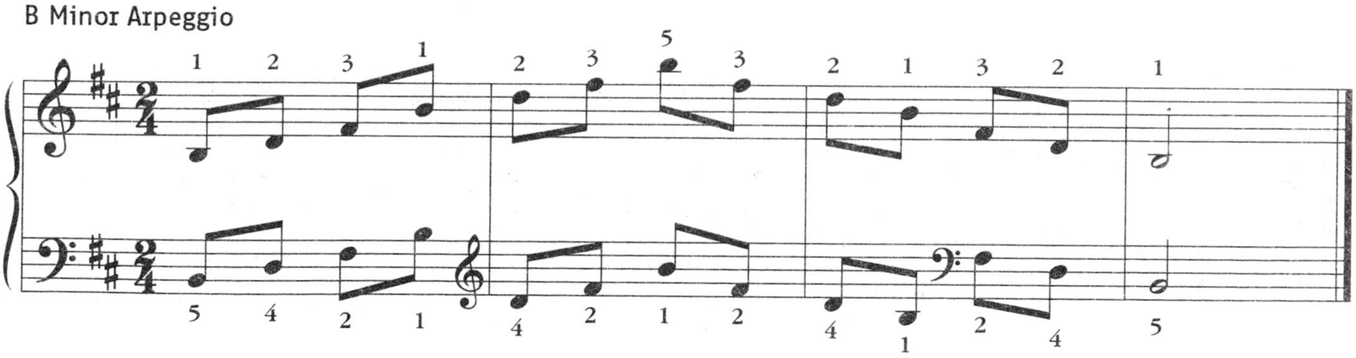

C appendix

Holiday Music

Leadsheets, Solo Arrangements and Duet Arrangements of Carols and Hanukkah Songs

LEAD SHEETS

JOLLY OLD SAINT NICHOLAS

Traditional

JOSEPH DEAREST, JOSEPH MINE

German

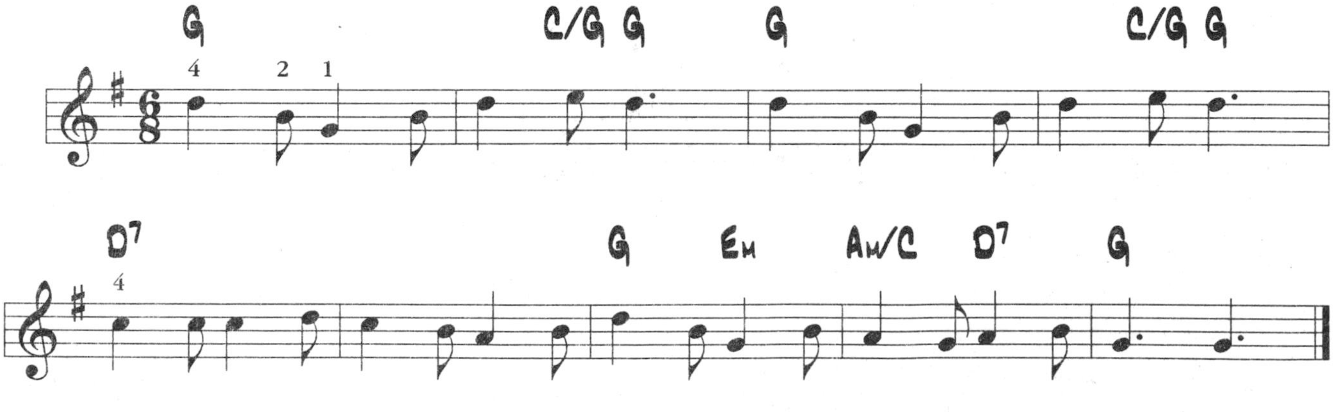

HANUKKAH SONG

Israeli

O CHRISTMAS TREE

German

HANUKKAH HYMN

Israeli

MID OX AND DONKEY

French

LULLABY MY LITTLE SON

Norwegian

BESIDE THY CRADLE

German

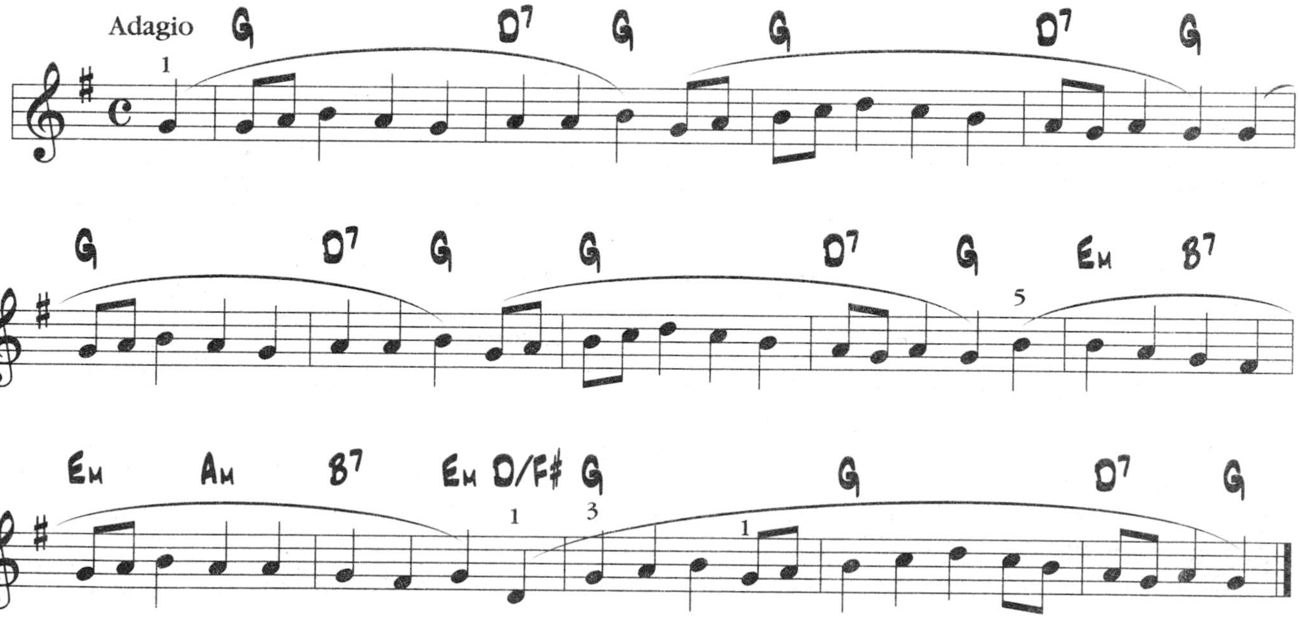

SOLO ARRANGEMENTS

I SAW THREE SHIPS

English
arr. James Lyke

Con spirito

PAT-A-PAN

French
arr. James Lyke

Quickly

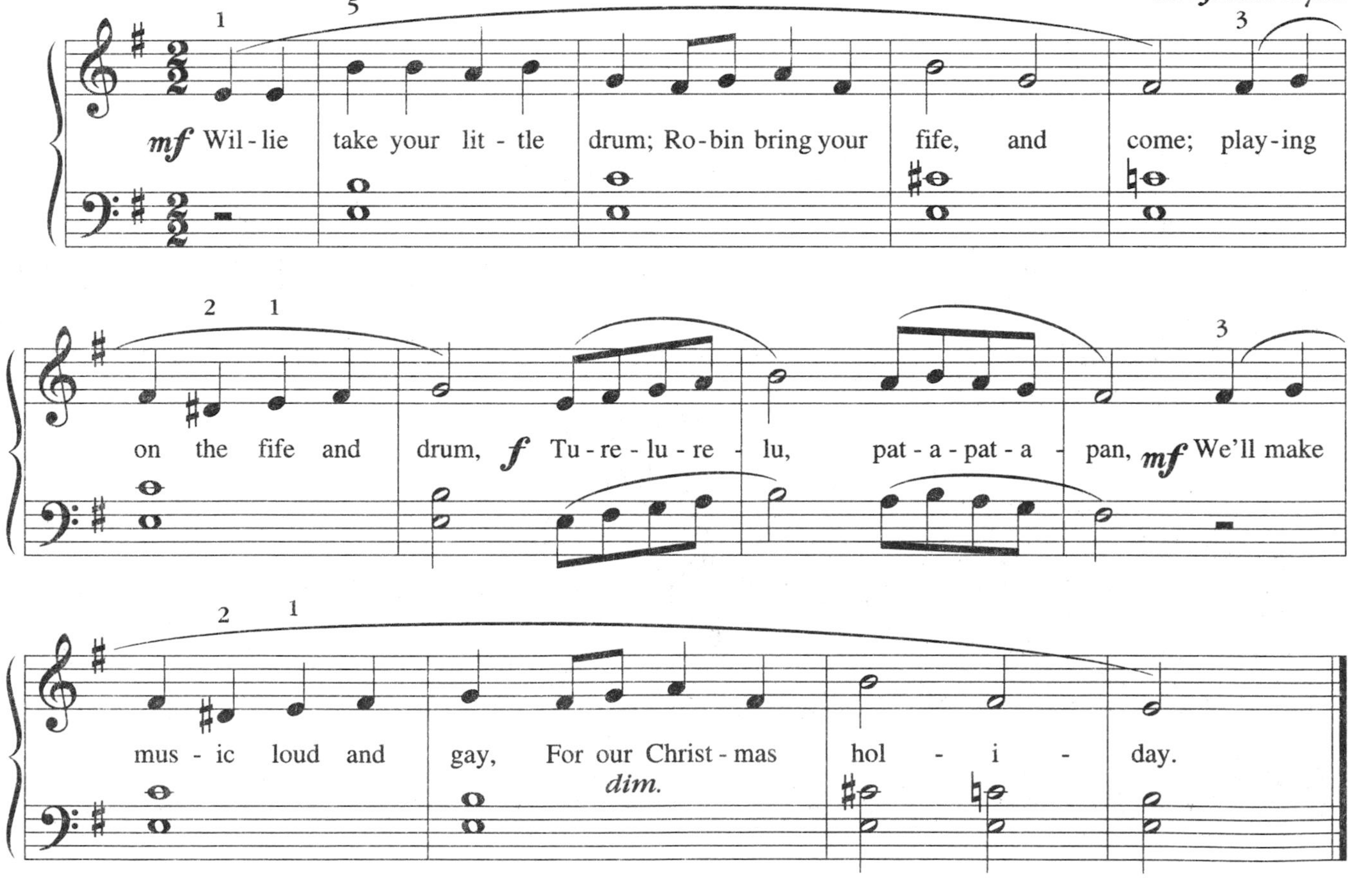

MY DREIDEL

Hebrew
arr. James Lyke

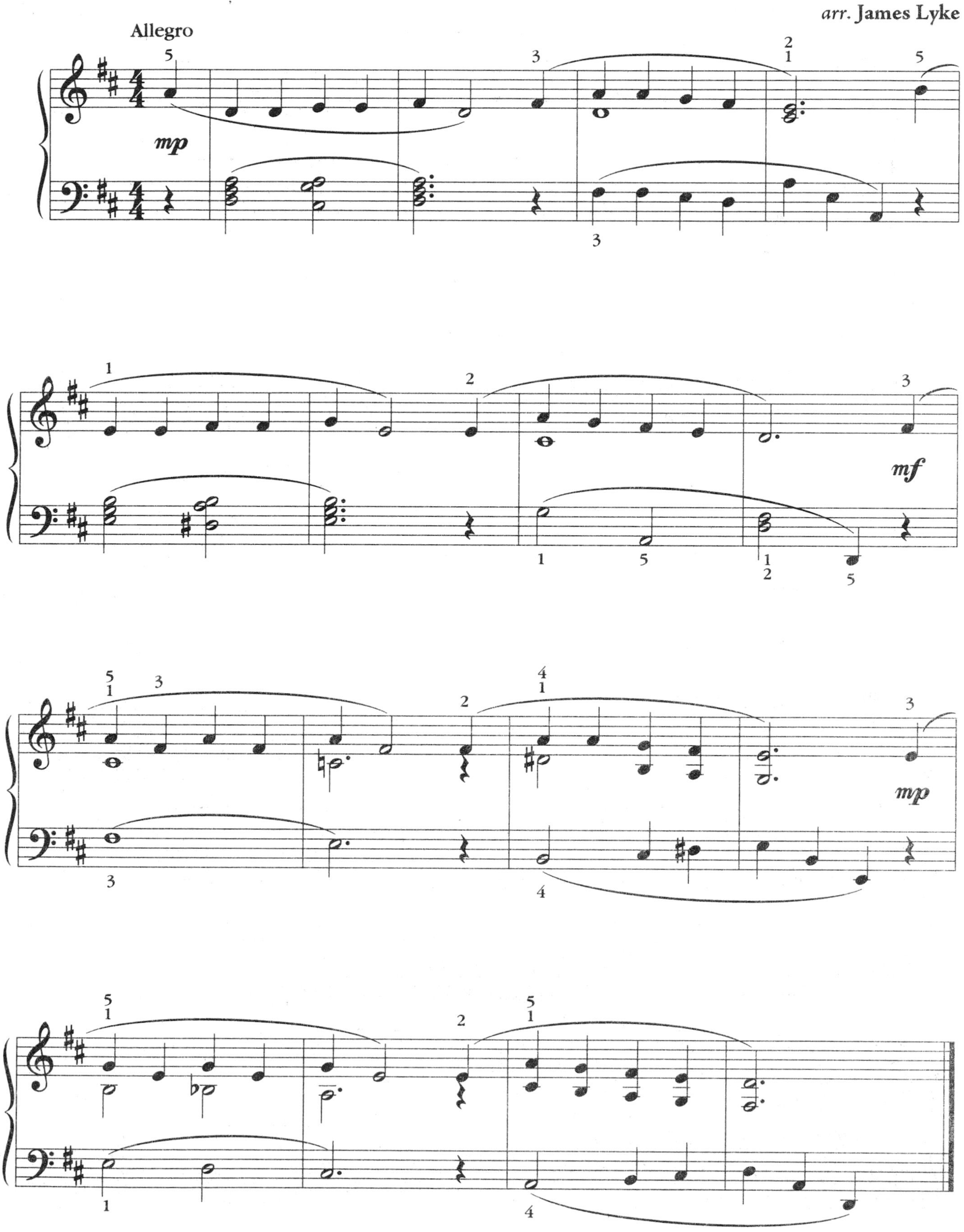

GOOD KING WENCESLAS

English
arr. **James Lyke**

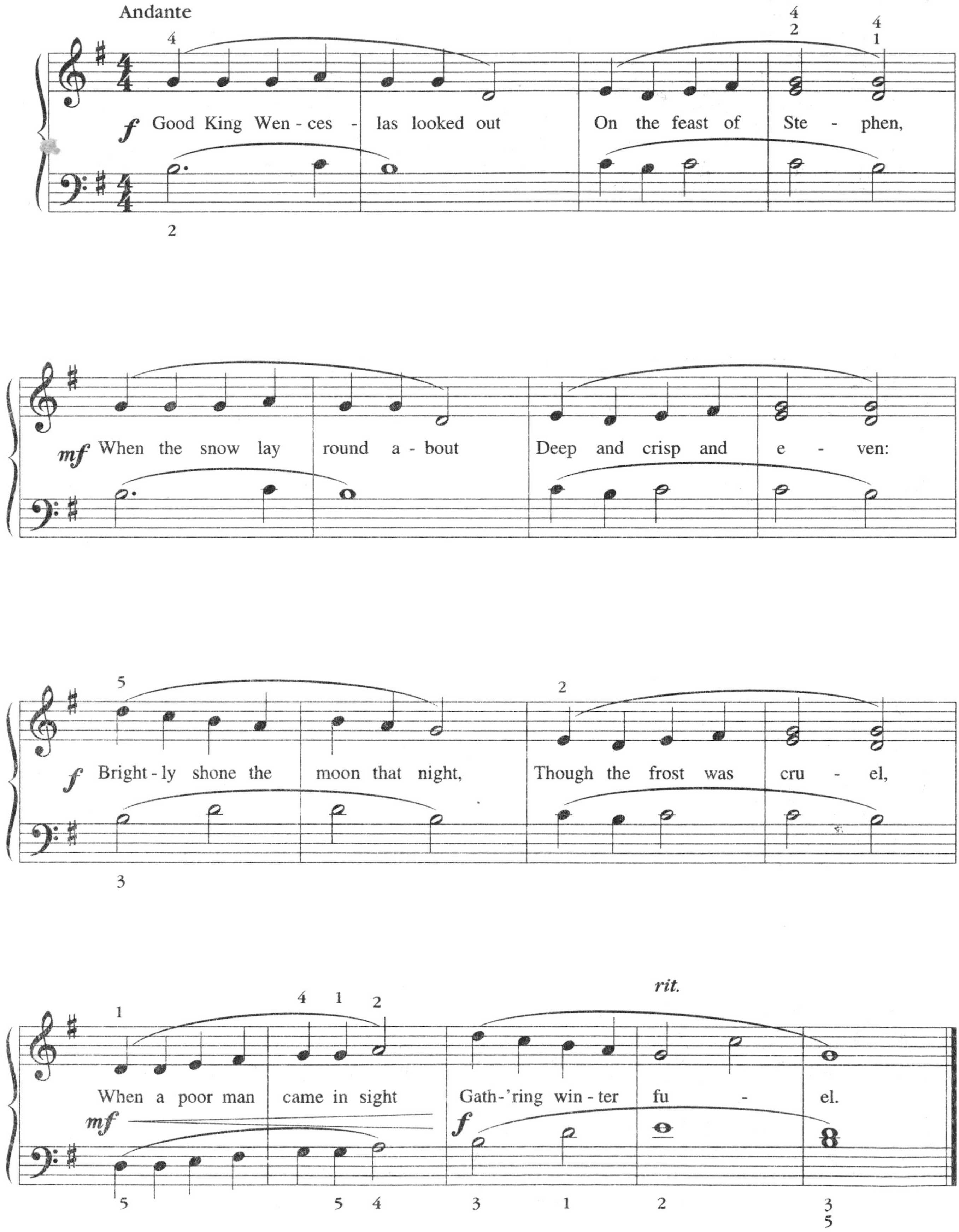

DING! DONG! MERRILY ON HIGH

French
arr. **Christos Tsitsaros**

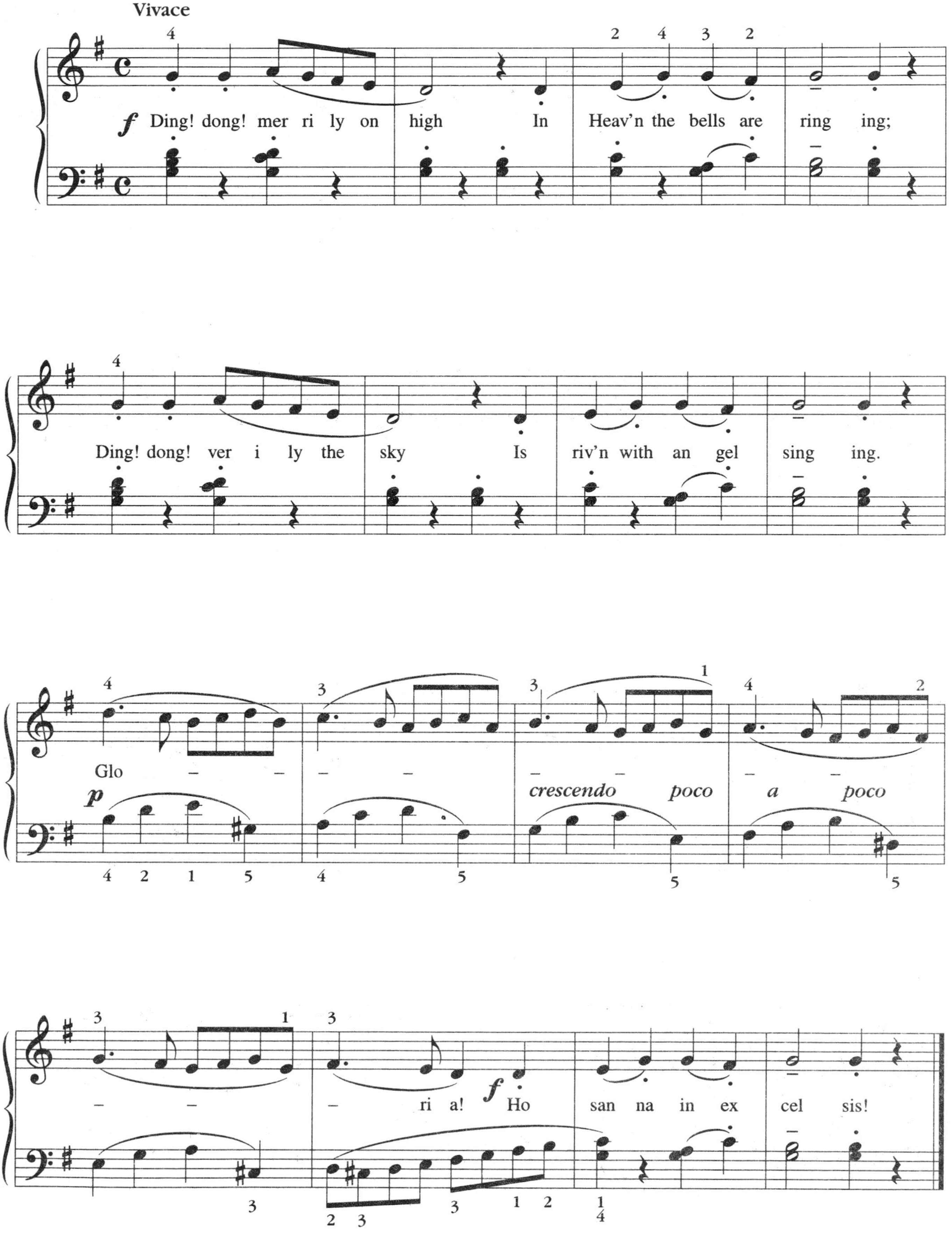

I WONDER AS I WANDER

Appalachian Carol
arr. **James Lyke**

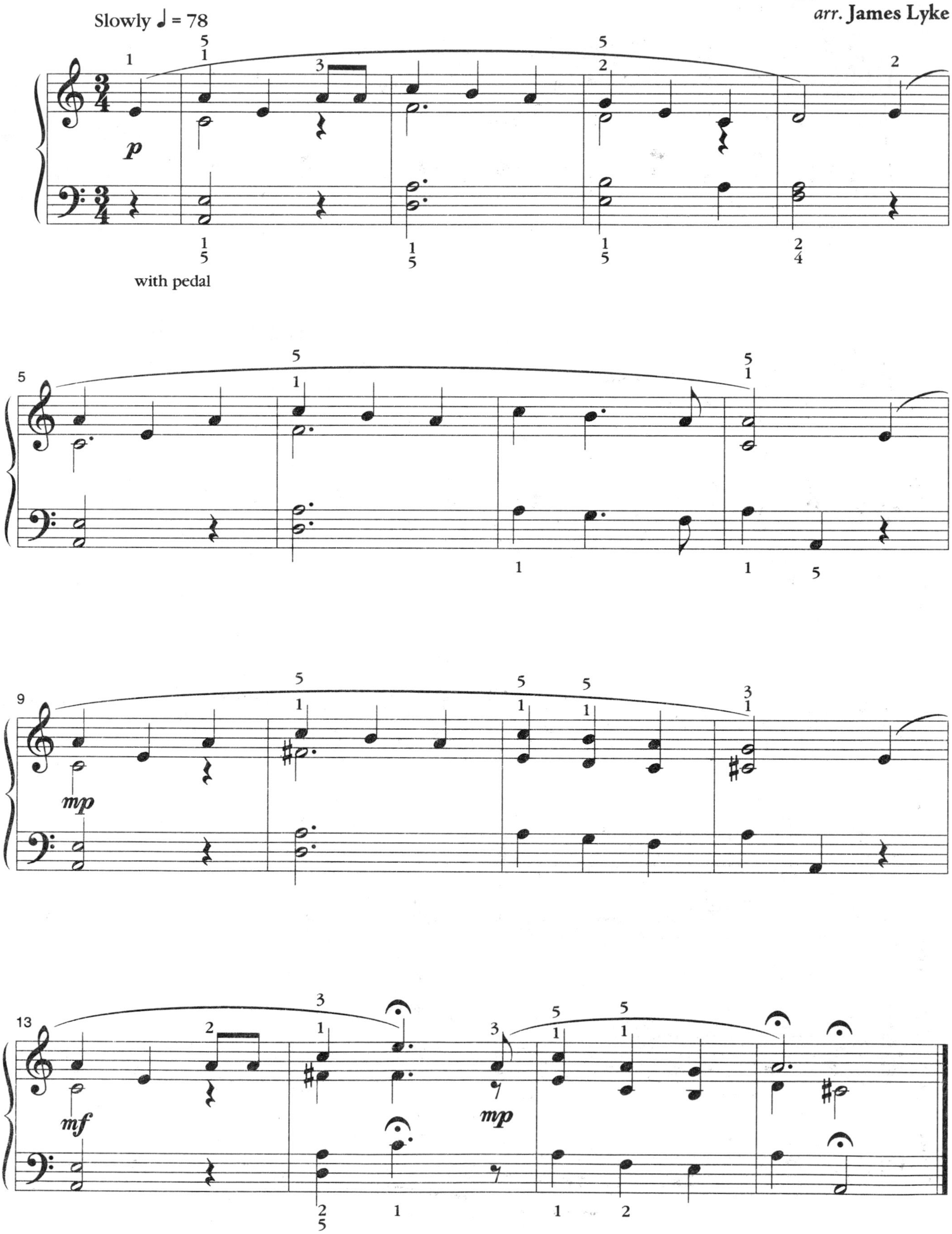

SILENT NIGHT

Franz Gruber
arr. Tony Caramia

DUET ARRANGEMENTS

55 CD

SEE THE DEAR LITTLE JESUS

Secondo – Teacher (or Student)

Polish Carol
arr. **James Lyke**

SEE THE DEAR LITTLE JESUS

Primo – Student (or Teacher)

Polish Carol
arr. **James Lyke**

56 CD

PARADE OF THE WOODEN SOLDIERS

Secondo – Teacher (or Student)

music by **Leon Jessell**
arr. **James Lyke**

56 CD

PARADE OF THE WOODEN SOLDIERS

Primo – Student

music by **Leon Jessell**
arr. **James Lyke**

March Tempo 𝅗𝅥 = 92

Secondo

Primo

57 CD

CHANUKAH

(2P4H)

Hebrew
arr. James Lyke

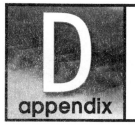

D appendix
Solo and Duet Literature

E appendix — Solo Arrangements of Folk and American Popular Songs, Accompaniments to Folk and American Popular Songs, Solo Arrangements of Holiday Songs

F appendix

CD / MIDI

Accompaniment Tracks

Each track contains a two-bar count-off; upbeat value(s) are included in the two measures. ASR = American Song Repertoire, acc. = Accompaniment, 1P4H = One Piano – Four Hands.